SQR in PeopleSoft and Other Applications
Second Edition

D

SQR in PeopleSoft and Other Applications Second Edition

PeopleSoft V.8

Galina Landres
Vlad Landres

MANNING
Greenwich
(74° w. long.)

For online browsing and ordering of this and other Manning books, please visit http://www.manning.com. The publisher offers discounts on this book when ordered in quantity. For more information, please contact:

Special Sales Department
Manning Publications Co.
209 Bruce Park Avenue   Fax: (203) 661-9018
Greenwich, CT 06830   email: manning@manning.com

Manning Publications Co.
209 Bruce Park Avenue
Greenwich, CT 06830

Copyeditor: Elizabeth Martin
Typesetter: Dottie Marsico
Cover designer: Leslie Haimes

ISBN: 1-932394-00-1
Printed in the United States of America
1 2 3 4 5 6 7 8 9 10 – VHG – 07 06 05 04 03

"It's never too late to be what you might have been."

—GEORGE ELIOT

To our dearest children Inna and Gene:
you are the world to us.

brief contents

contents

preface

Almost five years have passed since the first edition of this book arrived at bookstores and on the Internet. Since then, SQR has been upgraded to version 6 and many PeopleSoft developers are busy working with version 8.

The first edition had become dated and we faced the dilemma: to upgrade or not to upgrade. Almost 200 of our readers emailed and asked us to upgrade. Our publisher asked us to upgrade. Still we were hesitant. But when a friend bought the book and expressed puzzlement about a subchapter addressing the Year 2000 problem, we knew we were outvoted. The polls closed, the final count was 3 to 2: the readers, the publisher, and the friend vs. the two of us. Now, you have the result on your bookshelf (or maybe even on your desk).

So, what's new in the second edition? A lot.

The SQR language chapters have been upgraded to version 6. More real-life examples were added; for instance, how to generate Word documents from SQR. HTML enabling coverage was expanded to cover SQR features added since the time of the first edition release.

The PeopleSoft part was almost entirely redone to cover PeopleSoft version 8. We discuss the new PeopleSoft Internet Architecture (PIA). We added a separate chapter concerning the Process Scheduler recurrences and Job streams. Special attention was given to PeopleSoft security and how to handle profiles, roles, and permission lists. Finally, all navigation and screens that developers go through are for version 8.

preface to the first edition

After struggling to make an SQR program work one cold winter night in 1998, we searched through the vendor's manual for help. We were disappointed. Hoping to find a good book—maybe several books—on SQR, we hopped into a car and drove to a local Borders store. Both of us love the look and smell of today's superbookstores. We can spend endless hours browsing through the computer-book shelves in those miraculous stores, sometimes forgetting the original purpose of our visit, lost in reading and discovery. On that night, we were optimistic that we would be successful.

Well, guess what? We found nothing devoted to SQR. Not a single book! Shortly after our disappointing search, we began to notice we weren't alone. We read one frantic email after another from scores of SQR and PeopleSoft programmers, all lamenting the absence of books on SQR. As often happens in business, demand eventually gave birth to supply. After some agonizing, we decided to step up to fill the void. And after many long, hard-working nights, reams of paper and heaps of printer cartridges—as well as new, stronger glasses for Vlad—we finished the manuscript for this book.

Welcome to the world of SQR. The Structured Query Report Writer may not sound exciting at first, but where else can you find a programming tool, both robust and flexible, that works with nearly all known relational databases and operating systems, combines the power of SQL and the intelligence of procedural logic, and is easy to learn? "Come on," you may say, "there are other languages like that." That may be true, but there is something special about SQR: it is used as the main relational database reporting engine by PeopleSoft. Since PeopleSoft brought SQR to the front lines of today's ERP world, a number of other software package vendors have taken advantage of this language's unique capabilities. Recently, we read that another ERP software giant, SAP, is considering making SQR its report writing tool. Yes, this product definitely has a future!

We would not have done this language justice if we had limited our coverage to SQR's usage within PeopleSoft. So we decided to widen our presentation to include a discussion of all main features and capabilities of SQR outside of any specific connection to PeopleSoft.

We wrote this book for a broad audience. Readers who know nothing about SQR or PeopleSoft will find that it gives them a jump start. PeopleSoft developers will expand their knowledge of the SQR language. SQR programmers with little or no experience with PeopleSoft will be able to increase their scope. And readers who already have experience in both these areas will find many practical suggestions in over a hundred almost-real-life examples: this book is not just for beginners.

If you find this book interesting and useful, all the hard work and pain will have paid off for us. We hope that it will help SQR acquire new followers; that it will help our readers gain new and vital information; and that we will win new friends among them. Ultimately, these are our goals.

special thanks

It really took a village to shape our terribly imperfect manuscript into a real book.

We would like to thank the entire Manning Publications team for helping us to transform our pile of paper into this nice, neat volume. Our special thanks to Marjan Bace, Ted Kennedy, Mary Piergies, Adrianne Harun, Dottie Marsico, Leslie Haimes, and Sharon Mullins.

Our deepest appreciation goes to the following people who participated in the technical review of this book: Dia Barman, Bill McAllister, Steven Stein, George Jansen, Bob Talda, Peter Choi, Frank Monteleone, Vishwa Gaddamanugu, Early Stephens, and Tony DeLia. Not only did our reviewers help us to detect numerous glitches and inconsistencies in the original manuscript, but, even more importantly, they had the vision to recognize the value of our work, thereby encouraging us to continue.

Tony Delia, Isidor Rivera, Prakash Sankaran, and Bill McAllister deserve a special recognition for their continuous assistance and lots of invaluable suggestions.

To the entire team at Seagram—many thanks for your support and encouragement.

We also thank Ahmet Ackman, Ellen Tyvrovsky, and Henry Marx for helping us with this project.

And finally, this book would not have been possible without understanding and support from our children, Inna and Gene, our parents, relatives, and friends.

Our special thanks to those who helped us with the second edition

The second edition of this book obviously would not have happened without the first one. Therefore, our thanks to those who helped us with the first edition remain effective for the second edition.

For this edition, first and foremost, we would like to thank our readers who posted their reviews on Amazon, Barnes and Noble, Borders, and other booksellers' web sites and to those who sent us their feedback directly. Your comments were of tremendous importance to us.

The Manning team put a lot of effort on the second edition. Marjan Bace, Mary Piergies, Dottie Marsico, and Elizabeth Martin: we truly appreciate your assistance on every step.

Katherine Treiber from PeopleSoft Training: thank you for all your help. Ian Robinson from Brio Technology helped us with the software, Stan Quick from Brio Technology answered all of our questions about SQR version 6, and Wilbert Ngo spent so much time and effort reviewing our manuscript. Without this help, the second edition of this book would still be in our desk drawer.

We also would like to thank PeopleSoft Inc. and Brio Technology for endorsing our book and encouraging us to continue working on the second edition.

about the authors

Galina Landres has 20 years of professional experience as a full-time employee and consultant. She has developed multi-platform applications for a number of companies, including Waldenbooks, Siemens, Coopers & Lyband, and Seagram.

Vlad Landres has been involved in systems design and programming for 25 years. He has worked on both mainframe and client/server applications for the banking and insurance industries.

Galina and Vlad Landres are the founders of their consulting company SQRLand specializing in SQR and PeopleSoft applications. For more information about SQRLand, check its web page at www.sqrland.com.

about the cover illustration

The cover illustration of this book is from the 1805 edition of Sylvain Maréchal's four-volume compendium of regional dress customs. This book was first published in Paris in 1788, one year before the French Revolution. Its title alone required no fewer than 30 words.

> *Costumes Civils actuels de tous les peuples connus dessinés d'après nature gravés et coloriés, accompagnés d'une notice historique sur leurs coutumes, moeurs, religions, etc., etc., redigés par M. Sylvain Maréchal*

The four volumes include an annotation on the illustrations: "gravé à la manière noire par Mixelle d'après Desrais et colorié." Clearly, the engraver and illustrator deserved no more than to be listed by their last names—after all they were mere technicians. The workers who colored each illustration by hand remain nameless.

The colorful variety of this collection reminds us vividly of how culturally apart the world's towns and regions were just 200 years ago. Dress codes have changed everywhere and the diversity by region, so rich at the time, has faded away. It is now hard to tell the inhabitant of one continent from another. Perhaps we have traded cultural diversity for a more varied personal life—certainly a more varied and exciting technological environment. At a time when it is hard to tell one computer book from another, Manning celebrates the inventiveness and initiative of the computer business with book covers based on the rich diversity of regional life of two centuries ago, brought back to life by Maréchal's pictures. Just think, Maréchal's was a world so different from ours people would take the time to read a book title 30 words long.

about this book

Why SQR?

Structured Query Report Writer (SQR) is a programming language that combines the power of Structured Query Language (SQL) queries, the sophistication of procedural logic, and the freedom of multiple-platform development. Increasingly popular since PeopleSoft selected this language as its main SQL processing and reporting tool, SQR's unique combination liberates developers from the constraints of SQL and allows them to concentrate on the application aspects of their programs.

SQR is not just a language. It also includes an industrial-strength engine for extracting, transforming, and distributing data throughout the enterprise. It works equally well on both client and server, crosses almost seamlessly between different platforms, and covers nearly all relational databases.

Unlike most report writing tools, SQR is extremely flexible. With SQR you can extract data from and load data into the database, process complex file structures, print sophisticated reports with dynamic breaks at multiple levels, create interfaces between different systems, generate form letters with business charts, graphs and images, and perform many other tasks. At the same time, for those who used to work with drag-and-drop Graphical User Interface (GUI) development tools, SQR may look a little old-fashioned and Cobol-like (although an optionally purchased SQR Workbench eliminates this problem). The absence of a slick development environment is fully compensated by the robustness, scalability, and solid performance of this product: this is a serious tool for serious people.

Why this book?

We are presenting the only book about SQR available today. It provides a comprehensive guide to the SQR language covering all its elements and features, showing readers the best ways of utilizing SQR's capabilities, and demonstrating good programming habits.

But our book does not stop at this. It also covers all aspects of interaction between SQR programs and PeopleSoft. Many activities and tasks involved in PeopleSoft application development and maintenance are discussed in considerable depth, making the book a working manual for both SQR programmers and PeopleSoft developers.

The book is written as a "let's do it together" tutorial, starting with the basics and gradually progressing to fairly complex subjects. It guides a reader through its topics step by step, providing close-to-real-life examples along the way with the aim of ensuring the complete understanding of each subject. The discussion is not restricted to demonstrating a single technical solution to each problem, but challenges readers to explore various approaches while showing both the benefits and potential pitfalls of each option.

Who can use this book?

This book can be used by:

- programmers responsible for the systems analysis, development, and support of various SQR-based applications
- PeopleSoft developers and consultants who write new SQR programs or modify the existing ones, create interfaces between PeopleSoft and other systems, and convert legacy system data to PeopleSoft
- PeopleSoft support programmers responsible for maintaining PeopleSoft-delivered SQR programs and upgrading them to the next versions
- PeopleSoft functional users who would like to expand their technical background
- PeopleSoft database administrators
- database developers and administrators
- project leaders and managers responsible for SQR or PeopleSoft-related projects
- computer specialists who would like to learn about SQR and PeopleSoft by self-study

Our book requires no more than a basic understanding of programming and relational databases. At the same time, this book is not just for beginners. It presents SQR in considerable depth and will be useful for seasoned SQR developers. Most examples in this book are not light. They are close to real-life programs used in PeopleSoft-related SQR applications as well as other SQR-based applications.

As we mentioned, the book consists of three major parts. The first two describe the SQR language, both basic and advanced, while the third covers the integration of SQR programs with PeopleSoft. This should allow many readers who are familiar with only one of these two subjects to expand their knowledge of the other subject and to achieve proficiency in all areas:

- PeopleSoft developers who will read this book will benefit from learning all intricate details of the SQR language and will be able to write serious SQR programs using all capabilities of this language.
- SQR programmers with little or no knowledge of PeopleSoft will be able to learn PeopleSoft basics and how to make their programs run under PeopleSoft, thus expanding their professional horizons (and marketability).

What's in this book?

The book consists of three major parts. Part 1 introduces the basics of the SQR language; part 2 advances the reader's understanding of SQR by exploring its capabilities in greater depth; finally part 3 covers many aspects of PeopleSoft development involving integration of SQR programs with PeopleSoft.

Within each major part of this book, chapters are organized in such a way that every chapter introduces a group of related technical concepts and features like data elements, commands, methods, and techniques. Each chapter starts with a brief list of main topics covered in the chapter, follows with extensive discussions of these subjects, and concludes with a list of the chapter's key points.

Chapter 1 presents an overall picture of SQR and its main components. It includes a list of the databases and operating systems supported by SQR. This chapter also briefly describes the changes made to SQR in different versions.

Chapter 2 refreshes your knowledge about the basic concepts of the relational database model and SQL and also introduces a set of sample tables that will be used in examples throughout the book. Readers with solid SQL knowledge can skip this chapter; however, we suggest that every reader become familiar with the sample tables presented here.

Chapter 3 drives you through the process of building your first SQR program. In it we describe the SQR Dialog Box and show how to run SQR programs with the help of this tool. In addition, we introduce SQR program sections, procedures, and files, as well as an example SQR program with multiple procedures.

Chapter 4 introduces the building blocks of the SQR language: its data elements. The chapter covers all types of SQR data elements including: strings, dates, numerics, and SQR predefined variables, as well as different commands and built-in functions that are used to manipulate the data elements.

Chapter 5 discusses three fundamental topics: the SQR page, the structure of an SQR program, and SQR local and global procedures. Here we lay the foundation for a basic understanding of any SQR program no matter how complex. By dissecting the SQR page into its three main sections, we show you how these sections are used to produce a complete report page. We also discuss all five SQR program sections, and the difference between SQR local and global procedures.

Chapter 6 concerns the essence of SQR: the `Select` paragraph. Here is where you will see the source of SQR power in the combination of SQL and procedural logic that makes this product so different from many other reporting tools. In addition, we introduce the two SQR commands, `Lookup` and `Load-Lookup`, that let you pre-load frequently used tables into the computer memory, possibly saving precious processing time by reducing the number of database table lookups.

Chapter 7 sheds light on another SQR feature: the SQL paragraph. The SQL paragraph is the only place where you can use native SQL statements in SQR. You do not need to use native SQL to select data from the database, but if you want to update the content of certain tables or execute SQL Data Definition Language (DDL) commands to create, alter, or drop tables, the SQL paragraph is at your service.

In chapter 8 you learn how to use SQR logical expressions and operators to manage the program control flow. We show you how SQR handles elements common to any programming language: logical expressions, decisions, loops, etc.

Chapter 9 addresses the process of enhancing SQR-generated reports. While SQR is capable of performing many important tasks, printing reports is still its main job. We describe different methods of controlling the report appearance, including using edit format masks.

Chapter 10 covers one of the most difficult and confusing aspects of SQR—working with breaks. We cover this subject in-depth by presenting different techniques of controlling breaks. We use a number of examples to ensure a complete understanding of this important topic.

Chapter 11 deals with the issue of making your program flexible, using run-time variables and compile-time variables. We explain the difference between the usage of substitution variables and bind variables. We also discuss the difference between the Ask and Input commands as well as each command's appropriate usage. Another interesting subject covered in this chapter is building dynamic SQL statements and using the dynamic query variables.

Chapter 12 introduces SQR arrays. Arrays can be used to simplify your program and to improve its performance. They also serve as data sources for business charts and graphs. We show you how to create an array, populate an array with data, and to retrieve data from an array. We also demonstrate different techniques for sorting data elements in arrays and searching data in arrays.

Chapter 13 concentrates on multiple-report programs. We show you how to declare individual reports, define custom printer types, and direct output to specific reports. We also look at the naming conventions SQR uses to assign output file names to individual reports in a multiple-report program.

Chapter 14 explores SQR Portable Files (SPF). We discuss the advantages of using SPF files and different techniques that can be used to create, view, or print these files, including the SQR Viewer and the SQR Print tools.

Chapter 15 covers the Document paragraph, which is used to generate letters in SQR. We introduce document markers and show you how to use them to control the format and appearance of your letters. We talk about variable length sections in the Document paragraph and how to control pages in multiple-page letters. The main inconvenience of the Document paragraph is that it cannot cross over pages, and here we also will show you how to solve this problem.

In Chapter 16 you hopefully will have some fun by learning how to program graphics in SQR. The list of the graphical objects includes business charts and graphs, images, bar codes, lines, boxes, etc.

Chapter 17 addresses flat-file processing in SQR. We will discuss operations that are familiar to anyone who works with flat files in any programming language: opening and closing files, reading from and writing to files. SQR uses the `Print` and `New-Page` commands as a special way of outputting data to flat files, and we illustrate this simple technique.

Chapter 18 shows you how SQR interacts with other programs, products, and operating systems. The chapter covers submitting SQR programs from the operating system command line, running SQR in batch mode, invoking operating system commands and non-SQR programs from SQR, calling user functions from SQR, as well as calling SQR from various environments.

Chapter 19 extends the power of SQR to cyberspace. You learn how to convert the existing reports to HTML format without touching a single line in your programs, as well as how to write SQR programs specifically designed to generate Internet reports or webpages. We also show you how to place hypertext links into your reports and how an SQR program can accept input arguments from the Internet.

Chapter 20 talks about debugging SQR programs. Debugging in SQR is done in the old-fashioned way of tracing the program control flow and displaying the values of program variables with the help of the Show and Display commands. In addition, you can use SQR conditional compile directives to encapsulate the debugging logic in your program and keep this logic dormant until the need to re-activate debugging comes.

Chapter 21 concludes the SQR language part of our book. Instead of introducing new commands, concepts or features, we demonstrate how the already-explored methods can make your programs easier to build, test, maintain, and support. Do not expect ultimate solutions and carved-in-stone rules: they do not exist. Consider this chapter a set of ideas, suggestions, and recommendations that may be helpful for some developers.

Chapter 22 is the first PeopleSoft-related chapter. In it we show you how to run PeopleSoft-delivered SQR programs under the PeopleSoft Process Scheduler. We introduce basic PeopleSoft objects such as records, panels, panel groups, and menus. We also demonstrate how to schedule an SQR program execution under PeopleSoft and monitor this program's status via the Process Monitor.

In Chapter 23, we invite you for a brief tour that shows you what happens behind the scenes when users run their reports under PeopleSoft. Based on this knowledge, you will be able to figure out how to reuse the existing PeopleTools objects to run your own SQR programs under the PeopleSoft Process Scheduler.

Chapter 24 elaborates on the interaction between SQR programs and PeopleSoft by detailing the program changes that are necessary to make your programs Application Programming Interface (API) Aware. We discuss PeopleSoft-delivered SQC files, how to use the PeopleSoft API variables to communicate between your program and the Process Scheduler, and how to make the Process Scheduler aware of an error situation in your program.

Chapter 25 explores how an SQR program can accept input from PeopleSoft online panels. This chapter also includes writing your own SQC files, creating your own Run Control records and online panels, and granting your users access to the newly created or modified objects.

Chapter 26 describes the process of creating the Recurrence Definitions in PeopleSoft. The Recurrence Definitions are used to schedule programs for execution on a recurring basis. Starting from version 8, Recurrence Definitions are created under the Process Scheduler Manager. Chapter 26 also shows you how to create job streams that contain multiple processes.

Chapter 27 addresses implementing security in PeopleSoft. The chapter's main focus is how to use PeopleSoft security views in SQR to implement row-level security. In addition, this chapter teaches you how to prevent an SQR program from running outside the Process Scheduler.

Chapter 28 focuses on the concept of effective-dated data. Working with effective-dated tables presents certain challenges to SQR developers, and here we suggest a few techniques for solving problems common to many PeopleSoft developers.

The appendices of this book describe the sample database tables used in the examples throughout this book (appendix A); SQR command line flags (appendix B); SQR built-in functions (appendix C); and the SQR command syntax (appendix D).

What about the examples?

All the materials presented in the book are supported by over a hundred examples most of which are very close to real business situations and can be successfully used by application developers. All sample programs discussed in this book are freely available from http://www.manning.com/landres.

Most examples in our book are centered around the sample database presented in chapter 2 and appendix A. This database contains a few tables that are functionally similar to the corresponding PeopleSoft Human Resource Management Systems (HRMS) tables, but include only those columns which are essential to run our examples. Because of this similarity, many PeopleSoft developers will find our examples reflecting the situations that commonly occur in their business environments.

In most cases, the examples in this book were tested using Windows 98 or Windows NT as a client and HP UNIX as a server. We used the Oracle database under UNIX or SQLBase under Windows 95. While we did our best to make our examples as platform- and database-independent as possible, there is still a chance that a few examples may produce somewhat different results when run on different databases or under different operating systems.

PART 1

SQR basics

CHAPTER 1

Introducing SQR

IN THIS CHAPTER

- SQR architecture (the main components of SQR and their interrelationships)
- The databases supported by SQR
- Operating systems and platforms that SQR can run under
- SQR versions and releases

1.1 SQR architecture

Since Brio Technology became the SQR vendor, the names of some components have change. To ensure consistency with the previous edition of this book, we will keep SQR in the names of components that used to have this word in their names, but will name all newly added components the same as Brio calls them.

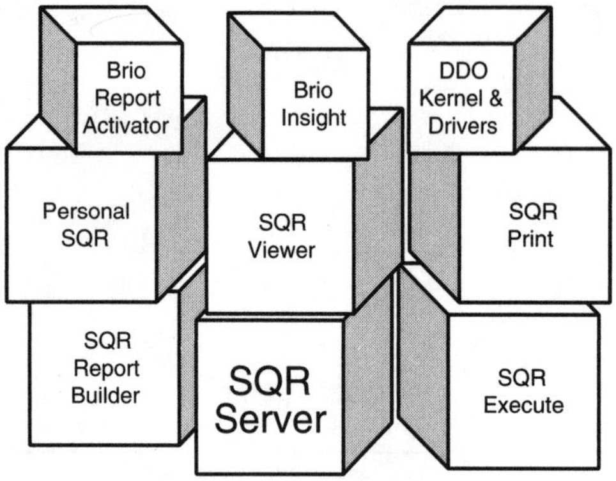

Figure 1.1 SQR main components

SQR components include SQR Server, Personal SQR, SQR Report Viewer, SQR Print, SQR Execute, SQR Report Builder (formerly SQR Workbench [SWRW]), Brio Report Activator, Brio Insight, DDO Kernel, and a set of DDO drivers (figure 1.1).

The Windows version of the SQR Server allows you to run SQR programs on your client machine under MS-DOS, Windows or Windows NT. SQR programs can be submitted from the operating system command line or via the SQRW Dialog Box. The program output can be directed to a printer, to a printer-specific file (or LIS file), to a printer independent file (SPF file), which later can be viewed via the SQR Viewer, to an Adobe PDF (Portable Document File) file, to a CSV (comma separate values) file, or to an HTML file.

The non-Windows versions of SQR Server are used to submit SQR programs on the server from the server operating system command line. Similarly to the Windows version, the program output can be directed to a printer, to a printer-specific file (*LIS* file), to a printer independent file (SPF file), to a PDF file, to a CSV file, or to an HTML file. The printerindependent files generated on server can be viewed via the SQR Report Viewer on Windows only.

Personal SQR is a single-user Windows-based emulation of SQR Server used for local reporting, technical training, or testing SQR programs prior to their deployment.

SQR Report Viewer (also known as *Brio Report Viewer*) is a Windows product that is used to view reports online. The reports must be generated in an SPF format. SPF reports can be generated on either client or server but can be viewed only on the client under Windows or Windows NT.

SQR Print is used to convert reports generated in SPF format to printer-dependent files (LIS files) that can be directed to a printer.

SQR Execute is a run-time version of SQR. It allows you to execute previously compiled SQR programs (sometimes, called SQT files) thereby eliminating the need to combine both compile and run stages in one step.

SQR Report Builder (also known as *Brio Report Builder*, formerly *SQR Workbench* or *VisualSQRIBE*) for Windows provides application developers, database administrators, and power users with a graphical development environment for rapidly building SQR applications using simple drag-and-drop facilities.

Brio Report Activator (formerly *InSQRIBE for SQR*) is a set of three ActiveX components that allow programmers to embed SQR functionality (print, view, or execute) into customer applications.

Brio Insight is a web browser plug-in that provides optional Brio interactive analysis capabilities for data delivered within SQR HTML output.

DDO Kernel and DDO drivers support Brio DDO (Direct Data Object) technology that may be optionally installed with SQR Server. DDO objects are used by SQR Server to access data from various relational and non-relational data sources. DDO drivers are tuned to read specific relational databases, ODBC, JDBC, as well as CSV files, XML data, multi-dimensional OLAP sources, OLEDB (Microsoft ADO OLEDB Client), and SAP BAPIs.

Figure 1.2 illustrates the interaction among SQR components.

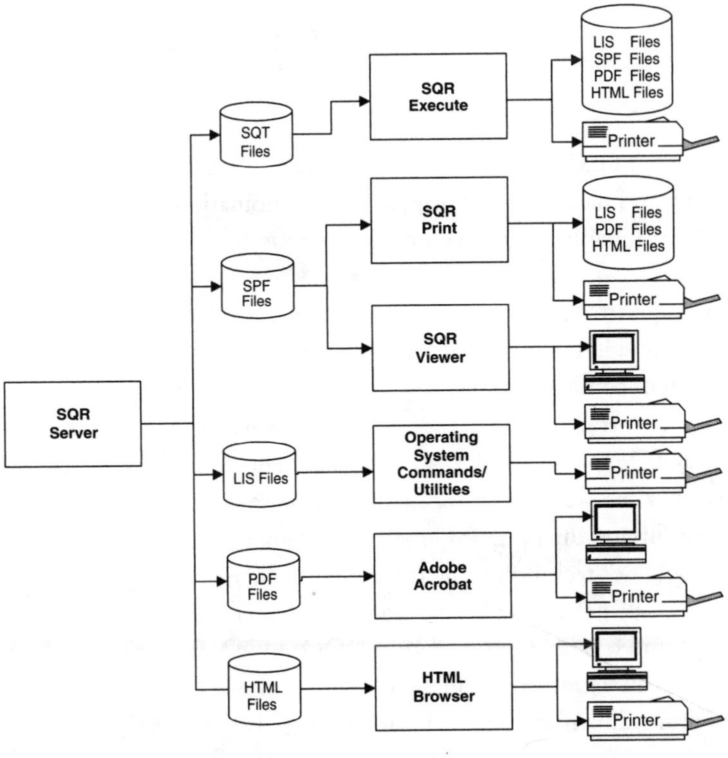

Figure 1.2 Interaction among different SQR components

1.2 Database support

SQR products are available for use with all major databases. The list of the databases includes Oracle, Sybase, Microsoft SQL Server, IBM DB2 (on mainframe and Windows/Windows NT), Centura SQLBase, Informix, Ingres, Red Brick, Rdb, and AllBase (figure 1.3).

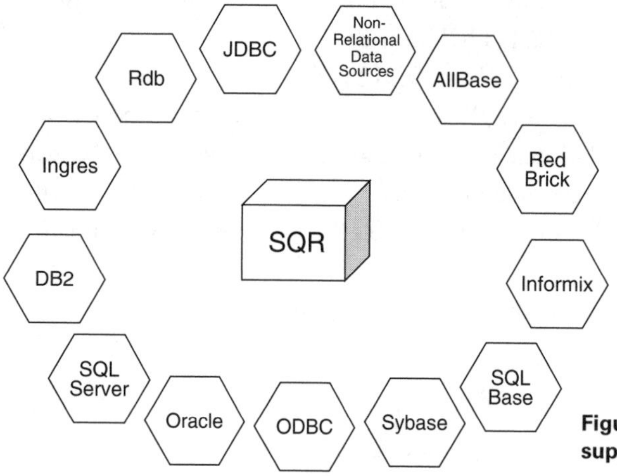

Figure 1.3 Databases supported by SQR

SQR native drivers ensure maximum performance for data extraction. SQR Server is optimized for more than 100 database/operating system combinations, with features such as direct array access and manipulation, as well as dynamic SQL support for both columns and tables.

In addition, SQR supports connections with Open Database Connectivity (ODBC) and JDBC, thus providing a potential for a further expansion of the available RDBMS and operating system combination list.

Native SQR language constructions that support database access are universal for all databases, which makes SQR programs database-independent. This does not mean that SQR program developers are restricted from using database-specific add-ons that can be instrumental in simplifying the program logic and improving data access performance. In such cases, a number of techniques are available to reduce or completely eliminate database dependency while preserving the optimal program efficiency.

New feature in SQR 5 and 6 is its support of Brio DDO. DDO drivers are used by SQR Server to access data from various relational and non-relational data sources such as CSV files, XML data, multi-dimensional OLAP sources (e.g., Essbase), OLEDB, and SAP R/3 BAPIs.

1.3 Operating system support

SQR Server runs on a wide variety of both desktop and enterprise operating systems, including MS-DOS, OS/2, Windows, Windows NT, UNIX, AS/400, VAX/VMS, MVS and, most recently, Red Hat Linux (figure 1.4).

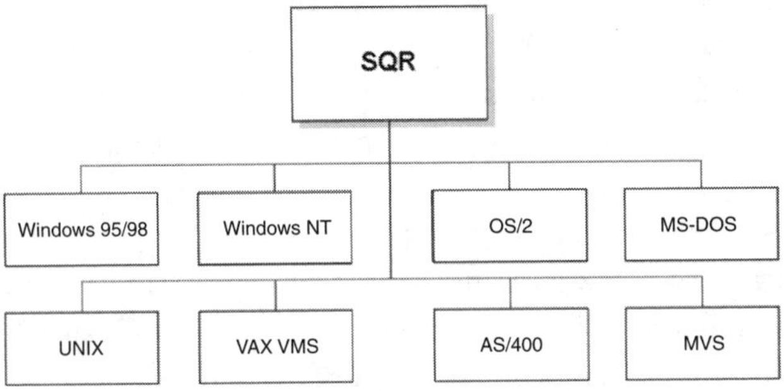

Figure 1.4 Operating systems supported by SQR

SQR programs are not distributed in the form of platform-dependent executables. They can be easily moved between platforms either at source level or as pre-compiled pseudo-code modules. All SQR commands, directives, and operators are platform-transparent and require no changes when the programs are moved across platforms. At the same time, programmers are free to invoke any operating system's specific commands or utilities if they feel the benefits of platform independence are outweighed by other considerations such as performance, ease of maintenance, or the need to integrate their programs into certain specific environments.

1.3.1 What's new in the recent releases

SQR products are rapidly changing. Release after release, the SQR vendor (presently, Brio Technology) keeps adding new features and eliminating bugs and inconsistencies.

Version 3 introduced SQR to the world of graphics by bringing in the `Declare-Chart`, `Print-Chart`, `Declare-Image`, `Print-Image`, and `Print-Bar-Code` commands. Another dramatic change was to allow multiple report programs. This change was implemented with another series of newly introduced commands: `Declare-Report` and `Use-Report`, as well as by adding new parameters to already existed commands such as the `For-Reports` parameter in the `Begin-Heading`, `Begin-Footing`, `Declare-Printer`, `Declare-Procedure`, and `Use-Procedure` commands.

Version 3 also added a number of useful built-in functions, including a newly introduced class of file manipulation functions (`delete()`, `exists()`, and `rename()`), the `array()` function, and a very useful `getenv()` function.

Other changes included allowing multiple report layouts (the `Declare-Layout` command), dynamic printer type change at run time (the `Alter-Printer` command), and a number of new printing options like the `Column` command; checking the status of input/output commands; invoking stored procedures (Ingres, Sybase, and Microsoft SQL Server), and so on.

Version 4 was equally revolutionary. First, it catapulted SQR into the cyberspace by Internet-enabling this product. The program developers were given a choice between an automatic conversion of SQR-generated reports without changing the source programs (by using the `PRINTER:HT` command line flag) or using a number of SQR HTML procedures to write programs specifically designed for the Internet, thereby taking advantage of the advanced HTML features.

Second, this version broke the language barriers by introducing SQR locales or sets of national preferences for language, currency, and presentation of dates and numbers. The `Alter-Locale` command introduced in Version 4 can be used to dynamically switch from one locale to another or to override certain characteristics of the current locale.

Third, the version introduced explicit declaration of SQR variables by using the `Declare-Variable` command. This allowed for the addition of date variables, a completely new variable type, and for the splitting the numeric variables into decimal, float, and integer variables. In conjunction with this change, version 4 brought in `Money`, `Date`, and `Number` default edit format masks.

Along with the date variables, came date built-in functions that support a wide range of string-to-date, date-to-string, and date and time manipulations. These functions included: `dateadd()`, `datediff()`, `datenow()`, `datetostr()`, and `strtodate()`. Prior to Version 4, programmers had to use database-specific SQL functions to handle date manipulations.

Other improvements in version 4 included adding GIF and JPEG image files to the list of available image file types.

Starting from Version 4.2, SQR can work with double-byte characters. The `ENCODING` environmental variable can be set to ASCII, SJIS, or JEUC. The two new double-byte string manipulation SQR commands, `Mbtosbs` and `Sbtombs`, carry out double-byte to single-byte and single-byte to double-byte conversions respectively. A number of built-in functions were added to facilitate double-byte string processing including `instrb()`, `lengthb()`, `substrb()`, `to_multi_byte()`, and `to_single_byte()`.

Two other unrelated to multiple-byte manipulation functions were added: `roman()`—converts its argument to lower-case roman numerals, and `wrapdepth()`—returns the number of print lines required to wrap a string.

The HTML-related improvements in version 4.2 included the new `Declare-Toc` and `Toc-Entry` commands. These commands allow developers of Internet-enabled reports to customize the table of contents portions of their reports. Without these commands, SQR generates standard tables of contents with basic page navigation for any report. In conjunction with this change, a number of SQR commands such as `Begin-Heading`, `Begin-Footing`, and `Declare-Report` were modified to include references to the related tables of contents.

The selection of SQR output formats was improved under version 4.3 by adding the CSV and Adobe PDF files.

Version 5 added support for Unicode (UCS-2 and UTF-8). All character set encodings are supported by one set of executables.

The HTML support was improved with more options of controlling the enhanced HTML output, including the support of HTML 4.

Starting from version 5, SQR supports Brio DDO. DDO objects are used by SQR Server to access data from various relational and non-relational data sources such as CSV files, XML data, multi-dimensional OLAP sources, OLEDB, and SAP BAPIs. This made SQR even a more robust tool in enterprise reporting. The same SQR operators can now be used to select and process data from a much wider variety of sources. SQR's strength of combining data row selection with procedural logic allows SQR programmers to use existing reports to query new data sources with minimal changes to the report's logic.

As a part of the DDO support, a new type of variables, list variables, can be used to create arrays in memory. These arrays can be passed as parameters when making selections from various DDO sources.

Another important feature of version 5 is the ability to generate the BQD (Brio Query Data) output. Programmers can place a special BQD icon in the navigation bar of their HTML output. Clicking on this icon invokes the Brio Query client that should be installed on your machine.

Version 6 brought expanded DDO functionality, different multi-byte encodings for the database, input files, output files, and report files and color printing support.

The expanded DDO functionality includes more database/platform combinations for both relational and non-relational datasources, datasource-specific aggregation functions for DDO-JDBC sources and multiple discrete connections to a given datasource.

SQR 6 supports random access to specific row elements in SQR list variables. You can now modify a specific row element of any list item.

You can define default colors globally and redefine colors using the RGB (red, green, blue) coding schema. You can also create your own color palette and use it when printing graphical charts.

Starting with this version, you can use a new SQR command, `Alter-Report`, to change report's heading or footing while report is running.

Another important improvement is a new keyword `Delay` of the `Print` command. This new keyword allows you to go back and change the value of a printed variable in the output buffer.

A new SQR function, `replace()`, will help you to replace all substrings within a string with a new value.

KEY POINTS

1 SQR components include SQR Server, SQR Viewer, SQR Print, SQR Execute, and SQR Workbench for Windows.

2 SQR products are available for use with all major databases including Oracle, Sybase, Microsoft SQL Server, DB2, SQLBase, Informix, Ingres, Red Brick, Rdb, and AllBase.

3 SQR server runs on a wide variety of both desktop and enterprise operating systems.

4 SQR programs are distributed at source level or as pre-compiled pseudo-code modules.

5 All SQR commands and functions are platform-transparent and require no changes when SQR programs are moved across platforms.

CHAPTER 2

Structured Query Language

IN THIS CHAPTER

- The concepts of the relational database model and the Structured Query Language or SQL
- A set of sample tables to be used in examples throughout this book
- SQL queries, subqueries, and table joins
- Relational and Boolean operators and aggregate functions
- Different techniques to improve the SQL query performance
- Referential integrity when table updates are done

SQR works with relational databases. It is therefore important to discuss the concepts of the relational database model and how information is retrieved from relational tables using the Structured Query Language (SQL). The usage of SQL statements in SQR programs is common practice, and SQR programmers with a solid understanding of SQL have a definite advantage when it comes to writing effective programs and reports.

This chapter is a brief description of SQL and is being presented to help readers with their understanding of SQR. Readers with solid SQL knowledge do not have to read this chapter. However, we suggest that every reader be familiar with the sample tables presented here since these tables are used in many examples throughout the book.

Please keep in mind that any kind of comprehensive coverage of SQL and relational databases is beyond the scope of this book. There are many books on this subject presently available on the market. Another important point is that, when discussing access to relational databases, we will not refer to any specific system like DB2, Oracle, or Sybase, but will rather try to present the subject in terms of the ANSI SQL, the subset of the SQL language defined by the American National Standards Institute. In some cases, however, we will be referring to certain product-specific features of SQL when it is necessary to use SQL expressions that are not supported by the ANSI SQL.

2.1 Relational database model

The relational database model concept was first proposed by Dr. E. Codd in his well known paper "A Relational Model of Data for Large Shared Data Banks" published in the Association for Computing Machinery magazine "Communications of the ACM" in 1970. However, until the mid-1980s, no commercial RDBMS existed on the market. The first commercial RDBMS products were offered by IBM under the name of DB2 and by Relational Software (now Oracle) under the name of Oracle. Later, a number of other companies joined the club of RDBMS vendors. Presently, the most significant players are IBM, Oracle, Sybase, Microsoft, and Informix.

The relational database model represents data as a set of tables. Tables are logical structures made up of columns and rows. Information in different tables may be interdependent. In other words, certain tables may have logical relationships to each other by having the same values in the data elements corresponding to similar columns. Any RDBMS product includes an engine to create, maintain, update, and query the table elements.

Let us consider an example of a few related tables. Since we will be using this set of tables in the examples throughout this book, it is important for our readers to become familiar with these tables. We modeled our tables after a few core tables that belong to the PeopleSoft HRMS system. When creating the tables, we included only those columns that were essential to run our examples. Therefore, while readers may find a resemblance between our sample tables and their PeopleSoft counterparts, the two sets of tables are different. There is a more detailed description of our sample tables in appendix A.

Take a look at figure 2.1. Every table here has an identifying column or a group of columns called *primary key*. In addition, a table may have columns whose values are also present in one or more columns of another table. These columns are called *foreign keys*. Primary and foreign keys help to maintain logical relationships between different tables. For example, the `Personal_Data` table has a primary key column `Emplid`. The

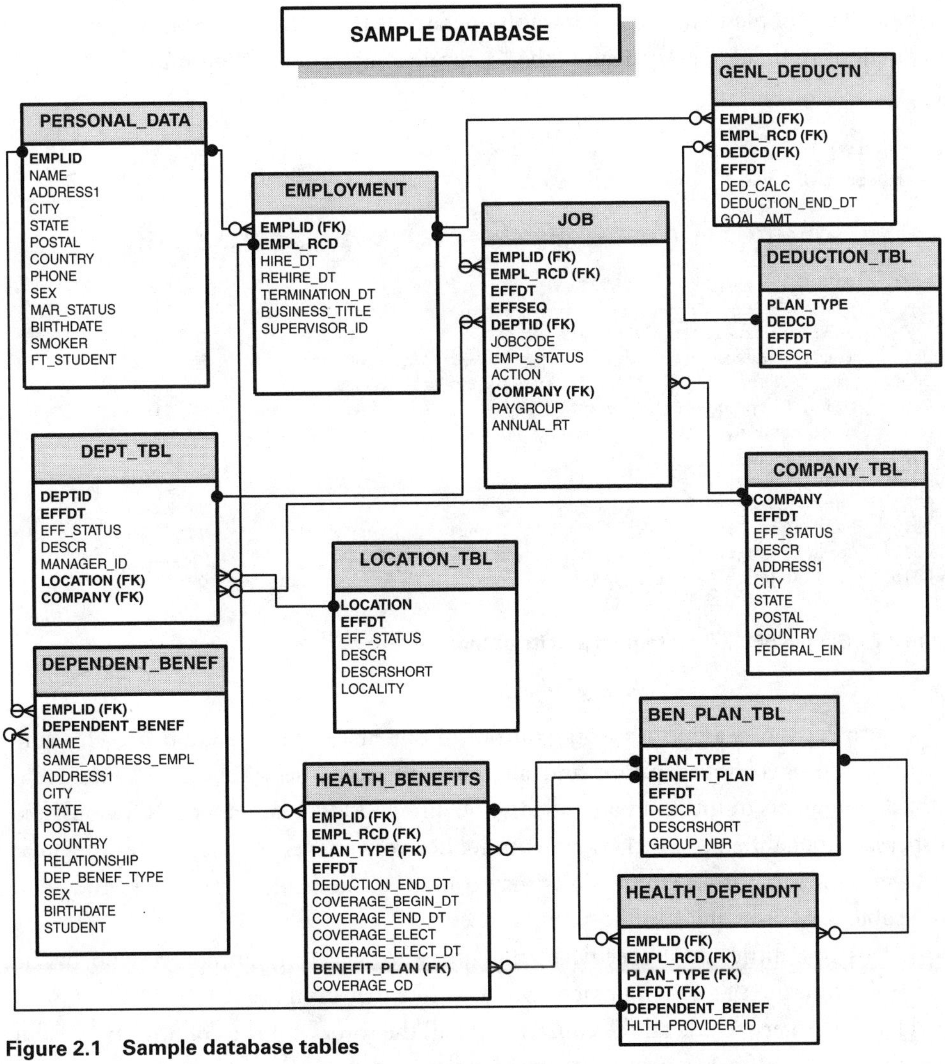

Figure 2.1 Sample database tables

Employment table has a primary key that is made up of two columns: Emplid and Empl_Rcd. At the same time, the Emplid column is a foreign key to this table. This column connects the Employment table to the Personal_Data table. The columns that participate in a logical relationship do not have to have the same name, but this is usually a convenient method of naming such columns.

2.2 Simple SELECT statements

SQL is a set of programming operators that support access to the elements of a relational database. The simplest and most common operator is the SELECT operator. We will use this operator to build a query against the Personal_Data table (figure 2.2).

```
SELECT *
FROM Personal_Data
```

```
EMPLID   NAME               ADDRESS1              CITY            ST POSTAL
-------- ------------------ --------------------- --------------- -- -------
KC0006   Jubinville,Pierre  3888 Rue St. Jean     Quebec City     QC G1P3C1
KC0007   Trudeau,Susan      28 Saunders Street    Fredericton     NB E3B1N1
KC0008   Wilson,Kenneth Joh 5755 Sackville Street Halifax         NS B3H2C9
KC0009   Mills,Stephanie A  9 Grafton Street      Charlottetown   PE C1A1K3
KC0010   Howe,Anthony R     38 Queen's Road       St. John's      NF A1C2A5
KC0011   Lau,Patrick        P.O. Box 262          Fort Simpson    NT X0E0N0
KC0012   Quency,Nancy J     P.O. Box 1998         Iqaluit         NN X0A0H0
KC0013   Tucker,Margaret    125 Main Street       Whitehorse      YT Y1A2B5
KC0014   Henderson,David M  2532 Cambie Street    Vancouver       BC V5Z2V2
KC0015   Campbell,Barry Rob 4928 Wildwood Place   Toronto         ON M8A1D3
KC0016   Vaillancourt,Paule 119 Rue Dalhousie     Quebec City     QC G1K9C8
```

Figure 2.2 Simple SELECT statement and its output

Figure 2.2 shows a portion of the output of our first SELECT statement. This simple query selects all the columns and all the rows from the Personal_Data table. SELECT statements of this kind are called unqualified SELECT statements. Obviously, in most cases, unqualified SELECT statements are not very convenient because a) they may produce too much output (some tables may contain millions of rows), and b) they may not be able to address any specific business needs.

Let us be a little more specific in our query by selecting employees who live in Montreal. Now, the SELECT statement will look like that in figure 2.3.

Here, the query selects all the columns and all the rows with the column City value equal to 'Montreal'. Our output has now become more manageable!

```
SELECT *
FROM Personal_Data
WHERE City = 'Montreal';
```

```
EMPLID NAME                   ADDRESS1                   CITY     STATE  POSTAL
------ ---------------------- -------------------------- -------- ------ --------
KC0019 Desmarais,Jean-Pierre  455 St. Catherine Street   Montreal QC     H2L2C4
KC0024 Maissoneuve,Louise     404 Rue Saint-Jean-Baptist Montreal QC     H2Y2Z7
KC0030 Millier,Joseph G       115 Rue de la Gauchetiere  Montreal QC     H2Z1Y2
KC0031 Saint-Amand,Marcel     357 Rue McGill             Montreal QC     H2Y2E8
```

Figure 2.3 A qualified SELECT statement

In most real projects, tables have many columns and selecting all table columns in one query may produce too much output. Another disadvantage of selecting all columns is that when a particular table structure is changed due to a column addition or deletion (yes, SQL allows you to do this!), the output of the same `SELECT` statement will also change.

The `SELECT` statement in figure 2.4 retrieves only columns `Name`, `Birthdate`, `Address1`, and `City` from the `Personal_Data` table. It also sorts the output rows by Name in ascending alphabetical order. By the way, when you list columns in the `SELECT` statement, you can list them in any order, not just in the order they appear in the table structure. Please note that in the `WHERE` clause, you can use columns that are not listed among the selected columns in the `SELECT` statement.

In some cases, the `SELECT` statement may produce duplicate values in the output rows. For example, let us select column `Supervisor_Id` values from the `Employment` table (figure 2.5).

```
SELECT Name,Birthdate,Address1,City
FROM Personal_Data
WHERE City = 'Montreal'
ORDER BY Name;
```

```
NAME                   BIRTHDATE ADDRESS1                    CITY
---------------------- --------- --------------------------- ----------
Desmarais,Jean-Pierre  14-MAR-60 455 St. Catherine Street    Montreal
Maissoneuve,Louise     03-MAY-67 404 Rue Saint-Jean-Baptiste Montreal
Millier,Joseph G       18-MAY-67 115 Rue de la Gauchetiere   Montreal
Saint-Amand,Marcel     26-AUG-51 357 Rue McGill              Montreal
```

Figure 2.4 Selecting only certain columns

```
SELECT Supervisor_Id
FROM Employment
ORDER BY Supervisor_Id;
```

```
SUPERVISOR_
-----------
KD0001
KF0001
KF0001
KF0001
KF0001
KF0002
KF0003
KF0003
KF0003
KF0003
KF0004
```

Figure 2.5 Duplicate rows in SELECT output

Our `SELECT` statement now produces duplicate rows because the `Employment` table has multiple rows with the same `Supervisor_Id` (some supervisors have more than one subordinate). If we want only unique records in the output (i.e., if we want to produce a list of unique `Supervisor_id` values), we can use the `SELECT` statement shown in figure 2.6.

```
SELECT DISTINCT Supervisor_Id
FROM Employment
ORDER BY Supervisor_Id;
```

```
SUPERVISOR_
-----------

KB0001
KB0002
KD0001
KF0001
KF0002
KF0003
KF0004
KF0008
KF0011
KG0001
```

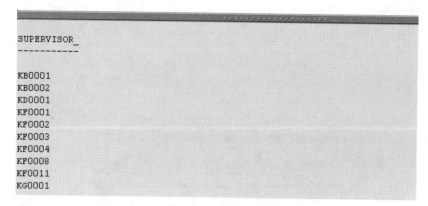

Figure 2.6 Using SELECT DISTINCT to eliminate duplicate rows

2.3 Using relational and Boolean operators in the WHERE clause

Selection conditions in the WHERE clause must, in many cases, meet a number of complex criteria. Relational and Boolean operators can be used to refine your SELECT statements and make them rather sophisticated. The following relational operators can be used in the WHERE clause: = (equal to), > (greater than), < (less than). You can also use combinations of two relational operators. For example, you can use >= (greater than or equal) or <> (not equal). In addition to the relational operators, you can also use the following Boolean operators: AND, OR, NOT. Let us consider the selection in figure 2.7.

```
SELECT Name,Birthdate,Address1,City,State
FROM Personal_Data
WHERE Birthdate >= '01-JAN-1944'
  AND Birthdate <= '31-DEC-1954'
  AND State = 'CA'
  AND NOT City ='Los Angeles';
```

```
NAME                 BIRTHDATE ADDRESS1                  CITY         STATE
-------------------- --------- ------------------------- ------------ ------
Jones,Susan          20-MAR-54 Box 200090                Castroville  CA
Mapin,George N       10-DEC-51 4816 Diaspo Blvd          San Ramon    CA
Stankowski,Martha    14-MAY-52 11308 Wildflower Lane     Grass Valley CA
Wicker,Frank         08-JAN-51 31 Jefferson St.          Napa         CA
Fraas,William        08-JAN-51 310 Dontell St.           Kernville    CA
Gardner,John         11-JUN-52 444 Glendale Ave.         Moraga       CA
Andrews,Frank        19-OCT-47 1303 Waverly Drive        Oakland      CA

7 rows selected.
```

Figure 2.7 Relational and Boolean operators in the SELECT statement

Here we select employees who were born between 1944 and 1954, reside in the state of California, and live outside of Los Angeles.

Note In this query, we use the date format of dd-mon-yyyy. Different RDBMS vendors use vendor-specific date formats, for example, 12/31/1970 can be coded '31-DEC-70' or '31-DEC-1970' for Oracle and '1970-12-31' for DB2.

You can also use parentheses in the WHERE clause expressions as in figure 2.8.

Another flavor of the WHERE clause is the LIKE operator which supports wildcard selections (figure 2.9).

```
SELECT Name,Birthdate,Address1,City,State
FROM Personal_Data
WHERE Mar_Status = 'M'
  AND (State = 'CA' OR State = 'CT');
```

```
NAME                 BIRTHDATE ADDRESS1             CITY           STATE
-------------------- --------- -------------------- -------------- ------
Roth,Calvin          24-FEB-69 5025 Sanders         Fresno         CA
Santos,Antonio       09-AUG-72 4689 Z Street        Sacramento     CA
Murkami,Bill         12-AUG-61 92 Pratt Street      Hartford       CT
McKinley,Larry J     03-MAR-40 1229 Glenwood Rd     Livermore      CA
Stankowski,Martha    14-MAY-52 11308 Wildflower Lane Grass Valley  CA
Wicker,Frank         08-JAN-51 31 Jefferson St.     Napa           CA
Fraas,William        08-JAN-51 310 Dontell St.      Kernville      CA
Tillotson,James                89 Jersey Street, #6 San Francisco  CA
Gardner,John         11-JUN-52 444 Glendale Ave.    Moraga         CA
Andrews,Frank        19-OCT-47 1303 Waverly Drive   Oakland        CA

10 rows selected.
```

Figure 2.8 Using parentheses in the WHERE clause

```
SELECT Emplid,Name
FROM Personal_Data
WHERE Name LIKE '%Frank';
```

```
EMPLID      NAME
----------- ---------------------
KUI001      Wicker,Frank
KUTR03      Andrews,Frank
```

Figure 2.9 Using the LIKE operator in the WHERE clause

As you can see, the `LIKE` operator allows you to select rows based on only partial knowledge of a column's content. In our case, by placing the percent sign in front of a search argument, we tell SQL to look for all values of column `Name` that are a combination of an unlimited number of any characters followed by the string "Frank." The query in figure 2.9 helps us find all employees with first name Frank although, strictly speaking, "Frank" could be a part of the last name. The percent sign could have been put anywhere in the search argument, not just at the beginning. The drawback of this kind of wildcard search is a poor search performance because the system does not know the exact starting position of the string to be searched. If you know for sure how many positions can be ignored during the search and where exactly these positions are, you can simply replace these positions with the underscores.

2.4 Aggregate functions

Aggregate functions apply to the entire `SELECT` statement output (also called the "result set"), not to specific rows. Each aggregate function summarizes information selected from a number of rows into one value. Here is a list of these functions:

`SUM(column name)` calculates the arithmetic sum of all selected values of a column. This function can work only with columns of the numeric format.

`AVG(column name)` calculates the average value of all selected values of a column. As with the `SUM` function, `AVG` can work only with columns of the numeric format.

`COUNT` counts the number of selected rows. There are different ways to use the `COUNT` function in `SELECT` statements and you will see some examples of this function in this chapter. `COUNT` can work with columns of any format.

`MAX(column name)` produces the largest of all selected values of a column. This function works with columns of any format.

`MIN(column name)` produces the smallest of all selected values of a column. This function works with columns of any format.

When functions `MAX` and `MIN` are applied to a non-numeric column, they produce the largest or the smallest binary value of the column.

In order to better illustrate the use of aggregate functions, let us discuss the `GROUP BY` clause. It allows you to define subsets of the `SELECT` statement output based on the values of a certain column. The query shown in figure 2.10 counts employees in each state. (In this query, we will process the Canadian provinces in the same way as the U.S. states.)

While it is possible to have multiple rows for some of the states, the query returns only one row per each state value. Please also note that we are ordering the output by `State` even though `State` is not included in the `SELECT` statement list.

Sometimes, you need to impose certain restrictions on the selection results obtained with the help of an aggregate function. This can be done by using the `HAVING` clause

```
SELECT COUNT(*)
FROM Personal_Data
GROUP BY State
ORDER BY State;
```

```
  COUNT(*)
----------
        22
         1
         3
         7
         9
         9
         1
         7
         3
         4
         5
```

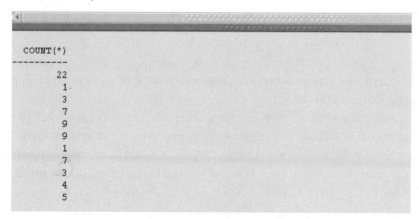

Figure 2.10 Using the aggregate function COUNT

which allows you to specify a logical expression that includes only certain aggregate rows in the query result set. Similarly to the logical expression in the `WHERE` clause, the expression in `HAVING` may include relational and Boolean operators. What is the difference between the `WHERE` and `HAVING` clauses? The `WHERE` clause limits the row selection prior to applying the aggregate functions. The `HAVING` clause applies to the results of the already-made selection thereby further refining the result set. Unlike the `WHERE` clause, the logical expression in the `HAVING` clause cannot include columns or aggregate functions that are not included in the `SELECT` statement.

In figure 2.11, we make some modifications to the previous query. We include the `State` column into the selection and use the `HAVING` clause to filter out states with only one employee. As you can see, the result set does not include one row with the `COUNT(*) = 1`.

```
SELECT State,COUNT(*)
FROM Personal_Data
GROUP BY State
HAVING COUNT(*) > 1
ORDER BY State;
```

```
STATE    COUNT(*)
------ ----------
               22
28              3
33              7
75              9
92              9
AB              7
AK              3
AL              4
AN              5
AZ              6
BA              3
```

Figure 2.11 Using the HAVING clause

If we would like to count the number of U.S. states with at least one employee, our query will look like that in figure 2.12.

Now, let us use the `MAX` aggregate function. The `Job` table contains multiple records per employee, and each record represents the employee status at a particular moment (not necessarily for a particular date because it is possible to have multiple records within the same date). If we need to know the last date of termination for an employee with `Emplid = 8146`, the query in figure 2.13 will do the job.

```
SELECT COUNT(DISTINCT State)
FROM Personal_Data
WHERE Country = 'USA';
```

```
COUNT(DISTINCTSTATE)
--------------------
                  53
```

Figure 2.12
A combination of COUNT and DISTINCT helped us to eliminate duplicate rows in the output and produce only one record.

```
SELECT MAX(Effdt)
FROM Job
WHERE Empl_Status = 'T'
  AND Emplid = 'C10001';
```

```
MAX(EFFDT
---------
15-JUL-00
```

Figure 2.13
Using the aggregate function MAX

We can use the same table to demonstrate how to use the AVG aggregate function (see figure 2.14).

```
SELECT Paygroup,AVG(Annual_Rt)
FROM Job
WHERE Empl_Status = 'A'
  AND Effdt BETWEEN '01-JAN-1990' AND '31-DEC-1995'
GROUP BY Paygroup
ORDER BY Paygroup;
```

```
PAY AVG(ANNUAL_RT)
--- --------------
KU2        40586.6
KU3          26000
KU4     31797.2571
KU6          70302
KU7     55188.5714
KU8     52965.3333
LBS       41196.48
LNP        60715.2
PAB          38300
PAM          39000
PJB          47000
```

Figure 2.14 Using the aggregate function AVG

The query produces a list of average annual rates for each pay group for the period between 1990 and 1995. We have to limit our selection to active employees only. Please note that the logical operator `BETWEEN` is used instead of two comparison operators to limit the value of the `Effdt` column.

2.5 Subqueries

The `SELECT` statements can be nested within one query. Usually, one query is used to perform the data selection while the result of another query execution determines the selection criteria for the first query. More than one table can be used in nested queries.

If we need to produce a list of all employees who were hired in 1996, the nested query shown in figure 2.15 will be of help.

```
SELECT Name
FROM Personal_Data
WHERE Emplid IN
  (SELECT Emplid
   FROM   Employment
   WHERE Hire_Dt BETWEEN '01-JAN-1996' AND '31-DEC-1996');
```

```
NAME
--------------------------------------------------
Jones,Susan
Nichta,Issac
Bergsten,Darlene
Aquilino,Beatrice
Justin,Clare
Hunsberger,Carlton
Brown,Jessica
Brown,Jennifer L
Gonzalez Izquierdo,Maria
De la Cruz Maroto,Angela
Breton,Jean-Claude
```

Figure 2.15 Nested SELECT statements

Let us analyze this query. The inner `SELECT` statement generates a list of employee Ids with the hire date within the year of 1996. This generated list is used to limit the output of the outer `SELECT` statement. Later in this chapter, we will see that the same result could have been achieved by executing just one `SELECT` statement against both `Personal_Data` and `Employment`, something called "table join." Please note that we use operator `IN` instead of an equal operator in the `WHERE` clause of the outer `SELECT` statement. This is because the inner `SELECT` might produce multiple values of column `Emplid`.

2.6 Table joins

One of the most important and exciting features of the relational databases is that you can join tables in your query based on the values of certain columns in these tables. SQL allows you to use multiple tables in one `SELECT` statement, taking advantage of logical relationships between the tables.

Consider the `SELECT` statement shown in figure 2.16. As you can see, the output of this query looks rather strange. This is called *a Cartesian product.* It contains all possible combinations of the rows from each table. In order to make sense of our join we need to refine our query.

```
SELECT Name,Hire_Dt
FROM Personal_Data,Employment
WHERE State = 'NY';
```

```
NAME                 HIRE_DT
-------------------- ---------
Baran,Charles        15-JUN-96
Parsons,Jean         15-JUN-96
Grafton,Ken          15-JUN-96
Aliverdi,Reza        15-JUN-96
Erickson,Arthur      15-JUN-96
Locherty,Betty       15-JUN-96
Di Benedetto,Rhonda  15-JUN-96
Rhett,Diandra        15-JUN-96
Smith,Maggie         15-JUN-96
Walker,Gail K        15-JUN-96
Ouren,Tom            15-JUN-96
```

Figure 2.16 A Cartesian product of two tables

In figure 2.17, the query output looks more intelligent. We just join our two tables by the key column `Emplid` in such a way that only rows with the same values of column `Emplid` in both tables are selected. Note that key columns used in the table join do not have to have the same name.

In our example, table `Personal_Data` and table `Employment` have a column with the same name, `Emplid`. Please note how we managed to differentiate between these columns from different tables by prefixing the column name with the table name. Unfortunately, this made our `WHERE` clause too lengthy. SQL allows us to simplify the `SELECT` statements by using table name aliases. With table name aliases, our query will look like that in figure 2.18.

```
SELECT Name,Hire_Dt
FROM Personal_Data,Employment
WHERE State = 'NY'
  AND Personal_Data.Emplid = Employment.Emplid;
```

```
NAME                 HIRE_DT
-------------------- ---------
Baran,Charles        15-JAN-82
Parsons,Jean         12-MAR-88
Grafton,Ken          02-APR-80
Aliverdi,Reza        22-MAR-85
Erickson,Arthur      12-MAY-87
Locherty,Betty       07-APR-89
Di Benedetto,Rhonda  11-OCT-90
Di Benedetto,Rhonda  12-MAR-93
Rhett,Diandra        21-OCT-90
Rhett,Diandra        12-MAR-93
Smith,Maggie         01-JAN-96
```

Figure 2.17 A table join

```
SELECT Name,Hire_Dt
FROM Personal_Data a,Employment b
WHERE State = 'NY'
  AND a.Emplid = b.Emplid;
```

```
NAME                 HIRE_DT
-------------------- ---------
Baran,Charles        15-JAN-82
Parsons,Jean         12-MAR-88
Grafton,Ken          02-APR-80
Aliverdi,Reza        22-MAR-85
Erickson,Arthur      12-MAY-87
Locherty,Betty       07-APR-89
Di Benedetto,Rhonda  11-OCT-90
Di Benedetto,Rhonda  12-MAR-93
Rhett,Diandra        21-OCT-90
Rhett,Diandra        12-MAR-93
Smith,Maggie         01-JAN-96
```

Figure 2.18 Using table name aliases

The aliases are especially useful when joining the same table. (Yes, a table can be joined to itself!) As with any other table join, when a table is joined to itself, each row of this table combines with itself and with every other row in the table. Then, assuming we use the proper WHERE clause, only certain rows are selected to the output of the query. The query in figure 2.19 joins table Employment to itself in order to produce a list of employees and their respective supervisors.

```
SELECT a.Emplid "EMPLOYEE ID",a.Business_Title "EMPLOYEE TITLE",
b.Emplid "MANAGER ID", b.Business_Title "MANAGER TITLE"
FROM Employment a, Employment b
WHERE a.Supervisor_id=b.Emplid
AND a.Empl_Rcd=0 and b.Empl_Rcd=0
AND a.Business_Title <>' '
AND b.Business_Title <>' ';
```

```
EMPLOYEE ID EMPLOYEE TITLE               MANAGER ID  MANAGER TITLE
----------- ------------------------ ----------- ------------------------
KF0021      Data Entry Clerk             KF0004      Manager HR
KF0022      Data Entry Clerk             KF0004      Manager HR
KF0023      Administrative Assistant     KF0004      Manager HR
KU0009      Data Entry Clerk             KU0042      Administrative Assistant
KU0035      Systems Analyst              KU0010      Payroll Clerk
KU0042      Administrative Assistant     KU0006      Manager-Employee Relation
KU0045      Administrative Assistant     KU0050      Manager-Employee Relation
KU0055      Manager-Employee Relation    KU0004      Director-Sales
```

Figure 2.19 Joining a table to itself

2.7 Table updates

SQL includes operators to support table field value updates: `INSERT`, `UPDATE`, and `DELETE`. These three operators are called Data Manipulation Language (DML) commands. Although SQR is used, for the most part, to generate reports, it supports the usage of DML commands.

The `INSERT` operator inserts rows into a table from the program's working storage or from another table. Figure 2.20's `INSERT` statement adds a row to table `Personal_Data`.

```
INSERT INTO Personal_Data
Values ('8299','John Smith','999 Main Street','Stamford','CT','06904',
'USA','203/111-1111','M','S','01-APR-1965','N','N');
```

```
1 row created.
```

Figure 2.20 Inserting a row into the Personal_Data table

The only output operator `INSERT` generates is the number of inserted rows. We recommend checking this number to make sure the operation was completed as planned. To successfully perform an insertion operation, SQL expects that all inserted column value types match the types that have been previously defined during the table creation. And, of course, the order of fields in the `VALUES` clause must be the same as the column order in the table.

Figure 2.21 illustrates how to insert rows from one table into another table. In this example, the `Employment` table from our sample database is populated with data from the `PS_Employment` table from the PeopleSoft database.

```
INSERT INTO Employment
Select Emplid,Empl_Rcd,Hire_Dt,Rehire_Dt,Termination_Dt,Business_Title,Supervisor_Id
FROM PS_Employment
WHERE Emplid between 'KB0001' and 'KC0001';
```

```
8 rows created.
```

Figure 2.21 Inserting multiple rows from another table

Take a closer look at this example. As you can see, the `SELECT` statement generates the input for `INSERT` from another table. You can limit the selection only to the values you need. This example also demonstrates that you do not have to insert all columns from one table into another one. You can specify only the columns you need. But wait a second! We know that the target table `Employment` has more columns than the ones listed in the `INSERT` statement. What values will be assigned to these columns? The columns not listed in the `INSERT` statement will be assigned their default values. The default values for each column are defined during the table creation stage. Some columns may have no default values and they are assigned special values called `NULL` values.

(Please note that when a table is created, certain columns may be defined as `NOT NULL` columns. This means that these columns cannot be assigned `NULL` values. When an insert operation is performed, all such columns must be listed in the `INSERT` statement.)

If we select the newly inserted rows from the `Employment` table now, we will see that column `Business_title` was assigned spaces even if this column was missing from the `INSERT` column list (figure 2.22).

If there is an insertion operator, is there also a deletion operator? Yes, there is, and it is simply called `DELETE`. It will help us to undo the previous `INSERT` operation (figure 2.23).

Take a close look at figure 2.23. What is the difference between the formats of `INSERT` and `DELETE` operators? The `INSERT` statement names the inserted columns while `DELETE` does not. This is logical. We are deleting the entire rows no matter how many columns these rows have and what the column values are.

```
SELECT Emplid,Hire_Dt,Business_Title,Supervisor_Id
FROM Employment
WHERE Emplid between 'KB0001' and 'KC0001';
```

```
EMPLID     HIRE_DT   BUSINESS_TITLE                 SUPERVISOR_
---------- --------- ------------------------------ ----------
KB0001     01-FEB-97
KB0002     15-APR-97                                KB0001
KB0003     15-SEP-98                                KB0001
KB0004     07-MAR-99                                KB0002
KB0004     01-FEB-00                                KN0007
KB0005     02-JUN-99                                KB0002
KBN001     12-FEB-00                                KB0002
KC0001     01-JAN-90

8 rows selected.
```

Figure 2.22 Column Business_title was assigned a default value (spaces)

```
DELETE FROM Employment
WHERE Emplid BETWEEN 'KB0001' AND 'KC0001';
```

```
8 rows deleted.
```

Figure 2.23 Deleting rows from a table

Note `DELETE` is a powerful and dangerous operation. If your `WHERE` clause is not precise enough, you can delete rows you never intended to delete. In fact, you can easily empty out an entire table! It is often recommended that a `SELECT` statement be executed with the same `WHERE` clause that will be used in the `DELETE` statement and that the selection output be reviewed prior to deletion just to make sure that you are deleting only the rows you want to delete.

We just learned how to insert and delete rows from a table but what if we want to change some column values in certain rows? SQL has the answer and—you guessed it—it is called `UPDATE`. This operator tells the RDBMS what rows are to be updated and what the new values should be. In figure 2.24, with just one SQL statement, we will promote all four data entry clerks to administrative assistants!

```
Update Employment
SET Business_Title='Administrative Assistant'
Where Business_Title='Data Entry Clerk';
```

```
4 rows updated.
```

Figure 2.24 Updating multiple rows

2.8 Referential integrity

We already noticed that the `INSERT`, `DELETE`, and `UPDATE` operators can create a mess if not used carefully. This is especially true when certain tables are logically related. Column value updates in one table may have an unexpected impact on other tables. For example, tables `Personal_Data`, `Job`, and `Employment` have the same column `Emplid`. Table `Personal_Data` is a parent to `Employment`. The `Employment` table is, in turn, a parent to `Job`. This type of relationship is called logical parent-child relationship. This means that rows with the same `Emplid` value in tables `Job` and `Employment` are dependent on rows in `Personal_Data`. Deleting a row from `Personal_Data` makes all rows with the same `Emplid` in the other two tables "orphans." What sense does it make to talk about an annual rate, business title, or job code of a non-existing employee? At the same time, we can, theoretically, delete one record in table `Job` and still keep the table relationship intact.

When a field in a table refers to a field in another table or even in the same table, it is called a *foreign key*; the field to which it refers is called its *primary key*. In our case, `Emplid` in the `Employment` table is a foreign key to the `Personal_Data` table, and `Emplid` in table `Personal_Data` is a primary key. The `Emplid` and `Empl_Rcd` columns in the `Job` table make up a foreign key to the `Employment` table whose primary key includes the two columns with the same names. The names of primary and foreign keys do not have to be the same; this is just a convenient way to emphasize their relationship.

Tables in a database are considered to be in a state of *referential integrity* when all rows with the same foreign key value in a child table refer to one and only one row in the parent table. A row in the `Employment` table can refer only to one row in the `Personal_Data` table. This means that column `Emplid` in `Personal_Data` must have unique values. At the same time, one row in the `Personal_Data` table may be referred to by more than one number of rows in the `Employment` table since one employee can have multiple jobs.

What happens to referential integrity when primary and foreign key values are changed or deleted? In that case, referential integrity can be broken. Therefore, it is necessary to impose certain restrictions on these values. For primary keys, the restrictions are relatively simple. They must be unique and contain no NULL values. Enforcing referential integrity for foreign keys means that every foreign key may contain only values that are present in the primary key or NULL values.

When an insert or update operation is performed to a foreign key column, any value assigned to this column must be already present in its primary key. The only exception is the NULL value. You can create a child record with its foreign key set to NULL and reassign its value sometime later. (Whether or not it makes business sense is a subject of a separate discussion.) There is no restriction on delete operations. You can delete any rows with foreign keys without affecting their primary key.

For the primary key value changes, the answer is a little less straightforward. According to the ANSI standards, primary key changes are restricted. No primary key value that is referenced by one or more foreign key values can be deleted or changed. Actual RDBMS implementations, however, are more liberal. You are given the following choices when changing or deleting primary key values: you can

- *restrict* primary key changes (ANSI standard)
- *cascade* primary key changes to foreign keys, in other words, changing primary key values will cause exactly the same changes in the corresponding foreign keys, deleting parent rows will cause automatic deletion of all their children rows
- set all corresponding foreign keys to their NULL values when the primary key is changed or deleted
- set all corresponding foreign keys to their default values when the primary key is changed or deleted

No restrictions are imposed on inserting new parent rows. You can insert as many new parent records as you want and you do not have to create their children right away. Specific business requirements, however, may call for immediate creation of foreign key rows once their primary keys are created.

Actual methods of maintaining referential integrity differ for different databases. For DB2, these methods can be a part of table declarations, while Oracle and Sybase use special program exits called triggers to handle primary key changes.

2.9 Performance considerations

Tables in a database can be very large, and selecting records from one or more tables may require substantial computer resources. An SQL query execution performance depends on table size, database design, and the way the SQL query is built. As far as an SQR programmer is concerned, nothing can be done to table sizes; occasionally, certain things can be done to the database design; and a lot can be done to improve SQL queries.

When an SQL operator is executed, the internal RDBMS engine selects the necessary rows by performing data search in tables involved in the query. There are two modes of this search: table scan and index scan. When table scan is done, the entire content of the tables is searched and selected rows are returned back to the user application. For index search, the RDBMS engine uses previously built indexes to select only necessary rows from the tables. In most cases, the second method proves more efficient.

Who creates table indexes? Usually, the database administrator does. It makes sense to create indexes on table columns that are frequently used in the WHERE clause. Indexes are always created on all primary and foreign keys. If you perform frequent SELECT statements and experience performance problems, you might want to discuss this with your database administrator to see if additional indexes can be of help.

In many cases, however, SQL statements can be improved to make the database engine work with indexes instead of doing table scans and to minimize repeatable table reads in correlated queries. Teaching the most effective SQL writing methods is certainly beyond the scope of our book, therefore, we just would like to include a few general suggestions:

- use the indexed columns whenever possible in the WHERE clause
- try to avoid ORDER BY, GROUP BY, and DISTINCT because these statements invoke internal sorts
- avoid Boolean NOT, use <> instead
- when joining tables, avoid using non-indexed columns in the WHERE clause
- when using sub-SELECT statements, use smaller tables in inner SELECT statements
- when possible, use the underscore instead of the percent sign in the WHERE clause for partial searches
- avoid using columns of different type and length in logical operators
- avoid arithmetic expressions in SELECT, WHERE, and HAVING
- minimize the usage of the HAVING clauses in SELECT statements. HAVING filters selected rows after all rows have been retrieved. Use WHERE instead of HAVING whenever possible
- use NOT EXISTS instead of NOT IN in subqueries
- avoid calculations on indexed columns

KEY POINTS

1. The relational database model represents data as a set of tables.
2. Tables are logical structures made up of columns and rows.
3. SQL is used to access the elements of a relational database.
4. The `SELECT` statement is used to retrieve entire rows or specific columns from one or more tables.
5. The `WHERE` clause in the `SELECT` statement is used to limit the retrieval based on certain criteria.
6. Relational and Boolean operators can be used to define the selection criteria in the `WHERE` clause.
7. Primary keys and foreign keys help to maintain logical relationships between different tables.

CHAPTER 3

Getting started

IN THIS CHAPTER

- The process of building your first SQR program
- The Program Section
- The `SQR Dialog Box` and how to run SQR programs with the help of this tool
- SQR output files
- SQR procedures
- An example of an SQR program with multiple procedures

3.1 Building your first SQR program

Are you ready for a ride? Buckle up and let's get moving. For some, Structured Query Report Writer sounds like a report generator, but you will soon learn that this fourth generation language can help you create rather complex programs.

What will you need to start? Not much! You will need the SQR product itself and any ASCII text editor of your choice to type in your program. Let's begin with creating a very simple SQR program. In this book, we will be using Microsoft Notepad as our text editor. Please keep in mind that, for large SQR programs, you may need some other editor, for example Microsoft WordPad. In fact, a more sophisticated editor that displays line numbers and supports convenient search/replace logic will save you time when it comes to working with complex programs. Make sure you save your program as a standard ASCII text format file.

Note Your editor will not know that you are writing an SQR program and, therefore, will not highlight syntax errors as you type. You will need to compile or run your program to have SQR inform you of errors (if any).

Our first program name will be `Test3A.sqr`. Extension `.sqr` is a default extension, and, with a few exceptions, we will be using this extension for SQR source program files throughout our entire book. (Of course, SQR executes program file with any extension, but we are just trying to adhere to a development standard.)

An SQR program consists of sections. Each section starts with the `Begin` statement, follows with SQR commands that make up the section body, and ends with the `End` statement:

```
Begin-<section_name>
  < Section body>
End-<section_name >
```

Typically, an SQR program may include a number of different sections, but the only required one is the `Program` section. Based on the above generic section format, the `Program` section should look like this:

```
Begin-Program
  < Section body>
End-Program
```

Note In earlier SQR versions the `Program` section was called the `Report` section. To maintain program compatibility, SQR still supports this section name, but in future releases the `Report` sections may become obsolete.

Now, let's just enter the text of our first program as shown in figure 3.1.

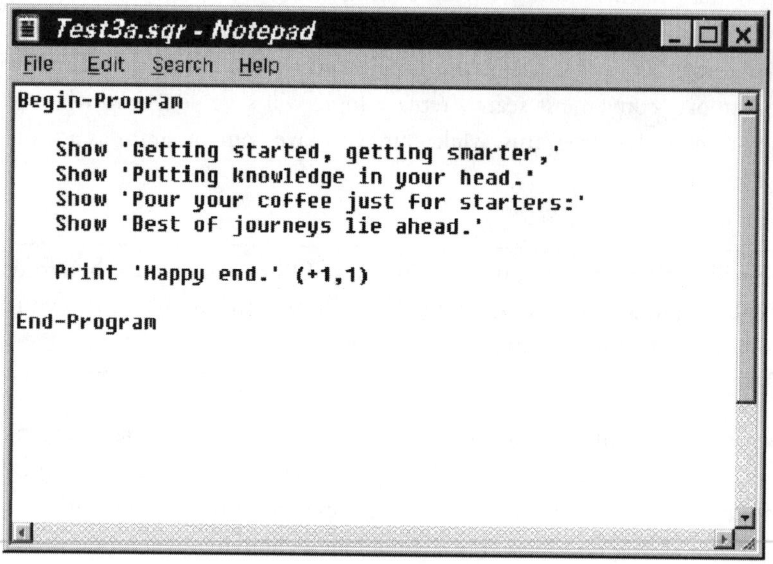


```
Begin-Program

   Show 'Getting started, getting smarter,'
   Show 'Putting knowledge in your head.'
   Show 'Pour your coffee just for starters:'
   Show 'Best of journeys lie ahead.'

   Print 'Happy end.' (+1,1)

End-Program
```

Figure 3.1 Your first SQR program Test3A.sqr

Looks simple? Sure! But this is a legitimate SQR program that can be executed using the `SQR Dialog Box`. Of course there are other ways of executing SQR programs besides the `SQR Dialog Box`, and we will discuss them later in this book.

3.2 SQR Dialog Box

The `SQR Dialog Box` provides the perfect means of running SQR programs under Windows. It also connects you to the database. The database you are using must be active and accessible. The `SQR Dialog Box` is very simple to use. The very first screen you receive will look like the one in figure 3.2 (it may look a little different to you depending on your setup parameters).

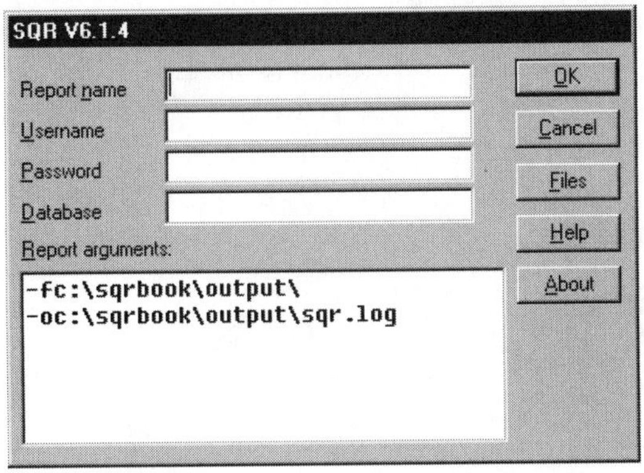

Figure 3.2
The SQR Dialog Box screen

Let us discuss the meaning of each screen component:

Report name Enter the name of your SQR program. The default file type is `.sqr`. Please note that you have to enter the fully qualified path before the program name (see figure 3.3). If you omit the program name or enter `?` in this field, SQR will prompt you for the program name. If you are not sure about the file name or location, click on the `Files` button and SQR will display a list of available drives, directories and files.

Database The name of the database which will be used in your SQR program.

Username Your user access ID. Please make sure you are granted access to all tables and views that you plan to use in your programs.

Password Your password to access the database.

Report arguments These are the SQR command line flags and arguments. Each report flag is preceded by a dash and, for some flags, may be followed by the flag arguments. We will discuss the report flags and arguments in detail later in this book. You can also find the list of the report flags in Appendix B. For the purpose of running our first program, we will need only two flags: `-F`, and `-O`. Flag `-F` defines the directory where SQR will place the report output file (in our case, the directory is `C:\sqrbook\output`). Flag `-O` defines the name of the SQR log file. As you can see, `SQR Dialog Box` uses certain default values depending on your initial setup.

In addition to the flags, there are report arguments that are used to supply an SQR program with information that was not originally hard-coded in the program. These are usually arguments used by the `Ask` and `Input` commands or files containing report parameters. We will discuss these arguments and parameters later in the book.

Note The report flag arguments must be entered without spaces between the flag and the argument.

Figure 3.3 shows the SQR Dialog Box screen after you have entered all the information necessary to run your program. (We changed the default `SQR.log` name to `TEST3A.log`).

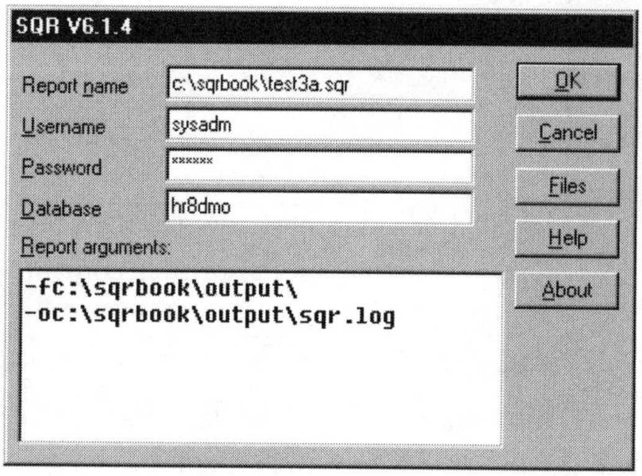

Figure 3.3
The SQR Dialog Box screen with user information

After you press the OK button, SQR will execute your report (figure 3.4). The program will run to the end and display the expected program log. (This is not the program output report file.)

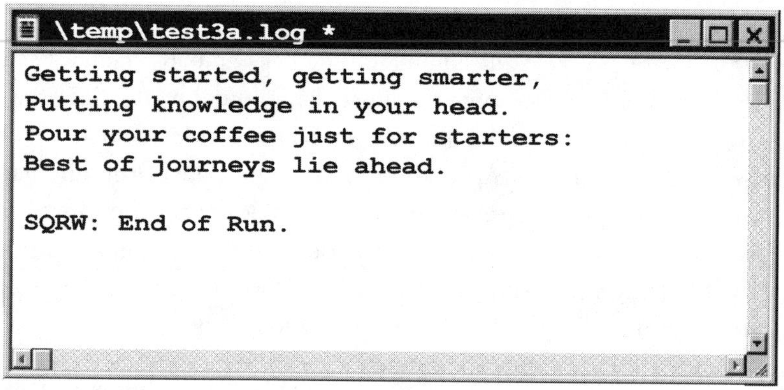

Figure 3.4 An SQR program log. (This is not the report file)

3.3 SQR output

SQR generates several output files. The most important output file is the actual report file. All `Print` commands direct their output to the report output file. By default, SQR creates an output file with the name of your program and the extension `.lis`. In our case, it will be `Test3A.lis`. Unless otherwise specified (as we did), SQR places the output file in the same directory with your SQR program. You can use the report flags to redirect output to any directory of your choice. As you can see from figure 3.3, the report output name will be `c:\temp\Test3A.lis`.

The default SQR report files (files with extension `.lis`) are basically designed for printing. If you try to view them on screen, you may see some special printer control characters. To make SQR report files more convenient for viewing, generate the `SPF` files in addition to or instead of regular report files. (`SPF` files will be covered in detail in chapter 14.) To have SQR generate an `SPF` output, you need to add one of the following flags to the list of the report flags: `-keep`, `-nolis`, or `-ziv` (Please see appendix B for a complete list of the report flags.)

Let us open and examine our program report file `Test3A.lis` as shown in figure 3.5.

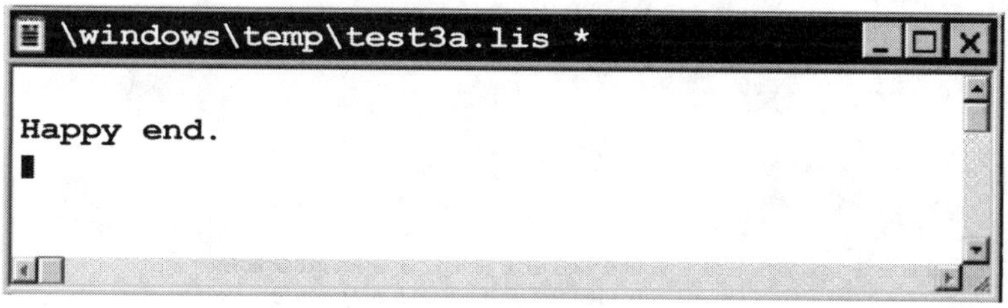

Figure 3.5 An SQR report file

When an SQR program runs under Windows, you can see the results of all your `Display` and `Show` statement executions on your screen. SQR will also display all compile errors on the same screen. All this screen information is actually written to your `.log` file. In our example, the name of the SQR log file is `c:\temp\Test3A.log`. You already saw our log file in figure 3.4.

Note If you do not specify different log file names for each SQR program run, the next program execution will overlay the previously created log file.

3.4 Adding more complexity

Now that we know how to run an SQR program, let us enhance it a bit to make it look more like a real program by introducing the `Procedure` section. An SQR program may include one or more SQR procedures. Procedures allow you to split your program into several logical pieces which makes the program easy to understand and maintain. Each SQR procedure is placed into a separate `Procedure` section.

Let's add several procedures to our program: procedures `Main` and `Print_Totals` will be called from the main program section, whereas procedure `Select_Employees` will be called from procedure `Main`. After adding the `Procedure` sections, the program becomes a little more serious:

```
!TEST3B.SQR
! A program with multiple procedures
!******************
Begin-Program
!******************
!This indicates a comment in SQR
! ...
  Do Main
  Do Print_Totals
End-Program

!******************************
Begin-Procedure Main
!******************************
   Show 'Main started.'
   Print 'Employee List' (1,4)
   Do Select_Employees
End-Procedure Main

!*********************************************
Begin-Procedure Select_Employees
!*********************************************
   Show 'Select Employees started.'
   Print 'Mary A. Jones     Secretary ' (+1,1)
   Print 'Alex S. Clarke    VP Marketing ' (+1,1)
   ! +1 in the first parameter of the Print command
   ! indicates next page line
End-Procedure Select_Employees

!*************************************
Begin-Procedure Print_Totals
!*************************************
   Print 'Total number of employees: 2' (+1,1)
End-Procedure Print_Totals
```

Two procedures are invoked in the `Program` section: `Main`, and `Print_Totals`

The `Select_Employees` procedure is invoked in the `Main` procedure

Let us run the program and examine its output files, that is, Test3B.lis (figure 3.6) and Test3B.log (figure 3.7). Please note that file Test3B.lis includes output from all three procedures: Main, Print_Totals, and Select_Employees. This is because all these procedures used the Print command. File Test3B.log, however, includes only output from Main and Select_Employees since only these two procedures had the Show statement coded.

Note SQR uses an exclamation sign to indicate the start of a comment line in the program.

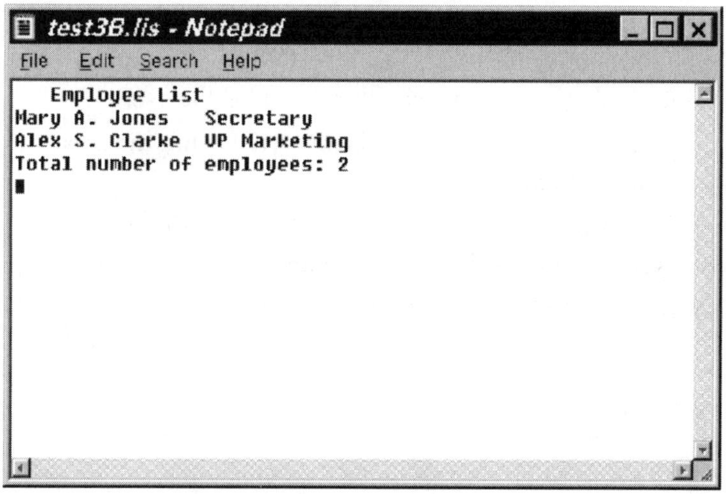

Figure 3.6 Program Test3B.sqr report file

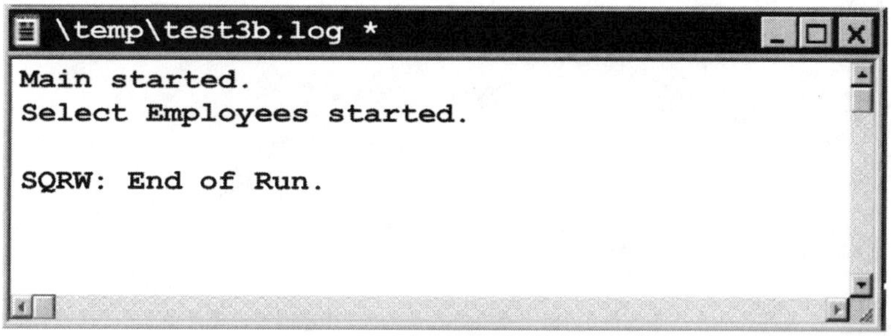

Figure 3.7 Program Test3B.sqr log file

KEY POINTS

1. You can use any ASCII text editor to type in your program.
2. The `SQR Dialog Box` can be used to submit your program for execution under Windows.
3. The following are commonly used extensions for different SQR files: .sqr for SQR programs, `.lis` for SQR report files, and `.log` for SQR log files.
4. All `Print` commands direct their output to the report file.
5. All `Show` and `Display` commands direct their output to the log file.
6. If you do not specify different log file names for each SQR program run, the next program execution will overlay the previously created log file.
7. An SQR program may include a number of different sections, but the only required one is the `Program` section.
8. An SQR `Program` section may call one or more procedures using the `Do` command. Procedures may, in turn, call other procedures.
9. SQR uses an exclamation mark to indicate the start of a comment line in the program.

C H A P T E R 4

SQR data elements and data manipulations

IN THIS CHAPTER

- Main types of SQR data elements
- SQR predefined variables
- Date variables
- Data elements manipulation
- The `Let` command
- Built-in functions

Any programming language deals with data elements. SQR has three main categories of data elements: SQR columns, variables, and literals. We will show you how SQR figures out each element's category and type by its name, and also what types can be used for the SQR data elements.

SQR has a number of reserved (or predefined) variables that are useful in monitoring your database selection status, checking the program execution platform, detecting the end-of-file condition, and so on. We will list all these variables in this chapter and will show how to use them in this and subsequent chapters.

Date variables are relatively new to SQR, and we will also talk about dates and date manipulation techniques in SQR.

Finally we will discuss different SQR data element manipulation techniques, including the arithmetic operations, string manipulations, the `Move` and `Let` commands as well as the usage of built-in functions.

4.1 SQR columns, variables, and literals

Just as a finite set of chemical elements can be combined into thousands of chemical compounds, the main SQR data elements—columns, literals, and variables—provide the basis of all SQR functionality. SQR data elements must be identified with a special character that specifies both the category and format of the data element. This special character must be placed at the beginning of each data element's name.

SQR columns are used to reference columns defined in the database. In order to reference a table column, SQR uses the symbol `&` as a prefix to the table column name. For example, `&Emplid` or `&Hire_Date`. SQR assigns types (character, number, or date) to columns based on their definition in the database. You do not have to declare SQR columns in your program. SQR will recognize them as long as they are valid SQL elements. (In chapter 6 we will show you how to assign a name to an SQL expression.)

SQR variables can be *string variables*, *numeric variables*, *date variables* (date variables are available starting from version 4), or *list variables* (available starting from version5). SQR uses the special character `$` for both string and date variables, the special character `#` for numeric variables, and the special character `%` for list variables. Examples: `$Name`, `#Count`, `#Number_Of_Pages`, `$Date_Of_Hire`, `%My_List`. SQR numeric variables can be floating point numbers (default), decimal numbers, or integers (decimal numbers and integers are available starting from version 4). Floating point variables may hold up to fifteen digits of precision. Decimal numbers are the most accurate, providing up to 38 digits of precision, but are slower to process. String variables can be of any length within the memory limitations of your computer.

In addition to string, numeric, and date variables, SQR uses special variables in the `Begin-Document` paragraph to define field positions for printing. These variables are called *document markers*. The symbol @ is used to identify document marker variables. Document markers are used only in the `Document` paragraph, and we will discuss them in chapter 15.

SQR literals are string, numeric, or date constants. String literals must be enclosed in single quotes, for example, `'This is a string literal'`. Numeric literals may include digits with optional decimal point and leading sign. You can also use the scientific notation for numeric literals. These are examples of numeric literals of different formats: `2043.44, -434.55, 0, 1234567, 5.6E5`. Like string literals, date literals must also be enclosed in single quotes, but the content of any date literal must be in one of the SQR date formats which will be discussed later in this chapter.

SQR variables do not have to be explicitly declared in the program. When a variable appears for the first time, SQR assigns this variable its type (based on the first character of the variable's name) and initial value. All string variables are initialized to the `NULL` value. All numeric variables are initialized to zeroes. All string variables have variable length. When a new value is assigned to a string variable, its length is automatically adjusted.

Prior to version 4, numeric variables were only floating point numbers. As of version 4, numeric variables can be *floating point* numbers (default), *decimal* numbers, or *integers*. In addition, version 4 introduced *date* variables. The first character of a variable name ($ or #) is no longer sufficient to define the variable. For example, floating point variables, decimals, and integers all have the same prefix: #. Similarly, both string and date variables have the same prefix: $. The problem can be solved by using the `Declare-Variable` command which allows you to explicitly declare variables (please see the command syntax in appendix D). In most cases, however, you can still declare variables (other than dates) implicitly by using the proper name prefixes. By the way, when date variables are declared, they are initialized to `NULL` values similarly to string variables.

Variable names are not case-sensitive; for example, `$Name` is the same as `$NAME` or `$name`. In our book we will be using, for the most part, word-cap variable names with the first letters of every word of the variable name typed in the upper case and the rest of the word typed in the lower case. We will use an underscore to connect words in multiple-word names of variables and procedure names. Variable names can be of any length, for example, `$Employee_Date_Of_Hire` is a valid name.

SQR variables can be *global* or *local*. We will give more detailed information about global and local variables when we discuss local and global procedures in chapter 5. For now, let's just keep in mind that *global variables* can be referenced throughout the entire program, whereas *local variables* are effective only within a local procedure. Please note that local variables are initialized only once when their respective procedures are invoked for the first time.

Figure 4.1 shows the SQR data element's hierarchy.

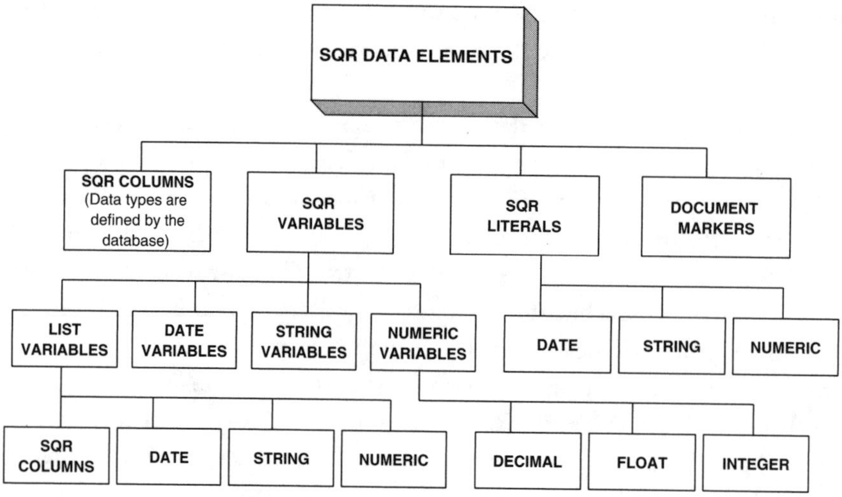

Figure 4.1 SQR data elements

4.2 Predefined SQR variables

It is important to know that SQR reserves a number of variables with special names. These variables are not declared in the program, but they can be used in the program logic.

Predefined SQR variables are extremely helpful and are used in programs extensively. We will be using different predefined variables in many examples throughout this book. Predefined variables are not write-protected, so you can change their values just as you would any other variable values. In some cases, you might want to change some predefined variables, such as `#current-line` or `#page-count` and use these changes in your program logic. In most cases, however, changing the values of SQR predefined variables won't make much sense. Why would you want to change the value of the `#sql-status` or `$sqr-platform` variables? You would rather check their values, wouldn't you?

Here is a list of SQR predefined variables:

- `#current-line` denotes the current line number within the current page. It is not, however, the current line in the report body. As we will discuss later, SQR page consists of a heading, a body, and a footing. Variable `#current-line` gives the number of the current line throughout the entire page.
- `#current-column` the current column number on the page.
- `#end-file` this numeric variable is set to 1 when the `Read` statement results in the end-of-file condition. Otherwise, `#end-file` is always 0.

- `#page-count` the current page number.
- `$current-date` the current date and time on the local machine when your program started running.
- `#return-status` this value will be returned by SQR to the calling program (in most cases, to the operating system). By default, this variable is initialized to the "success" return value for the operating system. It is, therefore, your responsibility to assign this variable the proper value in your SQR program.
- `#sql-count` the number of rows affected by any SQL DML statement (`Insert`, `Update`, or `Delete`). It is always a good idea to check the value of `#sql-count` in your program logic after each table update to ensure that the update has been actually performed as expected. Note that `#sql-count` cannot be used to check the number of selected rows. It is used only to verify updates.
- `$sql-error` this string variable contains an error explanation message from the database. Whenever a database error condition occurs, it is recommended to display variable `$sql-error` in your SQR program.
- `#sql-status` a status value returned from the database after each SQL statement is executed. Specific returned values differ for each database. You can find these values in your database manual.
- `$sqr-database` your SQR installation is set up to work with some database and this variable can be checked in an SQR program to determine what database you are working with. It is helpful if you want to make your program database-independent. Valid values are `'ALLBASE'`, `'DB2'`, `'INFORMIX'`, `'INGRES'`, `'ORACLE'`, `'RDB'`, `'SQLBASE'`, `'SYBASE'`, `'REDBRICK'`, `'ODBC'`.
- `#sqr-pid` the process Id of the current SQR run. This value is unique for each run of an SQR program and can be used to create unique composite file names.
- `$sqr-platform` this variable tells your SQR program which operating system the program is run under. Valid values are `'DOS'`, `'WINDOWS'`, `'WINDOWS-NT'`, `'UNIX'`, `'VM'`, `'VMS'`, `'MVS'`.
- `$sqr-locale` the name of the current locale. The SQR locale name is defined in the `SQR.ini` file. This variable controls the way SQR handles variables that may be displayed differently in different countries, for example, currencies, dates, time, names of days in the week, names of months, etc.
- `$sqr-dbcs` specifies whether SQR recognizes double-character strings (available starting from version 4.2). Valid values are `'Yes'` or `'No'`.

- `$sqr-encoding` the value of the SQR environmental variable `ENCODING` (available starting from version 4.2). Valid values are: `'ASCII'`, `'JEUC'`, `'SJIS'`,`'EBCDIC'`, `'EBCDIK290'`, `'EBCDIK1027'`, `'UTF-8'`, or `'UCS-2'`.
- `$sqr-encoding-console` the name of encoding for character data written to the log file or console (available starting from version 5). This value is defined by the SQR environmental variable `ENCODING-CONSOLE`. Can be used as a substitution variable.
- `$sqr-encoding-database` the name of encoding for character data retrieved from and inserted into the database (available starting from version 5). This value is defined by the SQR environmental variable `ENCODING-DATABASE`. Can be used as a substitution variable.
- `$sqr-encoding-file-input` the name of encoding for character data read from files used with the `Open` command (available starting from version 5). This value is defined by the SQR environmental variable `ENCODING-FILE-INPUT`. Can be used as a substitution variable.
- `$sqr-encoding-file-output` the name of encoding for character data written to files used with the `Open` command (available starting from version 5). This value is defined by the SQR environmental variable `ENCODING-FILE-OUTPUT`. Can be used as a substitution variable.
- `$sqr-encoding-report-output` the name of encoding for character data written to the report generated by SQR such as an `LIS` file (available starting from version 5). This value is defined by the SQR environmental variable `ENCODING-REPORT-OUTPUT`. Can be used as a substitution variable.
- `$sqr-encoding-source` the name of encoding for character data for SQR Source files and Include files (available starting from version 5). This value is defined by the SQR environmental variable `ENCODING-SOURCE`. Can be used as a substitution variable.
- `$sqr-program` the name of the SQR program file.
- `$sqr-report` the name of the report output file. This is the actual name specified in the `-F` flag parameter or in the `New-Report` command.
- `$sqr-ver` a string with your SQR version ID.
- `$username` the user name specified on the command line.
- `$sqr-hostname` the name of the computer on which your SQR program is executed (available starting from version 5). Can be used as a substitution variable.
- `#sqr-max-lines` the maximum number of lines for the current report (available starting from version 5).

- `#sqr-max-columns` the maximum number of columns for the current report (available starting from version 5).
- `#sqr-toc-level` the current TOC level (available starting from version 4.3.3).
- `#sqr-toc-page` the current TOC page number (available starting from version 4.3.3)
- `$sqr-toc-text` the current TOC text (available starting from version 4.3.3)

4.3 Working with dates

Date variables and date handling logic in SQR deserve a special discussion. In SQR, dates can be stored as character strings in string format variables or as dates in special date format variables (available starting from version 4). Like string variables, date variable names are prefixed with a dollar sign (`$`) but, unlike string variables, date variables must be explicitly declared as such with the help of the `Declare-Variable` command (available starting from version 4):

```
Begin-Setup
   Declare-Variable
          Date $Mydate
   End-Declare
End-Setup
```

In many cases, string variables are sufficient to hold dates. Generally, a variable gets populated with a date value by

- selecting this value from a database
- accepting user input via the `Input` command
- reading a date value from a flat file
- referencing the reserved SQR variable `$current-date`
- performing date manipulations using special SQR date functions.

When printing a date stored in a string variable, SQR column, or literal, the date must be in one of the following formats (unless a special date edit mask is specified):

- the format controlled by the SQR environmental variable `SQR_DB_DATE_FORMAT` or the corresponding setting in the `SQR.ini` file
- your database-specific format
- the date literal format `'SYYYYMMDD[HH24[MI[SS[NNNNNN]]]]'` (the square brackets denote optionality).

Table 4.1 lists the default date formats for different databases.

Table 4.1 Default date format masks for different databases in SQR

Database	Default Database Format
DB2	YYYY-MM-DD-HH:MI:SS.NNNNN YYYY-MM-DD
Informix	YYYY-MM-DD HH:MI:SS.NNN MM/DD/YYYY MM-DD-YYYY MM.DD.YYYY
Ingres	DD-MON-YYYY HH:MI:SS MM/DD/YYYY HH:MI:SS MM-DD-YYYY HH:MI:SS
ODBC	MM-DD-YY
Oracle	DD-MON-YY DD-MON-YYYY
Sybase	MON DD YYYY HH:MIPM MON DD YYYY [HH:MI[:SS[:NNN]][PM] MON DD YYYY [HH:MI[:SS[.NNN]][PM] YYYYMMDD [HH:MI[:SS[:NNN]][PM] YYYYMMDD [HH:MI[:SS[.NNN]][PM]
SQLBase	YYYY-MM-DD-HH.MI.SS.NNNNNN YYY-MM-DD HH.MI.SS.NNNNNN

4.4 List variables

List variables (available starting from version 5) contain ordered collections of SQR variables. These variables are not nested: you cannot include one list variable within another. List variables cannot be passed as parameters to local functions.

List variables are denoted with the special character %. Unlike other types of variables, list variables cannot be declared via the `Declare-Variable` command. They are created and manipulated using the Let command (see more about the Let command in 4.5.4). A list variable may include one or more SQR columns, variables or literals of any valid type except another list variable. You can use list variables to hold one set of variables or multiple rows of information of similar structure.

List variables are used in SQR for DDO in conjunction with the `Begin-Execute` command that uses list variables as parameters to pass them to external sources of information. SQR arrays cannot be used for this purpose.

4.5 Manipulating data elements

Every language has a set of data element manipulation commands that help to move information from one element to another, perform arithmetic, string, and logical operations, convert data elements from one data type to another, and perform other related operations. The following commands support data element manipulations in SQR: `Add`, `Subtract`, `Multiply`, `Divide`, `Move`, and `Let`. In addition, SQR provides a set of special string manipulation commands.

4.5.1 Arithmetic commands

The four arithmetic commands—`Add`, `Subtract`, `Multiply`, and `Divide`—are simple and straightforward. They work with two numeric fields, (a source field and a target field), perform the proper arithmetic operation, and store the result in the target field. A source field can be a variable, a column, or a literal; a target field can be only a variable; literals and SQR column variables cannot be modified. Let's take a look at some examples of the arithmetic commands:

```
Add #Employee_Salary To #Total_By_Department
Subtract 1 From #Employee_Count
Multiply &Rate_Increase Times #Total Round 2
Divide #Number_Of_Employees Into #Average_Salary Round 2 On-Error=Zero
```

The `Round` parameter rounds the result to the specified number of digits to the right of the decimal point. For float variables, this value can be between zero and fifteen. For decimal variables, this value cannot exceed the precision of the target variable. If the target variable is an integer, the `Round` parameter should not be used. (Please be aware that when dealing with money-related values, it is recommended to use decimals rather than float variables to avoid small inaccuracies in calculations.)

The `Divide` command has one special parameter, `On-Error`. It tells SQR how to handle a zero-division situation. In case of zero-division, you can set the result to a high value, to zero, or you can ask SQR to halt processing (the default option).

4.5.2 The Move command

The `Move` command is more versatile than the arithmetic commands. In addition to moving data from one field to another, it can also perform data conversions and data editing using special edit masks. (We will discuss different types of edit masks and their formats in chapter 9 when presenting the `Print` command because the `Print` command uses exactly the same types of masks as the `Move` command.)

As with the arithmetic commands, the Move command utilizes the source field—which can be an SQR column, variable, or literal as well as the target field, which can be only a variable.

Unlike the arithmetic commands, the Move command can handle data of any format. The source and target fields for the Move command can have different formats. For example, the source can be a numeric variable, and the target can be a string variable. In this case, the command not only moves data, but also performs the numeric-to-string conversion. Can the Move command move a string to a numeric field? Yes, but under one condition: the string must contain a valid number. Otherwise, the move will be performed incorrectly. Please be aware that SQR does not treat commas as valid separators in numbers. For example the following Move command

```
Move '15,995.00' To #Total  ! Results in incorrect move
```

will move 15.00000 to #Total. The command scans the source string up to the first non-numeric character (in this case, it is the comma) and converts only the scanned portion of the string. But the dot as a decimal part separator is processed correctly:

```
Move '15.99500' To #Total  ! Results in correct move
```

There is only one incompatible combination in the Move command: date and numeric fields cannot be converted into each other.

Let's consider a few examples of the Move command:

```
1. Move &Phone To $Disp_Phone (xxx)bxxx-xxxx
2. Move #Salary to $Disp_Salary $9,999,999.99
3. Move 'Month DD, YYYY' To $Date_Mask
   Move &Effdt To $Effective_Dt :$Date_Mask
4. Move &Counter To #Number_Of_Employees Number
5. Move &Annual_Rate To #Annual_Salary Money
6. Move $Hire_Date To $Start_Date Date
```

In the first line of the code, the value stored in the SQR column variable &Phone is moved to the string variable $Disp_Phone and is edited according to the specified edit mask. If the source field value is 2031234567, the target field after the move will be (203) 123-4567. The 'b' character in the edit mask denotes a space.

In the second line, the value in the numeric variable #Salary is converted to the string format according to the edit mask specified and moved to the string variable $Disp_Salary.

In these first two examples, edit masks were coded as literals. The third example demonstrates how you can build a mask dynamically, store the mask value in a string variable, and use this variable instead of a hard-coded literal. Please note that when you use a dynamic edit mask, you have to prefix the name of the corresponding string variable with a colon. The Move command in the third example uses a date format mask when moving the value of the source field &Effdt to the target field $Effective_Dt. The target field can be a string field or a date field; SQR will perform the move anyway. If the source field contains an invalid date, SQR will generate an error.

The fourth, fifth, and sixth examples demonstrate the Move commands' use of special SQR-reserved keywords in place of edit masks. These keywords, Number, Money, and Date, are used as the default masks for numeric, money, and date fields. The exact format of the default masks is controlled by the settings in the SQR.ini file. These settings can be changed dynamically with the help of the Alter-Locale command.

4.5.3 String manipulation commands

SQR has a few special commands to perform string manipulations. These commands are Find, Concat, Extract, Encode, String, Unstring, Uppercase, and Lowercase. SQR also has a number of string functions that offer a similar capability. These functions will be discussed later in this chapter. The string manipulation commands are helpful in finding portions of text within strings, extracting parts of a string into another string, concatenating multiple strings in one string, parsing a string into portions, and so on. You can find all the command descriptions and syntax in appendix D. It is worth mentioning that string manipulation commands work not only with strings but also with dates. In this case, date fields are converted internally to strings.

The Uppercase and Lowercase commands are pretty straightforward, therefore we will not discuss these two commands in this chapter.

The Find command helps you to locate the starting position of a sub-string within a string or date field. It returns the position of the first byte of the sub-string in a specially designated numeric variable. For example,

```
Find 'John' In $Full_Name 0 #Position
```

will look for the first occurrence of the character string 'John' in the $Full_Name starting from the leftmost byte of $Full_Name and, if found, will place the position of the found string into the numeric variable #Position. If the string you are looking for is not found, SQR moves –1 instead of the string position. What if the original string has more than one occurrence of the sub-string (as in 'John Johnston')? In this case, the Find command finds only the first occurrence of the sub-string unless you adjust the starting position in the Find command and repeat the search. By the way, the starting position can be coded as a literal or as a variable.

What happens if the sub-string or the target string are date fields? In this case, the Find command converts the date into a string before starting the search. The format of the string must be the format specified by the environmental variable SQR_DB_DATE_FORMAT, or, if no format is specified, your database-specific format (please see table 4.1), or the default date literal command.

The `Extract` command extracts a sub-string of specified length from a source string or date field and moves the sub-string to the specified target string or date variable. In the next example, the `Extract` command extracts a 3 byte-long area code from a string containing a telephone number and places the area code into the `$Area_Code` variable. The extraction starts from the second position of the source string (after the left parenthesis):

```
Extract $Area_Code From $Phone_Number 1 3
```

When the starting position of the sub-string is not known, the `Find` and `Extract` commands can work together: the `Find` command determines the location of a sub-string, then the `Extract` command uses the location as the starting point of the extraction. In the following example, the string `$Full_Name` contains last name (of variable length), comma, first name, and space. If we need to extract the first name from `$Full_Name`, our program will have to find the position of the comma in this string, then locate the ending space and calculate the length of the first name. Finally, the program will use the `Extract` command to extract the first name starting from the next position after the comma and using the calculated length of the first name:

```
Find ',' In $Full_Name 1 #Location
Move #Location To #Start_Location
Add 1 To #Start_Location
Find ' ' In $Full_Name #Start_Location #End_Location
Move #End_Location To #Length
Subtract #Start_Location From #Length
Extract $First_Name From $Full_Name #Start_Location #Length
```

When the source field in the `Extract` command is a date column or variable, the command converts this field to a string before extraction. The conversion is performed according to the format specified by the environmental variable `SQR_DB_DATE_FORMAT`, or, if not specified, according to your database-specific format (see table 4.1), or to the default date literal format.

The `Encode` command allows you to encode and place a sequence of special characters onto a string variable. The special characters can be non-display characters or escape sequence. For example, this command moves the code sequence that turns bold on to the `$Bold` string variable:

```
Encode '<27>L11233' Into $Bold
```

The Concat command appends one string to another string with optional editing if an edit mask is specified. The concatenated string can be a variable, a column, or a literal. The target string must be a variable. Here is an example of the Concat command:

```
Move 'bxxxxx-xxxx' To $Zip_Mask
Concat $Full_Zip With $Address :$Zip_Mask
```

In the example, the edit mask is built dynamically and stored in the string variable $Zip_Mask. When an edit mask is stored in a variable, the variable name must be prefixed with a colon. In the Concat command of this example, the $Full_Zip variable is edited using the mask specified and then is appended to the $Full_Address variable.

If you try to concatenate a number to a string, the Concat command will automatically convert the number to a string using the edit mask if specified.

If the concatenated field is a date variable or column and no edit mask is specified, the Concat command will convert the date into a string according to the format specified by the environmental variable SQR_DB_DATE_FORMAT, or, if not specified, according to your database-specific format, or to the default date literal format.

The String command is used to build a string from a list of sub-strings. The sub-strings in the newly-built string will remain separated from each other by one or more characters specified in the String command. This command is very convenient in creating comma-separated files that can be used in non-SQR applications, such as Microsoft Excel. In the following example, we build a comma-separated employee information record made up of different fields:

```
String $Emplid $Empl_Name $Birth_Dt $Address By  ','  Into $Empl_Record
```

What if you do not want to separate sub-strings when building your string? The syntax of the String command requires you to specify some sub-string separator. The problem can be solved by specifying a null delimiter ('').

The Unstring command is an opposite to the String command. It breaks a source string into a number of substrings using one or more specified characters as the substring separators. The command is very helpful in parsing composite fields into components. It can also be helpful in working with files created by non-SQR applications. Here is an example of the Unstring command:

```
Unstring $Empl_Name By '-' Into $First_Name $Mid_Initial $Last_Name
```

If you specify more substrings than can be found in the source strings, the extra substrings are set to empty strings. Conversely, if the source string has more substrings than specified in the Unstring command, the extra strings will be ignored. If one of the fields specified in either String or Unstring command is a date variable or column, it will be converted to a string according to the format specified by the environmental variable SQR_DB_DATE_FORMAT, or, if not specified, according to your database-specific format, or to the default date literal format.

4.5.4 The Let command

The Let command is much more complex and versatile than other data element manipulation commands. A single Let command may be capable of replacing a number of data manipulation and logic commands. The syntax of the Let command

```
Let  target_variable  =  expression
```

is very simple, but the expression in this command can be rather sophisticated.

Expressions in the Let command can be combinations of *operands*, *operators*, and *functions*. The command can perform variable assignments, string concatenations, numerical calculations, logical expression evaluations, function calls, and various combinations of these operations.

Operands in the Let command expressions can be variables, SQR columns, literals, or array fields (SQR array fields are covered in chapter 12). In certain cases, for example, in variable assignments, operands can be of different formats. SQR then performs the proper conversions. In other cases, such as calculations, operands must be only numeric. In the following example, the $Julian_Day string variable was extracted from the current date in the Julian format. The following sequence of two Let commands converts the $Julian_Day string variable into the numeric variable #Number_Of_Days and calculates the year-to-date daily expense payment average by dividing the year-to-date expense total amount by the number of days:

```
Let #Number_Of_Days = $Julian_Day
Let #Ytd_Expense_Average = #Ytd_Expense_Total / #Number_Of_Days
```

The first Let command is an assignment command and uses operands of two different formats: string and numeric. The second command is a calculation command and can use only numeric operands. If you were to try using $Julian_Day in the calculation without a prior conversion to numeric, an error would occur:

```
Let #Ytd_Expense_Average = #Ytd_Expense_Total / $Julian_Day   ! Error
```

If an expression contains numeric operands of different precisions, SQR converts operands with lower precision to match operands with higher precision. This way, SQR always preserves the number of significant digits when calculating an expression.

For example, if an expression contains float, integer, and decimal operands, the integer operands are considered the lowest in precision; the float operands are placed next in the precision hierarchy; and the decimal operands are considered the highest. Precision may be lost when the result of the expression is moved to the target variable and the precision of the target variable is lower than the precision of the calculated expression.

Let's consider the following two examples:

```
1. Let #Salary_Increase = #Salary * #Percent_Increase
2. Let #Dept_Rate_Increase = #Total_Salary_Increase / #Total_Salary
```

In the first line, a decimal variable `#Salary` is multiplied by a float variable `#Percent_Increase`. Prior to performing multiplication, the Let command converts `#Percent_Increase` from float to decimal to match the `#Salary` precision. The result of the calculation is moved to the decimal variable `#Salary_Increase` without any precision loss.

In the second line, the `Let` command performs a division on two decimal operands. The result of the division is of the decimal format and this result is converted to the float format and moved to the float variable `#Dept_Rate_Increase`. This variable has a lower precision than the intermediate result precision, and therefore, the `Let` command results in some precision loss.

Why did we use the `Let` command in the previous examples while the same operations could have been carried out by already familiar `Move`, `Multiply`, and `Divide` commands? One reason is that the `Let` command preserves the precision in calculations. Another reason is that the `Let` command allows the use of complex formulae, not just simple arithmetic operations.

Operators in the `Let` command can be *arithmetic*, *string*, or *relational*. The result of the `Let` command execution depends not only on operand values and operations performed on the operands, but also on the order of these operations. SQR assigns a precedence order to each operator. All relational operators have lower precedence than arithmetic and string operators. Operators of the same precedence are processed in the sequence they appear in the expression, from left to right. Tables 4.2 and 4.3 list separately relational SQR operators and arithmetic and string operators. The tables present operators in the descending precedence order with the lowest precedence number set to zero.

Table 4.2 Relational operators

Operator	Meaning	Precedence
>	Greater than	3
<	Less than	3
>=	Greater than or equal to	3
<=	Less than or equal to	3
<>	Not equal	3

Table 4.2 Relational operators (continued)

Operator	Meaning	Precedence
`!=`	Not Equal	3
`=`	Equal	3
`Not`	Logical NOT	2
`And`	Logical AND	1
`Or`	Logical OR	0
`Xor`	Logical XOR (Exclusive OR)	0

Table 4.3 String and Arithmetic Operators (have higher precedence than relational operators)

Operator	Meaning	Precedence
`||`	Concatenate 2 strings	4
`+`	Positive sign prefix	3
`-`	Negative sign prefix	3
`^`	Exponent	2
`*`	Multiplication	1
`/`	Division	1
`%`	Remainder	1
`+`	Plus	0
`-`	Minus	0

While the order of operations in the `Let` command is determined by the precedence rules, these rules can be overridden by using parentheses. Even if you do not need to override operator precedence, parentheses are recommended in complex expressions. Parentheses make your expressions more readable and easier to debug.

Let's take a look at a few examples of expressions in the `Let` command:

```
Let #A = (#K + #L / #M) * (2/#P - #Q)
Let #Vac_Balance = #Vac_Accrued + #Vac_Carryover - #Vac_Taken
Let #Total =
   #Total + (#Price * (100 - #Discount_Percent)/100) * #Quantity
Let $Full_Name = $First_Name || ':' || $Mid_Init || ':' || $Last_Name
Let #Flag = (#Total <= &Salary_Limit) Or (#Total <= #Special_Limit)
```

The last line of code deserves special discussion. The expression in the `Let` command in this example is a logical one. It returns one if the result of this expression is

True or zero if the result is False. Therefore the #Flag variable will be assigned one or zero, depending on the results of the comparisons in the logical expression (more about logical expressions in chapter 8).

The Let command can also be used to create and manipulate list variables (available starting from version 5). List variables contain ordered collections of SQR variables, literals and column variables. You can use list variables to hold one set of variables or multiple rows of information of similar structure. These variables are not nested: you cannot include one list variable within another. A list variable may include SQR columns, variables, or literals of any valid type except another list variable.

List variables are used in conjunction with the Begin-Execute command that uses list variables as parameters to pass them to external sources of information. SQR arrays cannot be used for this purpose.

Here is how you can create a list variable using the Let command:

```
Let %Customer = List(#Cust_Num, $Cust_Nm, $Cust_Birth_Dt)
```

The command creates a single-row list variable. To create a multiple-row list variable, use a slightly different format of the same command:

```
    Let %Customer[100] = List(NUMBER'.Cust_Num', TEXT'.Cust_Nm',
DATE'.Cust_Birth_Dt')
```

The number between the square brackets indicates the number of rows in the list.

The Let command is also used to manipulate a list's values. The following two Let commands demonstrate how to assign values to components of a list:

```
Let %Customer = List(#User_Id, $User_Nm, $User_Dob)
Let %Customer[#Row_Num] = List(#User_Id, $User_Nm, $User_Dob)
```

The first command assigns values to components of a single-row list. The second command assigns values to components of a row which number is stored in the #Row_Num variable. When assigning, the format and content of the source variables must be compatible with the types given in the definition. SQR will perform the necessary conversions between different data types. Assignments between date and numeric fields are prohibited.

To retrieve values stored in components of a list variable, use the following Let command:

```
Let $My_Cust_Name = %Customer[#Row_Num].Cust_Nm
```

As you can see, each `Let` command can replace a number of elementary arithmetic or string commands, but the real strength of the `Let` command is in its ability to use *built-in functions.*

4.6 Built-in functions in SQR

In addition to operands, the expressions in the `Let` command can include built-in functions. SQR provides a rich variety of numeric, string, date, file-related, and miscellaneous functions. You can use a function or an expression as an argument of another function as long as the inside function or expression returns a value of the proper type.

SQR Version 6 offers more than 50 different built-in functions. In addition, you can write your own functions in C using the supplied source file `ufunc.c`. All SQR built-in functions are listed in appendix C of this book. In this chapter, we will cover only the most frequently used functions. You will also have a chance to see a number of other SQR functions in examples throughout this book.

4.6.1 Numeric functions

The numeric built-in SQR functions are not used very frequently, but they may be helpful when you need to perform complex calculations in your program, for example, in financial forecasting. (A complete list of numeric functions can be found in appendix C.) We will present only one numeric function here, `abs()`, which returns the absolute value of the function's numeric argument. The argument can be an integer, float, or decimal literal, column, variable, or expression. Here is an example of the `abs()` function:

```
Let #Percent_Difference =
   (abs(#Average_Salary - &Salary) / #Average_Salary) * 100
```

The `abs()` function returns a value of the same type as its argument either integer, float, or decimal.

4.6.2 File-related functions

The SQR file-related functions are helpful in performing file maintenance, and can sometimes replace calls to the operating system. The following three functions are available: `delete()`, `exists()`, and `rename()`. All these functions return zero if the operation was successful; otherwise, they return the system error code (platform-specific). The following example uses all three of the SQR file-related functions:

```
!TEST4A.SQR
!Using file manipulation functions
Begin-Program
Move 'c:\temp\TESTA.LIS' To $File_Name
```

```
Move 'c:\temp\TESTB.LIS' To $New_File_Name
Let #Status = exists($New_File_Name)
If  #Status = 0
    Show 'File ' $New_File_Name ' exists. Will be deleted. '
    Let #Status = delete($New_File_Name)
End-If
Let #Status=rename($File_Name, $New_File_Name)
If #Status = 0
    Show 'File ' $File_Name ' successfully renamed to ' $New_File_Name
Else
   Show 'Error renaming ' $File_Name ' to ' $New_File_Name ', Status= '
   #Status
End-If
End-Program
```

In the `Test4A.sqr` program, we use the `exists()` function to check if the `TestB.lis` file presently exists. We check the function return value stored in the `#Status` variable. If it is zero, the file exists, and we use the `delete()` function to delete this file. Then, we use the `rename()` function to rename `TestA.lis` to `TestB.lis`.

4.6.3 Date functions

Beginning with version 4, SQR provides a number of date handling functions including `strtodate()`, `datetostr()`, `dateadd()`, `datediff()`, and `datenow()`.

Most string functions can also work with dates stored in string variables, but string functions handle dates as any other character sequences without recognizing their date-specific features. The date functions, however, offer additional features, for example, you can calculate the difference between two dates in any specified units from years to seconds.

Let's start with the simplest date function, `datenow()`. It returns the current date and time. This is how you use this function:

```
Let $Date_Time = datenow()
```

Looks simple, doesn't it? It is very simple, indeed. In fact, we could have also used the SQR predefined variable `$current-date` instead with one important difference: the `$current_date` variable contains the date and time when your program started while the `datenow()` function returns the current date and time.

Let us take a look at the function `strtodate()`. It helps to convert a text string to the date format. The conversion can be done with or without using a date edit mask. You can also use a specially reserved keyword `Date` in place of a mask to specify the default date mask.

SQR processes edit masks differently in the `strtodate()` function than in the `Move` command. In the `Move` command, the mask tells SQR the look of the target field after the conversion. In the `strtodate()` function, the mask tells SQR what to expect from the source field when doing the conversion. If no mask is specified, the source must be in the format specified by the `SQR_DB_DATE_FORMAT` environmental variable, in one of the database-specific formats (see table 4.1), or in the database-independent date literal format `'SYYYYMMDD[HH24[MI[SS[NNNNNN]]]]'`.

The following example demonstrates both ways of using the `strtodate()` function (with and without an edit mask):

```
!TEST4B.SQR
!Using the strtodate() function
Begin-Setup
   Declare-Variable
        Date $Mydate1
        Date $Mydate2
   End-Declare
End-Setup

Begin-Program
   Let $Mytext1 = '19980315'     ! Here, we use independent date
                                 ! literal format
   Let $Mytext2 = '98/03/15'     ! Here, we use mask-dependent format
   Let $Mydate1 = strtodate($Mytext1)! No mask, use independent date
                                 ! literal format
   Let $Mydate2 = strtodate($Mytext2, 'YY/MM/DD')
                                 ! Source content matches the mask
End-Program
```

The `datetostr()` function is an exact opposite of the `strtodate()`. It converts a date to a string. An edit mask specifying the look of the target string may be used in this function. The keyword `Date` in place of mask is used to specify the default date mask. If no mask is specified, the format specified by the `SQR_DB_DATE_FORMAT` environmental variable will be used. If this variable is not set, SQR will use one of the database-specific formats (see table 4.1), or the database-independent date literal format `'SYYYYMMDD[HH24[MI[SS[NNNNNN]]]]'`. This is an example of the `datetostr()` function:

```
Let $Date_String = datetostr($Mydate, 'MonbDD,bYY')
```

Another date function, `datediff()`, is convenient for calculating the difference between two dates. Before this function was made available, SQR programmers had to write rather sophisticated procedures to perform the task of converting years to months, months to days, accounting for the leap years, and so on. Now you need only the `datediff()` function to calculate the difference in required time units: years, quarters, months, weeks, days, hours, minutes, or even seconds! The function returns a float number that can be negative if the first date is earlier than the second date. Here is how you can use the `datediff()` function to calculate the difference between two dates in months:

```
Let #Diff_Months = datediff(&Effdt, $Calc_Date, 'MONTH')
```

Sometimes, after obtaining the difference between two dates as a number of specified time units, you need to convert this number back into years, months, days, etc. The current version of SQR does not have such a function. You will need to write a procedure or a user function to address this problem.

The `dateadd()` function adds the specified number of time units to a date. It returns another date as the result of the calculation. You can also perform a subtraction with the help of this command by specifying a negative number of the time units.

```
Let $Fifth_Anniversary_Dte = dateadd(&Hire_Dte,'YEAR',5)
```

4.6.4 String functions

String functions are extremely helpful and are widely used in SQR programs. There are sixteen string functions in SQR version 6: `instr()`, `isblank()`, `isnull()`, `length()`, `lower()`, `upper()`, `lpad()`, `rpad()`, `ltrim()`, `replace()`, `rtrim()`, `substr()`, `to_char()`, `to_number()`, `translate()`, and `edit()`. All these functions are described in appendix C. In this chapter we will discuss only a few frequently used ones.

The `length()` function is helpful in determining the number of characters in a string or date:

```
Let #Input_Length = length($Input)
```

The `ltrim()` and `rtrim()` functions use the specified set of characters (usually just one character) to trim the source string or date characters one by one from the left or right until the functions find a character that does not belong to the specified character set. At that moment, the trimming stops. The following example uses a space as a one-character set:

```
Let $Source_String = '     Smith    ,   John, Jr.    '
Let $New_String = ltrim(rtrim($Source_String, ' '), ' ')
! The result will be: 'Smith    ,   John, Jr.'
```

The source phrase in the example includes a number of spaces in the beginning, between the words, and in the end. The combination of the `ltrim()` and `rtrim()` functions eliminates all spaces in the beginning and end of the source string, but leaves the spaces between the words.

The `to_char()` function converts the source numeric literal, column, variable, or expression to the character format and preserves the precision of the source. This is an example of the `to_char()` function:

```
Let $My_String = to_char(#My_Number)
```

The `to_number()` function, an antipode of the `to_char()` function, converts the source string or expression to the numeric format. The function returns a float value, which is then converted to match the format of the target field (integer, float, or decimal). The source string or expression must contain a valid number:

```
Let #My_Number = to_number($My_String)
```

As with the `Move` command, the `to_number()` function scans the source string up to the first non-numeric character (commas are considered non-numeric) and converts only the scanned portion of the string, but the dot as a decimal part separator is processed correctly.

The `lower()` and `upper()` functions convert the contents of their argument to the lower or upper case, respectively (numbers and special characters are not converted), for example:

```
Let $Upper_String = upper($Mixed_String)
```

The `edit()` function is similar to the `Move` command, formatting the source field according to the specified edit mask. Here are a few examples of the `edit()` function:

```
Let $Soc_Sec_Number = edit(#SSN, 'xxx-xx-xxxx')
Let $Disp_Salary = edit((&Annual_Rte + #Bonus), '$$$,$$$,$$$.99')
Let $Disp_Date = edit(datenow(), 'DD/MM/YY')
```

Note You may be asking yourself why we need another function to do something that can be done by a simple `Move` command. The answer is that you cannot use `Move` or any other command in SQR expressions. SQR has a number of functions that do the same jobs as SQR commands, but these functions give you the advantage of being usable in expressions.

You can use a combination of string functions and commands. The following example will strip a carriage return character and a line feed character by using the `ENCODE` command and the `TRANSLATE` function:

```
encode '<13>' into $carriage_return
let $new_val1 = translate($old_val, $carriage_return, ")
encode '<10>' into $line_feed
let $new_val 2= translate($new_val1, $line_feed, ")
```

4.6.5 Miscellaneous functions

SQR has a number of functions that cannot be assigned to any distinct category: `array()`, `ascii()`, `asciic()`, `chr()`, `cond()`, `getenv()`, `nvl()`, `range()`. All these functions are described in detail in appendix C.

The `range()` function deserves a mention here. Use the `range()` function to check if the value of a literal, column, variable, or expression is between two specified boundary values. The boundary values can be specified as literals, columns, variables, or expressions. The function works with numbers, strings, or dates. If the checked argument is numeric, the boundary arguments must be numeric too. If the checked argument is a string, the boundary arguments can be strings or dates.

The function returns one if the checked value is within the range and zero if it is not. Please note that the second operand in the function must specify the lower boundary, whereas the third operand must specify the upper boundary of the range. Otherwise, the function will always return zero. The following three `Let` commands give you three different flavors of the `range()` function: numeric, string, and date.

```
Let #Flag = range(#Hourly_Rte, #Min_Rte, #Max_Rte)
Let #Flag = range(substr($Last_Name,1,1) 'A', 'M')
                                          ! Check if the first character
                                          ! is in range
Let #Flag = range($Date1, &Eff_Dte, datenow())
```

In the last line of the example, the `$Date1` variable is checked for being between the effective date and current date.

KEY POINTS

1. The three main SQR data elements are columns, variables, and literals.
2. SQR columns are fields defined in the database. SQR uses the symbol `&` as the first character of a table column name.
3. SQR variables can be either string variables or numeric variables. SQR uses the special character `$` for string variables and the special character `#` for numeric variables.
4. Starting from version 4, SQR introduced another type of variable: date variables. The numeric variables now can be integers, floats, or decimals.

KEY POINTS (CONTINUED)

5 SQR list variables (introduced in version 5) are ordered collections of SQR variables, literals or column variables.

6 SQR literals are string, date, or numeric constants.

7 SQR variables (except for date variables) do not have to be explicitly declared in the program; when a variable appears for the first time, SQR assigns this variable its initial value.

8 SQR variables can be global or local. Global variables can be referenced throughout the entire program while local variables are effective only within a local procedure.

9 SQR provides you with a number of data element manipulation commands, including arithmetic commands and string manipulation commands.

10 The `Move` command helps you to move data elements from one field to another with optional editing using special edit format masks.

11 The `Let` command has the most power allowing you the use of sophisticated expressions. As a result, one `Let` command can replace a number of elementary arithmetic or string commands.

12 SQR provides you with a rich variety of built-in functions

CHAPTER 5

Basic program structure

IN THIS CHAPTER

- SQR page
- SQR program sections
- SQR procedures

Mastering SQR pages is crucial when you design reports. Real business reports may sometimes be tricky. In the beginning of this chapter, we will discuss the concept of the SQR page without going into many details, but later we will add more information, and by the end of the chapter you will have become rather friendly with the SQR pages.

An SQR program consists of sections. We will discuss all five SQR program sections: the `Program` Section, the `Setup` Section, the `Heading` Section, the `Footing` Section, and the `Procedure` Section.

Finally, we will talk about local and global procedures and about the difference between these two procedure types.

You will encounter a number of unfamiliar words and expressions. Don't worry! Little by little, all these terms will be explained in this chapter or in the subsequent chapters.

All topics covered in this chapter will lay a foundation for a basic understanding of any SQR program no matter how complex the program might be.

5.1 SQR page

One of the most important SQR concepts is the way SQR builds its output pages. SQR does not print into its output file every time you use the `Print` command. Instead, SQR accumulates the entire page in the memory. The heading and footing sections are generated after the body of the page has been filled. Once the entire page is complete, it is written to the output file and is erased from the memory just in time to be replaced with the next page.

Figure 5.1 will help you to understand how SQR views a page.

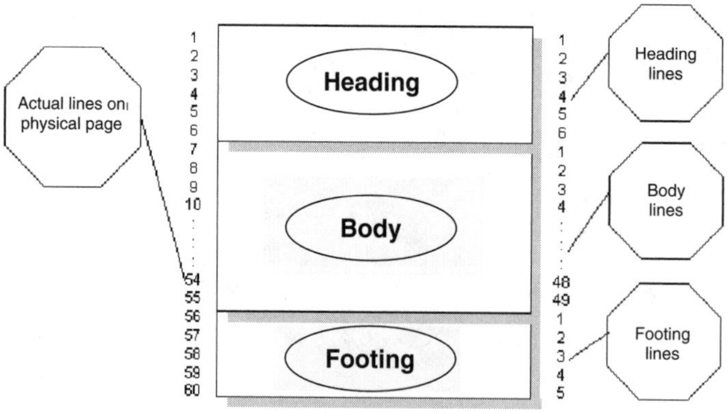

Figure 5.1 Main components of SQR page

5.2 How SQR processes the source program

SQR goes over the source program in two stages. The first stage is the compile stage, during which

- All external source files are inserted into the program source file.
- All compiler directives are evaluated. Compiler directives start with # and are processed during the compile stage, not the execution stage. These directives help to automatically change the program logic based on the values of certain variables (called substitution variables) without changing the source code of the program. It is achieved by making the SQR compiler ignore certain parts of the source code, depending on the values of certain substitution variables. This makes SQR programs more flexible and easier to maintain. (We will discuss compiler directives in chapters 11 and 20.)
- All substitution variables are resolved. These variables play the same role for parts of the source program as compiler directives do for the program logic. With just one key stroke, text substitution variables allow you to change variable names, literals, or even entire pieces of code, thus eliminating the need for a time-consuming search-and-replace.
- SQR executes all `Ask` commands that prompt the user for the values of some substitution variables not coded in the program (more about the `Ask` command in chapter 11).
- Program memory and work buffers are allocated. All memory arrays are created.
- SQR checks the syntax of the source program.
- SQR determines how to optimize the SQL data access.

The second stage comprises the actual program execution and takes place only if SQR finds no compile errors in your program. During the execution stage, SQR

- starts processing at `Begin-Program` and stops at `End-Program`
- calculates the size of the report working page
- processes the report body
- processes the report heading
- processes the report footing
- writes the entire page to the output file and gets ready for the next page.

Usually you won't separate the two stages when running the source program: SQR runs through the compile stage and, if no errors are found, immediately switches into the execution stage.

In some cases, though, you may not want to proceed directly to the execution stage. SQR does allow you to perform the compile step once, then save the pre-compiled version of the program, to rerun your report at a later date. Keep in mind, however, that if you use a pre-compiled version of a program, SQR will not re-execute all the above mentioned compile steps, including the `Ask` commands. SQR will use all external source files inserted during the compilation stage as well as all substitution variable values assigned. SQR does not compile your program into machine language: it will still run under SQR. The result of the compilation is portable between different hardware platforms. (Refer to chapter 18 for more details about running precompiled SQR programs.)

5.3 Five sections of an SQR program

An SQR program consists of the following five sections (also depicted in figure 5.2):

- `Program` section
- `Setup` section
- `Heading` section
- `Footing` section
- `Procedure` section

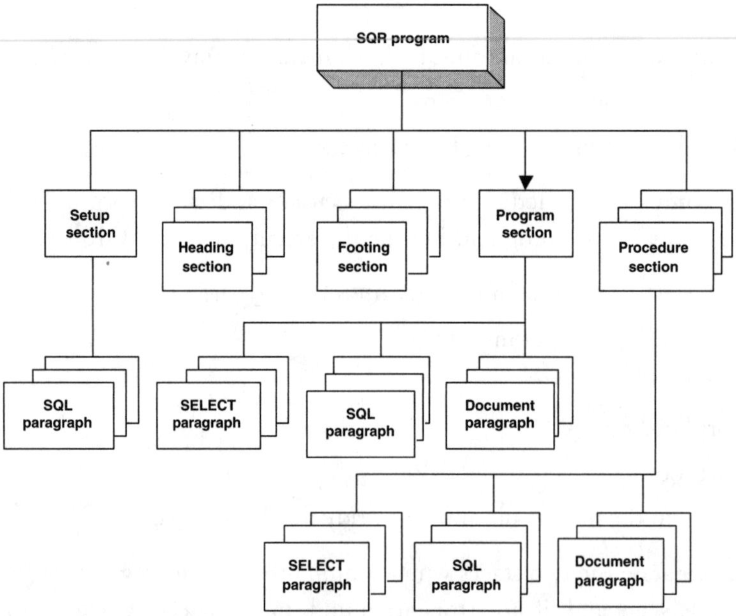

Figure 5.2 Different elements of an SQR program

Each section starts with the Begin command and ends with the End command. The Begin and End commands consist of the Begin or End verb followed by the hyphen and the section name, for example, Begin-Setup.

The only required section in SQR program is the Program section. All other sections are optional.

5.4 Program section

The Program section is the most important section in any SQR program. It defines the beginning and the end of the program. After SQR detects the Begin-Program statement in your source, it executes all other commands one by one, stopping only when the End-Program statement is read. This is how it looks:

```
Begin-Program
  ! Program section commands
End-Program
```

Place the Program section near the top of your program for better readability (if you have the Setup section and/or the Heading and Footing sections in your program, the Program section is usually located below these three sections). You can have only one Program section in a program and, for simple reports, it may be the only section you need. In complex programs, it may be a good idea to use the Program section to control the general flow of processing by calling different procedures (discussed later in this chapter). This approach is called modular programming, and it makes your programs easier to debug and maintain.

> **Note** In SQR versions prior to version 4, the Program section was also called the Report section.

5.5 Setup section

The Setup section contains commands that determine the overall characteristics of the program. This section is optional but, if included, must be placed at the beginning of the program. The Setup section is processed during the program compilation stage before actual program execution.

The following commands can be used in the Setup section (commands marked with an asterisk are used only in the Setup section)

- Ask *
- Begin-SQL
- Create-Array

- `Declare-Chart` *
- `Declare-Color-Map` *
- `Declare-Connection`
- `Declare-Image` *
- `Declare-Layout` *
- `Declare-Printer` *
- `Declare-Procedure` *
- `Declare-Report` *
- `Declare-TOC` *
- `Declare-Variable`
- `Load-Lookup`
- `Use` (Sybase and Microsoft SQL Server only) *

For a complete command syntax and usage, please see appendix D.

The following example illustrates how the `Setup` section is incorporated in an SQR program:

```
!TEST5A.SQR
!A Setup section
!****************************
Begin-Setup
!****************************
Declare-Layout Default
     Paper-Size=(8.5,11)
     Left-Margin=1.5
     Right-Margin=1.5
     Top-Margin=1
     Bottom-Margin=1
End-Declare
End-Setup
!****************************
Begin-Program
     ! ...
End-Program
```

In this `Setup` section, some default page layout parameters are overridden with parameters specified in the `Declare-Layout` command.

In `Test5A.sqr`, we use the `Setup` section to control the print parameters via the `Declare-Layout` command. In addition to paper size and margins, we could also have specified the maximum number of lines and columns as well as page orientation (the default orientation is portrait).

Take another look at our program. Note we use the `Default` as the layout name. SQR will take all the default layout parameters and substitute only the ones specified in the program. The final page layout parameter list will be a combination of default parameters and parameters specified in the program (paper size and margins are in inches).

```
Paper-Size = (8.5, 11)
Left-Margin = 1.5
Right-Margin = 1.5
Top-Margin = 1
Bottom-Margin = 1
Orientation = Portrait ! (default value)
Columns = 65 ! (default value)
Lines = 60 ! (default value).
```

5.6 Heading section

Commands in the `Heading` section are executed every time SQR generates a page. This section is used only when your report has a heading which is almost always the case for any business report. When an SQR program generates multiple reports, you can have more than one `Heading` section; however, there can be only one heading for each report. This does not mean that you have to code a `Heading` section for every single report. If some reports have identical headings, one `Heading` section can be shared by these reports.

Typically, report headings contain report title, date, page number, and similar information. The `Heading` section is processed just before the report page is written to the output file, after the page body is completed or a special command, `New-Page`, is issued.

The overall structure of the `Heading` section is rather simple:

```
Begin-Heading  #lines
     ! Heading section commands
End-Heading
```

Parameter *`#lines`* in the `Begin-Heading` statement defines the number of lines allocated for the heading. You must specify the number of heading lines to help SQR reserve enough room for heading at the page top, including the blank lines. SQR will calculate the number of lines available for the page body and footing by subtracting the `#lines` value from the `Max-Lines` parameter in the `Declare-Layout` command (if specified) or from the default value of the `Max-Lines` parameter.

Now, let us add the `Heading` section to our program:

```
!TEST5B.SQR
!A Heading section
!************************
Begin-Setup
!************************
     ! Setup section commands
```

```
End-Setup
!***********************
Begin-Heading 3
     Let $Date = datenow()
     Print $Date (1,1) Edit 'DD/MM/YYYY'
     Print 'Report TEST5B.SQR' (2,1)
     Page-Number (3,1) 'Page'
End-Heading
!************************
Begin-Program
!***********************
     ! Program section commands
End-Program
!***********************
```

This parameter specifies the number of lines reserved for the report heading.

Our program allocates three lines on each page for heading, and includes the date and time, report title, and page number in the heading area.

Take another look at figure 5.1. Line numbers within the heading, the body, and footing sections of the report are numbered separately, therefore, each section begins with its own line one. What would happen if the number of lines for the heading section was coded equal to two, but the `Print` commands in the `Heading` section use lines number three and four? In that case SQR would consider the first two lines as heading lines and the next two lines as report body lines, possibly causing the last two lines of the report page body to disappear from the output. It is, therefore, a good practice to always reserve enough lines for your headings.

Because SQR generates the heading and footing after the body of the page has been filled, by the time the heading and footing are processed, all variable values in the `Program` section have been assigned or calculated. You can take advantage of this fact and print in the `Heading` section any information selected from the database, or calculated, or derived some other way in the `Program` section as shown in the next example. (For a complete command syntax and usage, please see appendix D.)

```
!******************
Begin-Heading
    Print 'Report  TEST5B.SQR' (1,1)
    Print 'List of all active employees for company ' (2,10)
    Print $Company (2,+1)
End-Heading

!*****************
Begin-Program
!*****************
    Move 'ABCD Corporation' To $Company
End-Program

!****************
```

The value of `$Company` is assigned in the `Program` section but can be printed in the `Heading` section.

The value of `$Company` is assigned in the `Program` section and is available in the `Heading` and `Footing` sections.

5.7 Footing section

The general structure of the `Footing` section is as simple as that for the `Heading` section (the complete command syntax can be found in appendix D). All commands in this section are executed before the current page is written to the output file. Lines allocated for the footing, as well as lines allocated for the heading, reduce the number of lines available for the report body. Multiple-report programs may have multiple `Footing` sections.

```
Begin-Footing  #lines
     ! Footing section commands
End-Footing
```

Parameter *`#lines`* also defines the number of lines allocated for the footing. You must specify the number of footing lines to be reserved at the bottom of each page, including the blank lines. SQR will calculate the number of lines available for the page body and heading by subtracting the `#lines` value from the `Max-Lines` parameter in the `Declare-Layout` command (if specified) or from the default value of the `Max-Lines` parameter.

```
!TEST5C.SQR
!A Footing section
!***********************
Begin-Setup
!***********************
    ! Setup section commands
End-Setup
!***********************
Begin-Heading 3                      <-- 3 lines reserved for the report heading
     Print 'Report TEST5C.SQR' (1,1)
End-Heading
!***********************
Begin-Footing 2                      <-- 2 lines reserved for the report footing
     Page-Number (1,35) 'Page'
     Last-Page        ()   ' of ' '.'
End-Heading
!***********************
Begin-Program
!***********************
     ! Program section commands
End-Program
!***********************
```

In `Test5C.sqr`, we decided to print the current page number and the total of all pages at the bottom of the page. How does SQR know the total number of pages while generating a page in the beginning or in the middle of the report? The `Last-Page` command used in the `Footing` section allows SQR to accumulate the entire report without printing it until after the last page is processed.

Note You cannot use `Print` commands in the `Program` section to print in lines that belong to the `Heading` or `Footing` section. Only commands executed from the `Heading` or `Footing` section may place data in the corresponding areas of the page.

5.8 Procedure section

While the `Procedure` section is optional, it can be used to break your program into manageable and easy-to-maintain pieces. Consequently, the `Procedure` section is one of the most important parts of an SQR program. Multiple `Procedure` sections can exist in your program, but must have unique names and be invoked with the help of the `Do` command. Every procedure starts with the `Begin-Procedure` command (with an optional procedure name) and ends with the `End-Procedure` command. Procedures may contain commands and one or more of the following paragraphs: `Select`, `SQL`, or `Document`. (We will cover all these paragraphs in later chapters.)

Program `Test5D.sqr` is an example of the usage of SQR procedures:

```
!TEST5D.SQR
!Using the Procedure Sections
!****************************
Begin-Program
!****************************
   Do Main          <--  The Main procedure is invoked
End-Program              with the help of the Do command.

!****************************
Begin-Procedure Main
!****************************
    Do Select_Employee   <--  The Select_Employee procedure
End-Procedure                 is invoked in the Main procedure.

!*****************************************
Begin-Procedure Select_Employee
!*****************************************
Begin-Select
Emplid
Name
From Personal_Data
Where Company = 'ABC'
End-Select
End-Procedure
!**********************************
```

Procedures can be *global* or *local*. By default, all procedures are global; all variables and selected columns from a global procedure can be referenced in other procedures. To make a procedure local, you have to explicitly declare it local using the `Local` keyword (as shown in the next example), or to use arguments in the procedure. All procedures with arguments are considered local. All variables and selected columns created within a local procedure can be referenced only in this procedure and will not be recognized outside the procedure.

So far, all procedures in our previous examples have been global. The following example demonstrates how to explicitly declare a local procedure using the `Local` keyword:

```
Begin-Procedure List_Employees Local
    ! ...
End-Procedure
```

The second example of declaring a local procedure using the procedure arguments is

```
Begin-Procedure List_Employees($Company)
    ! ...
End-Procedure
```

The following rules apply to variables in local procedures:

- When a query is defined in a local procedure, all selected column names are considered local and cannot be referenced in other procedures.
- If a local procedure is called recursively, SQR will maintain only one copy of its local variables.
- To reference a global variable in a local procedure, you have to add an underscore to the variable name after its special character `$`, `#`, or `&`. Examples: `#_Count`, `$_Street`, `&_Emplid`.
- All SQR reserved variables are global. Therefore, when referencing SQR-reserved variables in a local procedure, you have to add an underscore to their names, for example, `$_sql-error` or `#_sql-status`.

Note When creating a *library procedure*, that is a procedure to be used later in other programs, it is always a good idea to declare it local. This will help you to avoid variable name conflicts that might arise when a calling program's variables have the same name as the library procedure variables. In that case SQR will not be able to differentiate between the variables. Declaring a variable local allows SQR to process local and global variables with the same names as different variables.

As you may have already noticed, global procedures are simpler to use than local procedures. You can use variables defined in other places of the program without special effort. At the same time, this flexibility may backfire when it comes to debugging a large program. It is easy to incorrectly reuse a variable which has already been defined somewhere else in the program. In a local procedure, this will not happen; different local procedures may use local variables with the same names without interfering with each other.

One of the local procedure's specialties is passing and accepting arguments. To better understand local procedures and their arguments, let us consider the following example:

```
!TEST5E.SQR
!Passing parameters between global and local procedures
!*******************
Begin-Program
!*******************

Do Main
End-Program

!*******************
Begin-Procedure Main
!*******************
Do Select_Employee

End-Procedure

!******************************
Begin-Procedure Select_Employee
!******************************
Begin-Select Distinct
A.Company
A.Emplid
Show 'Selected Emplid = ' &A.Emplid
 Let $Found = 'N'
 Do Select_Empl_Name(&A.Emplid, $Name)
 If $Found = 'Y'
 Do Print_Report_Line(&A.Company, &A.Emplid, $Name)
 End-If
From Job A
Where A.Effdt <= Sysdate
End-Select
End-Procedure

!************************************************************
Begin-Procedure Select_Empl_Name($Empl,:$Empl_Name)
!************************************************************
Begin-Select
B.Name
Show 'Found ' $Empl ' ' $Empl_Name
Move 'Y' To $_Found
Move &B.Name To $Empl_Name
From Personal_Data B
Where B.Emplid = $Empl
```

By default, the `Main` procedure is considered global.

By default, the `Select_Employee` procedure is considered global.

The `Select_Empl_Name` procedure is local: it uses input and output argument.

```
End-Select
End-Procedure

!******************************************************
Begin-Procedure Print_Report_Line($Company, $Empl, $Name)
!******************************************************
Print $Company    (+1,1)
Print $Empl       (,+2)
Print $Name       (,+2)
End-Procedure
!********************
```

The `Print_Report_Line` procedure is local: it uses input arguments.

> **Note** List variables may not be passed as parameters to local procedures.

In the example, the `Main` procedure is a global procedure that uses the `Do` command to invoke another global procedure, `Select_Employee`. Every database column value selected in `Select_Employee` is available throughout the entire program because this procedure is global. After the value of `Emplid` is found, it is passed to procedure `Select_Empl_Name` to obtain a name of the selected employee. Procedure `Select_Empl_Name` is local because it uses arguments. In our case, there are two arguments: variable `$Emplid` is passed to `Select_Empl_Name` as an input argument, whereas variable `$Empl_Name` is returned back to the calling procedure as an output argument. All output procedure argument names must be prefixed with a colon in the `Begin-Procedure` statement. Please note that when referencing global variable `$Found` in local procedure `Select_Empl_Name`, we added an underscore to the variable name after its special character `$`.

KEY POINTS

1. SQR page consists of a heading, a body, and a footing.
2. SQR accumulates all the report page lines in the memory and writes the entire page into the output file.
3. In most cases, SQR processes programs in two steps: the compile step and the execution step.
4. An SQR program may include the `Program` section, the `Setup` section, the `Heading` section, the `Footing` section, and the `Procedure` section. The only required section is the `Program` section.

KEY POINTS (CONTINUED)

5 The `Setup` section determines the overall characteristics of the program. This section is optional. The `Setup` section is processed during the program compilation stage before actual program execution.

6 Commands in the `Heading` and `Footing` sections are executed every time SQR generates a page.

7 The `Procedure` section is used to break your program into manageable and easy to maintain pieces. You can have multiple `Procedure` sections in your program. Each procedure is invoked with the help of the `Do` command.

8 Procedures can be global or local. By default, all procedures are global. To make a procedure local you have to explicitly declare it local or define procedure arguments.

9 All procedures that have arguments are local.

10 To reference a global variable within a local procedure, you have to add an underscore to the variable name after its type character `$`, `#`, or `&`.

11 All SQR reserved variables are global, therefore, when referencing SQR reserved variables in a local procedure, you have to add an underscore to their names.

CHAPTER 6

Working with data from a database

IN THIS CHAPTER

- The SQR `Select` paragraph
- SQR commands in the `Select` paragraph
- The print position parameters in the `Print` command
- Referencing SQL table columns and SQL expressions
- The two ways of printing selected columns in the `Select` paragraph: explicit printing and implicit printing
- The `Lookup` and `Load-Lookup` commands

6.1 The Select paragraph

The `Select` paragraph is the essence of an SQR program. It is crucial that you understand how it works. The beauty of the `Select` paragraph is that it is actually a combination of SQL `SELECT` statements and SQR processing; it allows you to apply SQR commands to the values of the selected rows.

The `Select` paragraph starts with the `Begin-Select` statement, followed by a list of all columns to be selected from the database as well as the table names and the selection criteria. It is very similar to the `SQL SELECT` statement. The `End-Select` command is coded at the end of the Select paragraph. All selected column names are placed one per program line at the beginning of each line with no comma. Alternatively, you can place multiple columns on one program line but, if this format is used, you have to separate the column names with commas. What makes the `Begin-Select` statement different from a plain `SQL SELECT` statement is that you can insert SQR commands in this statement. Here is an example:

```
Begin-Select
Emplid
Name
City
State
     Do Print_Row
From Personal_Data
Where Name like 'A%'
End-Select
```

You can insert SQR commands in the `Select` paragraph.

In the example, all rows from the `Personal_Data` table with the column `Name` values starting with `A` are selected from the database. Please note that all column names are coded at position one. All command lines, however, must be indented. This is how SQR distinguishes between column names and SQR commands. In our example, command `Do Print_Row` is indented relative to all column names.

> *Note* All selected columns must be listed in the `Select` paragraph; you cannot use an asterisk in the `Select` paragraph.

Let us see how this all works. What would happen if we did not have the `Do` command in our program? SQR would simply select the proper rows one by one and do nothing. Every selected row would overlay the previous row. Fortunately, SQR allows you to execute any number of SQR commands for each selected row. In our simple example, the `Do` command invokes the `Print_Row` procedure for each selected row. Later, in the following chapters, you will see that you can apply sophisticated logic when processing the selected rows. The `Select` statement actually creates a program loop and invokes the specified SQR commands in every loop iteration. Figure 6.1 explains the concept of the `Select` loop.

The loop will end when there are no more rows left to satisfy the `Where` clause criteria.

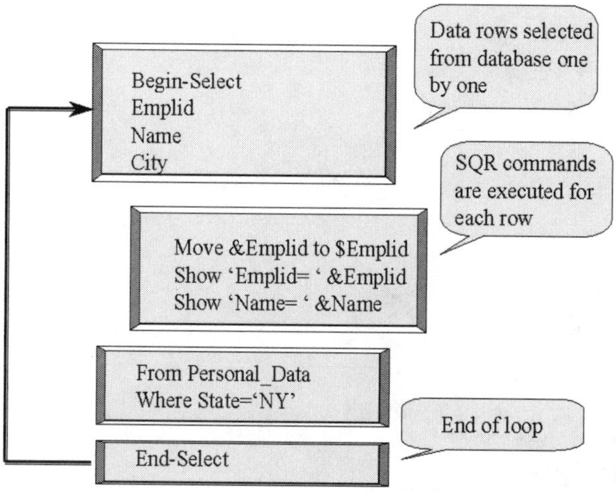

Figure 6.1
The Select paragraph with SQR commands

Since SQR commands are executed after all requested column values from a table row are selected, these commands can be placed anywhere in the `Select` paragraph (between `Begin-Select` and `From`) as long as they are indented. For example

```
Begin-Select
Emplid
     Move &Emplid to $Emplid
     Show 'Emplid = ' &Emplid
Name
     Show 'Name = ' &Name
City
     Do Get_Hire_Date
     Do Print_Row
From Personal_Data
Where State = 'NY'
End-Select
```

As you can see, two procedures—`Get_Hire_Date` and `Print_Row`—are called from the `Select` paragraph with the help of the `Do` command. You can have more than one `Select` paragraph in your program and the invoked procedures may also contain one or more `Select` paragraphs:

```
!TEST6A.SQR
!Using Nested Selects
!***********************************
Begin-Procedure Get_Employees
!***********************************
Begin-Select
Emplid
     Move &Emplid to $Emplid
     Show 'Emplid = ' &Emplid
Name
     Show 'Name = ' &Name
City
State
Zip
     Do Get_Hire_Date
     Do Print_Row
From Personal_Data
Where State = 'NY'
End-Select
End-Procedure

!***********************************
Begin-Procedure Get_Hire_Date
!***********************************
Begin-Select
Hire_Dt
From Employment
Where Emplid = $Emplid
End-Select
End-Procedure

!***********************************
Begin-Procedure Print_Row
!***********************************
Print $Emplid  (+1,1,11)
Print &Name    (,+2,30)
Print &City    (,+2,20)
Print &State   (,+2,15)
Print &Zip     (,+2,10)
Print &Hire_Dt (,+2,10)
End-Procedure
!***********************************
```

Invoked procedures may include one or more `Select` paragraphs.

The numbers in parentheses in the `Print` command indicate page line, page column, and output field length.

The numbers in parentheses in the `Print` command indicate the following: the first number defines the absolute or relative page line number; the second number defines the absolute or relative print column number; and the third number indicates the output field length (if omitted, the selected column length is used as the default). (We will discuss the `Print` command in detail in chapter 9 and subsequent chapters.)

Take a closer look at the example. In the Get_Employees procedure, for every row selected from Personal_Data, two procedures are called: one to obtain Hire_Dt and another to print all information selected for the employee. This is an example of the nested query technique. The bind variable $Emplid is used to join the inner query with the outer query. (See chapter 11 for a discussion of bind variables.)

What would happen if the inner query did not return any rows from table Employment? When a row is not returned from a query, none of the SQR commands in the Select paragraph are executed. In our case, variable &Hire_Dt for this particular employee would be set to the NULL value. All other variables, however, would be assigned their respective values, and the program would still generate an output line. To avoid the problem, our program needs some refinement. Let us initialize string variable $Hire_Date with spaces and print the hire date value from string variable $Hire_Date rather than from SQR column &Hire_Dt. Just a reminder: SQR column names start with & whereas string variable names start with $. This is how procedures Get_Hire_Date and Print_Row will look after the change:

```
!TEST6B.SQR
!Avoiding printing the NULL values
!****************************************
Begin-Procedure Get_Hire_Date
!****************************************
Move ' '          To $Hire_Date
Begin-Select
Hire_Dt
     Move &Hire_Dt To $Hire_Date
From Employment
Where Emplid = $Emplid
End-Select
End-Procedure

!****************************************
Begin-Procedure Print_Row
!****************************************
Print $Emplid (+1,1,11)
Print &Name (,+2,30)
Print &City (,+2,20)
Print &State (,+2,15)
Print &Zip (,+2,10)
Print $Hire_Date(,+2,10)        <----  Please note we print
End-Procedure                          $Hire_Date, not &Hire_Dt.
!****************************************
```

The first SQR command in procedure Get_Hire_Date just initializes variable $Hire_Date. If the SQL query returns a row, SQR will move the returned value to $Hire_Date; if no rows are returned, the Move operator (the only SQR command in the Select paragraph) will not be executed, and $Hire_Date will remain filled with spaces.

Another way to deal with empty SQL result sets is to use a switch variable. Let us change the `Get_Hire_Date` procedure

```
!TEST6C.SQR
!Using flags to check if any rows were selected
!*****************************************
Begin-Procedure Get_Hire_Date
!*****************************************
Move 'N' to $Found_Flag
Begin-Select
Hire_Dt
     Move 'Y' to $Found_Flag
From Employment
Where Emplid = $Emplid
End-Select
End-Procedure

!*****************************************
Begin-Procedure Print_Row
!*****************************************
Print $Emplid (+1,1,11)
Print &Name (,+2,30)
Print &City (,+2,20)
Print &State (,+2,15)
Print &Zip (,+2,10)
If $Found_Flag = 'Y'
  Print &Hire_Dt (,+2,10)
End-If
End-Procedure
!*****************************************
```

The value of `$Found_Flag` is checked to make sure the row has been selected.

After procedure `Get_Hire_Date` is executed, the `Print_Row` procedure checks the value of the `$Found_Flag` variable to make sure the row has been selected. It is always a good practice to check if your `Select` paragraph returns the expected rows.

When a `Select` paragraph contains a local procedure call, make sure that any variable, which may be used as a record count, is not defined in the local procedure. Otherwise, this record count will not be available to the calling procedure. If you need to update the record count in the local procedure, use a global variable defined outside of the local procedure and do not forget to use an underscore in the variable name. For example, if the name of a record count variable is `#Rec_Count`, it should be referred to as `#_Rec_Count` in the local procedure.

6.2 How to reference selected columns and SQL expressions

You already know that when a column value is selected from a database, SQR automatically creates a column variable for this column. The name of the column variable is the column name prefixed with an ampersand (&). You can use this name to reference the column variable later in your program. In our previous examples, all the selected table columns were automatically assigned their respective column variable names, for example, &Emplid, &Name, &Zip. If you use a table name alias in your Select paragraph, SQR will include the alias in the column variable name, for instance, &Personal_Data.Emplid or &A.Name. You can also have SQR assign a different name for a column variable by placing this new name right after the selected column in the Begin-Select statement. Why would someone want to rename a default column name? One reason is to avoid duplicate names. For example, table Personal_Data and table Employment both have the same column Emplid. You can use a different name for one of the column variables. Another possible use of name reassignment is to assign a name to an SQL expression or to an SQL aggregate function. Just one example:

Note Column variables are read-only variables. You cannot change column variable values or assign them new values.

```
Begin-Select
Count(*) &EE_Count
     Print 'Employee count = ' (1,1)
     Print &EE_Count (,+1)
From Employment_Data
Where Hire_Dt < Sysdate
And Empl_Rcd# = 0     ! We use this because
                      !there may be multiple employee records
End-Select
```

The $EE_Count column variable will hold the value of SQL function Count.

6.3 Explicit and implicit printing

In all previous examples we used the Print command to print the selected column values. This is called *explicit printing*. You may have SQR print a value of a selected column without issuing the Print command by placing a position parameter immediately after the column name. The printing will be performed at the moment of selection. This method of printing is called *implicit printing*. Let us change the Get_Employees procedure to print the employee information right after selection:

```
!TEST6D.SQR
!Implicit printing in the Select paragraph
!*****************************
Begin-Program
!*****************************
Do Get_Employees
End-Program
!*****************************
Begin-Procedure Get_Employees
!*****************************
Begin-Select
Emplid  (+1,1)        !Implicit Printing
    Move &Emplid to $Emplid
Name  (,+2)
City  (,+2)
State (,+2)
    Do Get_Hire_Date
From Personal_Data
Where State = 'NY'
End-Select
End-Procedure

!****************************************
Begin-Procedure Get_Hire_Date
!****************************************
Begin-Select
Hire_Dt  (,+2)
From Employment
Where Emplid = $Emplid
End-Select
End-Procedure
!****************************************
```

The print position parameters next to a table column cause the column value to be printed without using the `Print` command.

Notice the difference? We eliminate the entire `Print_Row` procedure by placing the print position parameters in the `Select` paragraph. SQR automatically executes the `Print` command for all selected columns with print position parameters specified. Figure 6.2 shows the program output using implicit printing.

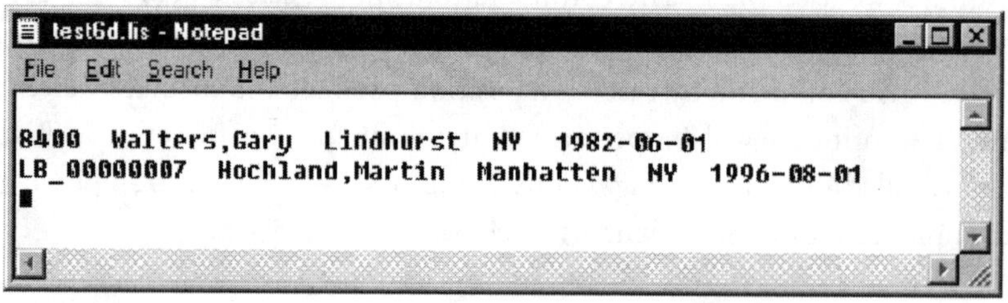

Figure 6.2 An output of a program that uses implicit printing

What would be the order of print commands execution in a `Select` paragraph with mixed implicit and explicit printing? To answer this question, let's run the following example and consider the results in figure 6.3.

```
!TEST6E.SQR
!Combining implicit and explicit printing in one Select paragraph
!******************************
Begin-Program
!******************************
Do Get_Employees
End-Program

!****************************************
Begin-Procedure Get_Employees
!****************************************
Begin-Select
Emplid  (+1,1)             !Implicit Printing
   Move &Emplid to $Emplid
   Print 'After Move Command. This is an example of explicit -
     printing' (+1,6)
Name  (+1,1)
City  (,+2)
State (,+2)
     Print 'About to call Get_Hire_Date procedure' (+1,6)
     Do Get_Hire_Date
From Personal_Data
Where State = 'NY'
End-Select
End-Procedure

!****************************************
Begin-Procedure Get_Hire_Date
!****************************************
Begin-Select
Hire_Dt  (+1,1)
From Employment
Where Emplid = $Emplid
End-Select
End-Procedure
!****************************************
```

Let's analyze figure 6.3. As you can see, the program printed the employee Id first. This was the result of the first implicit printing specified for the `Emplid` column. Next, the program printed the output of the `Print` command that was coded immediately after the `Emplid` column, followed by the results of an implicit printing for the `Name`, `City`, and `State` columns. As you can see, the output of the last explicit `Print` command concluded the sequence. Therefore, the order of both implicit and explicit print

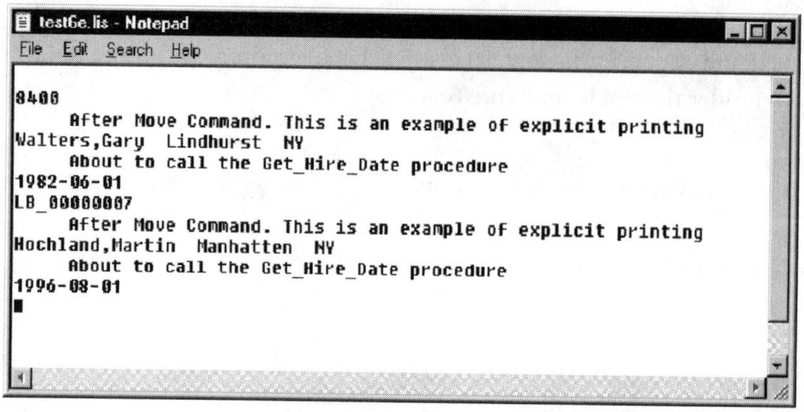

Figure 6.3 The order of both implicit and explicit print commands output is determined by the order in which these commands are coded in the Select paragraph.

commands output is determined by the order in which these commands are coded in the `Select` paragraph.

In addition to print position parameters, you can also include print edit parameters in your `Select` paragraph. These parameters define the output edit masks for each column, for example:

```
Begin-Select
A.Zip   (,+2) Edit 99999-9999
A.Phone   (,+2) Edit xxx/xxx-xxxxx
From Personal_Data
End-Select
```

See chapter 9 for a complete description of all `Print` command parameters.

6.4 Selecting data from multiple tables

You can select data from multiple tables by joining these tables in the main query. Let us rewrite our program and join table `Personal_Data` and table `Employment` in the main query:

```
!TEST6F.SQR
!Using table joins in the Select paragraph
!**************************************
Begin-Procedure Get_Employees
!**************************************
Begin-Select
A.Emplid (+1, 1)
A.Name    (,+2)
```

```
A.City          (,+2)
A.State         (,+2)
A.Postal            (,+2)
B.Hire_Dt       (,+2)
! Do Get_Hire_Dt
From Personal_Data A, Employment B
where A.Emplid=B.Emplid
And B.Empl_Rcd=0
End-Select
End-Procedure
!****************************************
```

We do not need to call the Get_Hire_Dt procedure.

Our program becomes simpler and smaller. Needless to say, simpler programs, although easier to maintain, are not always better. If records for a particular employee exist in one table, but not in the other, our simple join query would return no rows, and nothing would be printed for this particular `Emplid`. If, however, you need to print the information for every employee from the `Personal_Data` table (even if this employee has not been entered into the `Employment` table), you may use the nested query from our previous example instead of a table join, or use outer join.

6.5 Using the Load-Lookup and Lookup commands to improve performance

Another very useful technique of retrieving information from multiple tables employs the `Lookup` and `Load-Lookup` commands. Not only does this method significantly improve the program performance, but it may also simplify table joins.

The `Load-Lookup` command creates an internal memory array and populates this array with keys and the corresponding column values from a specified table. This command can be used in either the `Setup` section or any procedure, but it is important to remember that, if the `Load-Lookup` command is used in the `Setup` section, it is processed only once. When used in a procedure, the command is processed every time the procedure gets executed. `Load-Lookup` retrieves two fields from the database: the `Key` field and the `Return_Value` field. The `Key` field may be of the string or numeric format, and it must refer to a column with unique values in the table. No `NULL` values are allowed in the field. The `Return_Value` field may refer to just one table column or a combination of several table columns. In case of a column combination, the columns must be concatenated. You can have the `Load-Lookup` command populate its array with only certain records based on some specified selection criteria (see the example following).

> *Note* Please note that the `Return_Value` parameter in the `Load-Lookup` command is coded with an underscore! This is rather unusual for SQR. In most cases, SQR uses a hyphen in the names of its commands and parameters.

The `Lookup` command is used to search through internal memory arrays created and populated by the `Load-Lookup` command. It returns the `Return_Value` field value for each specified `Key` field value. SQR uses the binary search algorithm to search through the array. The following example shows how to use these two commands.

```
!TEST6G.SQR
!Using the Lookup and Load-Lookup commands
!**************
Begin-Setup
!**************
Load-Lookup Name =Company_Names
            Rows=200
            Table=Company_Tbl
            Key=Company
            Return_Value=Descr
     Where=Country='USA'
End-Setup
!********************************************
Begin-Program
!********************************************
Do Select_Employees
End-Program

!********************************************
Begin-Procedure Select_Employees
!********************************************
Begin-Select Distinct
Emplid (+1,1)
Company
   Lookup Company_Names &Company $Comp_Name
   Print $Comp_Name (,+1)
Where
From Job A
    A.Effdt =  (Select max(effdt) from Job
                 where Emplid    = A.Emplid
                 and   Empl_Rcd  = A.Empl_Rcd)
and A.Effseq =  (Select max(effseq) from Job
                 where Emplid    = A.Emplid
                 and   Empl_Rcd  = A.Empl_Rcd
                 and   Effdt     = A.Effdt)
End-Select
End-Procedure
!*******************************
```

The `Load-Lookup` command creates the `Company_Names` array and populates the array with data from the `Company` table.

The `Lookup` command retrieves the `$Comp_Name` value based on the key stored in `&Company`.

In this example, the `Load-Lookup` command creates an array named `Company_Names` and populates the array with the company names from the `Descr` column of the `Company_Tbl`. When populating the array, `Load-Lookup` uses the SQL `WHERE` clause to select only table rows with the `Country` column value equal to `'USA'`.

The Rows parameter specifies the initial size of our lookup array as 200 rows. This parameter is optional and, if omitted, a default value of 100 will be used. The Rows parameter value is not critical, it just helps SQR to manage memory more efficiently. When an array becomes full, another optional parameter, Extent, will be used to increase this array. If no Extent is specified, 25% of the initial size will be used as a default value. Note that the only limit to the size of a lookup table is the amount of memory available in your computer.

(The Load-Lookup command has a number of other useful parameters. For a complete list of the command parameters, please refer to the command description in appendix D.)

The Lookup command in the Select_Employees procedure is executed for each selected table row and retrieves from the Company_Names array the value of $Comp_Name based on the key value stored in &Company.

Let's consider a more complex example of the Lookup and Load-Lookup commands. Suppose you need to write field edit logic in a data extraction program for a payroll application. One of the input fields is the earning code for general deductions. This field verification can be done by performing the Deduction_Table lookup for each input record. For obvious reasons, this may not be the most efficient solution when the program input is large. This is a classic example of an instance in which the Lookup command may help to speed up processing. By loading the Deduction_Table into memory only once, and performing a binary search in the program memory (rather than reading the table to find the earning code), the processing time may be decreased ten-fold!

To make the program work even faster, you can limit the size of the lookup array by selecting only a certain type of deductions with Plan_Type = '00' (General Deductions) and loading only the most current rows into the lookup array.

This is how our code will look:

```
!TEST6H.SQR
!Using a complex Where clause with a subselect in the Load-Lookup
!*******************
Begin-Setup
!*******************
Load-Lookup name=Ded_Codes
Rows=500
Table='Deduction_Tbl A'
Key=Dedcd
Return_Value=DED_PRIORITY
Where='A.Plan_Type=''00'' and A.Effdt=
 (Select max(Effdt) from Deduction_Tbl
 Where Plan_Type=A.Plan_Type and Dedcd=A.Dedcd)'
End-Setup
!*******************
Begin-Program
```

```
!******************
!...
Let $Dedcd='NETPAY'
!...
Do Lookup_Dedcd
End-Program

!****************************
Begin-Procedure Lookup_Dedcd
!****************************
Lookup Ded_Codes $Dedcd $DED_PRIORITY
If Not Isnull($DED_PRIORITY)
   Show '$DED_PRIORITY=' $DED_PRIORITY
Else
   Let $Err = 'Dedcd '||$Dedcd ||' Not Found'
   Show $Err
End-If
End-Procedure
!...
```

As you can see, the `Load-Lookup` command allows for employing fairly complex `Where` clauses.

You can also build the `Where` clause in the `Load-Lookup` command dynamically by placing it into a string variable:

```
!TEST6I.SQR
!Using a dynamically built Where clause in the Load-Lookup command
!******************
Begin-Program
!******************
Let $Where = 'A.Plan_Type=''00'' and'
   ||' A.Effdt=(Select max (Effdt) from Deduction_Tbl'
   ||' Where Plan_Type=A.Plan_Type and Dedcd=A.Dedcd)'

Load-Lookup name=Ded_Codes
Rows=5
Table='Deduction_Tbl A'
Key=Dedcd
Return_Value='DESCR||'',''||DED_PRIORITY'
Where=$Where

Let $Dedcd='NETPAY'
Do Lookup_Dedcd
End-Program
!****************************
Begin-Procedure Lookup_Dedcd
!****************************
Lookup Ded_Codes $Dedcd $Return_Val
If Not Isnull($Return_Val)
   Unstring $Return_Val by ',' into $Descr $DED_PRIORITY
   Show '$Decscr=' $Descr
```

```
      Show '$DED_PRIORITY=' $DED_PRIORITY
   Else
      Let $Err = 'Dedcd '||$Dedcd ||' Not Found'
      Show $Err
   End-If
   End-Procedure
```

Did you notice that the `Load-Lookup` command in this example was moved from the `Setup` section to the `Program` section? The `Let` command used to build the `$Where` string is not allowed in the `Setup` section.

Please note another special feature in this example: the value in the `Return_Value` parameter includes not just one column name, but a comma-separated list of column names. We use a concatenation to store more than one column in the `Return_Val` string. In the `Lookup_Dedcd` procedure, we use the SQR `Unstring` command to parse the `$Return_Val` string to separate the column values. Figure 6.4. shows the `Test6I.sqr` execution log:

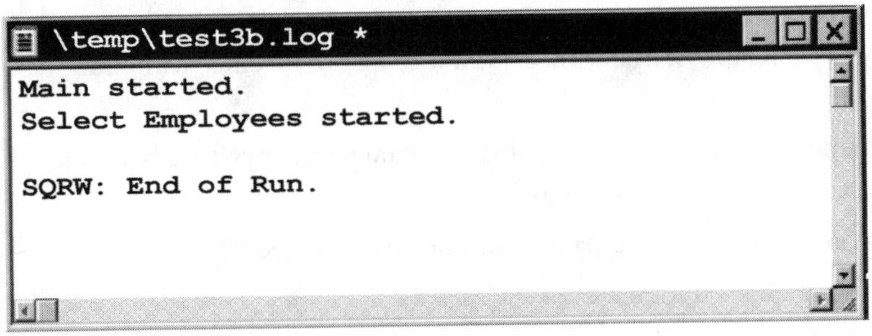

Figure 6.4 The Test6I.sqr program execution log

In `Test6I.sqr`, we used a hard-coded plan type value in the `Where` clause. If you want to use a string variable `$Plan_Type` instead of `'00'`, you cannot simply replace `'00'` with the `$Plan_Type`. SQR will not be able to interpret this string variable correctly in a quoted expression.

Here is the correct way to do this:

```
Let $Plan_Type='00'
Let $Where = 'A.Plan_Type='
 ||''''||$Plan_Type||''''
||' and A.Effdt=(Select max (Effdt) from Deduction_Tbl'
 ||' where A.Plan_Type=A.Plan_Type and Dedcd=A.Dedcd)'
```

In this example, the `$Plan_Type` string variable is surrounded with four quotes. If we did not enclose `$Plan_Type` in the quotes, this part of the `Where` clause would look like `A.Plan_Type = value`. The correct SQL syntax must be `A.Plan_Type = 'value'`. Therefore, we need to concatenate `$Plan_Type` with a quote on each side of this variable. Because a quote is considered a special character by the SQR compiler, we need to type it twice and enclose the double quote in single quotes.

Now that you know how to use the `Load-Lookup` and `Lookup` commands, let's discuss the benefits of their usage. In particular, let's consider whether table joins or lookups are more efficient. Generally, if your report is not too large and the number of table rows to be joined is also small, you would probably be better off using regular table joins because the `Load-Lookup` command loads selected table rows into the memory every time the report runs. However, for long program runs, `Load-Lookup` has proven to greatly improve performance. You may also consider using `Load-Lookup` when joining more than three large tables.

KEY POINTS

1. The `Select` paragraph starts with `Begin-Select` and ends with `End-Select`.
2. SQR commands can be placed in the `Select` paragraph anywhere between the column names and the `From` clause.
3. SQR commands in the `Select` paragraph must be indented.
4. `Select *` is not allowed in SQR.
5. SQR commands in the `Select` paragraph are executed for each selected row.
6. SQR column variables are read-only.
7. You can use an implicit `Print` command in the `Select` paragraph by placing the position qualifiers next to the selected columns.
8. There are many ways to select data from multiple tables. You can use SQL table joins, nested or hierarchical queries, or the `Load-Lookup` and `Lookup` commands.
9. Using the `Lookup` technique for long reports may significantly improve performance.
10. The `Load-Lookup` command can be used in the `Setup` section or in any procedure. It is used in conjunction with one or more `Lookup` commands.

CHAPTER 7

Taking full advantage of SQL

IN THIS CHAPTER

- Recommendations on the usage of native SQL statements in SQR
- The SQL paragraph
- How to execute more than one SQL statement in a single SQL paragraph
- The importance of handling error conditions in the `On-Error` procedure
- The difference between the update `DML` statements and the `DDL` statements and their usage in SQR
- Temporary tables and the usage of the SQL paragraph in the `Setup` section

7.1 Using the SQL paragraph in the procedure section

In chapter 6, we showed you how to use the SQR `Select` paragraph to retrieve data from your database. We learned that SQR `Select` is similar to SQL `SELECT`, but not exactly the same. You have to use strict SQR syntax to select data and to process each selected row, and cannot use native SQL `SELECT` statements in SQR.

What about other native SQL statements? Native SQL statements other than SQL `SELECT` are handled in the `SQL Paragraph`. For example, you may use this paragraph to load data into the database or to update certain records in the database. The `SQL Paragraph` can be used in one of the following three sections: the `Procedure` section, the `Program` section, or the `Setup` section.

You can reference any SQR column or variable in the `SQL Paragraph`. The following example shows how to use the `SQL Paragraph` in the `Procedure` section:

```
!**************************
Begin-Procedure Update-Zip
!**************************
Begin-SQL
Update Personal_Data
Set Postal = $New_Zip
Where Postal = $Old_Zip
End-SQL
End-Procedure
!**************************
```

As you see, the `SQL Paragraph` starts with the `Begin-SQL` command, ends with the `End-SQL` command, and has exactly the same syntax as that for native SQL. (Please be aware that native SQL syntax may be different for different databases. Use the one that corresponds to your environment.)

If you have more than one SQL statement in the same `SQL Paragraph`, the SQL statements must be separated by a semicolon:

```
!****************************************
Begin-Procedure Update_Delete
!****************************************
Begin-SQL On-Error=Db_Error
Update Personal_Data
Set Postal = $New_Zip
Where Postal = $Old_Zip;      <---  Multiple SQL statements in one SQL
Delete from Temp_Empl               paragraph are separated by a semicolon.
End-SQL
End-Procedure
!*****************************
Begin-Procedure Db_Error
```

```
!*****************************
Show 'SQL Error occured in Update_Delete proc'
End-Procedure
!**************************
```

The first SQL statement is terminated with a semicolon, whereas the last SQL statement does not have a semicolon at the end. In our example, we used the `On-Error` clause in the `Begin-SQL` statement. The `On-Error` clause specifies the name of the procedure to be executed if an error occurs during the SQL execution.

We will talk more about the importance of error-handling routines and the usage of the `On-Error` clause in chapter 21 of this book. A professionally-written program should always have error conditions handling, and, therefore, it is extremely useful to include the `On-Error` routines in your program. Many SQR commands and operators have optional `On-Error` clauses, an option not meant to be ignored.

Take another look at the previous example. It includes two unrelated table updates. The `Personal_Data` table is updated by changing zip codes for all records that satisfy the criterion in the `Where` clause. Separately, we delete all records from the `Temp_Empl` table. We wrote the program this way just to demonstrate how to place more than one SQL statement in one SQL paragraph. In real life, you would probably prefer to have two separate `SQL Paragraphs` for this type of processing to make debugging of your program much easier.

In this example, all table updates are placed into separate SQL paragraphs:

```
!*************************************************
Begin-Procedure Update_Delete_Insert
!*************************************************
Let $SQL_Error_Text='Updating Personal Data for ZIP = ' || $Old_Zip
Begin-SQL On-Error=Db_Error
Update Personal_Data          <--- Table Personal_Data is updated
                                   in a separate SQL paragraph.
   Set Postal = $Old_Zip
   Where Postal = $New_Zip
End-SQL
Show 'Rows Updated = ' #sql-count

Let $SQL_Error_Text='Deleting  Temp_Empl'
Begin-SQL On-Error=Db_Error
Delete from Temp_Empl      <--- The temporary table Temp_Empl is
End-SQL                         emptied in a separate SQL paragraph.
show 'Rows Deleted = ' #sql-count

Let $SQL_Error_Text='Inserting into Temp_Personal for Emplid='
   || $Emplid
Begin-SQL ON-Error=Db_Error
Insert Into Temp_Personal     <--- The temporary table Personal_Data is
(Emplid,                           populated in a separate SQL paragraph.
 Name ,
```

```
Phone)
Select
Emplid,
Name,
Phone
From Personal_Data
Where Emplid = $Emplid
And Country='USA'
End-SQL
If #sql-count=0
   Show 'No rows inserted into Temp_Personal'
Else
   Show 'Rows Inserted = '#sql-count
End-If
End-Procedure
!***********************************
Begin-Procedure Db_Error
!***********************************
Show 'SQL Error occurred in the Update_Delete_Insert procedure'
Show $SQL_Error_Text
If #sql-status = -9! If duplicate (this error code is for Oracle.
                   ! It is database specific)
   Show 'Insert Error: Duplicate row is not allowed for emplid='
    $Emplid
Else
   Show 'Error number: ' #sql-status
   Show 'SQL-Error = ' $sql-error
   Stop Quiet
End-if
End-Procedure
!*****************************
```

The `Quiet` parameter in the `Stop` command causes the program to stop instead of aborting with an error message.

Didn't we say that SQL `SELECT` statements cannot be used in SQR? What about the one in our example? This is not an independent SQL `SELECT` statement, but rather a part of a `DML` statement `Insert` and, as such, can be used in an `SQL Paragraph`.

In this example, we specify the same error handling procedure—the `Db_Error` procedure—in different SQL paragraphs. In order to have SQR print different error messages in different situations, we move the proper message text into the `$Sql_Error_Text` variable before executing an SQL statement. This useful technique helps to display error-specific messages while using the same routine. We also use another reserved SQR variable, `$sql-error`, that contains the error message returned from the database and is useful in analyzing the cause of the error.

If we did not specify the `On-Error` argument, SQR would, by default, display an error message and abort the program. By adding the `Db_Error` routine, we not only log the specifics about the error, but also let SQR continue with the program execution, unless a serious error occurs in which case the `Stop` command is executed. If the `Stop` command is not invoked, execution resumes at the statement following the SQL paragraph.

Note that after each SQL paragraph execution, we display the value of the SQR predefined variable `#sql-count`. It is a very good idea to always check this variable in order to make sure that the SQL statement has been executed correctly.

Please keep in mind that the `#sql-count` variable is only affected by DML statements (`Insert`, `Update`, or `Delete`). You cannot use it to find out how many rows were selected in a query. In order to do this in the `Select` paragraph, use your own counter and increment its value by 1 in the body of the `Select` paragraph.

When using the `Insert`, `Update`, or `Delete` statements, be aware that the RDBMS engines lock the changes made by these statements until the entire transaction is completed with the help of either the `Commit` operator or the `Rollback` operator. You can use either the SQR `Commit` command which should be used outside of the SQL paragraph, or your database-specific SQL `COMMIT` commands which can be used only within the SQL paragraph. If you use database-specific commands, keep in mind the following:

- for Sybase and Microsoft SQL Server, use `BEGIN TRANSACTION` and `COMMIT TRANSACTION`
- for Informix, use `BEGIN WORK` and `END WORK`
- for Oracle, it is recommended to use the SQR `Commit`.
  Please keep in mind that the `Commit` command in some databases (for example, Oracle) automatically closes all opened cursors. Therefore, this operation should not be performed while there are any active `Select` operations.

When your program finishes without errors, `Commit` is performed by SQR automatically.

7.2 DML vs. DDL statements

In previous examples, we demonstrated the use of SQL Data Manipulation Language (DML) in the SQL paragraph. `DML` operators include SQL table update statements such as `Insert`, `Update`, and `Delete`.

You can also use SQL Data Definition Language (DDL) statements such as `Create`, `Drop`, `Alter`, `Grant`, and `Revoke` in the SQL paragraph. Beware that SQR processes `DDL` statements differently from DML statements. DML statements are verified before the actual program execution. DDL statements, however, are not preprocessed prior to execution. If you happen to have a syntax error in a `DDL` statement, the error will not appear among the compilation errors.

Oracle users have to keep in mind that `DDL` statements cannot be executed while your `Select` queries are still active. `DDL` statement execution triggers the `Commit` operation which, in turn, closes all opened cursors. This could result in the loss of the next row content. Therefore, it is recommended to use DDL statements in the beginning or at the end of the program.

Sybase users should know that `Select ... Into ...` is considered a part of a DDL statement. It is, therefore, permitted in the SQL paragraph.

7.3 Using the SQL paragraph in the Setup Section

It may be a good idea to code your DDL statements in the `Setup` section of your program. In fact, both DDL and DML statements could be used in the SQL paragraph of the `Setup` section. We recommend, however, to help you differentiate between DML and `DDL` coding errors, that you keep the DML and DDL statements separate since only DML statements are preprocessed by SQR in the compile stage.

In SQR programs, `DDL` statements are often used with temporary tables. Temporary tables are handy to hold the intermediate results. If you want to create a temporary table, you may code the SQL paragraph in the `Setup` section as follows:

```
!***************
Begin-Setup
!***************
Begin-Sql On-Error=Warn
 Drop table Temp_Test_Tbl
 Create table Temp_Test_Tbl (Emplid char(11), Name char(30))
End-SQL
End-Setup
!***************************
```

The `Warn` value in the `On-Error` clause tells SQR to display a warning message.

We use the `Warn` parameter in the `On-Error` clause because, in the `Setup` section, the `On-Error` clause has a different syntax. In any other section, you have to specify an error-handling procedure name in the `On-Error` clause. In the `Setup` section, you can use the `On-Error` clause with one of the following parameters:

- `Stop` is used when you want to halt the program if an error occurs. Note that the rest of the program will be scanned for errors but will not be processed.
- `Warn` is used when you want a warning message to be displayed when an error occurs.
- `Skip` is used when you want to ignore all errors and to continue to run the program.

The default `On-Error` parameter in the `Setup` section is `Stop`. You may use more than one SQL paragraph in the `Setup` section, each with different error-handling routine.

KEY POINTS

1. You can use native SQL statements in SQR with the exception of the SQL `SELECT` statement.
2. It is a good idea to use the `On-Error` clause when updating tables.
3. SQR verifies SQL `DML` statements at the compile stage, but leaves SQL `DDL` statements unchecked.
4. The best place to create temporary tables is the `Setup` section.

CHAPTER 8

Loops and decision logic in SQR

IN THIS CHAPTER

- The three major elements in the SQR logical expressions
  - operands
  - relational, string, and numeric operators
  - built-in functions
- The order in which SQR evaluates different parts of a logical expression
- Different types of the `If` ... `Else` operators
- The `Evaluate` operator
- The `While` loop in SQR

8.1 Logical expressions

As with most programming languages, SQR includes basic program flow control logical operators. Each SQR operator (`If ... Else`, `Evaluate`, `While`) usually contains one or more logical expressions to be evaluated. After evaluation, logical expressions return a numeric value: zero if `FALSE` or non-zero if `TRUE`. Here are a few examples of logical expressions in SQR:

```
(#Salary >= #Max_Salary)
#Count
Not #sql-status = 0
Strtodate(&Effdte, 'MM-DD-YYYY') < $Calc_Date And &Paygroup = 'BW1'
```

An SQR logical expression can be a combination of three major elements: operands, operators, and functions.

Do not confuse SQR logical expressions with SQR expressions used in the `Let` command. Both types of expressions look alike and use the same named elements, but expressions in the `Let` command have different rules than those for logical expressions. For example, you can mix operands of different types in expressions used in the `Let` command, but you cannot do this in logical expressions:

```
If  #Num = $Char    ! Error: you cannot mix numeric and
                    ! string operands in a comparison
Let #Num = $Char    ! Correct
```

As you can see, the expressions in the two statements are identical, but the first statement results in an error because it includes a string-to-number comparison, while the second statement, in which it converts a string to a number is perfectly legal.

Another major difference between logical expressions and expressions in the `Let` command occurs when SQR processes logical expressions. SQR does not change the values of operands in these expressions, whereas the execution of an expression in the `Let` command may result in a change in the target operand value as in:

```
If  #Num1 = #Num2   ! The values of #Num1 and #Num2 are not changed
Let #Num1 = #Num2   ! The value of #Num1 is changed
```

8.2 Operands in logical expressions

Logical expressions can be simple elementary (atomic) expressions, such as comparisons of two variables, or combinations of atomic expressions. Operands in atomic SQR logical expressions must be of the same type, but you can mix different elements as long as they belong to different atomic expressions. For example, logical expression

```
$Char > #Num       ! Error
```

is incorrect because it mixes string and numeric operands in one atomic expression, but

```
$Char1 > $Char2 And #Num1 > #Num2 ! Valid
```

is a valid logical expression.

If a logical expression contains two numeric operands of different precision, SQR converts an operand with lower precision to match the operand of higher precision. Integer variables are considered the lowest in precision, followed by float variables, and then decimal variables as the highest in precision.

8.3 Relational, string, and numeric operators in logical expressions

A logical expression may include multiple operations on different operands. The result of the expression evaluation may depend not only on operand values, but also on the order of these operations, making it important to know the order in which SQR will execute operations in the expression. Normally, this sequence is defined by SQR precedence rules, but it can be overridden by using parentheses. Operators of the same precedence are processed in sequence, from left to right, within the logical expression.

Two types of logical operators exist:

- relational operators
- arithmetic and string operators

All relational operators have lower precedence to arithmetic and string operators. Refer to tables 4.2 and 4.3 in chapter 4. These tables list separately relational SQR operators and arithmetic and string SQR operators, respectively. The tables present operators in the descending precedence order with the lowest precedence number set to zero.

Expressions with relational operators look like this:

```
#Rate >= &Average_Rte And &B.Paygroup <> 'M01'
$Empl_Name = &A.Name
$Date1 <= &Effdt OR $Record_Num <= &B.Empl_Rcd#
(#Total = &Salary_Total) Or (#Total = #Calc_Total)
```

Here are examples of expressions with string and numeric operators:

```
&Company || &Paygroup <> $Security_Code
(#Ytd_Salary + #Ytd_Bonus) * #Soc_Sec_Rte > #Annual_Limit
-#Company_Match
datetostr($New_Date,'YYYY')>'1999'
```

Note The use of parentheses in complex expressions is recommended even if there is no need to override operator precedence. Parentheses make your expressions more readable and easier to debug.

8.4 Functions

You can use any number of built-in functions in a logical expression. You can also use a function within another function. (Note, though, that when a function uses another function as its argument, the inner function must return a value whose type is compatible with that of the outer function.) SQR provides a rich variety of numeric, string, date, file-related, and miscellaneous functions. Please refer to the `Let` command discussion in chapter 4 and to appendix C where all SQR functions are listed. The following are just a few examples of SQR logical expressions with built-in functions:

```
(Isnull(&Amount)) Or Not #sql-status = 0
To_char((#A + #B)*#C)
Length(&A.Name) >= 25
Upper(Rtrim(&A.Last_Name,' ')) || ' ' || &First_Name = $Input_Name
```

When calculating amounts, always use the `Round` function to maintain consistent decimal places.

8.5 Using If ... [Else] operators

The `If` operator is a backbone decision-making construct in any programming language. SQR is not an exception. In its simplest form of

```
If <Logical expression>
     <SQR commands>
End-If
```

the `If` operator allows your program to examine the logical expression and, based on the test result, designate courses of action. For example:

```
If (#Salary > #Salary_Limit)
 Do Print_Error
End-If
```

Sometimes, this form of the `If` operator is called a single-alternative `If` operator. If, however, we want to have more than one alternative courses of action, depending on the value of the tested logical expression, we will need another form of the `If` statement, a dual-alternative `If` operator:

```
If <Logical expression>
    <SQR commands>
Else
    <SQR commands>
End-If
```

SQR commands that follow the `If` and `Else` parts of the operator must start on a new line as in

```
If (#Salary > #Salary_Limit)
      Do Print_Error
Else
     Do Calculate_Bonus
End-If
```

The result of evaluation of the logical expression in the `If` statement is either `FALSE` (zero) or `TRUE` (non-zero). Remember that `TRUE` is not necessarily one. It can be any non-zero value. Therefore, instead of logical expression `(#Count<>0)` you can use `#Count` in the following example:

```
If  #Count
   Show 'Number of rows processed = ' #Count
Else
   Show 'There were no rows found'
End-If
```

Each `If` statement must also have a matching `End-If` statement to help SQR correctly parse nested `If` operators (if any):

```
If (&A.Empl_Status = 'T')
 Do Process_Terminated_Employees
Else
 If (&A.Empl_Status = 'L')
   Do Process_Leave_Of_Absence
   Do Print_LOA
 Else
   If  (&A.Empl_Status = 'A')
     Do Process_Active_EE
   End-If
 End-If
End-If
```

8.6 The Evaluate statement in conditional processing

Multiple-level nested `If ... [Else]` operators may look confusing and difficult to debug. The `Evaluate` statement offers a special form of multiple-alternative decision making that is useful when you have a large decision tree and all decisions depend on a value of the same variable.

We can rewrite the previous example of nested `If ... [Else]` operators to use the `Evaluate` statement:

```
Evaluate  &A.Empl_Status
 When = 'T'
   Do Process_Terminated_Employees
   Break
 When='L'
   Do Process_Leave_Of_Absence
   Do Print_LOA
   Break
 When='A'
   Do Process_Active_EE
   Break
 When-Other
   Show 'Unknown Empl, Status ' &A.Empl_Status
   Break
End-Evaluate
```

The argument in the `Evaluate` statement is compared with the value in the first `When` statement. If the result of the comparison is `TRUE`, SQR executes the commands below the `When`. If the expression is `FALSE`, the next `When` is evaluated. The optional `When-Other` statement is a "catch-all" clause that specifies the default actions when all previous `When` statements yield a `FALSE` result. The `Break` command is used to specify an immediate exit off the `Evaluate` statement. If `Break` is not coded, the comparison in the next `When` statement is executed, which takes additional processing time. It is a good habit to use `Break` after the processing commands to specify exit when needed.

In some cases, the `Break` command not only saves processing time, but can also spare you from a programming error. Let's consider the following code:

```
!...
Evaluate #Number
When = 5
   Do Proc_1
When = 6
   Do Proc_2
When = 7
   Do Proc_3
When-Other
   Do Proc_Other
End-Evaluate
!...
Begin-Procedure Proc_1
Let #Number = #Number + 1
End-Procedure
```

This is a typical SQR problem with the `Evaluate` statement, since it is easy to come to the conclusion that this logical construction works the same way as similar commands in C and some other languages. The difference is that, in every `When` statement, SQR evaluates not the original value of `#Number`, but the current one. In the example previous, if the `Proc_1` procedure changes the value in `#Number` from 5 to 6, the result of the logical expression evaluation in the next `When` statement will be `True`, and the `Proc_2` procedure will be also executed. Therefore, placing the `Break` command before the next `When` statement eliminates any possible problems.

There may be more than one `When` statement—sometimes, one after another—in which you need to specify multiple alternative values for comparison:

```
Evaluate  &A.Empl_Status
 When = 'T'
   Do Process_Terminated_Employees
   Break
 When='L'
 When='A'
   Do Process_Active_EE
   Break
 When-Other
   Show 'Unknown Empl, Status ' &A.Empl_Status
   Break
End-Evaluate
```

Procedure `Process_Active_EE` will be executed if `&A.Empl_Status='L'` or `&A.Empl_Status='A'`, i.e., if any of these conditions is `TRUE`.

Use the `When-Other` statement to specify the default process when all other `When` statements return `FALSE`. It must be the last argument.

8.7 Using the While command in loops

Loops are powerful computer language constructs that enable computers to perform many repetitive tasks. Without loops, computers might not exist. The `While ... End-While` statement is a classical loop construct used to process the body of the loop a number of times while the specified condition is `TRUE`. Once the condition becomes `FALSE`, the repetition terminates.

For example:

```
While #Max_Records < 100
 Do Load_Table1          ! This is the body of the
 Add 1 to #Max_Records   ! While loop statement
End-While
```

A logical expression in the `While` loop is tested for `TRUE` or `FALSE`. Logical expression `(#Max_Records<100)` is evaluated at the end of each loop iteration. As soon as this expression turns out `FALSE` (when the value of `#Max_Records` reaches the limit of 100), the `End-While` statement is reached and the loop ends.

Logical expressions in the `While` statement may include multiple conditions:

```
While ($Reprint <> 'Y') And ($Reprint <> 'N')
    Input $Reprint 'Is this a Reprint [Y/N] ?'
    Let $Reprint = Upper(Rtrim($Reprint, ' '))
End-While
```

To exit from the `While` loop before the `While` test condition returns `FALSE`, use the `Break` command:

```
While #I < #Total_Records_Read
 If &A.Empl_Stat = 'T'
   Break
 End-If
 If &A.Empl_Stat = 'A'
   Do Process_Active
 End-If
 Add 1 To #I
End-While
```

Note that the `Break` command causes an exit from the entire `While` loop, not from the `If` statement. The `Break` command cannot be used to exit from `If` statements.

You can have nested `While` statements each with its own `End-While` statement:

```
Begin-Program
Let $Input = 'Y'
While $Input <> ''
 Input $Input 'Please Enter Numeric code or Press Enter to Exit'
 Let #loc = 0
 While #loc < Length($Input)
   Extract $char from $Input #loc 1
   Evaluate $char
     when < '0'
     when > '9'
       Let $loc = edit((#loc+1),'999')
       Show 'Not Numeric Value found, char = ' $char ' loc = ' $loc
     break
   End-Evaluate
   Add 1 to #loc
  End-While
End-While
End-Program
```

Notice the two `While` loops. The outer loop checks for the end of user entry executing commands until the user enters an empty string. The inner loop examines every single character of the input string, checking for numbers and stopping after the last character in the input is checked. Have a look at the log file of the sample run in figure 8.1.

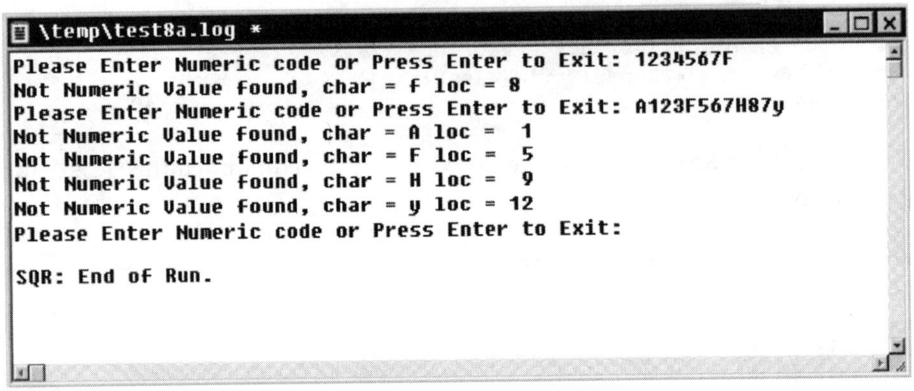

\temp\test8a.log *
Please Enter Numeric code or Press Enter to Exit: 1234567F
Not Numeric Value found, char = f loc = 8
Please Enter Numeric code or Press Enter to Exit: A123F567H87y
Not Numeric Value found, char = A loc = 1
Not Numeric Value found, char = F loc = 5
Not Numeric Value found, char = H loc = 9
Not Numeric Value found, char = y loc = 12
Please Enter Numeric code or Press Enter to Exit:
SQR: End of Run.

Figure 8.1 The Test8A.log file

KEY POINTS

1. An SQR logical expression can be a combination of three major elements: operands, operators, and functions.
2. There are two types of logical operators: relational operators, and arithmetic and string operators.
3. Parentheses in logical expressions help you to override operator precedence.
4. Parentheses in complex logical expressions make your expressions more readable and easier to debug.
5. You can use any number of built-in functions in a logical expression.
6. The result of a logical expression evaluation in the `If` statement is either `FALSE` (zero) or `TRUE` (non-zero).
7. The `Evaluate` statement is useful when you have a large decision tree, and all the decisions depend on a value of the same variable.
8. The `Break` command is used to exit from the `While` or `Evaluate` loops.

C H A P T E R 9

Enhancing your report

IN THIS CHAPTER

- Output formatting
- Using editing masks
  - text format masks
  - numeric format masks
  - date format masks
- Using the `Position` command
- Using the `Next-Listing` command to create detail groups in a report
- Vertical and horizontal spacing

In chapter 6, we introduce explicit and implicit printing of selected table columns. Since SQR's main job is to generate reports, one of the most important things SQR needs to know is where and how you want your data to appear on the page. The `Print` command places data on the page, indicating the row, the column, and the length. A second method—the `Document` paragraph—is useful for laying out the page and mixing it with data of different formats, for example, creating form letters. The `Document` paragraph will be covered in chapter 15.

9.1 Using the Print command

Because the `Print` command places data on the page grid, you must specify the position and length of each output field with the help of three parameters `(X, Y, Z)`. `X` signifies the line position of the page; `Y`, the column number; and `Z`, the number of positions allocated for the field. It is important to remember that the line position is always specified relative to the current page section, not to the entire report page.

If you use the `Print` command in the `Heading` section, you have to specify the line number within the heading portion of the page. If the `Print` command is used within any section other than the `Heading` or `Footing` section, the line number will be considered within the body of the report. The `Print` command used in the `Footing` section should refer to the line number in the footing portion of the report. For example

```
Begin-Heading 1
Print $Report_Name (1,1,20)
End-Heading
```

The `Print` command in the example places the value of the text variable `$Report_Name` in the first line of the heading portion of your report, starting from position one and allocating twenty positions in the page for this variable.

`X,Y,Z` can be numeric literals or variables. The position can be either absolute or relative. To indicate that a relative position is used, place the plus or minus sign before the position parameter `X` or `Y` (if you use a variable in place of `X` or `Y`, you can use only the plus sign). All relative positions are coded relative to the current position on the page. You can also use variables containing negative numbers to indicate relative negative positions, but you have to place the plus sign before the variable names. If you omit the position value or code a zero value instead, SQR will use the current position as default. If you specify zero for the length parameter `Z` or omit this parameter, the variable actual length will be used. The following illustrates the parameter rules:

```
!Different methods of coding the print position qualifiers
!in the Print command
```

```
Print  $Name (+1, 1, 20) ! Print $Name on the next line,
                         ! position 1,width=20

Print $Name (+2, +3)   ! Print $Name 2 lines below the current line,
                       ! starting from the current column + 3
                       ! and use width = actual length of $Name.


Let #Line=-2
Let #Column=5
Let #Length=10
Print $Name (+#Line,#Column,#Length)! Print $Name in the line that
                                    ! is 2 lines above the current
                                    ! line, from column 5, and
                                    ! allocate only 10  positions for
                                    ! field $Name.
Print $Name (,+3) ! Print at the current line position,
                  ! current column+3, use the actual length of
                  ! $Name for space allocation.
Print $Name ()    ! Print in the current line, current column,
                  ! use actual field $Name length
Print $Name(0,0,0)! Same as above

Let #i = -1
Let #j = -2
Print 'Error' (#i, #j)! This is incorrect, you must place a plus
                      ! before variables containing negative numbers
Let #i = -1
Let #j = -2
Print 'Error' (-#i, -#j) ! This is incorrect, you must place a plus
                         ! before variables containing negative
                         ! numbers
Let #i = -1
Let #j = -2
Print 'Correct' (+#i, +#j)     ! Now, this is correct.
```

All these rules are also valid for implicit printing (in the `Select` paragraph only). You can implicitly print a table column by specifying the print position coordinates `(X,Y)` and the space allocation `Z` to the right of the column name, as shown in this example.

```
!TEST9A.SQR
!Specifying print positions while using implicit printing
Begin-Program
Do Select_EE
End-Program

Begin-Procedure Select_EE
Begin-Select
Emplid  (+1, 1,11)
Name    (, +2, 20)
```

```
City (, +2, 15)
State  (, +2)
From Personal_Data
Where State = 'CA'
End-Select
End-Procedure
```

Figure 9.1 shows the output of our example.

6601	Jones,Gladys	Los Alamos	CA
6603	Pitman,Earl	Los Angeles	CA
7702	Atchley,Tamara	San Diego	CA
7705	Holt,Susan	La Mirada	CA
8001	Schumacher,Simon	Moraga	CA
8101	Penrose,Steven	Lafayette	CA
8102	Sullivan,Theresa	Moraga	CA
8105	DeHaven,Joanne	Danville	CA
8121	Gregory,Jan	Alamo	CA
8201	Rifkin,Cheri	Walnut Creek	CA
8202	Hadley,Charles	Lafayette	CA
8203	Webb,Floren	Concord	CA
8223	Buchanan,Cheryl	Danville	CA
8225	Sterling,Sharon	Danville	CA

Figure 9.1
Using print positions in implicit printing

You can also use substitution variables defined in the beginning of your program to code all printing parameters. The benefit of using substitution variables is that you can use the same variable in the `Print` commands throughout your program. Substitution variables (discussed in detail in chapter 11) can be used explicitly in the `Print` command or implicitly by using substitution variables in place of print parameters next to table column names. The following example shows how to combine the usage of substitution variables and implicit printing:

```
!Using substitution variables to specify print positions
Begin-Procedure Init
#Define col_emplid  1
#Define col_name   15
#Define col_city   30
#Define col_state  40
End-Procedure

! ...
Begin-Select
Emplid  (+1, {col_emplid})
Name    (, {col_name})
```

```
City  (, {col_city})
State (, {col_state})
From Personal_Data
Where State = 'NJ'
End-Select
```

9.2 Formatting your output

You can use a number of print format options to enhance the appearance of your report (see the complete list of options of the `Print` command in appendix D). In this chapter, we will cover the most commonly used format options.

You can use the `Bold` format qualifier to print a string in bold type:

```
Print $Name (+1, 1) Bold
```

Keep in mind, however, that for some printers, the `Bold` format may not work without some special effort. For example, for HP LaserJet printers, the appropriate boldface font must be loaded into the printer, and for some fonts, the bold option may not be available.

Note The commands `Declare-Printer` and `Alter-Printer` are used to control font selection. The `Print` command does not have this capability. We will discuss `Declare-Printer` and `Alter-Printer` in chapter 13.

To underline the printed string, use the `Underline` format qualifier:

```
Print $Header (2, 5) Underline
```

When printing the heading information, the `Center` format qualifier is really handy. You can use it for any line you want to print in the center of your report. When the `Center` option is used, the column positions are ignored. To determine column positions, SQR uses the `Page-Size` parameter in the `Setup` section. If you do not code the `Page-Size` parameter, SQR will use the default value.

```
Print 'Test Report' ()  Center
```

Often, it is necessary to fill a whole line or a part of a line with the same characters. You can save on keystrokes by using the `Fill` format qualifier for this purpose:

```
Print '*' (1,1,25)  Fill      ! Fills line with 25 asterisks
```

If you need to wrap a line, you may use the `Wrap` format qualifier.

```
Print $Comments (1,1) Wrap 15, 3
```

This command prints the value of string variable `$Comments` in several lines, fifteen characters per line for a maximum of three lines.

When using the `Wrap` qualifier, the `wrapdepth()` function introduced in version 4.2 can be helpful in controlling string wrapping dynamically. This function returns the number of print lines required to wrap the specified string, thus allowing you to avoid hard-coding this parameter.

`Match` is another interesting print format qualifier. It allows you to replace the original value with another value from a specified keyed value list thereby eliminating the need to write a conversion subroutine. For example, if we have an employee status code in the `$Empl_Status` variable but need to print the employee status instead of the code, the `Match` option will spare us the writing of a routine that will convert status code to status description:

```
Print $Empl_Status (0, 16) Match
        A 0 25 'Active'
        T 0 25 'Terminated'
        L 0 25 'On Leave'
```

When you use the `Match` format qualifier, if SQR finds a match, it will print the substituted value in the line and position specified in the `Match` parameters. Otherwise, SQR will print the original value in the line and position specified in the `Print` command. In our case, if a match is found, the corresponding substituted value (`'Active'`, `'Terminated'` or `'On Leave'`) will be printed in position 25 of the current line. If no match is found, an original employee status code will be printed in position 16 of the current line.

9.3 Using edit masks

The `Edit` argument is the most powerful among all `Print` command options. This option uses special format masks. When this argument is coded, the field is edited before it is printed. There are three types of edits: *Text Edit*, *Numeric Edit*, and *Date Edit*. Each of these three edit types has a different set of rules for mask coding. Let's take a look at mask types:

9.3.1 Text format masks

These special characters are used for text format masks:

- `X` place a character in the output:
  ```
  Move '123451234' To $Zip
  ```

```
Print $Zip     (1,1)    edit   xxxxx-xxxx
! the output will be 12345-1234
```

- `b` insert a blank in the output:

```
Move '2031231234' To $Phone
Print $Phone       (1,1) edit   (xxx)bxxx-xxxx
! the output will be (203) 123-1234
```

If you enclose the edit masks into quotes, you can use spaces to indicate blank characters.

- `~ (tilde)` skip a character in the output:

```
Print  'ABCDEFGH' (1,1) edit       xxxx~~xx
! the output will be ABCDGH
```

- `R` reverse the sequence of characters in the string for languages such as Hebrew
- any character can be used as a text constant in the output:

```
Move '12A' To $Apt
Print $Apt    (1,1)   edit  Apt.bxxxxx
! the output will be Apt. 12A
```

Note The characters `8`, `9`, `0`, `V`, and `$` are used as special indicators for numeric format masks, and therefore, cannot be used as parts of text format masks. If you need to use any special character as a part of a mask text, place a backslash ("\") before this character. This is true not only for special numeric characters, but for any other special character, for example, "b", "x", "~", etc.

9.3.2 Numeric format masks

The numeric format masks use a number of characters that create special editing effects to the output:

- `8` digit, zero fill to the right of the decimal point, trim leading blanks (left justify the number)
- `9` digit, zero fill to the right of the decimal point, space fill to the left

```
Let #Unit_Price = 10.459
Let #Quantity = 10
Let #Total = 104.59
Let #Credit_Balance = -50.00
Print #Unit_Price      (1,1)   edit 9999.99
Print #Quantity        (1,+3)  edit 9999.99
Print #Total           (1,+3)  edit 9999.99
Print #Credit_Balance  (1,+3)  edit 9999.99

! The output will be: 10.46     10.00      104.59     -50.00
! Please note that SQR performed decimal rounding for #Unit_Price
```

- `0` digit, zero fill to the left
- `B` treated as a "9" but if a value is zero the output is printed blank
- `$` dollar sign, optionally floats to the right

```
Let #Unit_Price = 10.459
Let #Quantity = 10
Let #Total = 104.59
Let #Credit_Balance = -50.00
Print #Unit_Price      (1,1)   edit  $$$$.99
Print #Quantity      (1,+3) edit        9999
Print #Total     (1,+3) edit $$$$.99
Print#Credit_Balance      (1,+3) edit $$$$.99

! The output will be: $10.46     10       $104.59      $-50.00
```

- `V` implied decimal point

```
Let #Total = 12104.59
Print #Total    (1,1)   edit  $,$$$,$$$V99

! The output will be:  $12,10459
```

- `MI` if placed at the end of the mask, causes a minus to be displayed at the right of a negative number
- `PR` if placed at the end of the mask, causes angle brackets (< >) to be displayed around a negative number
- `PS` if placed at the end of the mask, causes parentheses to be displayed around a negative number
- `NA` if placed at the end of the mask, causes "N/A" to be displayed if the numeric column variable is `NULL`
- `NU` if placed at the end of the mask, causes blanks to be displayed if the numeric column variable is `NULL`
- `E` denotes scientific format. The number of 9s after the decimal point determines the number of significant digits displayed
- . (dot) denotes decimal point
- , (comma) denotes comma.

9.3.3 Date and time format masks

Date format masks are used not only for printing, but also in the date manipulation built-in functions. As with the text or numeric masks, the date format masks use different characters to control the display of date format fields:

- `YYYY` 4-digit year; `YYY`, 3-digit year (the current millennium is assumed); `YY`, 2-digit year (the current century is assumed); `Y`, 1-digit year (the current century and decade are assumed)

- RR 2-digit year, the century is calculated as follows:
  - if RR is between 00 and 49 and the 2-digit current year is between 00 and 49, the current century is assumed
  - if RR is between 50 and 99 and the 2-digit current year is between 50 and 99, the current century is assumed
  - if RR is between 00 and 49 and the 2-digit current year is between 50 and 99, the next century is assumed
  - if RR is between 50 and 99 and the 2-digit current year is between 00 and 49, the century before the current one is assumed
- Q quarter of year (1–4)
- WW week of year (1–53). W week of month (1–5)
- DDD day of year (1–366). DD day of month (1–31). D day of week (1–7) starting from Sunday. DAY name of day. DY abbreviated name of day
- MONTH full name of month. MON abbreviated name of month. MM 2-digit month (1–12)
- RM Roman numeral month (I–XII)
- CC century
- BC or AD BC / AD indicator
- HH, MI, SS hour (based on 24 hour clock), minute (0–59), second (0–59).
- NNNNNN fractions of second (the precision depends on the computer, operating system, and database used)
- AM or PM meridian indicator
- | used to concatenate different masks

Any other characters in a date mask are treated as parts of a constant and will be included in the output field as text. If you would like to include in this text some characters that are special date mask characters from the previous list, you have to precede the entire text with a backslash (\).

Note The masks DAY, MONTH, MON, AM, PM, BC, and AD are case-sensitive and follow the case of the mask entered. For example, if the month is January, the mask MON results in JAN, the mask Mon results in Jan.

Let us summarize what we just learned about the print format masks in the following table (here, we use the literal date format for date source fields):

Table 9.1 Using print format masks

Edit Mask	Type	Source Field	Result
SSN:bbxxx-xx-xxxx	Text	123456789	SSN: 123-45-6789
Accountb#b~~~x-~xxxxx	Text	0001001234	Account # 1-01234
999,999.99	Numeric	123.4567	123.46
999V99	Numeric	123.4567	12346
9999	Numeric	123	123
9999	Numeric	-123	-123
9999	Numeric	-1234	**** (overflow)
9999	Numeric	12345	**** (overflow)
$$$,$$$,$$$.$$MI	Numeric	-500,000	$500,000.00-
B999,999.99	Numeric	0	(blank)
999,999.99	Numeric	0	0.00
999,990.99	Numeric	0	0.00
$$$,$$$,$$$.$$MINA	Numeric	NULL	N/A
$$$,$$$,$$$.$$MINU	Numeric	NULL	(blank)
9.999E	Numeric	123456	1.235E+005
MM/DD/YY	Date	19980115	01/15/98
MM:DD:YY	Date	19980115	01:15:98
MM/DD/YYYY	Date	19980115	01/15/1998
CC	Date	19980115	20
Q	Date	19980115	1
WW	Date	19980315	12
W	Date	19980115	3
D	Date	19980115	3
YYYYDDD	Date	19980115	1999015
Day,bMONTHbDD,YYYY	Date	19980115	Wednesday, JANUARY 15,1998
DAY,bDD-Mon-YY	Date	19980115	WEDNESDAY, 15-Jan-98
DD-RM-YYYY	Date	19981115	15-XI-1998
MM/DD/YY:HH:MI:SS	Date	19980115131545	01/15/98:13:15:45
HH:MI:SS	Date	131545	13:15:45

9.4 More about edit masks

In addition to the `Print` command, edit masks can be used in other SQR commands such as `Move`, `Concat`, `Display`, `Show`, as well as in some built-in functions.

Edit masks can be built and changed dynamically. You can assign a mask value to a text variable, and then reference this variable by its name, prefixed by a colon, for example:

```
Move '$999.99' to $My_Mask
Print #Test () edit :$My_Mask
```

SQR supports multiple language conversions for the following date format masks: MON, MONTH, DAY, DY, AM, PM, BC, and AD (see chapter 21).

Beginning with version 4, SQR provides three special keywords—Money, Date, and Number—that can be used in place of edit format masks.

Money is a special mask recommended for monetary fields. When this mask is used, SQR formats the output according to the current value of the environmental variable Money-Edit-Mask in the current locale. This is a good way to make your program country-independent. This mask cannot be used with date literals, variables or columns.

Number can be used as the default mask when printing or displaying numeric fields. When this mask is used, SQR formats the output according to the current value of the environmental variable Number-Edit-Mask in the current locale, making sure that the proper separator for thousands and the proper decimal place indicator are used, depending on the current locale (see chapter 21 for details and examples). This mask cannot be used with date literals, variables, or columns.

Date is a special keyword that can be used in place of date masks. When this keyword is used, SQR will format the output using the Date-Edit-Mask environmental variable in the current locale. If Date-Edit-Mask is not defined, the first database-dependent date format will be used. The source field must contain a valid date. As with the Money and Number keywords, the Date keyword is very helpful when writing programs designed for multiple language support: formatting all dates according to the national standards and using the names of months and days of week translated into the proper language, according to the current locale (see chapter 21).

Besides being used in the Print command, edit masks can also be used to move data from one field to another, thus supporting the conversion functionality:

```
Move #Count to $Row_Count 99999
Let $Amount = Edit(#Price * #Rate, '$99999.99')
```

9.5 Using the Position command

You can control the look of your printouts by coding a specific position on a page. The Position command will allow you to set the current position:

```
Position        (10,2) !Set the current position to line 10, column 2
Print    #Amount()     ! Print amount in the current position
Position        (+3, 1)! Set the current position 3 lines down
Print   #Total  ()     ! Print Total in current position
```

As you may have noticed in the example, you can use either absolute or relative positions. You can also use negative position numbers to move back from the current position on the page. When you indicate print positions using plus or minus signs, make sure you do not specify positions outside the page range.

The example next demonstrates the common practice of using the `Position` command in the `Select` paragraph:

```
Begin-Select
Emplid        (, 1, 11)
Name          (,+2, 20)
Position      (+1)     !Move the print position to the next line
From Personal_Data
End-Select
```

9.6 Controlling the vertical spacing

You can use the `Next-Listing` command to create detail groups in your report and to control the vertical spacing between detail groups on a page as in the following example. (The output of our example appears in figure 9.2.)

```
!Using the Next-Listing command
Begin-Program
Do Select_EE
End-Program

Begin-Procedure Select_EE
Begin-Select
Name        (1, 1, 40)
Address1    (2, 1, 30)
City        (3, 1, 15)
State       ( , +2, 2)
Postal      ( , +2,10)
 Next-Listing Skiplines=1 Need = 3
From Personal_Data
Where State = 'CA'
End-Select
End-Procedure
```

Here columns `Name`, `Address`, `City`, `State`, and `Postal` make up a *detail group* that is printed on three lines every time a row is selected. The `Next-Listing` command moves the current position to one line below the current line in the page body, skipping one line and starting the next detail group on the next line. The implicit print positions on the columns are, in fact, positions relative to the

> **Note** The `Next-Listing` command does not change the value of the SQR-reserved variable `#current-line` which holds the actual line number within the page body.

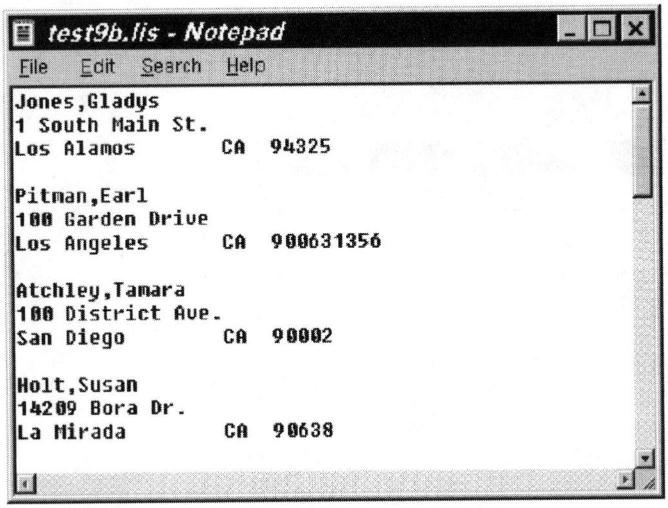

Figure 9.2
Using the Next-Listing command to create detail groups in a report

beginning of the new detail group. The `Need` parameter controls the end of the page printing, directing SQR to begin a new page if there are less than three lines on the current page left, thus eliminating a potential situation in which a detail group can be broken between two different pages.

You can also use the `Next-Listing` command when you need to create variable length detail groups by using the `Wrap` qualifier:

```
!Test9c.SQR
!Next-Listing command with variable length text paragraphs
Begin-Program
Do Select_EE
End-Program

Begin-Procedure Select_EE
Begin-Select
A.Emplid   (1,1,11)
A.Name     (2, 1, 20)    Wrap 15 2
B.Name     (2, +2, 20)   Wrap 15 2
 Next-Listing Skiplines=1 Need = 3
From Personal_Data A, Dependent_Benef B
Where A.Emplid=B.Emplid

End-Select
End-Procedure
```

After a wrapped string is printed, the current position on the page shifts one character to the right of the paragraph's bottom line. To avoid this, we specified the same starting line number (2) for both column `A.Name` and column `B.Name` in the example. For each detail group, both A.Name and B.Name will start on line 2 and may wrap into line 3 (figure 9.3).

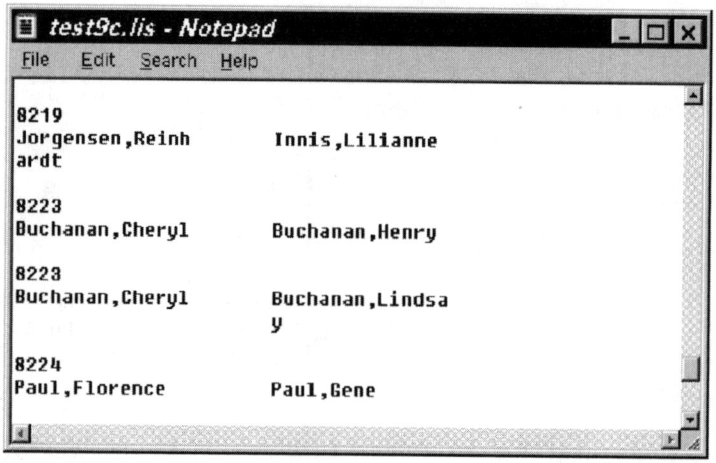

Figure 9.3 Using the Wrap command to create variable length detail groups

9.7 Controlling the horizontal spacing

The Columns, Next-Column and Use-Column commands are used to control the horizontal spacing in your report. They define and navigate logical columns on the page.

The Columns command defines one or more logical columns in the report. It also makes the first column of the group the current column.

```
Columns 10  20  30   !Define three columns in your report
```

This command defined three logical columns and made column 10 current. Now, if you use a Print command, it will shift the current column position from the left edge of the page and add ten (10) to the position qualifier in any Print command:

```
Columns 10 20 30
Print   $Name  (3, 2, 30)
```

$Name will be printed in the second position of the first logical column. What will be the actual SQR page position? The answer is: eleven.

In order to advance from one column to another, you use the Next-Column command.

```
Columns 10 20 30
Print   $Name  (3, 2, 30)
Next-Column
Print #Amount ()
```

The `Next-Column` command will move the current column position to the second declared logical column, that is the column located at absolute column position 20. Variable `#Amount` will be printed in the first position of the second logical column.

The `Use-Column` command sets a specific logical column as current or turns off column printing. To stop printing within logical columns simply specify 0 (zero) as a `Use-Column` parameter.

```
Columns 20 50
Use-Column 2           !The Columns command must be issued
                       !prior to Use-Column
Print $Last_Name () !Prints $Last_Name in the second column
Use-Column 0           !Stops printing within columns.
```

Even though your printing mode is reset to normal after issuing the `Use-Column 0` command, the logical columns you have previously defined are available, and you are able to go back to logical column printing by using the `Next-Column` or `Use-Column` commands.

9.8 Changing report's heading or footing

Starting with version 6, you can use a new SQR command, `Alter-Report`, to change a report's heading or footing sections while the report is running. You can change the size of heading or footing or switch from one heading or footing to another dynamically.

The `Alter-Report` command (please see the command reference in appendix D) has two pairs of operands, one pair for heading (`Heading` and `Heading-Size`) and another one for footing (`Footing` and `Footing-Size`). Let's see how you can change your report's heading dynamically. The `Heading` operand specifies the name of the heading section to be used in the report. This name must be coded in the `Name` operand of the `Begin-Heading` command (this operand is also new in version 6). You can also set the value of the `Heading` operand to `'NONE'` to disable the heading section for this report. The `Heading-Size` operand allows you to change the depth of your report's heading dynamically.

Here is an example:

```
Begin-Setup
Begin-Heading 3
   Name = Domestic
   Print ' North American ' (1,1,0) Center
```

```
      Print $current-date (1,50) Edit MM/DD/YYYY
   End-Heading

   Begin-Heading 3
      Name = International
      Print ' International ' (1,1,0) Center
      Print $current-date (1,50) Edit MM/DD/YYYY
   End-Heading
   ! . . .
   End-Setup

    Begin-Program
   ! . . .
      Alter-Report
         Heading='Domestic'
         Heading-Size=5
   ! . . .
      Alter-Report
         Heading='International'
         Heading-Size=4
   End-Program
```

The Footing and Footing-Size operands work similarly to that of Heading and Heading-Size.

If the Heading or Footing value is set to 'Default', SQR will revert to whatever was in effect when the report was initiated.

It is important to understand that the Alter-Report command affects the current report only. If anything has been placed on the page prior to issuing this command, the command will take effect for the next page; otherwise it takes effect for the current page.

Please note that the Alter-Report command does not switch to another report: it only changes the current report's heading or footing characteristics. To switch to another report in a multiple report program, use the Use-Report command (discussed in chapter 13).

9.9 Delaying printing of data

Starting with version 6, you can use a new keyword Delay of the Print command to delay the actual printing of data until the Set-Delay-Print command is issued. The Set-Delay-Print command allows you to go back and change the value of the printed variable in the output buffer based on the value of the With argument of this command. The Delay keyword is applied only to the data printed by the Print command the keyword is used with. All data printed by other Print commands without the Delay keyword are printed without a delay. The Print Delay and Set-Delay-Print commands work in pairs:

```
Print $Var1 (1,1,10) Delay
! . . .
Set-Delay-Print $Var1 With $Var2
```

It is important to understand that the `Delay` keyword impacts only the timing of your program's output, not the order in which print lines will appear on the page. How does SQR do this? The `Delay` keyword tells SQR to accumulate the entire report in a file without printing until the `Set-Delay-Print` command is issued. Then, SQR goes back and updates the value of the printed variable in the file. In order to achieve this, SQR in addition to its regular `LIS` output, creates a so-called `SPF` file (read more about `SPF` files in chapter 14).

When can this technique be useful? One example is when you need to print a report summary in the beginning of the report. Without the `Delay` option, you will have to write a multiple report program (see chapter 13) or access your database twice: first to print the summary data, second to print the detail report. With the `Delay` option, you can print your report's summary with empty totals using the `Print Delay` command, print the detail report and then, use the `Set-Delay-Print` command to update the report's summary with accumulated totals.

Here is an example of such a program. Let's say we need to print a list of employees and place certain employee summary information on the top of the report:

```
!****************************
!TEST9D.SQR
! Using the Print Delay and Set-Delay-Print Commands
!****************************
Begin-Program
!****************************
  Do Print_Summary
  Do List_Employees
  Do Release_Delay
End-Program

!****************************
Begin-Heading 2 Name = Summary
  Print 'Employee Status Summary' (1,1,30) Center
End-Heading
!****************************

!****************************
Begin-Heading 5 Name = Detail
  Print 'Active Employee List' (1,1,30) Center
  Print   '='                  (+1,1,50) Fill
  Print   'Company'            (+1,1 )
  Print   'Emplid'             (,+2 )
  Print   'Name '              (,+4 )
  Print   'Annual Salary'      (,+15)
```

```
  Print   '='                      (+1,1,50) Fill
End-Heading
!****************************

!****************************************
Begin-Procedure Print_Summary
!****************************************
Alter-Report
 Heading = 'Summary'
Print 'Number of Active Employees     : ' (+1, 1)
Print #Active      (,+1,10) Edit 9,999,999 Delay
Print 'Number of Terminated Employees : ' (+1, 1)
Print #Terminated (,+1,10) Edit 9,999,999 Delay
Print 'Number of Retired Employees    : ' (+1, 1)
Print #Retired     (,+1,10) Edit 9,999,999 Delay
New-Page
End-Procedure

!****************************************
Begin-Procedure List_Employees
!****************************************
Alter-Report
 Heading = 'Detail'

Begin-Select
B.Company
A.Emplid
A.Name
B.Empl_Status
B.Annual_Rt

  Evaluate &B.Empl_Status
    When='A'
      Add 1 to #Active_Total
      Print &B.Company      (,1,7)
      Print &A.Emplid      (,+2,8)
      Print &A.Name      (,+2,20)
      Print &B.Annual_Rt     (,+2,12) Edit $,$$$,$$$.00
      Position (+1)
      Break
    When='T'
      Add 1 To #Terminated_Total
      Break
    When='R'
      Add 1 To #Retired_Total
      Break
  End-Evaluate

From Ps_Personal_Data A, PS_Job B
Where  A.Emplid=B.Emplid
  And  B.Effdt = (Select Max(D.Effdt) From PS_Job D
          Where D.Effdt<=Sysdate
```

Use `Delay` argument to defer printing the totals

When using `Delay`, always code the field length explicitly

Changing heading from `Summary` to `Detail`

```
          And D.Emplid=B.Emplid
          And D.Empl_Rcd=B.Empl_Rcd)
   And  B.Effseq = (Select Max(C.Effseq) From Job C
            Where C.Emplid=B.Emplid
                   And C.Empl_Rcd = B.Empl_Rcd
              And C.Effdt=B.Effdt)
Order By B.Company, A.Emplid
End-Select
End-Procedure

!*****************************************
Begin-Procedure Release_Delay
!*****************************************
Set-Delay-Print  #Active with #Active_Total
Set-Delay-Print  #Terminated with #Terminated_Total
Set-Delay-Print  #Retired  with #Retired_Total
End-Procedure
```

Use `Set-Delay-Print` to go back and populate totals

In `Test9D.sqr`, we want to print a list of only active employees and place the total number of active, terminated and retired employees on the top of the report so that the company management will be able to see the totals first. Of course, there are many ways to print this report, but if we want to make it in one database pass, using the `Print Delay` command may be a good solution.

First, we define two headings for the report: one for the total part, another one for the detail part. We use the `Alter-Report` command to switch headings. The `Print_Summary` procedure prints the summary portion of the report, but uses the `Print Delay` command to defer printing the actual totals until the employee selection is complete.

The `List_Employees` procedure prints the list of active employees and accumulates the totals of active, terminated, and retired employees.

The `Release_Delay` procedure uses the `Set-Delay-Print` command to go back and populate the total fields in the report's summary. Please note that SQR will update these fields according to the positioning and formatting specified by the previous `Print Delay` commands.

Note The `Print Delay` and `Set-Delay-Print` commands always work in pairs: for each `Print Delay` command you have to code the corresponding `Set-Delay-Print` command.

9.10 Generating PDF files

Starting with version 4.3.2.2, SQR can generate Adobe PDF files. You don't have to change your program, all you have to do is to use the `-PRINTER:PD` SQR command line flag. The `SQR.INI` file has a new section called [PDF Fonts] which provides the mapping between SQR fonts and Adobe fonts. The name of the PDF file will be same as your report name with the `.PDF` extension.

Another SQR command line flag, `-EH_PDF` creates a PDF icon in the navigation bar when you generate HTML output.

KEY POINTS

1. The `Print` command controls the position and the length of each output field with the help of three parameters: the two coordinates on the page grid (line and column) and the number of positions allocated for the field.
2. Line positions are always specified relative to the current page section (header, body, or footer), not to the entire report page.
3. The position and length parameters in the `Print` command can be numeric literals or variables.
4. In the `Select` paragraph, you can implicitly print a table column by specifying the print position coordinates `(X,Y)` and the space allocation `Z` to the right of the column name.
5. You can use substitution variables to define all printing parameters at the beginning of your report.
6. The `Print` command format options help to enhance the appearance of your report.
7. There are three types of edit format masks: `Text Edit`, `Numeric Edit`, and `Date Edit`. Each of these three edit types uses its own set of special characters for mask coding.
8. Edit masks can be built and changed dynamically by assigning a mask value to a text variable, and then referencing this variable by its name prefixed by a colon.
9. The `Position` command will allow you to set the current position in the report page.
10. The `Next-Listing` command is handy when your report has groups of detail records.

KEY POINTS (CONTINUED)

11 The `Columns`, `Next-Column`, and `Use-Column` commands are used to control the horizontal spacing.

12 The SQR reserved variable `#current-line` always holds the actual line number within the page body.

13 The `Print Delay` command allows you to go back and change the value of an output variable before printing.

14 You can create PDF output without changing your program.

15 You can change report's heading or footing dynamically with the help of the `Alter-Report` command.

PART 2

Advanced features of SQR

CHAPTER 10

Using break logic in your SQR program

IN THIS CHAPTER

- Different print actions of the `On-Break` option
- Multiple-level breaks
- The `Before` and `After` qualifiers of the `On-Break` option
- The `Save` qualifier of the `On-Break` option
- The `Print=Never` option
- Controlling page breaks

In business reporting, when the value of a column is changed (that is, when a break occurs), it is common to do some special processing. You may need to skip lines, print a value only if changed, execute a special procedure before or after the break, print subtotals, etc.

SQR break handling commands allow you to do all of the above and more. Let us look at the following program, which, for every selected employee, prints the employee's name, his company, and the employee's salary. This example does not use any break logic. Figure 10.1 displays the program's output.

```
!****************************
!TEST10A.SQR
!An employee list program that uses no break logic
!****************************
Begin-Program
!****************************
      Do List_Employees
End-Program
!****************************
Begin-Heading 2
!****************************
   Print     'Company'         (1,1)
   Print     'Paygroup'        (,+2)
   Print     'Emplid'          (,+2)
   Print     'Name '           (,+4)
   Print     'Annual Salary'  (,+15)
   Print     ' '               (2,1)
End-Heading

!*****************************************
Begin-Procedure List_Employees
!*****************************************
Begin-Select
B.Company     (,1,7)
B.Paygroup    (,+2,8)
A.Emplid      (,+2,8)
A.Name        (,+2,20)
B.Annual_Rt   (,+2,12) Edit $,$$$,$$$.00
        Position   (+1)
From Personal_Data A, Job B
Where   A.Emplid=B.Emplid
        And B.Effdt=(Select Max(D.Effdt) From Job D
                     Where D.Effdt<=Sysdate
                     And D.Emplid=B.Emplid
                     And D.Empl_Rcd=B.Empl_Rcd)
        And B.Effseq = (Select Max(C.Effseq) from Job C
                        Where C.Emplid=B.Emplid
                        And C.Empl_Rcd = B.Empl_Rcd
                        And C.Effdt=B.Effdt)
Order By B.Company, B.Paygroup, A.Emplid
```

```
End-Select
End-Procedure
!****************************
```

Company	Paygroup	Explid	Name	Annual Salary
CBL	MN	B002	Maertens,Marianne	$769,392.00
CCB	BW0	E2301	Jacobs,Carol	$46,800.00
CCB	BW0	E2302	Gardner,John	$64,800.00
CCB	BW0	E2303	Andrews,Frank	$70,800.00
CCB	BW0	E2304	Jeffries,Anne	$31,200.00
CCB	BW0	E2305	Masterson,Marie	$8,195.20
CCB	BW0	G500	Miller,Robin	$26,000.00
CCB	BW0	G501	Caldwell,John	$38,400.00
CCB	BW0	G502	Downs,Megan	$19,448.00
CCB	BW0	G503	Castro,Mary	$36,000.00
CCB	BW1	G701	Cortez,Isabella	$4,825.60
CCB	BW1	G702	Jonas,Wendy	$4,825.60
CCB	BW1	G703	Lotta,Emmanuel	$4,825.60
CCB	BW1	G704	Dempsey,Elaine	$4,825.60
CCB	LT1	8530	Vierra,Gina	$19,344.00
CCB	LT1	LT001	Santos,Charles A.	$36,400.00
CCB	LT1	LT002	Hiromoto,Seiko	$46,904.00
CCB	LT1	LT003	Souza,Isobel	$72,800.00
CCB	LT1	LT005	Seca,Wenda A.	$34,645.00

Figure 10.1 List of employees by company and paygroup without using on-break logic

10.1 Using the On-Break option of the Print command

As you can see in figure 10.1, the report is just a list of employees sorted by company, paygroup, and employee Id. The look is not very appealing, but can be improved by using the `On-Break` option of the `Print` command.

The `On-Break` option causes the specified action to take place when the value of a certain output field is changed. It can be used for both explicit and implicit printing. You can specify a number of qualifiers of the `On-Break` option. These qualifiers define specific actions to be taken when the break occurs. The most popular qualifier is `Print` (not to be confused with the `Print` command). The `Print` qualifier is the default qualifier of the `On-Break` option: you do not have to specify this qualifier when coding the `On-Break` option. We will discuss other qualifiers later in this chapter.

When using the `Print` qualifier of the `On-Break` option, you can specify when the break field should (or should not) be printed:

- `Always` The break field will be printed for each detail group.
- `Change` The break field will be printed only when its value is changed. This is the default option.
- `Change/Top-Page` The break field will be printed when its value is changed plus at the top of each new page.
- `Never` The break field will not be printed.

The default action prints the break field only when its value changes.

Let us use the `On-Break` option in our program and see the difference:

```
!****************************
!TEST10B.SQR
!Using break logic in the employee list program
!****************************
Begin-Program
!****************************
      Do List_Employees
End-Program
!****************************
Begin-Heading 2
!****************************
   Print  'Company'        (1,1)
   Print  'Paygroup'       (,+2)
   Print  'Emplid'         (,+2)
   Print  'Name '          (,+4)
   Print  'Annual Salary'  (,+15)
   Print  ' '              (2,1)
End-Heading

!****************************************
Begin-Procedure List_Employees
!****************************************
Begin-Select
! We use the On-Break option below:
B.Company     (,1,7)  On-Break Print=Change/Top-Page Skiplines=1
B.Paygroup    (,+2,8)
A.Emplid      (,+2,8)
A.Name        (,+2,20)
B.Annual_Rt   (,+2,12) edit $,$$$,$$$.00
             Position  (+1)
From Personal_Data A, Job B
Where   A.Emplid=B.Emplid
        And B.Effdt=(Select Max(D.Effdt) From Job D
                     Where D.Effdt<=Sysdate
                     And D.Emplid=B.Emplid
```

Company is defined as a break field.

```
                      And D.Empl_Rcd=B.Empl_Rcd)
        And B.Effseq = (Select Max(C.Effseq) from Job C
                        Where C.Emplid=B.Emplid
                        And C.Empl_Rcd = B.Empl_Rcd
                        And C.Effdt=B.Effdt)
Order By B.Company, B.Paygroup, A.Emplid
End-Select
End-Procedure
!****************************
```

In `Test10B.sqr`, we defined `Company` as a break field and used the `On-Break` option for this field. In the `Print` qualifier, we chose to print the company ID 1) when its value is changed and 2) at the top of each new page even if the value is not changed.

In addition to the `Print` qualifier, we also used another qualifier: `Skiplines`. This qualifier specifies how many lines to skip when the break occurs.

Now, the output will look like that in figure 10.2.

Company	Paygroup	Explid	Name	Annual Salary
CBL	MN	B002	Maertens,Marianne	$769,392.00
CCB	BW0	E2301	Jacobs,Carol	$46,800.00
	BW0	E2302	Gardner,John	$64,800.00
	BW0	E2303	Andrews,Frank	$70,800.00
	BW0	E2304	Jeffries,Anne	$31,200.00
	BW0	E2305	Masterson,Marie	$8,195.20
	BW0	G500	Miller,Robin	$26,000.00
	BW0	G501	Caldwell,John	$38,400.00
	BW0	G502	Downs,Megan	$19,448.00
	BW0	G503	Castro,Mary	$36,000.00
	BW1	G701	Cortez,Isabella	$4,825.60
	BW1	G702	Jonas,Wendy	$4,825.60
	BW1	G703	Lotta,Emmanuel	$4,825.60
	BW1	G704	Dempsey,Elaine	$4,825.60
	LT1	8530	Vierra,Gina	$19,344.00
	LT1	LT001	Santos,Charles A.	$36,400.00
	LT1	LT002	Hiromoto,Seiko	$46,904.00
	LT1	LT003	Souza,Isobel	$72,800.00
	LT1	LT005	Seca,Wenda A.	$34,645.00

Figure 10.2 Using the On-Break option

10.2 Using Level qualifiers for multiple level breaks

As you can see from our previous example, employees may belong to multiple paygroups within the same company. We can add another break by paygroup to our report by adding the `On-Break` option to column `Paygroups`. In this case, we will have nested breaks. When dealing with nested breaks, use the `Level` qualifier to ensure that the breaks are properly nested and to control the order in which your break procedures are called (if any).

The parameter in the `Level` qualifier specifies the level of the break for reports containing multiple breaks. When coding the value of this parameter, you should number your breaks in the same order as that in the `Order By` clause. In our example, `Company` is the first level break, `Paygroup` is the second level break. After coding multiple breaks, our program will look as follows:

```
!****************************
!TEST10C.SQR
!Using the Level qualifier to define multiple level breaks
!****************************
Begin-Program
!****************************
      Do List_Employees
End-Program
!****************************
Begin-Heading 2
!****************************
   Print  'Company'        (1,1)
   Print  'Paygroup'       (,+2)
   Print  'Emplid'         (,+2)
   Print  'Name '          (,+4)
   Print  'Annual Salary'  (,+15)
   Print  ' '              (2,1)
End-Heading

!****************************************
Begin-Procedure List_Employees
!****************************************
Begin-Select
! We use the On-Break option with the Level qualifiers below:
B.Company (,1,7) On-Break Skiplines=1 Level=1
B.Paygroup (,+2,8) On-Break Level=2
A.Emplid   (,+2,8 )
A.Name     (,+2,20)
B.Annual_Rt(,+2,12) edit $,$$$,$$$.00
   Position  (+1)
From Personal_Data A, Job B
Where   A.Emplid=B.Emplid
```

`Company` is defined as a Level 1 break field.

`Paygroup` is defined as a Level 2 break field.

```
        And B.Effdt=(Select Max(D.Effdt) From Job D
                     Where D.Effdt<=Sysdate
                     And D.Emplid=B.Emplid
                     And D.Empl_Rcd=B.Empl_Rcd)
        And B.Effseq = (Select Max(C.Effseq) from Job C
                          Where C.Emplid=B.Emplid
                          And C.Empl_Rcd = B.Empl_Rcd
                          And C.Effdt=B.Effdt)
Order By B.Company, B.Paygroup, A.Emplid
End-Select
End-Procedure
!****************************
```

The output of the program with nested breaks is shown in figure 10.3.

Company	Paygroup	Explid	Name	Annual Salary
CBL	MN	B002	Maertens,Marianne	$769,392.00
CCB	BW0	E2301	Jacobs,Carol	$46,800.00
		E2302	Gardner,John	$64,800.00
		E2303	Andrews,Frank	$70,800.00
		E2304	Jeffries,Anne	$31,200.00
		E2305	Masterson,Marie	$8,195.20
		G500	Miller,Robin	$26,000.00
		G501	Caldwell,John	$38,400.00
		G502	Downs,Megan	$19,448.00
		G503	Castro,Mary	$36,000.00
	BW1	G701	Cortez,Isabella	$4,825.60
		G702	Jonas,Wendy	$4,825.60
		G703	Lotta,Emmanuel	$4,825.60
		G704	Dempsey,Elaine	$4,825.60
	LT1	8530	Vierra,Gina	$19,344.00
		LT001	Santos,Charles A.	$36,400.00
		LT002	Hiromoto,Seiko	$46,904.00
		LT003	Souza,Isobel	$72,800.00
		LT005	Seca,Wenda A.	$34,645.00

Figure 10.3 Using Level qualifiers in reports with multiple breaks

`On-Break` can only be used on string and date columns and variables. You cannot explicitly use the `On-Break` option directly on a numeric column or variable. To fool the system, move the numeric column value to a string variable, then code the `On-Break` option in the `Print` command for this new string variable:

```
!Using breaks for numeric columns
Begin-Select
```

```
Emplid  (+1,1)  On-Break Level=1
Annual_Rt
   Move &Annual_Rt To $Annual_Rate $,$$$,$$$.00
   Print  $Annual_Rate  On-Break Level=2
From Job
Order By Emplid, Annual_Rt
End-Select
```

Controlling multiple breaks may appear straightforward, but the internal SQR logic may get very tricky. When a break occurs at one level, it triggers breaks on variables with higher or equal `Level` qualifiers. For example, a break on `Company` triggers a break on `Paygroup` even if the value of this field did not change. At the same time, if both `Company` and `Paygroup` changed, SQR makes sure that a break on `Paygroup` does not happen twice. As we will learn later, a break on a variable (that is, a change in the value of this variable) may also result in a number of events such as the printing of the variable value, the skipping of a line, the invocation of a procedure, etc. Therefore, it is important for programmers to clearly understand the mechanics of break processing in SQR.

10.3 Using procedures when breaks occur

Many reports have fields or columns requiring special on-break processing, which is more complex than just a single action. SQR offers multiple ways of handling these situations. Using on-break procedures in your report allows you to customize break-processing logic, for example, to avoid printing redundant data, enhance the appearance of your report, perform conditional processing, print subtotals and totals when necessary, and so on.

When you use the `On-Break` option of the `Print` command, you can have SQR automatically call procedures before and after each break occurs. In order to accomplish this, use the `Before` and `After` qualifiers of the `On-Break` option of the `Print` command. The operands of the `Before` and `After` qualifiers specify the names of the procedures to be called. The `Before` qualifier will automatically call the specified procedure right before the column value is changed, including the processing of the first selected row. Similarly, the `After` qualifier will automatically call the specified procedure after the column value is changed including the last change, that is, when `Select` is completed. If no rows are selected, neither procedure will be called.

> *Note* The `Before` and `After` qualifiers can be used only within `Select` paragraphs.

Besides the procedure name operands in the `Before` and `After` qualifiers, there is a qualifier named `Procedure`. Do not confuse this qualifier with the procedure name operands. The parameter in this qualifier specifies the name of the procedure to be invoked when the break occurs. The `Procedure` qualifier is an old qualifier used in previous releases and cannot be used in combination with either `Before` or `After` procedures.

Before using `On-Break` procedures in the `Print` command, please read carefully the following sequence concerning events that occur when a query contains `Print` commands with `On-Break` qualifiers.

1. In the beginning of the query, all procedures specified in the `Before` qualifiers are invoked in the ascending `Level` order when the first row of the query is fetched. All break column values are printed in their respective positions unless `Print=Never` is specified
2. During the query execution, when a break occurs
   - all `After` procedures (if any) are invoked in descending `Level` order from the highest level down to the current break level of the break column. Please note that the previous values of the break columns are not available to the `After` procedures since they have been replaced with the new values. Use the `Save` qualifiers (covered in section 10.4) to keep the previous values after breaks occur.
   - all `Before` procedures (if declared) are processed in ascending `Level` order from the current break level to the highest break level.
   - if the `Procedure` qualifier was coded, the named procedure is invoked.
   - if `Skiplines` is specified, the current line position is advanced by the number of lines specified.
   - all break column values with the same or higher level are printed unless `Print=Never` is specified.
3. In the end of the query (at `End-Select`), all `After` procedures are processed once more in descending `Level` order.

To make sure that all these rules do not sound too confusing to you, let us enhance our previous program and include the `Before` and `After` break procedures in our SQR code. The `Show` operators located at certain strategic points in the program will help us trace the program control flow. We will use one `Before` break procedure named `Company_Name` to retrieve the company name from table `Company_Tbl` and to print a sub-header with the company name on each `Company` value break. We will also use two `After` break procedures named `Company_Totals` and `Paygroup_Totals` to calculate the number of employees and the total salary for each company and each paygroup within a company. Figure 10.4 shows a portion of the program's output.

```
!TEST10D.SQR
!Using the Before and After qualifiers of the On-Break option
!****************************
Begin-Program
```

```
!****************************
     Show 'Program Started'
     Do List_Employees
End-Program

!****************************
Begin-Heading 2
!****************************
   Print  'Company'        (1,1)
   Print  'Paygroup'       (,+2)
   Print  'Emplid'         (,+2)
   Print  'Name '          (,+4)
   Print  'Annual Salary'  (,+15)
   Print  ' '              (2,1)

End-Heading

!***************************************** *
Begin-Procedure List_Employees
!******************************************
Begin-Select
   Add 1 to #Row_Num
   Show  'Selected row# ' #Row_Num  '
   Comp='  &B.Company  '
   Paygrp='&B.Paygroup
B.Company    (,1,7)  On-Break Level = 1
 Before=Company_Name After=Company_Totals
              Skiplines = 1
B.Paygroup   (,10,8)  On-Break Level = 2
 After=Paygroup_Totals
A.Emplid      (,+2,8)
A.Name        (,+2,20 )
B.Annual_Rt   (,+2,12) edit $,$$$,$$$.00
  Position    (+1)

  Let #EE_Paygroup_Total= #EE_Paygroup_Total + 1
  Let #Sal_Paygroup_Total= #Sal_Paygroup_Total + &B.Annual_Rt
From Personal_Data A, Job B
Where   A.Emplid=B.Emplid
        And B.Effdt=(Select Max(D.Effdt) From Job D
                     Where D.Effdt<=Sysdate
                     And D.Emplid=B.Emplid
                     And D.Empl_Rcd=B.Empl_Rcd)

        And B.Effseq = (Select Max(C.Effseq) From Job C
                        Where C.Emplid=B.Emplid
                        And C.Empl_Rcd = B.Empl_Rcd
                        And C.Effdt=B.Effdt)
Order By B.Company, B.Paygroup, A.Emplid
End-Select
End-Procedure
```

`Company` is defined as a Level 1 break field with `Before` and `After` procedures.

`Paygroup` is defined as a Level 2 break field with an `After` procedure.

```
!*************************************
      Begin-Procedure Company_Name
!*************************************
Show 'Before Procedure Company_Name is invoked'
Begin-Select
C1.Descr
   Print 'Company Name: ' (+1,1)
   Print &C1.Descr (,+2)
   Position (+1)
From Company_Tbl C1
Where C1.Company = &B.Company
And C1.Effdt = (Select Max(Effdt) From Company_TBL
                Where Company = C1.Company)
End-Select
End-Procedure
```

Company_Name is defined as a Before procedure on Company break.

```
!*************************************
Begin-Procedure Company_Totals
!*************************************
Show 'After Procedure Company_Totals is invoked'
Print 'Number of Employees in Company = ' (+1,5)
Print   #EE_Company_Total () edit 999999
Print 'Total Annual Salary Paid for Company = ' (+1,5)
Print  #Sal_Company_Total () edit $$$,$$$,$$$.00
Let  #EE_Company_Total = 0
Let  #Sal_Company_Total = 0

End-Procedure
```

Company_Totals is defined as an After procedure on Company break.

```
!*************************************
Begin-Procedure Paygroup_Totals
!*************************************
Show 'After Procedure Paygroup_Totals is invoked'
Print 'Number of Employees in Paygroup = ' (+1,5)
Print   #EE_Paygroup_Total () edit 999999
Print 'Total Annual Salary Paid for Paygroup = ' (+1,5)
Print  #Sal_Paygroup_Total () edit $$$,$$$,$$$.00
Position (+1)

Let  #EE_Company_Total = #EE_Company_Total + #EE_Paygroup_Total
Let  #Sal_Company_Total = #Sal_Company_Total +  #Sal_Paygroup_Total

Let #EE_Paygroup_Total = 0
Let #Sal_Paygroup_Total = 0

End-Procedure
!********************************
```

Paygroup_Totals is defined as an After procedure on Paygroup break.

Figure 10.4 shows a portion of the program output.

The program run log in figure 10.5 will help us to better understand the sequence of different events during the program execution.

```
Company Name:   Continental Commerce - Belgium
CBL MN    B002   Maertens,Marianne  $769,392.00

   Number of Employees in Paygroup =      1
   Total Annual Salary Paid for Paygroup =    $769,392.00

   Number of Employees in Company =      1
   Total Annual Salary Paid for Company =    $769,392.00
Company Name:   Continental Commerce&Business

CCB BW0    E2301   Jacobs,Carol        $46,800.00
           E2302   Gardner,John        $64,800.00
           E2303   Andrews,Frank       $70,800.00
           E2304   Jeffries,Anne       $31,200.00
           E2305   Masterson,Marie     $8,195.20
           G500    Miller,Robin        $26,000.00
           G501    Caldwell,John       $38,400.00
           G502    Downs,Megan         $19,448.00
           G503    Castro,Mary         $36,000.00

   Number of Employees in Paygroup =      9
   Total Annual Salary Paid for Paygroup =    $341,643.20
    BW1    G701    Cortez,Isabella  $4,825.60
           G702    Jonas,Wendy      $4,825.60
           G703    Lotta,Emmanuel   $4,825.60
           G704    Dempsey,Elaine   $4,825.60

   Number of Employees in Paygroup =      4
```

Figure 10.4 Using the Before and After procedures in reports with breaks

Let us examine figure 10.5 and retrace the sequence of events that took place during the program run:

1. After the program initiation, when the very first row is fetched, the `Company_Name` procedure specified in the `Before` qualifier for the `Company` column is invoked. The procedure retrieves the company name from table `Company_Tbl` using the `Company` column value from the first row as a key and returns control back to procedure `List_Employees`. No `Before` qualifier is specified for the `Paygroup` column and, therefore, no procedure is invoked.
2. As the subsequent rows in the `List_Employees` Select paragraph are being fetched, SQR keeps its tabs on the values of `Company` and `Paygroup`.
3. If `Paygroup` is changed, SQR identifies this event as a *Break Level 2*. This, in turn, triggers the invocation of procedure `Paygroup_Totals` specified in the `After` qualifier for the `Paygroup` column. `Paygroup_Totals` prints the number of

employees and the salary total for the paygroup. If the `Before` qualifier were specified for `Paygroup`, the proper procedure would have been invoked following the `Paygroup_Totals` procedure.

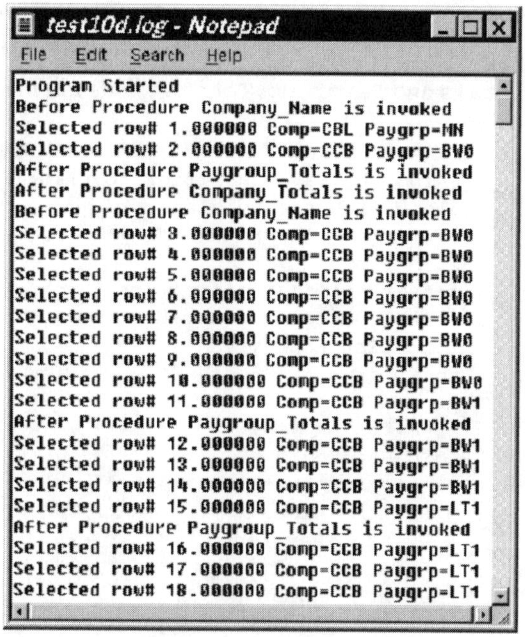
test10d.log - Notepad
File Edit Search Help
Program Started
Before Procedure Company_Name is invoked
Selected row# 1.000000 Comp=CBL Paygrp=MN
Selected row# 2.000000 Comp=CCB Paygrp=BW0
After Procedure Paygroup_Totals is invoked
After Procedure Company_Totals is invoked
Before Procedure Company_Name is invoked
Selected row# 3.000000 Comp=CCB Paygrp=BW0
Selected row# 4.000000 Comp=CCB Paygrp=BW0
Selected row# 5.000000 Comp=CCB Paygrp=BW0
Selected row# 6.000000 Comp=CCB Paygrp=BW0
Selected row# 7.000000 Comp=CCB Paygrp=BW0
Selected row# 8.000000 Comp=CCB Paygrp=BW0
Selected row# 9.000000 Comp=CCB Paygrp=BW0
Selected row# 10.000000 Comp=CCB Paygrp=BW0
Selected row# 11.000000 Comp=CCB Paygrp=BW1
After Procedure Paygroup_Totals is invoked
Selected row# 12.000000 Comp=CCB Paygrp=BW1
Selected row# 13.000000 Comp=CCB Paygrp=BW1
Selected row# 14.000000 Comp=CCB Paygrp=BW1
Selected row# 15.000000 Comp=CCB Paygrp=LT1
After Procedure Paygroup_Totals is invoked
Selected row# 16.000000 Comp=CCB Paygrp=LT1
Selected row# 17.000000 Comp=CCB Paygrp=LT1
Selected row# 18.000000 Comp=CCB Paygrp=LT1

Figure 10.5 The execution log of Test10D.sqr with the Before and After procedures

4 If `Company` is changed, SQR identifies the event as a *Break Level 1.* All procedures specified in the `After` qualifiers from the highest break level to Break Level 1 are invoked. In our case, procedure `Paygroup_Totals` (Break Level 2) is invoked first, procedure `Company_Totals` (Break Level 1) is invoked second. Please note that in our case, both `Company` and `Paygroup` changed at the same time. SQR triggers a break on `Paygroup` every time a break on `Company` occurs. To avoid double-breaking, the break on `Paygroup` is cleared. Then, all procedures specified in the `Before` qualifiers from the highest break level to Break Level 1 are invoked. In our case, there is only one procedure: `Company_Name`.

5 After the query execution is finished, all `After` procedures from the highest break level to Break Level 1 are invoked. The `Paygroup_Totals` procedure is called first, the `Company_Totals` procedure is called second.

10.4 Using the Save qualifier of the On-Break option

Sometimes it is necessary to use or print the previous break value of a print variable in the `After` procedure. Since `After` procedures are executed after the values of the `On-Break` columns have been changed, the columns will already hold their new values. The problem can be solved by using the `Save` qualifier of the `On-Break` option. This method allows you to store the previous column value in a specially designated variable when a break on this column value occurs.

Let us change our test program to demonstrate the `Save` qualifier. Suppose we want to print `Paygroup` and `Company` along with totals in both `After` procedures (`Company_Totals` and `Paygroup_Totals`). This will involve some changes to our program:

```
!TEST10E.SQR
!Using the Save qualifier to print Paygroup and Company
!along with the totals
!****************************
Begin-Program
!****************************
   Show 'Program Started'
   Do List_Employees
End-Program

!****************************
Begin-Heading 2
!****************************
   Print  'Company'        (1,1)
   Print  'Paygroup'       (,+2)
   Print  'Emplid'         (,+2)
   Print  'Name '          (,+4)
   Print  'Annual Salary'  (,+15)
   Print  ' '              (2,1)
End-Heading

!****************************************
Begin-Procedure List_Employees
!****************************************
Show 'Procedure List_Employees Started'

Begin-Select
    Add 1 to #Row_Num
    Show  'Selected row# ' #Row_Num ' Comp=' &B.Company
      ' Paygrp=' &B.Paygroup
    ! We use the Save qualifiers below:
B.Company        (,1,7)   On-Break Level = 1
 After=Company_Totals Skiplines = 1
                          Save=$Prev_Comp
B.Paygroup     (,10,8) ON-BREAK Level = 2
 After=Paygroup_Totals Save=$Prev_Paygrp
A.Emplid       (,+2,8)
A.Name         (,+2,20 )
B.Annual_Rt    (,+2,12)  edit $,$$$,$$$.00
   Position    (+1)
   Let #EE_Paygroup_Total= #EE_Paygroup_Total + 1
   Let #Sal_Paygroup_Total= #Sal_Paygroup_Total + &B.Annual_Rt

From Personal_Data A, Job B
where   A.Emplid=B.Emplid
        And B.Effdt=(Select Max(D.Effdt) from Job D
                     Where D.Effdt<=Sysdate
```

The `Save` qualifiers are used to save pre-break values of `Company` and `Paygroup`.

```
                    And D.Emplid=B.Emplid
                    And D.Empl_Rcd=B.Empl_Rcd)
         And B.Effseq = (Select Max(C.Effseq) From Job C
                      Where C.Emplid=B.Emplid
                      And C.Empl_Rcd = B.Empl_Rcd
                      And C.Effdt=B.Effdt)
Order By B.Company, B.Paygroup, A.Emplid
End-Select
End-Procedure

!******************************************
Begin-Procedure Company_Totals
!******************************************
Show 'After Procedure Company_Totals is invoked'
Print 'Number of Employees in Company ' (+1,5)
! We print the saved Company value below:
Print $Prev_Comp  (,+1)
Print   #EE_Company_Total (,+1) edit 999999
Print 'Total Annual Salary Paid for Company = ' (+1,5)
Print  #Sal_Company_Total () edit $$$,$$$,$$$.00
Position (+1)

Let   #EE_Company_Total = 0
Let  #Sal_Company_Total = 0

End-Procedure
!******************************************
Begin-Procedure Paygroup_Totals
!******************************************
Show 'After Procedure Paygroup_Totals is invoked'
Print 'Number of Employees in Paygroup  ' (+1,5)
! We print the saved Paygroup value below:
Print $Prev_Paygrp (,+1)
Print   #EE_Paygroup_Total (,+1) edit 999999
Print 'Total Annual Salary Paid by Paygroup = ' (+1,5)
Print  #Sal_Paygroup_Total () edit $$$,$$$,$$$.00
Position (+1)

Let   #EE_Company_Total = #EE_Company_Total + #EE_Paygroup_Total
Let  #Sal_Company_Total = #Sal_Company_Total +  #Sal_Paygroup_Total

Let #EE_Paygroup_Total = 0
Let  #Sal_Paygroup_Total = 0

End-Procedure
!***********************
```

Saved pre-break `Company` value is printed in the `After` procedure.

Saved pre-break `Paygroup` value is printed in the `After` procedure.

As you can see from figure 10.6, which illustrates the output of `Test10E.sqr`, using the `Save` qualifier of the `On-Break` option helps us retain the previous values of the company code and paygroup when breaks on these column values occurred. The

```
Company  Paygroup  Emplid    Name                       Annual Salary

CBL      MN        B002      Maertens,Marianne          $769,392.00

     Number of Employees in Paygroup   MN       1
     Total Annual Salary Paid by Paygroup =    $769,392.00

     Number of Employees in Company  CBL       1
     Total Annual Salary Paid for Company =    $769,392.00

CCB      BW0       E2301     Jacobs,Carol                $46,800.00
                   E2302     Gardner,John                $64,800.00
                   E2303     Andrews,Frank               $70,800.00
                   E2304     Jeffries,Anne               $31,200.00
                   E2305     Masterson,Marie              $8,195.20
                   G500      Miller,Robin                $26,000.00
                   G501      Caldwell,John               $38,400.00
                   G502      Downs,Megan                 $19,448.00
                   G503      Castro,Mary                 $36,000.00

     Number of Employees in Paygroup   BW0      9
     Total Annual Salary Paid by Paygroup =    $341,643.20
         BW1       G701      Cortez,Isabella              $4,825.60
                   G702      Jonas,Wendy                  $4,825.60
                   G703      Lotta,Emmanuel               $4,825.60
                   G704      Dempsey,Elaine               $4,825.60

     Number of Employees in Paygroup   BW1      4
 Total Annual Salary Paid by Paygroup =      $19,302.40
```

Figure 10.6 The output of Test10E.sqr which used the Save qualifier

saved values were used in the `After` procedures for each break to print the totals by paygroup or company along with the paygroup or the company code.

10.5 Using Print=Never option in the Print command

By default, break column values are printed automatically. In certain cases, you may choose not to print a break column value when a break occurs. You might prefer, for instance, to print the company name instead of printing the company Id when a company break occurs. In our previous `Company` break examples, SQR prints the value of the `Company` column, which is a three-character company Id, not a full company name. The following example shows how to use the `Print=Never` option of the `Print` command to print company names on `Company` break (figure 10.7 shows the output of our example):

```
!TEST10F.SQR
!Using the Print=Never to suppress on-break column values
!***************************
Begin-Program
!***************************
   Show 'Program Started'
      Do List_Employees
End-Program

!********************************
Begin-Heading 2
!********************************
Print 'Emplid'          (1,21)
Print 'Name '           (,+4)
Print 'Annual Salary'   (,+15)
Print ' '               (2,1)
End-Heading

!*****************************************
Begin-Procedure List_Employees
!*****************************************
Show 'Procedure List_Employees Started'
Begin-Select
   Add 1 to #Row_Num
   Show 'Selecting Row#=' #Row_Num 'Comp=' $B.Company
      'Paygroup=' &B.Paygroup
! We use the Print=Never option below:
B.Company ()  On-Break Level = 1 Before=Company_Name Print=Never
B.Paygroup()  On-Break Level = 2 Before=Paygroup_Code Print=Never
A.Emplid     (,21,8)
A.Name       (,+2,20)
B.Annual_Rt  (,+2,12)  edit $,$$$,$$$.00
   Position  (+1)
From Personal_Data A, Job B
Where   A.Emplid=B.Emplid
        And B.Effdt=(Select Max(D.Effdt) from Job D
                     Where D.Effdt<=Sysdate
                     And D.Emplid=B.Emplid
                     And D.Empl_Rcd=B.Empl_Rcd)

        And B.Effseq = (Select Max(C.Effseq) From Job C
                        Where C.Emplid=B.Emplid
                        And C.Empl_Rcd = B.Empl_Rcd
                        And C.Effdt=B.Effdt)
Order by B.Company, B.Paygroup, A.Emplid
End-Select
End-Procedure

!*********************************************
 Begin-Procedure Company_Name
!*********************************************
Show 'Procedure Company_Name is invoked'
```

Using `Print=Never` to suppress on-break column prints

```
Begin-Select
C1.Descr
    Print 'Company Name: ' (+1,1)
    Print &C1.Descr (,+2)
    Position (+1)
From Company_Tbl C1
Where C1.Company = &B.Company
And C1.Effdt = (Select Max(Effdt) From Company_Tbl
                Where Company = C1.Company)
End-Select
End-Procedure
```

Company name is printed in the **Before** procedure.

```
!******************************************
Begin-Procedure Paygroup_Code
!******************************************
Print 'Paygroup Code: ' (+1,1)
Print &B.Paygroup (,+2)
Position (+1)
End-Procedure
!*****************
```

Paygroup is printed in the **Before** procedure.

```
                  Emplid      Name                      Annual Salary

Company Name:   Continental Commerce - Belgium

Paygroup Code:   MN
                  B002       Maertens,Marianne            $769,392.00

Company Name:   Continental Commerce&Business

Paygroup Code:   BW0
                  E2301      Jacobs,Carol                  $46,800.00
                  E2302      Gardner,John                  $64,800.00
                  E2303      Andrews,Frank                 $70,800.00
                  E2304      Jeffries,Anne                 $31,200.00
                  E2305      Masterson,Marie                $8,195.20
                  G500       Miller,Robin                  $26,000.00
                  G501       Caldwell,John                 $38,400.00
                  G502       Downs,Megan                   $19,448.00
                  G503       Castro,Mary                   $36,000.00

Paygroup Code:   BW1
                  G701       Cortez,Isabella                $4,825.60
                  G702       Jonas,Wendy                    $4,825.60
                  G703       Lotta,Emmanuel                 $4,825.60
```

Figure 10.7 Using the Print=Never option for Company and Paygroup

In Test10F.sqr, we use the Print=Never option for the columns Company and Paygroup to suppress automatic printing of these column values when breaks occur. Instead, we call the Company_Name procedure to retrieve the company name, to print this name whenever a Company break occurs, and to call the Paygroup_Code procedure to print the text literal 'Paygroup Code' together with the Paygroup value whenever a Paygroup break occurs.

10.6 Controlling page breaks

Now that you understand how to deal with multiple break columns, it will take you only a minute to incorporate page breaks into your report, won't it? Well, it may take a little bit more than a minute ...

Let us try to incorporate page breaks into our previous example. Suppose we want to start a new page every time Paygroup or Company is changed. In addition, we would like to print the company code and name along with the paygroup code in the header.

The task may sound trivial, but your program has to take care of a multitude of details, and avoiding page breaking within one detail record is only one of them. For example, inserting a page break (with the help of the New-Page command) in the After procedure for Company and the After procedure for Paygroup will cause a problem when Company is changed: you will have two new pages instead of one.

We recommend that, in order to avoid incorrect new page processing, you

- carefully plan all your On-Break events
- place all On-Break columns in the Select statement ahead of other columns
- place all On-Break columns in the Select statement in the ascending level order
- avoid using Wrap and On-Break on the same column.

The following example will show you one of the ways of incorporating page breaks into your report correctly:

```
!TEST10H.SQR
!Controlling page breaks in your report
!****************************
Begin-Program
!****************************
      Let $First='Y'
      Show 'Program Started'
      Do List_Employees
End-Program
!****************************
Begin-Heading 7
!****************************
   Do Company_Name
```

```
   Print  'LIST OF EMPLOYEES ' (1,1)  Center
   Print  'Page'               (,90)
   Print  #page-count          (,+1) edit 999
   Print  'Company'            (+2,1)
   Print  $Company             (,+1)
   Print  $Company_Name        (,+1)
   Print  'Paygroup'           (+1,1)
   Print  $Paygroup            (,+1)
   Print  'Emplid'             (+2,1,8)
   Print  'Name '              (,+2,20)
   Print  'Annual Salary'      (,+2,13)
   Print  '='                  (+1,1,45) fill
End-Heading
!*****************************************
Begin-Procedure List_Employees
!*****************************************
Begin-Select
   Add 1 to #Row_Num
B.Company ()  On-Break Print=Never Level = 1 After=Company_Totals
                       Save=$Prev_Comp
B.Paygroup()  On-Break Print=Never Level = 2 After=Paygroup_Totals
                       Before=Before_Paygrp Save=$Prev_Paygrp
A.Emplid  (+1,1,8)
A.Name    (,+2,20)

B.Annual_Rt    (,+2,12) edit $,$$$,$$$.00
  Let $Company=&B.Company
  Let $Paygroup=&B.Paygroup
  Let #EE_Paygroup_Total= #EE_Paygroup_Total + 1
  Let #Sal_Paygroup_Total= #Sal_Paygroup_Total + &B.Annual_Rt
From Personal_Data A, Job B
Where A.Emplid=B.Emplid
     And B.Effdt=(Select Max(D.Effdt) From Job D
                  Where D.Effdt<=Sysdate
                  And D.Emplid=B.Emplid
                  And D.Empl_Rcd=B.Empl_Rcd)
     And B.Effseq = (Select Max(C.Effseq) From Job C
                     Where C.Emplid=B.Emplid
                     And C.Empl_Rcd = B.Empl_Rcd
                     And C.Effdt=B.Effdt)
Order By B.Company, B.Paygroup, A.Emplid
End-Select
End-Procedure

!*****************************************
Begin-Procedure Company_Name
!*****************************************
Begin-Select
C1.Descr
   Move &C1.Descr to $Company_Name
   show '$Company_Name=' $Company_Name
From Company_Tbl C1
```

Use the `Before` procedure to handle page breaks.

```
Where C1.Company=$Company
And C1.effdt=(Select Max(Effdt) From Company_Tbl
   Where Company = C1.Company)
End-Select
End-Procedure

!******************************************
Begin-Procedure Company_Totals
!******************************************
Move $Prev_Comp to $Company       ! Will be used in the Header
Print 'Number of Employees in Company = ' (+1,5)
Print $Prev_Comp      (,+1)
Print   #EE_Company_Total       () edit 999999
Print 'Total Annual Salary Paid for Company = ' (+1,5)
Print  #Sal_Company_Total       () edit $$$,$$$,$$$.00
Let  #EE_Company_Total = 0
Let  #Sal_Company_Total = 0

End-Procedure

!******************************************
Begin-Procedure Paygroup_Totals
!******************************************
Move $Prev_Paygrp to $Paygroup    ! Will be used in the Header

Print 'Number of Employees in Paygroup = ' (+1,5)
Print $Prev_Paygrp      (,+1)
Print   #EE_Paygroup_Total       () edit 999999
Print 'Total Annual Salary Paid for Paygroup = ' (+1,5)
Print  #Sal_Paygroup_Total       () edit $$$,$$$,$$$.00
Position (+1)

Let  #EE_Company_Total = #EE_Company_Total + #EE_Paygroup_Total
Let  #Sal_Company_Total = #Sal_Company_Total +  #Sal_Paygroup_Total

Let #EE_Paygroup_Total = 0
Let #Sal_Paygroup_Total = 0

End-Procedure
!******************************************
Begin-Procedure Before_Paygrp
!******************************************
If $First='Y'
   Let $First='N'
Else
   New-Page
End-If
End-procedure
!********************************
```

Print the current page and start a new page.

In our enhanced version of the program, `Test10H.sqr`, we added a new `Before` procedure named `Before_Paygrp` to create a page break by using the `New-Page` command when necessary. Why do we place the `New-Page` command into this procedure? Here, the sequence of events that you've learned in this chapter comes into its own. If you remember, the `Before` procedure is first invoked in the very beginning of the query. We use the `$First` variable as a switch to determine whether or not to issue the `New-Page` command. In the beginning, we do not need to switch a page, therefore, in our procedure, we check the `$First` switch, bypass the `New-Page` command this time, and set `$First` to `'N'`. The procedure is invoked again when a new value for `Paygroup` or `Company` is selected, after all totals in the `After` procedures are printed—a perfect place to open a new page. Remember, when the `New-Page` command is called, the current page is being written to the output file, and the new page has been started.

In `Test10H.sqr` we also improve the appearance of our report by printing a header with the report name, company code and name, and paygroup code. The header is printed automatically every time the current page is printed. We want to make sure that when a new row is selected on `Paygroup` or `Company` break, the header from the current page still contains the previous value, not the newly selected one, so we move the saved `Company` and `Paygroup` values in the `After` procedures to the variables used in the `Heading` section.

And now, as you can see in figure 10.8 our report looks much more professional:

```
LIST OF EMPLOYEES                        Page    1

Company M04 Midwest Manufacturing
Paygroup MMN

Emplid     Name                        Annual Salary
=============================================
M001       Bradford,James             $155,520.00
M002       Fernandez,Michael Ra        $69,060.00
M003       Evans,Lawrence              $43,080.00
M009       Payne,James Rocco           $35,100.00
    Number of Employees in Paygroup =  MMN        4
    Total Annual Salary Paid for Paygroup =     $302,760.00
```

Figure 10.8 A multiple page output in a program with breaks (continued on next page)

```
LIST OF EMPLOYEES                    Page   2

Company M04 Midwest Manufacturing
Paygroup MWK

Emplid    Name                       Annual Salary
=============================================
M004      Firestone-Marcus,Han     $26,416.00
M005      Hamasaki,Lewis Georg     $26,000.00
M006      Bottswell,Brian Jack     $29,120.00
M007      Carlos,Tomas Massimo     $22,048.00
M008      Van der Camp,Petros      $28,392.00
M010      Cardella,Sharon Anne     $17,940.00
    Number of Employees in Paygroup =  MWK      6
    Total Annual Salary Paid for Paygroup =    $149,916.00

    Number of Employees in Company =  M04     10
    Total Annual Salary Paid for Company =    $452,676.00
```

```
LIST OF EMPLOYEES                    Page   3

Company MDB Multi Dimensional Business
Paygroup MO2

Emplid    Name                       Annual Salary
=============================================
MD0001    Koontz,Stephan            $278,604.00
MD0002    Limburg,James             $130,320.00
MD0003    Kean,Betsy                $100,752.00
MD0004    Miller,Jacqueline          $54,528.00
MD0007    Bershas,James              $81,456.00
MD0008    Grissom,Jane Frances       $63,936.00
MD0009    McGregor,Julie             $36,920.00
MD0010    Habeggar,Cary             $120,000.00
    Number of Employees in Paygroup =  MO2      8
    Total Annual Salary Paid for Paygroup =    $866,516.00

    Number of Employees in Company =  MDB      8
    Total Annual Salary Paid for Company =    $866,516.00
```

Figure 10.8 A multiple page output in a program with breaks (continued)

KEY POINTS

1. You can greatly enhance your report by using the `On-Break` option of the `Print` command.
2. You can write special procedures to be invoked before and after column breaks. The `Before` and `After` qualifiers tell SQR when to call these procedures.
3. The `Level` qualifier of the `On-Break` option is used to arrange multiple breaks in hierarchy, and to specify the sequence of events.
4. Use the `Skiplines` qualifier to insert the necessary number of lines between detail groups.
5. When a break occurs, the previous column value is overridden with the new one. Use the `Save` qualifier to save a previously selected value to be used in the `After` procedures.
6. `On-Break` can only be used on string and date columns and variables.
7. In the beginning of a query, all `Before` procedures are processed in ascending `Level` order when the first row of the query is fetched.
8. All `After` procedures are processed in descending `Level` order from the highest level to the current break level of the field where the break occurred.
9. All `Before` procedures are processed in ascending `Level` order from the current break level to the highest break level.
10. The `Procedure` qualifier can not be used in a combination with either `Before` or `After` qualifiers.
11. After the query execution (at `End-Select`), all `After` procedures are processed once more in descending `Level` order.
12. If a query returns no rows, neither `Before` nor `After` procedures is invoked.

C H A P T E R 1 1

Run-time and compile-time variables

IN THIS CHAPTER

- Run-time variables and compile-time variables
- The difference in the usage of the substitution variables and the bind variables
- Technical aspects of working with substitution variables
- `Ask` and `Input` commands
- Dynamic query variables and how to construct dynamic SQL statements using these variables

SQR allows one to create very flexible and truly dynamic reports. This may include not only accepting report parameters as a part of user dialogs, but also dynamically changing your SQL statements based on user input. The following three types of special variables are used to make SQR reports flexible:

- SQR bind variables
- Substitution variables
- Dynamic query variables

11.1 SQR bind variables

SQR bind variables are used when a query includes parameters defined outside of this query. These parameters may come, for example, from user input, another query, or procedure. Using these variables is a very common technique in SQR; in fact, we have already employed SQR bind variables in examples throughout the previous chapters. SQR bind variables are *run-time variables*: their values are assigned and changed during the program execution stage. When you use a bind variable in an SQL statement, SQR "binds" the variable before the SQL is executed. The only thing that changes between SQL executions is the value of this variable.

The following code gives an example of the usage of SQR bind variables:

```
!TEST11A.SQR
!Using SQR Bind variables
!****************************
Begin-Procedure Main
!****************************
While  #Stat <> 3          !Status=3 indicates the Null String
                           !(not available prior to 4.0)
      Input $Emplid 'Please Enter Employee ID '
        Type=Number Status=#Stat
      Do Get_Empl_Info
End-While

End-Procedure

!*******************************
Begin-Procedure Get_Empl_Info
!*******************************
Let $Found='N'
Begin-Select
Name          (+1,1,20)
Birthdate     (,+2,10)
      Let $Found ='Y'
From Personal_Data
Where Emplid=$Emplid
```

The value of `$Emplid` is obtained from user input.

`$Emplid` is used as a bind variable.

```
End-Select
End-Procedure

!****************************
```

In our main procedure, we prompted the user for an employee Id, placed the response into the `$Emplid` variable, and then called the `Get_Empl_Info` procedure. In `Get_Empl_Info`, we simply selected and printed the selected employee information. We actually used `$Emplid` in our `Select` statement as a bind variable. Every time `Select` statement is executed, the current value of the variable `$Emplid` will be used, and therefore, the requested employee information will be printed.

In the previous example, we used bind variables to link a procedure to a query in another procedure. Bind variables can also be used to link one query to another. One typical situation occurs when you use hierarchical or nested queries. Another instance takes place when a main query selects certain rows, (obtains values for, let's say, columns A and B) and uses those values as parameters (bind variables) in the subordinate query. In the example below, we select and print the names of employees terminated from their job in 1998, and had at least one promotion prior to termination.

```
!TEST11B.SQR
!***************************
Begin-Program
!***************************
Do Main
End-Program

!***************************
Begin-Procedure Main
!***************************
Begin-Select
A.Emplid
A.Empl_Rcd
A.Effdt
A.Company
B.Name
   Do Check_Prior_Rows
   If $Found='Y'
     Do Print_Selected_Row
   End-If
From Job A, Personal_Data B
Where A.Empl_Status='T'
And To_Char(A.Effdt,'YYYY') = '1998'   ! To_Char is an
                                       ! Oracle-specific function
And A.Emplid=B.Emplid
End-Select
End-Procedure
```

```
!*******************************
Begin-Procedure Check_Prior_Rows
!*******************************
Let $Found='N'
Begin-Select
C.Emplid
C.Effdt
   Let $Found='Y'
From Job C
Where C.Emplid=&A.Emplid
And      C.Empl_Rcd=&A.Empl_Rcd
And      C.Empl_Status = 'PRO'
And      C.Effdt < &A.Effdt
End-Select
End-Procedure
!*******************************
```

The bind variables `&A.Emplid`, `&A.Empl_Rcd#`, and `&A.Effdt` link two SQL queries.

Two queries exist in our example. In the main query, we select all employees terminated in 1998 by joining the tables `Job` and `Personal_Data`. The next logical step is to check if every employee did, in fact, have a promotion some day prior to termination. We use a subordinate query in the `Check_Prior_Rows` procedure to select all rows containing effective dates prior to the employee termination date as well as `Empl_Status = 'PRO'` for each employee selected in the main query. (Please note that we used an Oracle built-in SQL function `To_Char` to extract the year from a date format column `Effdt`. Similar functions are available from other RDBMS vendors.)

We know that the rows selected in the subordinate query belong to the employee selected in the main query because the `&A.Emplid` bind variable gets populated in the main query. Two other bind variables, `&A.Empl_Rcd#` and `&A.Effdt` help to refine the subordinate query result set.

For every employee selected in the main query, our `Check_Prior_Rows` procedure selects table `Job` rows that satisfy the criteria in the `Where` clause of the subordinate query. For our particular business purpose, the selection of multiple rows is fine since the goal is to find at least one. We accomplish this selection by setting the global variable `$Found` to `'Y'`. There may be situations in which you have to make sure that your query returns only one row, for example the last one row, or the first one, or the one prior to the last row. There are many different techniques used to accomplish this. Since PeopleSoft is heavily involved in working with effective-dated or historical information, we will discuss different techniques for those situations in our PeopleSoft-related chapters.

11.2 Substitution variables

Substitution variables are used to specify SQR elements in several program locations at compile time. Substitution variables are *compile-time variables*. The values of substitution variables are set during the compilation stage and checked for syntax errors before the execution begins. They cannot be changed during the program execution. The `#Define` statement and the `Ask` command present two ways to define substitution variables and to assign values to these variables.

Substitution variables make your SQR program easier to maintain. Let us take a look at the following example:

```
!TEST11C.SQR
!Using substitution variables
#Define col_emplid     12      !Employee ID
#Define col_empl_name 30       !Name
#Define col_company     7      !Company
#Define col_hire_dt    10      !Hire Date
#Define col_sep         2      !Column Separator
```

The widths of variables are defined as substitution variables.

```
!********************
Begin-Heading 5
!********************

Print ' '            (+2,1,{col_emplid})
Print 'Emplid'       (0,1,{col_emplid})
Print 'Name  '       (0,+{col_sep},{col_empl_name})
Print 'Hire Date '   (0,+{col_sep},{col_hire_dt})
Print 'Company'      (0,+{col_sep},{col_company})
```

Using substitution variables in `Print` statements.

```
!***************
Begin-Program
!***************
Do Get_Employee_Info
Do Print_Emplyee_Info
...
End-Program

!*******************************************
Begin-Procedure Print_Employee_Info
!*******************************************
Print 'Emplid' (+1,1,{col_emplid})
Print 'Name  ' (0,+{col_sep},{col_empl_name})
Print 'Hire Date '(0,+{col_sep},{col_hire_dt})
Print 'Company'(0,+{col_sep},{col_company})
 ...
End-Procedure
!*******************************
```

At the beginning of our program, we use substitution variables to define the width of all the variables we want to print. Please note that we define these variables only once, but use them in more than one place in the program. After defining the column widths at the beginning of our program, we use them in the `Heading` section and the `Print_`

Employee_Info procedure. When referenced in the program, substitution variable names must be enclosed in braces "{}".

Is there an advantage in using the substitution variables? Well, let us assume that you want to change the appearance of your report by printing four spaces, instead of two, between columns. If you use substitution variables as we do in Test11C.sqr, all you have to do is to change the statement #Define col_sep 2 to #Define col_sep 4. Without the #Define statement, you would have to go over your program and change every single Print command.

It is common practice to define substitution variables in an *external source file*. Usually you put together some commonly-used variables in a separate file (called *include file*), then add this file to your SQR program with the help of the #Include statement. This method allows you to share one include file between multiple programs: you can change only this file without changing all other programs. SQR supports nested #Include statements: one include file may have a #Include statement referencing another include file, allowing up to four levels of nesting.

Another way to utilize substitution variables is to use the Ask command. The Ask command, always coded in the Setup section, prompts the user for the value which is placed into a substitution variable. The important fact to remember is that the value is input and substituted at compile time, before actual execution of the program begins. This substitution variable in the Ask command can later be used to replace any command, SQL statement, or argument.

Because scanning of substitution variables takes place before the #Include statement is processed, your program logic may change the included file's name depending on some substitution variable value taken, for example, from the user's response to an Ask command preceding the #Include statement. This allows you to take another step towards increasing your program's flexibility. Remember, this is all done at compile time as in the following example:

```
!****************************
Begin-Setup
!****************************
Ask  Printerid 'Please Enter Printer ID '
#Include 'printer{Printerid}.dat'
End-Setup
!****************************
```

A substitution variable obtained from user input defines which printer control file to use.

The Ask command should not be confused with the Input command, another user dialog command. The Input command is processed at execution time, whereas the Ask command is processed at compile time. Remember our first bind variable example, Test11A.sqr? Let us use this example again, but this time, instead of the Input command, we will use the Ask command. Since there are some limitations on where and how the Ask command can be used, we will change our program accordingly:

```
!TEST11D.SQR
!Using substitution variables in the Select paragraph
!***************
Begin-Setup
!***************
Ask  Emplid 'Please Enter Employee ID'
End-Setup

!****************************
Begin-Program
!****************************
Do Get_Empl_Info
End-Program

!***************************************
Begin-Procedure Get_Empl_Info
!***************************************
Let $Found='N'
Begin-Select
Name
Birthdate
      Let $Found='Y'
From Personal_Data
Where Emplid='{Emplid}'
End-Select
End-Procedure
!****************************
```

The Select criteria is obtained from user input with the help of a substitution variable.

Notice the difference? First, we use the Ask command in the Setup section, the only section where you can use this command. Since Ask is executed at compile time, no program loops can be used, therefore, we prompt the user only once in our example. Although there are cases (explored later in this chapter) when Ask is more powerful than Input, in this particular example we just want to demonstrate the difference between the Ask and Input commands. As with any substitution variable, when referencing a substitution variable used in the Ask command, the variable name must be placed in braces, for example, {Emplid}.

Ask commands have to be issued prior to any use of their substitution variables. If the Ask command references a variable that has already been defined by the #Define statement, the user will not be prompted for the value, and Ask will use the defined value.

Occasionally, as in the following example, the use of substitution variables is necessary. Let us assume that, depending on user input, you need to modify the appearance of the report. In addition, you want to prompt for the array characteristics:

```
!TEST11E.SQR
!****************
Begin-Setup
!****************
Ask Header_Lines 'Enter Number of lines for Heading '
Ask Footer_Lines 'Enter Number of lines for Footing '
Ask Array_Name   'Enter Array Name '
Ask Array_Size   'Enter Array Size '

Create-Array Name={Array_Name} Size={Array_Size}
   Field = Emplid:char
   Field = Name:char
   Field = Zip:char
End-Setup

Begin-Heading {Header_Lines}
Print 'The Use of Substitution Variables' () center
End-Heading

Begin-Footing {Footer_Lines}
page-number (1,1) 'Page '
End-Footing

Begin-Report
Print 'Test' (1,1)
End-Report
!*****************
```

Substitution variables help to modify array name and size. These parameters cannot be modified dynamically from the `Input` command.

Substitution variables help to change the `Heading` and `Footing` parameters. These parameters cannot be modified dynamically via the `Input` command.

As you can see, substitution variables help us to modify command lines which are normally quite restrictive. The `Input` command can't do this. This is an example when the `Ask` command has more power than the `Input` command. Another benefit of using substitution variables is that, since substitutions take place at compile time, any possible errors can be checked before execution starts. In many cases, however, `Input` is more convenient than `Ask`. With `Input`, for instance, you can validate user input and re-prompt if it is not valid, something you cannot do with the `Ask` command.

11.3 Dynamic query variables

Dynamic query variables are used to build dynamic SQL code. Sometimes called dynamic SQL variables, or simply, dynamic variables, dynamic query variables are text variables whose values are used as parts of SQL statements. When referenced in SQL statements, their names must be enclosed in square brackets, for instance, `[$By]`, or back slashes in MVS, AS/400, for instance, `\$By\`. You can use dynamic query variables to substitute columns and other parts of SQL statements or to dynamically change the `Where` clause or an entire SQL statement. The important thing to remember is that when you use dynamic variables in your SQL statement, SQR cannot check your syntax at compile time as it usually does. Therefore, each SQL statement will be constructed and checked at run time. Run-time errors will occur if a dynamic variable or the `Where` clause syntax are incorrect. Good error-handling routines in your programs are always important, but when SQL statements are modified at run time, such routines are a must.

If we need to select all active employees who live in states specified in user input, dynamic query variables will be of great help:

```
!TEST11F.SQR
!Using Dynamic Where clauses
!***************************
Begin-Program
!***************************

Do Main
End-Program

!***************************
Begin-Procedure Main
!***************************
Let $State_Error = 'Y'
While $State_Error='Y'
   Input $State_List
    'Enter a list of comma separated state codes (ex. NY,CT,MI)'
   Let $State_List=Rtrim($State_List,' ')
   If $State_List = ''
      Show 'Incorrect Input'
   Else
      Let $State_Error = 'N'
      Do Build_Where
      If $State_Error = 'N'
         Do Get_Employees
      Else
           Show 'Invalid State, please re-enter'
      End-If
   End-If
End-While
End-Procedure

!*************************************
Begin-Procedure Build_Where
!*************************************
!Construct the Where statement
Let $Where= 'B.State In (' ! Init Where
Let #Length=Length($State_List)! Get the Length
Let #Start=1               ! Start position for Substring
Let $Quote = ''''
Let $Comma = ''            ! Initialize to null string

While #Length > 0
   Let $Sti = Substr($State_List,#Start,2)
```

A portion of the SQL WHERE clause is constructed based on user input.

```
   Do State_Lookup
   If $State_Error = 'Y'
     Break                        !Break from the while loop
   End-If
   Let $Where=$Where ||$Comma||$Quote|| $Sti || $Quote
   Let $Comma = ','
   Let #Start = #Start + 3
   Let #Length = #Length - 3

End-While
Let $Where= $Where || ')'
Show '$Where=' $Where

End-Procedure
!*****************************************
Begin-Procedure Get_Employees
!*****************************************
Begin-Select On-Error=Invalid_Select
A.Emplid
A.Hire_Dt
B.Name
B.State
   Show &A.Emplid ' In ' &B.State
From Employment A, Personal_Data B
Where A.Emplid=B.Emplid
And A.Termination_Dt is Null
And [$Where]
End-Select
End-Procedure
```

Previously created portion of the SQL `WHERE` clause is used in a query with the help of a dynamic query variable.

```
!*****************************************
Begin-Procedure Invalid_Select
!*****************************************
Show 'Error in Select Statement. Check your Where clause = ' $Where
End-Procedure

!*****************************************
Begin-Procedure State_Lookup
!*****************************************
Let $State_Error = 'Y'
Begin-Select
State
   Let $State_Error = 'N'
From STATE_NAMES_TBL
Where State=$Sti
End-Select
End-Procedure
!******************************
```

In `Test11F.sqr`, we prompt the user for a list of two-character state codes. The input is used to build a portion of the `Where` clause in the following format: "`B.State` in ('XX','YY','ZZ')". In the Get_Employees procedure, we use the dynamic query variable [$Where] from the main procedure whose value is changed depending on user input. As the result, a portion of the Where clause of the Select statement in the program will be changed during program execution depending on user input.

11.4 More about dynamic query variables

Dynamic query variables can be instrumental in building rather sophisticated generic utilities to select information from the database, or insert new records into the database. For example, depending on user input, you can dynamically construct an entire SQL statement.

The process may seem straightforward: just use the method employed in generating the Where clause when building the remaining parts of the entire SQL statement. There is one problem: SQR must know the types of all columns used in the Select paragraph at compile stage. This necessitates the usage of a somewhat tricky logic when working with columns of different types.

We will start with an example that demonstrates how to build SQL statements with columns of the character type only:

```
!TEST11G.SQR
!Using Dynamic variables to build SQL
!****************************
Begin-Program
!****************************
Input $Table_Name 'Enter table name for Select Statement (eg. Job)'
Input $Column_Names
 'Enter char type colmns for Select stmnt comma sep.(eg. Emplid,Company)'
Input $Where 'Enter the Where clause (eg. Company=''XYZ'')'
Input $Order_By 'Enter Order By Statement'
Unstring $Column_Names By ',' Into $Column_Name1 $Column_Name2
  $Column_Name3 $Column_Name4

If Rtrim($Where,' ')<>''
   Let $Where='Where '||$Where
End-If

If Rtrim($Order_By,' ')=''
   Let $Order_By= 'Order by '|| $Order_By
End-If

Show  $Table_Name '   ' $Column_names '   ' $Where '   ' $Order_By
Do Execute_Select
End-Program

!******************************************
Begin-Procedure Execute_Select
```

```
!*****************************************
Begin-Select On-Error=Select_Error
[$Column_Name1] &colmn1=Char (+1,1)
[$Column_Name2] &colmn2=Char (,+1)
[$Column_Name3] &colmn3=Char (,+1)
[$Column_Name4] &colmn4=Char (,+1)

  Show &Colmn1 ' ' &Colmn2 ' ' &Colmn3 ' ' &Colmn4

From [$Table_Name]
[$Where]
[$Order_By]
End-Select
End-Procedure

!*************************************
Begin-Procedure Select_Error
!*************************************
Show 'SQL ERROR: in Select ' $Column_Names ' From ' $Table_Names  ' '
 $Where  ' ' $Order_By
Show 'SQL-status=' #sql-status
End-Procedure
```

This query uses dynamic table and column names and hard-coded column types.

The resulting program may look a little artificial since its only purpose is to demonstrate the usage of dynamic variables in building all parts of the SQL paragraph.

At the beginning, we prompt user to enter the input parameters. In a production environment, it may be a good idea to verify every part of user input against your database. The table name, for example, can be verified against the system catalog (the names of the catalog table vary for different databases) that contains all table names. Similarly, you can verify the entered column names.

As you can see, the above example uses a hard-coded column type, and therefore, will work only with columns of the character type. If you need to build a query that uses different types of columns, you can use a number of techniques.

One method is to continue using the hard-coded character type for all the columns in the `Select` paragraph, but to also employ the database-specific built-in conversion functions to convert each column value to the character format:

```
!TEST11L.SQR
!Building Dynamic SQL with various column data types
!**************************
Begin-Program
!**************************
Do Get_Input
If Not IsNull($Input_Table_Name)
   Do Build_Dynamic_Vars
   Do Execute_Select
Else
   show 'No Entries found. Program Ended'
```

```
End-If
End-Program
!********************************
Begin-Procedure Get_Input
!********************************
Let $End='Y'
While Upper($End) = 'Y'
   Let $End='N'
   Input $Input_Table_Name
        'Enter table name for Select Statement (e.g. Job)'
   Do Verify_Table_Name
   If $Table_Exists = 'N'
      Input $End 'Table is not found. Retry? (Y/N) ' type=char
   End-If
End-While
If Not IsNull($Input_Table_Name)
    Input $Column_names
   'Enter valid colmns, comma sep.,max=3 (e.g. Emplid,Company)'
   Input $Where
   'Enter the Where statement criteria (e.g. Company=''XYZ'')'
   Input $Order_By
   'Enter the Sort Order (e.g. 1,2 or Emplid,Company)'
End-If
End-Procedure
!********************************
Begin-Procedure Verify_Table_Name
!********************************
Let $Table_Exists = 'N'
Let $Input_Table_Name = Upper($Input_Table_Name)
Begin-Select
Table_Name
  Let $Table_Exists = 'Y'
From All_Tables
where Table_Name=$Input_Table_Name
End-Select
End-Procedure
!**********************************
Begin-Procedure Build_Dynamic_Vars
!**********************************
Do Build_Dynamic_Colmns

if rtrim($Where,' ')<>''
   Let $Where='Where '||$Where
End-If

if rtrim($Order_By,' ')=''
   Let $Order_By='1'
End-If
End-Procedure
!**********************************
Begin-Procedure Build_Dynamic_Colmns
!**********************************
```

Verifying table name in the systems catalog.

```
Let $q=''''
unstring $Column_names by ',' into $Column_Name1 $Column_Name2
         $Column_Name3
Do Convert_To_Char($Column_Name1,$Dyn_Column_Name1)
show $Column_Name1 $Dyn_Column_Name1
Do Convert_To_Char($Column_Name2,$Dyn_Column_Name2)
show $Column_Name2 $Dyn_Column_Name2
Do Convert_To_Char($Column_Name3,$Dyn_Column_Name3)
show $Column_Name3 $Dyn_Column_Name3
End-Procedure

!*************************************************************
Begin-Procedure Convert_To_Char($Column_Name,:$Dyn_Column_Name)
!*************************************************************

Let $Input_Column_Name = Rtrim($Column_Name,' ')
If $Input_Column_Name <> ''
   Let $Input_Column_Name = Upper($Input_Column_Name)
   Do Get_Data_Type($Input_Column_Name,$Data_Type)
   If $Data_Type <> ''
      Evaluate $Data_Type
      When = 'DATE'
        Let $Dyn_Column_Name = 'To_Char('||$Column_Name||','
                               ||$_q ||'YYYYMMDD' ||$_q||')'
     Break
      When = 'NUMBER'
        Let $Dyn_Column_Name = 'To_Char('||$Column_Name||')'
     Break
      When-Other
        Let $Dyn_Column_Name = '' || $Column_Name
      End-Evaluate
   End-If
   show '$Dyn_Column_Name=' $Dyn_Column_Name
Else
   Let $Dyn_Column_Name =''
End-If
End-Procedure

!*************************************************************
Begin-Procedure Get_Data_Type($Input_Column_Name,:$Data_Type)
!*************************************************************
Let $Data_Type=''
Begin-Select
Column_Name
Data_Type
  Let $Data_Type=&Data_Type
From All_Tab_Columns
where Table_Name=$_Input_Table_Name
and   Column_Name=$Input_Column_Name

End-Select
End-Procedure
```

Depending on the data type, building the data conversion string

Obtaining data type from systems catalog

```
!********************************
Begin-Procedure Execute_Select
!*********************************
Begin-Select On-Error=Select_Error
[$Dyn_Column_Name1] &colmn1=char (+1,1)
[$Dyn_Column_Name2] &colmn2=char (+1,1)
[$Dyn_Column_Name3] &colmn3=char (+1,1)
  show &colmn1 ' ' &colmn2 ' ' &colmn3
From [$Input_Table_Name]
[$Where]
Order by [$Order_By]
End-Select
End-Procedure
```

The actual Select statement with Dynamic variables

```
!**************************
Begin-Procedure Select_Error
!**************************
Show 'SQL ERROR:' 'Select ' $Column_Names ' From ' $Input_Table_Name
     ' ' $Where
show '$Dyn_Column_Names=' $Dyn_Column_Name1 ' ' $Dyn_Column_Name2 ' '
      $Dyn_Column_Name3
Show 'SQL-status=' #sql-status
End-Procedure
```

In `Test11L.sqr`, the program uses the Oracle system catalog tables `All_Tables` (which contains all table names) and `All_Tab_Columns` (which contains all column names and types for each table) to verify the entered table name and to determine the type of each column entered by the user. Depending on the column type, the program then uses the proper format of the Oracle-specific function `to_char()` to convert the column value to the character type. This way, the column types for all columns in the `Select` paragraph can be coded as character. Later, all converted-to-character type column values may be reconverted back if required by the application logic.

If you work with a database other than Oracle, you can use your database-specific system catalog tables and type conversion functions.

Beware: using dynamically built SQL gives you lots of power. Use it with caution. The syntax of dynamically generated SQL statements is not checked at compile time. While using simple hard-coded SQL statements may seem less fancy (and sometimes increases the size of your program), in many cases, it is more reliable and efficient than generating dynamic SQL.

KEY POINTS

1. The three special types of variables that increase flexibility of SQR programs are: bind variables, substitution variables, and dynamic query variables.
2. Bind variables and dynamic query variables are run-time variables.
3. Substitution variables are *compile time variables*: their values cannot be changed at run time.
4. Bind variables are used in SQL statements in the `SQL` or `Select` paragraphs.
5. Bind variables can be used in correlated `Select` statements to link one query to another.
6. Substitution variables can be used to alter any part of SQR programs.
7. Substitution variable values are set at compile time by either the `#Define` compile directive or the `Ask` command.
8. The `Ask` command can be used only in the `Setup` section.
9. When referenced in a program, substitution variable names must be enclosed into braces; e.g., `{Subst_Var}`.
10. A change to just one substitution variable may cause multiple changes in the program.
11. Dynamic query variables are variables whose values are used as parts of SQL statements.
12. When referencing dynamic query variables you should enclose their names in square brackets; e.g., `[dynamic_var]`.
13. Dynamic query variables can be used to substitute any part of an SQL statement.
14. When dynamic query variables are used to generate SQL statements, SQR can not check the SQL syntax at compile time.
15. When using dynamic query variables to generate SQL statements, it is very important to code error-handling routines.

CHAPTER 12

Working with arrays

IN THIS CHAPTER

- Creating an array
- Populating an array with data
- Retrieving data from an array
- Referencing individual array elements
- Multiple-occurrence fields in SQR arrays
- Using the generic SQR `Let` command and SQR array-specific commands to access array elements.
- Sorting arrays
- Searching data in arrays

12.1 SQR arrays

Arrays can be found in many programming languages. They are instrumental to success when a program needs to work with a number of identical groups of fields in the program memory. Instead of referring to each field by its unique name, arrays allow you to take advantage of the fact that all these groups have an identical or similar layout. A typical array is a collection of similar groups of fields in the program memory wherein each group can be referred to by its relative position number in the array (figure 12.1).

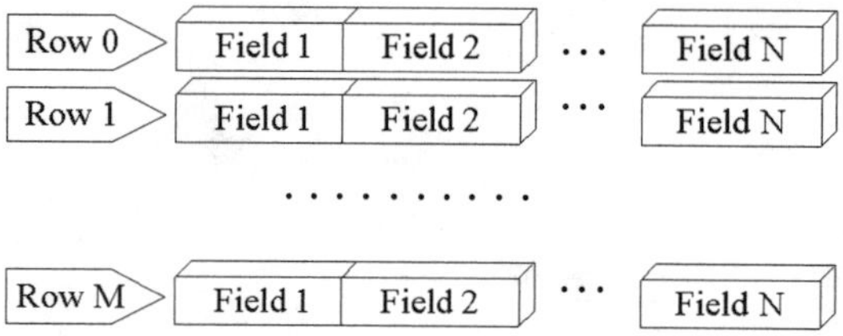

Figure 12.1
A typical SQR array

An SQR array is a memory structure that consists of rows and fields. When no arrays are used, in most cases, an SQR program processes its input records one by one. After a record is processed, it is overlaid with the next record, making the first record's contents inaccessible. Because it is sometimes necessary to process all or some records at once, SQR arrays can serve as buffers where the data can be temporarily stored. Oftentimes, it is not only a convenient method of temporarily storing information, but also a good way of developing an efficient program.

In addition to storing data in the program memory, arrays are also used by the `Print-Chart` command to generate graphical charts. (See chapter 16.)

Do not confuse arrays with relational tables: arrays are temporary structures created in the program memory, whereas tables reside on discs.

SQR has a specific set of commands used to create and populate arrays and to access information stored in arrays. The following commands work with arrays:

- `Create-Array`
- `Clear-Array`
- `Get`
- `Put`
- `Array-Add`
- `Array-Subtract`
- `Array-Multiply`
- `Array-Divide`

In addition to the above array-specific commands, you can use the already familiar SQR command `Let` to manipulate array elements.

12.2 How to create an array

In SQR, arrays are created during the compile stage, before the program is executed. The `Create-Array` command is used to create an array in any section of your program. For example

```
Create-Array Name=Dependents Size=25
   Field=Dependent_Id:Char
   Field=Dependent_Name:Char
   Field=Dependent_Birthday:Date
   Field=Relationship:Char
```

Table 12.1 shows the elements of our array.

Table 12.1 Array elements

Array element	Dependent_Id	Dependent_Name	Dependent_Birthday	Relationship
Dependents(0)	01	Smith,Maria	01-Jan-1960	SP
Dependents(1)	02	Smith,Albert	02-Feb-1982	S
Dependents(2)	03	Smith,Marsha	03-Mar-1984	D
Dependents(3)	04	Smith,Lisa	04-Apr-1940	M

In the above example, we created an array named `Dependents` with a size of twenty-five rows. Each row holds a record representing one dependent. There are four fields in every row of our array: `Dependent_Id`, `Dependent_Name`, `Dependent_Birthday`, and `Relationship`. Please note that no special characters are used to denote array fields formats: formats in the `Declare-Array` command are declared explicitly.

The `Size` in the `Create-Array` command specifies the maximum number of rows in the array. If you do not know the expected number of rows in an array, it is better to over-allocate rather than under-allocate the memory for your array. In our example, most employees will probably have two or three dependents, but we allocated room for twenty-five dependent rows just in case an unusual situation exists.

If the array subscript value exceeds the maximum array size, SQR aborts the program execution and displays the following message:

```
(SQR 1500) Array element out of range (25) for array
   'Dependents' on line 28.
SQRW: Program Aborting.
```

In this case, our program attempted to address row 25 which is beyond the maximum number of rows (row numbers start with row zero).

Each field in an array must be assigned a type:

- `Char` for character strings
- `Number` for default numeric type fields
- `Decimal` for decimal numbers with an optional precision qualifier
- `Float` for double precision floating point numbers
- `Integer` for integer numbers
- `Date` for dates declared as date variables.

Please note that in SQR version 3.0 (and earlier versions) you can only use either `Number` or `Char` types, with `Char` used to store both strings and dates.

In many instances, a row in an array may contain a field, consisting of a number of repeated portions of the same type, for example, three different employee phone numbers: a work phone number, a home phone number, and a beeper number. These fields are called *multiple-occurrence* fields. Instead of coding each portion of a multiple-occurrence field as a separate field, you can define only one field and specify the number of occurrences for this field:

```
Create-Array Clients Size=100
Field=Name:Char
Field=Phone:Char:3
```

In the above example, we defined an array of one hundred rows; each row includes the `Name` field and the three-occurrence field `Phone`.

Figure 12.2 is a graphical illustration of an array where `Field2` is a two-occurrence field.

Once an array is dynamically created, any array field can be referenced by specifying the field name, the field row number starting from number zero, and, for multiple-occurrence fields, the field occurrence number starting from occurrence number zero. In the `Clients` array, the rows are numbered from zero to 99, and the field `Phone` occurrences are numbered from zero to 2.

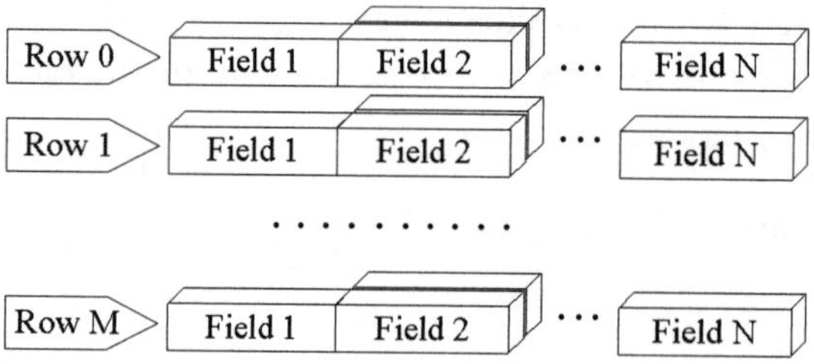

Figure 12.2
An array with multiple-occurrence

All SQR arrays are created before the program is executed. While the Create-Array command can be used in any section of your program, it is a good practice to place it into the Setup section. Also, we recommend the Size parameter be defined as a substitution variable, and placed at the top of your program. This way, if you need to change the size of an array, you will not have to go over your program to find the location of the proper parameter.

Let's use a substitution variable in our Create-Array statement:

```
#Define Max_Dependents 25
Begin-Setup
   Create-Array Name=Dependents Size = {Max_Dependents}
   Field=Dependent_Id:Char
   Field=Dependent_Name:Char
   Field=Dependent_Birthday:Date
   Field=Relationship:Char
End-Setup
```

The Create-Array command just allocates and initializes memory for an array. It is still a programmer's job to populate the array with information by reading data from the database tables or some other input, and moving the selected data into the array. When an array is created, its fields are automatically initiated to their default values based on the following rules:

- all numeric fields (with types equal to Number, Decimal, Float, or Integer) are set to zero
- all string fields (with type equal to Char) are set to NULL
- all date fields (with type equal to Date) are set to NULL.

You can specify an initial value for an array's field in the Create-Array command, as in the following example where all three occurrences of the Phone field are set to an initial value of 'None'.

```
Create-Array Name=Clients Size=100
Field=Name:Char
Field=Phone:Char:3='None'
```

12.3 Placing data into arrays

There are two methods of placing data into an array. You can reference the array elements in the Let command or use the array-specific command Put.

Here are several examples using the Let command:

```
1 Let Dependents.Dependent_Id(10) = '01'
2 Let Dependents.Dependent_Id(#Row_Num) = &A.Dependent_Benef
3 Let Clients.Phone(#i,#j) = &A.Phone
```

In the example's line 1, the string literal `'01'` is moved into field `Dependent_Id` of the 11th row (counting from row number zero) of the `Dependents` array. The row number does not have to be coded as a constant; numeric variables can be used to store and dynamically change row numbers.

In line 2, the row number is stored in the numeric variable `#Row_Num`, which can be changed by the program.

> **Note** When using variables to refer to row numbers or occurrence numbers, be sure to keep the variable values within the boundaries defined in the `Create-Array` command.

In line 3, the field `Phone` in the `Clients` array is a multiple-occurrence field. The numeric variables `#i` and `#j` store the row number and the field `Phone` occurrence number, respectively. The `Let` command moves the value of `&A.Phone` to the field `Phone` of the `Clients` array with the row number stored in `#i` and the occurrence number stored in `#j`.

The `Put` command was designed specifically to work with arrays, and offers more flexibility in placing data into arrays. You can move values to all of the array fields at once using just one `Put` command, or you can move data to one or more specified fields. For example

```
1 Put '01' Into Dependents(5)
2 Put '01' 'Smith,Maria' Into Dependents(#i)
3 Put &A.Dependnt_Benef &Birthday Into Dependents(#Row_Sub)
  Dependent_Id Dependent_Birthday
4 Put &Name $Phone into Clients(#Row_Num) Name Phone(#Sub_Num)
5 Put $Phone1 $Phone2 $Phone3 into Clients(0) Phone(0) Phone(1)
  Phone(2)
```

In line 1 of the above examples, a string literal `'01'` is moved into the first field of the 6th row of the `Dependents` array (row numbers are counted from row zero). We do not specify the name of the target field, and, therefore, SQR automatically places the data into the first field of the row.

In line 2, two literals—`'01'` and `'Smith,Maria'`—are moved into a row in the `Dependents` array. The row number is stored in the numeric variable `#i`. As in the first example, no particular target fields are specified, and SQR moves both literals into the first two consecutive array fields in the order they were defined in the `Create-Array` statement. In this case, `'01'` is moved into `Dependent_Id` field, and `'Smith,Maria'` is moved into `Dependent_Name`.

In line 3, the values of SQR columns &A.Dependnt_Benef and &Birthday are moved into the two specified target fields, Dependent_Id, and Dependent_Birthday, in a row with the number stored in #Row_Sub. If we did not specify the target field names, &A.Dependnt_Benef would be moved into the first field in the row; Dependent_Id, and &Birthday would be moved into the next one, Dependent_Name.

We recommend you use the form of the Put statement used in the third line of the example code even if you do not have to specify the target fields: it is preferable from the program maintenance point of view. If the array row layout is changed, the Put statement in the third example will not have to be modified, as long as fields Dependent_Id and Dependent_Birthday remain parts of the array row.

In line 4, the value of SQR column &Name is moved into field Name of the Client's row with the number controlled by #Row_Num. String variable $Phone is moved into field Phone of the same row of the array. Phone is a multiple-occurrence field and the numeric variable #Sub_Num stores the occurrence number in the target field Phone.

Finally, in line 5, the string variables $Phone1, $Phone2, and $Phone3 are moved into the zero, first, and second occurrences of the Phone field in the first row of the Clients array.

12.4 Initializing arrays

As we have already mentioned, when an array is created all its field values are automatically initialized. Sometimes you need to re-initialize an array after some or all of its fields have been populated. It is a good practice to always reinitialize your array after its use. The Clear-Array command resets each field of an array to its initial value. Field initial values are specified in the Create-Array command. If no initial value was specified for a field, the field is set to its default value.

Here is an example of the Clear-Array command:

```
Clear-Array Name=Dependents
```

12.5 Retrieving data from arrays

Two methods of retrieving data from an array are very similar to the two previously described methods of placing data into an array. You can use the Let command or the array-specific command Get.

The examples next illustrate the use of the Let command when retrieving data from an array:

```
Let $Dep = Dependents.Dependent_Id(#i)
Let $Phone = Clients.Phone(#i,#j)
```

The Get command is similar to the Put command and gives you more flexibility in retrieving data from arrays than the Let command. You can retrieve all the array's fields at once using one Get command. You can also move data from one or more specified fields or occurrences of a field:

```
1 Get $Dep_Id From Dependents(10)
2 Get $Dep_Id $Dep_Name From Dependents(#i)
3 Get $Dep_Id $Dep_Bday From Dependents(#Row_Sub) Dependent_Id
  Dependent_Birthday
4 Get $Client_Name $Client_Phone From Clients(10) Name Phone(#j)
5 Get $Phone1 $Phone2 $Phone3 From Clients(#i) Phone(0) Phone(1)
  Phone(2)
```

In line 1 of our example, $Dept_Id is populated from the first field of the Dependents array's row number 10 (counting from row number zero). Since we did not code a specific field name of the row, SQR automatically retrieves the content of the first field in the row.

In line 2, the values of $Dept_Id and $Dept_Name are retrieved from the first two fields of the Dependents array element with the row number stored in #i.

In line 3, the values of the Dependent_Id and Dependent_Birthday fields from the row with the number stored in #Row_Sub are moved to $Dep_Id and $Dep_Bday respectively. As we already mentioned, this method of explicit coding of the row field names is preferable from the program maintenance point of view.

In line 4, field Name from the 11th row is moved into the string variable $Client_Name. In addition, the Phone field, which occurs in row j, is moved into the specified variable $Client_Phone.

In the last line of this example, the zero, the first, and the second occurrences of the Phone field in the row with the number stored in #i are moved into string variables $Phone1, $Phone2, and $Phone3.

12.6 Performing arithmetic operations on elements of an array

You can perform addition, subtraction, division, and multiplication operations on elements of an array by using the Let command or one of the following four array-specific commands.

- Array-Add
- Array-Divide

- `Array-Multiply`
- `Array-Subtract`

In order to use these commands, the array must be previously created by the `Create-Array` command. All fields used in these operations must be declared as `Number`, `Decimal`, `Float`, or `Integer`.

The following examples will show you how to use these commands:

```
1 Let Employees.Salary(10) = Employees.Salary(10) + #Bonus
2 Array-Add #Count To Clients(#i) Count
3 Array-Subtract 1 From Books(500) Books_Received
4 Array-Multiply #Incr1 #Incr2 #Incr3 Times Empl(1) Rate(0) Rate(1)
  Rate(2)
5 Array-Divide 5 Into Empl(#M)
```

In line 1, the `Let` command is used to add the value in `#Bonus` to the `Salary` field in the 11th row (counting from row number zero) of the `Employees` array.

In line 2, the value of numeric variable `#Count` is added to the value of `Count` in the `Clients` array's row with the number stored in `#i`.

In line 3, we subtract one from the value in the `Books_Received` field in the 501st row (counting from row number zero) of the array `Books`.

In line 4, the occurrences 0, 1, and 2 of the field `Rate` of the second row of array `Empl` are multiplied by the values stored in `#Incr1`, `#Incr2`, and `#Incr3`, respectively. The result is stored in the same occurrences of the field `Rate` in the same row of the array.

In line 5, the very first field of the row with the number stored in `#M` is divided by five. Note that if a zero-division occurs, SQR is smart enough to intercept it. A warning message will be displayed, and the program execution will continue without changing the result field.

Now let's create a program using some of the commands we have learned in this chapter. Suppose, for example, we need to produce an employee listing by department and print the following departmental statistical information: the number of active employees, the number of women, the number of men, and an average salary for the department.

Of course, this task can be accomplished without using an array. We would just need to select employees sorted by department, accumulate separate female and male count totals as well as the department salary total, and, on department break, print the tabs accumulated during the select process. But the real business environment sometimes brings additional challenges. We may be asked to print a list of employees by the department, and, at the same time, departmental statistics for each department at the bottom of the report. We can develop two separate SQR programs for these two different tasks, but wouldn't it be more efficient to avoid accessing the database twice? Keeping this in mind, let's write our program:

```
!TEST12A.SQR
!Using arrays in SQR

#Define Stat_Array_Size 100
!***********************
Begin-Setup
!***********************
Create-Array Name=Statistics Size ={Stat_Array_Size}
   Field=Deptid:Char='999999'
Field=Active_EE:number
Field=Women:Number
Field=Men:Number
Field=Total_Salary:number
End-Setup

!********************
Begin-Heading 3
!********************
Print 'Employee Statistics by the Department' (1,10)
Print 'Department Id' (2,1,)
Print 'Employee Id' (,+2)
Print 'Status' (,+2)
Print 'Sex' (,+2)
Print 'Annual Rate' (,+2)
Print ' ' (3,1)
End-Heading
!********************
Begin-Program
!********************
Let #i=0
Do Select_Employees
Do Print_Summary
End-Program

!***********************************
Begin-Procedure Select_Employees
!***********************************
Begin-Select
A.Deptid (+1,1,13) On-Break
A.Emplid (,+2,11)
A.Empl_Status (,+2,6)
B.Sex (,+2,3)
A.Annual_Rt (,+2,12) Edit $,$$$,$$$.00
   Do Update_Array
From Job A, Personal_Data B
Where
A.Emplid=B.Emplid
And A.Empl_Status='A'
```

The array **Statistics** is created.

```
And A.Deptid in ('10200','21700')
And   A.Effdt=(Select Max(Effdt) From Job
      Where     Emplid=A.Emplid
      And       Empl_Rcd=A.Empl_Rcd
      And       Effdt<=Sysdate)
And   A.Effseq=(Select Max(Effseq) From Job
      Where     Emplid=A.Emplid
      And       Empl_Rcd=A.Empl_Rcd
      And       Effdt = A.Effdt)

Order By  A.Deptid,A.Emplid
End-Select
End-Procedure

!******************************
Begin-Procedure Print_Summary
!******************************
Print 'Summary by Department' (+2,10)
Let #i=0
While #i <= {Stat_Array_Size}
   Get $Deptid #Active #Women #Men #Total_Salary
     From Statistics(#i)
   If $Deptid='999999'
     Break
   Else
     If #Active <> 0
       Let  #Average_Salary = #Total_Salary / #Active
     End-If

      Print 'Department ' (+1,1)
      Print  $Deptid (,+1)
      Print 'Number of Active Employees     = ' (+1,1,33)
      Print  #Active  (,+1) edit 9,999,999
      Print 'Number of Women                = ' (+1,1,33)
      Print  #Women (,+1) edit 9,999,999
      Print 'Number of Men                  = ' (+1,1,33)
      Print  #Men (,+1) edit 9,999,999
      Print 'Average Salary                 = ' (+1,1,33)
      Print  #Average_Salary  (,+1) Edit $$$,$$$,$$$.99
      Next-Listing Need=4 Skiplines=1
   End-If
   Add 1 to #i
End-While

End-Procedure

!******************************
Begin-Procedure Update_Array
!******************************
!Find an element in the array with Deptid = Selected Deptid
!If it's not there, create a new element in the array
```

The `Get` command is used to retrieve the values of the array's fields.

```
Let $Found='N'
Let #j=0
While #j < {Stat_Array_Size}
   Get $Deptid From Statistics(#j) Deptid
   If $Deptid='999999'
      Let #i=#j
      Put &A.Deptid Into Statistics(#i) Deptid
      Let $Found='Y'
      Break
   Else
      If &A.Deptid = $Deptid
         Let #i=#j
         Let $Found = 'Y'
         Break
      End-If
   End-If
   Let #j=#j+1
End-While

If $Found='N'
   Display 'ERROR: There are more than {Stat_Array_Size}
      departments in the array'
   Stop
End-If
Array-Add 1 To Statistics(#i)  Active_EE
Array-Add &A.Annual_Rt To Statistics(#i) Total_Salary
If &B.Sex='M'
   Array-Add 1 to Statistics(#i) Men
Else
   Array-Add 1 to Statistics(#i) Women
End-If

End-Procedure
!*****************************
```

The `Put` command is used to place `&A.Deptid` into the array.

The `Array-Add` command is used to update the array's field values.

Figure 12.3. shows the output report of our program.

In the `Setup` section of `Test12A.sqr`, we use the `Create-Array` command to create an array of a hundred rows. Arrays are preallocated in memory, therefore, we do not want to overestimate array sizes. That is, we assume that there will not be more than a hundred departments. Since we define the upper boundary, we have to make sure that it is not exceeded during the program run. The `Select` paragraph in the main procedure, `Select_Employees`, joins the `Job` table and the `Personal_Data` table to select department ID, employee ID, employee status, employee sex, and employee salary. The selected rows are ordered by the department ID and the employee ID. For every record selected, the procedure `Update_Array` is invoked.

The `Update_Array` procedure looks for an element in the array `Statistics` with `Deptid` equal to the `&Deptid` selected for each employee selected in the main

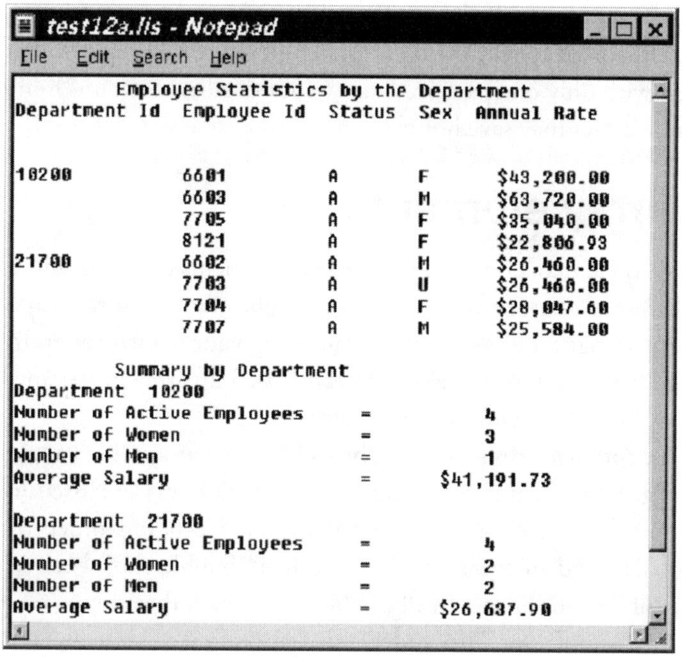

test12a.lis - Notepad

File Edit Search Help

```
          Employee Statistics by the Department
Department Id  Employee Id  Status  Sex  Annual Rate


10200             6601         A      F      $43,200.00
                  6603         A      M      $63,720.00
                  7705         A      F      $35,040.00
                  8121         A      F      $22,806.93
21700             6602         A      M      $26,460.00
                  7703         A      U      $26,460.00
                  7704         A      F      $28,047.60
                  7707         A      M      $25,584.00

          Summary by Department
Department  10200
Number of Active Employees     =        4
Number of Women                =        3
Number of Men                  =        1
Average Salary                 =   $41,191.73

Department  21700
Number of Active Employees     =        4
Number of Women                =        2
Number of Men                  =        2
Average Salary                 =   $26,637.90
```

Figure 12.3 List of employees by the department with departmental statistics at the bottom

query. If not found, a new row is added to the array. The value of the `Deptid` field in the row is set to the selected department Id value with the help of the `Put` command. When the array was created, all the `Deptid` values were set to `'999999'`. This helps to identify empty array rows. Another method of checking for empty rows is to save the subscript to the last loaded element and to check for this value when performing the search. In this case, the initial value for `Deptid`, will be set to `NULL`. After exiting from the search loop, we make sure that the array row number does not exceed its upper boundary. If so, the program displays an error message on the screen, logs the error into the log file, and stops the program execution. Alerting those responsible for program execution about this and other serious error possibilities would be a wise precaution and good programming practice.

When the row is found in the array, the `Array-Add` command is used to update the following array fields: `Active`, `Women`, `Men`, and `Total_Salary`. When all employees are selected, our array will be filled with all the information necessary to print the departmental totals. In the `Print_Totals` procedure, the program uses the `Get` command to retrieve every row of the array and prints the statistical information for each department. Note that we use the `Let` command to calculate the average salary for the department.

As you can see from the example, SQR arrays offer a lot of ways to create effective programs. You can eliminate the need to sort the data, and combine several reports into one by using multiple arrays with only one pass on data. If your database contains hundreds of thousands of records, arrays may save hours of computing time.

12.7 Sorting array elements

When working with an array, there may be a need to sort array elements by one or more fields within the array. There are many reasons why you might want to sort arrays. Often, sorting may help to rearrange an array to make generating your reports easier. In other cases, you may need to use certain search algorithms to speed up array processing. Most of these algorithms can work only with pre-sorted arrays.

There are many different sort algorithms that can be used to sort arrays. Let's apply the classical "bubble sort" algorithm to the `Dependents` array which was discussed in the beginning of this chapter. We will sort our array in the ascending order by `Dependent_Id`. The approach used in the algorithm is called "bubble sort" because rows with the smaller values of `Dependent_Id` will bubble up through the array.

`Test12B.sqr` uses the "bubble sort" to order the `Dependents` array by the Dependent Ids:

```
!Test12B.SQR  Bubble Sort Example
!Using the "bubble sort" algorithm to sort an array
!********************************
#Define Max_Dependents 25
!********************************
Begin-Setup
!********************************
   Create-Array Name=Dependents Size = {Max_Dependents}
   Field=Dependent_Id:Char
   Field=Dependent_Name:Char
   Field=Dependent_Birthdate:Date
   Field=Relationship:Char
End-Setup
!********************************
Begin-Program
!********************************
Let #I=0
Do Main
End-Program
!********************************
Begin-Procedure Main
!********************************
Begin-Select
A.Emplid
      Let #Ind = 0
      Do Load_Dep_Array
```

```
      Do Sort_Dep_Array
      Do Print_Array
From Personal_Data A
Where A.Emplid In ('8001','8360')    !Limit selection for
                                     !testing purpose
Order By A.Emplid
End-Select
End-Procedure
!*******************************
Begin-Procedure Load_Dep_Array
!*******************************
Begin-Select
B.Emplid
B.Dependent_Benef
B.Name
B.Birthdate
B.Relationship
      Show &B.Emplid
      Show &B.Dependent_Benef
      Put  &B.Dependent_Benef
           &B.Name &B.Birthdate
           &B.Relationship
      Into Dependents (#ind) Dependent_Id Dependent_Name
        Dependent_Birthdate Relationship
      Add 1 to #Ind
      If #Ind >= {Max_Dependents}
        Show 'Array size is exceeded the Max of ' '
        {Max_Dependents}' ' for Emplid = ' &B.Emplid
         Exit-Select
       End-If
From Dependent_Benef B
Where B.Emplid = &A.Emplid
Order By B.Dependent_Benef DESC
End-Select
Let #Count = #Ind
Show '#Count =' #Count
End-Procedure

!*******************************
Begin-Procedure Sort_Dep_Array
!*******************************
Let #Ind_Out = 0
While #Ind_Out < #Count
   Let #Ind_In = #Ind_Out + 1

   While #Ind_In < #count
      Let $Dep_Out = Dependents.Dependent_Id(#Ind_out)
      Let $Dep_In = Dependents.Dependent_Id(#Ind_in)
      If $Dep_Out > $Dep_In
        Do Swap_In_Out
      End-If
      Add 1 to #Ind_In
```

Populating the Dependents array

Sorting the Dependents array using the "bubble sort" algorithm

```
   End-While
   Add 1 to #Ind_Out
End-While
End-Procedure
!*******************************
Begin-Procedure Swap_In_Out
!*******************************
Get $Dependent_Id_Temp $Name_Tmp $Birthdate_Tmp $Relationship_Tmp
   From Dependents (#Ind_In) Dependent_Id Dependent_Name
   Dependent_Birthdate Relationship
Let Dependents.Dependent_Id(#Ind_In) =
   Dependents.Dependent_Id(#Ind_Out)
Let Dependents.Dependent_Name(#Ind_In) =
   Dependents.Dependent_Name(#Ind_Out)
Let Dependents.Dependent_Birthdate(#Ind_In) =
 Dependents.Dependent_Birthdate(#Ind_Out)
Let Dependents.Relationship(#Ind_On) =
   Dependents.Relationship(#Ind_Out)

Put $Dependent_Id_Temp $Name_Tmp $Birthdate_Tmp $Relationship_Tmp
   Into Dependents (#Ind_Out) Dependent_Id Dependent_Name
   Dependent_Birthdate Relationship
End-Procedure

!*******************************
Begin-Procedure Print_Array
!*******************************
Let #Ind = 0
While #Ind < #Count
   Let $Dependent_Id = Dependents.Dependent_Id(#Ind)
   Let $Name = Dependents.Dependent_Name(#Ind)
   Let $Birthdate = Dependents.Dependent_Birthdate(#Ind)
   Let $Relationship = Dependents.Relationship(#Ind)
   Show &A.Emplid
   Show $Dependent_Id
   Show $Name
   Show $Birthdate
   Show $Relationship
   Add 1 To #Ind
End-While
End-Procedure
!*******************************
```

Swapping two elements of the array

The program starts with selecting data from the `Personal_Data` table, and, for each selected row, calls the `Load_Dep_Array` procedure to populate the `Dependents` array with data from the `Dependent_Benef` table. Once the array is populated, the `Sort_Dep_Array` procedure is called to sort the array by the `Dependent_Id` field, and the `Print_Array` procedure is called to print information about the dependents of each selected employee.

Let's take a closer look at the `Sort_Dep_Array` procedure. The processing starts with the first row of the array. The goal is to place the element with the smallest `Dependent_Id` into this row. The procedure goes over all remaining elements of the array, starting from the second element, and, if it finds an element which has a smaller `Dependent_Id` than the element in the first row, the logic swaps the two elements by calling the `Swap_In_Out` procedure.

Once the element with the smallest `Dependent_Id` is put into the first row, the procedure will try to put the element with the next smallest `Dependent_Id` into the second row by going over all remaining elements starting from the third element and swapping any element that has a smaller `Dependent_Id` with the element currently in the second row. The process will continue until the entire array is sorted.

The procedure has a nested two-level loop. The outer loop determines which array element is used as the basis of comparison. The inner loop goes over the list of array elements, starting from the one located after the element currently used as the basis, and compares the value of `Dependent_Id` in each element to the value in the basis.

While the "bubble sort" algorithm is straightforward and easy to program, it is not the most efficient one when dealing with very large arrays. Depending on the array size and the importance of your program performance, you may want to try other popular sorting algorithms. Another classical sorting algorithm, called *QuickSort*, is demonstrated in Brio's SQR User's Guide (version 4).

An interesting comparison of three different sorting algorithms can be found on the website http://www.sqrtools.com, created by Tony DeLia. In his website, Tony discusses the following three algorithms: Bubble sort, Insertion sort, and QuickSort, and compares their performance by sorting the same array using each of these algorithms.

12.8 Searching data in arrays

Searching data in an array is even more important then sorting. SQR does not have special commands to carry out array searches; you have to program this logic yourself. There are many popular algorithms that can be used to search in arrays. Some of them are very simple to implement, while others may require some effort. As with sorting, you need to select an algorithm depending on your array size and the required program performance. Here we will discuss two algorithms: *sequential search* and *binary search*.

The sequential search algorithm is very straightforward: when looking for an element with a particular value in a certain field, your program has to go over every single array element until it hits the right one. Not a very efficient method of searching, but very simple to program. In most non-time critical applications this method is quite sufficient. The sequential search was already used in `Test12A.sqr`, therefore we will not bother you with another example of an SQR code that will implement this algorithm. Please note that this method does not require a presorted array.

The binary search algorithm is more efficient than the sequential search, but it has one very important limitation: it works only with presorted arrays. Depending on the order of sorting—ascending or descending—you may need to slightly modify this algorithm.

The main idea of the binary search algorithm is very simple: it compares the target value to the value of the search field of the middle element of the array's current search area. The search starts when the current search area is equal to the entire array. The search fields in the array are ordered in a predefined sequence, therefore, if the target value is less than the value in middle element, the search focuses on the lower half of the array, otherwise the search concentrates on the upper half. The remaining half of the array becomes the current search area. The next step is to compare the target value to the middle element of the current search area. This process of dividing the current search area in two continues until the element is found or the current search area is empty (element not found).

As you can see, the binary search does not involve searching through the entire array. For large arrays, this algorithm may result in substantial savings. If you use the sequential search algorithm, on average, your program will have to compare the search key with half of the elements of the array. On the other hand, using the binary search algorithm for an array of one billion elements will require only a maximum of 30 comparisons to find the key!

Here is an SQR program that uses the binary array search:

```
!Test12C.SQR
!Binary Search Example
!**********************************
#Define Max_Companies 2000
!********************************
Begin-Setup
!********************************
   Create-Array Name=Companies Size = {Max_Companies}
   Field=Company_Cd:Char
   Field=Company_Name:Char
   Field=Count:Number
End-Setup

!********************************
Begin-Program
!********************************
Do Load_Comp_Array
Do Main
End-Program

!********************************
```

```
Begin-Procedure Main
!******************************
   Do Update_Comp_Array
   Do Print_Comp_Totals
End-Procedure

!******************************
Begin-Procedure Load_Comp_Array
!******************************
Let #Idx = 0
Begin-Select
Company
Descrshort
   Let $Company = Rtrim(&Company,' ')
   Put $Company &Descrshort into Companies (#Idx)
     Company_Cd Company_Name
   Let #Idx = #Idx + 1
   If #Idx > {Max_Companies}
     Show 'Array size is exceeded the Max of ' '{Max_Companies}'
     Move #Idx to $Idx 9999
     Show 'Number of Companies loaded = ' $Idx
     Exit-Select
   End-If
   Show 'idx = ' #Idx
From Company_Tbl
Order By Company
End-Select
Let #Max_Loaded = #Idx - 1
Show 'Loaded:' #Max_Loaded
End-Procedure

!******************************
Begin-Procedure Update_Comp_Array
!******************************
Begin-Select
A.Emplid
A.Company
   Let $Found = 'N'
   Let $Ee_Company = Rtrim(&A.Company,' ')
   Do Search_Comp_Array
     If $Found = 'Y'
       Let Companies.Count(#Idx) = Companies.Count(#Idx) + 1
     Else
       Show 'Company not found in array for Emplid/Company ---> '
         &A.Emplid '/' &Company
     End-If
From Job A
   Where
A.Empl_Status = 'A'
And A.Effdt=(Select Max(Effdt) From Job
   Where Emplid=A.Emplid
   And Empl_Rcd=A.Empl_Rcd
```

Populating the Companies array

Calling the search subroutine

```
And Effdt<=Sysdate)
And A.Effseq=(Select Max(Effseq) From Job
Where Emplid=A.Emplid
And Empl_Rcd=A.Empl_Rcd
And Effdt = A.Effdt)
Order By A.Emplid
End-Select
End-Procedure

!********************************
Begin-Procedure Search_Comp_Array
!********************************
Let #Idx = 0
Let #Start = 0
Let #End = #Max_Loaded
While (#Start <= #End) and $Found = 'N'
   Let #Mid = Trunc((#Start+#End)/2,0)
   Let $Comp = Companies.Company_Cd(#Mid)
   If $Ee_Company < $Comp
      Let #End = #Mid - 1
   Else
      If &A.Company > $Comp
         Let #Start = #Mid + 1
      Else
         Let $Found = 'Y'
      End-If
   End-If
End-While
Let #Idx = #Mid
End-Procedure

!********************************
Begin-Procedure Print_Comp_Totals
!********************************
Let #Idx = 0
Print 'Number Of Employees per Company'  (1,1) Center
While #Idx <= #Max_Loaded
   Get $Company $Name #Count From  Companies (#Idx) Company_Cd
      Company_Name Count
      If #Count > 0
         Print $Company   (+1,1,5)
         Print $Name      (,+1,20)
         Print #Count     (,+1,5)   Edit 99999
      End-If
   Add 1 To #Idx
End-While
End-Procedure
!********************************
```

Using the binary search algorithm (annotation at Begin-Procedure Search_Comp_Array)

Dividing the current search area in half (annotation at Let #Mid = Trunc((#Start+#End)/2,0))

The purpose of `Test12C.sqr` is to print an employee headcount report per company. In the beginning, the `Load_Comp_Array` procedure populates each element of the Company array with the company code and company name from the Company_Tbl table. The Count field in each element of the Company array remains initialized to zero.

Next, the Update_Comp_Array procedure reads the Job table, and for each selected employee record, searches the row with the proper company code in the Company array and increments the Count field in this row. The actual search is carried out by the Search_Comp_Array procedure that employs the binary search algorithm. This algorithm can be used because the Load_Comp_Array procedure populates the Company array in the ascending company code order.

KEY POINTS

1. The Create-Array command creates an array of fields in the memory.
2. The Create-Array command can be used in any section of your SQR program.
3. You can specify an initial value for each field in an array.
4. Some fields in an array can be defined as multiple-occurrence fields.
5. Row numbers and field occurrence numbers in arrays start from zero.
6. Row numbers and field occurrence numbers can be numeric literals or numeric variables.
7. When using variables to refer to row numbers or occurrence numbers, be sure to keep the variable values within the boundaries defined in the Create-Array command.
8. All SQR arrays are created during the program compile stage.
9. The following commands can be used when working with arrays:
   - Create-Array
   - Clear-Array
   - Get
   - Put
   - Array-Add
   - Array-Subtract
   - Array-Multiply
   - Array-Divide
   - Let

KEY POINTS (CONTINUED)

10 All fields used in arithmetic operations must be declared as `Number`, `Decimal`, `Float`, or `Integer`.

11 The `Get` command is used to retrieve one or more fields from an array.

12 The `Put` command is used to move one or more fields into an array.

13 The `Clear-Array` command is used to initialize an array.

14 Commonly known sort and search algorithms can be used to sort or search array elements. Specific algorithm selection should be made based on the array size and the program performance requirements.

C H A P T E R 1 3

Creating multiple reports

IN THIS CHAPTER

- Declaring individual reports
- Defining custom printer types
- Directing the `Print` command output to specific reports
- Naming conventions for the output report files

So far, we have discussed only single-report SQR programs, that is, programs that generate only one output report. There are cases however, when an SQR program may need to create more than one report. For efficiency's sake, you may choose to produce multiple reports in a single program.

With today's databases covering thousands of megabytes of data, generating several reports with one pass on the database may result in substantial savings. (This is especially true when your program accesses remote databases over the network connections.) Another reason you might want to generate multiple reports in a single program would be if you needed to direct program reports to different printers. For instance, a payroll detail report might need to go to a secured printer, a check printing report to a special printer, while a payroll summary report could go to a shared printer.

In many cases, writing one program that generates several business-related reports may also result in savings on the future program maintenance since you'll have to support only one program. Be careful though. If multiple report logic makes your program too complex and difficult to understand, you may be better off with a few single report programs.

In this chapter we'll create a program that produces two different reports using one pass on data, but first, let's look at some SQR commands that are used for creating multiple reports in one program.

13.1 Defining multiple reports

In a multiple-report SQR program, each report must be defined with a separate `Declare-Report` command. This command is coded in the `Setup` section.

In the `Declare-Report` command, you specify the following attributes:

- the name of the report
- the name of the layout to be used for this report
- the type of the printer to be used for this report.

Depending on the specific business requirements, each report can use its own layout or printer definitions, or some reports can share the same layout or printer definitions. If no `Printer-Type` is specified, the default is the `LINEPRINTER` for this report. If no layout is specified in the `Declare-Report` command, the `Default` layout is used. (See the command reference in appendix D for a complete description of the `Declare-Report` command.)

Here is an example of coding the `Declare-Report` command:

```
Declare-Report My_Report1
Layout=My_Layout1
```

```
Printer-Type=PS
End-Declare
```

Valid values for the `Printer-Type` argument in the `Declare-Report` command are `HTML` (`HT`), `HPLASERJET` (`HP`), `POSTSCRIPT` (`PS`), and `LINEPRINTER` (`LP`).

The `Declare-Layout` command is also coded in the `Setup` section. This command allows you to specify the attributes of the layout for your output file and define as many layouts as you need for your application. If you do not code the `Declare-Layout` in your SQR program, a default layout with the name `Default` will be created. If you need to override its attributes, you can define a layout called `Default` in your program and list only the attributes you need to change. If you are defining multiple layouts in your program, each layout name must be unique.

The following example shows the use of the `Declare-Layout` and `Declare-Report` commands when multiple reports are created in one SQR program:

```
!Using the Declare-Layout and Declare-Report commands
Begin-Setup
Declare-Layout Empl_Layout
Left-margin=1
Right-margin=1
End-Declare

Declare-Layout Summary_Layout
End-Declare

Declare-Report Empl_Detail
Layout=Empl_Layout
Printer-Type=HP
End-Declare

Declare-Report Empl_Summary
Layout=Summary_Layout
Printer-Type=Postscript
End-Declare
End-Setup
...
```

Each printer type specified in the `Declare-Report` commands has a set of default attributes. If you need to override some of the default printer attributes, use the `Declare-Printer` command. This command is also coded in the `Setup` section. The `Declare-Printer` command allows you to create your own customized printer type and assign it a name. In order to make a `Declare-Printer` command applicable to a specific report, you have to use the `For-Reports` parameter with a specific report name defined in a `Declare-Report` command. If the `For-Reports` parameter is not coded, the printer type attributes specified in the `Declare-Printer` command will apply to all reports that use the printer type specified in the Type argument of this Declare-Printer command.

The Declare-Printer command does not specify a physical printer, it defines only a printer type. In most cases, reports are written to output files (under Windows, you have an option to direct your report to the Windows default printer without using an intermediate file). In order to print a report produced for a specific printer type, use the appropriate operating system commands.

You can use only one Declare-Printer command for each printer type specified in Declare-Report commands.

```
!Using the Declare-Printer command
Declare-Printer My_HP_Printer   ! for all reports that use HP printers
Type=HP
Font=4                          ! Helvetica
End-Declare

Declare-Printer My_PS_Printer
For-Reports=(My_Report)! only for the My_Report report
Type=PS                         ! (this report must use PS printer)
Font=5   ! Times-Roman
End-Declare
```

If no Declare-Printer is specified, the following default printer type names will be used: DEFAULT-LP for line printer, DEFAULT-HP for HP LaserJet, or DEFAULT-PS for PostScript.

Please note that the names of custom printer types defined in the Declare-Printer commands are not referred to explicitly in the Printer-Type parameter of the Declare-Report command. The Declare-Report command can specify only standard printer types. If you want a custom printer type to be used in certain reports, you have to use the For-Report parameter of the Declare-Printer command. Here is an example of using custom printer types in the Declare-Report commands:

```
!Using custom printer types in the Declare-Report command
Begin-Setup

Declare-Printer HP1
   For-Reports = (Total_Report)
   Type = HP
   Font = 4
End-Declare

Declare-Printer HP2
   For-Reports = (Detail_Report)
   Type = HP
   Font = 5
End-Declare
```

```
Declare-Report Total_Report
   Printer-Type = HP
End-Declare

Declare-Report Detail_Report
   Printer-Type = HP
End-Declare
```

You can change the printer type dynamically by using the `Use-Printer-Type` command. This command allows you to change the printer type used in the report currently being processed. Be aware that the `Use-Printer-Type` command must be issued before the first line of the output report is written, otherwise the command will be ignored.

```
!Using the Use-Printer-Type command to specify printer type
Use-Report My_Report
Use-Printer-Type PS
print (1, 1) 'Testing My Report '
```

If you are using the same printer type for all reports, you can specify this printer type in the SQR command line `-Printer:xx` flag. This will cause your SQR program to produce all your report output files for the specified printer type. For example, you can specify `-Printer:HP` to produce all output for HP LaserJet printers.

Please keep in mind that if the `-Printer` command line flag is specified, it will override the printer types for all reports in your program.

If you need to change certain printer characteristics for the current printer type used in the current report in any part of the program except the `Setup` section, you can use the `Alter-Printer` command.

(Please refer to appendix D for a full description of the above discussed commands.)

13.2 Handling multiple reports in one program

If your program generates multiple reports, the `Print` commands need to know which report to direct their output to. The `Use-Report` command will allow your program to switch between reports. When this command is used, all `Print` commands issued after the `Use-Report` command will write the output to the specified report file, until the next `Use-Report` command is issued. For example, in the following code, the first `Print` command will direct its output to the `Empl_Detail` report. The second `Print` command will direct its output to the `Empl_Summary` report:

```
!Using multiple Use-Report commands to redirect the output
Use-Report Empl_Detail
  Print 'Emplid' (1,1)
```

```
...
Use-Report Empl_Summary
  Print 'Total Employees:'  (+1,1)
  Print  #Tot_Recs (,1)
```

The above technique is used to print the report body in multiple report programs. Headers and footers are printed using a different approach. Technically, the same header or footer can be shared by multiple reports. In real business life, however, different reports usually have different information in their headers and, sometimes, footers. In these cases, you should code separate `Heading` and `Footing` sections for each report and use the `For-Report` parameter to assign each section to a specific report, for example:

```
!Using the For-Reports argument in the Heading and Footing sections
Begin-Heading 5 For-Reports=(Empl_Detail)
   Print 'Employee Detail Report' (1) Center
   Print …
End-Heading
Begin-Heading 3 For-Reports=(Empl_ Summary)
   Print 'Employee Summary Report' (1) Center
   Print …
End-Heading
   Begin-Footing 1 For-Reports=(Empl_Detail)
   Print 'End Of Report' (1,1)
End-Footing
```

13.3 An example of a multiple report program

Suppose you are assigned a task to develop a program that will print two reports. The first report will list all employees who currently participate in any health benefit plan along with their plan type and coverage codes. In addition, the report will indicate which employees had their dependent's coverage terminated. The second report will list only those employees and their dependents who had their benefits coverage terminated within the reporting period. In the following example, we will create the two separate reports in one program:

```
!**********************************************
! TEST13A.SQR
!A multiple report program
!**********************************************
!Set report column widths
#Define col_emplid    11       !Employee ID
#Define col_empl_name 15       !Employee Name
#Define col_plan_type  5       !Plan Type
#Define col_cov_cd        8     !Coverage Code
#Define col_cov_drop_flag 5     !Dependent Coverage Termination
#Define col_effdt        12     !Effective Date
#Define col_dep_id        6     !Dependent Beneficiary ID
#Define col_dep_name     15     !Dependent Name
```

```
#Define col_sep           1      !Column Separator
!**********************
Begin-Setup
!**********************

   Declare-Layout EE_Data
     Left-Margin=1
   End-Declare

   Declare-Layout Term_Dependents
     Orientation=Landscape
     Left-Margin=0.3
   End-Declare

   Declare-Report EE_Data
     Layout=EE_Data
   End-Declare

   Declare-Report Term_Dependents
     Layout=Term_Dependents
   End-Declare
End-Setup

!*********************************
Begin-Program
!*********************************
   Do Process_Main
End-Program

!*********************************
Begin-Heading 4 For-Reports=(EE_Data)
!*********************************
   Print 'List of Employees by Plan Type' (1) Center
   Print 'Page'           (,+9)
   Print #page-count         (,+1) edit 999

   Print 'EMPLID'                   (+1,1,{col_emplid})
   Print 'Name  '                   (0,+{col_sep},{col_empl_name})
   Print 'Plan  '                   (0,+{col_sep},{col_plan_type})
   Print 'Effdt'                    (0,+{col_sep},{col_Effdt})
   Print 'Coverg'                   (0,+{col_sep},{col_cov_cd})
   Print 'Dep.  '                   (0,+{col_sep},{col_cov_drop_flag})
   Print '      '                   (+1,1,{col_emplid})
   Print '      '                   (0,+{col_sep},{col_empl_name})
   Print 'Type  '                   (0,+{col_sep},{col_plan_type})
   Print '      '                   (0,+{col_sep},{col_Effdt})
   Print 'Code  '                   (0,+{col_sep},{col_cov_cd})
   Print 'Term  '                   (0,+{col_sep},{col_cov_drop_flag})
   Print '-'                        (+1,1,60)  Fill

End-Heading
```

Annotations:
- Declaring a layout for each report (at `Declare-Layout Term_Dependents`)
- Using the **`Declare-Report`** command for each report (at `Declare-Report Term_Dependents`)
- Using the **`For-Reports`** parameter to specify the report name (at `Begin-Heading 4 For-Reports=(EE_Data)`)

```
!****************************************
Begin-Heading 4 For-Reports=(Term_Dependents)
!****************************************
   Print 'List of Terminated Dependents' (1) Center
   Print 'Page'                     (,+15)
   Print #page-count                (,+1) edit 999
   Print 'EMPLID'                   (+2,1,{col_emplid})
   Print 'Name  '                   (0,+{col_sep},{col_empl_name})
   Print 'Plan Type'                (0,+{col_sep},{col_plan_type})
   Print 'Effdt'                    (0,+{col_sep},{col_Effdt})
   Print 'Dep ID '                  (0,+{col_sep},{col_dep_id})
   Print 'Dep Name'                 (0,+{col_sep},{col_dep_name})
   Print '-'                        (+1,1,65)  Fill

End-Heading

!************************************
Begin-Procedure Process_Main
!************************************
!Select and print all Employees
!who are currently covered by any Health Benefits
!and who have Family, or Empl+1 Coverage

Begin-Select
A.Emplid
A.Plan_Type
A.Effdt
A.Covrg_Cd
B.Name

   Do Check_Dep_Termination
   If $TERM ='N'
     Let $TERM = ' '
   End-If
   Do Print_EE_Data

From Health_Benefit A, Personal_Data B

Where   A.Effdt  =(Select Max(Effdt) From Health_Benefit
               Where  Emplid    =   A.Emplid
               And    Plan_Type =   A.Plan_Type
               And    Effdt    <=   Sysdate)
And    A.Coverage_Elect Not In ('T','W')
And    A.Emplid = B.Emplid
Order By  A.Emplid, A.Plan_Type

End-Select

End-Procedure
!**********************************************
Begin-Procedure Check_Dep_Termination
!**********************************************
```

Printing a heading for the **Term_Dependents** report (annotation on Begin-Heading line)

If terminated dependent is found, the record will go to the **Term_Dependents** report. (annotation on Do Check_Dep_Termination)

Print the **EE_Data** report record. (annotation on Do Print_EE_Data)

```
! For each row retrieved in Step 1, compare between the previous
! maximum effective dated record and the current effective dated
! HEALTH_DEPENDNT row to determine a dependent that is no longer
! covered
! If dropped dependents are found, print the record to a
! separate report

Move 'N' to $TERM

Begin-Select
C.Emplid
C.Plan_Type
C.Effdt
D.Dependent_Benef

   Move 'Y' to $TERM
   Do Print-Terminated-Dependents
   Show 'Dep Term found=' &D.Dependent_Benef ' for Employee '
     &A.Emplid
   From Health_Benefit C,
     Health_Dependnt D
 Where     C.Emplid    = &A.Emplid
 And       C.Plan_Type = &A.Plan_Type
 And       C.Emplid    = D.Emplid
 And       C.Plan_Type = D.Plan_Type
 And       C.Effdt     = D.Effdt
 And       C.Effdt     = (Select MAX(E.Effdt)
   From Health_Benefit E
   Where  C.Emplid    = E.Emplid
   And  C.Plan_Type    = E.Plan_Type
   And  E.Effdt  < &A.Effdt)
 And  D.Dependent_Benef Not In
   (Select F.Dependent_Benef
   From Health_Dependnt F
   Where  C.Emplid    = F.Emplid
   And    C.Plan_Type = F.Plan_Type
   And    F.Effdt     = &A.EFFDT)

End-Select
End-Procedure

!***********************************
Begin-Procedure Print_EE_Data
!***********************************
  Use-Report EE_Data
  Let $EmplID=&A.Emplid
  Let $Date_Str= Datetostr(&A.Effdt,'mm/dd/yyyy')
  Print &A.Emplid (+1,1,{col_emplid})  On-Break Print=Change/Top-Page
  Print &B.Name  (0,+{col_sep},{col_empl_name})  On-Break
                Print=Change/Top-Page
  Print &A.Plan_Type(0,+{col_sep},{col_plan_type})
  Print $Date_Str(0,+{col_sep},{col_effdt})
```

The `Use-Report` command tells SQR to direct all output to the `EE_Data` report.

```
  Print &A.Covrg_Cd(0,+{col_sep},{col_cov_cd})
  Print $Term     (0,+{col_sep},{col_cov_drop_flag})

  Add 1 to #ee_rcds

End-Procedure
!*******************************************
Begin-Procedure Print-Terminated-Dependents
!*******************************************
  Use-Report Term_Dependents
  Let $EmplID=&A.Emplid

  Do Get_Dependent_Name
  Let $Date_Str= Datetostr(&A.Effdt,'mm/dd/yyyy')
  Print &A.Emplid          (+1,1,{col_emplid})
     On-Break Print=Change/Top-Page
  Print &B.Name            (0,+{col_sep},{col_empl_name})
     On-Break  Print=Change/Top-Page
    Print &A.Plan_Type(0,+{col_sep},{col_plan_type})
    Print $Date_Str    (0,+{col_sep},{col_effdt})
    Print &D.Dependent_Benef(0,+{col_sep},{col_dep_id})
    Print $DEP_NAME    (0,+{col_sep},{col_dep_name})

  Add 1 to #Dep_Rcds

End-Procedure

!**************************************************
Begin-Procedure Get_Dependent_Name
!**************************************************
Let $Dep_Name=' '
Begin-Select
Name
  Move &Name to $Dep_Name
From Dependent_Benef
Where EMPLID=&A.Emplid
And Dependent_Benef=&D.Dependent_Benef
End-Select
End-Procedure
!************************** End of Report ***************************
```

The `Use-Report` command tells SQR to direct all output to the `Term_Dependents` report.

In the `Setup` section, we declare two reports and the layout for each report. If the layouts were the same as the `Default` layout, we could have omitted these declarations. When creating multiple reports, however, it is a good idea to keep the layouts separate. It gives you better flexibility for future changes and uniquely identifies both reports, along with the report declarations.

A separate heading is defined for each report. There are two `Begin-Heading` commands in the program. Each command specifies its report name using the `For-Report` parameter.

In the Process_Main procedure, the Health_Benefits and Personal_Data tables are joined to select employee information required for the employee report. For each row selected, the Check_Dep_Termination procedure and Print_EE_Data procedure are called.

The Check_Dep_Termination procedure contains a little tricky WHERE clause in its SQL. This code is a good example of "effective-dated" logic, which allows the program to compare the effective dates in the current and prior rows to determine a dependent no longer covered by a health plan.

For each row selected from the Health_Benefit table in the Process_Main procedure, the program selects the prior record in the Health_Benefit table and the matching Health_Dependent record, and also checks to make sure that this Dependent is not in the current Dependent_Benef record. If the terminated dependent record is found, the program calls the Print_Terminated_Dependents procedure.

The Print_Terminated_Dependents procedure issues the Use-Report command to direct all print output into the Term_Dependents report. From this moment on, all Print commands will direct their output to this report until another Use-Report command overrides this setting.

In the Print_EE_Data procedure, another Use-Report command directs all output to the EE_Data report until the next Use-Report command is issued.

The results of the program are the two report files: Test13a.lis (figure 13.1) and Test13a.l01 (figure 13.2).

```
                    List of Employees by Plan Type        Page   1
EMPLID     Name                Plan    Effdt          Coverg  Dep.
                               Type                   Code    Term
---------------------------------------------------------------------
6601       Jones,Gladys         10     06/01/1996     1
                                11     06/01/1996     1
                                14     06/01/1996     1
6602       Peppen,Jacques       10     02/01/1997     1       Y
                                11     06/09/1996     1
                                14     06/09/1996     1
6603       Pitman,Earl          10     06/01/1996     4
                                11     06/01/1996     4
                                14     06/01/1996     4
7702       Atchley,Tamara       10     06/01/1996     1
                                11     06/01/1996     1
                                14     06/01/1996     1
7704       Riall,Alphonsin      10     12/21/1997     1
                                11     12/21/1997     1
                                14     12/21/1997     1
```

Figure 13.1 A portion of the Employee List report

```
              List of Terminated Dependents                    Page   1

EMPLID Name                 Plan    Effdt        Dep ID Dep Name
--------------------------------------------------------------------


6602     Peppen,Jacques    10       02/01/1997   03       Peppen,Annalise
                           10       02/01/1997   02       Peppen,Ronald
                           10       02/01/1997   01       Peppen,Marie
7705     Holt,Susan        10       02/01/1997   03       Holt,Jarrett
8200     Albright,Arnold   10       01/01/1998   01       Arnold,Judy
8553     Jackson,Sonya     11       12/24/1995   03       Jackson,Rachel
                           11       12/24/1995   02       Jackson,Anna Li
                           11       12/24/1995   01       Jackson,Gregory
G011     Sherwood,Steven   11       04/01/1998   01       Sherwood,Nancy
G040     O'Leary,Mary      10       12/01/1995   01       O'Leary,Lloyd
                           11       12/01/1995   01       O'Leary,Lloyd
G200     Monroe,Henry      10       01/04/1998   02       Monroe,Brett
                           11       12/21/1997   02       Monroe,Brett
G400     Sharpe,James      10       01/04/1998   02       Sharpe,Jason
                           11       12/28/1997   02       Sharpe,Jason
```

Figure 13.2 A portion of the Terminated Dependents report

13.4 Output files in SQR programs with multiple reports

We know that our program generates two report files, `Test13a.lis` and `Test13a.101`, but which file name will be assigned to each program report? The file names are assigned in the order in which the `Declare-Report` commands are coded in the program. The first `Declare-Report` command in our program defines the `EE_Report`. Therefore, this report is written to the `Test13a.lis` file. The report defined in the second `Declare-Report` command goes to `Test13a.101`.

By default, SQR creates output report files with the same names as your program name, but with different extensions. For single report programs, the extension is usually `.lis` or `.spf`. For multiple report files, the report file names are still the same as the program name, but the file extensions will be `.lis`, `101`, `102`, and so on. In case of the `.spf` output files (see chapter 14), the names will be same as the program name with the extensions: `.spf` , `.s01`, `.s02`, and so on.

SQR version 4 offers an improved file naming scheme: the default report file names are controlled by the `OUTPUT-FILE-MODE` environmental variable in the `Default-Settings` section of the SQR.ini file. If this variable is set to `SHORT` (the default setting), SQR uses the previously described naming conventions. If the variable is set to

LONG, the first report file name will be the same as the program name; the second report file name will be the program name post-fixed with _01; the third file name will be the program name post-fixed with _02, and so on. All file extensions in this case will be the same: .lis. In our program, the report file names will be Test13A.lis and Test13A_01.lis.

Based on the described naming conventions, you may guess that you can have up to a hundred reports in a program, but who would need this many reports in one program, anyway?

You can use the -F flags in the SQR command line to override the default file names with your own file output names. For example, if you want the Test13A.sqr program to generate the Empl.lis and Depd.lis report files, use the following -F flags:

```
-FEmpl.lis -FDepd.lis
```

Similarly, you can use the -F flag to create multiple .spf files. Keep in mind, however, that you must still specify the .lis extensions for these files. SQR will automatically rename the files to Empl.spf and Depd.s01. (More about SPF files in chapter 14.).

KEY POINTS

1 In multiple report programs, each report must be defined with a separate Declare-Report command.

2 The Declare-Report and Declare-Layout commands must be coded in the Setup section.

3 Each report can use its own layout or printer type definitions, some reports can share the same layout and (or) type definitions. If no layout is specified, the Default layout is used.

4 If you define multiple layouts in your program, each layout name must be unique.

5 The Use-Report command allows your program to switch between reports.

6 SQR allows you to specify the Heading and Footing sections for each report using the For-Report argument in the Begin-Heading and Begin-Footing commands.

KEY POINTS (CONTINUED)

7 When creating multiple output files, the default names of the report files will be the program name with the extensions `.lis`, `l01`, `l02`, and so on. In case of the `SPF` output files, the file extension will be: `.spf`, `.s01`, `.s02`, and so on.

C H A P T E R 1 4

Creating SQR Portable Files

IN THIS CHAPTER

- How to create `SPF` files
- The advantages of using `SPF` files
- The `SQR VIEWER`
- Using the `SQR PRINT` to convert `SPF` files to printer-specific files

In our examples to this point, the SQR programs have directed their report output to the regular SQR report output files with the `.lis` extension. This extension is a default extension for a single report program output file. (For multiple report programs, the file extensions are `.lis`, `.l01`, `.l02`, and so on.) `LIS` files are printer-specific output report files. In order to print these files, you have to use the proper operating system command or utility, for example, `lp` for UNIX, or `copy` to printer port for DOS. You have probably already noticed that this kind of output is not always convenient, especially if you would like to view the file before printing, or to email it to your users for review. In many cases, `LIS` files are impossible to preview without printing them and are very difficult to refine and, sometimes, quite a few trees may be destroyed before you can make your report perfect.

SQR allows you to create SQR Portable Files (`SPF`); these files help to resolve all of the above-mentioned problems and add a great deal of flexibility to the task of creating SQR reports. The main idea of `SPF` files is that, with their help, your program can create printer-independent output files. These files can be viewed and printed by the `SQR Viewer`, or converted back to `LIS` files with the help of the `SQR Printer`. Both the `SQR Viewer` and `SQR Printer` will be discussed later in this chapter. End users can use `SPF` files to view, e-mail, fax, or print them on any available printing device.

14.1 How to create an SPF file

`SPF` output files can be produced by SQR on any platform.

You do not have to change your program to make it generate `SPF` output. All you need to do is to use one of the following flags in the SQR command line or the SQR Dialog Box:

- `-NOLIS` will create `SPF` file output instead of `LIS` file output
- `-KEEP` will allow you to create `SPF` output in addition to `LIS` output
- `-ZIV` will invoke the `SQR Viewer` after creating an `SPF` file. This flag automatically invokes the `-KEEP` flag to create an `SPF` file. If your program creates multiple output files, the `SQR Viewer` will automatically display only the first report file. The other `SPF` files can be viewed or printed by using the `SQR Viewer`'s file selection option.

Here are some considerations for you to keep in mind when creating printer-independent reports:

- When creating a report for different printers, make sure you are using fonts that are common among printers that may be used to produce your report. You may have to limit the fonts used to font numbers 3, 4, and 5 (Courier, Helvetica, and Times Roman, respectively) or PostScript, HP LaserJet printers in Windows environment.

On some HP printers font 4 is not available, which leaves you with font 3 and 5 as common fonts. When in doubt, use font 3 to test your report.

- There may be variations in the implementation of some graphical features between different printer types.
- The best way to make sure that your program works with different printer types is to test it.

For our readers who would like to take a look "behind the scenes," it may be of some interest to know that, in many cases, SQR generates `SPF` output even when it is not asked to do so. When SQR needs to accumulate its output before creating the final reports, (for example, in multiple-report programs) it uses `SPF` files as intermediate output file storage. Another example occurs when the `Last-Page` command is used in a program (see chapter 5). As you already know, this command causes SQR to accumulate the entire report without printing it until the last page is processed. In these and other cases, SQR automatically creates `SPF` files and deletes them upon the program's completion (unless the `-KEEP` flag is specified).

By the way, `SPF` files generated by SQR behind the scenes may be a source of the following confusing error message:

```
"(SQR 6003) Unexpected End-of-File while processing the
   printer file".
```

This may happen when `LPT1` is used in place of a report file name with the `-F` SQR command flag. In most cases, using this value in the `-F` flag is not a problem except when `SPF` output is created. When SQR creates `SPF` output, it takes the current output file name (in our case, it is `LPT1`) and adds the `.spf` extension to this name. As soon the `LPT1.spf` is created, Windows sends this file to the printer. Unfortunately, SQR considers `LPT1.spf` a normal file name and will try to open and read the file. To avoid this problem, direct your output to a file and print this file in a separate step.

14.2 Advantages of SPF files

`SPF` files allow you to generate a report and store the produced `SPF` output for subsequent electronic distribution or on-site printing. You do not have to know the type of printer belonging to each potential recipient.

`SPF` files also permit you to view, search, or email the text portions of a graphic output by rendering a line-printer output.

In addition, many problems with printing graphical objects on certain printer types can be solved by generating `SPF` files rather than directing the program output to a printer.

You can also separate printing from report execution. For example, you might want to run the report on the database server computer, and then print it on another computer. The overhead associated with producing the graphics will be shifted to the computer where the report is printed. Since SPF format reports can be produced by SQR on any platform, you can take advantage of the Windows printing capabilities even though you created the SQR report file on another platform. For example, you can run a report on a UNIX server and then print the output on a PC using Windows.

14.3 Using the SQR Viewer

The `SQR Viewer` allows you to view your report online before you print it. You can also take advantage of the `Viewer's Print Preview`, `Print Setup`, `Find`, and `Zoom` options as well as the capability to email the report to your users (presently supported are Lotus Notes, E-mail, and Microsoft Mail).

To view a report through the `SQR Viewer`, the report must be in the `SPF` format. These files normally have `.spf` or `.snn` extensions.

In order to demonstrate the use of `SPF` files and the `SQR Viewer`, we will take an SQR program that we developed in the previous chapter and, without changing its code, create the `SPF` output.

Figure 14.1 shows a snapshot of the SQR dialog box with the `-NOLIS` flag, which allows us to create `SPF` output for the `Test13A.sqr` program.

We use the `-NOLIS` command line flag to create `SPF` output. Since the `Test13A.sqr` program creates two output files, the `NOLIS` option will make the program generate two `SPF` files: `Test13A.spf` and `Test13A.s01`. (If the `OUTPUT-FILE-MODE`

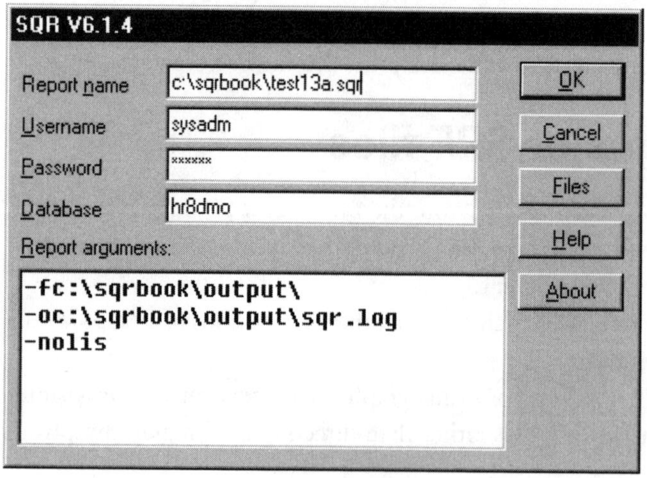

Figure 14.1
Using the NOLIS flag to generate SPF output

environmental variable in the `SQR.ini` file is set to `LONG`, the SPF file names will be `Test13A.spf` and `Test13A_01.spf`.) In order to view these files online, you can either double-click on the file in the appropriate directory, or invoke the `SQR Viewer` and open each file from the `SQR Viewer` menu. Figure 14.2. shows the `Test13A.spf` file viewed with the help of the `SQR Viewer`.

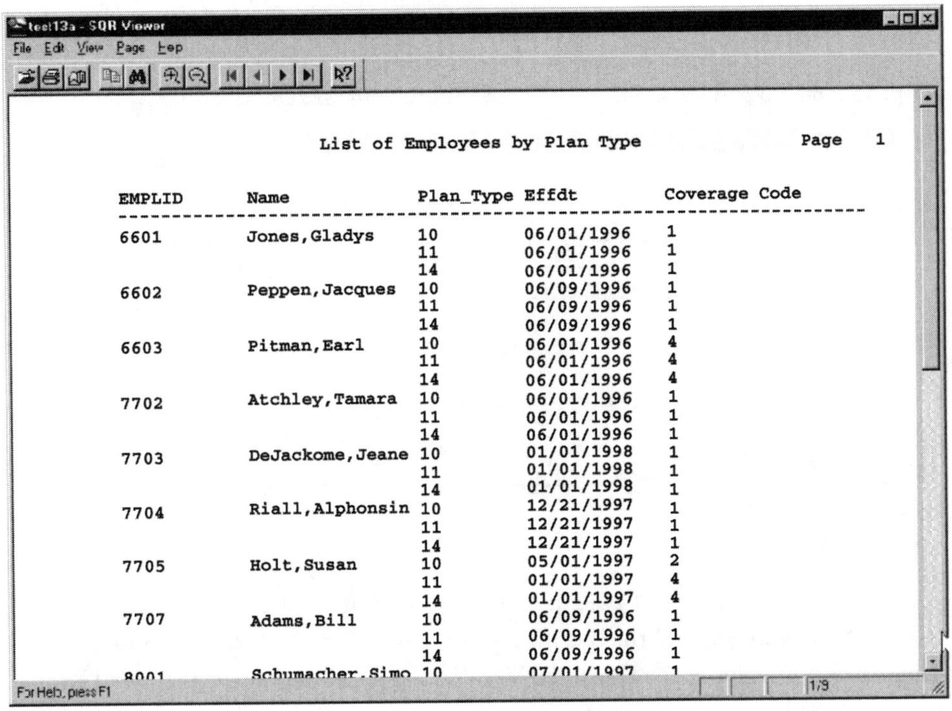

List of Employees by Plan Type   Page 1

EMPLID	Name	Plan_Type	Effdt	Coverage Code
6601	Jones,Gladys	10	06/01/1996	1
		11	06/01/1996	1
		14	06/01/1996	1
6602	Peppen,Jacques	10	06/09/1996	1
		11	06/09/1996	1
		14	06/09/1996	1
6603	Pitman,Earl	10	06/01/1996	4
		11	06/01/1996	4
		14	06/01/1996	4
7702	Atchley,Tamara	10	06/01/1996	1
		11	06/01/1996	1
		14	06/01/1996	1
7703	DeJackome,Jeane	10	01/01/1998	1
		11	01/01/1998	1
		14	01/01/1998	1
7704	Riall,Alphonsin	10	12/21/1997	1
		11	12/21/1997	1
		14	12/21/1997	1
7705	Holt,Susan	10	05/01/1997	2
		11	01/01/1997	4
		14	01/01/1997	4
7707	Adams,Bill	10	06/09/1996	1
		11	06/09/1996	1
		14	06/09/1996	1
8001	Schumacher,Simo	10	07/01/1997	1

Figure 14.2 Using the SQR Viewer to view an SPF file

As you can see, it is very convenient to look at your report on-line. You can then print the report or send it to your users. (To exit from the `SQR Viewer`, select EXIT from the `File` menu.)

Another convenient way of using the `SQR Viewer` is to run your program with the `-ZIV` command line flag. When you use this flag, SQR creates `SPF` output, automatically invokes the `SQR Viewer`, and opens the first `SPF` file created in the program.

It is important to keep in mind that while `SPF` files can be created on any platform, the `SQR Viewer` can be used only on Windows. What if your program ran on a non-Windows platform, but you or your users need to view the `SPF` files generated by the program? The simplest way to solve the problem is to use a file transfer tool (such as the FTP) to transfer the files to the Windows environment.

Another option for programs run on UNIX is to use the UNIX uuencode and mail commands to email the SPF output to the client site. An example of an SQR code that can carry out this task is shown here:

```
!TEST14A.SQR
!Sending SPF output from UNIX to Windows
Begin-Program
 Print 'My test email with ' (1,1)
 Unstring $sqr-report By '.' Into $Filename $Extension

 New-Report 'temp.lis'

 Let $Spf_File = $Filename || '.spf'
 Let $Command = 'uuencode ' || $Spf_File || ' ' || $Spf_File ||
   > '  mailfile'
 Call System Using $Command #Status
 If #Status <> 0
    Show 'Problem with redirecting SPF file'
 End-If
 Call System Using 'mail "SPF Mail" John_User@abcd.com < mailfile'
    #Status
 If #Status <> 0
     Show 'Problem with sending SPF file=' #status
 End-If
End-Program
```

The code shown in Test14A.sqr demonstrates how to use the UNIX uuencode and mail commands to send the SPF files generated on UNIX directly to a user's email system. If the SQR Viewer is a registered Windows application, the recipient will be able to start it from his/her email package.

14.4 Converting SPF files to printer-specific files

When an SQR program which contains printer type specific commands generates an SPF file, the file becomes printer-independent. All printer type specific features are lost. Another product called SQR Print allows you to convert printer-independent SPF files to printer-specific LIS files.

To invoke the SQR Print in the Windows environment, enter the following:

```
SQRWP [file_name] [command_flags]
```

where file_name is the SPF file name (possible flag values are listed in appendix B). If you run the SQR Printer on a server, use SQRP instead of SQRWP.

Despite its name, SQR Print's main job is not to print its output, but rather to generate an LIS file with the same name as the report, using the .lis extension. You can override this name with the -F command line flag.

You can use the -PRINTER command line flag to specify the type of printer for your LIS output. The available printer types are: Line Printer (LP), HP LaserJet (HP), HTML (HT), PostScript (PS), and Windows (WP). If your report includes graphics and you choose an LP, the graphic elements such as lines, boxes, and charts will be skipped. Only text portions of the report will be printed.

Instead of invoking the SQR Print via a command line on Windows, you can use the SQR Print Dialog Box as in figure 14.3.

Figure 14.3 Using the SQR Print Dialog Box

As you can see, the product is very simple. You select FILE, PRINT, and the system will prompt you for other parameters as shown in figure 14.4.

In FILE NAME, you specify the input SPF file to be converted. In Generate Output For, you specify the printer type. This is the equivalent of using the Declare-Printer or Use-Printer-Type command. The default is SPF file.

By default, the output file will be written to the same directory and have the same name as the input file but with the .lis extension. If you need to use a different output file name or directory, select PRINT TO FILE, and the system will prompt you for an output file name.

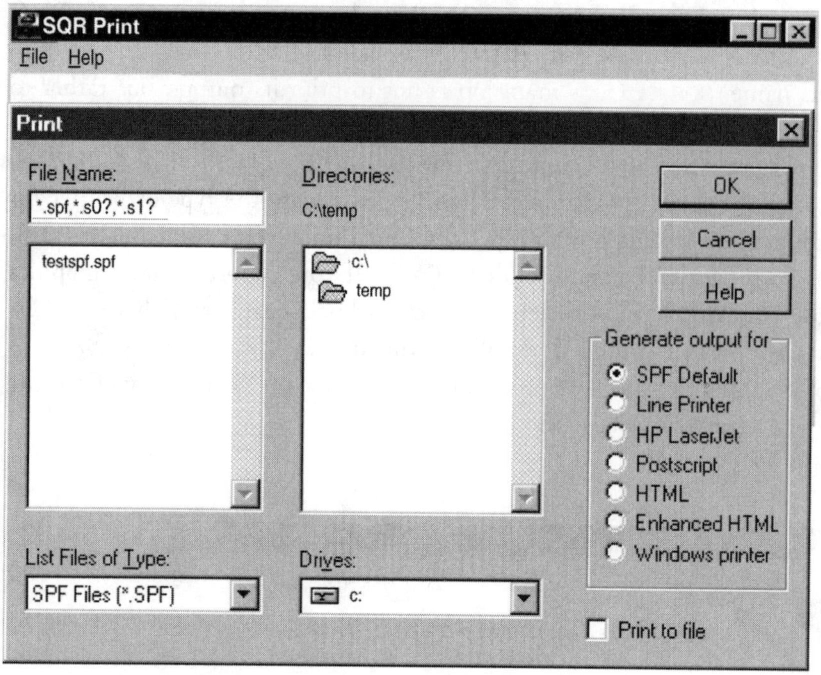

Figure 14.4 Generating an LIS file via the SQR Print Dialog Box

KEY POINTS

1. SQR Portable Files (`SPF` files) are printer-independent and offer a higher degree of flexibility for both program developers and end users.
2. You do not have to change your program to make it generate `SPF` files: it can be achieved by using the proper SQR command line flags.
3. `SPF` files can be generated on any platform.
4. The `SQR Viewer` allows you to view, print, and email `SPF` files. This product works in the Windows environment only.
5. The `SQR Print` converts `SPF` files to printer-specific files. This is a multiple-platform product.

CHAPTER 15

Generating letters

IN THIS CHAPTER

- The `Document` paragraph's format
- Using the `Document` paragraph in SQR programs
- Document markers
- Variable length sections in the `Document` paragraph
- How to control pages in multiple page letters
- How to use multiple `Document` paragraphs

Every time you need to generate a line in a report (even when the line consists of a plain text), you have to use the `Print` command. Often, your report may contain large portions of text with very few variables. In these cases, you may use the SQR `Document` paragraph to code the text portions of the report without using the `Print` commands.

The SQR `Document` paragraph allows you to put information onto a report page as if you were using a word processor. This technique is especially useful when creating form letters. You can design your business forms or letters, and automatically populate them with data from the database.

Suppose you are a company Human Resources (HR) Administrator, and you need to send a letter to every employee inviting them to a holiday party. The task may seem as simple as generating a standard letter template and inserting an employee name and address into each letter. But what if your employees have different party locations? In that case, your program will have to select a department Id for each employee and add program logic to determine the party location for each individual employee. We will show you how to accomplish this and similar tasks in this chapter.

15.1 Using the Document paragraph to create form letters

As we learned in our earlier chapters, in order to print a document page, SQR first builds the page in the memory buffer. We were using the `Print` command to put information onto a report page, explicitly specifying the location (row, column, and length) on the page. There is, however, another way to do it. The `Document` paragraph allows you to combine the body of your standard letter with the values of variables or database columns.

The `Document` paragraph can be used in an SQR `Procedure` section or in the `Program` section. It is advisable to place it in the `Procedure` section. It starts with the `Begin-Document` command and ends with the `End-Document` command. You can have multiple `Document` paragraphs in a single procedure. In the following example, we use a `Document` paragraph in the `Print_Letter` procedure:

```
!Coding the Document paragraph
Begin-Procedure Print_Letter
Begin-Document (1,1)
Dear friend:
.b                    <---| Use .b to print a blank line.
This letter is written to let you know how simple it is to use the SQR
Document Paragraph.
.b
Sincerely yours,
.b
.b
```

```
End-Document
End-Procedure
```

Coding the `Document` paragraph is somewhat different from using the `Print` command. There are certain rules you have to adhere to when using the `Document` paragraph:

- Use spaces (not tabs) to indent text or field.
- Use `.b` to indicate an entire blank line.
- Use fixed or relative position to indicate the start of the paragraph on the page.
- SQR commands (including the `Print` command) are not allowed within the `Document` paragraph.
- A `Document` paragraph must fit within a single report page.

In order to place a variable or column into your document, simply specify the variable or column name at the desired location as in the following example:

```
!Placing a variable in a Document paragraph
Begin-Procedure Print_Letter
Let $My_String = 'My Document'

Begin-Document (1,1)
.b
$My_String     <---|  The value of $My_String will be
                   |  printed at this location of the document.
.b
End-Document
End-Procedure
```

Now, that we better understand the purpose of using the `Document` paragraph, let's put on our HR Administrator's hat and create a program to generate the invitation letters mentioned earlier:

```
!TEST15A.SQR
!Using logic to assign values to variables in the Document paragraph
!********************************
Begin-Program
!********************************
   Do Process_Employees
End-Program

!************************************************
Begin-Procedure Process_Employees
!************************************************
Begin-Select
A.Name
A.Address1
A.City || ' '||A.State|| ' ' ||A.Zip &Addr
B.Company
```

```
B.Deptid
   Do Get_Location(&B.Deptid,$Location)
   Let $Location = Upper(Rtrim($Location,' '))
     Show 'Location=' $Location
     Evaluate $Location
       When = 'CORP HQ'
         Let $Restaurant = 'Planet Hollywood'
         Break
       When = 'DP Center'
         Let $Restaurant = 'Hard Rock Cafe'
         Break
       When = 'PARIS'
         Let $Restaurant = 'Moulin Rouge'
         Break
       When-Other
         Let $Restaurant = 'Home'
     End-Evaluate

   If Rtrim($Restaurant,' ') <> 'Home'
     Let $Restaurant = Rtrim($Restaurant,' ')|| '.'
     Do Convert_Name(&A.Name,$First_Last_Name)
     Let $First_Last_Name_Col = $First_Last_Name|| ':'
     Do Print_Letter
     New-Page
   End-If

From   Personal_Data A, Job B
Where A.Emplid=B.Emplid
   And B.Empl_Status = 'A'
   And   B.Effdt =(Select Max(Effdt) From Job
                   Where Emplid=B.Emlid
                   And Empl_Rcd=B.Empl_Rcd)
End-Select

End-Procedure

!**********************************************************
Begin-Procedure Get_Location($Deptid,:$Loc)
!**********************************************************
Begin-Select
L.Descrshort
   Move &L.Descrshort to $Loc
From Dept_Tbl C, Location_Tbl L
Where C.Deptid=$Deptid
And C.Effdt=(Select Max(Effdt) From Dept_Tbl
             Where Deptid=C.Deptid
             And Effdt<=Sysdate)
And C.Location=L.Location
And L.Effdt=(Select Max(Effdt) From Location_Tbl
             Where Location=L.Location
             And Effdt<=Sysdate)
End-Select
```

```
End-Procedure

!***********************************************************************
Begin-Procedure Convert_Name($Last_First,:$First_Last)
!***********************************************************************
!Input parameter includes:  Last name,First name, MI
!Output parameter includes: First name, MI, Last name

Let $Last_Name=Substr($Last_First,0,instr($Last_First,',',0)-1)
Let First_Name=Substr($Last_First,instr($Last_First,',',0)+1,
   Length($Last_First)- instr($Last_First,',',0))
Let $First_Last=Rtrim($First_Name||' '||$Last_Name,' ')
Show '$First_Last=' $First_Last

End-Procedure
!****************************************
Begin-Procedure Print_Letter
!****************************************
Begin-Document (1,1)
.b
.b
.b
$First_Last_Name
&A.Address1
&Addr
.b
.b
.b
Dear $First_Last_Name_Col
.b
.b
You are cordially invited to attend our annual Holiday party.
It will be held at $Restaurant
Please feel free to bring as many guests as you think is appropriate
for the occasion.
.b
.b
.b
Best wishes to you and your family in the coming Holiday season.
.b
Sincerely,
HR Administrator
.b
.b
/Mrs. Bayer/
.b
End-Document
End-Procedure
```

The employee name and address

The party location

In Test15A.sqr, we select all active employees in the Process_Employees procedure. We join the Personal_Data table with the Job table in order to select the

```
Gladys Jones
1 South Main St.
Los Alamos CA 94325



Dear Gladys Jones:


You are cordially invited to attend our annual Holiday party.
It will be held at Planet Hollywood.
Please feel free to bring as many guests as you think is appropriate
for the occasion.



Best wishes to you and your family in the coming Holiday season.

Sincerely,
HR Administrator


/Mrs. Bayer/
```

Figure 15.1 An example of the holiday party invitation letter

company and employee name, and to make sure that employee status is active. We use the `Evaluate` command to select the restaurant the employee is invited to attend. After all information is prepared, we are ready to print the letter. Note that in the `Document` paragraph we use string variables as well as column variables, and place them exactly where we wanted them to be printed.

Be careful with your letter space planning: if you place a variable in a `Document` paragraph, make sure it gets enough room for printing. If another variable must follow the first one, and you want to avoid blank spaces, concatenate your variables outside the `Document` paragraph. In `Test15A.sqr`, we use this technique to concatenate the employee full name stored in `First_Last_Name` with a colon and store the result of concatenation in the `First_Last_Name_Col` variable.

15.2 Document markers

Another method of placing the values of variables or columns into your document involves using *document markers*. A document marker is a special variable whose name begins with an `@`. It marks a location in the document where you place data from areas external to the Document paragraph parts of the program. Document markers defined in Document paragraphs can be referenced in the Position command outside the Document paragraph to establish the next printing position. (Remember, SQR commands cannot be used inside the Document paragraph). The use of document markers may be helpful in many cases. Let's say you would like to print some portions of your document in bold. You may employ the following technique to accomplish this:

```
!TEST15B.SQR
!Using document markers
!********************************
Begin-Program
!********************************
   Do Print_Doc
   Do Print_Bold
End-Program

!**********************************
Begin-Procedure Print_Doc
!**********************************
Begin-Document (1,1)
Dear colleague:
This document is created just for a demo purpose.
The following lines will be printed in Bold letters.
.b
@Start_Bold          <---   Using a document marker to identify a
                            starting position in the Document paragraph
.b
The following lines will be printed underlined.
@Start_Underline
.b
End-Document
End-Procedure
!**********************************
Begin-Procedure Print_Bold
!**********************************
Position () @Start_Bold
Print 'Printing the Bold Text' () Bold
Position () @Start_Underline
Print 'Printing the Underline Text' () Underline
End-Procedure
```

In this example, we create two document markers inside the Document paragraph. Then, in the Print_Bold procedure, we position our line at the location indicated by the @Start_Bold document marker, and use a regular Print command with the Bold qualifier to print at the current location. Another document marker, @Start_Underline, is used to print an underlined text. Note that just naming a document marker @Start_Bold does not make SQR print the following text in bold. It is the Print command with the Bold qualifier that places data in bold at the location marked by our document marker. Now our program output will look like that in figure 15.2.

```
Dear colleague:

This document is created just for a demo purposes.
The following lines should be printed in Bold letters.

Printing the Bold Text

The following lines should be printed underlined.
Printing the Underline Text
```

Figure 15.2 Using document markers and Print commands to format output

The next example demonstrates another way of using document markers. We hope you did not put your HR Administrator's hat too far away as you will need it again. Let's say you, as an HR Administrator, are going to send every department manager a list of all employees up for review. The list will include the review date printed for each employee. The program may look like the following:

```
!TEST15C.SQR
!An Employee Review Date Notification program
!*******************************
Begin-Program
!*******************************
   Do Process_Main
End-Program

!***************************************
Begin-Procedure Process_Main
!***************************************
Begin-Select
A.Manager_ID       <--- The main query selects department managers.
A.Deptid
A.Descr
B.Name
   Let #Rcds = 0
   Show &A.Manager_Id ' ' &A.deptid
   Do Convert_Name(&B.Name,$First_Last_Name)
   Let $First_Last_Name_Col = $First_Last_Name|| ':'
   Do Print_Letter
   Do Get_Employees      <--- Get an employee list for each department manager.
   New-Page

From Dept_Tbl A, Personal_Data B
   Where A.Manager_Id=B.Emplid
   And   A.Company='CCB'
   And   A.Effdt=(Select max(Effdt) from Dept_tbl
                  where Deptid=A.Deptid
                  and Effdt<=Sysdate)
Order by A.Deptid
```

```
End-Select
End-Procedure
!*********************************
Begin-Procedure Get_Employees
!*********************************
Show 'Get_Empl started...'
Position () @EE_List          <----  Set position with the help
                                     of the document marker.

Begin-Select
C.Name  (0,1,20)
D.Review_Dt(0,+2)
   Add 1 to #Rcds
   If #Rcds >= 10          <----  Maximum ten employees
                                  per page
     Let #Rcds=0
     New-Page
     Do Print_Letter
     Show 'There are more than 10 Employees in Department:' &A.Deptid
       Position () @EE_List
   Else
     Position (+1)    !Advance to the next line
   End-If
From Personal_Data C, Job D
Where   C.Emplid=D.Emplid
   And D.Deptid=&A.Deptid
   And C.Emplid<>&A.Manager_Id
   And D.Empl_Rcd = 0
   And D.Effdt = (Select Max(Effdt) From JOB
     Where Emplid=D.Emplid
     And Empl_Rcd=D.Empl_Rcd)
End-Select

End-Procedure

!*****************************************************
Begin-Procedure Convert_Name($Last_First,:$First_Last)
!*****************************************************
!Input parameter includes:  Last name,First name, MI
!Output parameter includes: First name, MI, Last name

Let $Last_Name=Substr($Last_First,0,instr($Last_First,',',0)-1)
Let $First_Name=
Substr($Last_First,instr($Last_First,',',0)+1,Length($Last_First)-
Instr($Last_First,',',0))
Let $First_Last=Rtrim($First_Name||' '||$Last_Name,' ')

End-Procedure

!****************************************
Begin-Procedure Print_Letter
!****************************************
Begin-Document (1,1)
.b
.b
```

```
$First_Last_Name
Manager of &A.Descr Department
.b
.b
.b
Dear $First_Last_Name_Col
.b
.b
This is a reminder that the following employees of your department
will have  their annual reviews:
.b
@EE_List
.b
.b
.b
.b
.b
.b
.b
.b
.b
.b
.b
.b
Please prepare the appropriate documentation by their respective
review dates.
.b
.b
.b
Sincerely,
HR Administrator
.b
.b
/Mrs. Bayer/
.b
End-Document
End-Procedure
```

In the Main procedure of Test15C.sqr, we first select all managers of the company's departments, one by one, with the company Id = 'CCB'. In order to obtain the manager's names, we join Dept_Tbl with Personal_Data. For each selected row in the main query, we execute the Convert_Name procedure to rotate the employee name to the printable format. Then we call the Print_Letter procedure. This procedure contains a Document paragraph, which begins with the Begin-Document command and ends with the End-Document command. In the paragraph, we use the string variable $First_Last_Name, the column variable &Descr, and the document marker @EE_List to mark the beginning of the employee list. Please note that we have not yet selected the list of employees, but we have already printed the document into a buffer. This is an important consideration: you must print a document before referencing a document marker, since SQR may not know the actual marker location until the document is placed on the page. After the body of the document is created, we call the `Get_Employee` procedure that selects all employees for the specific department, and prints each employee name and review date at the position specified by the `@EE_List` document marker.

There are several important points to mention. First, as you may have already noticed, we allocated ten blank lines for our employee list in the document paragraph. What will happen if the number of selected employees exceeds ten? If we did not have special logic to check the number of selected employees, the program would keep on printing employee names and review dates, thus overlaying next lines in the document. Therefore, we check the number of selected employees beforehand. If the number exceeds ten, we issue the `New-Page` command, which prints the current page and prepares the new one. Then, on the next page, we generate our document, reset the record count, and make sure that the next print position starts at the document marker. The output of the program will look like that in figure 15.3.

```
Simon Schumacher
Manager of the Office of the President

Dear Simon Schumacher:

This is a reminder that the following employees of your department
will have their annual reviews:

Bennett,William D.     1998-12-31
Elias,Jan              1998-10-30
Campenhout,Marc        1998-10-20
Dahling,Irene          1998-01-22
Rossalini,Bartholome   1998-02-12
Wagner,Gretchen        1998-02-18
Jordan,Robert          1998-03-28
Austin,Caroline        1998-03-28
Kidd,Kenneth           1998-04-15
Bird,Douglas           1998-04-30

Please prepare the appropriate documentation by their respective
review dates.



Sincerely,
HR Administrator
/Mrs. Bayer/
```

Figure 15.3 The output of the Employee Review Date Notification program
(continued on next page)

```
Simon Schumacher
Manager of Office of the President

Dear Simon Schumacher:

This is a reminder that the following employees of your department
will have their annual reviews:

Smith,John               1998-05-10
Bronte,Katherine         1998-05-18
Fletcher,Leslie          1998-05-31
Drew,Suzanne             1998-06-10
Reagan,Deidre            1998-06-12
Alomar,Samuel            1998-03-16
Barfield,John            1998-02-28
Cone,Alton               1998-09-10
Bell,Anna                1998-12-15
Gruber,Jennifer          1998-08-24

Please prepare the appropriate documentation by their respective
review dates.



Sincerely,
HR Administrator
/Mrs. Bayer/
```

Figure 15.3 (continued) The output of the Employee Review Date Notification program

Let's review the output of `Test15C.sqr` in figure 15.3. We avert the danger of printing employee names and review dates over the lower portion of the document body when the number of employees exceeds ten, but the program output still does not look right. Instead of generating one letter to each department manager, the program produces multiple letters on the same subject to the same department manager if the number of employees exceeds the limit. In section 15.3, we will employ another technique to fix this problem.

What if you know for sure that the variable portion of your document will never exceed the designated space? Why bother with all these tricks of preventing something which will never happen? Our note of caution is this: despite present numbers, never assume that the maximum number of employees in every department will never exceed the limit. If your letter includes variable length parts, you need to include some page change control logic similar to the one presented in the previous example to provide for the future expansion.

15.3 Using variable length sections

As you see from our examples, using the `Document` paragraph can be a simple and straightforward method of creating form letters, but it has certain limitations. The main inconvenience is that one `Document` paragraph cannot cross over pages. You may solve this problem by taking advantage of the fact that there could be multiple `Document` paragraphs in one SQR program or even in one SQR procedure.

The next example illustrates the use of multiple `Document` paragraphs for fixed portions of a letter, as well as how to print variable length information between different `Document` paragraphs. We will code the beginning of the letter in one `Document` paragraph in the `Print_Letter_Beginning` procedure, and the ending portion of the letter in another `Document` paragraph in the `Print_Letter_Ending` procedure. For the purposes of demonstration, we assume a maximum page length of thirty lines in this example. Let's rewrite the previous example, using the multiple `Document` paragraph technique:

```
!TEST15D.SQR
!Using multiple Document paragraphs in one Procedure section
Begin-Setup
Declare-Procedure
Before-Page=Before_Page_Proc
End-Declare
Declare-Layout Default
Max-Lines=30
End-Declare
End-Setup
!*******************************
Begin-Program
!*******************************
   Do Process_Main
End-Program

!*******************************
Begin-Procedure Before_Page_Proc
!*******************************
If #page-count > 1
   Print '(Continued)'   (1,1)
   Print 'Page: '        (+0,+2)
   Page-Number           (0,+1)
   Position (+1)
End-If
End-Procedure
!*******************************
Begin-Procedure Process_Main
!*******************************
Begin-Select
A.Manager_ID
```

```
A.Deptid
A.Descr
B.Name
   Let #Rcds = 0
   Show &A.Manager_Id ' ' &A.Deptid
   Let #page-count=1
   Do Convert_Name(&B.Name,$First_Last_Name)
   Let $First_Last_Name_Col = $First_Last_Name || ':'
   Do Print_Letter_Begining
   Do Print_Employees
   If #current-line > 19
     New-Page
   End-If
   Do Print_Letter_Ending
   New-Page

From Dept_Tbl A, Personal_Data B
   Where A.Manager_Id=B.Emplid
   And   A.Company='CCB'
   And   A.Effdt= (Select Max(Effdt) From Dept_Tbl
                 Where Deptid=A.Deptid
                 And Effdt<=Sysdate)
Order By A.Deptid
End-Select
End-Procedure

!*****************************************
Begin-Procedure Print_Employees
!*****************************************
Show 'Get-empl started...'

Begin-Select
C.Name    (0,1,20)
D.Review_Dt  (0,+2)
   Add 1 to #Rcds
   Position (+1)

From Personal_Data C, Job D
Where   C.Emplid=D.Emplid
   And D.Deptid=&A.Deptid
   And C.Emplid<>&A.Manager_Id
   And D.Empl_Rcd = 0
   And D.Effdt = (Select Max(Effdt) From JOB
                  Where Emplid=D.Emplid
                  And Empl_Rcd=D.Empl_Rcd)
End-Select

End-Procedure

!****************************************************
Begin-Procedure Convert_Name($Last_First,:$First_Last)
!****************************************************
```

Making sure there is enough room on the page for the second Document paragraph (annotation pointing to `If #current-line > 19`)

```
!Input:  Last,First MI
!Output: First MI Last

Let $Last_Name=Substr($Last_First,0,instr($Last_First,',',0)-1)
Let
$First_Name=Substr($Last_First,instr($Last_First,',',0)+1,-
   Length($Last_First) instr($Last_First,',',0))
Let $First_Last=Rtrim($First_Name||' '||$Last_Name,' ')

End-Procedure

!*************************************************
Begin-Procedure Print_Letter_Begining
!*************************************************
Begin-Document (1,1)    <---| First Document paragraph
.b
$First_Last_Name
Manager of &A.Descr Department
.b
Dear $First_Last_Name_Col
.b
This is a reminder that the following employees of your department
will have their Annual reviews:
.b
End-Document
End-Procedure

!****************************************
Begin-Procedure Print_Letter_Ending
!****************************************
Begin-Document (+1,1)    <---| Second Document paragraph
.b
Please prepare the appropriate documentation by their respective
review dates.
.b
Sincerely,
HR Administrator
.b
/Mrs. Bayer/
End-Document
End-Procedure
```

In `Test15D.sqr`, contrary to the previous test, we do not have to count how many employees have been selected. We simply print the first `Document` paragraph in the procedure `Print_Letter_Beginning`, then all employees from the selected department, and (upon finishing printing the employee list) the second `Document` paragraph in the procedure `Print_Letter_Ending`.

In the `Print_Employee` procedure, SQR takes care of the page overflow situation: whenever an end of the current page is reached, SQR opens a new page automatically.

We still have to make sure that there are enough lines left for the second `Document` paragraph at the end of the entire letter. We do this by checking the SQR reserved variable `#current-line` and issuing the `New-Page` command if there is not enough room for the second `Document` paragraph on the current page.

The output of our program will look like that in figure 15.4.

```
Simon Schumacher
Manager of Office of the President

Dear Simon Schumacher :

This is a reminder that the following employees of your department
will have their Annual review:

Bennett,William D.      1998-12-31
Elias,Jan               1998-10-30
Campenhout,Marc         1998-10-20
Dahling,Irene           1998-01-22
Rossalini,Bartholome    1998-02-12
Wagner,Gretchen         1998-02-18
Jordan,Robert           1998-03-28
Austin,Caroline         1998-03-28
Kidd,Kenneth            1998-04-15
Bird,Douglas            1998-04-30
Smith,John              1998-05-10
Bronte,Katherine        1998-05-18
Fletcher,Leslie         1998-05-31
Drew,Suzanne            1998-06-10
Reagan,Deidre           1998-06-12
Alomar,Samuel           1998-03-16
Barfield,John           1998-02-28
Cone,Alton              1998-09-10
Bell,Anna               1998-12-15
Gruber,Jennifer         1998-08-24
King,Russell            1998-08-03
Lamp,Claire             1998-07-27
```

Figure 15.4 Using multiple Document paragraphs to generate letters with unlimited employee lists (continued on next page)

```
(Continued)  Page:  2

McGriff,Frank          1998-08-24

Please prepare the appropriate documentation by their respective
review dates.

Sincerely,
HR Administrator

/Mrs. Bayer/

Hugh Aitken
Manager of Retail Servicesment

Dear Hugh Aitken      :

This is a reminder that the following employees of your department
will have their Annual review:

Vierra,Ginaual         1998-07-31
Ling,David             1998-08-05


Please prepare the appropriate documentation by their respective
review  dates.

Sincerely,
HR Administrator

    /Mrs. Bayer/
```

Figure 15.4 Using multiple Document paragraphs to generate letters with unlimited employee lists (continued)

You may now be asking yourself these questions: was the usage of the `Document` paragraph justified in this specific case? Was it worth the trouble? Wouldn't we be better off using the regular SQR report printing technique?

The purpose of `Test15D.sqr` was to demonstrate how to deal with situations when the variable portion of the document exceeds the designated page space. It is up to our readers to decide how practical this approach is and if the standard SQR report generation technique is appropriate in a particular case.

KEY POINTS

1. Use the `Document` paragraph to create form letters.
2. The `Begin-Document` and `End-Document` commands are used to define the `Document` paragraph.
3. The `Document` paragraph may be used inside any procedure. There may be multiple `Document` paragraphs within a program.
4. Do not use tabs inside a `Document` paragraph. Use spaces instead. For a full line of spaces specify `.b`.
5. SQR commands are not allowed within the `Document` paragraph.
6. A printed `Document` paragraph must fit into a single report page.
7. You can use document markers to designate special locations in the `Document` paragraphs where you can place data from external to the paragraph parts of the program. The `Position` and `Print` commands are used to move data to the `Document` paragraph from outside of the paragraph.
8. You must generate a document before placing information at the locations marked by document markers.
9. You can separate your letter into variable length sections to achieve greater flexibility.

C H A P T E R 16

Using graphics

IN THIS CHAPTER

- Printing business graphics charts
- Controlling parts of an SQR graphics chart
- Using SQR arrays to feed data into business charts
- Using images in reports
- Printing bar codes and address labels
- Changing fonts and letter sizes
- Drawing boxes, horizontal lines, and vertical lines
- Controlling the position on the page when working with graphical objects

As a reporting tool, SQR supports a rich variety of different graphical objects that can enhance the appearance of your reports as well as add a number of valuable features such as business graphs and charts, bar codes, address labels, signatures, and so on.

Not all printer types will support all these features. In some cases, you may get a shadow box or just an empty space instead of the nice image you expected. Only PostScript printers or HP printers with HPGL support (generally, HPLaserJet 3 and higher) are capable of printing the image outputs. The surest way to generate your graphics is to direct the program output to an `.spf` file (more about `.spf` files in chapter 14).

Another problem with printing most graphical objects in SQR is controlling the object's position on the page. After a graphical object is printed, SQR brings the current position on the page back to the upper left hand corner of the object. If you do not take this into consideration, the subsequent `Print` commands may simply overlay the object. We will learn how to deal with these problems later in the chapter. Let's start with the most exciting graphical objects: business graphs and charts.

16.1 Declaring a business chart

Business charts, graphs, and histograms are very useful when you need to present complex quantitative data in the simplest and most cohesive way. Generally, readers of reports equipped with graphical charts read and understand the presented information more quickly and make fewer mistakes analyzing the printed materials. It is certainly worthwhile to make the extra effort of adding these useful features. This is especially true when your report includes tabular information with repeated rows of similar structure containing numerical data with values that depend on one or two parameters (sometimes called dimensions) such as time, geographical region, type of merchandise, and so on. Beware, however, of the fact that if the tabular information to be displayed with the help of a chart has too many cells, the graphical chart may become difficult to analyze. Segments in a bar or pie chart may overlay each other. In this case, you may be better off with the conventional tabular presentation.

Depending on your program structure and the number of charts to be printed in one program, printing a business chart may be a one-step or a two-step procedure. The one-step approach uses the `Print-Chart` command; the two-step approach uses a combination of the `Declare-Chart` and `Print-Chart` commands.

If your program has only one chart or a few different charts that have very little in common, you can utilize the one-step approach: use a fully-coded `Print-Chart` command to print each chart. The problem with this technique is that since you have to define all features of the graphical object to be printed in each `Print-Chart` command, you have a lot of coding to do. A mere syntax definition of this command takes more than a page in the SQR language reference manual (see appendix D). Of course, not all the command parameters have to be coded, you can use the default values for certain parameters, but it is still a big job to code a business chart in an SQR program.

The two-step approach comes in very handy when you have a number of same or similar charts in one program. In this case, you can use just one `Declare-Chart` command to define all basic features of the chart, and multiple `Print-Chart` commands to print each specific graphical object. When all the basic features of a chart are already defined by the `Declare-Chart` command, there is no need to code all the `Print-Chart` parameters; you only have to code a few necessary ones.

To better understand how to declare a business chart, let us consider the following situation: You need to produce a report that will list the number of employees in different regions during different time periods. The report should include a business chart depicting the number of employees by geographical region (Northeast, South, Central, West) from January 1998 to June 1998. In our particular case, we have two dimensions: regions and time. Before we start coding the chart, let us select the chart type. SQR offers a good choice of types, including

- line graph
- different kinds of bar charts
- histogram
- area / stacked area / 100%-area charts
- XY-scatter plot
- high-low-close graph

A regular bar chart will do a very good job of displaying the employee numbers distribution. Let us use the `Declare-Chart` command to code our chart. As any other declarative command, the `Declare-Chart` command must be coded in the `Setup` section.

```
!An example of the Declare-Chart command
Begin-Setup
Declare-Chart  Employees_By_Region     <---| Declaring a chart
      Title='Employees by Region by Month'
      Type=STACKED-BAR
      Legend=Yes
      Legend-Placement=Upper-Right
      X-Axis-Label='Months'
      Y-Axis-Label='Number of Employees'
End-Declare
End-Setup
```

In the example, we declare a chart named `Employees_By_Region`. We assign our chart a title as well as labels to be displayed along the `X` and `Y` axes. We define the chart legend placement: the legend will be placed in the upper-right corner of the chart. The chart type is defined as STACKED-BAR, but later it will be redefined as BAR just to demonstrate how the chart parameters can be dynamically redefined. We did not code all the command parameters. The omitted ones will either be assigned their default values or be supplemented with the Print-Chart parameter values later. If you have been following us with coding and then tried to run the program, you were probably disappointed: nothing came up. The Declare-Chart command does not print charts, it is the Print-Chart command that performs the actual printing.

16.2 Creating an array

No, this is not a misplaced subchapter. You will need to refresh your memory on the material covered in chapter 12. We are going to create an array. In SQR, arrays serve as data sources for charts, and there is a good reason for this: arrays contain repeated rows of similar structure. Let's create an array to hold the employee numbers by region and months. We will use the Create-Array command to create an empty array, and a number of Put commands to populate the array with the chart data. This will be a two-dimensional array with the following dimensions: month and region.

```
!Creating and populating an array as a data source for a bar chart
Begin-Setup
Create-Array  Name=Number_Of_Employees
       Size=12
       Field=Month:Char
       Field=Empno:Number:4
End-Setup
Begin-Program

Put 'Jan' 20 22 28 32 Into Number_Of_Employees(0)
        Month Empno(0) Empno(1) Empno(2) Empno(3)
Put 'Feb' 10 16 12 18 Into Number_Of_Employees(1)
        Month Empno(0) Empno(1) Empno(2) Empno(3)
Put 'Mar' 12 15 18 22 Into Number_Of_Employees(2)
        Month Empno(0) Empno(1) Empno(2) Empno(3)
Put 'Apr' 30 26 19 23 Into Number_Of_Employees(3)
        Month Empno(0) Empno(1) Empno(2) Empno(3)
Put 'May' 23 20 15 12 Into Number_Of_Employees(4)
        Month Empno(0) Empno(1) Empno(2) Empno(3)
Put 'Jun' 20 16 12 10 Into Number_Of_Employees(5)
        Month Empno(0) Empno(1) Empno(2) Empno(3)
End-Program
```

Creating an array to feed data to the chart. Each array row will contain employee numbers in four regions for the month.

In real business, the array is usually populated with data from the database or from an external file. Each particular chart type needs its own specific array structure. In case of the BAR type (both the regular BAR and STACKED-BAR), the array's structure, as well as the data placed into the array, must fit the two-dimensional pattern. The first dimension (the month name) value is moved to a single-occurrence field `Month` of each row and the number of employees for each region is moved to each occurrence of the multiple-occurrence field `Empno` where every occurrence corresponds to one region (the region is the second dimension). Please note that while the first dimension values (months) are stored in the array explicitly, the second dimension values (regions) are not stored in the array: they are just implied based on their occurrence numbers. If we were to display a different type of chart, for instance, a pie chart, the array structure would be different. We will show you an example of a pie chart later in this chapter.

Now with our array created, we are ready to print our chart.

16.3 Printing a chart

In order to print a chart, SQR needs to know the chart's graphical characteristics, the chart size and location on the page, and the source of data for the chart.

The chart's characteristics can be defined (fully or partially) in the `Declare-Chart` command. Later, this definition is finalized with the help of the `Print-Chart` command. The `Print-Chart` command defines the following:

- all the chart characteristics if the chart has not been previously-defined or adds/overrides previously defined characteristics
- the chart location on the page and the chart size
- the array which holds the data source for the chart.

Let's code the proper `Print-Chart` command to display the employee distribution by geographical region:

```
!TEST16A.SQR
!A bar chart generating program
!***************
Begin-Setup
!***************

Declare-Chart  Employees_By_Region
      Title='Employees by Region by Month'
      Type=STACKED-BAR
      Legend=Yes
      Legend-Placement=Upper-Right
      X-Axis-Label='Months'
      Y-Axis-Label='Number of Employees'
End-Declare

Create-Array  Name=Number_Of_Employees
      Size=12
      Field=Month:Char
```

```
      Field=Empno:Number:4

End-Setup

!*******************
Begin-Program
!*******************

Put 'Jan' 20 22 28 32 Into Number_Of_Employees(0)
       Month Empno(0) Empno(1) Empno(2) Empno(3)
Put 'Feb' 10 16 12 18 Into Number_Of_Employees(1)
       Month Empno(0) Empno(1) Empno(2) Empno(3)
Put 'Mar' 12 15 18 22 Into Number_Of_Employees(2)
       Month Empno(0) Empno(1) Empno(2) Empno(3)
Put 'Apr' 30 26 19 23 Into Number_Of_Employees(3)
       Month Empno(0) Empno(1) Empno(2) Empno(3)
Put 'May' 23 20 15 12 Into Number_Of_Employees(4)
       Month Empno(0) Empno(1) Empno(2) Empno(3)
Put 'Jun' 20 16 12 10 Into Number_Of_Employees(5)
       Month Empno(0) Empno(1) Empno(2) Empno(3)
Print-Chart  Employees_By_Region (2,5)
      Chart-Size=(50,30)
      Data-Array= Number_Of_Employees
      Data-Array-Row-Count=6
      Data-Array-Column-Count=5
      Legend-Presentation=Outside
      Data-Array-Column-Labels=
       ('NORTH EAST','SOUTH','CENTRAL','WEST')
      Type=BAR
```

In addition to previously defined chart parameters, the `Print-Chart` command specifies the chart size and location on the page, names the data array, and overrides some of the previously declared chart parameters.

```
End-Program
```

In the `Test16A.sqr` program, we define our chart characteristics with the help of the `Declare-Chart` command, create an array to feed the chart with data, and use the `Print-Chart` command to print the chart. The `Print-Chart` command specifies the location of the chart on the page (2, 5) and the chart size (the first number in the `Chart-Size` parameter specifies the chart horizontal length in SQR page columns; the second number specifies the vertical height of the chart in SQR page lines). Please note that the `Print-Chart` command overrides the value of one of the parameters defined in the `Declare-Chart`. The `Type` is defined as `STACKED-BAR` in `Declare-Chart` and is overridden as `BAR` in `Print-Chart`. In addition, the `Print-Command` specifies the location, the size, and the data source for the chart. The two parameters `Data-Array-Row-Count` and `Data-Array-Column-Count` can limit the amount of data fed to the chart from the array. If the values of these parameters are lower than the corresponding array parameters, only the specified number of rows and/or columns will be used to feed the array data to the chart. In our case, the array `Number_Of_Employees` was defined with twelve rows to hold data for all twelve months of the year, but the `Print-Chart` command uses only the first six rows.

Please note that we specified `Data-Array-Column-Count=5` even if the corresponding array definition included only two array fields, `Month` and `Empno`. When SQR generates a chart, it counts every array field as well as every occurrence of a field as a separate column. In our example, the four occurrences of the `Empno` field are considered four separate columns.

The `Data-Array-Column-Labels` parameter tells SQR what values must be placed in the chart legend. In our case, the legend should display the regions. Finally, we add another parameter, `Legend-Presentation`, which places the chart legend outside the area defined by the two chart axes (but still inside the chart border). The output of our program is shown in figure 16.1.

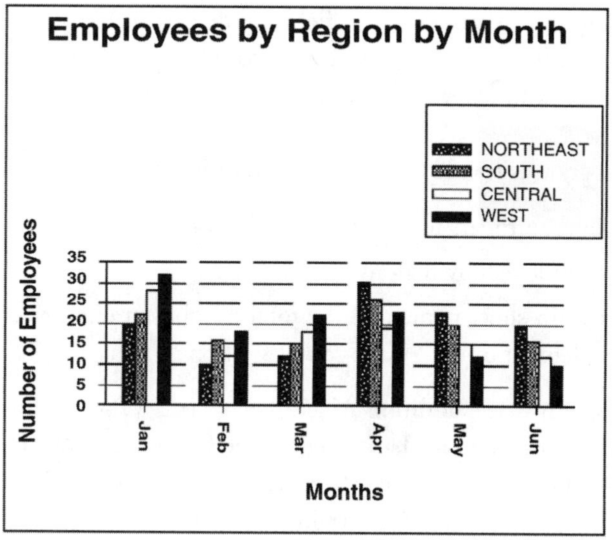

Figure 16.1
Generating a bar chart

If we were to print some additional information below our chart or to add another chart, where do you think the current print position would be? Based on common sense, one would expect the position to be next to the chart's lower right hand corner. Actually, after the chart is generated, the current position jumps back to the page position it occupied prior to the start of the chart generation. To solve this problem, you have to adjust the page position by adding the number of lines and columns occupied by the chart to the proper SQR page position parameters. This is true for all SQR graphical objects, not just for business charts.

We will demonstrate the page position controlling technique in the following example. In this example, we will print a small report using the regular `Print` commands at the top of the page, then add two business charts, one beneath the other. The report will display the employee statistics by region and time in a tabular format. The first chart located under the report will be exactly the same as the one on figure 16.1. The second chart will be a pie chart displaying the total employee headcount for all regions for each month.

We will need to make a number of modifications to our program:

First, we define another array, `Employees_By_Month`, which will feed data into the pie chart. Every array element includes three fields: `Month`, `Empno`, and `Explode`. As we mentioned earlier, each chart type needs its special array organization. In case of the pie chart, every row in the array corresponds to one pie chart segment. The `Month` field is pretty similar to the `Month` field of the `Number_Of_Employees` array. The values of this field will be displayed in the chart legend. The `Empno` field will hold the total number of employees for every month. The values of this field will determine the size of each chart's segment; these values will also be displayed next to every segment. The `Explode` field, special for pie charts, indicates whether the corresponding pie chart segment should be exploded.

The second change to the program is to add a `While` loop in order to

- print a table displaying employee numbers for every month by regions
- calculate the total number of employees by regions for every month
- for every month, move the month short name and the total number of employees by all regions into the proper element of the `Employees_By_Month` array.

The third change to the program is the addition of another `Print-Chart` command to print the second business chart, the pie chart. As does the first `Print-Chart` command, the second `Print-Chart` command will reference the previously defined `Declare-Chart` command, and will add or override certain chart parameters.

```
!TEST16B.SQR
!Adjusting the print position after printing a business chart
!********************
Begin-Setup
!********************
Declare-Chart  Employees_By_Region
      Title='Employees by Region by Month'
      Type=STACKED-BAR
      Legend=Yes
      Legend-Placement=Upper-Right
      X-Axis-Label='Months'
      Y-Axis-Label='Number of Employees'
End-Declare
```

```
Create-Array  Name=Number_Of_Employees
      Size=12
      Field=Month:Char
      Field=Empno:Number:4

Create-Array Name=Employees_By_Month
      Size=12
      Field=Month:Char
      Field=Empno:Number
      Field=Explode:Char
End-Setup

!*******************
Begin-Program
!*******************
Do Create_Array
Do Print_Table
Do Print_Charts

End-Program

!*************************************
Begin-Procedure Create_Array
!*************************************
Put 'Jan' 20 22 28 32 Into Number_Of_Employees(0)
        Month Empno(0) Empno(1) Empno(2) Empno(3)
Put 'Feb' 10 16 12 18 Into Number_Of_Employees(1)
        Month Empno(0) Empno(1) Empno(2) Empno(3)
Put 'Mar' 12 15 18 22 Into Number_Of_Employees(2)
        Month Empno(0) Empno(1) Empno(2) Empno(3)
Put 'Apr' 30 26 19 23 Into Number_Of_Employees(3)
        Month Empno(0) Empno(1) Empno(2) Empno(3)
Put 'May' 23 20 15 12 Into Number_Of_Employees(4)
        Month Empno(0) Empno(1) Empno(2) Empno(3)
Put 'Jun' 20 16 12 10 Into Number_Of_Employees(5)
        Month Empno(0) Empno(1) Empno(2) Empno(3)
End-Procedure

!************************************
Begin-Procedure Print_Table
!************************************
Print '            Employees By Region by Months' (1,1)
Print ' ' (+1,1)
Print 'Month North East      South    Central       West ' (+1,3)
Print ' ' (+1,1)
While #i < 6
   Get $Month #Emp1 #Emp2 #Emp3 #Emp4 From Number_Of_Employees(#i)
       Month Empno(0) Empno(1) Empno(2) Empno(3)
   Print $Month (+1,3,5)
   Print #Emp1 (,+6) Edit 9,999
   Print #Emp2 (,+6) Edit 9,999
   Print #Emp3 (,+6) Edit 9,999
```

```
   Print #Emp4 (,+6) Edit 9,999
   Let #Emp_Total = #Emp1+#Emp2+#Emp3+#Emp4
   Put $Month #Emp_Total 'N' Into Employees_By_Month(#i)
   Let #i = #i + 1
End-While
Print ' ' (+1,1)
End-Procedure

!**************************************
Begin-Procedure Print_Charts
!**************************************
Print-Chart  Employees_By_Region (+1,5)
       Chart-Size=(50,25)
       Title='Employees by Region by Month'
       Data-Array= Number_Of_Employees
       Data-Array-Row-Count=6
       Data-Array-Column-Count=5
       Legend-Presentation=Outside
       Data-Array-Column-Labels=('NORTH EAST','SOUTH','
          CENTRAL','WEST')
       Type=BAR

Print-Chart  Employees_By_Region (+27,5)
       Chart-Size=(50,15)
       Title='Total Headcount by Month'
       Data-Array= Employees_By_Month
       Data-Array-Row-Count=6
       Data-Array-Column-Count=3
       Legend-Placement=Lower-Right
       Legend-Presentation=Outside
       Data-Array-Column-Labels=Employees_By_Month
       Type=PIE

End-Procedure
```

Adjusting the current page position from the upper left corner to under the bottom of the previous chart

Please note the difference between coding the print position parameters in the first and second `Print-Chart` commands. In the first `Print-Chart` command, the page line number is coded as +1, pretty much the same way as it would have been coded in a regular `Print` command when you need to start printing on the next line. In the second `Print-Chart` command, however, the page line number is coded as +27 even though the intent is to print the chart starting just two lines below the first chart. The reason is that SQR does not move the current position after printing any graphical object. You need to account for the number of lines occupied by the object (in our case the number of lines is twenty-five) and adjust the current page position accordingly. Now, let's run the modified program and see the output in figure 16.2.

Employees By Region by Months

Month	North East	South	Central	West
Jan	20	22	28	32
Feb	10	16	12	18
Mar	12	15	18	22
Apr	30	26	19	23
May	23	20	15	12
Jun	20	16	12	10

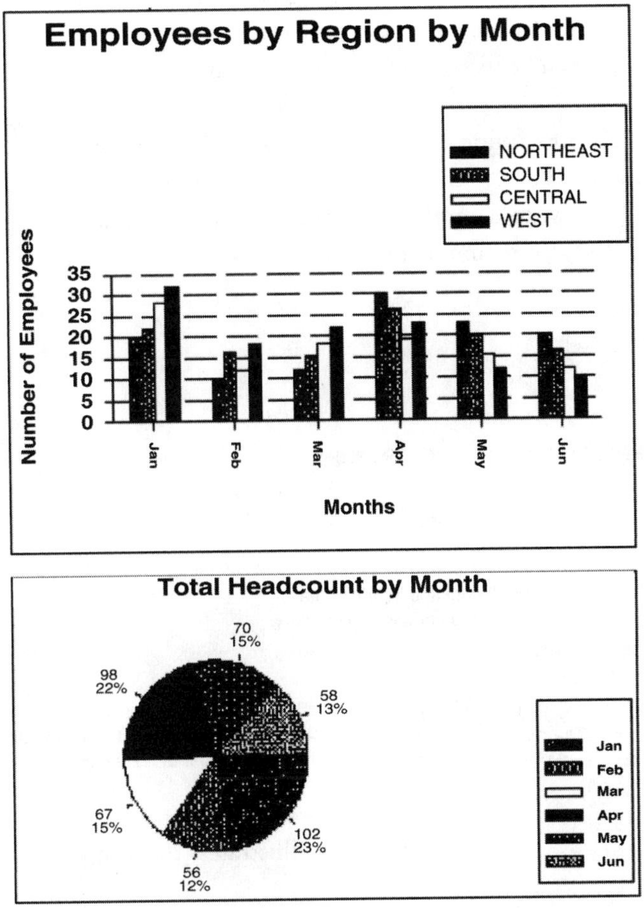

Figure 16.2
Using the previous chart size to adjust the starting position of the next chart

16.4 Using images in reports

Image is another popular graphical object in SQR. You can use images to print corporate logos, signatures, pictures, and so on. As with business graphs and charts, you have a choice between a one-step process and a two-step process when programming images in your report. An image characteristics can be defined (fully or partially) in the

Declare-Image command, and later this definition can be finalized with the help of the Print-Image command. Alternatively, images can be printed in one step using only the Print-Image commands. Because both image processing commands have substantially fewer operands, you save almost nothing by declaring an image and printing the image later, unless your program logic calls for printing exactly the same image in many places in the report (for example, a corporate logo). Another case when the two-step approach can prove useful is when several programs share the same image. In this case, it would make sense to declare the image only once and to place this declaration into a shared file. The file can be inserted into many programs using the #Include compile directive.

Declare-Image and Print-Image have identical operands with the exception of the page position operand of the Print-Image command, which the Declare-Image command does not use. Let's write a sample program to print an image using the Declare-Image and Print-Image commands:

```
!TEST16C.SQR
!An image printing program
Begin-Setup
Declare-Image Flower
   Type=BMP-FILE
   Source='C:\MSOFFICE\CLIPART\FLOWER.BMP'
End-Declare
End-Setup

Begin-Program
Let #Image_Length = 6
Let #Image_Height = 8
Print 'Look at this flower: ' (2,2)
Print-Image Flower (+2,5)
    Image-Size=(#Image_Length,#Image_Height)
Let #Curr_Line_Adj = #Image_Height +3
Print 'Isn''t it lovely?' (+#Curr_Line_Adj,2)
End-Program
```

The length and height of the image are defined dynamically.

Adjusting the current page position from the upper left corner of the image

Look at this flower:
Isn't it lovely?

Figure 16.3 Printing an image

Figure 16.3 illustrates the output of our program.

Please note that as with other graphical objects, SQR brings the current page position back to the upper lefthand corner of the image after printing the image. Therefore, the next Print command needs to account for the image height to adjust the current line number. In our example, instead of using a hard-coded image height, we use the numeric variable `#Image_Height` and calculate the necessary adjustment dynamically.

Note `EPS` images can only be printed on PostScript printers. `BMP` images can only be printed using Windows. `GIF` and `JPEG` images are only suitable for HTML output (more about HTML output in chapter 19).

16.5 Printing bar codes

SQR supports a wide variety of bar code types. Bar codes are printed with the help of the `Print-Bar-Code` command. This command has a number of operands, the most important one being `Type`. Table 16.1 lists the available bar code types and their characteristics. Please note that some bar code types use only numbers while other types are more liberal and allow you to encode almost everything. The content of the text to be encoded by the `Print-Bar-Code` command must correspond to the bar code type.

Some bar code types use check sums that can be calculated and printed in the bar code. In these cases, you need to code `Checksum=Yes` in the `Print-Bar-Code` command (for a complete syntax of the `Print-Bar-Code` command, please refer to appendix D). The text encoded in the bar code is specified by the `Text` operand. You can also specify some additional text to be printed without encoding with the help of the `Caption` operand.

Table 16.1 Types of bar codes

Type	Description	Text Length	Text Type	Checksum Y/N
1	UPC-A	11, 13, or 16	Numbers only	N
2	UPC-E	11, 13, or 16	Numbers only	N
3	EAN/JAN-13	12, 14, or 17	Numbers only	N
4	EAN/JAN-8	7, 9, or 12	Numbers only	N
5	3 of 9 (Code 39)	1 to 30	Numbers, Upper Case Letters, Punctuation	Y
6	Extended 3 of 9	1 to 30	Numbers, Upper / Lower Case Letters, Punctuation, Control Characters	Y
7	Interleaved 2 of 5	2 to 30	Numbers only	Y

Table 16.1 Types of bar codes (continued)

Type	Description	Text Length	Text Type	Checksum Y/N
8	Code 128	1 to 30	Numbers, Upper / Lower Case Letters, Punctuation, Control Characters	N
9	Codebar	1 to 30	Numbers only	Y
10	Zip+4 Postnet	5, 9, or 11	Numbers only	N
11	MSI Plessey	1 to 30	Numbers only	Y
12	Code 93	1 to 30	Numbers, Upper Case Letters, Punctuation	Y
13	Extended 93	1 to 30	Numbers, Upper / Lower Case Letters, Punctuation	Y
14	UCC-128	19	Numbers only	N
15	HIBC	1 to 30	Numbers only	Y

The following example shows how to generate a bar code with the type HIBC:

```
!TEST16D.SQR
!Generating an HIBC type bar code
Begin-Program
Print ' The type of this bar code is HIBC ' (2,2)
Move '123456789' To $Text
Let $Caption='ABCDEF - ' || $Text
Print-Bar-Code (+2, 2)
   Type=15    ! Type=HIBC
   Height=0.5
   Text=$Text
   Caption=$Caption
   Checksum=Yes
Print 'End of bar code area' (+5, 2)
End-Program
```

In `Test16D.sqr`, the `Print-Bar-Code` command specifies the starting position of the bar code, the height of the bar code in inches, the text to be encoded and printed on the bar code, and an additional text to be printed under the bar code area (this text is not to be processed by bar code scanners).

Please note that, as with other graphical objects, SQR will not adjust the current page position after generating the bar code. Subsequent `Print` commands must account for the bar code area height (including the caption area) when calculating the next print position. The height of bar code graphical objects is defined in inches, not in SQR print lines. The height must be between 0.2 and 2 inches. The `Print-Bar-Code` command

```
The type of this bar code is HIBC

ABCDEF - 123456789

End of bar code area
```

Figure 16.4 Printing a bar code

does not specify the length of the bar code because the bar code scanners are tuned to certain distances between the lines, depending on the bar code type.

Figure 16.4 shows the output of our program.

16.6 Drawing boxes and solid lines

The `Graphic` command can be used to draw boxes as well as horizontal or vertical lines. It can also be used to change fonts, but this use of the `Graphic` command may be obsolete in the next SQR versions. Therefore, we recommend using the `Declare-Printer` or `Alter-Printer` commands to change fonts and letter sizes. We will demonstrate the font and letter size change technique in this subchapter.

First, though, let's use the `Graphic` command to print address labels for an employee mailing list. In the following example, our program will select employees from the `Personal_Data` table and, for each selected employee, generate an address label with a ZIP+4 Postnet bar code to support pre-sorted mailing. The address labels will be printed in rows, two labels per row, and every label will be framed in a box. To demonstrate the font and letter size change technique, the employee names will be printed using one letter font, while the address portion will be printed using a different font and letter size. In addition, we will demonstrate the line drawing technique by creating a solid frame around the entire page. The frame will be made up of two vertical and two horizontal lines:

```
!TEST16E.SQR
!Using the Graphic command
!******************
Begin-Setup
Declare-Procedure
      Before-Page=At_Page_Start
End-Declare
End-Setup

!*******************
Begin-Program
!*******************
   Use-Printer-Type HP
   Columns 3 33
   Do Main_Proc
End-Program
```

```
!**********************************
Begin-Procedure Main_Proc
!**********************************
Begin-Select
Name
Address1
City
State
Zip
   Do Convert_Name(&Name,$First_Last_Name)
   Do Generate_Label
From Personal_Data
Where State = 'CA'
End-Select
End-Procedure

!**********************************************************
Begin-Procedure Convert_Name($Last_First,:$First_Last)
!**********************************************************
!Input parameter includes:  Last name,First name, MI
!Output parameter includes: First name, MI, Last name

Let $Last_Name=Substr($Last_First,0,instr($Last_First,',',0)-1)
Let $First_Name=
Substr($Last_First,instr($Last_First,',',0)+1,
   Length($Last_First)-Instr($Last_First,',',0))
Let $First_Last=Rtrim($First_Name||' '||$Last_Name,' ')

End-Procedure
```

```
!*********************************
Begin-Procedure Generate_Label
!*********************************
Let #Label_Count = #Label_Count+1
Graphic (3,2,28) Box 10 5
Print ' ' (+1,1,27) Fill
! Set the font to Times Roman
Alter-Printer Font=5 Point-Size=12
Print $First_Last_Name (+1,3) Bold
! Change the font to Courier
Alter-Printer Font=3 Point-Size=12 Pitch=16.66
Print &Address1 (+1,3)
If length(&Zip) < 6
   Let $Display_Zip = &Postal
Else
     Let $Display_Zip = substr(&Zip,1,5) || '-' || substr(&Zip,6,4)
End-If
Let $City_State_Zip = &City || ', ' || &State || ' ' || $Display_Zip
Print $City_State_Zip (+1,3)
Print ' ' (+1,1,26) Fill
Print '-' (+1,3,25) Fill
Print ' ' (+1,1,26) Fill
```

Drawing a box around the address label

Setting the font to Times Roman

After drawing the box, the print position remains at the upper left of the box thus allowing for printing inside the box.

Changing the font to Courier Roman

```
Print-Bar-Code (+1,4)
    Type=10        ! Type = Zip+4 Postnet
    Height=0.8
    Text=&Postal
Next-Column
If #Label_Count = 2
   Let #Label_Count=0
   Next-Listing Need=12
End-If
End-Procedure

!****************************************
Begin-Procedure At_Page_Start
!****************************************
   Graphic (1,1,60) Horz-Line 20
   Graphic (1,1,58) Vert-Line 20
   Graphic (1,61,58) Vert-Line 20
   Graphic (59,1,60) Horz-Line 20
   Print ' ' (2,2,58) Fill
End-Procedure
```

Drawing a page frame using vertical and horizontal lines

In the `Test16E.sqr` we use all three types of the `Graphic` command.

The `Graphic Box` command specifies the box position and length in parentheses and the box height and rule width following the `Box` keyword. The position, length, and height are coded in SQR print lines and columns. The rule width is coded in decipoints (there are 720 decipoints per inch). You can also code an additional positional parameter right after the width to specify shading. The shading is coded in percentage, from 1 (very light) to 100 (black).

The `Graphic Horz-Line` and `Graphic Vert-Line` commands specify the position of the starting point of the line and the line length in the parentheses while the width is specified after the `Horz-Line` or `Vert-Line` keyword. The position and line length are coded in SQR print lines and columns, and the width is coded in decipoints. The same result could have been achieved by using the `Graphic Box` command, but we wanted to demonstrate the usage of the `Graphic Horz-Line` and `Graphic Vert-Line` commands.

In addition to drawing boxes and lines, two `Alter-Printer` commands are used to control the fonts and letter sizes in the mailing labels.

Due to the large output size, only a portion of the `Test16E.sqr` output is shown in figure 16.5.

Please note that, in our program, we take advantage of the fact that SQR does not adjust the current page position after printing graphical objects. Our program first prints a box, and then places the address label information inside the box.

Figure 16.5 Generating address labels using the Graphic, Alter-Printer, and Print-Bar-Code commands

KEY POINTS

1. SQR offers a rich variety of graphical objects.
2. Not all printer types are capable of supporting all graphical objects, the surest way to generate graphical objects is to direct the program output to an `.spf` file.
3. You can print a business chart using the `Print-Chart` command without declaring the chart, or you can declare the chart using the `Declare-Chart` command and print this chart later using the `Print-Chart` command.
4. Business charts receive data from SQR arrays. Each chart type needs its special array organization.
5. When SQR prints a graphical object, it leaves the current page position at the upper left-hand corner of the object where the printing started.
6. When printing images, you can use the `Declare-Image` command to define an image in one source file and share this file between multiple programs. In this case, the `Print-Image` command performs actual printing of the previously defined image.

KEY POINTS (CONTINUED)

7 SQR supports a wide variety of bar code types.
8 The `Graphic` command draws vertical or horizontal lines or boxes.
9 You can control fonts and letter sizes with the help of the `Declare-Printer` or `Alter-Printer` commands.

C H A P T E R 1 7

Working with flat files

IN THIS CHAPTER

- The `Open`, `Read`, `Write`, and `Close` commands
- Working with fixed length records and variable length records
- Checking the end-of-file condition
- Reading into and writing from strings, binary data, and dates
- Creating interface files for external applications
- Using the `Print` and `New-Page` commands to output data to flat files
- Using interface files to upload data into databases
- Sorting flat files

17.1 Files in SQR

Many situations exist where, in addition to working with database tables and arrays, you may want to take advantage of regular sequential (often called "flat") files. SQR supports all necessary input/output operations on flat files, including opening and closing files and reading from and writing to files. Please note that SQR does not provide random access input/output commands; all records are processed sequentially.

You can use sequential files to

- import data from other systems into your database tables
- unload data from your database tables into sequential files, and use the files as interfaces to external systems
- sort your data using the operating system commands or utilities.

Flat files created in SQR are frequently used as interfaces between PeopleSoft applications and other systems. They are also used for generating comma-delimited (or any other symbol-delimited) files compatible with the Excel Spreadsheet format, or for creating inputs to Lotus Notes or E-mail.

17.2 Using the input/output operations in SQR

Like most programming languages, SQR uses the `Open`, `Read`, `Write`, and `Close` commands to handle sequential files.

17.2.1 Opening a file

Before accessing a file in SQR, you have to open it. A file can be opened as an input file for reading from an existing file, or an output file for writing to a new file or appending data to an existing file. The maximum number of open files at any time is 256. If your program includes more than 256, close the files you do not need at the moment.

When a file is opened for reading, the record length specified in the `Open` command must be equal to or greater than the length of the longest record used in the file. The maximum record length is (32K - 1) bytes (32767).

When a file is opened for writing, a new file is created unless the `For-Append` parameter is specified. If the same file already exists and no append mode is specified, the existing file will be overwritten.

To better understand all the `Open` command operands, let us consider a few examples of the `Open` command:

```
1 Open 'My_File_1' as 1 For-Reading Record=80:Vary
2 Open 'c:\temp\My_File_2' as 2 For-Reading Record=88:Fixed
3 Open $File_1 as 3 For-Reading
4 Open $File_2 as #k For-Writing Record=100
5 Open $File_3 as 4 For-Append Record=70
6 Open &A.File_Name as 5 For-Reading Record=120:Fixed_Nolf
7 Let $File_4='c:\files\input\My_File_3'
   Open $File_4 as 6 For-Reading Record=150:Vary
   Status=#FileStatus
   If #FileStatus != 0
         Show 'Error Opening File: '  $File_4
   Else
         Show 'File ' $File_4 'Opened Successfully'
   End-If
```

In the example in line 1, we opened a file named `'My_File_1'` for `Reading`. The file name in SQR can be coded as a literal or stored in a string variable or column variable. The file name can be specified as a fully qualified name, including the drive and directory, or as a file name only. If the drive and directory are not specified, SQR will use the current directory as a default. The number `1` next to the file name in the `Open` command is the file number (often called the file handle), which is used by other input/output commands to reference the file in the program. You can use any literal, variable, or column variable to specify the file number. File numbers are used in the program in the `Read`, `Write`, and `Close` commands instead of file names. These numbers can be any positive integers less than 64,000. The maximum record size in our example is eighty, which means that all bytes in the input record beyond eighty will be ignored. Since our record type was defined as `Vary`, all records in the file must be terminated by a line terminator (platform-dependent). It is important to note that files with `type=Vary` should not contain binary data.

In line 2, the file `'c:\temp\My_File_2'` is opened as a `Fixed Length` file. This means that all the records in this file have the same length=88. Each record is terminated with a line terminator. You can use this type of file to read binary data. Note that, for files with type `Fixed`, record length does not include the line terminator characters.

In line 3, we opened a file with the name stored in the SQR variable `$File_1`. It is a good practice to use variables instead of hard coding file names. Doing so gives you the flexibility to change the file name in the program before you use the `Open` command.

In line 4, the file with a name stored in the SQR variable `$File_2` is opened for `Writing` with the file handle stored in the SQR numeric variable `#k`. The maximum record length is 100. Since the file type is not specified, SQR will be using the `Vary` type as a default.

In line 5, the file with the name stored in the SQR variable `$File_3` is opened for `Append`. This means that all output information will be placed at the end of the file. If the file does not exist, a new file will be created with the specified attributes: `Record`

Length=70, File Type=Vary (default file type). If the file does exist, make sure the file attributes specified in the Open command match the existing file attributes. Failure to do so may lead to unpredictable results.

In line 6, the file with the name stored in the column variable &A.File_Name is opened for Reading. The file type is specified as Fixed_Nolf, which indicates that all the records in the file are 120 bytes in length with no line terminator at the end of the record. This file type is very useful when writing or reading binary data. Please note that the Fixed_Nolf qualifier is coded with an underscore rather than with a hyphen. This is one of just a few SQR command arguments that are coded with an underscore.

The last example, in line 7, shows the way to check if your Open command was successfully executed. It is not only a good practice to check the Open command status, but it *must* become your programming habit. In most cases, when the returned status is not zero, it means that the file was not found. Verify that your file is, in fact, in the specified directory, and has the correct name and extension. Make sure that the correct syntax is used when specifying the directory. For example, you may want to run your program in both UNIX and Windows environments. When specifying the file directory, keep in mind that in Windows you use backslashes while in UNIX the directory must be specified with forward slashes, for example

```
c:\Temp\Myfile.dat        ! in Windows environment
/tmp/Myfile.dat           ! in UNIX environment
```

17.2.2 Closing a file

SQR files stay opened until the Close command is used or your program successfully terminates.

The SQR Close command is very simple. Here are a couple of examples:

```
Close 1
Close #k
```

As you can see, the Close command uses only one argument, the file number, which is the number assigned to the file in the corresponding Open command.

17.2.3 Reading from a file

SQR will allow you to read an input file only if the file was opened For-Reading. The Read command reads the next record from the file into the variable or variables specified in the command.

Read Into

There are several ways to read a record from a file, and, depending on your program needs, you may choose the proper approach. Each record can be either read into one SQR string variable or a number of individual variables. To illustrate the point, let's look at the following example:

```
Read 1 Into $Input_Record:80
```

In this example, we read the whole record into a string variable `$Input_Record`. This gives us flexibility and, with the help of string functions, we can easily extract the needed fields, or parse the record by a field separator. This approach is especially useful when dealing with records containing variable length fields. Here are some parsing examples:

```
Unstring $Input_Record  By  ','  Into $Last_Name $First_Name $Address
Extract $First_Name from $Input_Record 0 20
Let $Last_Name=Substr($Input_Record,1,20)
```

Another method of using the `Read` command is when the input record is read directly into the specified fields. Please note that this method is mostly used when you know the exact length of every field. Here is an example of this flavor of the `Read` command:

```
Read 1 into $Last_Name:20
            $First_Name:10 $Address:50
```

Detecting end of file

When reading a file you should always check if the End-Of-File condition is reached. SQR internal variable `#end-file` is set to 1 when there are no more records to read. You should make sure that this condition is checked after each record is read. A common practice is to place the `Read` statement into a loop, then break from the loop when the End-Of-File condition is detected. Please note that not breaking from the loop will cause an extra record process.

Here are some examples of how this check can be accomplished:

```
...
!***********************************
Begin-Procedure Read-File
!***********************************
While 1
 Read 1 Into $Record:80
 If #end-file = 1
   Break                 !Break from the While Loop
 End-If
 Do Process-Input-Record
```

Check if the `End-Of-File` condition is reached.

```
End-While
!At this point all the records are read from the file
Close 1
End-Procedure
```

In this example, we use the `Read` command within an infinite loop. After each record is read, we check for the End-Of-File condition, and, when `True`, exit from the `While` loop with the help of the `Break` command.

Many C programmers would probably frown at this example. Using an infinite loop is often considered to be a bad programming technique. Even though `While 1` expressions are widely used in SQR, we can easily avoid them. Let's rewrite our previous example using the SQR reserved variable `#end-file` in the `While` expression:

```
...
!**********************************
Begin-Procedure Read-File
!**********************************
While Not #end-file
 Read 1 Into $Record:80
         If #end-file
         Break
         End-If
 Do Process-Input-Record
End-While
!At this point all the records are read from the file
Close 1
End-Procedure
...
```

Check for `End-Of-File` condition in the `While` Statement.

Our procedure becomes smaller and perhaps more acceptable for those who like to program with style.

Verifying read status

As an option you can designate a numeric variable in the `Read` command in order to obtain the read status from the operating system. The name of the variable is specified in the `Status` parameter of the `Read` command. SQR returns zero if the read is successful, otherwise, a system-dependent error number is returned. The following example illustrates the use of the `Status` parameter in the `Read` command:

```
!**********************************
Begin-Procedure Read-File
!**********************************
While Not #end-file
 Read 1 into $Record:80 Status=#Read_Stat
 If #end-file
   Break
 End-If
```

```
 If #Read_Stat <> 0
    Show 'Bad return from the Read command, errno=' #Read_Stat
    ' Record # = ' #Rcds
 Else
    Add 1 to #Rcds
    Do Process-Input-Record
 End-If
End-While
!At this point all the records are read from the file
Close 1
End-Procedure
```

Reading text data

When reading text data (any string of characters), you should specify the variable name and number of bytes you want the program to read. Keep in mind that the trailing blanks are omitted when the record is read.

The total length specified for all your read variables must be less than or equal to the length of the entire record read.

Reading binary data

In order to read binary data, the file must be opened as a file with record type equal to `Fixed` or `Fixed_Nolf`. Binary fields can be one, two, or four bytes in length. When reading binary numbers, they must be placed into numeric variables.

> **Note** If you use binary numbers, the file may not be portable across platforms, since binary number representation is platform dependent.

Binary numbers hold only integers. If you need to maintain a decimal portion of a number, convert the number to a string variable.

The following is an example of reading binary numbers:

```
Read 1 Into #Amount:2 #Hours:1
```

Reading date fields

If a date field was written to a file in the SQR date variable format, you can read this field to either a date or a string variable. The date variable must be in one of the following formats:

- the format specified by the `SQR_DB_DATE_FORMAT` environmental variable
- your database specific format
- the database independent format `'SYYYYMMDD[HH24[MI[SS[NNNNNN]]]]'`.

Here is an example of reading a date field into a date variable:

```
Declare-Variable
   Date $Input_Date
End-Declare

!**********************************
Begin-Procedure Read-File
!**********************************
While Not #end-file
Read 1 Into $Input_Date:18 $Record    <-- Reading a date into a date variable declared above
If #end-file
 Break
End-If
End-While
End-Procedure
....
```

When a date field is read into a text variable, you may use the `strtodate()` function to convert a string to a date.

```
Declare-Variable
   Date $Date1
End-Declare

!********************************* *
Begin-Procedure Read-File
!**********************************
While Not #end-file
Read 1 Into $String_Date:18 $Record    <-- Reading a date field into a string variable, and converting a string to a date
               If #end-file
                    Break
               End-If
Let $Date1 = strtodate($String_Date)
End-While
End-Procedure
```

17.2.4 Writing to a file

SQR will allow you to write a record to a file only if the file was opened `For-Writing` or `For-Append`. The `Write` command writes a record to a file from the variable or variables specified in this command.

When using SQR `Write` command, you can write to a file from a single literal, variable, or column, or from a list of literals, variables, or columns. The command operands are very similar to those of the `Read` command. You have to specify the file number, the source field(s), the length of the source field(s), and a variable to hold the `Write` command status. Only the file number and source field names are required parameters. The source field length and the status variable are optional. Let's look at the following examples:

```
1 Write 1 From $Record:80 Status=#Write_Stat
2 Write #H From $Record_2
3 Write 2 From $Last_Name:20 ',' $First_Name:10 ',' &Address:50
4 Write 3 From #Amount:2 #Number:1
5 Write 4 From $Date:18
```

In line 1 of our example, we write an entire record from the string variable `$Record`. Since the record length of eighty bytes is specified, only the first eighty bytes will be written. If `$Record` is longer than eighty bytes, the record will be truncated. If `$Record` is shorter than eighty, the remaining part of the record will be padded with spaces. Also, since the `Status` keyword is coded, SQR will move a zero to `#Write_Stat` if `Write` is successful, or, in case of a `Write` command failure, a system-dependent error number will be moved to `#Write_Stat`.

In line 2, the record is written from the string `$Record_2`. Since the length is not specified, the current length of the variable `$Record_2` will be used. The file number previously specified in the `Open` command is stored in the `#H` variable.

In line 3, the record is written from the three specified fields. Since we wanted this file to be comma-separated, we placed commas between the data fields.

Line 4 illustrates the use of numeric variables as sources. In this case, the length argument is mandatory, and only one- two- or four-byte binary integers are allowed by SQR. If you need to write decimal or floating point numbers, you can convert them to string variables, then write from the string variables.

In line 5, we write from a date variable. Before being written to a file, the date is converted to a string using the format specified by the `SQR_DB_DATE_FORMAT` environment variable, or if not set, your database-specific format.

What would happen if the file record length specified in the `Open` command differs from the record length specified in the `Write` command? If the length in `Open` is smaller than the length in `Write`, an error will occur. If the record length in the `Write` command is smaller than the length in the `Open` command, the length in the `Write` command will be used. Please note that if you don't specify the length of each field in your record, SQR will treat the file as having variable length records. Also, it is important to know that you cannot read or write `NULL` values to and from an ASCII file, since SQR strings are `NULL`-terminated.

17.3 Different techniques for creating flat file output

One of the most popular uses of flat files is downloading information from a database into a flat file. The file created can later be used by other applications outside the SQR environment. You can use one of two major approaches to accomplish this task:

- the Write command
- the Print and New-Page commands.

Using the Write command is a more traditional way of creating flat files. It is also a more flexible method. It involves the following steps:

1. Open a file For-Output or For-Append.
2. Select the required data from your database tables in the Begin-Select paragraph.
3. Perform the necessary data conversions and manipulations.
4. Use the Write command to place data into the file.
5. Repeat steps 2, 3, and 4 until the end of selection.
6. Close the output file.

17.3.1 Using input/output commands

Let's assume, that we want to create a list of all active employees and their phone numbers, to download this list to a file, and to use the resulting file as an interface to the E-mail system:

```
!TEST17A.SQR
! The E-Mail Interface program
!********************
Begin-Program
!********************
  If    $sqr-platform = 'WINDOWS-NT '
        Let  $FileName='c:\appldir\Employee.dat'
  Else   ! UNIX
        Let  $FileName='/tmp/appldir/Employee.dat'
  End-If
  Open $FileName as 1 For-Writing Record=100 Status=#OpenStat
  If #OpenStat != 0
   Show 'Error Opening ' $FileName
  Else
   Do Process_Employees
   Close 1
  End-If

  Display 'Total records exported: ' Noline
  Display #Tot_Recs 999,999,999

 End-Program
!*******************************************
Begin-Procedure Process_Employees
!*******************************************
Move 0 To #Tot_Recs
Begin-Select
```

Checking the platform and setting the right file path

Open output file, and check its status.

```
A.Emplid
A.Deptid
B.Name
B.Phone
   Do Write-Output-Record
From Job A, Personal_Data B
Where   A.Emplid=B.Emplid
And A.Empl_Rcd=0
And A.Empl_Status = 'A'
And A.EFFDT = (Select MAX(Effdt)
            From    Job
            Where   Emplid   = A.Emplid
            And     Empl_Rcd = A.Empl_Rcd
            And     Effdt    <= Sysdate)
And A.Effseq =  (Select MAX(Effseq)
            From    Ps_Job
            Where   Emplid     = A.Emplid
            And     Empl_Rcd = A.Empl_Rcd
            And     Effdt = A.Effdt)
End-Select
End-Procedure
!**********************************************
Begin-Procedure Write-Output-Record
!**********************************************
 Write 1 From
  &A.Emplid:11
  &A.Deptid:10        Write SQR columns with
  &B.Name:30          fixed lengths
  &B.Phone:10
  Add 1 to #Tot_Recs

End-Procedure
```

In `Test17A.sqr`, we open a file for writing, select data from the `Personal_Data` and `Job` tables row by row in the `Process_Employees` procedure, and, for every record read from `Job` and `Personal_Data`, we call the `Write_Output_Record` procedure to output the record to the file. Please note that, at the beginning, the program checks the SQR predefined variable `$sqr-platform` to determine the platform under which it is running, in order to specify the correct fully qualified file name. This piece of logic makes your SQR program less platform-dependent and allows you to run it in UNIX or Windows environments without changing the program. Another important point to remember is to use the `Status` argument when opening a file. Why bother with checking the status when opening an output file? Wouldn't SQR just create the file if it didn't exist? Sure, but if the file name you specified is not valid, for example, if the directory or folder you coded in your program does not exist you would probably want to notify the operator and stop the program. A good program has to address all possible "if" questions.

Figure 17.1 illustrates a sample portion of our output file.

```
6601     10200    Jones,Gladys
6602     21700    Peppen,Jacques
6603     10200    Pitman,Earl
7702     11000    Atchley,Tamara
7703     21700    DeJackome,Jeanette
7704     21700    Riall,Alphonsine
7705     10200    Holt,Susan
7706     P9300    Quabin,Mark
7707     21700    Adams,Bill
8001     10100    Schumacher,Simon       415/376-38
8052     20100    Avery,Joan             604/376-38
8101     10500    Penrose,Steven         415/284-72
8102     10900    Sullivan,Theresa       415/376-29
8113     20500    Frumman,Wolfgang       604/284-72
8120     20900    Jones,Theresa          604/376-29
8121     10200    Gregory,Jan            415/837-44
```

Figure 17.1 A portion of the E-Mail Interface program output

The `Open` statement in `Test17A.sqr` did not specify `Record=Fixed`, but the output file generated by the program came out with fixed length records because we specified the exact length for each variable in the output record. The total record length was simply calculated as the sum of all the record components.

17.3.2 Creating comma-separated file output

Some applications, like the Microsoft Excel, work with comma- or other symbol-separated files. We can easily change our previous SQR program to create such a file. In order to do this, we would only need to rewrite the `Write_Output_Record` routine to look like this

```
!**************************************************
Begin-Procedure Write_Output_Record
!**************************************************
 Write 1 from
  &A.Emplid ','
  &A.Deptid  ','      <---| Creating a comma-separated file
  &B.Name  ','
  &B.Phone

  Add 1 To #Tot_Recs

End-Procedure
```

We use a hard-coded string literal `','` as a field separator. It may be a better idea to define the separator as a variable at the beginning of the program, and then to use the variable instead of the literal. In this case, if you later decide to use another character for field separation, you would have to change it only once. In fact, in our particular example, it might be better to use a character other than a comma. Why? Let's run the program, examine the output, and we'll see the answer right away.

As you probably noticed, the column variable `&B.Name` in figure 17.2 already contains a comma. Therefore, it would be better to use another character for field separation. The best solution depends, of course, on your business requirements. By now, you have probably recognized the ability of SQR to meet your business needs.

```
6601,10200,Jones,Gladys,
6602,21700,Peppen,Jacques,
6603,10200,Pitman,Earl,
7702,11000,Atchley,Tamara,
7703,21700,DeJackome,Jeanette,
7704,21700,Riall,Alphonsine,
7705,10200,Holt,Susan,
7706,P9300,Quabin,Mark,
7707,21700,Adams,Bill,
8001,10100,Schumacher,Simon,415/376-3848
8052,20100,Avery,Joan,604/376-3847
8101,10500,Penrose,Steven,415/284-7229
```

Figure 17.2 A portion of the comma-delimited file

Starting with version 4.3, SQR offers a set of command flags (`-EH_CSV`, `-EH_CSV:`*`file_name`*, `EH-CSVONLY`) that make SQR generate CSV output without making any changes to the program. These flags, however, still do not convert your report into a CSV file automatically. If you run an SQR program that was designed to generate a regular report with headers, footers, totals and so on, and use one of these flags, SQR will generate CSV output and will place all these headers, footers, and other unnecessary information into the output using every `Print` command output as a separate comma-separated field. Therefore, generating a program report and CSV output as two separate files is still a good idea. However, if your program generates only field-oriented output, the `-EH_CSV*` flags will save your time plus you will have an option to place an Excel icon pointing to your CSV file on your HTML output (please see chapter 19 and appendix D for details).

17.3.3 Using the Print command to create a flat file

Using the `Write` command to create an output file is the traditional way of creating a flat file. Many programming languages use very similar approaches. SQR allows you to employ another technique of writing data to an output file: using the `Print` command with which you have already become familiar. Keep in mind, however, that this method is not as flexible as using the `Write` command; it has a number of limitations which we will discuss later in this chapter.

To use the `Print` command to output data to a file:

- specify `Max-Lines = 1` in the `Declare-Layout` command
- define the `Width` in the `Declare-Layout` command equal to record size (the size of your output record)
- specify `Formfeed=No` in the `Declare-Layout` command to make sure that SQR will not output form-feed characters
- use explicit length in your `Print` command, thus placing each field at a fixed location in the record
- use the `New-Page` command after each record is processed.

The following example demonstrates the second technique of creating an output file with fixed length records:

```
!TEST17B.SQR
! Using the Print and New-Page commands to generate and output file
!********************
Begin-Setup
!********************
Declare-Layout  Default
Formfeed=No     ! Prevent form feeds between records.
Max-Lines = 1   ! Output will be 1 line deep by 80 columns wide.
Max-Columns=80
Left-margin=0   ! Make sure we start from the top
Top-margin=0
End-Declare

End-Setup
!********************
Begin-Program
!********************
  Do Process_Employees
  Display 'Total records exported: ' Noline
  Display #Tot_Recs 999,999,999

End-Program
```

```
!*********************************************
Begin-Procedure Process_Employees
!*********************************************
Move 0 To #Tot_Recs

Begin-Select
A.Emplid            (1,1,11)
A.Deptid            (0,0,10)
B.Name              (0,0,30)
B.Phone             (0,0,10 )
 New-Page                  <-------| Use the New-Page command after each record.
 Add 1 to #Tot_Recs
From Job A, Personal_Data B
Where A.Emplid=B.Emplid
   And A.Empl_Rcd=0
   And A.Empl_Status = 'A'
   And A.Effdt = (Select Max(Effdt)
                From   Job
                Where Emplid  = A.Emplid
                And  Empl_Rcd = A.Empl_Rcd
                And  Effdt    <= Sysdate)
And  A.Effseq =  (Select Max(Effseq)
                From  Job
                Where  Emplid     = A.Emplid
                And  Empl_Rcd     = A.Empl_Rcd
                And  Effdt        = A.Effdt)
End-Select
End-Procedure
```

As you can see from `Test17B.sqr`, our program becomes much simpler. We do not have to deal with any input/output commands. We just select the required data from the tables, and print them into a file. Note that your file will be created as an `LIS` file unless you use the `-F` SQR command line flag to specify another name for your program report file. This technique is very useful when you need to create a fixed-length character output, but will not work for variable or binary output. Also, if you need to print an audit report in addition to your output file, it may be a better idea to use regular input/output commands in order to distinguish between your report output and the file output. It is possible, however, to create more than one `LIS` file output by using techniques described in chapter 13.

17.4 Using flat files to import data into your database

Another frequent task involves uploading data from a flat file into a database. You can develop a simple program that reads the file and inserts the information into your database. Some business needs require the designing of more complex programs that not only read and insert, but also verify the information read from the file, and populate multiple tables at once. Your SQR program can do many things, including the following:

- read records from the input file
- edit input fields using SQR functions, table lookups, and queries
- build logic to insert data into different tables based on the specified criteria
- check for duplicates
- print an audit report.

The next program demonstrates the standard technique of loading data into a database table. You can easily modify it, depending on your business needs. PeopleSoft programmers may find this example useful when working on data conversion or interface projects.

```
!TEST17C.SQR
! Using flat files to populate the database
!************************
Begin-Program
!************************
  Open 'c:\temp\job.dat' As 1 For-Reading Record=3000
      Status=#FileStat
  If #FileStat !=0
   Show 'Error Opening Input File'
  Else
   Do Read_Input_File
  End-If
End-Program

!***********************
Begin-Setup
!***********************
  Begin-SQL On-Error=Stop
Create Table Temp_Job_Tbl
(
Emplid Varchar2 (11) Not Null,
Empl_Rcd Number Not Null,
Effdt Date Not Null,
Effseq Number Not Null,
Deptid Varchar2 (10) Not Null,
Jobcode Varchar2 (6) Not Null,

Empl_Status Varchar2 (1) Not Null,
Annual_Rt Number (18,3) Not Null,
Monthly_Rt Number (18,3) Not Null,
Hourly_Rt Number (18,6) Not Null
)
```

```
  End-Sql
End-Setup

!****************************************
Begin-Procedure Read_Input_File
!****************************************
Display 'Inserting records from file c:\temp\job.dat into-
           Temp_Job_Tbl ...'
Move 0 to #Inserts
Move 0 to #Tot-Recs
While Not #end-file
  Read 1 Into $Input:1000
  If #end-file
     Break
  End-If
  Unstring $Input By $Sepchar Into -
  $Emplid -
  $Empl_Rcd -
  $Effdt -
  $Effseq -
  $Deptid -
  $Jobcode -
  $Empl_Status -
  $Annual_Rt -
  $Monthly_Rt -
  $Hourly_Rt

  Do Insert_Temp_Job

End-While

Close 1
Display 'Total records inserted: ' Noline
Display #Tot_Recs 999,999,999
End-Procedure

!****************************************
Begin-Procedure Insert_Temp_Job
!****************************************
Begin-Sql On-Error=Insert_Error

  Insert Into Temp_Job_Tbl
(
 Emplid,
 Empl_Rcd,
 Effdt,
 Effseq,
 Deptid,
 Jobcode,
 Empl_Status,
 Annual_Rt,
 Monthly_Rt,
```

```
 Hourly_Rt)

Values
(
 $Emplid,
 $Empl_Rcd,
 $Effdt,
 $Effseq,
 $Deptid,
 $Jobcode,
 $Empl_Status,
 $Annual_Rt,
 $Monthly_Rt,
 $Hourly_Rt
)
End-Sql
If #sql-count=1
 Add 1 to #Inserts
 If #Inserts >= 500
   Commit
   Move 0 to #Inserts
 End-If
 Add 1 to #Tot_Recs
End-If

End-Procedure

!*************************************
Begin-Procedure Insert_Error
!*************************************
If #sql-status = -9 ! if duplicate (this code is for ORACLE only)
   Show 'Insert Error: Duplicate row is not allowed for emplid='
    $Emplid
Else
   Show 'Insert Error: ' $sql-error
   Show 'Error number: ' #sql-status
   Stop    ! Halt Program and Rollback
End-If
End-Procedure
```

17.5 Using operating system commands to sort files

Often a need arises to sort the same data in two different ways within your program. Sometimes, internal arrays are used for this purpose, but you can also use a flat file when the required array exceeds the available memory. Also, with external files, you can use operating system commands or utilities to perform the sorting task rather than writing the sorting logic yourself.

For example, suppose you need to produce a list of all employees in your organization sorted by their names. At the same time, you need to have another report sorted by ZIP codes. One way to accomplish this is to use two `Select` paragraphs with different `Order By` clauses, but, in this case, you would have to select your data twice. If we want to avoid double-reading the database, the task can be approached with the following code:

```
!TEST17D.SQR
! Using the UNIX Sort command instead of selecting from the database
! twice. This Program Demonstrates the use of files for Sort purposes
! The UNIX Sort is used and is being invoked from SQR program
!*******************
Begin-Program
!*******************
  Do Main
End-Program

!**************************
Begin-Procedure Main
!**************************
Open 'file1.dat' as 1 For-Writing Record=80:Vary

Begin-Select
Emplid  (+1,1)
Name    (,+1)
State   (,+1)
Postal  (,+1)
    Write 1
    From
        &Emplid ':'
        &Name:25  ':'
        &State:2  ':'
        &Postal
From  Personal_Data
Order By Name
End-Select

! Close the file and call the UNIX Sort command
Close 1
! Sort the file starting at field # 4 using a colon as separator
Call System Using 'sort -t: +3 file1.dat > file2.dat' #Status

! Open the newly created file and read it in.
Open 'file2.dat' As 2 For-Reading Record=80:Vary

New-Page
Print '       Employee List by Zip Code     ' (1,1)
Print ' Zip Code  Employee Id  Employee Name                State '
      (+1, 1)
```

```
While Not #end-file
   Read 2 Into $String:80
   If #end-file
     Break
   End-If
Unstring $String By ':' Into $Emplid  $Name  $State  $Zip
Print $Emplid  (+1, 1, 8)
Print $Name  (, +1, 25)
Print $State   (, +1, 5)
Print $Zip     (, 1, 8)

End-While
Close 2

End-Procedure
```

In `Test17D.sqr`, we select data from the `Personal_Data` table, print the selected information into a report, and, at the same time, use the `Write` command to output each selected record into a flat file named `file1.dat`. When the selection is over, we close the file, and then call the UNIX `Sort` utility to sort our `file1.dat`. The result of the sort is placed into `file2.dat`. Since ZIP code is the third field in the record, the `Sort` utility sorts the file by ZIP codes. After the file is sorted, we simply read the file, record by record, and print the report in the sorted order. With this approach, our program creates two different reports with just one pass on data in the database.

KEY POINTS

1. SQR provides the following Input/Output commands: `Open`, `Read`, `Write`, and `Close`.
2. Before accessing a file, it must be opened. If you are reading a file, it should be opened `For-Reading`. If you are writing to a file, it should be opened `For-Writing`.
3. The open `For-Append` parameter is used when you need to append the records to an existing file. If a file does not exist, it will be created.
4. The record type may be defined as `Fixed`, `Vary`, or `Fixed_Nolf` (fixed with no line terminator). The `Fixed_Nolf` type is often used for accessing binary data.

KEY POINTS (CONTINUED)

5 When reading from or writing to a file, you refer to the file by the file number rather than by the file name. File names are specified only in the `Open` command.

6 SQR internal variable `#end-file` is set to `1` when there are no more records to read.

7 When reading text data, the trailing blanks are omitted.

8 In order to read binary data, the file must be opened as `Fixed` or `Fixed_Nolf`.

9 You cannot read or write `NULL` values from or to an ASCII file.

10 The `Print` and `New-Page` commands can be used to create flat files with fixed length records.

11 You can use the operating system commands to sort files.

12 Files are closed either by the `Close` command, or upon the successful termination of your program.

C H A P T E R 1 8

Interacting with operating systems and other applications

IN THIS CHAPTER

- Submitting SQR programs from the operating system command line
- Creating and executing pre-compiled programs
- Running SQR programs in batch mode
- Issuing operating system commands from SQR programs
- Invoking non-SQR programs from SQR
- Invoking SQR programs from other SQR programs
- Invoking SQR programs from non-SQR programs
- Calling user functions from SQR programs
- Generating Word documents from SQR

An SQR program can be invoked in a number of different ways. You already know how to start your program from the `SQR Dialog Box` in the Windows environment. You can also execute SQR programs from the operating system command line or call them from other programs. As an alternative, SQR programs can be run in batch mode under VAX/VMS, MVS, UNIX, MS-DOS, Windows NT, Windows 95 and OS/2 using DCL (VAX/VMS), JCL (MVS), shell scripts (UNIX), or batch files (MS-DOS, WINDOWS, OS/2).

18.1 Executing an SQR program from the command line

When executing an SQR program from the operating system command line, you need to enter

- the name of the SQR engine (`SQRW` in Windows, `SQR` in UNIX, etc.)
- your program name
- the database connectivity string
- SQR command line flags
- application-specific arguments.

Since `.sqr` is the default extension for all SQR source programs, you don't have to specify it, unless your program has another extension.

The *database connectivity string* contains important information needed to connect your program to the database, including user Id and password. The exact format of this string is database-specific.

18.1.1 SQR command line flags

SQR allows you to change its default behavior by using the command line flags. Some of the flags have arguments. Please do not confuse the SQR command line flag arguments with command line arguments.

SQR command line flag arguments are simply parameters related to each specific flag, for example, flag `-ZIF` (alternative `INI` file directory) requires the directory name as its argument.

Command line arguments are application-specific input parameters that are retrieved by your program from the command line using the `Input` or `Ask` command. Examples include `state code`, `as-of-run date`, and so on.

Command line flags always start with a dash (`-`). If a flag has arguments, the arguments must follow the flag with no spaces between the flag and its arguments. All SQR command line flags are described in appendix B. In this chapter, we will discuss some of the most frequently used flags.

Some command line flags are used to specify a directory, a file name or a path. In the following example, the `-F` flag is used to override the default SQR output file name and directory. By default, SQR names the output report file the same as your program name with an `.lis` extension and places this file into the current directory.

The following examples show the usage of the `-F` flag in Windows and UNIX:

```
1 sqrw test01.sqr sqrbook/passwd -Fc:\temp\                !Windows
2 sqrw test01.sqr sqrbook/passwd -Fc:\temp\Mysqr.lis       !Windows
3 sqrw test01.sqr sqrbook/passwd -Fc:\temp                 !Windows
                                                            !(Incorrect Path)
4 sqrw test01.sqr sqrbook/passwd -fc:\temptst              !Windows
5 sqr test01.sqr sqrbook/passwd -F/home/output/            !UNIX
6 sqr test01.sqr sqrbook/passwd -F/home/output/output.lis    !UNIX
7 sqrw test02.sqr sqrbook/passwd -freport1.lis -freport2.lis -freport3.lis
                                                            !Windows
8 sqrw test02.sqr sqrbook/passwd -Keep -fc:\temp\          !Windows
9 sqrw test03.sqr sqrbook/passwd -Keep -freport1.lis -freport2.lis
                                                            !Windows
```

In line 1 of our example, when the `test01.sqr` program is executed, the `test01.lis` output file will be created in the c:\temp directory.

In line 2 when the `test01.sqr` program is executed, the output report will go to the `c:\temp\Mysqr.lis file.`

In line 3 (during the program execution), when the output file is about to open, SQR will display the following message: "Cannot open the report output file c:\temp. Permission denied. Program aborted." What happened? Since the backslash character at the end of the path was missing, SQR decided that `temp` is the output file name and tried to open the `temp` directory as an output file for writing, thus triggering the "Permission denied" error.

In line 4, the program output was directed to the `c:\temptst` file. Note that, in this case, the file is created with no `.lis` extension because the file name was explicitly specified with no extension.

In line 5, the `test01.lis` file is created in the UNIX directory `/home/output.`

In line 6 we wanted to redirect the output file to the `output.lis` file in the `/home/output` directory.

In line 7, a multiple report program, `test02.sqr` creates three output report files in the current directory. The first one goes to the `report1.lis` file; the second file is created as `report2.lis`; and the third file name is `report3.lis`. All three files are created in the current directory.

In line 8, the same multiple report program is executed with the command line flag `-KEEP`. As we discussed in chapter 14, this flag tells SQR to create an `SPF` file in addition to the regular LIS file. Since the program generates three output report files, the following six files will be created in the c:\temp directory: test02.lis, test02.l01, test02.l02, and test02.spf, test02.s01, test02.s02. Please note that, from SQR version 4 on, you may see different report file names. The report file names and extensions are now controlled by the OUTPUT-FILE-MODE parameter in the SQR.ini file. If the value of the OUTPUT-FILE-MODE parameter is set to SHORT, the output file names would be: test02.lis, test02.l01, test02.l02, and test02.spf, test02.s01, test02.s02. If the value of the OUTPUT-FILE-MODE parameter is set to LONG, the output file names would be: test02.lis, test02_01.lis, test02_02.lis, and test02.spf, test02_01.spf, test02_02.spf.

In line 9, the following four files will be created in the current directory: report1.lis, report2.lis, report1.spf, report2.s01. Please note, that in this example, the -F flag arguments specify their respective file names with the .lis extensions even though the program will generate both the regular and the SPF output. Also, note some inconsistency in the file naming scheme for LIS files and SPF files.

Like the -F flag, the -I flag specifies a list of directories where SQR will search for files specified in the #Include statements. If the #Include statement in your SQR program does not specify the search path, SQR will first look for the file in the current directory. If the files are not found in the current directory, SQR will search in the directory specified in the -I flag. You can specify multiple directory paths. The directory names must be separated by semicolon or comma. For example:

```
-Ic:\sqr\user\include\;c:\sqr\include\              !Windows
-I/$HOME/sqr/inc/,/$HOME/mysqr/inc/                 !UNIX
```

When you specify the directory for both -F and -I flags, you must use the right sub-directory separation character at the end. For Windows, it is a backslash, for UNIX, it is a forward slash.

In order to override the directory and/or the name of the SQR.ini file, use the -ZIF flag with the file name following the flag. The default name is SQR.ini. This file contains the default settings and parameters used by SQR.

The -O flag is used to override the default program log file name. If this flag is not used, the program log will be placed in the current directory. The default log file name is your program name with the .log extension. Please note that this flag can be used only in Windows. Use the standard file redirection method (">") in UNIX.

In chapter 20, we will discuss the flags that may be used in testing and debugging, including: -Debug, -S, -T, -E, -C.

18.1.2 SQR command line arguments

SQR command line arguments are the values that your SQR program expects to receive from the command line via the Ask or Input commands. Since all Ask commands in your SQR program are processed first, all arguments for the Ask commands should be listed before arguments for the Input command. All the arguments must be listed in the order they are prompted for in your SQR program. In the following example, the program reads two arguments from the command line: File_Name and As_Of_Date. The first argument is retrieved by the Ask command, the second one is read by the Input command:

```
!TEST18A.SQR
!Retrieving SQR command line arguments
...
Begin-Setup
 Ask File_Name 'Please Enter Input File Name'
End-Setup
Begin-Program
 Input $As_of_Date type=date
...
End-Program
...
```

The command line for this example will look like

```
SQRW Test18a.sqr test/pswrd -Fc:\temp\ 'My_File' '09/01/1998'
```

When retrieving arguments from the command line, SQR uses the following logic:

- attempts to read the arguments from the command line
- if no arguments are found in the command line, SQR looks for an argument file
- if no argument file is found, SQR will prompt the user for input.

Note that when the Input command uses the Batch-Mode parameter, SQR will not prompt the user for input. Specifying the command line arguments eliminates the need to prompt an operator. This is especially useful when you execute your SQR program in the batch mode or schedule your process to run automatically at night.

18.1.3 Using the argument files

You can use a text file to pass arguments to your program in the command line. Each argument should be entered in the argument file, one argument per line. An argument file may include an unlimited number of arguments. SQR will process the arguments one by one. The argument file name must be specified on the command line with the @

character preceding the file name. For example, if `test18A.sqr` program is invoked from the command line using an argument file to pass two parameters to this program, the command line may look like

```
sqr test18A.sqr test/pswrd @arg1.dat
```

where `arg1.dat` is an argument file containing

```
!SQR argument file
my_file
09/01/1998
```

In addition to program input parameters, SQR allows you to put your program name and the database connectivity string into the first two lines of an argument file. This comes in handy when you wish to execute your program from a command file or a batch script, and do not want to expose your database access password. The following example shows how to execute your program from the command line while keeping the program name, user name, and password in your argument file:

```
sqr @arg2.dat
```

where `arg2.dat` is an argument file containing

```
!Placing both the user Id and password in an argument file
test18a.sqr
test/pswrd
my_file
09/01/1998
```

You can optionally specify a question mark in your command line to prompt user for some of the command line arguments. For example, in the command

```
sqr test18a.sqr ? @arg1.dat
```

the program prompts the user for the database/password instead of reading this information from an argument file.

SQR argument file can also be generated as an output from another SQR program, allowing two different programs to communicate via an argument file. One last note: when putting parameters in the argument file, do not include them in quotes.

18.2 Executing a precompiled SQR program

In chapter 5, we explained that SQR goes over the source program in two steps. The first step is compiling the program, and the second step is actual program execution. So far, we have been compiling and executing our SQR programs in one step, but SQR allows you to separate these two steps.

In order to compile an SQR program without executing, use the `-RS` SQR command line flag which allows you to create a pre-compiled version of your program. Pre-compiled programs are usually assigned the extension `.sqt` and are sometimes called `SQT` programs. After an `SQT` program is created, you can execute it at any time with the help of either the `-RT` SQR command line flag, or via the `SQR Execute` (`SQRT` for UNIX or `SQRWT` for Windows) program. The `SQR Execute` program performs only program execution. It allows you to specify most command line flags similar to the flags you specify when executing your program in two stages. Please refer to appendix B for a complete list of the SQR command line flags. The following examples show you how to pre-compile and then execute an SQR program:

```
  !Creating a pre-compiled SQR program and
  !executing this program in a separate step
1 sqrw test01.sqr sqrbook/passwd -RS                !compile test01.sqr
2 sqrw test01.sqt sqrbook/passwd -RT -Fc:\temp\     !execute test01.sqt
3 sqrt test01.sqt sqrbook/passwd -F/tmp/            !execute test01.sqt
                                                    !via sqrt program
```

In line 1 of our example, we compile the `test01.sqr` program and save the compiled version of the program in the `test01.sqt` file.

Line 2 shows how to execute a pre-compiled program using the `SQRW` and the `-RT` command line flag.

Line 3 demonstrates how to execute a pre-compiled program using the `SQR Execute` or `SQRT` program.

Compiling an SQR program once, and then executing the already-compiled file could improve the performance of your SQR program to some degree. However, there are some limitations that have to be taken into consideration when running a program in two separate steps. When your program is compiled and executed at the same time, it is not so important to know what is done at which stage, but as soon as you separate the two steps, you must be aware of what happens during each stage. A clear understanding of what SQR actually does during each of these two steps is very important. For example, all compiler directives (`#Define`, `#If`, `#Include`, etc.) as well as the commands in the `Setup` section (`Ask`, `Declare-Layout`, etc.) are processed at compile time. This means that when a pre-compiled program is executed, all `Ask` commands will be ignored. You will have to use the `Input` command, instead of the `Ask` command, to prompt for user input at run time.

18.3 Executing your SQR programs in batch mode

SQR programs can be executed in batch mode under MS-DOS, Windows, UNIX, VAX/VMS, or MVS. For example, an SQR command line can be included into a batch file or a UNIX shell script. PeopleSoft users are, probably, familiar with a special script named `PRCS_SQR`. This script was developed by PeopleSoft to run PeopleSoft SQR programs in the UNIX environment. It takes all user parameters from PeopleSoft on-line panels with the help of the PeopleSoft Process Scheduler, and dynamically builds the regular SQR command line described above.

18.4 Issuing operating system commands from an SQR program

You can issue operating system commands within an SQR program. This feature gives you a great deal of flexibility, allowing you, for example, to use the same operating system commands that work with files and directories. This is as simple as issuing the same commands from the operating system command line. For example, if your program runs under UNIX and you would like to make a copy of a file, you may use the following code in your program:

```
!Executing a UNIX command from an SQR program
Let $Command_String='cp /usr/tmp/file1.dat /usr/tmp/file2.dat'
Call System Using $Command_String  #Status
If #Status<>0
   Show 'Error executing the command in Unix: '$command
End-If
```

As you can see, all you need to do is to move the command to a string variable using exactly the same syntax as you would use in the UNIX system command line. In fact, it's always a good idea to test this command separately from a command line before you put the code into your program. After the string is built, use the `Call System` SQR command to execute the command in the `$Command_String` variable. The operating system returns the status of the command execution in the `#Status` numeric variable. The value returned in the status variable is system-dependent. (Please see the complete description of the `Call System` command and return statuses in appendix D.)

You do not have to move the operating system commands to a string, you can hard-code them right in the `Call System` command. In the next example, the UNIX `cp` command is explicitly coded in the `Call System` command.

```
Call System Using 'cp /usr/tmp/file1.dat /usr/tmp/file2.dat' #status
```

In order to execute a similar command in the Windows environment, the following command may be used:

```
!Executing Windows commands from an SQR program
Let $COMSPEC=getenv('COMSPEC')
Let $Command=$COMSPEC||
   ' /C copy c:\temp\testdate.lis c:\myoutput\testdate.lis'
Call System using $Command #Status
If #Status<>0
   Show 'Error executing the command in Windows: '$Command
End-If
```

The following example shows how to print a report output file from an SQR program. The program checks for the platform and, depending on the result, executes the corresponding operating system command.

```
!Printing a file from SQR on different platforms
*******************************************************************
Begin-Procedure Print-file
!******************************************************************
Show '$sqr-platform=' $sqr-platform
Print $sqr-platform (+1,1)
Move $sqr-report to $Save_Report
! to Close the current report output file
New-Report 'new.lis'
Let $Eval_Platform = substr($sqr-platform,1,7)
Show $Eval_Platform
Evaluate $Eval_Platform
   When = 'DOS'
   When = 'VMS'
      Let $command='print'||$Save_Report
      Break
   When='UNIX'
      Let $Command='lp '||$Save_Report
      Break
   When = 'WINDOWS'
      Let $Command=getenv('COMSPEC')|| '/C print '||$Save_Report
      Break
   When-Other
      Show 'Do not know how to print for ' $Eval_Platform
   End-Evaluate
Call System Using $Command #Status
End-Procedure
```

The `Call System` command can also help you to create new directories and files, check for the existence of a specified file; delete, rename, and move directories and files; or perform other tasks. If your program runs under UNIX, you can take advantage of the rich variety of the UNIX operating system commands and utilities, such as `sort`, grep, and others. Be careful, however, if your program is written to run on multiple platforms. Before issuing a specific operating system command, it is always a good idea to check if the command matches the current platform.

The `Call System` command can be invoked in either synchronous mode or asynchronous mode. If you would like to run an operating system command and execute the next SQR command in your program without waiting for the completion of the operating system command, specify the `Nowait` parameter in the `Call System` command. If SQR commands that follow the `Call System` command depend on the results of the `Call System` command execution, use the `Wait` parameter. Not every operating system will allow you this kind of flexibility: only Windows 95/98/2000, Windows NT, or VMS support both the synchronous mode and asynchronous mode of the `Call System` command. In UNIX, you can use only the `Wait` parameter. In Windows 3.1, you can only use `Nowait`. The default behavior of the `Call System` command also depends on the operating system used. In Windows 95/98/2000 and Windows NT, the default is `Nowait`, whereas in VMS, the default is `Wait`.

Please keep in mind that SQR offers a few file manipulation functions: `exists()`, `rename()`, and `delete()`. If these SQR functions are sufficient for your task, use them instead of the operating system's specific commands to ensure platform independence for your program. For instance, if you need to change a file name from `file1.dat` to `file2.dat`, there are two different ways to do this. The following code includes two SQR procedures: the first one renames a file using the UNIX `mv` command; the second one performs the same task with the help of the SQR `rename()` function:

```
!Two methods of renaming a file using a UNIX command or an
!SQR function
!**************************************
Begin-Procedure Unix_Rename
!**************************************
Let $Command_String='mv /usr/tmp/file1.dat /usr/tmp/file2.dat'
Call System Using $Command_String  #Status
If #Status<>0
 Show 'Error executing the command in Unix: '$Command_String
End-If
End-Procedure
...

!**************************************
Begin-Procedure SQR_Rename
!**************************************
Let $File3='/usr/tmp/file3.dat'
Let $File4='/usr/tmp/file4.dat'
Let #Ret_Cd = exists($File4 )
If #Ret_Cd = 0
 Let #Ret_Cd = delete($File4)
```

Using the `Call System` command to rename file `File1.dat` to `File2.dat`

Using an SQR function to re-name `File3.dat` to `File4.dat`

```
End-If

 Let #Ret_Cd = rename($File3,$File4)
If #Ret_Cd <> 0
 Show 'Error Renaming ' $File3 ' to ' $File4 ' Ret_cd=' #Ret_Cd
End-If
End-Procedure
```

In the `Unix_Rename` procedure from the preceding example, the UNIX `mv` command is used to rename `file1.dat` to `file2.dat`. In the `SQR-Rename` procedure, we take advantage of the platform-independent function `rename()` to carry out the same task. Before calling this function, the program checks if the output file already exists, and if so, deletes it. We use two more SQR functions to do this: `exists()` and `delete()`. Using the SQR functions alone does not warrant platform independence. Perhaps you've already spotted a problem in this procedure that will prevent its successful run on Windows. The file names are coded with forward slashes making the procedure only good for UNIX. The problem can be easily fixed by generating fully-qualified file names depending on the current platform. Another way of solving this problem is to accept file names from user input.

In chapter 17 we used the UNIX `sort` command in one of the chapter's examples. You can use this command to sort `file1.dat` and place the result into `file2.dat` by using the following command:

```
Call System Using 'sort file1.dat > file2.dat' #Status
```

Another popular UNIX command, `grep`, can help you extract records from a file based on the record's content. In the following example, this command is used to extract all records that contain a specific Paygroup code in any record position.

```
!Using the UNIX grep command to extract records that
!contain the specified text
!**********************************************************************
Begin-Procedure Extract_Paygroup($FileIn,$FileOut,$Paygroup)
!**********************************************************************
Let $Redirect=' >'
Let $Command_Line= 'grep '||$Paygroup || ' '||$FileIn||
   $Redirect||$FileOut
Show '$Command_Line=' $Command_Line
Call system using $Command_Line #status
If #status <> 0
       Show 'Unsuccessful Call to execute Unix Extract, #status='
         #status
End-If
End-Procedure
...
```

The above example shows a local procedure that accepts the following input parameters: input file name, output file name, and Paygroup code. The value in the `$Paygroup` variable defines the selection criterion. The procedure does not specify the position of the `Paygroup` field in the record. The `grep` command will search over the entire record, and, if it finds a string that matches the value in `$Paygroup`, the record will be selected. Isn't this amazing? We select records from a file without even opening the file! Try it on your system, and you will also notice that the processing time is unbelievable: this procedure can crunch a fairly large file in less than a second. The above procedure is capable of replacing an entire SQR program: leaving no need to open files, read and write records, use the string comparisons, and so on. You can also save on writing the error handling code.

Hopefully, you are convinced by now that using the `Call System` command can be a good and efficient alternative to writing your own subroutines .

18.5 Calling external programs from SQR

As you just learned, the `Call System` command is used to execute the operating system commands. SQR, however, sees no difference between an operating system command and any executable program that can be invoked from the command line. You can use the same command to execute any application program, compiled as executable file, to be run from the command line. You can also execute a batch file or a shell script from an SQR program. One important thing to consider is how the invoked external program gets connected to the database (in most cases, it is necessary).

18.5.1 Calling a Pro-Cobol program from an SQR program under UNIX

The following example shows how to execute a program written and compiled in Pro-Cobol:

```
!Using the Call System command to execute a
!program written in Pro-Cobol
Call System Using '/home/user/cbl/PRG01' #Status
  If #Status <> 0
   Show 'Unsuccessful Call to execute PRG01, #status=' #Status
   Let $Error_Msg = 'Unable to execute COBOL PRG01'
   Let #Ret_Cd=#Status
  End-If
...
```

In this example, the invoked program does not need to connect to a database, nor does it accept input parameters. If your program uses input parameters and works with a database, the program call will have to include the database name, user Id, and password as well as the program input parameters. The following example shows one way of doing this:

```
!Passing input parameters and database connectivity information
!in a program written in Pro-Cobol
Let $Connect_String=' user01/mypasswd@hrdev'
Let  $My_Command = '/home/user/cbl/prg002 '||$Company || ','
                                           ||$Paygroup || ','
                                           ||$Pay_End_Dt || ','
                                           ||$Connect_String

Call System Using $My_Command   #Status
Show 'Return from Call ' #Status
 ...
```

One thing that could be improved in the above example, is to get rid of hard-coded database connectivity information. The calling SQR program has already received these parameters so if the called program works with the same database, it can use the same parameters.

There are several methods you may choose to pass the connectivity string from the main program to a subroutine. The method chosen depends on the method of the main SQR program invocation. If you call your SQR program from the command line, you can place the connectivity information in an argument file, and then read this file in your SQR program, get the database connectivity string, and pass it to the subroutine. If the main program is executed from a batch file or shell script, the connectivity string can be saved in a temporary environment variable for use in your program. The following example demonstrates this technique for an SQR program invoked from the PeopleSoft Process Scheduler. The Process Scheduler uses the `prcs_sqr` UNIX script to parse input parameters including the connectivity string, and then dynamically builds a command line to submit the SQR program. We made a few simple modifications to this script by saving the database connectivity string in an environment variable `MYENV`.

```
#Saving the database connectivity string in an environmental variable
# Parse and interpret parameters in the command line.
parse_command_line()
{
  CMDF_SYNTAX="Syntax: <process> <signon> <+p>|<+P>|
   <sqr option>[ <+p>|<+P>|<sqr option>]..."
    if [ $# -lt 3 ]
    then
        error_exit 1 "Too few arguments in command file" $CMDF_SYNTAX
    fi
    # Get the report parameter and go to the next argument.
    rpt='downshift_string $1'
```

Suppose the connectivity string is saved in the MYENV variable. Now we can retrieve the value of the MYENV variable in our SQR program with the help of the getenv() SQR function. The connectivity string obtained from this variable is passed to the calling program:

```
!Passing the connectivity string from main program to a subroutine
Let $Connect_String = getenv('MYENV')
```

The getenv() SQR function retrieves saved connectivity string.

18.5.2 Calling an SQR program from another SQR program under UNIX

Just as we did when calling Pro-COBOL programs from SQR programs, we can use the connectivity information derived from either an argument file or a batch file. If we use the same technique to save and use an environment variable, calling an SQR program from another SQR program in UNIX environment may look like the following:

```
Let $Out_Dir =  '/usz/tmp/'
Let $Connect_String = getenv('MYENV')
Let  $My_Command = '/opt/sqr/ora/workbench/bin/sqr '
                                  || 'PS_HOME/sqr/mysqr.sqr '
                                  || $Connect_String
                                  || ' -m $PS_HOME/sqr/allmaxes.max'
                                  || ' -F' || $Out_Dir || 'mysqr.lis'
Call System Using $My_Command   #Status
Let $Print_Command =  'lp -d mp_mis1 ' || $Out_Dir || 'mysqr.lis'
Call System Using $Print_Command #Status
```

This example looks somewhat like the previous one. Please note, however, the difference: the command line contains an invocation of the SQR itself rather than the program name. This command line looks exactly like the one you would use to execute your program from the command line. The second Call System command is used to print the program output report.

18.5.3 Calling a PeopleSoft Cobol program from SQR

This subchapter is intended for PeopleSoft developers only. It shows some tricks that may be used to run PeopleSoft Cobol programs from SQR. Why would someone ever want to call a PeopleSoft Cobol program from an SQR program? In some cases, it may be necessary. Let's take for example the *Leave Accrual* process. This process must be run separately for every plan type. To speed up processing, users may want to specify all plan types at once, and submit all the processes together. In this and similar cases, calling PeopleSoft Cobol programs from SQR may prove useful.

There are several things that we have to take into consideration. First, the PeopleSoft Cobol programs are usually called from a batch file or shell script which, in turn, is executed from the Process Scheduler. Second, these programs usually work with databases, and, therefore, require the database connectivity string. The following example shows how an SQR program obtains all necessary parameters from PeopleSoft, saves these parameters in a temporary parameter file, builds a UNIX command line, and then uses this command line in the `Call System` command to invoke a PeopleSoft Cobol program:

```
!TEST18B.SQR
!Calling a PeopleSoft Cobol program from SQR
!**************************************
Begin-Procedure Process-Main
!**************************************
...
  Do Build-Command-Line
...     !The actual logic of a Select loop is omitted
   Do Call-PSPACCRL          !This procedure is called in a Select loop
  ...
   Do Delete-Param-File
End-Procedure Process-Main

!**************************************
Begin-Procedure Build-Command-Line
!**************************************
  !Process Instance
  Move #prcs_process_instance to $Cur_Prcs_Inst 999999
  Let $Cur_Prcs_Inst= Rtrim (Ltrim($Cur_Prcs_Inst,' '),' ')
  !Process Run Control
  Let $prcs_run_cntl_id=Rtrim(Ltrim($prcs_run_cntl_id,' '),' ')
  !Operator ID
  Let $prcs_oprid= Rtrim(Ltrim($prcs_oprid,' '),' ')
  !Database name
  Do Get-DBNAME
  !Operator password
  Let $PSWD = getenv('OPRPSW')
  Do Create-Param-File

  !Command line
  Let  $subroutine = 'PSRUN PSPACCRL <leave.par'
  End-Procedure
!**************************************
Begin-Procedure Get-DBNAME
!**************************************
Begin-Select
dbname
   Let $DB_Name = &dbname
from psprcsrqst
   where prcsinstance=$Cur_Prcs_Inst
```

Preparing command line parameters

Creating an argument file

Building a command line to invoke the PSPACCRL program and to pass the program input parameters in the leave.par argument file

```
End-Select
End-Procedure
!*****************************************
Begin-Procedure Create-Param-File
!*****************************************
 Let $subroutine='cd $PS_HOME/bin'
 Call System using $subroutine   #status
  If  #status <> 0
     Let $Error_Msg = 'Unable to change Unix directory to '
      ||$subroutine
     Do Error
  End-If
Let $OpenError='N'
Let #tot-recs-out = 0
Let $Param_File='leave.par'
open $Param_File as 1 for-writing record=100:vary status=#filestat1
Move #filestat1 to $FileStat 9999
If #filestat1 <> 0
   Let $Error_Msg = 'Error Opening File: '|| $Param_File||': '
   || $filestat
    Do Error
End-If
If $OpenError='N'
    Write 1 from $sqr-database
    Write 1 from $DB_Name
    Write 1 from $prcs_oprid
    Write 1 from $PSWD
    Write 1 from $prcs_run_cntl_id
    Write 1 from $Cur_Prcs_Inst
    Close 1
End-If
End-Procedure
!*****************************************
Begin-Procedure Call-PSPACCRL
!*****************************************
  Let #status = 0
  Call system using $subroutine   #status
  show 'Return from Call ' #status
  If  #status <> 0
     Let $Error_Msg = 'ERROR in COBOL Prgm PSPACCRL'
     Show $Error_Msg
  Else
     Print 'Records were successfully processed by PSPACCRL' (+1,1)
  End-if
End-Procedure

!*****************************************
Begin-Procedure Delete-Param-File
!*****************************************
  Let #status = 0
  Let $del = 'rm leave.par'
  Call System Using $del #status
```

Using the `Call System` command to change the current directory (annotation for `Call System using $subroutine #status`)

Creating an argument file containing the database name, operator ID, password, the run control ID, and the process instance ID (annotation for the `Write 1 from` lines)

Using the `Call System` command to delete the argument file (annotation for `Call System Using $del #status`)

```
    If  #status <> 0
      Show 'ERROR Deleting leave.par file '! not a critical error,
                                          ! do not stop execution.
    End-if
  End-Procedure
  ...
```

The main idea behind this example is to dynamically build a command line that is similar to the command line used by the PeopleSoft Process Scheduler. The Process Scheduler submits Cobol programs via its PSRUN utility. In our code we dynamically build the command line

PSRUN PSPACCRL <leave.par,

where PSPACCRL is the name of the *Leave Accrual* Cobol process, and leave.par is a parameter file built to run this process. The logic in the example may seem straightforward except for the method of passing the database password to the Cobol program. The program reads the password from the environmental variable OPRPSW using the SQR getenv() function. The trick is to set this environmental variable prior to the SQR program execution. In order to do this, the PeopleSoft-delivered PRCS_SQR UNIX shell script was changed to retrieve the password from the command line and save it in OPRPSW. (The PRCS_SQR script is used by the Process Scheduler to run SQR programs on UNIX.) When the process finishes, the OPRPSW variable will be deleted. As you can see from the example, the program dynamically builds a parameter file named leave.par to pass all the input parameters to the COBOL program. At the end of the process, this parameter file is deleted due to security reasons.

18.6 Calling SQR from other programs

In order to call SQR programs from non-SQR applications, you can use the SQR Application Program Interface: SQR API.

18.6.1 Using SQR API

In Windows environment, you can use SQR API via the Dynamic Link Library (DLL) calls. Any program in Windows environment that is capable of using DLL calls can invoke SQR with the help of SQR API. If an SQR program is called from a C or C++ program, a header file sqrapi.h has to be included in the program.

In UNIX, a static link library SQR.a or SQR.lib is provided. Programs written in C or C++ must include a header file, sqrapi.h. When linking C or C++ applications, both the SQR API library and your database library must be included as well as two additional libraries: Bcl.a and Libsti.a.

You can call SQR programs from PowerBuilder, Visual Basic, Microsoft Access, and other applications that support VBA. SQR programs can also be invoked from Oracle Forms. Please refer to the application-specific technical documents for the detail steps required to link your application with SQR.

The following steps are needed to invoke an SQR program from a C program on UNIX platform:

1 Code an SQR program call within your C program. Include the `sqrapi.h` header file in your program. Build the proper SQR command line parameters to support the call. Include the user ID, database password, and application-specific input parameters into the command line as in

```
//Calling SQR from a "C" program in UNIX
#include <sqrapi.h>
my_func()
{
   int stat = 0;
   stat = sqr ("mysqr userid/psswd@testdb");
   if (stat == 0)
      printf ("\n\t\tSuccessfull SQR call\n");
   else
      printf ("\n\t\tSQR call failed\n");
   sqrend();
}
```

Call an SQR program via the SQR API. The call status is returned by the API upon program completion.

Releases the memory and closes the cursors

2 Compile your C program.

3 Change your `make` file to include all necessary SQR API libraries: `Bcl.a`, `Libsti.a`, `SQR.a`, plus other libraries required by your application.

4 Run the `make` file to link the programs to create an executable file.

18.6.2 Using PeopleCode to schedule an SQR program execution from PeopleSoft

In PeopleSoft, SQR programs are usually submitted from a menu under the PeopleSoft Process Scheduler. In this case, the Process Scheduler performs actual program invocation, as well as passing parameters to the program. We will discuss this process in detail in part 3.

Sometimes you may need to submit an SQR program from PeopleSoft in some nontraditional way, (if, for instance, a program call is triggered by certain events). Or you may want to give users an option to push a button and initiate an SQR program directly from the current PeopleSoft page, thereby avoiding the need for users to switch to the Run Control page and the Process Scheduler Request page that are normally used to submit an SQR program. By the way, in PeopleSoft, programs and jobs (sets of related programs that have to run in a certain order) are called processes. In order to implement this, a PeopleCode function, `ScheduleProcess`, is used. This function accepts the program input parameters, validates them, and inserts a record into the PeopleSoft `Process Request` table, forcing the system to execute the process automatically.

You can optionally schedule your process to run at any specified moment. You can also create recurring processes that can be scheduled to run automatically at specified intervals. If there are several related processes that have to be run sequentially or in parallel, you can create a job where you specify the individual SQR processes and the order in which they run. (Note, jobs are not supported on the client. Only API Aware processes are allowed in job definitions. Please refer to chapter 24 for detailed explanations on how to make your SQR program API Aware.)

There are eight parameters that can be used when scheduling an SQR process from PeopleCode. The `Process Type` and `Process Name` are the only required parameters of the `ScheduleProcess` function. The complete `ScheduleProcess` function parameters are:

- `Process_Type` (*string*), a required parameter that specifies the process type. Use `"SQR Report"` to schedule a single SQR program or `"PSJob"` to schedule a job.
- `Process_Name` (*string*), a required parameter that specifies your SQR process or job name, as defined in your Process definition. Please note that the Process or Job definition must be created prior to scheduling this process. (Refer to chapter 23 for details on how to create Process definitions.)
- `Run_Location` (*string*), an optional parameter that specifies where the process is run: "1" = client; "2" = server. Please note that depending on where your PeopleCode is running, you may or may not be able to change the run location. For example, if the PeopleCode script runs on client, your SQR processes can run on either client or server. If, however, the PeopleCode script is run on server, then your SQR process cannot be scheduled to run on client.
- `Run_Cntl_Id` (*string*), an optional parameter that specifies a `Run Control Id` (a string that identifies your process for the Process Scheduler).
- `Process_Instance` (*number*), a temporary variable which you provide as a placeholder to be filled by the `ScheduleProcess` function. This is an optional parameter, and if not passed, the process instance number is not returned to your PeopleCode script.
- `Run_Dttm` (*DateTime*), an optional parameter that specifies the date and time to schedule your process.
- `Recurrence_Name` (*string*), an optional parameter that specifies the recurrence name. (Refer to chapter 24 for details).
- `Server_Name` (*string*), an optional parameter that specifies the server name (if any).

Here is an example of a PeopleCode script that schedules an SQR process:

```
!Using PeopleCode to schedule an SQR program
&PROCESS_NAME = "my_sqr";
&PROCESS_TYPE = "SQR Report";
&RUN_CNTL_ID= "My_Run_ID";
&RC = ScheduleProcess(&PROCESS_TYPE, &PROCESS_NAME, "2",
  &RUN_CNTL_ID, &PRCS_INST);
IF &RC != 0
WinMessage("Error: Error Scheduling SQR Process, rc="|&RC);
End-If;
```

In the preceding example, the value in `&RC` informs your code whether or not the process was successfully scheduled to run. Do not confuse it with a return code from your SQR program: your program has not even started to run yet. As soon as the `PeopleCode` function `ScheduleProcess` inserts a record into the `Process Request` table, `PeopleCode` returns to the next command and does not know anything about your SQR process execution. You can see your program run status on the Process Monitor page.

The next example shows you how to use *inline bind variables* in the `ScheduleProcess` function. Inline bind variables allow you to avoid hard-coding some of the `ScheduleProcess` function parameters and to use the pertinent parameters from the current page. You can reference any parameter from the current component by using a combination of the record name and the parameter name and prefixing this combination with a colon. For example, to pass the value of `Run Location` and the `Report` name stored in the record `MY_RECORD`, use

```
/*Using inline bind variable to schedule a process from PeopleCode*/
&PROCESS_NAME = :MY_RECORD.REPORT;
&PROCESS_TYPE = "SQR Report";
&RUN_CNTL_ID= "My_Run_ID";
&RUN_LOCATION=:MY_RECORD.LOCATION
&RC = ScheduleProcess(&PROCESS_TYPE, &PROCESS_NAME,
  &RUN_LOCATION,&RUN_CNTL_ID, &PRCS_INST);
IF &RC != 0
  WinMessage("Error: Error Scheduling SQR Process, rc="|&RC);
End-If;
...
```

Keep in mind that before you schedule any SQR program to run from `PeopleCode`, you must create a Process definition for this program. Starting from PeopleSoft version 8, you can also use the `CreateProcessRequest PeopleCode` function instead of the previous method.

18.7 Linking with a user function written in C

SQR offers a rich variety of commands and built-in functions. Still, there are some functions or features that are native to other programming languages, but may be very difficult or even impossible to implement using SQR commands and functions. Fortunately, SQR provides a way to extend itself by integrating your own functions written in standard languages like C or utilizing libraries of vendor-supplied functions.

SQR provides two ways of linking an SQR program with a function written in C. You can add your function to either the `Ucall.c` or `Ufunc.c` file. Depending on where the function was placed, there are two methods of the function invocation:

- If the function was placed into `Ucall.c`, it can only be invoked via the SQR `Call` command (do not confuse this command with the `Call System` command).
- If the function was placed into `Ufunc.c`, it must be used in the SQR `Let` command similarly to any native SQR function.

For example:

```
!Two methods of invoking a user function
! my_func1 was placed into the UCALL.C file:
Call My_Func1 Using $Parm_In $Parm_Out

! my_func2 was placed into the UFUNC.C file:
Let #Status = my_func2($Parm_In, $Parm_Out)
```

The first method involves creating your subroutine, adding the code and function prototype to `Ucall.c` file, recompiling the `Ucall.c`, and re-linking it with SQR.

In this chapter, we will concentrate on the second method of user function invocation, that is, calling the new user functions from SQR the same way you would call native SQR functions.

Creating custom functions for SQR involves some effort. The most difficult part of the effort happens outside of SQR. In the next subchapter, we will create a sample C function, and then go over all steps that are necessary to incorporate this function into the SQR environment.

18.7.1 Creating a user function

Our sample function will convert its input to a hexadecimal format. It may prove especially useful when working with file interfaces from non-SQR applications. Sometimes, developers working with programs written in different programming languages have problems with interpretation of the file interfaces between these programs. In other cases, technical documentation from interfacing systems may include inaccurate input record layouts. This is especially frustrating when dealing with complex records containing mostly numeric data. The new function will help you to quickly produce a dump of any string, which may prove extremely helpful when debugging your programs.

Our new function will accept an input string and return a string containing the input string in the hexadecimal format. This way, we will be able to demonstrate how custom-made functions read their input parameters and how they return the output results. After the function is created, it will be added to SQR as a user function and may be called within an SQR program as follows:

```
Let $HexString= showsashex($Input_String)
```

where `$HexString` represents the result string and `$Input_String` contains the function input string.

We will start by writing a C function that will convert its input to the hexadecimal format. Thanks to C language flexibility, this task can be accomplished in a number of ways. The example which follows shows just one possible way (many readers will probably come up with different implementations of this logic):

```
//An example of a user function written in "c"
static void showashex CC_ARGL((argc,argv,result,maxlen))

CC_ARG(int, argc) /* Number of actual arguments */
CC_ARG(char*, argv[]) /* Pointers to arguments: */
CC_ARG(char*, result) /* Where to store result */
CC_LARG(int, maxlen) /* Result's maximum length */

{
 char *pIn,*pOut;
 int iLen;
   pIn=argv[0];
   pOut=result;
   iLen=0;
   while (*pIn && iLen<maxlen)
   {
     sprintf(pOut,"%2.2x",*pIn);
     iLen+=2;
     pIn++;
     pOut+=2;
   }
   *pOut=0;
   return;
}
```

Note that the C function's type is `void` even though we planned that the corresponding SQR function will return a string. As you will see later, communicating between SQR and the underlying C functions is done indirectly using the standard SQR interface.

18.7.2 Integrating a user function with SQR

SQR has a source file named `Ufunc.c` that contains all user-defined C functions. In order to integrate our new function with SQR, we need to perform the following steps:

- create the function prototype and add this prototype to the function declaration list
- add an entry to a global array `USERFUNC` to describe the new function
- add the function code to `Ufunc.c`
- re-link SQR using the supplied `make` file
- test your new function.

18.7.3 Adding a function prototype

In order to add a function prototype to `Ufunc.c`, we will be using the `CC_ARGS` macro that makes your code portable between different compilers. This is how it is done:

```
static void showashex CC_ARGS((int, char *[], char *, int));
```

This line will be added to already defined prototypes in `Ufunc.c`:

```
//Adding a function prototype
static void max          CC_ARGS((int, double *[], double *));
static void split        CC_ARGS((int, char *[], double *));
static void printarray   CC_ARGS((int, char*[], double *));
static void showashex    CC_ARGS((int, char *[], char *, int));
                         /* new function prototype */
...
```

As you can see, our function prototype is somewhat different from the three function prototypes. The reason is that there is a difference in passing parameters to functions that have string output (string functions) and functions that have numeric output (numeric functions). You have to adhere to the following rules:

String functions must include:

- the number of arguments (`int`)
- an array of argument pointers to either `char[]` or `double (char *)`, or `(double *)`
- the address of the result `string (char *)`
- the maximum length of the result string, in bytes (`int`).

Numeric functions must include:

- the number of arguments (int)
- an array of argument pointers to either `char[]` or `double` `(char *)` or `(double *)`
- the address of the result numeric value `(double *)`.

As you can see from the description, the difference between the numeric and string functions, is that string functions have one additional argument: the maximum length of the result string. This argument prevents memory corruption by limiting the length of the output string. Another difference between string and numeric functions is that string functions return a character pointer address of the result string, whereas numeric functions return a double pointer to the address of the resulting numeric value.

18.7.4 Adding an entry to the USERFUNCS array

In order to describe our function, we need to add an entry to an array of structures in `Ufunc.c`. The name of the array is `USERFUNCS`. Each array structure contains five entries for every function. We will add a structure for our new function and then explain each structure element.

The following is the `USERFUNCS` array in `Ufunc.c` after the addition of the new function:

```
//The USERFUNCS array
userfuncs[] =
{
"max",          'n',      0,   "n",     PVR max,
"split",        'n',      0,   "C",     PVR split,
"printarray",   'n',      4,   "cnnc",  PVR printarray,
"showashex",    'c',      1,   "c",     PVR showashex,
/* Last entry must be NULL—do not change */
 "",       '\0',      0,    "", 0
 };
```

Let's discuss each element in the array's structure:

The first element is the name of a user-defined SQR function. This is the name that will be used in the `Let`, `If` and `While` commands in the SQR program. The name must be in the lower case. Our function name will be `showashex`. Note that in SQR you will be able to code it in any case.

The second element is the function's return type: `'n'` = numeric, `'c'` = character. Our function will return a string; therefore the entry indicates `'c'`.

The third element specifies the number of input arguments. If a function has a variable number of arguments, set this element to `0`. Our function accepts `1` argument: the input string.

The fourth element is a string that specifies the input argument types. Since our function accepts string arguments, this element must be coded `"c"`. Please note that the order in which argument types are specified is important: first, you specify the type of the first argument, then the type of the second argument, and so on.

The fifth element is a pointer to the C function. We are using the PVR macro that provides the proper cast for the pointer. For our function, the entry is `PVR showashex`. This entry refers to the function prototype that we defined in the first step.

18.7.5 Adding your C function to Ufunc.c

The next step is to add your C function source code to `Ufunc.c`. Make sure the function is unit-tested outside of Ufunc.c, and then simply add the code of your function to `Ufunc.c`. Note that the `CC_ARGL`, `CC_ARG`, and `CC_LARG` macros are used to make our code portable.

18.7.6 Re-linking SQR and testing your new function

Since we have modified the `Ufunc.c` file, we have to recompile this file and re-link it with SQR. SQR provides the `make` file that contains both the compilation and the linkage steps. The `make` file is located in the `LIB` (UNIX) or `LIBW` (Windows) sub-directory of SQR.

After the program is compiled and linked successfully, let's test our new function. We can create the following simple test program for this purpose:

```
!Testing the new user-defined function called from SQR
Begin-Program
Let $InString = 'ABCD &^$#@!!(),.;'
Let $HexString = ShowAsHex($InSring)
Show 'Input string = ' $InString
Show 'Hex   string = ' $HexString
End-Program
```

Figure 18.1 shows the program run log.

18.7.7 Adding user-defined functions in Windows NT

The process of adding a user-defined function in Windows NT is similar to that in Windows and UNIX. When integrating the new function with SQR under Windows NT, you need to use the `Extufunc.c` file instead of `Ufunc.c`. Although all basic steps are the same as described earlier, there are some specifics. For example, you will need to

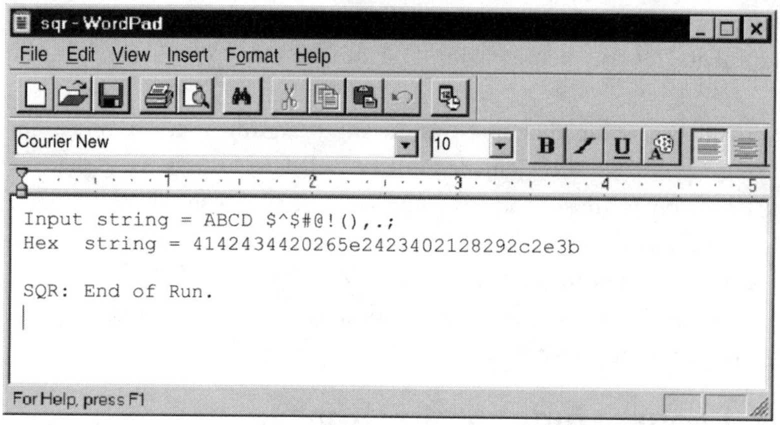

Figure 18.1 The new user-defined function test log

use different functions and different DLL files. Please refer to the `Extufunc.c` file for more information. In the beginning of this file, there are extensive comments and directions. The name of the SQR-provided `make` file under Windows NT is `SQREXT.MAK`. This file is used to compile and link your new function with `SQREXT.DLL`.

18.8 Generating a Word document

Generating Word documents from SQR is a fairly popular task. In this subchapter, we will generate PIN numbers that employees will use to access their HR records via a self-service application. Our program will generate a letter in Word to each employee informing the employee about his/her new PIN number.

We will need three main components: a Word file with the letter template, another Word file containing a macro that will carry out the mail merge and printing functions, and our SQR program.

Let's start with the template. This is the letter that we are going to send each employee (we will name it `Tmp18C.DOC`):

Welcome to the ABCD Employee Self Service Center.

In order to keep your personal information secure when accessing the telephone or online system, you will be required to enter your Employee ID and Personal Identification Number (PIN). Your PIN is provided below:

Your PIN: «Pin»

After you access the system for the first time, you will need to change your PIN to one of your choice. You will be prompted to enter a new four-digit PIN. Please be sure to make it something not known to other people.

«Name»
«Address1»
«Address2»
«City», «State» «Zip»

In our template letter named `Tmp18C.DOC`, we inserted seven MAILMERGE fields that will be populated with the employee PIN number, employee name, and various parts of the employee address.

The second component is the Word macro:

```
Sub TEST18CM()
'
' TEST18CM Macro
'
Dim DirOut$
Dim DirDoc$
Dim OutFiles$
Dim DocFile$
Dim filenm$
Dim DataFiles$
Rem ==============================================
Rem Employee PIN Notification Letter
Rem ==============================================
DirOut$ = "c:\sqrbook\output"
DirDoc$ = "c:\sqrbook\examples"
OutFiles$ = DirOut$ + "\TEST18C*.*"
DocFile$ = "\TEST18C.doc"
WordBasic.ChDir DirOut$
filenm$ = DirDoc$ + DocFile$
WordBasic.FileOpen Name:=filenm$, ReadOnly:=0
DataFiles$ = DirOut$ + "\TEST18c.lis"
WordBasic.MailMergeOpenDataSource Name:=DataFiles$, ReadOnly:=0
WordBasic.MailMerge MergeRecords:=0, Destination:=0, MailMerge:=1

Rem Print the document
Rem WordBasic.FilePrintDefault

Rem Set cursor to top field
WordBasic.StartOfDocument

DataFiles$ = DirOut$ + "\EmplPIN.doc"
WordBasic.FileSaveAs Name:=DataFiles$, Format:=0, LockAnnot:=0,
Password:="", AddToMru:=1, WritePassword:="", RecommendReadOnly:=0,
EmbedFonts:=0, NativePictureFormat:=0, FormsData:=0,
SaveAsAOCELetter:=0
```

```
On Error Resume Next

End Sub
```

This macro reads the in `Test18C.LIS` file that will be generated by our SQR program, and, for each employee, populates the mail merge fields in the template (PIN number, employee name, and employee address) from `Test18C.LIS` and generates the PIN notification letter, then, after the entire file of letters is complete, prints the complete file and closes the file and the Word template document.

Therefore, the main task of our SQR program is to generate the right `Test18C.LIS` file with PIN, employee name, and employee address for each employee and to invoke the Word executable.

This is our SQR program:

```
!TEST18C.SQR
!Calling Word from SQR
!***************************
Begin-Setup
!***************************
Declare-Layout Default
Formfeed=No
Max-Lines=1
Max-Columns=150
Left-Margin=0
Top-Margin=0
End-Declare
End-Setup
!***************************
Begin-Program
!***************************
  Let #Seed = 1
  Do Process_Main

  If #Record_Count > 0
    ! Close the current report by opening dummy report
    New-Report 'dummy.lis'
    Do Invoke_Word
  End-If
End-Program

!*****************************************
Begin-Procedure Process-Main
!*****************************************
  Do Write_Heading
  Do Extract_Data
End-Procedure

!*****************************************
Begin-Procedure Write_Heading
```

```
!****************************************
! Write Word Mail Merge Column Headings

  Let $Ioarea = 'Pin,Name,Address1,Address2,'
  Let $Ioarea = $Ioarea || 'City,State,Zip,End'
  Print $Ioarea (1,1)
  New-Page

End-Procedure

!*******************************************
! Get employee data
!*******************************************
Begin-Procedure Extract_Data

Begin-Select

P.Name
P.Address1
P.Address2
P.City
P.State
P.Postal

  Let $Name     = &P.Name
  Let $Address1 = &P.Address1
  Let $Address2 = &P.Address2
  Let $City     = &P.City
  Let $State    = &P.State
  Let $Zip      = &P.Postal
  Do Generate_Pin ! Generate random PIN, move to $Pin
  Add 1 to #Record_Count
  Do Print_Data

From Job A,
     Personal_Data P
     Where A.Emplid        = P.Emplid
       And A.EMPL_Rcd      = 0
       And A.EFFDT = (Select Max(Effdt)
         From  Job
             Where Emplid = A.Emplid
             And Empl_Rcd = A.Empl_Rcd
              And Effdt    <= Sysdate)
      And A.Effseq = (Select Max(Effseq)
                     From  Job
                      Where Emplid    = A.Emplid
                      And   Empl_Rcd = A.Empl_Rcd
                      And   Effdt    = A.Effdt)
      And A.Action In ('HIR', 'REH')
      And A.Action_Dt = Sysdate
      And A.Empl_Status = 'A'
Order by P.Name
```

```
End-Select
End-Procedure

!*******************************************
Begin-Procedure Generate_Pin
!*******************************************
  Let #Next_Pin = (#Seed * 1103515245) + 12345
  Let #Next_Pin = #Next_Pin / 65536
  Let #Next_Pin = mod(#Next_Pin, 32768)
  Let $Pin      = edit(#Next_Pin,'9999')
  Let #Seed     = #Seed + 1
End-Procedure

!*******************************************
Begin-Procedure Print_Data
!*******************************************
  Print '"'            (+1,1)
  Print $PIN           ()
  Print '","'          ()
  Print $Name          ()
  Print '","'          ()
  Print $Address1      ()
  Print '","'          ()
  Print $Address2      ()
  Print '","'          ()
  Print $City          ()
  Print '","'          ()
  Print $State         ()
  Print '","'          ()
  Print $Zip           ()
  Print '","'          ()
  Print 'END'          ()
  Print '"'            ()
  New-Page

End-Procedure
!*******************************************
Begin-Procedure Invoke_Word
!*******************************************
! Run Winword to Create the Form in Word
 Let $WinWord='c:\Progra~1\Micros~3\office\winword.exe
            || 'c:\sqrbook\examples\TEST18C.doc
            || /mTEST18CM'
 Show 'winword=' $winword
 Call System Using $WinWord #Dos_Status
 Show 'Return code from Word = ' #Dos_Status
End-Procedure
!**************************************************************
```

In `Test18C`, we start with writing the mail merge headings to the output file. This will be the first record in the file. Next, we select the most current employee name and address information for each employee from the database. These data are used to populate the pertinent mail merge data fields in the output record for each employee. In addition, the `Generate_Pin` procedure is used to generate a pseudo-random PIN number for each employee.

As you can see, we use a combination of the `Print` and `New-Page` commands in place of the `Write` command to generate the output file. After the program's output `LIS` file has been created, we use the `New-Report` command to close this file so that SQR could release the file before the program's completion. Then the `Invoke_Word` procedure calls the Word executable and passes the name of a Word file that stores the mail merge macro and the name of the macro itself. The macro, in turn, reads in the output of our program (`Test18C.LIS`) and generates the PIN notification letters using the Word template named `Text18C.DOC`.

As the result, our program will generate an output Word document partially shown here:

Welcome to the ABCD Employee Self Service Center.

In order to keep your personal information secure when accessing the telephone or online system, you will be required to enter your Employee ID and Personal Identification Number (PIN). Your PIN is provided below:

Your PIN: 00909

After you access the system for the first time, you will need to change your PIN to one of your choice. You will be prompted to enter a new four-digit PIN. Please be sure to make it something not known to many people.

Adams, Cynthia
812 Central Avenue

Great Falls, MT 59405

Welcome to the ABCD Employee Self-Service Center.

In order to keep your personal information secure when accessing the telephone or online system, you will be required to enter your Employee ID and Personal Identification Number (PIN). Your PIN is provided below:

Your PIN: 17747

After you access the system for the first time, you will need to change your PIN to one of your choice. You will be prompted to enter a new four-digit PIN. Please be sure to make it something not known to many people.

Aliverdi, Reza
201-7421 Fullerton St

Syracuse, NY 132052011

After this document is generated, the macro automatically prints and saves the document in `EmplPIN.doc`.

KEY POINTS

1. You can execute an SQR program from a command line, start this program from the SQRW Dialog Box in the Windows environment, or call the program from other programs.
2. SQR allows you to change its default behavior by using its command line flags. SQR command line flags always start with a dash (-). Some flags may have additional arguments. In this case, the arguments must follow their respective flags immediately with no intervening spaces.
3. When flag arguments specify file directories, they must be ended with the operating system-specific directory character. For Windows, it is a backslash; for UNIX, a forward slash.
4. SQR command line arguments are the values that your SQR program expects to receive from the command line via the `Ask` command at compile time or the `Input` command at run time.
5. You can use an argument file to pass arguments to your program on the command line. Each argument must be entered in the argument file on a separate line.
6. SQR processes the program in two stages: the compilation stage and the actual program execution. You can use the `-RS` command flag to create a pre-compiled version of your program (with the `.sqt` extension). You can execute a pre-compiled version of an SQR program by specifying the `-RT` command flag or using the `SQR Execute`.

KEY POINTS (CONTINUED)

7 You can issue any operating system command within your SQR program. The `Call System Using` command is used to execute the operating system commands.

8 In addition to issuing the operating system commands, the `Call System Using` command can be used to invoke any executable program.

9 In order to call SQR programs from other applications, you can use `SQR API`.

10 SQR programs can be scheduled for execution from `PeopleCode`.

11 You can extend the SQR built-in functions spectrum by writing your own functions in "C" or "C++".

C H A P T E R 1 9

Internet enabling

IN THIS CHAPTER

- The three ways to generate HTML from an SQR program output
- HTML procedures
- Controlling the output positioning in Internet-enabled SQR programs
- Formatting the HTML output
- Hypertext links and hypertext link anchors
- Accepting arguments from the Internet environment

In this chapter you will learn how to convert existing SQR reports into the HTML compatible format and how to write SQR programs specifically designed to generate Internet reports or Web pages. Please keep in mind that our book is not about the Internet or HTML, we just touch some Internet topics related to SQR program Internet enabling. For any kind of comprehensive coverage of the Internet, please refer to the special books on this subject.

19.1 SQR and the Internet

One of the new features in SQR version 4 is Internet enabling. You can generate program reports in an HTML compatible format and publish these reports on the Internet or an intranet. You can place hypertext links in your report, thus allowing the report viewers to switch from place to place within the report, or to jump to another report, or, even, to a different website. Alternatively, you can create hypertext link anchors in key places inside your report so that other web pages will be able to include pointers to these specific portions in the report.

For example, you can include hypertext links and link anchors in two related reports. This way, the viewers will be able to jump back and forth between the two reports and better understand the relationships between the report data.

There are three methods of generating HTML output from an SQR program. Each method requires a different programming effort—from very minimal effort, involving no program source changes, to rather substantial program code modifications. And, of course, different efforts bring different results. The more changes you make to your program the better functionality you'll receive.

Not all SQR features are presently supported by the Internet conversion. The following graphical features cannot be converted to HTML:

- font selection
- bar codes
- lines and boxes
- charts and graphs.

19.2 No program code changes

Too good to be true? Actually, if your goal is just to publish an SQR-generated report on the Internet or an Intranet without any changes or special features, you do not need to touch a single line in your program! All you have to do is to run the program using the SQR command flag `-PRINTER:HT`. SQR will automatically convert the program output into the HTML format and will take care of positioning, HTML tags, font and letter size mapping, and so on.

Another alternative involving a very minimal program change is to use the `Declare-Printer` command with the argument `Type=HT` or the `Use-Printer-Type HT` command.

When you use this technique, the program output is positioned on the web page according to the position coordinates specified in the `Print` or similar native SQR commands. The text is displayed using a fixed-width font such as Courier even if your program uses a different font. If your program code includes special characters that are used by HTML, such as < or >, the characters are converted into the corresponding HTML sequences.

When converting your program output to HTML, SQR will create the same number of HTML pages as that for the regular SQR output: the pages will be generated automatically, based on the report layout page length or according to the SQR page control commands used.

When you use the `-Printer:HT` command line flag, SQR automatically generates the following three output files: an HTML frame file, a report body file, and a table of contents file. The file names are generated as follows:

The frame file name is your program name post-fixed with `_frm`; the table of contents file name is your program name post-fixed with `_toc`; the report body file name is your program name. The extensions to all three files are set to `.htm`. What if your program has more than one output report? In that case, SQR will generate three more files for each additional report and will insert `_01`, `_02`, and so on, into the file names of each file triplet. You can override the file names using the `-F` SQR command line flag.

After the output files have been generated, you need to use the `FTP` utility, or a similar file transfer tool, to move these files to the appropriate web server directory. If users will be linked to your report from an HTML index file or from another web page, the links should be pointing to the frame file.

The frame file displays the report in the following `HTML FRAMESET` format: the left frame shows pointers to all the report pages, whereas the right frame shows the report body with pointers to the first, previous, next, and last report pages displayed on the top of the report. You can point the cursor to any page pointer and the web browser will bring you to the selected report page. You can also scroll down the report using the browser's scroll-down control. Your web browser must support the `FRAMESET` format. (Most browser products, including both the Netscape Navigator and the Microsoft Internet Explorer, support this format.)

Let's take one of the programs created in chapter 13, `Test13A.sqr`, and run this program with the `-Printer:HT` SQR command line flag to produce an HTML output (figure 19.1).

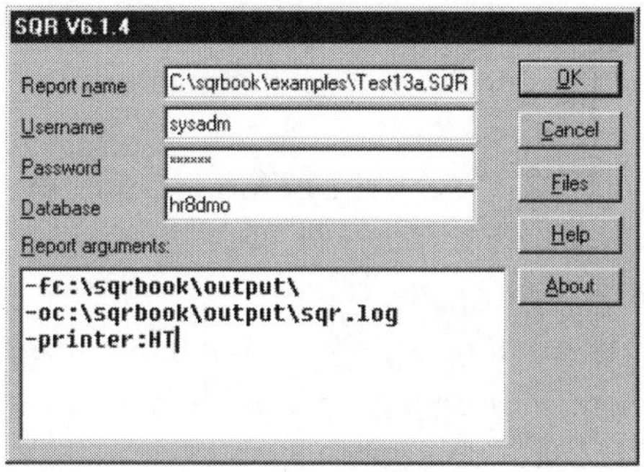

Figure 19.1 Submitting an SQR program to generate HTML output

Because the `Test13A.sqr` program produces two output reports, it will generate the following six output files: `Test13A.htm`, `Test13A_frm.htm`, `Test13A_toc.htm`, `Test13A_01.htm`, `Test13A_01_frm.htm`, and `Test13A_01_toc.htm`.

The `Test13A.htm` file is an HTML body file; the `Test13A_frm.htm` is an HTML frame file; and `Test13A_toc.htm` file is an HTML table of contents file for the first `Test13A.sqr` report. Figure 19.2 shows how the `Test13A_frm.htm` file is viewed on a web page. Because the program output report includes multiple pages, SQR automatically generates pointers to every report page and places these pointers in the left frame of the report. The report body is placed in the right frame of the report.

Similarly, the other file triplet: `Test13A_01.htm`, `Test13A_01_frm.htm`, and `Test13A_01_toc.htm` belongs to the second program report.

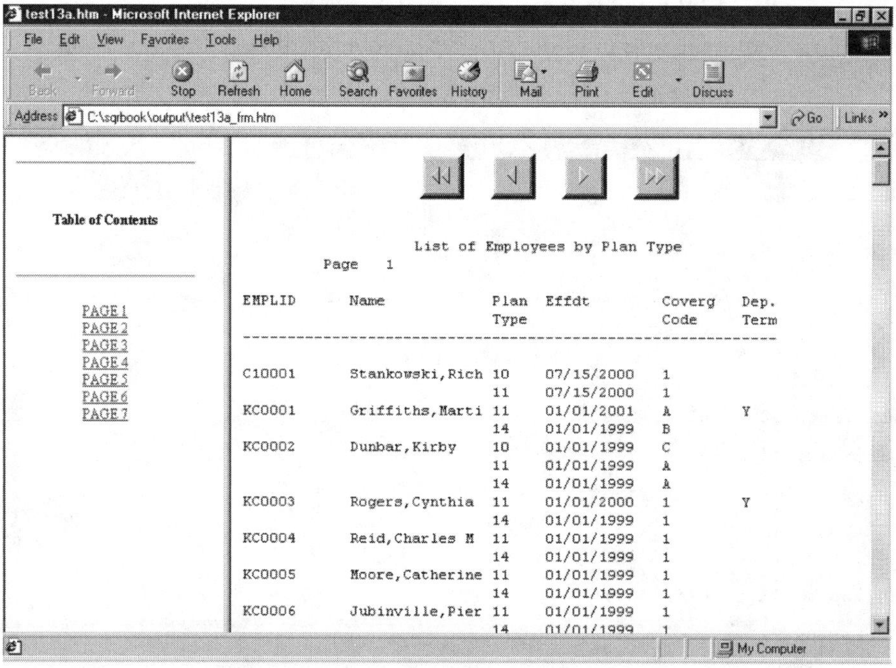

Figure 19.2 Viewing an SQR-generated HTML frame output via a web browser.

As you can see, SQR uses a standard design to build the table of contents frame automatically. If you do not like this design, use the `Declare-Toc` command (introduced in version 4.2) to build your own table of contents.

If your browser does not support the HTML `FRAMESET` format use the `Test13A.htm` file instead of that in `Test13A_frm.htm`. You will not see the page pointers, but the browser will still display the entire report body.

Starting with version 4.3.1, you can use another SQR command flag, `-PRINTER:EH`, to generate HTML output without making any changes to your program. This flag allows you to generate enhanced HTML 3 output.

The enhanced HTML output flag can also be used in conjunction with a number of new features available starting from version 4.3.2. You can have SQR generate a CSV file or a PDF file, specify the directories where an HTML browser should look for the referenced icons or images, set the language for the HTML navigation bar, move or copy the program output to a Zip file, define a scaling factor for your HTML output, and so on. For the complete description of all SQR command flags please see appendix B.

Let's run the `Test13A.sqr` program with the following SQR flags: `-PRINTER:EH`, `EH_PDF`, `EH_CSV`, `EH_BQD`. We are hereby requesting SQR to generate enhanced HTML output and place the three icons on the top of the report: an Adobe PDF icon, an Excel CSV icon, and a Brio BQD (Brio Query Format File) icon.

Figure 19.3 shows the output of our program. Note the three icons on the top.

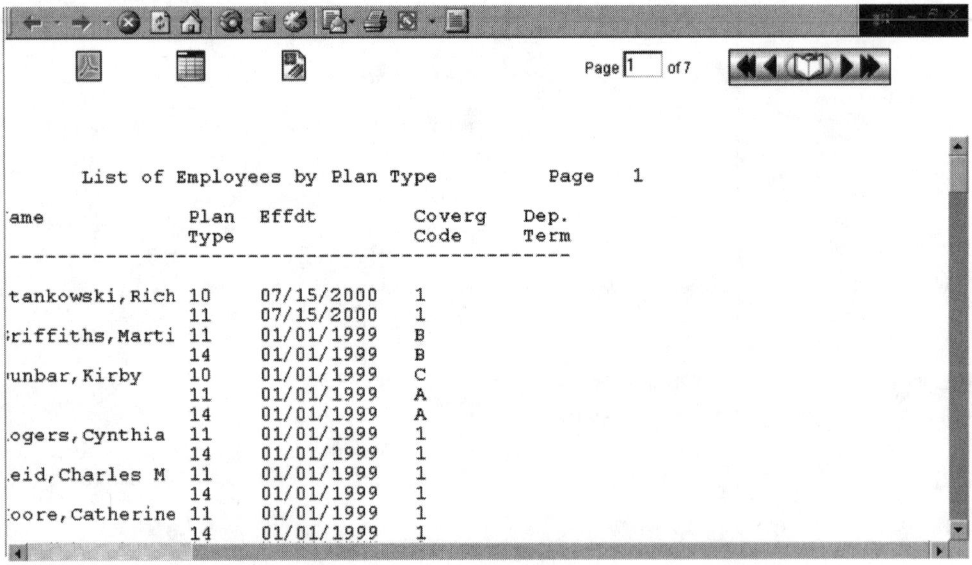

Figure 19.3 Using the –PRINTER:EH flag to generate enhanced HTML output

19.3 Using a table of contents

Strictly speaking, tables of contents are not just features of HTML-enabled reports. SQR allows you to generate a table of contents for any report. For example, you can generate a table of contents for a PDF-formatted report, for an SPF report or for a regular LIS report.

But with an HTML-enabled report, you can take advantage of the hypertext links that SQR places in a table of contents. These links help report viewers with navigating between different portions of their reports.

SQR automatically generates a rudimentary table of contents for any HTML-enabled report by dividing the report into pages (see figure 19.2.). You can use a combination of the `Declare-Toc` and `Toc-Entry` commands to divide your report into logical portions and build a symbolic table of contents for the report based on the report specifics. Depending on the report structure, you can build rather complex tables of contents with various levels of chapters and subchapters.

In order to demonstrate full capabilities of this feature, we need an SQR program that generates output with multiple levels of data so that we would be able to build a table of contents with multiple levels. Let's employ the `Test10C.sqr` program used in chapter 10 to generate a list of employees by company and paygroup. In chapter 10, we used this program to create breaks in the program output at two levels: level 1 breaks by company and level 2 breaks by paygroup within the same company. Now, we will modify it to build a table of contents with company names as chapters and paygroup codes as subchapters.

This is the modified program renamed as `Test19A.sqr`:

```
! TEST19A.SQR
! Using Table of Contents
!****************************

Begin-Setup

  Declare-Report Report19A
  End-Declare

  Declare-Toc Test19A
    For-Reports = (Report19A)
    Before-Toc=Print_Toc_Header
  End-Declare

End-Setup

Begin-Program
!****************************
     Show 'Program Started'
     Do List_Employees
```

```
End-Program

!****************************
Begin-Heading 3
!****************************
     Print 'List of Employees by Company, Paygroup' (1,1)
     Print 'Page'            (,+3)
     Print #page-count       (,+1) edit 999
     Print Company'          (+1,1)
     Print  'Paygroup'       (,+2)
     Print  'Emplid'         (,+2)
     Print  'Name '          (,+4)
     Print  'Annual Salary' (,+15)
     Print  '                (+1,1)
End-Heading

!***********************************
Begin-Procedure Print_Toc_Header
!***********************************
  Position (+1,1)
  Print 'Employees by Company, Paygroup' () Bold
  Position (+1,1)
End-Procedure
!********************************
Begin-Procedure List_Employees
!********************************
Begin-Select
  Add 1 to #Row_Num
  Show 'Selected row# ' #Row_Num ' Comp=' &B.Company  ' Paygrp='
      &B.Paygroup
B.Company   (,1,7)  On-Break Level = 1 Before=Company_Name
            After=Company_Totals Skiplines = 1
B.Paygroup(,10,8) On-Break Level = 2 Before=Paygroup_Group_Code
            After=Paygroup_Totals
A.Emplid(,+2,8)
A.Name(,+2,18)
B.Annual_Rt(,+1,13) edit $$,$$$,$$$.00
  Position(+1)

    Let #EE_Paygroup_Total= #EE_Paygroup_Total + 1
  Let #Sal_Paygroup_Total= #Sal_Paygroup_Total + &B.Annual_Rt
From Personal_Data A, Job B
Where A.Emplid=B.Emplid
And B.Effdt=(Select Max(D.Effdt) From Job D
   Where D.Effdt<=Sysdate
   And D.Emplid=B.Emplid
   And D.Empl_Rcd=B.Empl_Rcd)

And B.Effseq = (Select Max(C.Effseq) From Job C
   Where C.Emplid=B.Emplid
                  And C.Empl_Rcd = B.Empl_Rcd
   And C.Effdt=B.Effdt)
```

```
Order By B.Company, B.Paygroup, A.Emplid
End-Select
End-Procedure

!************************************
Begin-Procedure Company_Name
!************************************
Show 'Before Procedure Company_Name is invoked'

Begin-Select
C1.Descr
   Print 'Company Name: ' (+1,1)
   Print &C1.Descr (,+2)
   Position (+1)
From Company_Tbl C1
Where C1.Company = &B.Company
And C1.Effdt = (Select Max(Effdt) From Company_TBL
                Where Company = C1.Company)
End-Select

Move &C1.Descr To $Company_Name
Let $Toc_Caption='Company: '||$Company_Name
Toc-Entry Text=$Toc_Caption Level = 1

End-Procedure

!************************************
Begin-Procedure Paygroup_Group_Code
!************************************
Show 'Procedure Paygroup_Group_Code is invoked'
Move &B.Paygroup To $Paygroup
Let $Toc_Caption='Paygroup: '||$Paygroup
Toc-Entry Text=$Toc_Caption Level = 2
End-Procedure

!************************************
Begin-Procedure Company_Totals
!************************************
Show 'After Procedure Company_Totals is invoked'
Print 'Number of Employees in Company = ' (+1,5)
Print  #EE_Company_Total () edit 999999
Print 'Total Annual Salary Paid for Company = ' (+1,5)
Print  #Sal_Company_Total () edit $,$$$,$$$,$$$.00

Let  #EE_Company_Total = 0
Let  #Sal_Company_Total = 0

End-Procedure

!************************************
Begin-Procedure Paygroup_Totals
!************************************
```

```
Show 'After Procedure Paygroup_Totals is invoked'
Print 'Number of Employees in Paygroup = ' (+1,5)
Print   #EE_Paygroup_Total () edit 999999
Print 'Total Annual Salary Paid for Paygroup = ' (+1,5)
Print  #Sal_Paygroup_Total () edit $,$$$,$$$,$$$.00
Position (+1)

Let  #EE_Company_Total = #EE_Company_Total + #EE_Paygroup_Total
Let  #Sal_Company_Total = #Sal_Company_Total +  #Sal_Paygroup_Total

Let #EE_Paygroup_Total = 0
Let #Sal_Paygroup_Total = 0

End-Procedure
!********************************
```

In `Test19A.sqr` we made the following modifications:

- added the `Declare-Toc` command in the `Setup` section
- added the `Toc-Entry` command in the `Company_Name` section to generate level 1 table of contents entries
- added another `Toc-Entry` command in the `Paygroup_Group_Code` section to generate level 2 table of contents entries.

The `Declare-Toc` command defines the look of the table of contents, relates program reports to the table of contents, and allows you to specify procedures that will be called before and after generating the table of contents, before and after generating every page, or before generating each entry of the table of contents. For a single-report program, you need only one `Declare-Toc` command. For a multiple-report program, you may still use one `Declare-Toc` command if the look and structure of the table of contents can be same for all reports or you may specify separate tables of contents for each report or for the groups of reports.

In our case, we use the `Before-Toc` operand of the `Declare-Toc` command to specify a name of the procedure that will be invoked before generating the table of contents. We use this procedure to print a title for our table of contents. It is really a "nice to have" feature: SQR would have generated the table of contents without the `Before-Toc` operand, but a table of contents with a title looks more professional, plus this is a good chance to demonstrate how to use this operand.

The `Toc-Entry` command makes SQR generate an entry in the table of contents. The `Text` argument of this command defines the exact content of this entry. SQR generates each table of contents entry automatically at the level specified and takes care of indentation, inserting the proper HTML hypertext link, building the hierarchy, tree and so on.

If you want to build your table of contents entries yourself, you can use the `Entry` argument of the `Declare-Toc` command. This argument specifies the name of a procedure that is invoked to process each entry of the table of contents. SQR passes the text of each entry (generated by the `Toc-Entry` command) in the `$SQR-Toc-Text` reserved variable. SQR also passes the level of entry in the `#SQR-Toc-Text` reserved variable and the current page number in the `#SQR-Toc-Page` reserved variable. In most cases, you do not need to use this argument: you can trust SQR with generating table of contents entries.

Figure 19.4 shows the HTML output of `Test19A.sqr`.

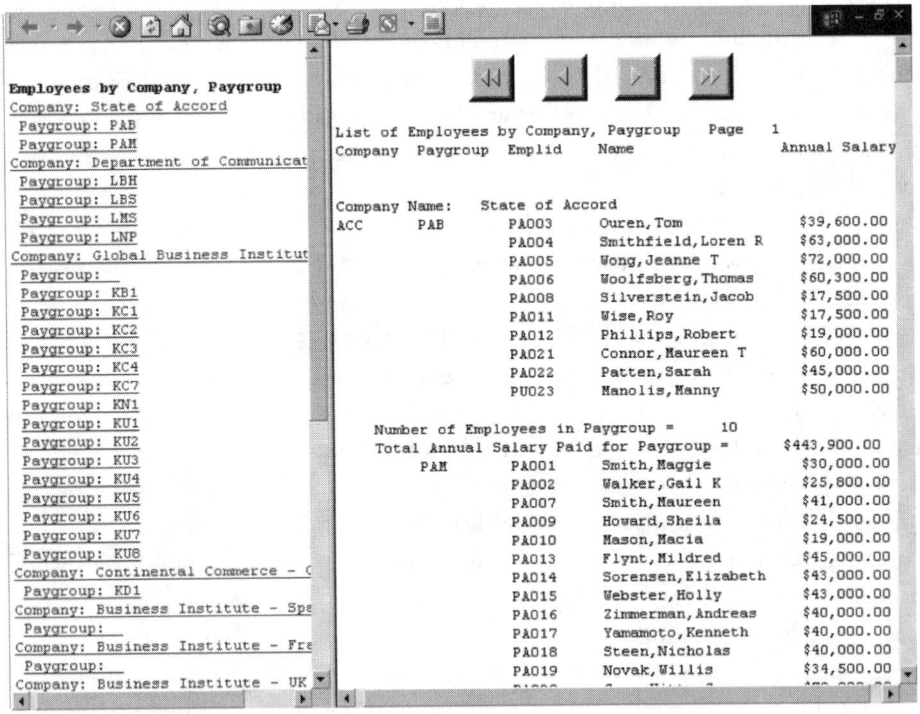

Figure 19.4 Using table of contents

19.4 Bursting your HTML output

When you generate output without using the bursting option, SQR creates the report body as one HTML file. When viewing the report via an HTML browser, the entire report body is loaded into the memory. To speed the process of loading and opening of large reports, SQR allows you to divide the report body into pages or other logical pieces. This way, your users will be able to preview the report's table of contents without opening the entire report. By clicking on specific pages or other entries in the table of contents, they will cause the loading of only selected pieces of the report.

Generating your report by pieces is called *bursting*. When using this option, you can divide the entire report into many pieces and have SQR generate only the pieces you need. You can divide your report into physical pages and have SQR generate only certain pages or page ranges (this option is called *demand paging*). Another option is to use the `Declare-Toc` command to generate the report's table of contents and burst your report on a desired level: generate only table of contents, table of contents and level 1 entries, table of contents and level 2 entries, and so on.

To use report bursting, you need to use two SQR command flags: `-PRINTER:HT` (or `-PRINTER:EH`) and `-BURST`. The arguments of the `-BURST` flag control the level of bursting. For example, you can ask SQR to generate pages 1, 2, 10, 11, and 12 by specifying `-BURST:P1,1,2,10-12`. The first argument of the `-BURST` flag (`P`) denotes how many changes each HTML output file will have, the second argument lists the page numbers to be generated.

Another option that can be used only if your report has a table of contents is to have SQR generate only the table of contents by using `-BURST:T` or the table of contents and report entries at the desired level by using `-BURST:Si` where `i` is the level number.

Let's run `Test19A.sqr` with the `-PRINTER:HT` and `-BURST:P2,1-6` flags. This means that SQR will generate only first six pages of the report and split the output into three files containing two pages each. Figure 19.5 shows the output in this case. You can see that although SQR generated the entire table of contents for the report, only entries representing pages from 1 to 6 have hypertext links to the report body (these entries are underlined). The report body frame shows only the first two pages of the report. To see the remaining pages, you have to use the page controls on the top. The output directory will have three report body files, `test19A_1.HTM`, `test19A_2.HTM`, and `test19A_3.HTM`, each file will be two pages long.

Let's run the `Test19A.sqr` program with the `-PRINTER:HT` and `-BURST:S1` flags. This will make SQR generate a table of contents file and split the report body into separate HTML files with each file containing only data for a specific company. The program output will look like that shown in figure 19.6. Please note that when you open the report, SQR loads only the report's table of contents and the first report body file. When you click on some entry in the table of contents, only this portion of the report body is loaded into the memory by the browser. Also note that all table of contents entries have links to all parts of the report body because with this option, we do not limit the size of the report body.

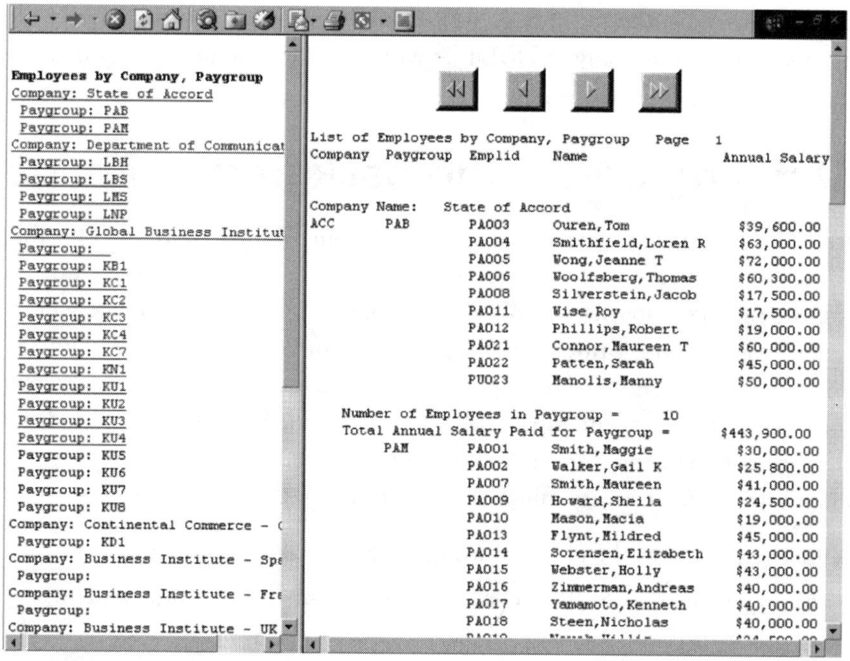

Figure 19.5 Using demand paging

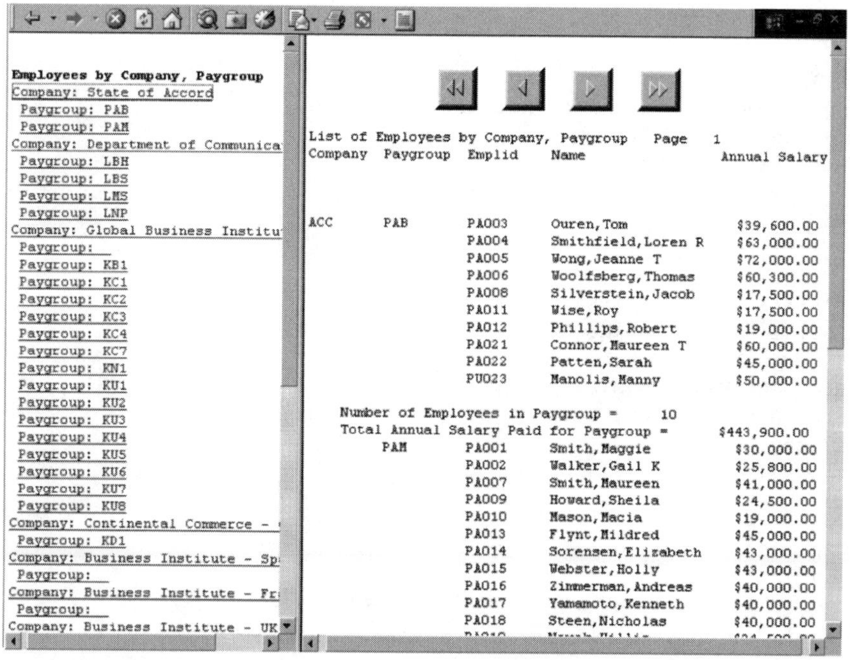

Figure 19.6 Bursting the Test19A.sqr program output on the company level

If we were to use the `-BURST:S2` flag, SQR would generate a table of contents file and split the report body into many HTML files with each file containing only data for a specific paygroup.

19.5 Defining a title and background image

Now we are going to make a few improvements to our HTML output. The first improvement will be a visual one: we are going to define a background for the report to make it better fit the rich Internet graphical environment. The second change will be more important: we will add a title to the report. Do not confuse this title with the report header. In some browsers, the title appears in the title bar of the browser window; in others, the title is centered at the top of the screen. The title is used in search indexes as well as in the browser's history lists and bookmarks.

Both improvements require very minimal program changes. All you will have to do is:

- add the `Html.inc` file to the program using the `#Include` command
- invoke the following two SQR procedures: `Html_Set_Head_Tags` and `Html_Set_Body_Attributes`.

The procedures should be invoked at the program start using the SQR `Do` command. For example, in case of `Test13A.sqr`, the beginning and the end of the program will look like that in `Test19B.sqr`.

```
!TEST19B.SQR
!Adding webpage title and background
Begin-Setup
!***********************
  . . .
End-Setup
!**********************************
Begin-Program
!**********************************
  Let $Title = '<TITLE>ABCD Company. List of Employees by -
     Health Plan</TITLE>'
  Do Html_Set_Head_Tags($Title)
  Do Html_Set_Body_Attributes('Background="bkgrnd2.GIF"')
  Do Process_Main
End-Program
  . . .
#Include 'html.inc'
```

Note When selecting a background image for a report, avoid sharp pictures, text, or any distinct objects as parts of the image. Otherwise, they will multiply over the page and reduce the visibility of your report.

The input parameter for the `Html_Set_Head_Tags` procedure is a string that includes the title text surrounded by the `<TITLE>` and `</TITLE>` tags and, optionally, the META information about your document. The META information may contain several sections, including the keywords used by search engines, document description, rating, etc. An example of the `Html_Set_Head_Tags` procedure with the META section is:

```
Html_Set_Head_Tags('<TITLE>My Title </TITLE>
 <META NAME="keywords" CONTENT="SQR, SQL, PeopleSoft">
 <META NAME="description" CONTENT="A comprehensive guide to SQR">
 <META NAME="rating" CONTENT="General"> ')
```

The input parameter for the `Html_Set_Body_Attributes` procedure is a string that includes the name of the report background image file. You can use `GIF` or `JPEG` files for images. All image files used in your reports must be placed in the same directory with the reports. Alternatively, you can place the image files in a separate directory and specify this directory name in the `-EH_IMAGES` SQR command flag (see appendix D).

As an alternative to a background image, you can use the same procedure to specify a background color for your report, for example:

```
Html_Set_Body_Attributes('BGCOLOR=SILVER')
```

In order to convert the program output to the HTML format, you still have to run the program using the SQR command line flag `-PRINTER:HT`. SQR will use the same approach to print positioning, font and letter size mapping, special HTML character replacement, etc., as the approach used in the previous method involving no program changes. The `Test19B.sqr` program will generate the same number of output files: `Test19B.htm`, `Test19B_frm.htm`, `Test19B_toc.htm`, `Test19B_01.htm`, `Test19B_01_frm.htm`, and `Test19B_01_toc.htm`.

After adding the title and the background, the program output now will look as shown in figure 19.7.

As you can see, the specified title is displayed on the browser title bar, not on the report. The report is shown in the HTML Frameset format with pointers to the report pages shown on the left frame.

Please keep in mind that there must be one, and only one, title in each HTML document. If your program generates more than one report, each report will carry the same HTML title, but you can generate different headers for each report.

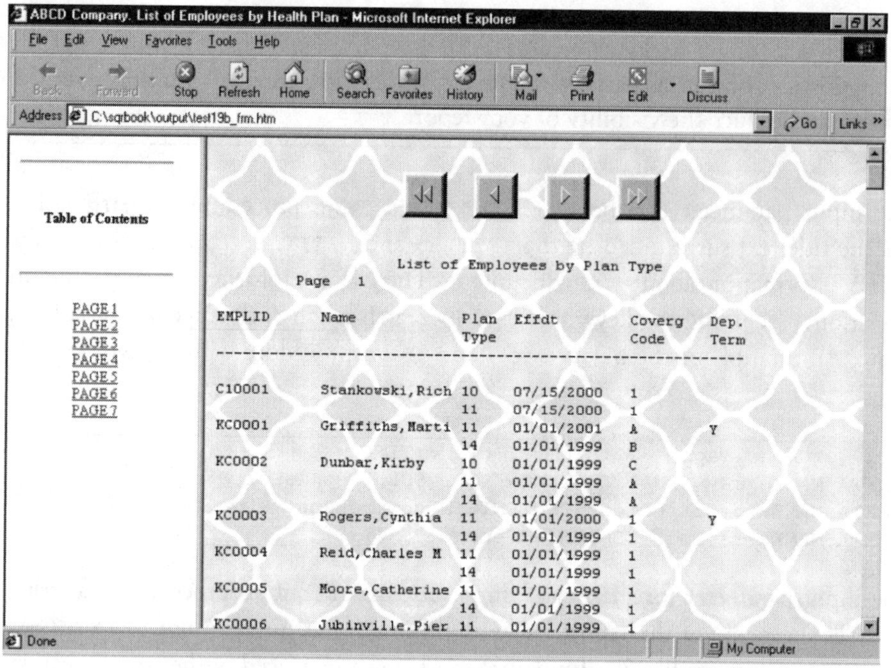

Figure 19.7 Adding a title and a background image to your report

---

Note Avoid foreign letters or special characters in the title. Use the HTML reserved names or number codes instead. For example, use `&amp` or `&#38` in place of the ampersand symbol (&). Please refer to special HTML manuals for a complete list of HTML reserved names and codes for foreign letters or special characters.

19.6 Adding more HTML features

In the previous examples, the look of our report did not change much, the only change made was adding the report background. Now we are going to add more HTML features to the report, which will enhance the report appearance and allow you to use HTML graphics and hypertext link pointers and anchors.

To add more HTML features to your program, you have to use the SQR HTML procedures. These procedures are delivered in the `Html.inc` file. Additionally, you have to run your program with the already mentioned SQR command line flag:

```
-PRINTER:HT
```

The SQR HTML procedures are turned on by calling the `Html_On` procedure in the beginning of the program. Invoking this procedure alone changes your program behavior drastically. All position qualifiers in the native SQR printing commands are ignored, and if you do not account for this, the output of your program will be messed up as in figure 19.8.

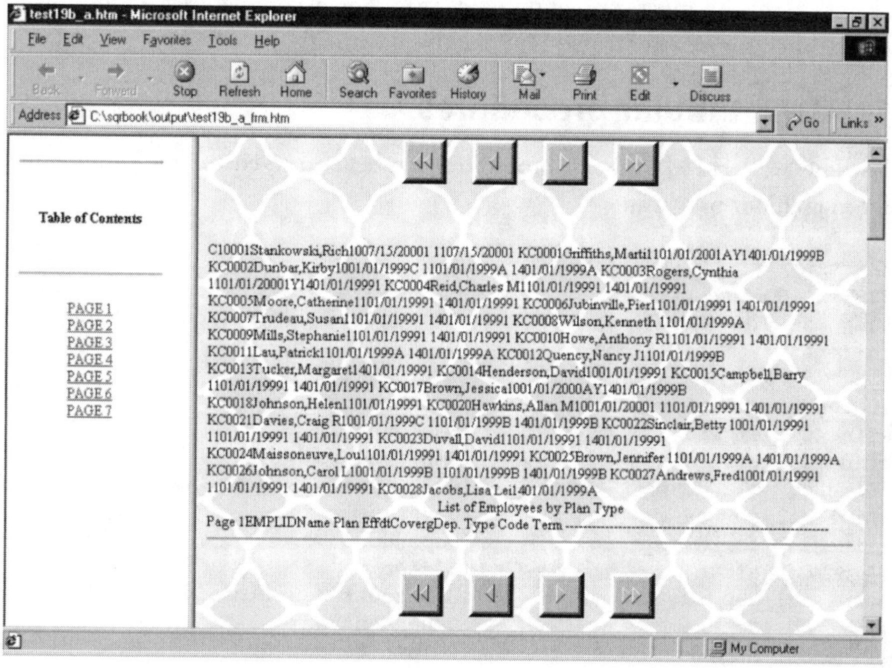

Figure 19.8 Invoking the Html_On procedure makes SQR ignore all print positioning qualifiers.

To fix the problem, you have to use the SQR HTML tabular procedures to control the field positions on your report by converting the report into an HTML table. Also, the `Max-Lines` parameter of the `Declare-Layout` command must specify a very large number of lines per page because SQR automatically inserts the page navigation hypertext links and HTML page break tags at page breaks. If this happens somewhere inside an HTML table, the output may display incorrectly.

In addition to the SQR HTML tabular procedures, a number of other HTML procedures can help in controlling the report output on the web page. These procedures fall into the following categories:

- general purpose procedures
- heading procedures

- tabular procedures
- highlighting procedures
- list procedures
- hypertext links procedures.

For obvious reasons, we will not be able to discuss all SQR HTML procedures in this book, but only the most frequently-used ones. For a complete list of the SQR HTML procedures, please refer to the SQR technical manuals.

19.6.1 HTML tabular procedures

This is how the SQR HTML tabular procedures can be used to ensure the correct output positioning in our program:

```
!*************************
! TEST19C.SQR
!Using the HTML tabular procedures to control output positioning
!*************************

!Set report column widths
#Define col_emplid         11     !Employee ID
#Define col_empl_name      20     !Employee Name
#Define col_plan_type       5     !Plan Type
#Define col_cov_cd          8     !Coverage Code
#Define col_cov_drop_flag  20     !Dependent Coverage Termination
#Define col_effdt          12     !Effective Date
#Define col_dep_id          6     !Dependent Beneficiary ID
#Define col_dep_name       15     !Dependent Name
#Define col_sep             1     !Column Separator
!***********************
Begin-Setup
!***********************
 Declare-Layout EE_Data
   Max-Lines=3000
   Left-Margin=1
 End-Declare

 Declare-Layout Term_Dependents
   Max-Lines=200
   Orientation=landscape
   Left-Margin=0.3
 End-Declare

 Declare-Report EE_Data
   Layout=EE_Data
 End-Declare

 Declare-Report Term_Dependents
   Layout=Term_Dependents
```

Specify a very large number of lines in a page to make the entire report one page.

```
 End-Declare
End-Setup

!**********************************
Begin-Program
!**********************************
   Do Html_On()
   Do Html_Set_Head_Tags('<TITLE>ABCD Company. List of -
     Employees by Health Plan</TITLE>')
   Do Html_Img(' SRC="edition.GIF" ')
   Do Html_Set_Body_Attributes('Background="bkgrnd2.GIF" ')

   Do Process_EE_Heading
   Do Process_Dep_Heading
   Do Process_Main
End-Program

!*************************************************
Begin-Procedure Process_EE_Heading
!*************************************************
  Use-Report EE_Data
  Do Html_Table('BORDER')
  Do Html_Caption(' ')
  Print 'List of Employees by Plan Type' (1) Center
  Do Html_Caption_End
  !Print 'Page'                  (,+15)
  !Print #page-count            (,+1) edit 999
  !Print ' '                     (+2,1,{col_emplid})
  Do Html_Tr(' ')
  Do Html_Th(' ')
  Print 'EMPLID'                 (+1,1,{col_emplid})
  Do Html_Th(' ')
  Print 'Name  '                 (0,+{col_sep},{col_empl_name})
  Do Html_Th(' ')
  Print 'Plan'                   (0,+{col_sep},{col_plan_type})
  Do Html_Th(' ')
  Print 'Effdt'                  (0,+{col_sep},{col_Effdt})
  Do Html_Th(' ')
  Print 'Cov Type'               (0,+{col_sep},{col_cov_cd})
  Do Html_Th(' ')
  Print  'Dep Cov Terminated'    (0,+{col_sep},{col_cov_drop_flag})
  Do Html_Th_End
  !Print '-'                     (+1,1,70)  Fill

End-Procedure
!************************************************************
Begin-Procedure Process_Dep_Heading
!************************************************************

Use-Report EE_Data

  Use-Report Term_Dependents
```

Define the report title.

Define an image ribbon and a background for the report.

Use the SQR HTML procedures to define the table characteristics.

Define the table header cells.

```
   Do Html_Table('BORDER')
   Do Html_Caption(' ')
   Print 'List of Terminated Dependents' (1) Center
   Do Html_Caption_End
   !Print 'Page'                    (,+15)
   !Print #page-count               (,+1) edit 999
   !print ' '                       (+2,1,{col_emplid})

   Do Html_Tr(' ')
   Do Html_Th(' ')
   Print 'EMPLID'                   (+1,1,{col_emplid})
   Do Html_Th(' ')
   Print 'Name  '                   (0,+{col_sep},{col_empl_name})
   Do Html_Th(' ')
   Print 'Plan_Type'                (0,+{col_sep},{col_plan_type})
   Do Html_Th(' ')
   Print 'Effdt'                    (0,+{col_sep},{col_Effdt})
   Do Html_Th(' ')
   Print 'Dep ID '                  (0,+{col_sep},{col_dep_id})
   Do Html_Th(' ')
   Print 'Dep Name'                 (0,+{col_sep},{col_dep_name})
   !Print '-'                       (+1,1,70)  Fill
End-Procedure
!***************************************
Begin-Procedure Process_Main
!***************************************
!Select and print all Employees
!who are currently covered by any Health Benefits
!and who have Family, or Empl+1 Coverage

Begin-Select
A.Emplid
A.Plan_Type
A.Effdt
A.Covrg_CD
B.Name

    Do Check_Dep_Termination
    If $Term =  'N'
        Let $Term =  ' '
    End-If
    Do Print_EE_Data

From Health_Benefit A, Personal_Data B

Where   A.Effdt  =(Select Max(Effdt) From Health_Benefit
                 Where   Emplid          =  A.Emplid
                 And     Plan_Type       =  A.Plan_Type
                 And     Effdt          <=  Sysdate)
 And    A.Coverage_Elect Not In ('T','W')
 And    A.Emplid = B.Emplid
 Order By  A.Emplid, A.Plan_Type
```

```
End-Select
End-Procedure
!**************************************************
Begin-Procedure Check_Dep_Termination
!**************************************************
! For each row retrieved in Step 1, compare between the previous
! maximum effective dated record and the current effective dated
! HEALTH_DEPENDNT row to determine a dependent that is no longer
! covered. If dropped dependents are found, print the record to a
! separate report

Move  'N' To $Term

Begin-Select
C.Emplid
C.Plan_Type
C.Effdt
D.Dependent_Benef

    Move 'Y' to $Term
    Do Print_Terminated_Dependents
    Show 'Dep Term found=' &D.Dependent_Benef '
        for Employee '&A.Emplid
 From Health_Benefit C,
      Health_Dependnt D
 Where   C.Emplid          = &A.Emplid
 And     C.Plan_Type       = &A.Plan_Type
 And     C.Emplid          = D.Emplid
 And     C.Plan_Type       = D.Plan_Type
 And     C.Effdt           = D.Effdt
 And     C.Effdt           = (Select Max(E.Effdt)
                             From Health_Benefit E
                             Where  C.Emplid    = E.Emplid
                             And    C.Plan_Type = E.Plan_Type
                             And    E.Effdt     < &A.Effdt)
 And  D.Dependent_Benef Not In
     (Select F.Dependent_Benef
       From Health_Dependnt F
       Where  C.Emplid      = F.Emplid
       And    C.Plan_Type   = F.Plan_Type
       And    F.Effdt       = &A.EFFDT)

End-Select
End-Procedure

!*******************************************
Begin-Procedure Print_EE_Data
!*******************************************
  Use-Report EE_Data
  Let $EmplID=&A.Emplid
  Let $Date_Str= Datetostr(&A.Effdt,'mm/dd/yyyy')
  Do Html_Tr(' ')
```

```
Do Html_Td(' ')
Print &A.Emplid      (+1,1,{col_emplid})
           On-Break Print= Change/Top-Page
Do Html_Td(' ')
Print &B.Name        (0,+{col_sep},{col_empl_name})
           On-Break Print=Change/Top-Page
Do Html_Td(' ')
Print &A.Plan_Type   (0,+{col_sep},{col_plan_type})
Do Html_Td(' ')
Print $Date_Str      (0,+{col_sep},{col_effdt})
Do Html_Td(' ')
Print &A.Covrg_Cd    (0,+{col_sep},{col_cov_cd})
Do Html_Td (' ')
Print $Term          (0,+{col_sep},{col_cov_drop_flag})
Do Html_Td_End
Do Html_Tr_End

 Add 1 to #Ee_Rcds

End-Procedure
!*****************************************************
Begin-Procedure Print_Terminated_Dependents
!*****************************************************
 Use-Report Term_Dependents
 Let $EmplID=&A.Emplid
 Do Get_Dependent_Name
 Let $Date_Str= Datetostr(&A.Effdt,'mm/dd/yyyy')
 Do Html_Tr(' ')
 Do Html_Td(' ')
 Print &A.Emplid              (+1,1,{col_emplid}) On-Break
                              Print=Change/Top-Page
 Do Html_Td(' ')
 Print &B.Name                (0,+{col_sep},{col_empl_name})  On-Break
                              Print=Change/Top-Page
 Do Html_Td(' ')
 Print &A.Plan_Type           (0,+{col_sep},{col_plan_type})
 Do Html_Td(' ')
 Print $Date_Str              (0,+{col_sep},{col_effdt})
 Do Html_Td(' ')
 Print &D.Dependent_Benef     (0,+{col_sep},{col_dep_id})
 Do Html_Td(' ')
 Print $DEP_NAME              (0,+{col_sep},{col_dep_name})
 Do Html_Td_End
 Do Html_Tr_End

  Add 1 to #Dep_Rcds

End-Procedure

!***********************************
Begin-Procedure Get_Dependent_Name
!***********************************
```

Define each table detail column cell.

```
Let $Dep_Name=' '
Begin-Select
Name
  Move &Name to $Dep_Name
from Dependent_Benef
where EMPLID=&A.Emplid
and Dependent_Benef=&D.Dependent_Benef
End-Select
End-Procedure

#include 'html.inc'
```

In `Test19C.sqr`, we made a number of program changes. These changes helped to improve the report appearance and eliminated the problem of positioning the report elements.

The first improvement we made was to place an image on the top of the report. The image can be a corporate logo, a picture, a banner, or simply a multiple-color ribbon. Use the `Html_Img` procedure to insert an image in your report. For example, this is how we placed the Online Edition banner on the top of the report:

```
Do Html_Img(' SRC="edition.GIF" ')
```

The `Html_On` procedure is called at program start to turn all other SQR HTML procedures on. For each of the program's two reports, the `Declare-Layout` command is used to make the number of lines in the page exceed the entire report length, placing all output into one large page.

A number of SQR HTML tabular procedures is used to control the output field positions. Let's discuss these procedures in more detail.

- The `Html_Table` and `Html_Table_End` procedures are used to mark the start and end of the table. The `BORDER` argument of the `Html_Table` procedure causes a border to be displayed around each table cell.
- The `Html_Caption` and `Html_Caption_End` procedures specify the table caption. Immediately after the `Html_Caption` procedure call, you have to use the `Print` command to display the table caption.
- The `Html_Tr` and `Html_Tr_End` procedures mark the start and end of a new table row. You need to code these procedures for each table row, including the header row, the detail rows, and the total row (if there is one).
- The `Html_Th` and `Html_Th_End` procedures mark the start and end of each table column header. You have to code as many `Html_Th` procedures as the number of columns in the table. The `Print` command following the `Html_Th` procedure call must display the column heading. You do not have to change the `Print` command position parameters. They will be ignored anyway.

- The Html_Td and Html_Td_End procedures mark the start and end of each column cell in the table detail body. As with column headers, you have to code as many Html_Td procedures as the number of columns in the table. The Print command following the Html_Td procedure call must display the content of the column cell.

Figure 19.9. shows how a portion of the first program report will look on a web page. (The second report will look similar.)

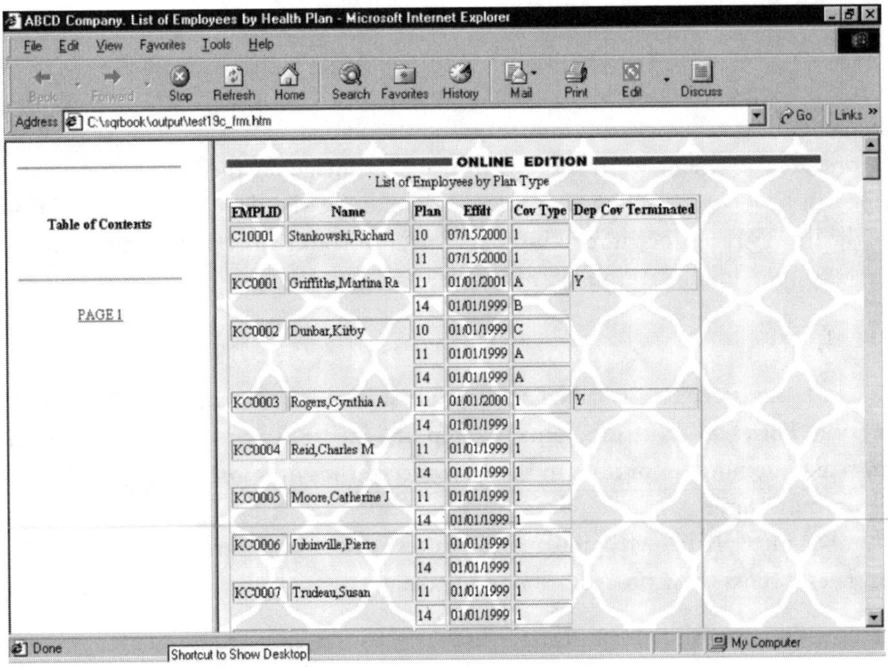

Figure 19.9 Using the SQR HTML tabular procedures

Please note that the web browser displays the report as one table with no page breaks and no page navigation pointers. This is because we defined the entire report as one large page.

19.6.2 HTML heading procedures

The SQR HTML heading procedures help you to display certain portions of the report more prominently than other portions. You can use up to six header levels, with level one as the most prominent and level six as the least prominent. Most reports will seldom need more than three levels of headers. You do not have to start from level one heading. Use the level which best fits your report design.

The `Html_Hn` and `Html_Hn_End` (where *n* can be from 1 to 6) procedures are used to specify the start and end of each level heading. You can also specify the proper HTML heading attributes as the `Html_Hn` procedure parameters as shown in `Test19C.sqr`. In this example, we are using two heading levels: level one and level two. Place the `Print` command between the `Html_Hn` and `Html_Hn_End` procedures to specify the heading text.

```
!*************************
! TEST19D.SQR
!Using HTML headings
!*************************
  . . .
!**********************************
Begin-Program
!**********************************
   Do Html_On()
   Do Html_Set_Head_Tags('<TITLE>ABCD Company. List of Employees by-
                        Health Plan</TITLE>')
   Do Html_Img(' SRC="edition.GIF" ')
   !Do Html_Set_Body_Attributes('Background="bkgrnd2.GIF" ')

   Do Process_EE_Heading
   Do Process_Dep_Heading
   Do Process_Main
End-Program

!*************************************************
Begin-Procedure Process_EE_Heading
!*************************************************
  Use-Report EE_Data
  Do Html_H1(' ')    <----| Define level one header.
  Print 'Employee Health Benefit Coverage Report' (1,1)
  Do Html_H1_End
  Do Html_Table('BORDER')
  Do Html_Caption(' ')
  Do Html_H2(' ')    <----| Define level two header.
  Print 'List of Employees by Plan Type' (+1) Center
  Do Html_H2_End
  Do Html_Caption_End
  . . .
End-Procedure
!*************************************************************
Begin-Procedure Process_Dep_Heading
!*************************************************************

  Use-Report Term_Dependents
  Do Html_H1(' ')
  Print 'Employee Dependents with Health Benefit Coverage Terminated'
               (1,1)
  Do Html_H1_End
```

```
  Do Html_Table('BORDER')
  Do Html_Caption(' ')
  Do Html_H2(' ')
  Print 'List of Terminated Dependents' (+1) Center
  Do Html_H2_End
  . . .
End-Procedure
!**************************************
  . . .
#include 'html.inc'
```

Figure 19.10 shows how both these headings will look on a web page.

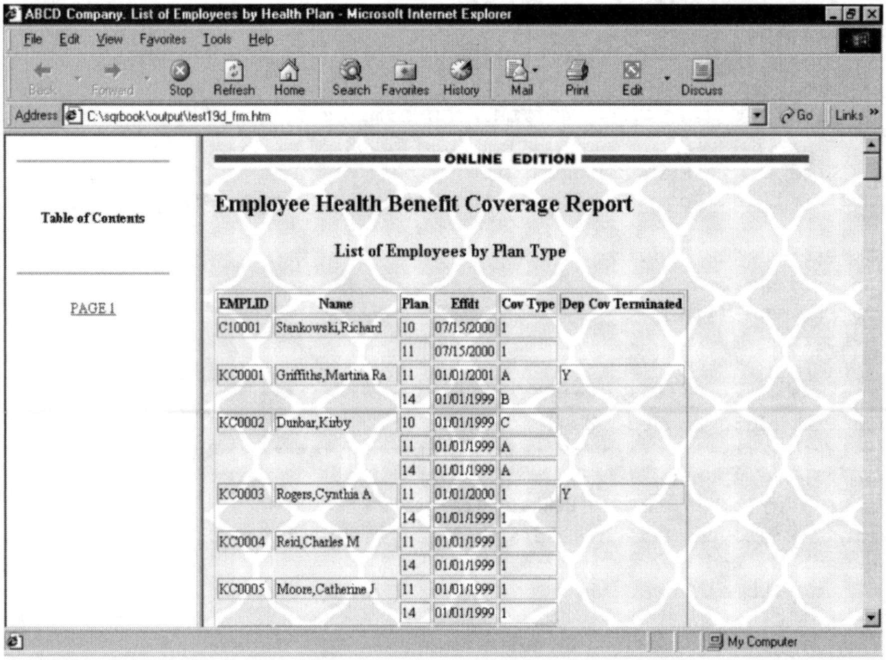

Figure 19.10 Using the SQR HTML heading procedures

Note SQR HTML procedures can be made transparent: if you do not use the `PRINTER:HT` SQR command flag, all HTML procedures in your program will be ignored, and SQR will generate regular `LIS` files as output reports.

19.6.3 HTML hypertext link procedures

The SQR HTML hypertext link procedures make your report look like a true web report. You can use them to either:

- specify a link to another part of the current web page or an external web page or
- define an anchor within your report so that the same or another web page can have a link to this part of your report.

The same pair of SQR HTML procedures, `Html_A` and `Html_A_End`, can perform either of the previously mentioned functions. What the procedures actually do depends on the `Html_A` procedure's input argument.

To define a hypertext anchor in your report, use the `NAME` argument in the `Html_A` procedure. This argument specifies the name of the anchor. For example, the following code defines an anchor named `TAGB` in the program output report:

```
Do Html_A('NAME=TAGB')
Do Html_A_End
Print 'Annual Report. Section B' ()
```

Please note that, if other documents include links to the `TAGB` anchor, clicking on these links will bring viewers right to the beginning of the `'Annual report. Section B'` statement.

To define a hypertext link to another place, use the `HREF` argument in the `Html_A` procedure. There are two possible methods of coding hypertext links.

If the point of reference is at the beginning of a separate document, use an absolute or relative URL address of the entire document. For example, the following code specifies a hypertext link to the ABCD company home page which is external to your program report:

```
Do Html_A('HREF=http://www.abcd.com')
Print 'Return to ABCD company home page' ()
Do Html_A_End
```

To define a hypertext link to some place inside a document, you need to specify the name of a previously defined anchor located in this place in the document. You can code hypertext links pointing to anchors within the same document or anchors defined in web pages external to your program report.

The following example demonstrates the use of the `Html_A` procedure to create a pointer to the anchor `Anchor1` defined in another web page:

```
Print 'Click below to review the employment opportunities at -
   ABCD company: '
```

```
Do Html_A('HREF="http://www.abcd.com/homepage/-
   employment.htlm#anchor1" ')
Print 'The current list of openings' ()
Do HtmlA_End
```

We will use HTML hypertext links and anchors to connect the two output reports in our program. Let's recall that the first program report lists all employees and their health benefit plans. The second report includes only those employees whose dependents lost their benefits within the period covered by the report. In the first report, employees listed in the second report are marked with a "Y" in the "Dep Cov Terminated" column. Wouldn't it be nice to insert hypertext link pointers in the first report so that, for the employees with terminated dependent health benefits, the links would bring the viewer to the corresponding places in the second report? Also, we can walk an extra mile and place similar link pointers in the second report that will bring the viewer back to the first report, right to the previously viewed portion in this report!

The improvement will require a few additional changes to our program:

```
!**************************************
! TEST19E.SQR
!Using HTML hypertext links procedures
!**************************************

!Set report column widths
#Define col_emplid          11      !Employee ID
#Define col_empl_name       20      !Employee Name
#Define col_plan_type        5      !Plan Type
#Define col_cov_cd           8      !Coverage Code
#Define col_cov_drop_flag   20      !Dependent Coverage Termination
#Define col_effdt           12      !Effective Date
#Define col_dep_id           6      !Dependent Beneficiary ID
#Define col_dep_name        20      !Dependent Name
#Define col_sep              1      !Column Separator
!***********************
Begin-Setup
!***********************
 Declare-Layout EE_Data
   Max-Lines=3000
   Left-Margin=1
 End-Declare

 Declare-Layout Term_Dependents
   Max-Lines=200
   Orientation=landscape
   Left-Margin=0.3
 End-Declare

 Declare-Report EE_Data
   Layout=EE_Data
```

```
 End-Declare

 Declare-Report Term_Dependents
   Layout=Term_Dependents
 End-Declare
End-Setup

!***********************************
Begin-Program
!***********************************
   Do Html_On()
   Do Html_Set_Head_Tags('<TITLE>ABCD Company. List of Employees by -
      Health Plan</TITLE>')
   Do Html_Img(' SRC="edition.GIF" ')
   !Do Html_Set_Body_Attributes('Background="bkgrnd2.GIF" ')

   Do Process_EE_Heading
   Do Process_Dep_Heading
   Do Process_Main
End-Program

!**************************************************
Begin-Procedure Process_EE_Heading
!**************************************************
  Use-Report EE_Data
  Do Html_H1(' ')
  Print 'Employee Health Benefit Coverage Report' (1,1)
  Do Html_H1_End
  Do Html_Table('BORDER')
  Do Html_Caption(' ')
  Do Html_H2(' ')
  Print 'List of Employees by Plan Type' (+1) Center
  Do Html_H2_End
  Do Html_Caption_End

  Do Html_Tr(' ')
  Do Html_Th(' ')
  Print 'EMPLID'                (+1,1,{col_emplid})
  Do Html_Th(' ')
  Print 'Name  '                (0,+{col_sep},{col_empl_name})
  Do Html_Th(' ')
  Print 'Plan'                  (0,+{col_sep},{col_plan_type})
  Do Html_Th(' ')
  Print 'Effdt'                 (0,+{col_sep},{col_Effdt})
  Do Html_Th(' ')
  Print 'Cov Type'              (0,+{col_sep},{col_cov_cd})
  Do Html_Th(' ')
  Print  'Dep Cov Terminated'   (0,+{col_sep},{col_cov_drop_flag})
  Do Html_Th_End

End-Procedure
!***************************************************************
```

```
Begin-Procedure Process_Dep_Heading
!*************************************************************
  Use-Report Term_Dependents
  Do Html_H1(' ')
  Print 'Employee Dependents with Health Benefit Coverage Terminated'
              (1,1)
  Do Html_H1_End
  Do Html_Table('BORDER')
  Do Html_Caption(' ')
  Do Html_H2(' ')
  Print 'List of Terminated Dependents' (+1) Center
  Do Html_H2_End

  Do Html_Tr(' ')
  Do Html_Th(' ')
  Print 'EMPLID'    (+1,1,{col_emplid})
  Do Html_Th(' ')
  Print 'Name  '    (0,+{col_sep},{col_empl_name})
  Do Html_Th(' ')
  Print 'Plan_Type' (0,+{col_sep},{col_plan_type})
  Do Html_Th(' ')
  Print 'Effdt'     (0,+{col_sep},{col_Effdt})
  Do Html_Th(' ')
  Print 'Dep ID '   (0,+{col_sep},{col_dep_id})
  Do Html_Th(' ')
  Print 'Dep Name'  (0,+{col_sep},{col_dep_name})

End-Procedure
!*************************************
Begin-Procedure Process_Main
!*************************************
!Select and print all Employees
!who are currently covered by any Health Benefits
!and who have Family, or Empl+1 Coverage

Begin-Select
A.Emplid
A.Plan_Type
A.Effdt
A.Covrg_CD
B.Name

    Do Check_Dep_Termination
    If $Term =  'N'
        Let $Term =  ' '
    End-If
    Do Print_EE_Data

From Health_Benefit A, Personal_Data B
Where   A.Effdt  =(Select Max(Effdt) From Health_Benefit
                  Where  Emplid     =  A.Emplid
                  And    Plan_Type  =  A.Plan_Type
```

```
                And     Effdt      <=  Sysdate)
 And     A.Coverage_Elect Not In ('T','W')
 And     A.Emplid = B.Emplid
 Order By  A.Emplid, A.Plan_Type

End-Select
End-Procedure
!************************************
Begin-Procedure Check_Dep_Termination
!************************************
! For each row retrieved in Step 1, compare between the previous
! maximum effective dated record and the current effective dated
! HEALTH_DEPENDNT row to determine a dependent that is no longer
! covered. If dropped dependents are found, print the record to a
! separate report

Move  'N' To $Term

Begin-Select
C.Emplid
C.Plan_Type
C.Effdt
D.Dependent_Benef

    Move 'Y' to $Term
    Do Print_Terminated_Dependents
    Show 'Dep Term found=' &D.Dependent_Benef '
      for Employee '&A.Emplid
 From Health_Benefit C,
    Health_Dependnt D
 Where  C.Emplid       = &A.Emplid
 And    C.Plan_Type    = &A.Plan_Type
 And    C.Emplid       = D.Emplid
 And    C.Plan_Type    = D.Plan_Type
 And    C.Effdt        = D.Effdt
 And    C.Effdt  = (Select Max(E.Effdt)
               From  Health_Benefit E
               Where  C.Emplid     = E.Emplid
               And    C.Plan_Type  = E.Plan_Type
               And    E.Effdt      < &A.Effdt)
 And  D.Dependent_Benef Not In
   (Select F.Dependent_Benef
     From Health_Dependnt F
     Where  C.Emplid    = F.Emplid
     And    C.Plan_Type = F.Plan_Type
     And    F.Effdt     = &A.EFFDT)

End-Select
End-Procedure

!******************************************
Begin-Procedure Print_EE_Data
```

```
!*******************************************
  Use-Report EE_Data
  Let $EmplID=&A.Emplid
  Let $Date_Str= Datetostr(&A.Effdt,'mm/dd/yyyy')
  Do Html_Tr(' ')
  Do Html_Td(' ')
  Print &A.Emplid     (+1,1,{col_emplid})  On-Break
                        Print=Change/Top-Page
  Do Html_Td(' ')
  Print &B.Name       (0,+{col_sep},{col_empl_name})  On-Break
                        Print=Change/Top-Page
  Do Html_Td(' ')
  Print &A.Plan_Type  (0,+{col_sep},{col_plan_type})
  Do Html_Td(' ')
  Print $Date_Str     (0,+{col_sep},{col_effdt})
  Do Html_Td(' ')
  Print &A.Covrg_Cd   (0,+{col_sep},{col_cov_cd})
  Do Html_Td(' ')
  Print $Term         (0,+{col_sep},{col_cov_drop_flag})
  If $Term = 'Y'

      Let $Emp_Anchor_Str='NAME='||'"'||'Ea' || &A.Emplid||'"'
      Do Html_A($Emp_Anchor_Str)
      Do Html_A_End
      Let $Dep_Anchor = 'HREF='||'"'
         ||'TEST19D_01.HTM#Da' ||  &A.Emplid || '"'
      Do Html_A($Dep_Anchor)
      Print 'Go to Dependents List' ()
      Do Html_A_End
  End-If
  Do Html_Td_End
  Do Html_Tr_End

   Add 1 to #Ee_Rcds

  End-Procedure
!*********************************************************
Begin-Procedure Print_Terminated_Dependents
!*********************************************************
  Use-Report Term_Dependents
  Let $EmplID=&A.Emplid
  Do Get_Dependent_Name
  Let $Date_Str= Datetostr(&A.Effdt,'mm/dd/yyyy')
  Do Html_Tr(' ')
  Do Html_Td(' ')
  Print &A.Emplid  (+1,1,{col_emplid}) On-Break Print=Change/Top-Page
  Let $Dep_Anchor =  'NAME=' ||'"'|| 'Da' || &A.Emplid || '"'
  Do Html_A($Dep_Anchor)
  Do Html_A_End

    If  $Emplid <> $Save_Emplid
     let $Save_Emplid = $Emplid
```

Defining an anchor in the Employee Benefits report

Defining a link to the Dependents report

Defining an anchor in the Dependents report

```
    Let $Emp_Anchor =  'HREF='||'"'
    ||'TEST19D.HTM#Ea' || &A.Emplid  || '"'
    Do Html_A($Emp_Anchor)
    Print 'Go back to Employee List' ()
    Do Html_A_End
  End-If

    Do Html_Td(' ')
  Print &B.Name              (0,+{col_sep},{col_empl_name})  On-Break
                                                  Print=Change/Top-Page

  Do Html_Td(' ')
  Print &A.Plan_Type         (0,+{col_sep},{col_plan_type})
  Do Html_Td(' ')
  Print $Date_Str            (0,+{col_sep},{col_effdt})
  Do Html_Td(' ')
  Print &D.Dependent_Benef (0,+{col_sep},{col_dep_id})
  Do Html_Td(' ')
  Print $DEP_NAME            (0,+{col_sep},{col_dep_name})
  Do Html_Td_End
  Do Html_Tr_End

  Add 1 to #Dep_Rcds

End-Procedure

!**************************************
Begin-Procedure Get_Dependent_Name
!**************************************
Let $Dep_Name=' '
Begin-Select
Name
  Move &Name to $Dep_Name
from Dependent_Benef
where EMPLID=&A.Emplid
and Dependent_Benef=&D.Dependent_Benef
End-Select
End-Procedure

#include 'html.inc'
```

Defining a link to the Employee Benefits report

As you can see, the program inserts HTML hypertext anchors in the second report for each listed employee. When this employee record is processed in the first report, the program inserts a hypertext link to the corresponding anchor in the second report. Similarly, the program generates anchors in the first report for employees listed in the second report and inserts links to these anchors in the second report. Both the anchor names and the hypertext links include the employee Id, thus ensuring uniqueness of each pair of references.

Figure 19.11 shows a portion of the first report with a pointer to the second report for employee Martina Griffiths whose dependents lost their benefits during the reporting period.

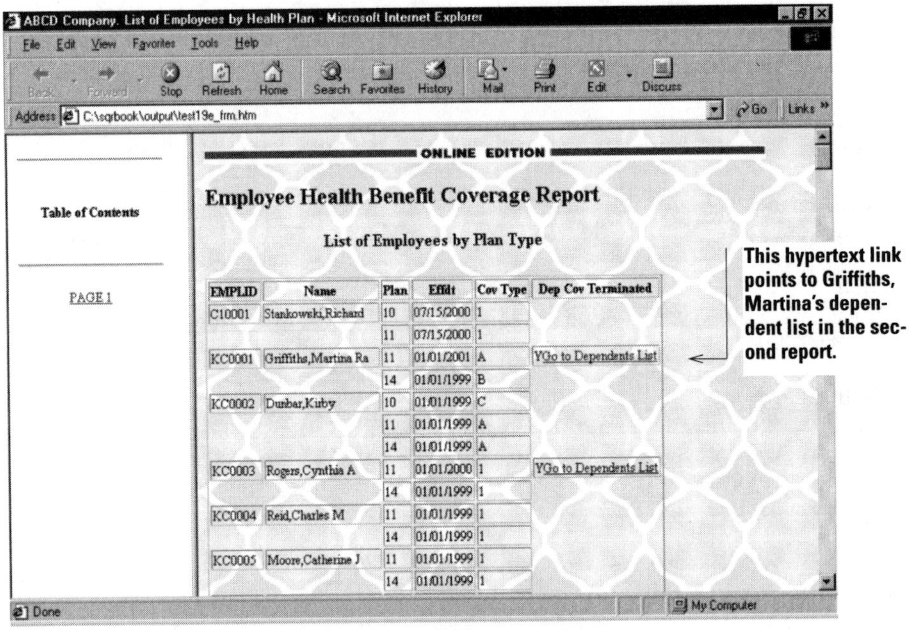

Figure 19.11 A hypertext link points from employee Griffiths, Martina in the first report to her dependents' information in the second report.

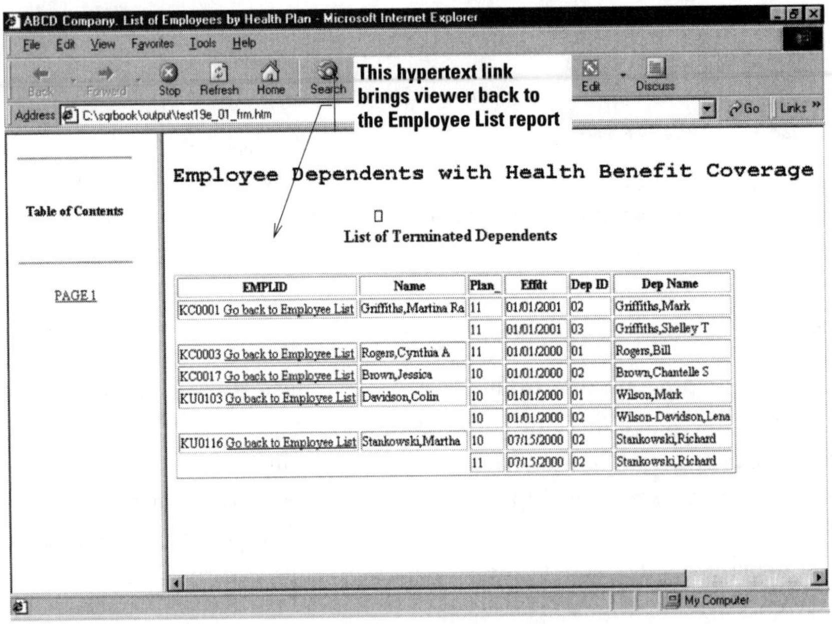

Figure 19.12 After clicking on the link in the first report, the viewer is brought to this place in the second report. Clicking on the link next to the employee name brings the viewer back to the employee information in the first report.

If the report viewer clicks on the link, the browser will bring the viewer to the corresponding place in the second report where the employee dependents with terminated benefits are listed. To return back to the first report, one just needs to click on the link to the first report next to the employee name as in figure 19.12.

19.7 How an SQR program accepts parameters from the Internet

You can use the regular SQR `Input` command to accept input parameters from a CGI (Common Gateway Interface) script. Passing input parameters to an SQR program over the Internet involves creating an HTML fill-out form and writing a CGI script to call your SQR program and to pass input parameters to the program. After the SQR finishes, the CGI script copies the program output file to the standard output.

Let's modify our program to limit the employee selection to the specified state only and to accept `State` as an input parameter.

```
!*************************
! TEST19F.SQR
! Accepting input parameters from a CGI script
!*************************
Begin-Setup
!***********************
  . . .
End-Setup

!******************************
Begin-Program
!******************************
 DoHtml_On()
 Input $State Maxlen=2 ' '       <-- Accepting State as an input parameter from a CGI script
 Do Html_Set_Head_Tags('<TITLE>ABCD Company. List of Employees by -
      Health Plan</TITLE>')
 Do Html_Img(' SRC="edition.GIF" ')

 Do Process_EE_Heading
 Do Process_Dep_Heading
 Do Process_Main
End-Program
 . . .
!*************************************
Begin-Procedure Process_Main
!*************************************
!Select and print all Employees
!who are currently covered by any Health Benefits
!and who have Family, or Empl+1 Coverage

Begin-Select
```

```
A.Emplid
A.Plan_Type
A.Effdt
A.Covrg_CD
B.Name

    Do Check_Dep_Termination
    If $Term =  'N'
        Let $Term =  ' '
    End-If
    Do Print_EE_Data

From Health_Benefit A, Personal_Data B
Where   A.Effdt  =(Select Max(Effdt) From Health_Benefit
                  Where Emplid     =  A.Emplid
                  And   Plan_Type  =  A.Plan_Type
                  And   Effdt     <=  Sysdate)
 And    A.Coverage_Elect Not In ('T','W')
 And    B.State = $State
 And    A.Emplid = B.Emplid
 Order By  A.Emplid, A.Plan_Type

End-Select
End-Procedure
!************************************
  . . .
#include 'html.inc'
```

The program selects only employees who reside in the state specified.

In `Test19F.sqr`, the modified program accepts `State` as input parameter, moves this value to the `$State` string variable, and uses `$State` as a bind variable in the `Select` paragraph of the `Main` procedure. The logic used to read input parameter is not different from any regular input parameter read code in an SQR program.

The next step is to create an HTML fill-out form. This form will include a drop-down selection list to help the user to select the state. The following example presents a sample of a simple HTML fill-in form that can serve our purpose:

```
<HTML><HEAD>
<TITLE> Employee Health Benefit Report </TITLE></HEAD>
<BODY>
<FORM METHOD=POST ACTION="http://yoursite.com/cgi-bin/-
   benefit_report.sh">
<HR>
<STRONG>Please select the State to run the report by:  </STRONG>
<SELECT STATE="State" Size="3">
<OPTION VALUE="CA">California
<OPTION SELECTED VALUE="CA">California
 <OPTION VALUE="CT">Connecticut
<OPTION VALUE="NY">New York
</SELECT><HR>
```

```
<INPUT TYPE="submit" VALUE="Submit report">
<INPUT TYPE="reset">
</FORM>
</BODY></HTLM>
```

Figure 19.13 shows how our HTML fill-in form will look on a web page.

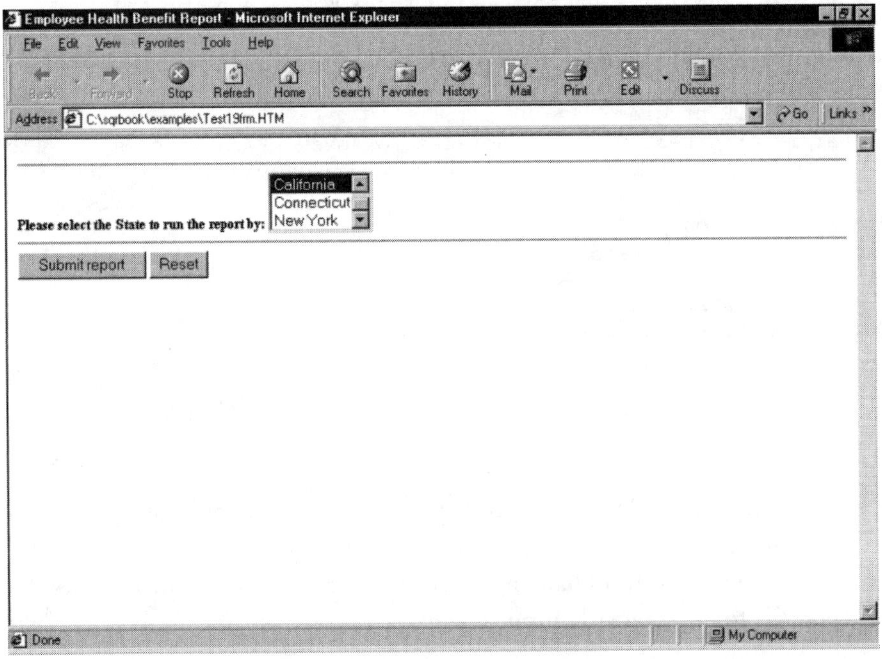

Figure 19.13 An HTML fill-in form that is used to pass input parameters to a CGI script

As you can see, the form contains a state selection drop-down list and a button to submit the report after the user selects the state. The form calls the `benefit_report.sh` CGI script and passes the selected state code to this script. The script, in turn, calls our SQR program and passes the selected value to this program as input parameter.

CGI scripts can be written in different languages: Perl, Visual Basic, C++, UNIX Shell script, and so on. Next we present an example of a UNIX shell script that sets the ORACLE environmental variables, accepts the state code value from the HTML fill-out form, invokes our SQR program via the command line method, and passes the state code as input parameter to the program.

```
#! /bin/sh
#Set the appropriate ORACLE environment variables
ORACLE_SID=oracle7;
```

```
export ORACLE_SID
ORACLE_HOME=/usr2/oracle7;
export ORACLE_HOME
SQRDIR=/usr2/sqr/bin;
export SQRDIR
#identify the output as being HTML format
echo "Content-type: text/html"
echo ""
# get values from fill-out form using the POST method
read TEMPSTR
STATE=`echo $TEMPSTR | sed "s;.*STATE=;;
s;&.*;;"`
#invoke the SQR program
sqr /usr/reports/test19e.sqr dbaorauser/orapssw -F/usr/tmp/emprpt.lis
 -F/usr/tmp/deprpt.lis "$STATE" >/usr/tmp/test19e.out 2>&1 < /dev/null
if [ $? -eq 0 ]; then
  # display the output
  cat /usr/tmp/emprpt.lis
else
  # display the error
  echo "<HTML><BODY><PRE>"
  echo "failed to run SQR program"
  cat /usr/tmp/test19e.out
  echo "</PRE></BODY></HTML>
fi
```

The script retrieves the selected state code into the `STATE` variable and passes this parameter to the SQR program. The script also redirects the standard input from `/dev/null` to prevent the program from hanging when it requires any input, then copies the generated report file to the standard output stream.

KEY POINTS

1 You can generate program reports in an HTML compatible format and publish these reports on the Internet.

2 There are three main methods to generate HTML from an SQR program output.

3 You always have to use the `-PRINTER:HT`, `-PRINTER:EH`, or `-EH_*` SQR command line parameter to have your program generate HTML output.

KEY POINTS (CONTINUED)

4 All SQR HTML procedures are delivered in the `Html.inc` file.

5 Executing the `Html_On` procedure turns on all SQR HTML procedures, but causes SQR to ignore all print position qualifiers.

6 The SQR HTML table procedures can be used to control the report-element positioning.

7 The SQR HTML hypertext link procedures allow you to specify links to other parts of the current web page or to an external web page. Alternatively, you can use these procedures to define anchors within your report so that the same or other web pages can have links to these anchors.

8 Your program can use the regular SQR `Input` command to accept input parameters from another HTML script.

9 If you run an SQR program without the `PRINTER:HT`, `-PRINTER:EH`, or `-EH_*` command flag, SQR will ignore all SQR HTML procedures in the program and will generate regular `LIS` files as the program's output.

C H A P T E R   2 0

Debugging techniques

IN THIS CHAPTER

- The `Show` and `Display` commands
- Methods of debugging encapsulation
- SQR command line flags that are frequently used in debugging

As happens with any programming language, working with SQR frequently involves tracking down errors, especially when your program logic is complex. Even if your program runs to the end without an abend, you still may want to make sure that all the program variables were assigned the expected values. It is a good idea to display the content of some variables at the important points of your program, or just to trace the program control flow at certain strategic places. We always think that this can be done later, after the program is created, but the best time to plan on program debugging is the time when you write the program.

20.1 Using the Show and Display commands

When it comes to debugging an SQR program, there are no fancy step-through debuggers. Your main weapons are the two SQR commands: `Show` and `Display`. You can use these commands anywhere in your program except the `Setup` section. Both the `Show` and `Display` commands display the specified texts and variables on the screen and also write the same information into the program log file.

If, for example, you ran and completed a program successfully, but your output is not what you expected, then you need to find out whether your program had some logic flaws, or whether the unexpected results have been caused by an incorrect selection in the program's query. The simplest way to find this out is to add some `Show` or `Display` commands to the program:

```
!Using the Show command to display selected columns
Show 'Select Started'
Begin-Select
A.Emplid
A.Name
     Show 'Selected Emplid = ' &A.Emplid ' Name= ' &A.Name
From PERSONAL_DATA
Where Name Like 'Abr%'
End-Select
```

In the example, each selected record is displayed on the screen and written to the program log file. If you do not see any records displayed on the screen, you may have a problem with your `Select` statement. There can be many reasons: the selection criteria in the `Where` clause may be too restrictive; the database tables do not have the expected information; or (most likely), your `Select` statement is incorrect. At this point, the `Display` or `Show` commands are not very helpful, and the best way to track down the problem is to use a database on-line access tool like `SQL Plus` for Oracle, SQL Programmer for Sybase, or `QMF` for DB2. In PeopleSoft, you can use the `PS Query` tool to debug your query, and then paste the `Select` statement into your SQR program. Please keep in mind that because different databases have slightly different `Select` statement syntax, this statement may need some minor adjustments after you paste it into an SQR program.

The `Display` command is somewhat similar to the `Show` command, but it has less power: you cannot display multiple fields in one `Display` command. For example, to display the same information as we did in the preceding example using the `Display` command, you may need four `Display` commands (the `Noline` qualifier prevents the line advancement; thereby keeping all four displayed fields on one screen line):

```
Display 'Selected Emplid = '  Noline
Display &A.Emplid  Noline
Display ' Name= ' Noline
Display &A.Name
```

In addition to its ability to display multiple fields, the `Show` command allows you to control the cursor position on screen, send beeping signals, make the screen fields blink, display the screen fields in bold, underline the screen fields, and so forth. In fact, it may be used as a crude screen design tool, although it cannot compete with today's systems like PowerBuilder or Visual Basic.

As you can see, the `Show` command is more convenient to use, but no matter what command you use for debugging—`Display` or `Show`—they both can be instrumental in program testing. Careful planning and placement of the `Display` or `Show` commands in your program will help you to identify potential problems while spending as little time and effort as possible.

> **Note** Both the `Display` and `Show` commands allow you to use edit format masks when displaying the content of the program variables.

20.2 Using conditional compiler statements

Conditional compiler statements allow you to modify your program based on the values of certain SQR command line flags or substitution variables. Note that these statements are checked at compile time, not at run time.

20.2.1 The #Debug command

You can optionally use the `#Debug` conditional compiler directive by executing the `Display`, `Show`, `Print`, or other commands in your program during testing, and then deactivating them when the program is released to production. This approach is called *debugging encapsulation.*

Any SQR command that immediately follows the `#Debug` statement will be compiled only when the corresponding `-Debug` flag is specified in the SQR command line. The `#Debug` command may be appended (suffixed) with one or more letters or numbers, e.g.; `#Debugxy`, to provide additional flexibility in debugging. You may optionally specify up to ten different suffix letters or numbers.

When you use a specific suffix letter in the `-Debug` command line flag, all `#Debug` statements with the same suffix in the program will be activated by the compiler. This is in addition to all `#Debug` statements with no suffix.

For example, if the flag `-DEBUGxyz` is used on the command line, SQR automatically creates four substitution variables: `debug`, `debugx`, `debugy`, and `debugz`. This causes all commands following the `#Debug`, `#Debugx`, `#Debugy`, or `#Debugz` statements to be activated:

```
#Debug Show 'Start Proc1'
#Debugx Show 'Start Proc2'
#Debugy Display 'Start Proc3'
#Debugz Display 'Start Proc4'
```

If a statement like: `#Debuga Show 'Test Started'` is coded in the program, and no `-DEBUGa` flag is specified in the command line, then this statement will not be processed during the compile stage, and therefore, will not be executed.

Table 20.1 shows the examples of the `-Debug` flag in the SQR command line, `#Debug` statements, and the results of compilation.

Table 20.1 Using the #Debug commands

Debug flag	#Debug statement in the program	The result of program compilation	Comment
-DEBUG	#Debug Show 'A'	Show 'A'	The -DEBUG flag was defined with no suffix, the command following the #Debug command is activated.
-DEBUG	#Debuga Show 'B'		Because no -DEBUGa flag was specified the command following the #Debuga command is ignored.
-DEBUGabcd	#Debuga Show 'A' #Debugb Show 'B' #Debugc Show 'C' #Debugd Show 'D' #Debug Show 'N' #Debugx Show 'X'	Show 'A' Show 'B' Show 'C' Show 'D' Show 'N'	All commands except #Debugx are activated.

20.2.2 Other conditional compiler directives

When using the `#Debug` directive, you have to place this command before any SQR statement that you would like activated or deactivated. The `#Debug` directive is not very convenient when you need to turn entire sections of code on or off for debugging. It can be achieved by using the following commands:

```
#Ifdef or #Ifndef /#End-If
#If/#Else/#End-If
```

In fact, it is a good idea to code the program control flow trace statements and encapsulate them into the conditional compiler directive blocks when you write a program. For example, a code such as the following can be very useful to trace down potential problems that may occur in the future:

```
!Using the #Ifdef command
Begin-Procedure Get-Employees
#Ifdef Debug
  Show 'Procedure Get Employees Started'
#Endif
Begin-Select
Select
Emplid
Name
SSN
  #Ifdef Debug
     Show 'Employee:' &Emplid ' Name: ' &Name ' Selected '
     Add 1 to #Rcds_selected
  #End-If

From Personal_Data
Where
...

End-Select
End-Procedure
...
```

In the example, we used the conditional compiler directives `#Ifdef/#End-If` to encapsulate SQR statements that we want executed only if the `Debug` substitution variable is defined in the program. This variable can be defined explicitly using, for instance, the `#Define Debug 1` statement in the beginning of your program, or implicitly by specifying the `-DEBUG` flag in the command line. The second option is preferable, especially after your program is released to production, since, in this case, you will not have to change the program every time you want to run it in the debugging mode.

Remember, you can specify the `-DEBUG` flag with a suffix, thereby creating not only one substitution variable `Debug`, but also a few additional substitution variables. For example, the `-DEBUGabc` flag in the command line causes the creation of four substitution variables: `Debug`, `Debuga`, `Debugb`, and `Debugc`. All these variables can be checked by the `#Ifdef` commands, thus providing a good deal of flexibility during both the program testing and maintenance.

As with the `#Ifdef/#End-If` directive, you can use `#If/#Else/#End-If` conditional compiler directives to split the encapsulated code into conditional blocks:

```
!Using the #If/#Else/#End-If command
#Define Test 'Y'
...
#If  Test = 'Y'
   Show 'Test Started'
#Else
   Show 'This is a Production Run'
#End-If
...
```

20.3 Using SQR command line flags to enable SQR debugging information

In addition to the `-DEBUG` command line flag, a few other command line flags may prove helpful in tracking down different problems. Depending on the particular situation, you can use the SQR command line flags or their combinations shown in table 20.2.

Table 20.2 Additional SQR command line flags used in debugging

SQR Command Line Flag	Purpose	Comments
-S	To show the status of all program cursors.	Upon program completion, displays the following information: • text of each SQL statement • number of times each SQL statement was compiled and executed • total number of rows selected All this information will be displayed on the screen and placed into the program log file (see figure 20.1). Note that the bind variables will not be shown.
-T*nn*	To generate only *nn* pages of the program output report.	All `ORDER BY` clauses in the `SELECT` statements will be ignored. For multiple report programs, only the first *nn* pages of the first program report are produced.
-C	To create the Cancel Dialog Box during the program run.	This option will enable you to cancel the program execution when necessary (and avoid using CNTRL-ALT-DELETE).

Table 20.2 Additional SQR command line flags used in debugging (continued)

SQR Command Line Flag	Purpose	Comments
-E[*file*]	To direct all the error messages to a file.	You can direct all SQR-generated messages to a specified file. The default file name will be the name of your SQR program with an extension .err, e. g., `Test01.err`. This way, you can direct all the Show and Display command output to a LOG file and all SQR-generated messages to an ERR file. If SQR generates no messages, no ERR file is created.

To illustrate the use of the `-S` flag, let's run one of the programs created in chapter 11, `Test11F.sqr`. with this flag. After the program finishes, the program log file will have the information shown in figure 20.1.

```
Cursor Status:

 Cursor #1:
   SQL = select A.Emplid, A.Hire_Dt, B.Name, B.State From Employment A,
        Personal_Data B Where A.Emplid=B.Emplid And A.Termination_Dt is
          Null And [$Where]
 Compiles = 2
 Executes = 1
 Rows     = 175

    SQR: End of Run.
```

Figure 20.1 A program log file with cursor information

As you can see from the log file displayed in figure 20.1, the information about cursors can be helpful in identifying potential problems with SQL statements in your program. Unfortunately, it is not very comprehensive. For example, the report does not show the SQL statement as it is passed to your database engine for execution.

Depending on the problem that needs debugging, you may need to supplement the `-S` flag with a few `Show` or `Display` commands, or use other techniques described earlier in this chapter, but do not discard the output produced with the help of the `-S` flag. It could help you, not only in finding SQL-related problems, but also in tuning your program's performance. Your data base administrator may use this report to find a way to increase the database efficiency.

You may find the -T*nn* command flag useful when testing large reports. It allows you to generate only the specified number of pages for your report output. The program will stop execution after the first *nn* pages of output are created. Note that because this flag suppresses all Order By clauses in the Select statements, your database records will not be sorted when using this option. This may lead to incorrect processing. For example, if you use the break logic in your report, this flag may cause incorrect processing of breaks.

KEY POINTS

1 The Display and Show commands are the main instruments in debugging SQR programs.

2 The -DEBUG SQR command line flag in combination with the #Debug, #IfDef, and #IfNdef statements, can help to encapsulate the debugging logic in your program.

3 The -S, -T, -C, and -E SQR command line flags can provide additional help during the debugging process.

CHAPTER 21

Good programming practices

IN THIS CHAPTER

- Supporting multiple national environments
- Developing and maintaining platform and database independence
- Handling error conditions
- Making your programs easier to build, test, and maintain

In this chapter, we will not introduce any new commands, parameters, or flags. Instead, we are going to discuss a few programming techniques designed to address a number of problems and challenges that many SQR programmers may face while working on real projects.

The approaches and techniques presented in this chapter should be viewed as suggestions and ideas rather than strict technical recommendations. We are sure that our readers will be able to come up with alternative solutions to the discussed problems (perhaps, even better ones), and possibly, add to the list of the subjects discussed in this chapter. Your actual business environment will determine your particular priorities and programming standards. We feel, however, that at least, some of the discussed problems are common, and, therefore, worthy of discussion.

21.1 Going global

Today's business trend towards a global economy puts additional pressure on business software developers. Many large corporations have scores of subsidiaries in different countries involving different languages, alphabets, currencies, ways of displaying dates, times, and so forth. Obviously traditional methods of writing programs designed for just domestic use are becoming outdated. In today's world, any computer language not capable of addressing these issues puts itself at risk of losing market share and, ultimately, becoming obsolete.

SQR addresses the problems of global development by arming both program developers and system administrators with a number of options. The available options include special system settings that can be used to control the system defaults, as well as commands that allow program developers to dynamically switch from one set of system parameters to another. In addition, the most recent releases of SQR (4.2 and higher) include support for double-byte character manipulations and the Japanese Imperial Era calendar.

SQR provides different ways to write programs capable of working in different national environments. Which way is the best depends on a number of factors. The most important factor concerns the programming standards at your site and the stringency of their enforcement. SQR provides program developers with a high degree of flexibility when it comes to printing or manipulating data. When printing or manipulating dates, money, or numbers, programmers can choose between the endless combinations of different edit format mask characters. This flexibility may backfire if you need your program to switch from one national environment to another without program changes, depending on some input parameter of system settings.

For example, if you use hard-coded currency format masks, like `$,$$$,$$$V99`, switching to another currency sign or another way of displaying decimals will involve making changes to the program or, worse yet, creating different versions of the same program. Another example occurs when your program uses hard-coded date format masks, for example, `'MONTHbDD,YYYY'`. This is the traditional American way of displaying dates, and will display the New Year's date as `JANUARY 1, 1998`. In France, the same date will be more likely displayed as `1 janvier 1998`. If your program uses a hard-coded date mask (common in the USA) `MM/DD/YYYY`, April 10, 1998 will be displayed as `04/10/1998`. In most European countries, the recipients of this report will read this date with the month and date transposed, i.e. October 4, 1998: they expect the day's portion of a date to precede the month's portion. As with hard-coded currency format masks, hard-coded date masks make multiple language support very difficult.

The best way to eliminate the problem is to use special SQR keywords `Date`, `Money`, and `Number` when printing or manipulating dates, monetary fields, or numbers. These are preset edit masks that format dates, money or numbers according to the settings in the `SQR.ini` file. The downside of using the keywords is that they impose certain limits on the way your programs will display and manipulate data. For example, if `DATE-EDIT-MASK` is defined in your `INI` file as `Mon-DD-YYYY`, you will need to make an additional effort to squeeze this date into an 8-character field to make it fit some of your overly populated reports. On the other hand, if you are involved in a global development project, using these keywords must be a part of the programming standards in your team.

Assuming that the use of edit format keywords is enforced, you can use *SQR locales* to make your programs automatically adapt to national environments. An SQR locale is a set of local preferences for language, currency, and presentation of dates and numbers.

For example, the US locale will use English names for days and months, the dollar sign for currency, the American way of inputting dates (month first, day second), the American way of displaying dates, the twelve-hour cycle for time, numbers with commas separating the thousands, and a period for the decimal place. The French locale will use French names for days and months, `F` (French franc) for currency, the French way of inputting dates (day first, month second), military time, and the European way of displaying numbers (periods separating thousands, and a comma for the decimal place).

If you use this approach, switching to another national environment will require no programming changes. All you need to do is to make sure that users running your reports have the right `INI` files on their machines. SQR provides predefined locales such as US-English, UK-English, German, French, Spanish, or Japanese. If this is not enough, you can easily create additional locales and place them into the `SQR.ini` file. For example, this is how the US-English locale looks:

```
NUMBER-EDIT-MASK        = '999,999,999.99'
MONEY-EDIT-MASK         = '$$9,999,999.99'
MONEY-SIGN              = '$'
```

```
MONEY-SIGN-LOCATION    = Left
THOUSAND-SEPARATOR     = ','
DECIMAL-SEPARATOR      = '.'
EDIT-OPTION-NA         = 'n/a'
INPUT-DATE-EDIT-MASK   = 'MM/DD/YYYY'
DATE-SEPARATOR         = '/'
TIME-SEPARATOR         = ':'
EDIT-OPTION-AM         = 'am'
EDIT-OPTION-PM         = 'pm'
EDIT-OPTION-BC         = 'bc'
EDIT-OPTION-AD         = 'ad'
DAY-OF-WEEK-CASE       = Edit
DAY-OF-WEEK-FULL       = ('Sunday','Monday','Tuesday',
                          'Wednesday','Thursday', 'Friday','Saturday')
DAY-OF-WEEK-SHORT      = ('Sun','Mon','Tue','Wed','Thu','Fri','Sat')
MONTH-CASE             = Edit
MONTH-FULL             = ('January','February','March','April','May',
                         'June','July','August','September','October',
                         'November','December')
MONTH-SHORT            = ('Jan','Feb','Mar','Apr','May','Jun',

                          'Jul','Aug','Sep','Oct','Nov','Dec')
```

Usually, the `SQR.ini` file contains a few locales. One locale is considered a default locale, and its name is specified in the `[Default-Settings]` section of the `SQR.ini` file. If the name of the default locale is not specified in the `SQR.ini` file, SQR will use a locale named `System`. This locale is also present in the `SQR.ini` file. By assigning users in different countries to different locales, you can make your programs switch automatically to the necessary environment without changing a single line of code. Of course, your program will only change the way it displays dates, money, and numbers. You will still have to take care of things like social security numbers, postal codes, addresses, telephone numbers, and so on, but these, too, can be automated by storing the relevant edit format masks in a database and using the current locale name as a key to retrieve the proper masks. The SQR predefined variable `$sqr-locale` can be used to determine the name of the current locale. A similar approach can be employed by storing report headers and other text strings translated into different languages in a database.

In many cases, your program may need to switch to another locale dynamically. This may happen when SQR programs are run on a server and share the same `INI` file, or when the same program must generate multiple reports for different countries. These programs may accept the country code as an input parameter or they may read it from an input file or a database. The `Alter-Locale` SQR command then can be used to change the current locale assignment at any moment. You can use this command as many times as you want. In addition to switching the current locale, you can also use this command to override certain parameters in the existing locales. The example next demonstrates the use of this command:

```
! TEST21A.SQR
!Dynamically changing locales
Begin-Setup
Declare-Variable
   Date $Date_Time
End-Declare
End-Setup

Begin-Program

Let $Date_Time = datenow()
Let #Salary = 120000

Alter-Locale Locale = 'US-English'  ! Switching to US locale
 DATE-EDIT-MASK        = 'Month DD, YYYY'
Print 'Country USA                  ' (1, 1)
Print 'Date, Time: ' (+1, 1)
Print $Date_Time (, +1) Date
Print 'Salary: ' (, 35)
Print #Salary (, +1) Money
Alter-Locale Locale = 'UK-English'  ! Switching to UK locale
Print 'Country Great Britain ' (+1, 1)
Print 'Date, Time: ' (+1, 1)
Print $Date_Time (, +1) Date
Print 'Salary: ' (, 35)
Print #Salary (, +1) Money

Alter-Locale Locale = 'German'          ! Switching to German locale
Print 'Country Germany        ' (+1, 1)
Print 'Date, Time: ' (+1, 1)
Print $Date_Time (, +1) Date
Print 'Salary: ' (, 35)
Print #Salary (, +1) Money

Alter-Locale Locale = 'French'          ! Switching to French locale
Print 'Country France         ' (+1, 1)
Print 'Date, Time: ' (+1, 1)
Print $Date_Time (, +1) Date
Print 'Salary: ' (, 35)
Print #Salary (, +1) Money

Alter-Locale Locale = 'French'          ! Making French locale European
     Money-Sign = '  EU'                ! switching currency to euro
Print 'European Market        ' (+1, 1)
Print 'Date, Time: ' (+1, 1)
Print $Date_Time (, +1) Date
Print 'Salary: ' (, 35)
Print #Salary (, +1) Money

Alter-Locale Locale = 'Spanish'         ! Switching to Spanish locale
Print 'Country Spain          ' (+1, 1)
Print 'Date, Time: ' (+1, 1)
```

```
Print $Date_Time (, +1) Date
Print 'Salary: ' (, 35)
Print #Salary (, +1) Money
End-Program
```

The output of `Test21A.sqr` appears in figure 21.1.

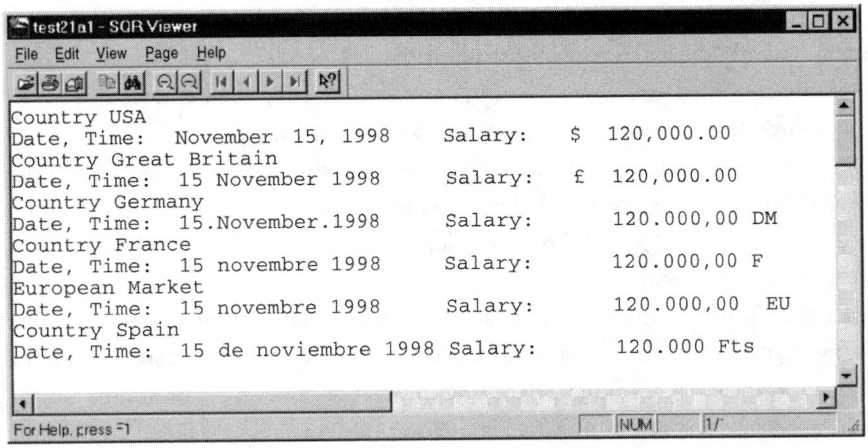

Figure 21.1 Using different locales to print dates and money in different languages

Starting with version 4.2, SQR made another step in supporting multiple languages by introducing double-byte character manipulations. To enable this feature, the `ENCODING` environmental variable in the `SQR.ini` file must be set to either `SJIS` or `JEUC`. The default value of this variable is `ASCII`. Two new SQR commands, `Mbtosbs` and `Sbtombs`, can be used to convert double-byte strings to their single-byte equivalents, and single-byte strings to their double-byte equivalents, respectively (please see appendix D). A number of double-byte string manipulation and conversion functions have been added to the list of SQR built-in string functions.

In addition, two new date edit format codes can now be used in the `Print` command to support the Japanese Imperial Era calendar. Both codes are supported only when the `ENCODING` environmental variable is set to enable double-byte character manipulations. The `ER` format code returns the name of the Japanese Imperial Era in the appropriate kanji (e.g., "Heisei" is the current era). The `EY` format code returns the current year within the Japanese Imperial Era.

21.2 Creating platform-independent programs

One of the strong points of SQR is its ability to run on multiple platforms. Today's corporate-wide enterprise systems usually include components running on different operating systems from Windows to mainframe. Making a program portable between different platforms has always been a developer's dream.

SQR is inherently designed to support platform independence. Because SQR programs are usually compiled and executed in one invocation, they can be moved between platforms at source level, thereby requiring no changes (at least in theory). Even precompiled SQR programs remain portable: when an SQR program is pre-compiled, the resulting `SQT` file is not a true executable file. It represents a pseudo-code, interpreted by the `SQR Execute` (`SQRT` or `SQRWT`). For example, you can use `SQRT` on UNIX to run an `SQT` file created on Windows.

The fact that SQR is capable of producing multiple platform programs does not mean that any SQR program can be moved between different operating systems without special effort. Certain program functionality requirements can limit a program's portability, sometimes making it nearly impossible due to numerous technical difficulties and high development costs.

To avoid possible confusion, let's call a program platform-independent if it is portable across a few of the most popular operating systems. In fact, many developers would consider an SQR program platform-independent when the program can be executed on both client and server without any changes.

Making an SQR program platform-independent involves careful planning and self-discipline. At times you won't need to do anything to make your program portable. In other cases, creating platform independence will require additional programming effort. Let's talk about a few major factors that may affect your program's platform independence.

When an SQR program contains fully qualified file names, they should not be hard-coded. This is true for input/output files, `#Include` files, image files, printer startup files, report files used in the `New-Report` command, file names used in SQR built-in functions, and so on. Hard-coded fully qualified file names include file directories which are platform-specific. For example, a fully-qualified file name must be coded differently for different operating systems:

```
c:\temp\myfile        ! DOS, Windows, Windows NT
/temp/myfile          ! UNIX
dsn=temp.myfile(      ! MVS
```

A few relatively simple techniques exist to solve the problem.

One method is to include all required file names in the program's input parameter list. The parameters can be input via user entry (not the best idea since it involves an extra load for users and a high likelihood of entry mistakes) or placed into the program's argument file. This method works well when your program deals with a small number of files. When the number of files is substantial, the number of input parameters becomes equally substantial (a fact that your data center administrator may not appreciate).

Another method for addressing coding differences for fully qualified file names is to define a directory for all files as a substitution variable in an `SQC` file. Depending on the platform, the proper platform-specific `SQC` file can be placed in the program working directory. This approach is used, for example, by PeopleSoft in its `Setenv.sqc` file. The program logic in this file checks the current platform defined in the platform-specific `SQC` files and sets a substitution variable `{Fileprefix}` based on the platform. For example, for Windows NT, the substitution variable is set to '`c:\temp`', whereas, for UNIX, this variable is set to '`/usr/tmp`'. The fully qualified file names can be built into the program by concatenating the directory and file names. You can define more than one directory: for example, one directory for image files, and another directory for input/output files. Here is an example of using three substitution variables to define file directories:

```
Let $My_File   = '{fileprefix}' || $My_File || '.OUT'
Let $Input_File   = '{io_dir}' || $File_In
Let $Logo_File = '{image_dir}' ||$Logo
```

Please keep in mind that, if you use a substitution variable for a directory, the fully qualified file names will be resolved at compile stage, therefore, you cannot use this method to create a pre-compiled program on one platform and later run it on another platform. The problem can be easily solved by using input parameters instead of substitution variables.

The third method used when working with full file names is to check the `$sqr-platform` SQR predefined variable that contains the operating system name. Use the `Evaluate` command to build the proper file names depending on the value of this variable.

Rule number one: *avoid hard-coded fully qualified file names in platform-independent programs.*

In chapter 18, we discussed the `Call System` command, which allows you to issue native operating commands from an SQR program. While this command increases your program's power and flexibility, you should try to avoid using it in platform-independent programs. SQR provides a few functions that perform a similar task to that of many platform-specific operating system commands. These SQR functions are platform-independent and you should definitely choose them over the `Call System` command. We hope that SQR will add more functions in its future releases. One SQR function you have to be careful about is: `getenv()`. This function allows you to retrieve the value of the specified environmental variable. If you use this function, make sure that you specify only variables that are valid for any operating system your program might run on.

This suggests your rule number two: *avoid calling operating system commands from SQR programs. Use similar SQR functions instead.*

What if SQR functions cannot do what you need? Use a method similar to the file name building technique: check the `$sqr-platform` SQR predefined variable and, depending on its value, use the appropriate platform-specific operating system command. This approach does not make your program platform-independent from a purely scientific point-of-view, but, practically speaking, the program can still be considered portable. If, for example, you can improve your program performance by calling a sort utility, do not discard this just because this call will make the program platform-dependent. It is worth the extra programming effort to call the proper sort utility, depending on the `$sqr-platform` variable value.

There are many other factors that may affect your program portability: not all printer types are supported by all operating systems; not all databases can run on any platform; not all image file types are valid across different platforms; and the return codes from SQR file processing commands are platform-specific. Only a comprehensive testing of your program on different platforms can ensure your program platform independence. Rule number three: *test your programs on different platforms.*

21.3 Database-independent programs

Many programming tools claim that they can work with any database, but SQR is one of the few that can really do this. Its database versatility is phenomenal: SQR can work with Oracle, MS SQL Server, Sybase, SQLBase, DB2, Informix, Ingres, Allbase, Rdb, as well as with other databases via the ODBC.

Does this make your program database-independent automatically? You probably already know the answer. As with platform independence, database independence involves additional programming effort.

Rule number one: *do not use database-specific functions.* This rule was a bit difficult to follow in prior versions of SQR. Version 4 introduced a number of date-processing functions that eliminated the need to use similar database-specific functions. Even with prior versions, you could use a combination of SQR commands and built-in string functions to replace nearly all database-specific functions.

One limitation on the use of SQR commands and built-in functions remains: they cannot be used in the `Where` clause. If you need to use data conversions and other built-in functions in the `Where` clause, your choice is limited to database-specific SQL functions. Rule number two: *avoid using built-in functions in the `Where` clause.*

Please keep in mind that in many cases, built-in functions in the `Where` clause can be very instrumental in reducing the SQL query sizes and improving performance. A reasonable compromise can be found in coding separate SQL logic for each database used in your company and calling the appropriate code, depending on the value of the `$sqr-database` predefined variable.

The following two examples are designed to demonstrate the pros and cons of using database-specific functions. Both programs do the same job of selecting all employees who were hired or rehired during the specified year.

`Test21B.sqr` uses the `datetostr()` SQR built-in function to convert dates to strings, and therefore, is database-independent:

```
!***********************************
!Test21B.SQR
!A database-independent SQR program
!***********************************
Begin-Program
!*********************
Do Main
End-Program
!*********************
Begin-Procedure Main
!*********************
Begin-Select
Emplid
Hire_Dt
Rehire_Dt
   If &Hire_Dt > &Rehire_Dt
     Let $Serv_YYYY=datetostr(&Hire_Dt,'YYYY')
   Else
     Let $Serv_YYYY=datetostr(&ReHire_Dt,'YYYY')
   End-If

   If $Serv_YYYY = '1998'
     Print &Emplid        (+1,1,10)
     Print &Hire_Dt       (,+1,10)
     Print &Rehire_Dt     (,+1,10)
   End-If
From Employment
End-Select
End-Procedure
```

The second program `Test21C.sqr`, employs the Oracle database functions `To_Char` and `Decode` to carry out date-to-string conversions. Both functions are placed in the `Where` clause:

```
!****************************************
!Test21C.SQR
!Using Oracle database-specific functions
!****************************************
Begin-Program
!*********************
Do Main
End-Program
!*********************
Begin-Procedure Main
!*********************
Begin-Select
Emplid    (+1,1,10)
Hire_Dt   (,+1,10)
Rehire_Dt (,+1,10)
From Employment
Where to_char(decode(rehire_dt,Null,hire_dt,rehire_dt),'YYYY')=
    '1998'
End-Select
End-Procedure
```

As you can see, the second program is much smaller and straightforward. It is also more efficient because it restricts the employee selection in its `Where` clause. But it is not database-independent!

Today's RDBMS offer ever-improving performance and flexibility. Strong competition between the relational database vendors has forced the vendors to offer more and more database-specific features to attract new customers and retain the existing ones. This has resulted in less compatibility between different databases. If you want your programs to be database-independent, stick to the common denominator: ANSI SQL standards. This way, you can be sure that at least the SQL parts of your programs will work the same way on different databases. This is your rule number three: *use the ANSI standards in your SQL.* So why doesn't everyone use ANSI standards? For two reasons: first, the ANSI standards are too restrictive, and second, many programmers do not know them.

Working with dates presents another problem for database independence. As we mentioned earlier in this chapter, using hard-coded date masks makes it difficult for your program to work in different language environments. Using no edit mask in date-to-string conversions will make SQR utilize the default date mask. This default date mask is controlled by the SQR environmental variable `SQR_DB_DATE_FORMAT`. If this variable is not defined, SQR will use the first database-specific default date format. Consequently, the `String` command may produce different results, depending on the database-specific format used:

```
String &Emplid &Name &Effdt &Address Into $Empl_Record
```

Assuming the `&Effdt` value is March 15, 1998, the command will move the value shown in table 21.1 to the date portion of the output record.

Table 21.1 Database-dependent default date formats

Database	Output
Oracle	15-MAR-1998
Sybase	MAR 15 1998
DB2	1998-03-15-00.00.00.000000
Informix	1998-03-15 00:00:00.000
SQLBase	1998-03-15-00.00.00.000000

To avoid problems, move `&Effdt` to a string variable using an edit mask (same for all databases) prior to invoking the `String` command. Rule number four: *do not rely on database-specific default date formats.*

It is always a good idea to check the database return code after each SQL operation. But can you always expect the same return codes when working with different databases? Will the databases return the same error messages? The answer is no! It may be a good idea to code separate error-handling routines for different databases and to use the `$sqr-database` predefined variable to call the right routine. Rule number five: *do not assume that all databases return the same error codes and messages.*

Many SQR commands have database-specific parameters and flags or use different syntax with different databases. Here are a few examples:

- `-C`, `-XP`, `-NR`, `-SORT`, `-DB`, `-LOCK` flags in the `Begin-Select` and `Begin-SQL` commands
- `-B` flag in the `Begin-Select` command
- the `Execute` command.

Rule number six: *avoid database-specific parameters and flags in SQR commands.*

21.4 SQL or procedure calls?

In some cases, your program may include rather complex database queries. Should you go crazy by making your SQL more and more complex or should you take advantage of SQR procedure calls instead?

There is no single answer to this question. Each of these approaches may have both advantages and disadvantages, depending on your specific situation.

In many cases, confining all database queries to one SQL may result in a better program performance by reducing the number of open cursors and minimizing the communication between SQR and the database. It also makes your program shorter.

On the other hand, there may be a number of advantages of making your main SQL simpler by shifting a substantial portion of work to procedures that you can invoke from the main SQL.

One of the main drawbacks of very complex "one covers all" SQL statements is that they tend to be very difficult to program and debug. By its nature, SQL is not a procedural language and when your query involves complex logic, you have to create numerous sub-selects, thus increasing a possibility of making an error. It also makes your program difficult to read and understand by other programmers. One single change to your SQL may cause unexpected changes in the query results.

Another problem is that complex SQL statements may have to join many large tables, choking your database engine, especially when you have many outer joins performed against large tables. And in many cases you need outer joins to ensure no data loss when records in joint tables do not match.

Employing one SQL also causes programmers to use more database-specific functions, which makes your program less database-independent.

Using SQR procedure calls from main SQL can make your program much simpler to debug. It will also improve the program's readability. Changes to the program logic are much easier to make and these changes are much more predictable. After all, didn't we say that the main strength of SQR is its ability to combine SQL and procedural logic? Why not use this approach all the time? The main problem is performance. Each query in a called procedure creates a database connection and opens a cursor, which slows your program.

In many cases, you may face this dilemma when working on a master-detail program. In this case, a reasonable compromise may be found in using the `Load-Lookup` command to load the necessary detail data into the program memory and call an SQR procedure to retrieve these data from memory instead of making another SQL call.

21.5 Using the top-down approach

In most examples in our book, we have tried to demonstrate the modular approach to writing SQR programs. We usually started with the main procedure that called other procedures. Each called procedure encapsulated certain functionality, thereby avoiding creating spaghetti-like code. Limiting each procedure to just one function is very important when it comes to program maintenance. Another suggestion is to never combine the `Select` and `SQL` paragraphs in one procedure: this makes your program difficult to test and debug.

Using procedures allows you to create programs by starting from the main procedure and gradually adding lower level procedures. This approach is called *top-down* construction. What is good about this method is that you do not have to code the entire program at once. The yet-to-be-written procedures can be made *dummy* by coding the `Begin-Procedure` and `End-Procedure` statements and hard-coding variables that will be populated in these procedures. This way, you can start testing your program's top-level functionality almost from the moment you start the program code. This is especially important if your program is just one of several related programs in a job or script. Another benefit of the top-down construction is that it forces you to think of the program-testing process well before you have finished with coding. If you work in a team, other team members do not have to wait until you deliver your program—you can give them an unfinished program that may support certain application's functions while you continue working on the remaining procedures.

One problem with the top-down approach is that different procedures often communicate by using shared variables. This creates a good deal of confusion and may be one of the main sources of programming errors. A good way to solve this problem is to use local procedures.

21.6 Local procedures vs. global procedures

Depending on your previous programming experience, you may have differing opinions about the benefits of using local and global procedures. C programmers usually prefer to use local procedures as much as possible. Others may argue that using local procedures involves too much overhead. We shall discuss advantages and disadvantages of local procedures, and let our readers be the final judges.

As you already know, all procedures in SQR are considered global by default. In order to make a procedure local, it must have parameters or must be explicitly declared local. Variables that appear in local procedures are not available outside of their respective procedures. This way, the same variable name can be used in different local procedures without creating an error situation. At the same time, local procedures can communicate with other local and global procedures via parameters. Since global variables defined outside of a local procedure can be accessed only by using special naming conventions (see chapter 5), there is no risk that some variable values can be accidentally overridden. As you can see, local procedures can be instrumental in top-down construction. On the other hand, they have not become popular among the SQR programming community.

Using local procedures is definitely the way to go when:

- the same procedure is called more than once from other procedures (or is called recursively) and uses only its parameters to communicate with the outside world

- a procedure resides in an `#Include` file and is designed to be used by different programs.

In other cases, the use of local procedures by inexperienced programmers may result in additional programming effort and problems with debugging.

If you decide to try using local procedures, please keep in mind the following:

- All variables defined within local procedures are considered local variables, and are not available to other procedures. If you use a variable name that was defined in another local procedure, SQR will not alert you and will consider this variable a new local variable.
- In order to access global variables or columns, they have to be prefixed with an underscore (_) between the first character and the variable or column name (e.g., `&_A.Emplid`, or `$_FileName`).
- Local variables are not initialized every time the procedure is called, but retain their values from the previous procedure call.

Taking these rules into consideration, it's very easy to misspell a variable name or forget about the underscore, making your program prone to errors that are sometimes difficult to trap. Keep in mind that SQR will not alert you since declaring variables is not enforced in SQR. A misspelled variable will simply be considered a new one.

21.7 Handling error conditions

Coding error-handling routines allows you to alert users of any unusual situation, avoid system crushes, and prevent a possible database corruption. A well-written program should have enough error-condition handling to cover both programming errors and unexpected external environmental problems (erroneous input, server crushes, etc.).

A number of SQR commands allow you to use the `On-Error` argument to explicitly specify the name of an error-handling procedure. Among these commands are

- `Begin-Select`
- `Begin-Sql`
- `Connect`
- `Execute` (For Sybase, Microsoft SQLServer and Ingres)

The procedure specified in the `On-Error` argument will be called if the command fails. If no procedure name is specified, and the command fails, SQR halts with an error message.

If your Select paragraph does not contain dynamic variables, there is no need to code the On-Error argument, since it will be checked for syntax errors at the compile stage. When dynamic variables are used, this argument is recommended.

If the Begin-SQL command is used in the Setup section, the On-Error argument specifies the action (Stop, Warn, or Skip), rather than the name of an error-handling procedure.

The On-Error argument in the Divide command works differently. It allows you to set the result to High or Zero when a zero-division occurs. If this argument is omitted, and a zero-division is attempted, SQR halts with an error message. Since zero-division could also happen in the Let command by simply using the "/" sign, you should either check the divisor before division, or use the Divide command with the On-Error argument instead of /. Please note that the Array-Divide command does not have the On-Error argument.

In addition, the following SQR commands use the Status argument to return the status of their execution: Input, Open, Read, Write, Call System. You should check the status variable after executing these commands.

SQR built-in functions do not have the Status argument, but many return a numeric value that can be checked for the status of their execution. Use the Let command to assign this value to a numeric variable, for example:

```
Let #File_Exists = exists($File_Name)
If   #File_Exists <> 0
     Show 'File '  $File_Name '  ' does not exist. '
Else
     Do Main_Process
End-If
```

It is difficult to overstate the importance of error handling. The effort spent to code the error-handling routines is never a wasted time. You will be awarded by a lower maintenance cost, and a higher degree of your data integrity.

21.8 Other useful suggestions

Every SQR programmer has his/her own programming style, usually an amalgam of the programmer's personality and experience, as well as the business and technical environment. It is impossible to present any sort of carved-in-stone rules and recommendations. Perfect programs do not exist nor do absolutely correct ones. Often, budget constraints and time pressures prevail and programmers have to cut corners. It is hard to follow all rules when you have just two hours to write a program.

Throughout this book, we tried to emphasize the importance of error handling, thorough testing, and other good programming habits. Here are a few additional suggestions:

- Do as little hard-coding as possible. Try to make your programs flexible by using substitution variables, dynamic columns, and argument files. Use the SQR predefined variables instead of hard-coded values (see chapter 4 for examples).
- Place encapsulated debugging statements in your program when you write it, not after you have a problem. Using the `-DEBUG` SQR command flag will allow you to turn the debugging on when necessary; otherwise, these debugging statements will be simply ignored by the compiler (see chapter 20 for details and examples).
- Do not forget about comments. Do not rely on program documentation: it gets lost or misplaced and, sometimes, does not provide the necessary answers to specific questions about the program code.
- Use meaningful variable names. Avoid assigning program variables the same names as database columns. For instance, someone could easily confuse `&Effdt` for `$Effdt`.

KEY POINTS

1 To support global development:
   - avoid hard-coding date, currency, and numeric edit format masks: use SQR special keywords `Date`, `Money`, and `Number` instead
   - use SQR locales.

2 To ensure your program's platform independence:
   - do not use fully qualified hard-coded file names
   - use the `$sqr-platform` predefined variable to determine the current platform
   - avoid calling operating system commands from SQR programs; use similar SQR functions instead
   - test your programs on both client and server.

KEY POINTS (CONTINUED)

3 These rules will help you to write database independent programs:

- do not use database-specific functions, use similar SQR functions instead
- avoid using built-in functions in the `Where` clause
- use the ANSI standards in your SQL
- do not rely on database-specific default date formats
- do not assume that all databases return the same error codes and messages
- do not use database-specific command parameters and flags.

4 Using SQR procedures in the `Begin-Select` instead of sub-queries gives your move flexibility and improves readability of your program, but may negatively impact performance.

5 The *top-down* approach to writing programs allows you to write and test high-level procedures while deferring the creation of some lower-level procedures. It is a good idea to limit every program procedure to just one function.

6 Local procedures may help to avoid errors caused by incorrect usage of previously defined variables.

7 Coding error-handling routines allows you to alert users of any unusual situation, avoid the system crushes, and prevent a possible database corruption.

8 Avoid hard-coding in your programs.

9 Place encapsulated debugging statements in the program code.

10 Do not forget about comments.

11 Use meaningful variable names.

PART 3

SQR and PeopleSoft

CHAPTER 22

Running SQR in PeopleSoft applications

IN THIS CHAPTER

- Running SQR programs in PeopleSoft applications
- Monitoring the execution of SQR programs submitted from PeopleSoft
- Viewing the log file and output of your SQR program

22.1 SQR and PeopleSoft

PeopleSoft belongs to a few companies that develop enterprise resource planning and management software. PeopleSoft packages or modules present comprehensive solutions capable of supporting business functionality of an entire corporate structure or large parts of it.

PeopleSoft applications offer a wide range of query and reporting tools that enable users to access the necessary information for both day-to-day and long-term business decisions. For each product (HRMS, Payroll, Financials, etc.), PeopleSoft delivers a set of standard canned reports as a part of its basic package. At the same time, PeopleSoft offers a number of tools designed to help developers with customizing existing reports as well as creating new ones.

PeopleSoft has selected SQR as one of its main reporting and processing tools because SQR provides a flexible and robust report-writing environment. SQR works beautifully when your report needs complex procedural logic or a tricky database manipulation; when you need to run your report on multiple platforms; when your report structure is complex with multiple breaks; or when you need to combine data base retrieval with special row processing.

SQR is included with all PeopleSoft packages. As you learned earlier in this book, you can run your SQR programs from the SQR dialog box, or you can execute them from the operating system command line. PeopleSoft-delivered reports are usually executed from an online page and run with the help of the PeopleSoft Process Scheduler. This does not mean that you cannot execute PeopleSoft-delivered SQR programs from the SQR dialog box or a command line. You just need to have access to the database and to include the proper flags and arguments into the dialog box or the command line.

Programs in PeopleSoft can be written in different languages: SQR, Crystal Reports, Cobol, Application Engine, etc. All these programs can run under the PeopleSoft Process Scheduler. The Process Scheduler works with *processes* and *job streams.*

A *process* is any program that runs under PeopleSoft Process Scheduler. It can be a reporting program, a file generation program, a database update program, or a combination of all three. You can run processes on your workstation or a server. The PeopleSoft Process Scheduler can help you to schedule the execution of processes so that they can run automatically. Previously, we used to call SQR programs "programs" or "reports". In this and subsequent chapters, we will be using the terms "process," "program," and "report" interchangeably to mean any SQR program that runs under PeopleSoft.

The PeopleSoft Process Scheduler allows you to bundle processes into *job streams* and schedule them to run at a specific date and time.

Let's go over the PeopleSoft's standard way of initiating and running SQR programs, monitoring the program execution and analyzing the results. We'll start with the user's view of the process. In subsequent chapters, you will learn what happens behind the scenes, as well as how to create your own Process Scheduler definition in order to allow execution of your SQR program from a PeopleSoft page. Please note that starting from release 8, online panels are called pages and panel groups are called components.

22.2 A high-level view

Let's start by discussing the way PeopleSoft interacts with SQR programs at a very conceptual level without going into many details. (Subsequent chapters will cover every part of this process at a more detailed level.)

In most cases, PeopleSoft users initiate their requests for reports via PeopleSoft pages. These pages can be delivered by PeopleSoft or developed by application programmers.

When a page information is filled in, PeopleSoft generates process request parameters. These parameters usually include `User Id`, `Run Control Id`, `Run Location`, `Output Destination`, `File/Printer` name, plus application-specific parameters, for example, `Company Id`, `FromDate`, `To Date`, and so on.

After the process request parameters have been read from a page, PeopleSoft passes them to the Process Scheduler (please see figure 22.1):

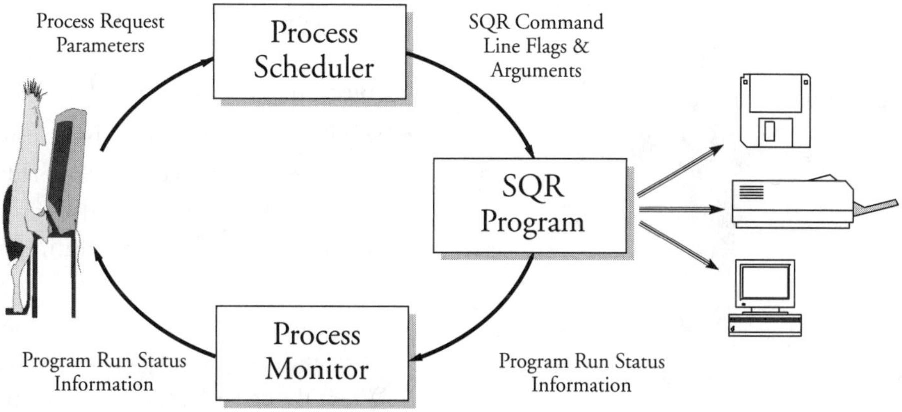

Figure 22.1 Interaction between PeopleSoft and SQR

The Process Scheduler generates the SQR command line with flags and arguments that are required to run the requested SQR program, invokes SQR, and passes the flags and arguments to SQR. When the input from the page is saved, the system updates a number of tables that are used by SQR to communicate with the Process Scheduler and the Process Monitor via the special PeopleSoft API.

The requested SQR program is executed. It may generate reports, update the database, create flat files, or print its reports directly on the specified printer. Users are kept informed about the program status with the help of the PeopleSoft Process Monitor. The Process Monitor receives the program feedback via the PeopleSoft API parameters and displays the program status on the Process Monitor page.

22.3 PeopleSoft objects

PeopleSoft uses a number of objects to control both user-interface and internal processing of the invoked SQR programs. These objects are shown in figure 22.2.

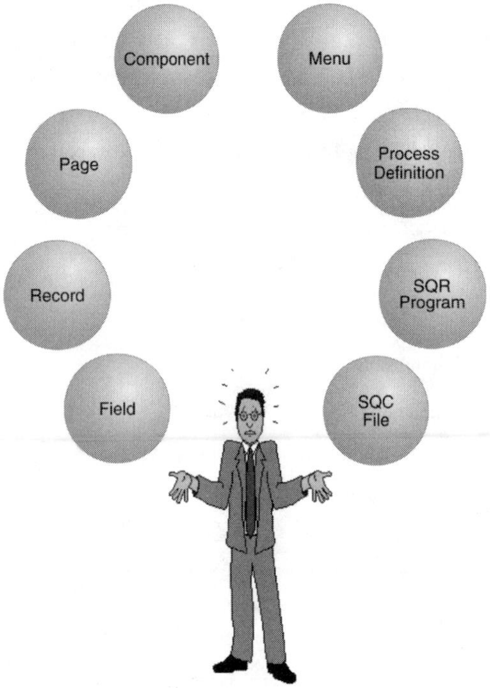

Figure 22.2 PeopleSoft objects

All these objects will be discussed in this or subsequent chapters. Here, we will just present a brief overview of each one:

- *PeopleSoft fields* are basic units of information. In PeopleSoft, fields are defined as stand-alone objects. If any of a field's properties (size, data type, description, etc.) is changed, the change will affect all PeopleSoft objects that include this field.
- *PeopleSoft records* are built by grouping PeopleSoft fields together. Building a record definition is the first step in creating a PeopleSoft record. In this step, you define some basic record characteristics and the record key structure. When the record definition is complete, you can use a special PeopleSoft tool to execute an SQL `CREATE` statement to build the corresponding database table.
- *PeopleSoft pages* are used for data entry and view purposes. In our discussion we will be focusing only on one category of pages: the Run Control pages. These pages are used to enter application-specific parameters necessary to execute your SQR program.

- *PeopleSoft components* are used to link pages to PeopleSoft menus. Once a page is created, it must be added to a component. A component can be composed of a single page or a set of pages. All pages in a component must have the same key structure.
- *PeopleSoft menus* help users to select the report they need to run. When an SQR program is added to the system, it can be attached to an existing menu or to a new menu.
- *PeopleSoft Process definitions* contain information that is necessary to schedule and run your process. They specify the process type, name and description, and the components for which the report is selected.
- an *SQR program* can be a PeopleSoft-delivered program or a custom-written program. In theory, any SQR program can run under the Process Scheduler, however, as you will learn later, in order to maintain a productive two-way communication between your program and PeopleSoft, you have to make certain changes to the program.
- *SQC files* are the `#Include` files that can be added to your SQR program source code. PeopleSoft-delivered `SQC` files help you to standardize interfaces between your program and the Process Scheduler. In addition, you can write your own `SQC` files.

22.4 Selecting a menu

PeopleSoft-delivered reports are usually displayed under the Report or Process menu bar item. In most cases, programs that generate output for printing or displaying are listed under Report, while programs that manipulate the database records or generate flat files are listed under Process. This is not a carved-in-stone rule: some programs marked as reports may update the databases, and some programs marked as processes may generate reports. Many programs do many jobs: print reports, update the databases, and generate files.

> **Note** Please do not confuse the programs listed under the Process on the menu bar with the PeopleSoft Process Scheduler processes: *any program run under the Process Scheduler is considered a process.*

To run a report, select it from the appropriate menu: the Report menu or the Process menu. First, you have to know, of course, which report you need to execute. The HR Manager's hat will help you with this task. Once you put it on, you will immediately realize that you would like to take a look at all available reports within the Administer Workforce (GBL) menu.

To begin, navigate to the following page:

Navigation: Home ➡ Administer Workforce ➡ Administer Workforce (GBL) ➡ Report (figure 22.3).

To print a list of all employee birthdays, for example, click on the Employee Birthdays hyperlink (figure 22.3).

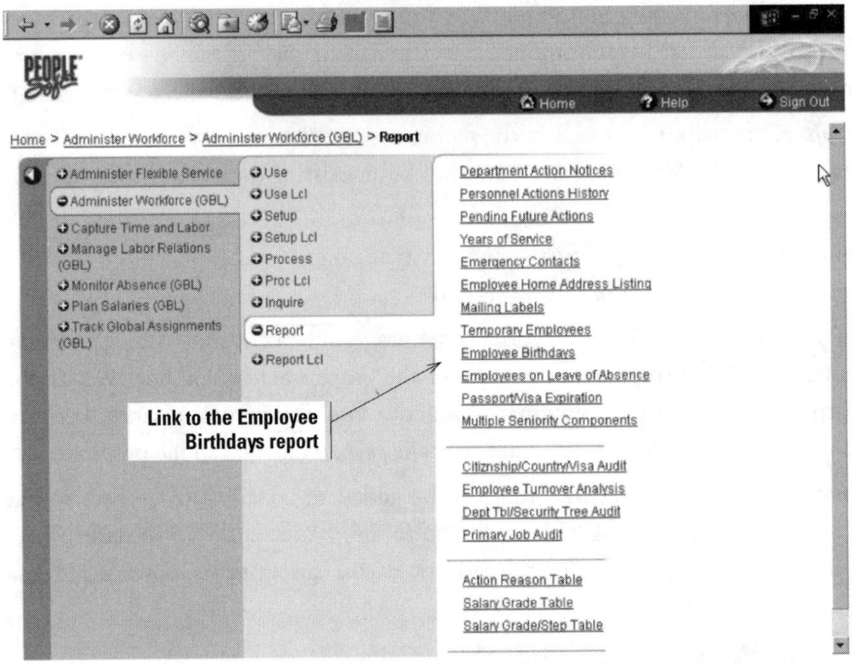

Figure 22.3 Selecting a list of all reports available in Administer Workforce (GBL) menu

At this point the system asks you to specify the Run Control ID value or to add a new value (figure 22.4). The PeopleSoft system is using a special Run Control ID that along with your User ID and a Process Instance, uniquely identify this report.

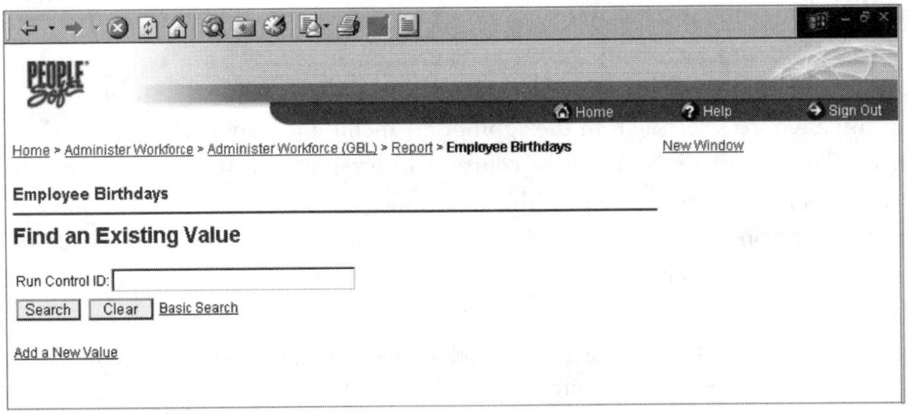

Figure 22.4 Selecting the Employee Birthdays report for execution

22.5 Run control

When we run a process via the Process Scheduler, we need to supply it with a number of parameters like: the run location, output destination, output format, file/printer name, etc. This information is stored in the PeopleTools Run Control record `PSPRCSRUNCNTL`.

In addition, each process maintains its own Application Run Control record to store the process-specific input run-time parameters, for example, `As-Of-Date`, `Company Code`, or `State`. The `Run Control Id` along with the `Operid` are the key fields in both Application Run Control records and PeopleTools Run Control records.

Let's get back to our previous page (figure 22.4). In this page, the system asks you to create a PeopleTools Run Control record or to select an existing one. If an existing record fits your process execution requirements, find the proper record, and reuse it. Otherwise, you will need to click on the Add a New Value link, and add a new `Run Control Id`. Let's select the Add action (figure 22.5).

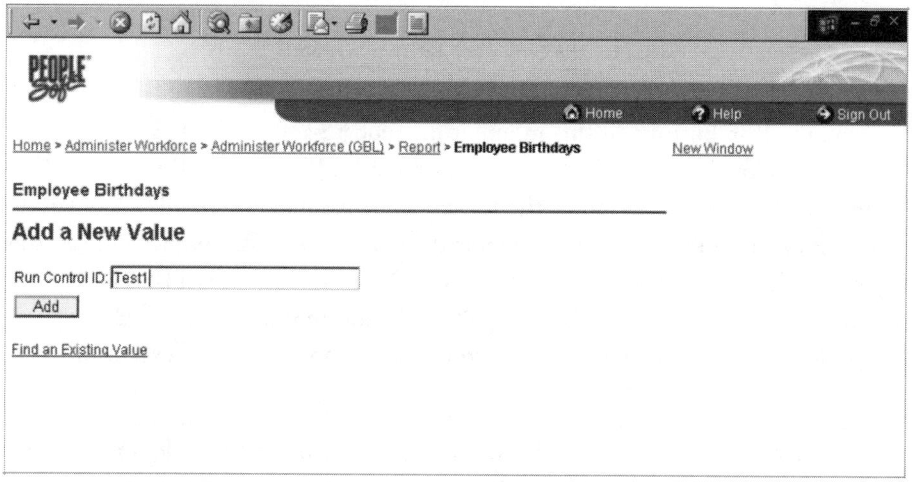

Figure 22.5 Adding a new Run Control record

The system prompted for a Run Control ID. Let's enter TEST1 as shown in figure 22.5 and click on Add. If you already established a Run Control ID, enter it or use the Find an Existing Value link to search for it.

The system displays the next screen called the Run Control page (figure 22.6).

What you see in figure 22.6 is the Run Control page for the Employee Birthdays report. The Run Control ID is the TEST1 value you entered in the previous page.

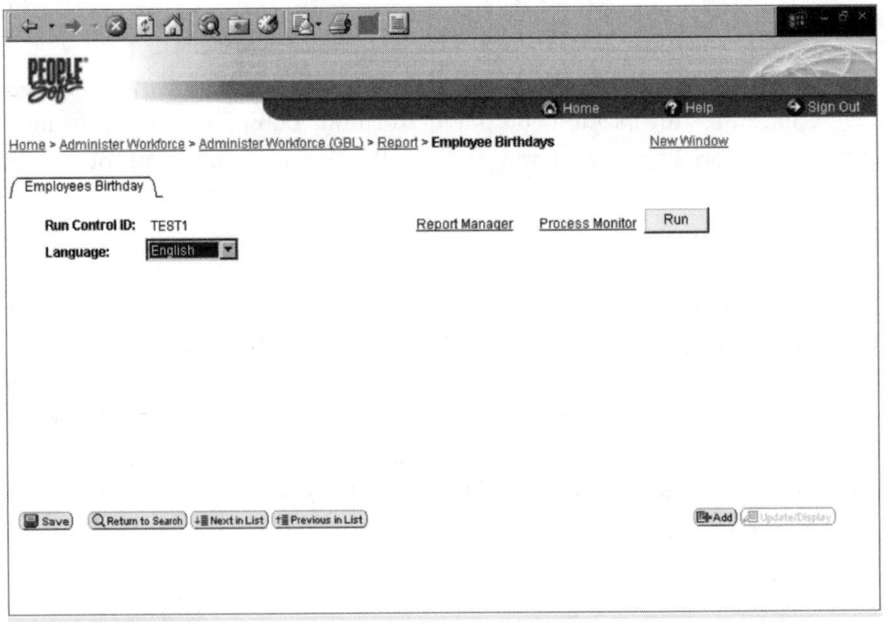

Figure 22.6 The Run Control page for the Employee Birthdays report

Click on the Run button. At this moment the report parameters are saved, and the Application Run Control record is created. This record, identified by Run Control ID TEST1 and Operator ID (PS), stores the report input parameters. It will allow you to reuse these parameters in the subsequent report runs. The next time you need to run this report, you simply select the proper Run Control ID (in our case, it is TEST1), and the system automatically retrieves the settings. (Please be aware that some HRMS applications may delete their Application Run Control records upon successful execution).

Note Note that clicking on the Run button in the Run Control page does not submit the report yet. It brings us to the Process Scheduler Request dialog page.

22.6 The Process Scheduler Request dialog

The Process Scheduler Request dialog (figure 22.7) is used to specify where you want to run your report, the destination type and format of your output, and the time of the report execution. Let's take a closer look at this page and its parameters.

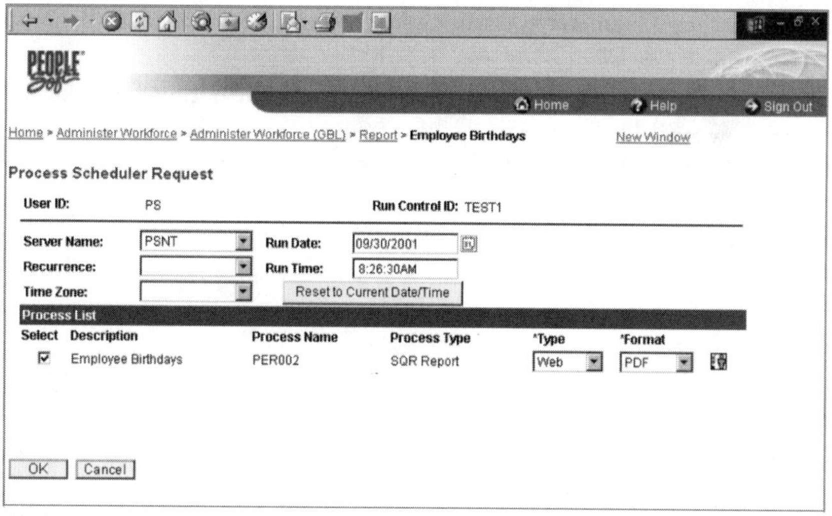

Figure 22.7 Process Scheduler Request dialog

In this page (figure 22.7) you tell the system how to handle your process request. You select the `Server Name` you run your report on, the Recurrence definition, the `Run Date`, and `Time`. The `Recurrence` parameter allows you to define your process as a recurring process that may be executed on a periodic basis. By default, the `Run Date` and `Run Time` parameters are set to the current run date and time. You can change these parameters to indicate that you want to execute your process at a later time.

You can specify a `Time Zone` in which your process will run. For instance, you could be in Eastern Standard Time (EST) zone and schedule a process to run in PST (Pacific Standard Time) zone.

The Reset to Current Date/Time button will set the `Run Date` and `Run Time` to current date and time.

Please note that starting from release 8.0, the setup control for Recurrence has been removed from this page. You can still select an existing Recurrence definition for your process but in order to add or modify one, you need to use the development environment. We'll discuss this in details in chapter 26 of this book. This change was made to simplify the Process Request dialog for end users.

Let's examine the Process List portion of the Process Scheduler Request page. Under Process List you could have more than one process as long as they all share run-time parameters specified in the same Run Control record and page. The Select check box lets you chose one or more processes to run together. If this box is not checked, the process will not be included into the run.

By changing the `Type` parameter you can choose to send your output to the Web (default), a file, a printer or email.

The Format box will allow you to specify the format of your output file. The following formats are now available as output types for SQR:

- Adobe Acrobat (`*.pdf`)
- Comma Delimited (`*.csv`)
- PostScript (`*.ps`)
- HP (`*.lis`)
- HTML (`*.htm`)
- Line Printer(`*.lis`)
- SQR Portable (`*.spf`)

The default output format for SQR with output type Web is Adobe Acrobat (`.pdf`).

As you can see there are several kinds of file output types that you can choose for your process. There is a variety of possible output formats depending on what output type you have selected. Table 22.1 shows formats you can choose for each Type selected.

Table 22.1 Output file types and the corresponding file formats

	File	Email	Printer	Web
PDF - Acrobat (*.pdf) (Must have Acrobat Reader installed to read these files.)	X	X		X
HP - (*.lis)	X	X	X	X
LP - Line Printer (*.lis)	X	X	X	X
SPF - SQR Portable Format (*.spf)	X	X		X
PS - PostScript Files (*.ps)	X	X	X	X
CSV - Comma Delimited (*.csv)	X	X		X
HTML (*.htm)	X	X		X

If you select File or Printer as your output type, you will be able to specify the Output Destination that will appear on the screen once the File or Printer is selected.

For Email or Web you will be able to specify the destination on the Distribution Detail page by clicking on the Distribution icon that appears only when output type is Web or Email. The Distribution Detail page allows you to select the recipients of your process output. If the process that you are running allows output that can be emailed (for example, Adobe Acrobat [`.pdf`] files), you can enter an email subject and message and send the output to a group of email addresses.

Those who used the system prior to version 8 may also notice that the Run Location box is not available when submitting your report from a browser. The Windows version of the Process Scheduler Manager still exists for a backward compatibility and you can submit your reports on the client when using the application in Windows. PeopleSoft recommends that you run your processes from a browser using the PeopleSoft Internet Architecture (PIA). During the course of this book, we will be executing our processes from a browser using PIA. This architecture gives you more flexibility in distributing and viewing your output in Report Manager. If you submit your process using the Windows client, the Process Request Dialog page appears after you select File, Run or click on the traffic light button from a PeopleSoft application. When you submit a process request from PIA, you execute the request using the Process Scheduler Server Agent. If you use Windows, you still have the option of submitting your request through the Server Agent or running it locally on your workstation.

After your Process Scheduler Request page is filled, click on the OK button (figure 22.7.) The PeopleTools Run Control record (PSPRCSRUNCNTL) is updated. Also a record is inserted into the PSPRCSRQST table (Process Request Table) and other PeopleTools tables. This gives the Process Scheduler the necessary information to run and monitor the process request.

How does it work? The Process Scheduler Server Agent polls the PSPRCSRQST table for incoming process requests. When the row is found, the Server Agent invokes the special program, called PSSQR wrapper, which then calls `SQRW.EXE` or `SQR.EXE` depending on the platform the SQR Report runs on. The Process Scheduler Server Agent also updates the Run Status of this process instance to Initiated and the Session ID with the process instance of that process.

Figure 22.8 shows you that the report is submitted for execution. How can we be sure that the report has been submitted? Take a look at the line under the Run button. It shows the Process Instance number. As soon as your report is submitted, the system automatically generates the Process Instance value.

Note A Process Instance number displayed under the Run button indicates that your process has been submitted for execution.

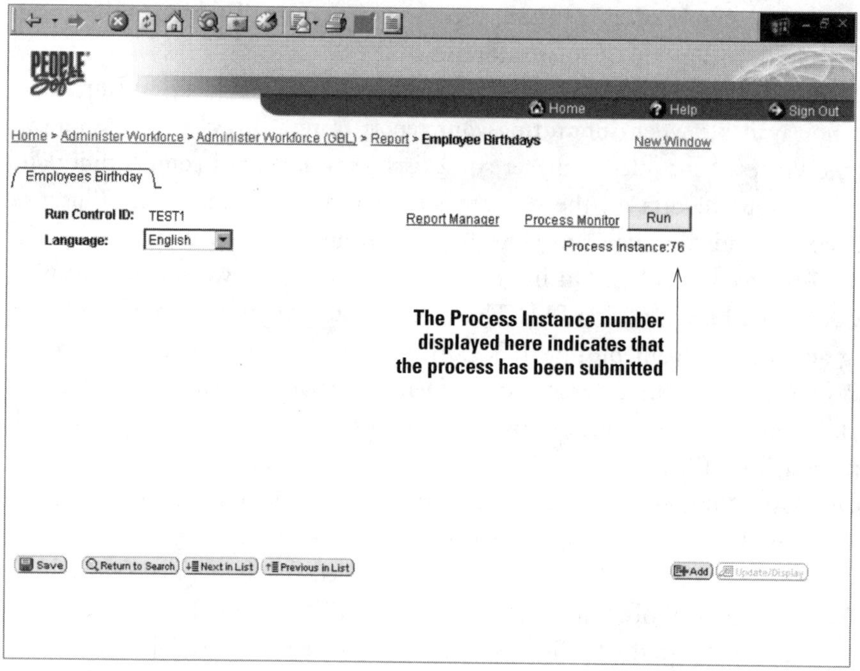

Figure 22.8 The Employee Birthdays report is submitted for execution.

22.7 The Process Monitor

The Process Monitor not only allows you to check the status of your process, but also to delete completed report requests from the queue or cancel process requests that are currently running or have been initiated.

If you click on the Process Monitor hyperlink (figure 22.8), the system will bring you to the Process Monitor page as shown in figure 22.9.

The Refresh button is used to update this page. The Process Monitor shows the processes by User (Operator ID). You can modify this process list by narrowing the selection down to a specific Server, Type (SQR Report, SQR Process, Application Engine, Crystal, etc.), or Run Status (Success, Error, Initiated, Canceled, etc.). Also, you can use the `Last` edit box to see your reports within a specified time range in Days, Hours, Minutes. Usually, you view by your own user ID. But if you leave this field blank the system lets you view all the processes that you are authorized to see.

The View Job Items checkbox lets you view the individual items, or process requests, that make up a job. If you want to see the entire job and not the process requests within it, leave this checkbox blank.

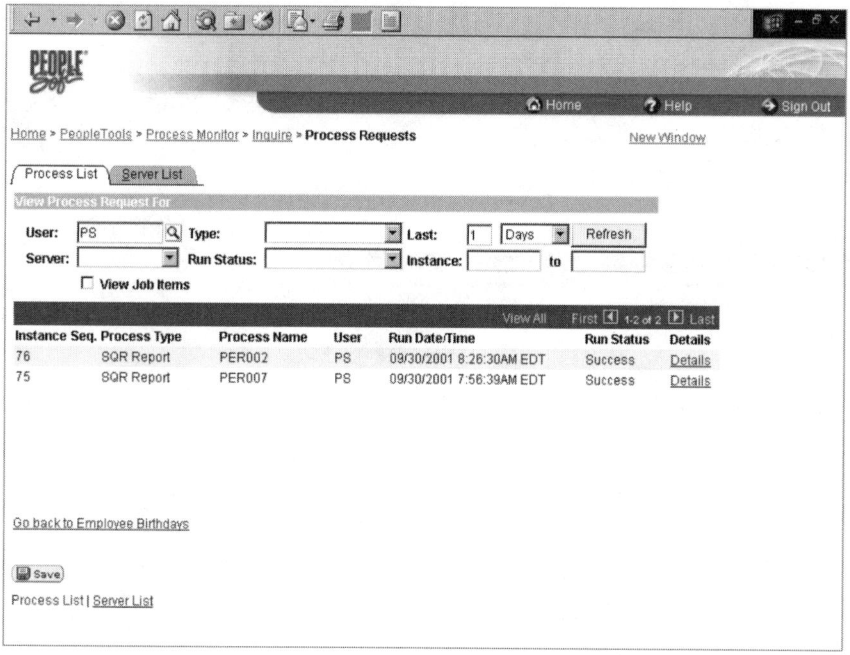

Figure 22.9 The Process Monitor page

Sometimes, if the process you started just sits in the input queue with its status equal to Initiated or Queued, and you wonder what's going on, the first thing to do is to click on the Details link to find the Server name your process was assigned to. Then you can check to see whether the appropriate Server Agent is up and running by selecting the Server List tab (figure 22.10).

As you can see, the PSNT Server Agent is up and running. But if it is down, you would need to contact your systems administrator to start the right Server Agent for your process.

Let's go back to the Process List tab (figure 22.9). Our process has been successfully executed. Click on the Details link. The system will display the Process Detail page as shown in figure 22.11.

This page (figure 22.11) gives you more information about the process request. The Process Detail page shows the process Description, Type, the Run Control ID, and the Server name. You can check to see how long your report took to run by looking at the begin and end date/time stamps. Knowing these details can be very useful in troubleshooting.

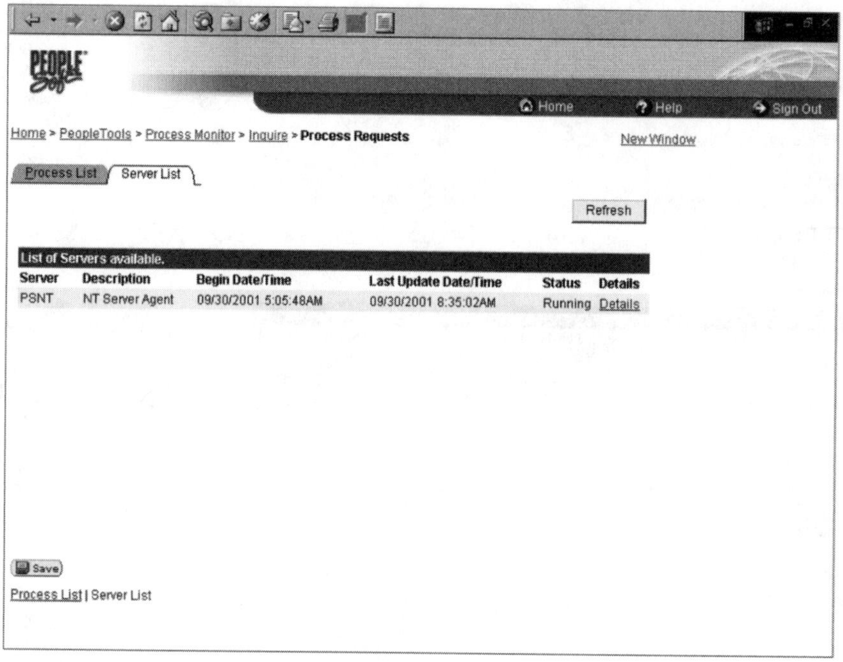

Figure 22.10 The Server List tab

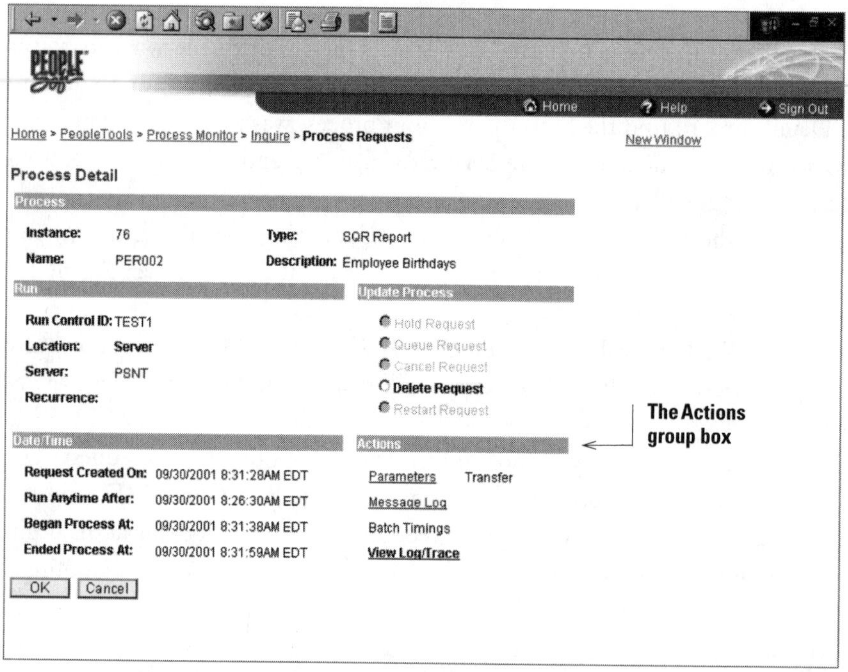

Figure 22.11 The Process Detail tab

22.7.1 Deleting, cancelling, or putting on hold report request

The Process Detail page gives you a certain level of control over your process. You can cancel, delete, restart or put the process on hold. Depending on the current status of your process, the system will allow you to select a valid action.

You will be able to:

- `Delete` the process request if its current status is one of the following: `Error`, `Cancelled`, `Successful`, `Unsuccessful`, `Not Posted`.
- `Cancel` the process request if its current status is `Hold`, `Queued`, `Initiated`, `Processing`
- `Hold` process requests that are `Queued`.
- `Queue` process requests you've put on `Hold`.
- `Resend` the `Not Posted` process requests.

Since our process has been successfully executed, the system will allow us to delete the request. All other actions are grayed-out.

In order to update the Process Request status, you have to select the valid action and then click on the OK button.

Depending on your system security setup, you may be able to update the status of the processes submitted by other operators.

22.7.2 Viewing the Process Request parameters

In the lower right corner of the Process Detail page (figure 22.11) there is an Actions group box. It contains links to other pages that display additional details about your process request. Click on the Parameters link. The system will show you the Process Request Parameters page as in figure 22.12.

Figure 22.12 displays all parameters that are passed to your process, as well as the command line used during the process execution.

Take a closer look at the Command Line entry. It shows the exact command line that your operating system uses to launch `PSSQR.EXE` to run SQR. As we already mentioned, starting from release 8, SQR is executed with the help of the wrapper program `PSSQR.EXE`.

This very useful information will help you to eliminate any configuration problems you might have. You could copy these parameters and then try to run the process outside Process Scheduler to isolate a problem. Please note that you would have to manually provide the access ID and password since they are not exposed on this page for security reasons. Also keep in mind that some delivered PeopleSoft programs prevent you from

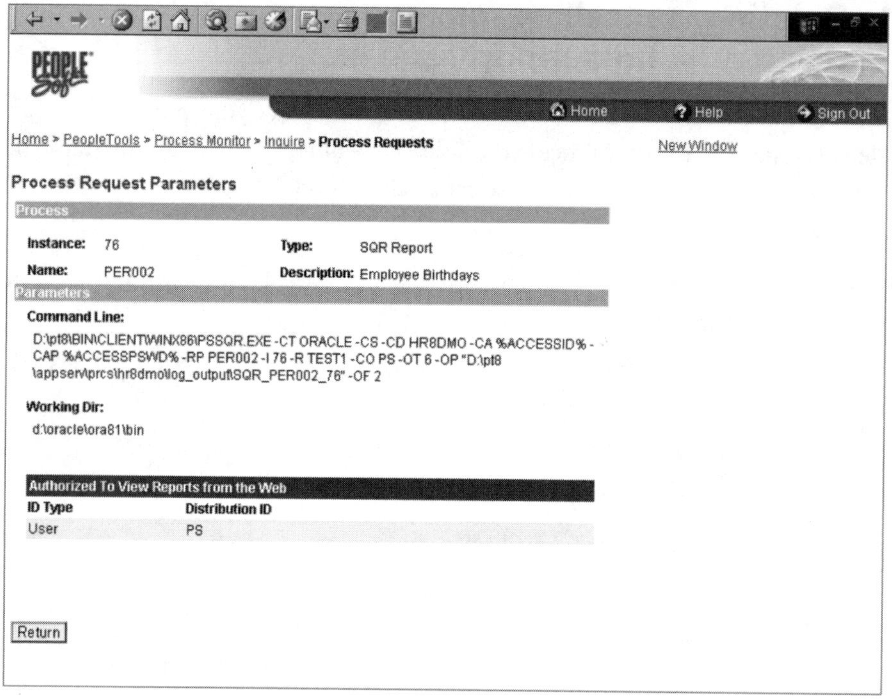

Figure 22.12 The Process Request Parameters page

executing them outside the Process Scheduler for security reasons. We'll discuss this in chapter 27.

The Working Dir displays the directory in which the database connectivity software is installed.

Click on the Return button to get back to the Process Request Detail page.

22.7.3 Reviewing the Message Log and Trace files

From the Process Detail page (figure 22.11) click on the View Log/Trace link. The system will display the Report/Log Viewer page as shown in figure 22.13.

This lets you view the message log, trace file, or the output of the report in PDF format.

Please note that the View Log/Trace link appears on the Process Detail page (figure 22.11) when the following two conditions are met:

- the process request output destination is set to Web
- the report and log files were successfully posted to the Report Repository by the Distribution Agent. The process must have a run status of `Successful`.

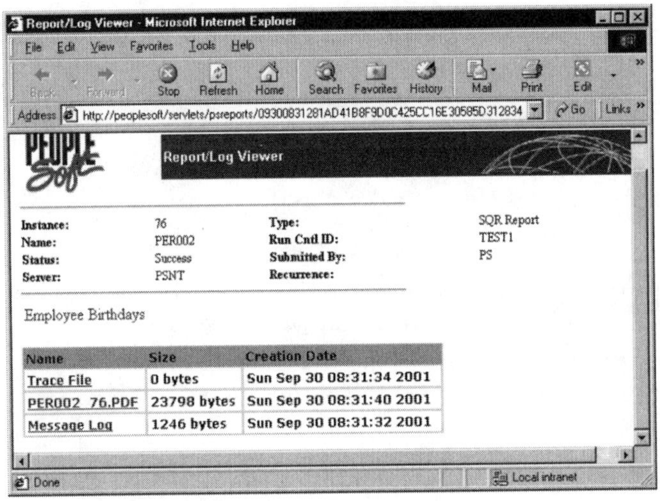

Figure 22.13
The Report/Log Viewer page

In case the report hasn't been transferred to the Report Repository, the run status of the process request will remain `Posting` and the View/Log link will not be active. In this case you can check the Message Log for any messages from the Distribution Agent indicating if there were problems transferring files to the Report Repository.

Note The View Log/Trace link is only available from the Web. If you are accessing the Process Detail from Windows version of PeopleTools this option will not be available.

Let's click on the Message Log link (figure 22.11). The system displays a page as shown in figure 22.14.

This page (figure 22.14) gives you more detailed information about your process including the database name and type, run control parameters and flags, output destinations, etc. It also can be very useful in troubleshooting.

Let's get back to the Report/Log Viewer page (figure 22.13) by selecting the Back arrow on the Internet Browser menu bar, or by closing this page.

The Trace File link brings you a page with the log file. Any `Display` or `Show` statements used in your SQR program will be shown in this file. It will also show you any errors produced by the program. If your SQR program has no `Display` or `Show` statements and runs with no errors, you may see an empty file in this case. This is exactly what happened in our case. As you may have noticed, the size of the trace file in figure 22.13 is zero.

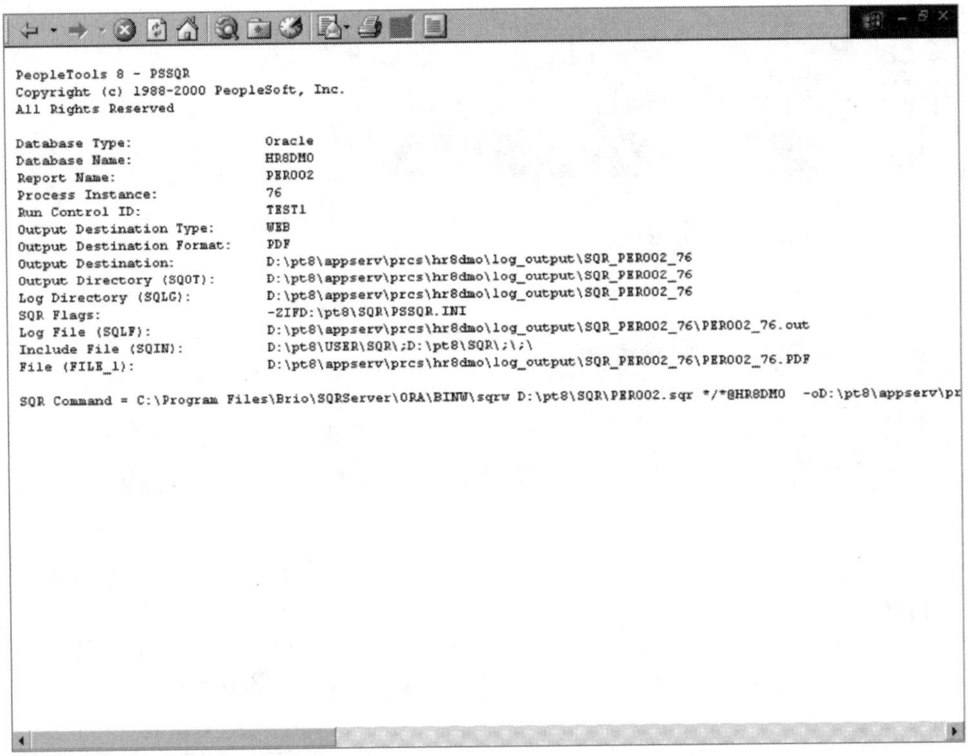

```
PeopleTools 8 - PSSQR
Copyright (c) 1988-2000 PeopleSoft, Inc.
All Rights Reserved

Database Type:                      Oracle
Database Name:                      HR8DMO
Report Name:                        PER002
Process Instance:                   76
Run Control ID:                     TEST1
Output Destination Type:            WEB
Output Destination Format:          PDF
Output Destination:                 D:\pt8\appserv\prcs\hr8dmo\log_output\SQR_PER002_76
Output Directory (SQOT):            D:\pt8\appserv\prcs\hr8dmo\log_output\SQR_PER002_76
Log Directory (SQLG):               D:\pt8\appserv\prcs\hr8dmo\log_output\SQR_PER002_76
SQR Flags:                          -ZIFD:\pt8\SQR\PSSQR.INI
Log File (SQLF):                    D:\pt8\appserv\prcs\hr8dmo\log_output\SQR_PER002_76\PER002_76.out
Include File (SQIN):                D:\pt8\USER\SQR\;D:\pt8\SQR\;\;\
File (FILE_1):                      D:\pt8\appserv\prcs\hr8dmo\log_output\SQR_PER002_76\PER002_76.PDF

SQR Command = C:\Program Files\Brio\SQRServer\ORA\BINW\sqrw D:\pt8\SQR\PER002.sqr */*@HR8DMO  -oD:\pt8\appserv\pr
```

Figure 22.14 The Message Log page

22.7.4 Viewing the report output

If your program produced a report with an output destination type of Web, you should be able to click on the report link from the Report/Log Viewer page (figure 22.13) and view your report via a browser as shown in figure 22.15.

Another way to view your report is by using the Report Manager. You can use the following path: PeopleTools>Report Manager>Inquire>Report List. The page will display all reports you (or all operators that are authorized to view) have executed within the specified time interval. For example, figure 22.16 shows all reports executed by operator PS within the last 2 days.

From this page you can also view your report output by choosing the View link for the report you'd like to view.

Have you noticed that the status of our report on figure 22.16 is `Posted`? Don't be alarmed. `Status` on the Report Manager page is different from `Run Status` on the Process Request page. `Posted` here indicates that our report file has been successfully posted to the Report Repository.

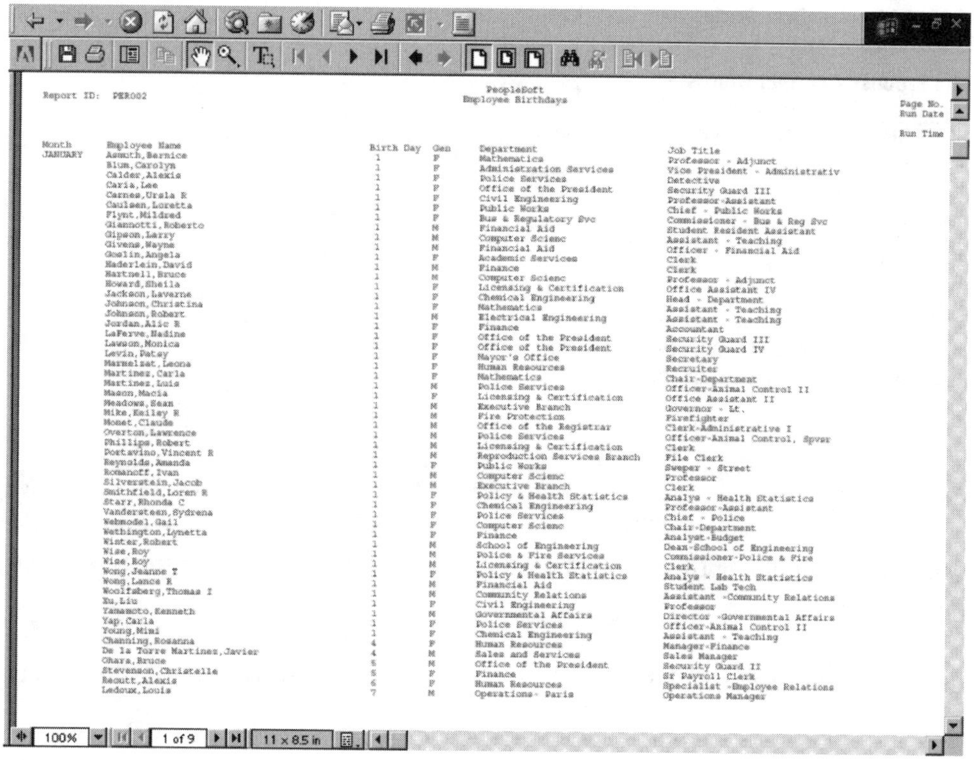

Figure 22.15 The output report file

In fact, a process with an output destination type of Web will have several different statuses during the time between the process initiation and report posting. These run statuses are described in table 22.2.

Table 22.2 The Run Status and Distribution Status

The Process Request Status	Run Status in Process Monitor	Distribution Status in Report Manager
New Process Request created.	Queued	Scheduled
Process Request is initiated by a Process Scheduler Server Agent.	Initiated	Processing
The program for the process request started.	Processing	Processing
Program has completed.	Posting	Generated
Distribution Agent attempts to transfer the files to the Report Repository.	Posting	Posting

Table 22.2 **The Run Status and Distribution Status (continued)**

The Process Request Status	Run Status in Process Monitor	Distribution Status in Report Manager
Distribution Agent failed to transfer file to the Report Repository and hasn't reached the Maximum of Transfer Retries.	Posting	Posting
All files are successfully transferred to the Report Repository	Successful	Posted
The Distribution Agent failed to transfer files to the Report Repository and has used up the Maximum of Transfer Retries.	Not Posted	Not Posted

Note that status changes described in table 22.2 apply to process requests that have output destination type of Web. Log files are transferred to the Report Repository when you select the option of transferring log files to the Report Repository in the Server Definition page.

For process types with output destination other than Web, you can track status through the Message Log. For example, if you execute the same report with the Output

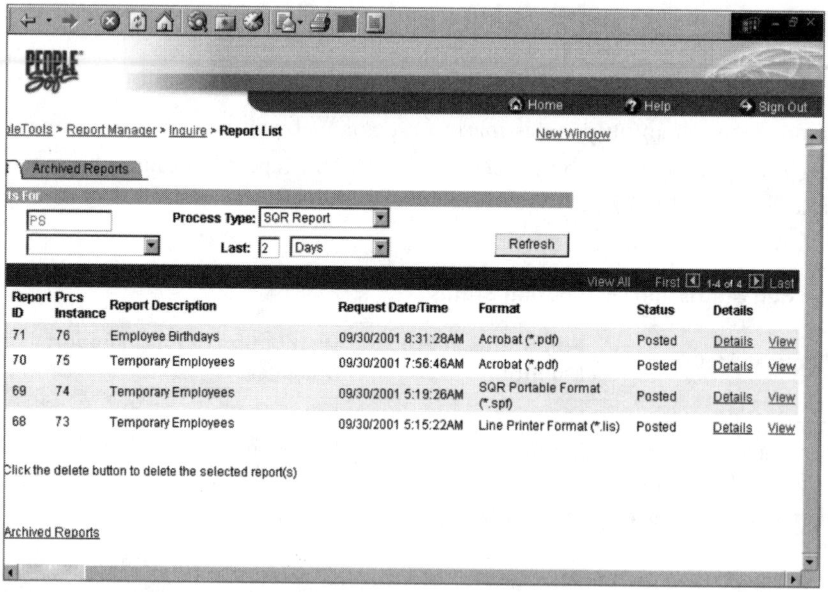

Figure 22.16 All reports in the Report Manager submitted by Operator PS within the last 2 days

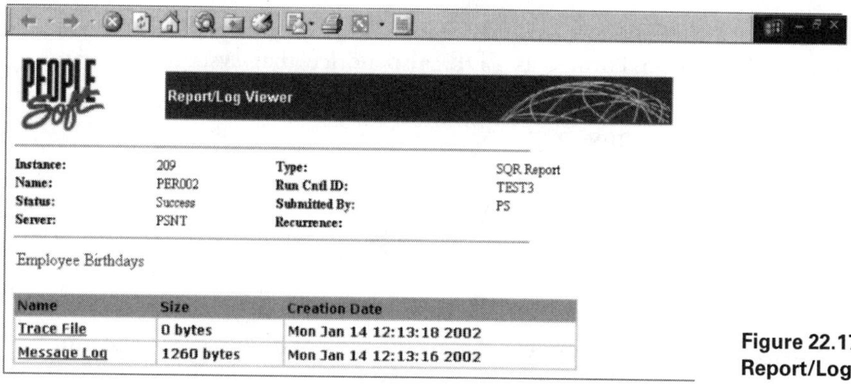

Figure 22.17 Report/Log Viewer

Destination as File and then look at the Report Log/Viewer page, you will not find any links to your output report as shown in figure 22.17.

When a report's output type is other than Web, the Report/Log Viewer does not show a link to the report's output file.

In order to find the output destination, just click on the Message Log link as shown in figure 22.17. The next page (figure 22.18) shows that the report output destination is PDF.

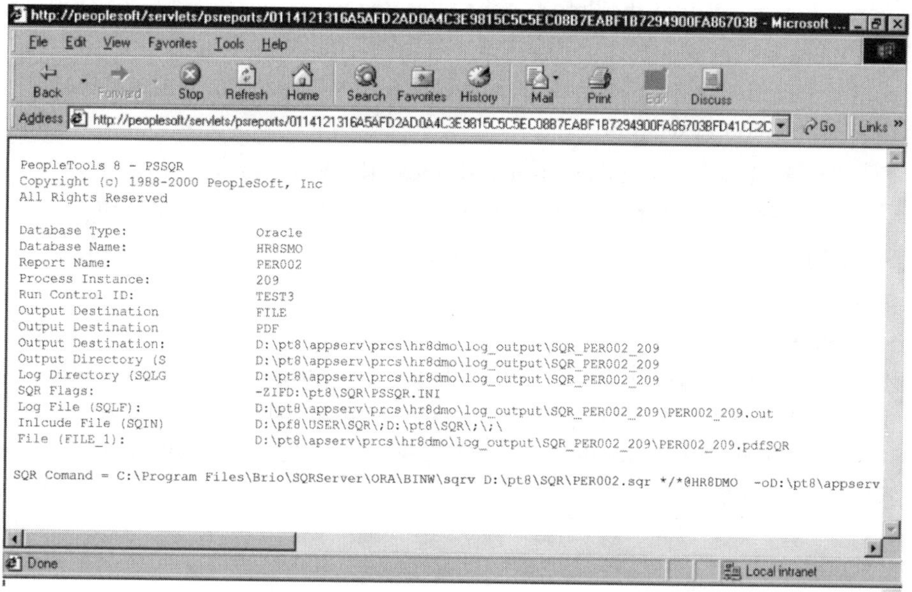

Figure 22.18 The Message Log contains output destination and other important parameters

Figure 22.18 shows that we executed our report with Output Destination Type of File and Output Destination Format as PDF. Also notice that system automatically assigned the output report name in the following format: ProcessName_Instance.Format, in our case, it is `PER002_209.PDF`.

KEY POINTS

1. PeopleSoft-delivered reports are usually executed from online pages and run with the help of the PeopleSoft Process Scheduler.
2. The Process Scheduler works with processes and job streams.
3. PeopleSoft recommends executing processes and jobs via the PeopleSoft Internet Architecture (PIA). It allows you more flexibility in distribution and viewing the report output in Report Manager.
4. The Process Scheduler controls process execution with the help of the control records: PeopleTools Run Control and the Application Run Control. The Run Control ID along with the Operator ID are the key fields in these records.
5. Clicking on the Run button in the Run Control Page does not submit a report. It brings you to the Process Scheduler Request page.
6. The Process Scheduler Request page is used to specify where you want to run your report, the destination and the type and format of your output, and the time of the report execution.
7. The Process Instance number displayed under the Run button on the Run Control page indicates that your process has been submitted for execution.
8. SQR is executed by the wrapper program `PSSQR.EXE`. This is an executable module of a program written in C that is responsible for handling your process request.
9. The Trace File hyperlink in the Report/Log Viewer page brings you a page with the log file. Any `Display` or `Show` statements used in your SQR program will be shown in this file. It will also show you any errors produced by the program.

KEY POINTS (CONTINUED)

10 The View Log/Trace link appears on the Process Monitor Detail page if the following two conditions are true:

- the process request output destination is set to Web
- the report and log files were successfully posted to the Report Repository by the Distribution Agent. The process must have a run status of Successful.

11 If your program produced a report with an output destination type of Web, you would be able to click on the report link from the Report/Log Viewer page and view your report online. For process types with output other than Web, you can track their status through the Message Log.

12 The Status on the Report Manager page differs from the Run Status on the Process Request page

CHAPTER 23

Attaching an SQR program to PeopleSoft objects

IN THIS CHAPTER

- The PeopleSoft Internet Architecture and the development environment
- Selecting Run Control records
- Selecting Run Control pages
- Selecting components and adding pages to the components
- Selecting a menu for your report
- Granting security access to the newly created menu items
- Creating a Process definition for your program
- Testing your changes

23.1 Behind the scenes

In the previous chapter, you learned how to run the PeopleSoft-delivered SQR reports from the web pages using the Process Scheduler. Now we will take a look at what is happening behind the curtain and learn how you can attach your own reports to the PeopleSoft Process Scheduler. You will need to use PeopleSoft PeopleTools, an application development environment that allows programmers to develop, customize, maintain, and implement pages, components, records, and menus. Please be advised that while we will touch on aspects of PeopleTools pertinent to SQR, a thorough discussion of PeopleSoft objects would go beyond the scope of our book. Here we will concentrate on PeopleTools objects that are used in attaching an SQR program to the PeopleSoft Process Scheduler. To learn more about the PeopleSoft development process, please refer to the corresponding PeopleSoft technical manuals.

PeopleSoft delivers a number of standard reports, records, pages, and menus, and has always recommended that the best way to add new functionality is to clone already developed similar application objects. We will be using this commonly accepted approach in attaching custom reports to PeopleSoft.

In the previous chapter, we discussed the process of selecting, scheduling, running, monitoring, and viewing an existing report. What steps are necessary to add a new report to the PeopleSoft Process Scheduler? The best way to answer this question is to use one of the sample programs created in the previous chapters of this book.

In chapter 17, we created the E-Mail Interface program, `Test17A.sqr`. With this as our custom SQR program, we will determine what needs to be done so that users can run this program under PeopleSoft. Let's review how an existing program (for example, the Employees Birthdays report) is accessed in PeopleSoft, and, also what PeopleTools objects are involved in this process. These or similar objects will be the ones you need to create or modify for the new program.

To access any report under PeopleSoft, you need to know the menu to which this report belongs. For the Employees Birthdays report, the menu is Administer Workforce (GBL). When you go to Administer Workforce (GBL) and select Reports (see figure 22.3 in chapter 22), all reports relevant to this task are listed under this menu. For a new report, you either have to create a new menu or attach the report to an existing menu.

Let's go back to figure 22.3. When you select the Employees Birthdays report and specify a `Run Control Id` for the report, the system displays the Run Control page for the selected report. Every report needs this kind of page, which contains the Operator ID, the Run Control ID, and the application-specific parameters (if any). Therefore, the new report will either need a new Run Control page or use an existing one.

In PeopleSoft, a page is linked to a menu with the help of a component. Therefore, a new component has to be created or an existing one can be modified.

After all application-specific parameters (if any) are entered and the Run Control page is saved, the system inserts this information into the Application Run Control record for the report.

In order to attach your report to a Run Control page, a Process definition has to be created for this report.

To summarize, the following PeopleTools objects have to be created or reused when you need to attach a custom report to the PeopleSoft Process Scheduler:

- Menu
- Run Control page
- Component
- Application Run Control record
- Process definition

Now, that you know all the steps involved in attaching a program to PeopleSoft, let's do this for the E-Mail Interface program. One special feature of this program is that it uses no input parameters. Later, we will discuss how to handle input parameters in programs run under the Process Scheduler.

Note that the listed objects do not have to be created in the order shown. In fact, our steps in attaching the E-Mail Interface program to the Process Scheduler will have to be taken in a different order as we'll explain later in this chapter.

23.2 PeopleSoft Internet Architecture

In PeopleSoft 8, access to the system by end users is based on the PeopleSoft Internet architecture (PIA). In PIA, end users do not have any PeopleSoft-specific software installed on their machines. They use standard Internet browsers to connect to their respective Web server, which, in turn, interacts with the Application server.

The PeopleSoft Web server handles the standard tasks of communication between the Application server and user's browser, such as sending data back and forth, encryption, hosting of static web pages and images, and so on. In addition to the standard tasks, this server hosts a number of PeopleSoft-specific Java servlets designed to handle various PeopleSoft-specific transactions.

The Application server hosts most of the processing logic. There are two main parts of this server: the Tuxedo middleware and the PeopleSoft server processes. Tuxedo's Java-enabled component Jolt manages communication between the Web server and Application server. The PeopleSoft server processes run the bulk of the PeopleSoft business logic. When processing each user request, the Application server processes connect to the Database server, submit the database query, and receive the query result set. The Application server processes then analyze and process the result set, generate the output stream, and send it to the Web server via Jolt, which ultimately sends it back to the browser (see figure 23.1). The Application server also communicates with the Batch server.

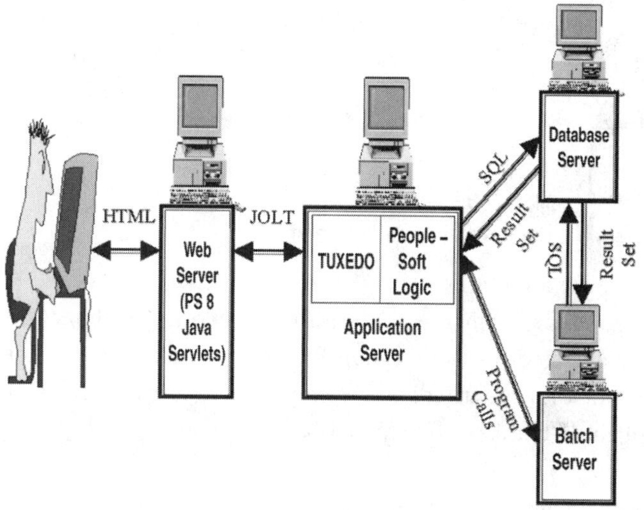

Figure 23.1
The PeopleSoft Internet Architecture (PIA)

The Database server stores all PeopleSoft tables. There are three main types of tables on this server: system catalog tables, PeopleTools tables and PeopleSoft application data tables.

The Batch server controls the execution of batch processes. The most important component of this server is the Process Scheduler. The Process Scheduler submits and monitors your SQR programs as well as various other processes such as Application Engine processes, Cobol programs, etc. Depending on your specific environment, the Batch server may be a separate physical server or a part of the Application server.

The PIA schema supports the most reliable and secure business environment for end users. PeopleSoft developers and system administrators do not need such a complex schema. They can use the traditional client/server two-tier architecture for development or system administration and use the PIA mostly for testing purposes (a three-tier architecture may also be a part of this schema). In this case, all PeopleSoft software is installed on developers' machines or networks. This approach reduces much of the PIA overhead while providing developers with access to all system catalog tables, PeopleTools tables, and application tables (see figure 23.2).

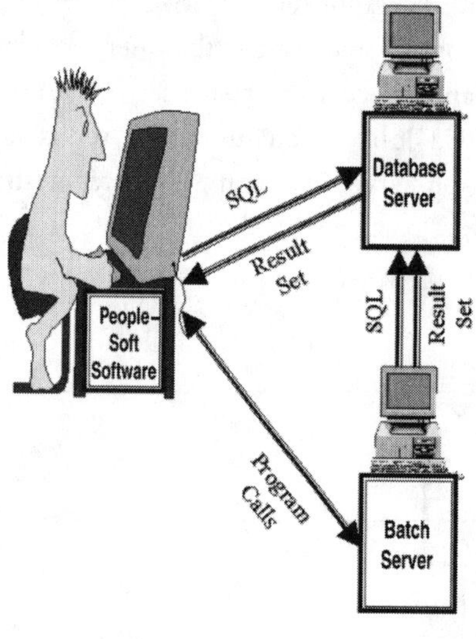

Figure 23.2
The development environment

The fact that PeopleSoft developers can use the traditional two-tier architecture does not mean that nothing has changed. In fact, version 8 is so revolutionary that not only the architecture changed, but tools, methods of development and even names of some PeopleTools objects changed. What used to be panels are now pages, panel groups are now components.

In this and subsequent chapters, we will be using the development environment to create or modify various PeopleTools objects and the PIA to access the PeopleSoft utilities, administer the PeopleSoft security, or run your processes.

23.3 Selecting a Run Control record

As you have learned, the Application Run Control records are used to save the input parameters for processes. PeopleSoft developed a number of Application Run Control records that can be used if these records have the necessary fields for your program. For example, the Temporary Employees report uses `As-Of-Date` as an input parameter. This report uses an Application Run Control record named `RUN_CNTL_HR`. The structure of this record is shown in figure 23.3.

Are you surprised to see many more fields than just `ASOFDATE`? Yes, this record is a placeholder for most HRMS report input parameters. This does not mean that all the record fields have to be used in every single report. If you know that your report input parameters are among the fields in this record, you can safely use the record as your report Application Run Control record.

Can we use the `RUN_CNTL_HR` record for the E-Mail Interface program that needs no input parameters? Yes, we can, but using this record may impact the performance.

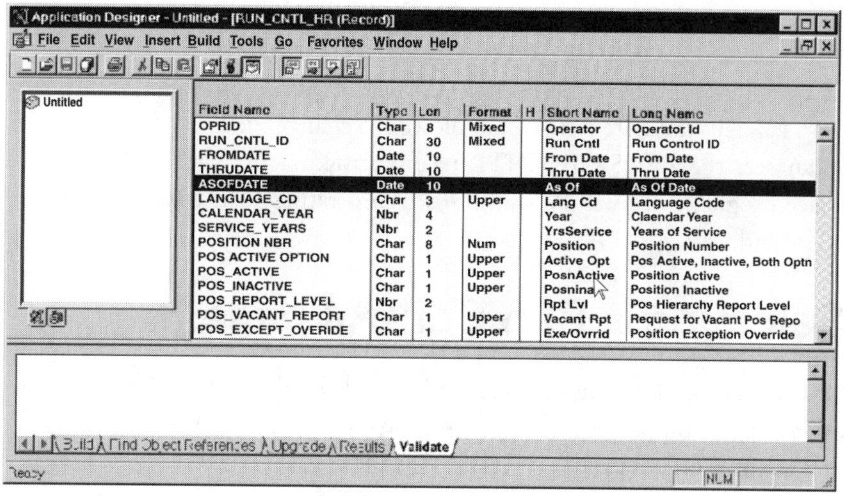

Figure 23.3 The RUN_CNTL_HR Run Control record

There is always some overhead with handling a long list of input parameters in an Application Run Control record. If a process uses no input parameters, it is more efficient to use the PeopleSoft-delivered Application Run Control record designed for this kind of process. The record name is PRCSRUNCNTL. Many standard PeopleSoft reports, for example the Emergency Contacts report, use this record. Figure 23.4 shows the record structure.

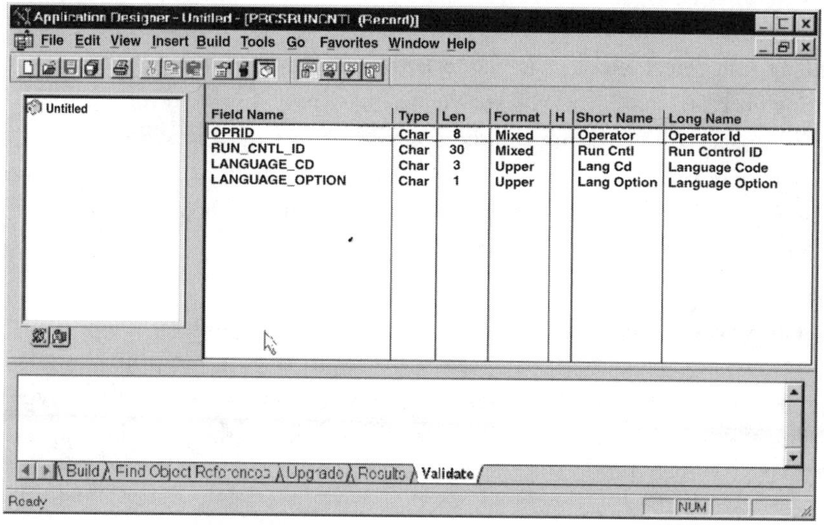

Figure 23.4 The standard Run Control record with no input parameters

The fields `OPRID` and `RUN_CNTL_ID` are the PRCSRUNCNTL record key fields. The `LANGUAGE_CD` and `LANGUAGE_OPTION` fields are used in global development projects. The default value of the `LANGUAGE_CD` field depends on your `OPRID`. The `LANGUAGE_OPTION` tells the system if you are allowed to change the `LANGUAGE_CD` field.

As you can see, the PRCSRUNCNTL record structure fits the purpose of the E-Mail Interface program. We will be using this record rather than creating a custom `Run Control` record.

23.4 Selecting a Run Control page

Instead of creating an Application Run Control record for the E-Mail Interface program, we have managed to find an existing PeopleSoft-delivered one. A similar approach can be used for a Run Control page.

We will try to find an existing standard Run Control page that suits our purpose and will reuse the page for the E-Mail Interface program.

One way to select a page is to choose one that you have already worked with since you will be familiar with its input parameters and Run Control record.

If you are not sure about the page name, find a page associated with a report that uses the same input parameters as your program does. For example, we can take advantage of the fact that the Emergency Contacts report does not accept input parameters. This gives us a hint that the page used in this report can be good for the E-Mail Interface program. All we need to do is to obtain the page name for the Emergency Contacts report and make sure that this page works with the same Application Run Control record. Select the Emergency Contacts report from the Administer Workforce (GBL) menu and enter any Run Control ID. The Run Control page for the Emergency Contacts report will appear. Select View, Page Name as shown in figure 23.5.

After clicking on Page Name, you will see the necessary page displayed (figure 23.6).

You can see the page name at the bottom right portion of the page: PRCSRUNCNTL.

If we want to reuse this page for the E-Mail Interface program, it must (1) use no input parameters and (2) be linked to the same Run Control record (in our case, it is PRCSRUNCNTL).

We already know that the page uses no input parameters.

To make sure that the page we are going to use for our program is linked to the PRCSRUNCNTL record, let's check the page structure in the Application Designer. Select Go, PeopleTools, Application Designer. Do File, Open, enter Page as object type, and enter `PRCSRUNCNTL` as a page name. Click Enter. You will see the page that appears in figure 23.7.

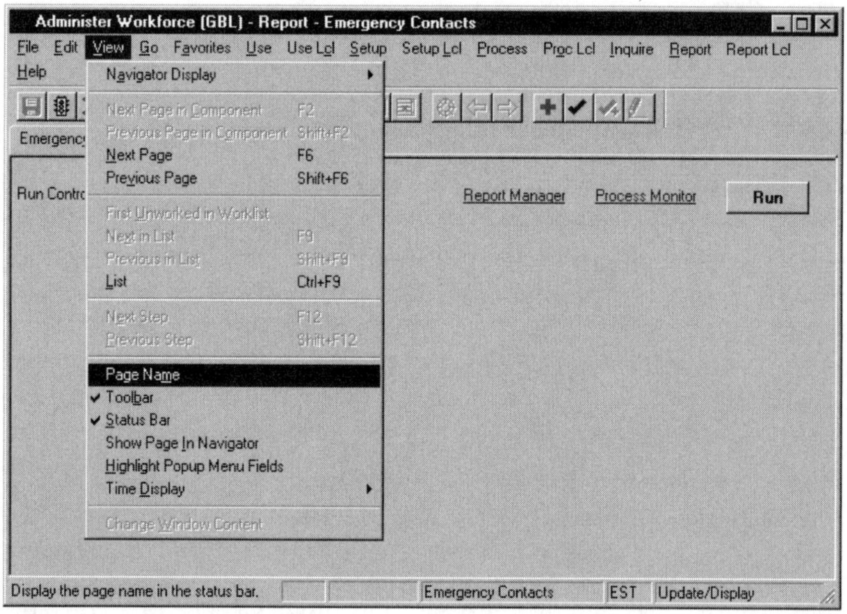

Figure 23.5 Displaying a page attached to a report

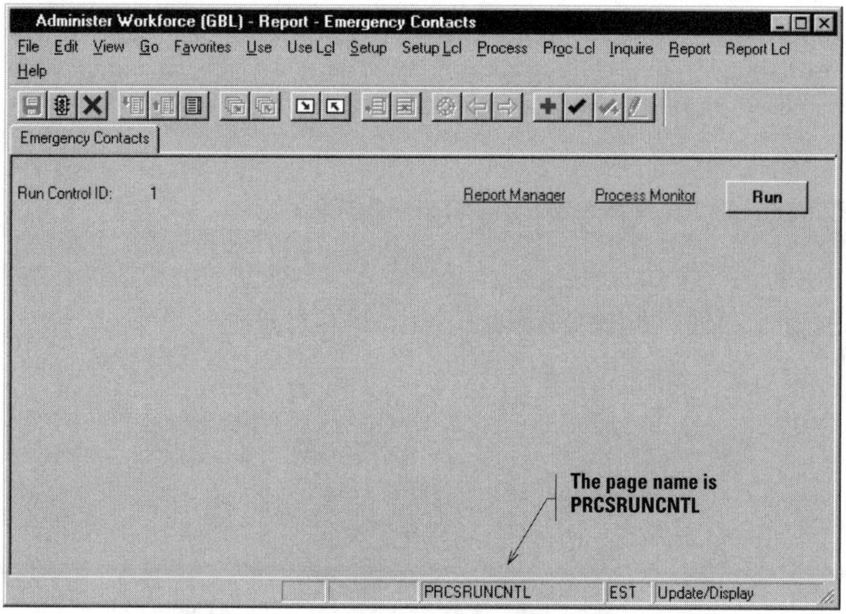

Figure 23.6 The PRCSRUNCNTL Run Control page

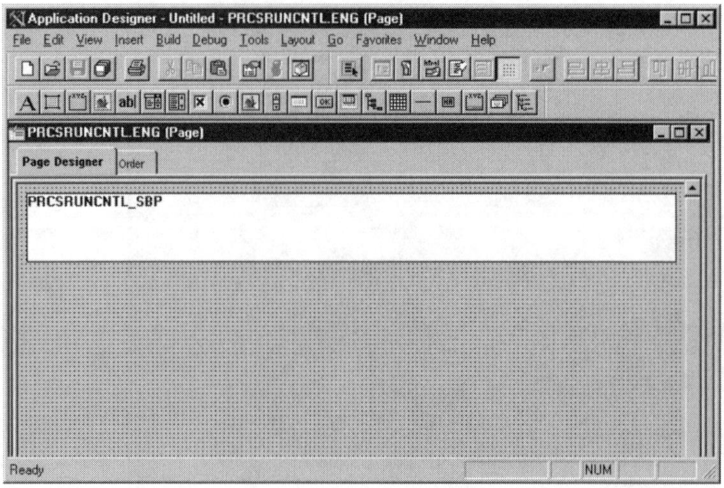

Figure 23.7 The standard Run Control page with no input parameters

The page contains a subpage named PRCSRUNCNTL_SBP. All the PRCSRUNCNTL page fields are located inside of this sub-page. If you select Layout, Test Mode, or click on the Test Mode button, you will be able to see all the page fields (see figure 23.8).

Let's find out what records are behind this sub-page. First you need to get out the Test mode. To accomplish this, click on the Test Mode button again. Then point your mouse on the sub-page and right mouse-click. Select the first option, View Definition.

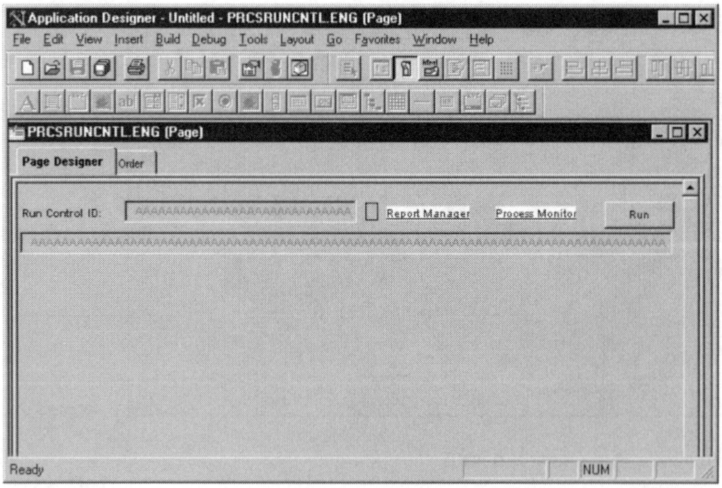

Figure 23.8 The PRCSRUNCNTL page in Test mode

You can achieve the same by selecting the sub-page and using the toolbar: View ➡ View Definition as shown in figure 23.9

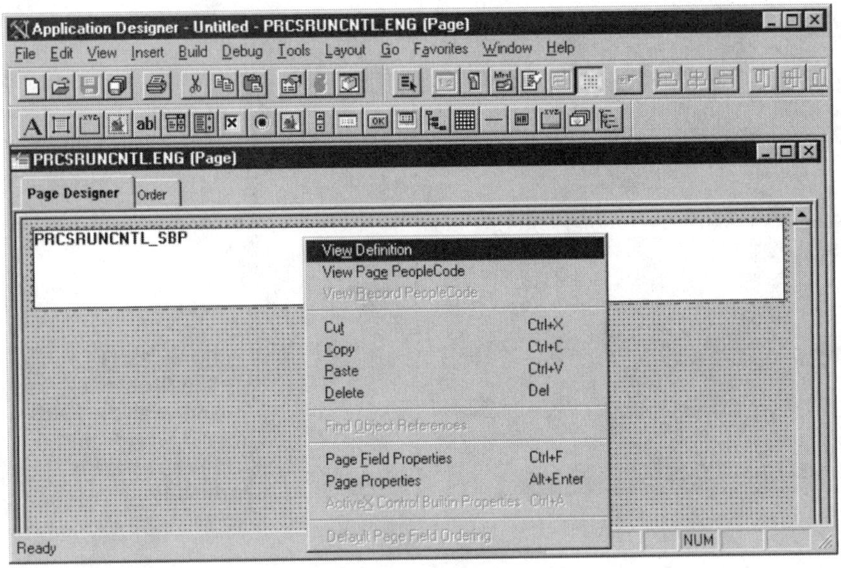

Figure 23.9 Viewing the definition of the sub-page

The definition contains two tabs: Page Designer and Order tab. The Page Designer tab is shown in figure 23.10.

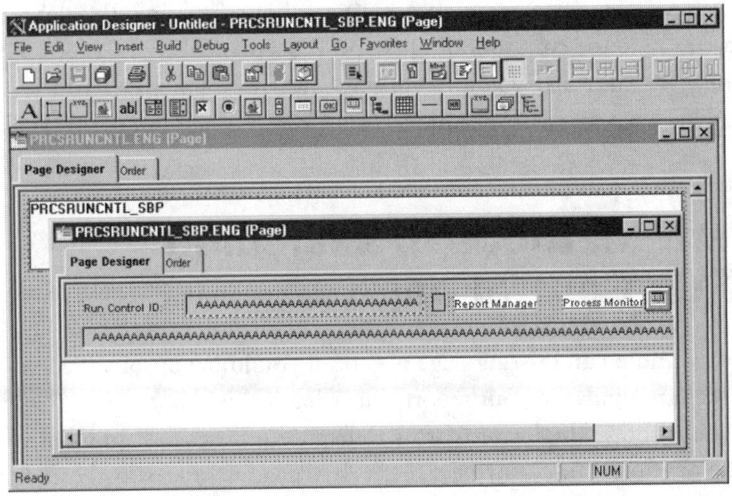

Figure 23.10 Displaying the Page Designer tab of the sub-page

Let's select the Order tab and examine the fields and records that are behind this page (figure 23.11).

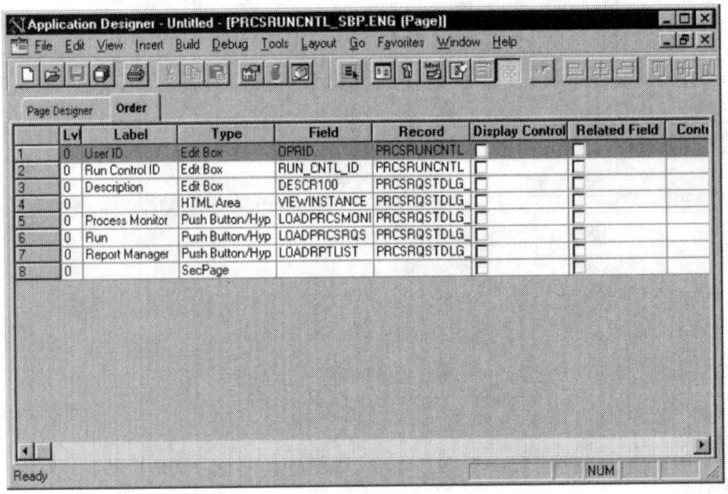

Figure 23.11 The Order tab shows all the fields and records that the sub-page is built from

As you can see from figure 23.11, the Process Run Control sub-page contains two key fields from the PRCSRUNCNTL record and the links to Report Manager, Process Monitor, and Run Control dialog.

At last, we verified that this Run Control page is linked to the PRCSRUNCNTL Run Control record. Note that both the record and the page have the same name. This is not a requirement. In most cases, the names are different, and often, a page is linked to not one, but several records. (For more information about building PeopleSoft records and pages please refer to the corresponding PeopleTools manuals.)

Now that you know for sure that you are working with the right page, you can use the PRCSRUNCNTL page as an Application Run Control page for the E-Mail Interface program.

23.5 Different methods of searching for a Run Control page

The preceding method of finding an existing page is good if you know of some PeopleSoft-delivered reports that are similar to your report. But what if this is not the case?

One helpful method is to use the Record Cross Reference utility. All Run Control pages are linked to one or more Run Control records. If a page is linked to the right record, you can use it. For example, if your report uses the `As-Of-Date` as its input parameter, you can look for standard pages that are linked to the RUN_CNTL_HR Run Control record and contain the `Asofdate` field.

The Record Cross Reference utility can be accessed via the PIA or the development environment. Let's use the PIA.

Navigation: PeopleTools ➟ Utilities ➟ Use ➟ Record Cross Reference.

Enter RUN_CNTL_HR as the Record name (figure 23.12). Click the Search button.

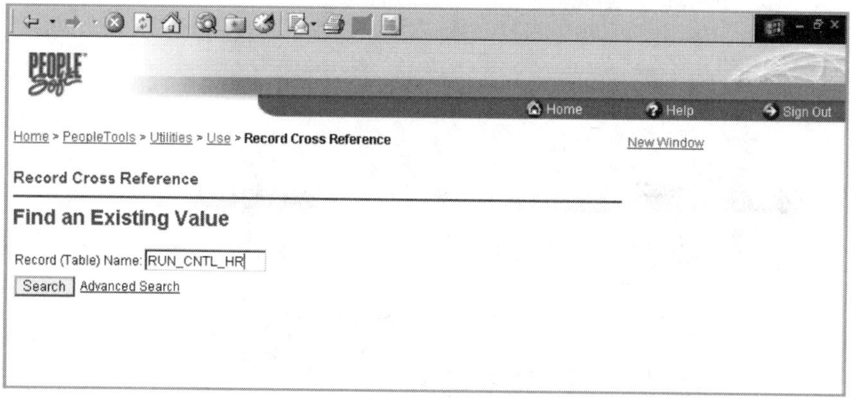

Figure 23.12 Selecting record cross reference list for RUN_CNTL_HR

Figure 23.13 shows all objects that use the RUN_CNTL_HR record.

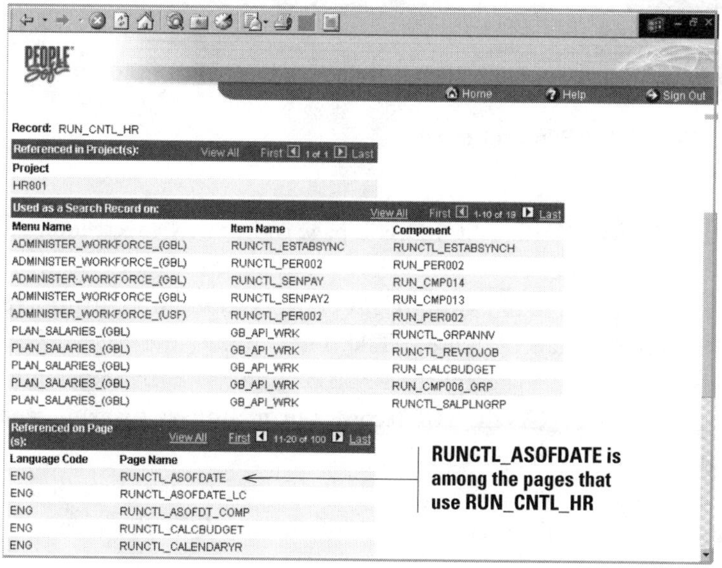

Figure 23.13
All pages that use the RUN_CNTL_HR record

If you scroll down the Referenced on Pages scroll area on the cross-reference page, you will see a lot of pages that use the RUN_CNTL_HR record. This is because this record, besides the `As-Of-Date`, has a number of other fields. The fact that a page is listed here does not necessarily mean that it has the fields you need to use. For example, not all the listed pages display the `As-Of-Date` field. Our obvious choice is the RUNCTL_ASOFDATE page because the page name suggests that it has the `Asofdate` field. In order to make sure that this page is the right one, let's open the page via the development environment and review it (figure 23.14).

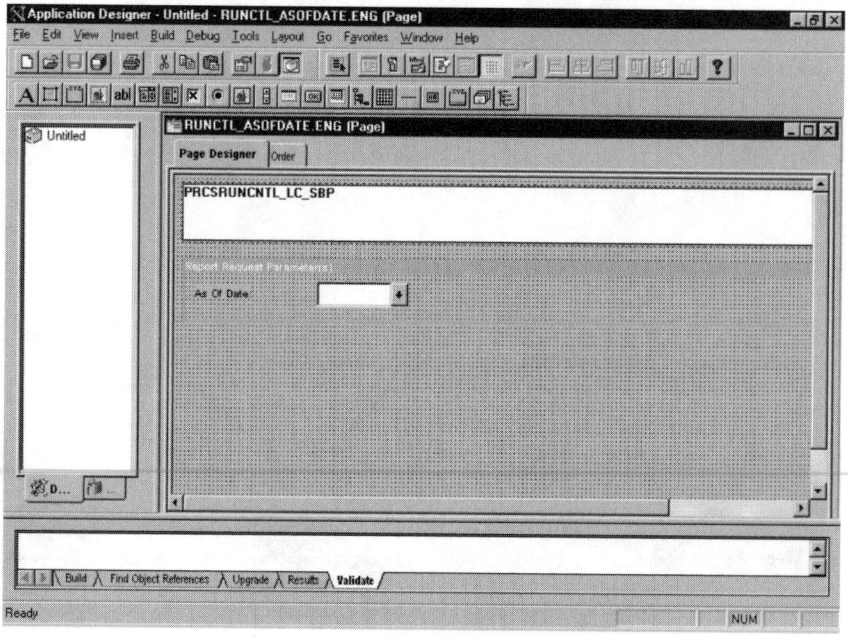

Figure 23.14 The RUNCTL_ASOFDATE Run Control page

Now you can see that the RUNCTL_ASOFDATE page is the one we were looking for: it includes the right input parameter.

Let's go back to figure 23.13 and scroll down the list of pages. You can see that there are other standard HR pages that can be reused. Take for example, the RUNCTL_FROMTHRU page. It was developed to accept the `FromDate` and `ThruDate` parameters. This page uses the same RUN_CNTL_HR record, but it displays two different parameters from the record as shown in figure 23.15.

As figure 23.16 illustrates, Run Control pages work like filters between the user and Run Control records: they show only the necessary fields of the records on the screen.

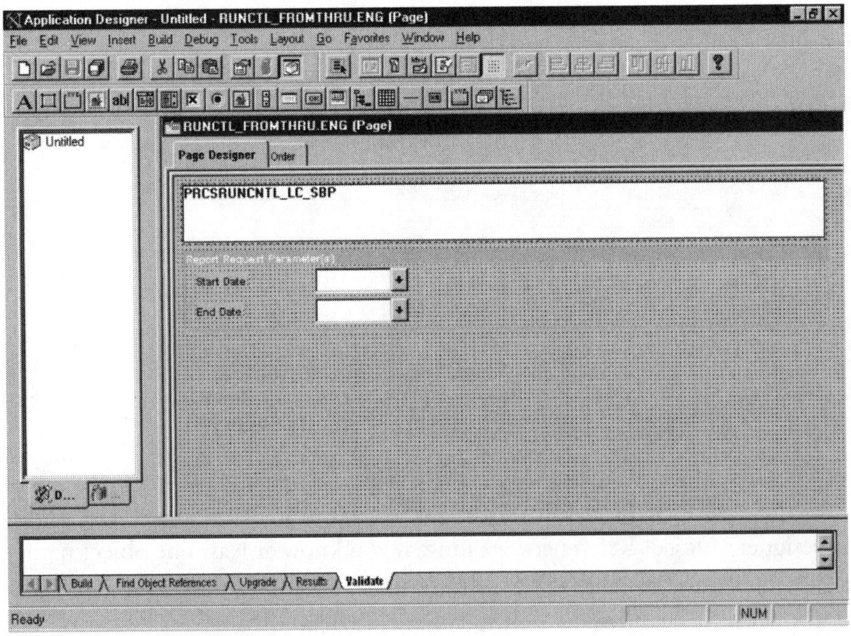

Figure 23.15 The RUNCTL_FROMTHRU page

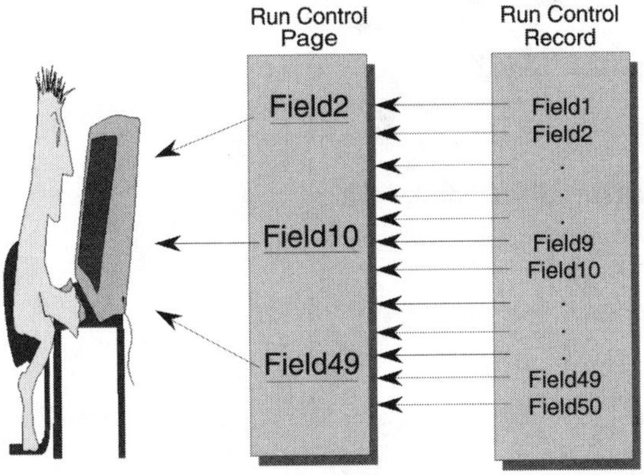

Figure 23.16
Run Control pages show only some fields of the entire Run Control record.

Another way to find a Run Control Page for reuse is to search the entire list of all available pages. You can do partial name search. For example, if you need to list all pages with names starting with RUN, go to Application Designer, Open, Page. Type RUN in the Name and press Enter. The list of all pages with names starting with RUN will appear. Browse through the list (figure 23.17) to find a match for your program.

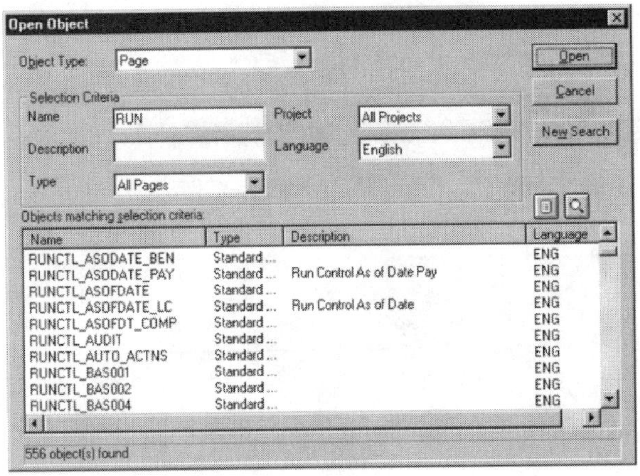

Figure 23.17
List of available pages with names starting with Run

The third, and probably the fastest way to find a page you are looking for, is to use Application Designer's Object References. As long as you know at least one object name, for example the field name, you can select Edit, Find Object References, and all objects that contain this field will be listed, as shown in figure 23.18.

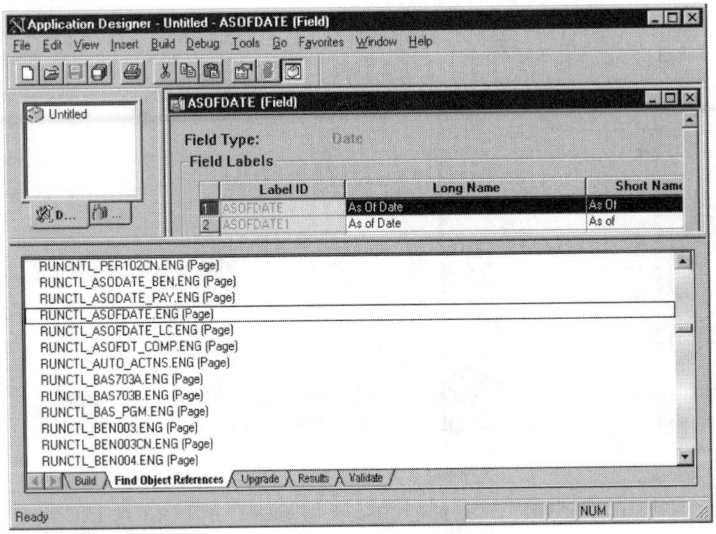

Figure 23.18 Using the Application Designer's Object References to find the page that contains the AsOfDate field

23.6 Creating a component

After a page is selected or created, it must be added to a component before you can attach it to a menu. Component is actually a link between a Run Control page and a menu.

Until now, we were trying to reuse the existing PeopleSoft delivered objects. This time we will create a new custom component for our report. Why couldn't we follow the same PeopleSoft recommendation and try to find a suitable delivered component for our page? Let's think for a moment and get back to the design stage. How do we want to execute our report? Most probably we would want to access our report in a way similar to the way we selected the Employee Birthdays or Emergency Contacts reports. And therefore, it will have to have its own place in the menu. And since we already know that a component is a bridge between a page and a menu, we need to create a component. The page will be added to the component, and then the component will be added to the menu.

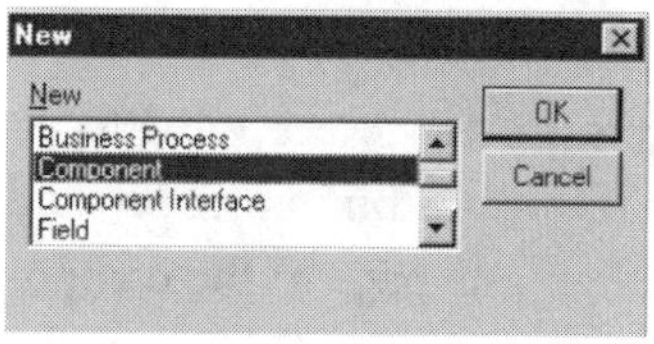

Figure 23.19
Creating a component

Let's create a component by selecting File, New (in the Application Designer), and double-clicking on Component in the New dialog (figure 23.19).

Now, we need to add our page (PRCSRUNCNTL) to the component in figure 23.20.

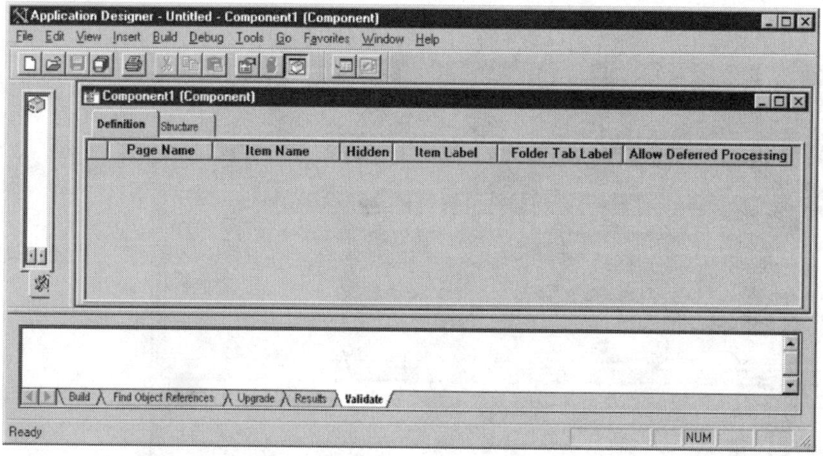

Figure 23.20 The Component screen

To do this, click on the Insert Page button on the toolbar, or select Insert, Page into Component (figure 23.21).

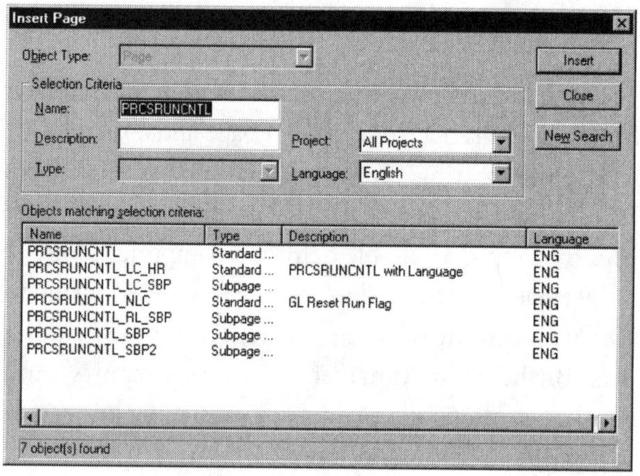

Figure 23.21 Selecting a page to add it to a component

Enter PRCSRUNCNTL as the page name, and press Enter. Select the PRCSRUNCNTL page from the list of all pages and click on the Insert button in order to add this page to the new component. If you need to add more than one page to the component (in our case, it is not necessary), repeat the preceding steps for all additional pages. When all the pages you wanted to add to your component have been inserted, click on the Close button. You will see all the pages in your new component (in our case, it is just one page, PRCSRUNCNTL) (figure 23.22).

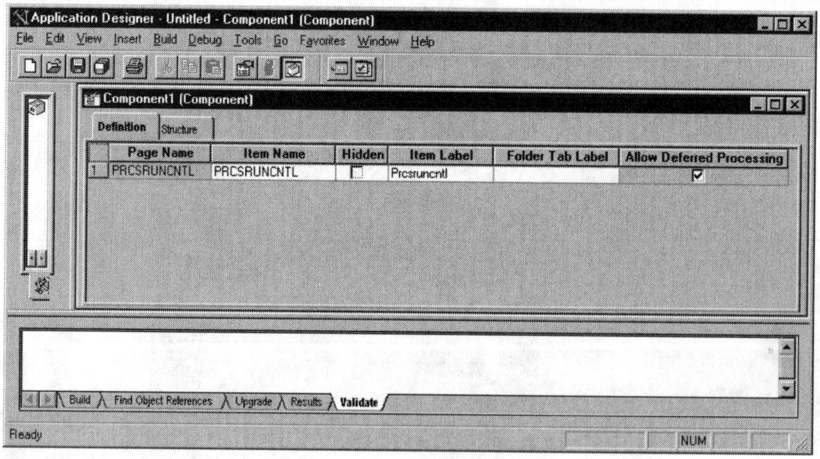

Figure 23.22 The PRCSRUNCNTL page is added to the new component

Each page in a component has a set of properties. The PRCSRUNCNTL page has been added to the component with its properties set to their default values. Let's change these values to make them more meaningful.

The Item Name (figure 23.22) is used for informational purposes only, but it must be unique within the component. We'll leave it the same as the page name (the default value).

The next column is Hidden. You only set this value `On` if you need the page to be hidden from user's view. We'll leave the value of this column `Off`. You can have several pages in a component with the Hidden value set to `Off`, and one or more pages with the value set to `On`. This technique is used when you need to bring to the buffer certain fields from some pages, but you don't want to display these pages to users.

The Item Label column is your page name as it will appear on the menu. It will also be displayed at the bottom of the page and as the default folder tab label. Right now it is named PRCSRUNCNTL, which is not very meaningful. Let's call it E-mail.

The Folder Tab Label is used to identify the folder tab when the component is selected. Let's name it E-Mail Interface for our task.

The last column, Allow Deferred Processing, indicates whether the deferred processing has been turned off or on at the Page Properties level. On this page it is for information purposes only, and therefore it is marked as read-only field.

PeopleSoft created the deferred processing mode to increase the efficiency of processing transactions. To maximize online performance, PeopleSoft sets the default for both page fields and pages to allow for deferred processing.

After we enter all the values, our component definition will look like the one in figure 23.23.

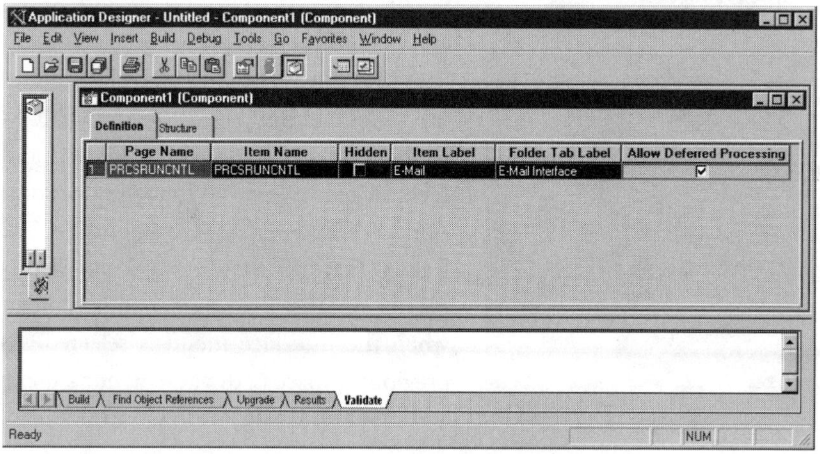

Figure 23.23 Setting page properties for the new component

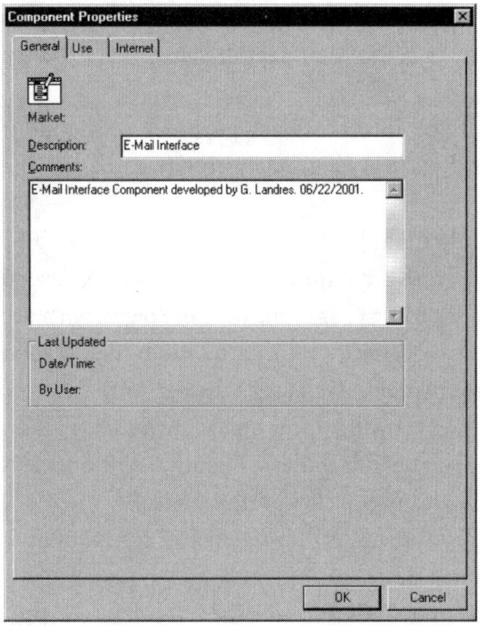

Figure 23.24 The Component Properties dialog (the General tab)

Before you save the newly created component, we need to add additional important information. We have to set the properties for the entire component, including: search records, update and data entry actions, and detail page information.

Select File, Object Properties, or click on the Properties button in the toolbar, or right-click on the Component definition and select Component Properties from the pop-up menu.

You will see the Component Properties dialog window. The window has three tabs: General, Use, and Internet. Let's fill in the first tab as shown in figure 23.24.

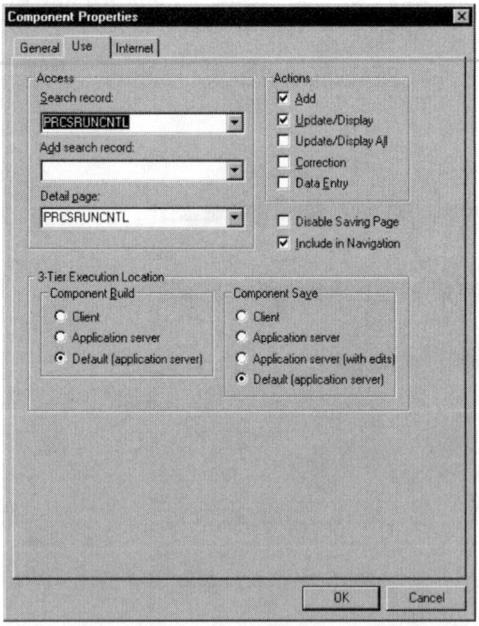

Figure 23.25 The Component Properties dialog (the Use tab)

The second and the third tab of the component shown in figure 23.25 require more knowledge to fill in. Please refer to the PeopleTools technical documentation for more information about the Search Records, Three Tier Execution, and Detail Page selections.

Let's do the following selections in the Use tab page: select PRCSRUNCNTL as both Search Record and Detail Page. Allow the following actions: Add and Update/Display (figure 23.25). Remember, that these actions will be displayed on the Process Scheduler menu when the interface menu is selected. As previously discussed, these actions mean adding or updating a Run Control record.

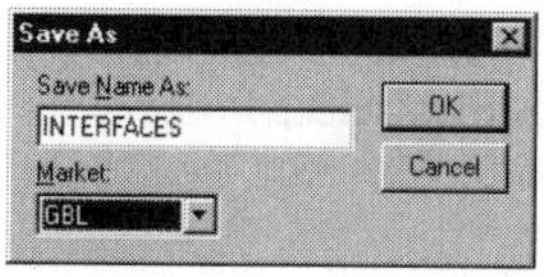

Figure 23.26 Saving the Interfaces component

Now is the time to save our component. Let's select File, Save, and enter the new Component name as Interfaces (figure 23.26).

23.7 Selecting a menu for your report

The next decision is which menu to run your report under. In order to find an appropriate menu for your report, let's discuss what options you have and the advantages and disadvantages of each option.

The first option is to add your new report to an existing menu item with the same input parameters. If you use this option, your report will be added to the existing report list in the Process Scheduler Request page similar to the one shown in figure 23.27.

This option is the simpler one to implement. You don't need to create a menu or component. You only have to create a Process definition, that links your SQR program to an existing component. The disadvantage of this method is that, because the new report or process is not going to be a separate item in a menu, users may find

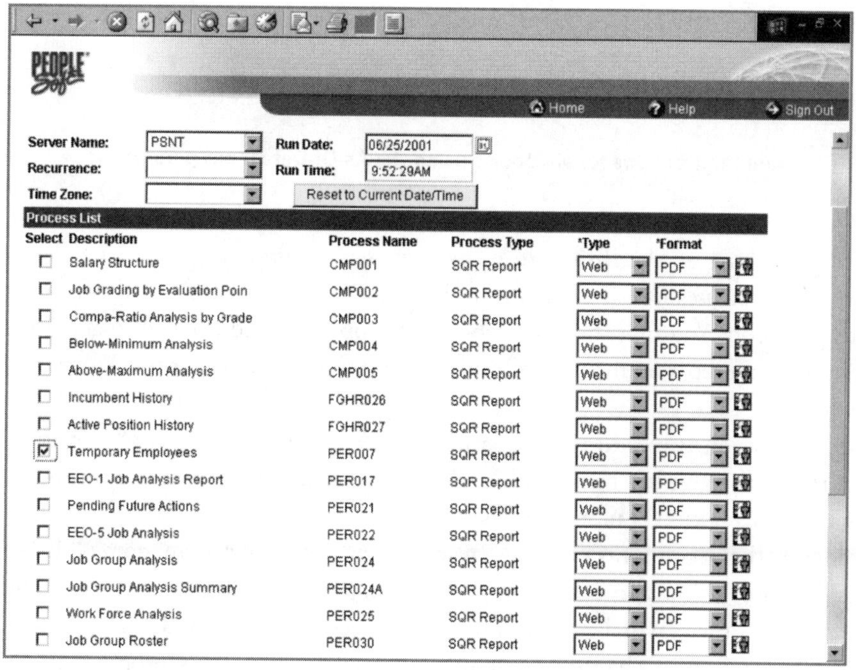

Figure 23.27 The Process Scheduler Request page

navigation to this report rather difficult. For example, in order to get the Process Scheduler Request page for the Temporary Employees report, users need to select Process, As-Of-Date Request.

Users then have to enter the proper Run Control ID, and get the Run Control page, which will not yet show a list of reports or processes (figure 23.28).

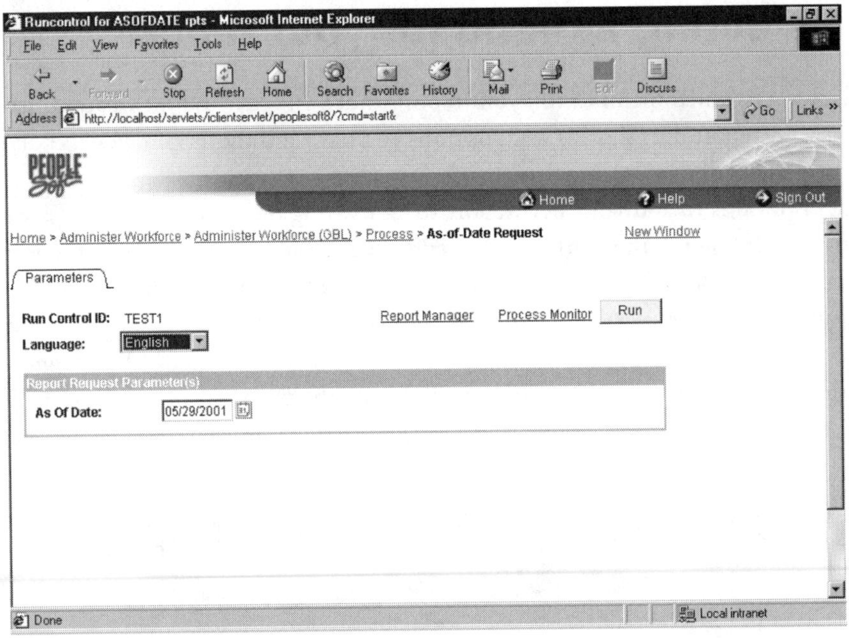

Figure 23.28 The Run Control page for all reports using the As-Of-Date input parameter

Only after clicking on the Run button can users see the Process Scheduler Request page with all the processes listed, as shown in figure 23.27. As you can see, this is not a very intuitive method. You may, however, choose this option in addition to placing the new program under a separate menu (as PeopleSoft did, for example, for the Temporary Employees report).

The second option is to add your report or process as a separate menu item to an appropriate menu and give it a meaningful name to make sure the report or process can be easily found. This option is more user friendly.

We can use the second option and create a separate menu item named Interfaces, attaching our E-Mail Interface program to it. We should also keep in mind that, in the future, there will be some other interfaces attached to the same menu item. Per our discussion in chapter 22, it makes sense to attach this program under

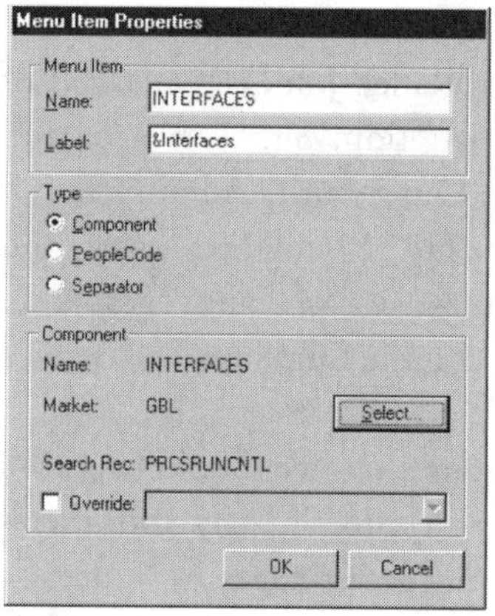

Figure 23.29 Adding a new menu item to the Process menu

the Process menu rather than attaching it under the Report menu.

We are going to add a new menu item named Interfaces to the menu Process in the Administer Workforce (GBL) menu.

To create a new menu item, switch to the development environment. Then, go to the Application Designer, and select File, Open, Menu, Administer Workforce (GBL). Click on the Process menu bar item, and then double-click on the empty rectangle at the bottom of the menu.

The Menu Item Properties dialog will appear as shown in figure 23.29.

On Menu Item Properties, click on Select and add our Interfaces component to the Interfaces menu item.

After the new menu item is created, you have to decide who will be able to see it. Only users who belong to the proper operator class should be granted access to the new menu item.

23.8 Granting security access to a new menu item

Since we created Interfaces under the Process menu in the Administer Workforce GBL page, we have to allow certain users to access this menu item and the corresponding page. Let's see how to use the PeopleSoft Security maintenance tools to accomplish this task.

PeopleSoft delivered a robust application that allows us to create and maintain multiple levels of security. For our specific task, we will be concerned with online security, and, particularly, with user security. This type of security is managed with the help of security definitions.

In order to sign on to PeopleSoft, each user ID must be associated with a user security definition. User security definition includes three related types: user profile, roles, and permission lists.

Each PeopleSoft user has an individual profile. This profile is linked to one or more roles (employee, supervisor, manager, security administrator, etc.). Permission lists control access to menus, components and pages for each role. It also controls user's actions such as Add, Update, Correction. Roles act as links between user profiles and permission lists.

In order to make it clear, let's consider the following example. Suppose we have three employees, John Smith, Simon Schumaker, and Ann Rader. John is a manager of Human Resources, he also takes care of security administration, Simon is a payroll supervisor and Ann is a computer programmer in Finance. Our Security Administration created the following four roles: Security Admin, Manager HR, Payroll Supervisor, and Employee. Let's assume that our very small HRMS system consists of eight pages: A, B, C, D, E, F, G, H. Pages A through F belong to HR, including the Employee Self Service pages A, B, C. Pages E, F, G, H belong to Payroll.

Let's see who is linked to what role and what permissions each role should have. We will start with permissions. Security Admin should have access to all pages and, therefore, should be linked to all permissions. Employee can only access pages A, B, and C: this role should only be linked to the Employee Self-Service permission. Manager HR should have access to all HR pages and will be linked to the HR permission. Finally, Payroll Supervisor should have access to pages E, F, G, H and be linked to the Payroll permission. All users are employees no matter what positions they hold, therefore, Ann, John, and Simon are linked to the Employee role. In addition, John is linked to the Security Admin and HR manager roles while Simon is linked to the Payroll Supervisor role.

Figure 23.30 will show how the three security objects, permission lists, roles, and user profiles are linked together:

Of course, our picture is much simplified. Permission lists are lists of authorizations that you assign to roles. Besides access to pages, Permission lists store Sign-On times,

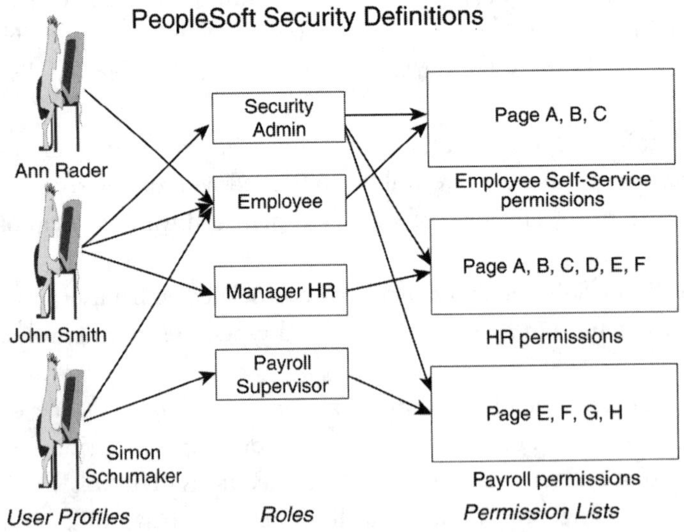

Figure 23.30 PeopleSoft security objects

menus (or components), access to PeopleTools. Be aware that changes to permission Lists will impact all users that are linked to that permission list via their roles.

And now that we understand the concept of user security definitions, let's use PeopleTools to grant security to our new menu item.

As we just discussed, we need to grant access to users by assigning our new pages and components to permission lists. Each permission list should be linked to one or more roles.

Let's see how to find these three components and link them.

Let's assume that user IDs and roles already exist. We know, for example, that at least the PS user ID exists because we used it to login and execute the delivered PeopleSoft reports. This PS user ID and its profile may be linked to a number of roles. Our first step, therefore, is to identify a role that is appropriate. Then, we will have to link this role with the proper permission list to grant security access to our new component.

Login into PeopleSoft (in PIA mode) and take a look at the User Profiles for the PS user ID (figure 23.31).

Navigation: Home ➠ PeopleTools ➠ Maintain Security ➠ Use ➠ User Profiles

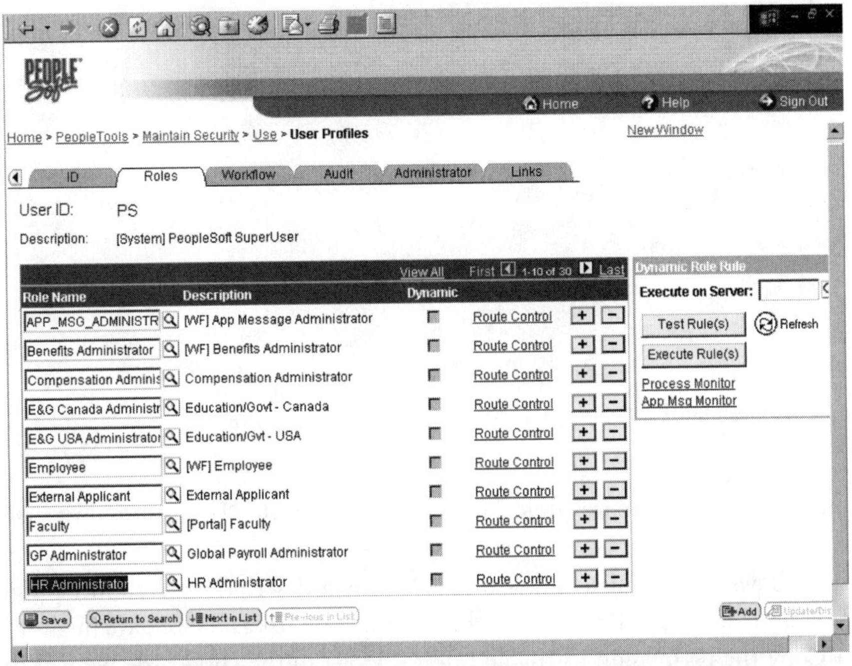

Figure 23.31 Identifying a role to use for security access to our new page

Let's switch to the Roles tab and see the roles that are assigned to this user profile. Since our new page belongs to HR, the HR Administrator role seems appropriate. Our goal is to find a permission list that we will use for our newly created component. If one does not exist, we can create a new permission list for our new component, and then link this list to the HR Administrator role.

Our next step is to examine the permission lists linked to the HR Administrator role (figure 23.32).

Navigation: Home ➟ PeopleTools ➟ Maintain Security ➟ Use ➟ Roles

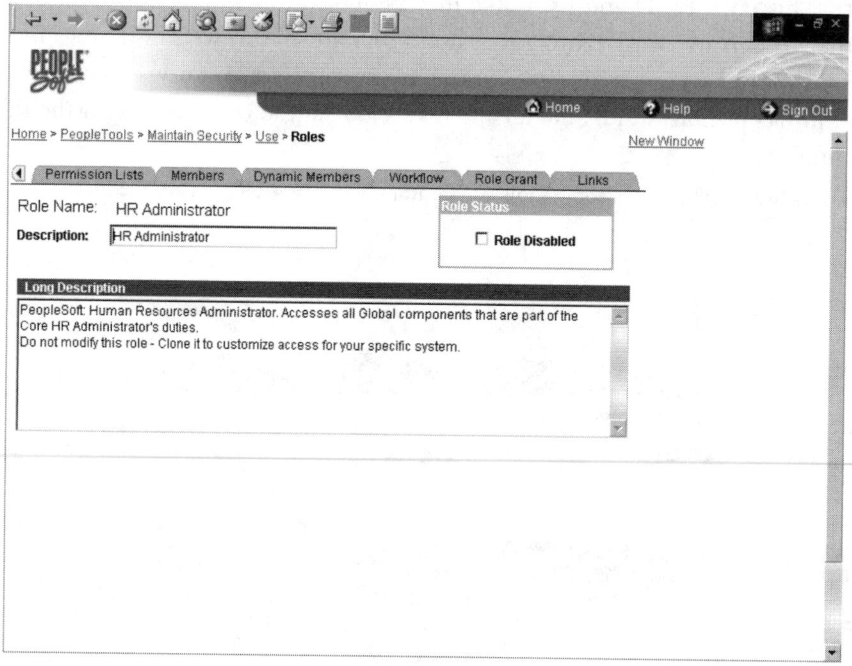

Figure 23.32 Selecting the HR Administrator role

From the HR Administrator Role tab let's switch to the Permission Lists tab (figure 23.33).

If we scroll down the permission lists and look at their descriptions as shown in figure 23.33, we can identify the Report Workforce permission list as the one we might be able to use. Copy the permission list name (CPHR3350) to the clipboard. We will be using it in a moment. Our next step is to modify the permissions in this list. Let's go to the Permission Lists (Home>PeopleTools ➟ Maintain Security ➟ Use ➟ Permission Lists), and paste our clipboard value into the Permission Lists search dialog (Figure 23.34).

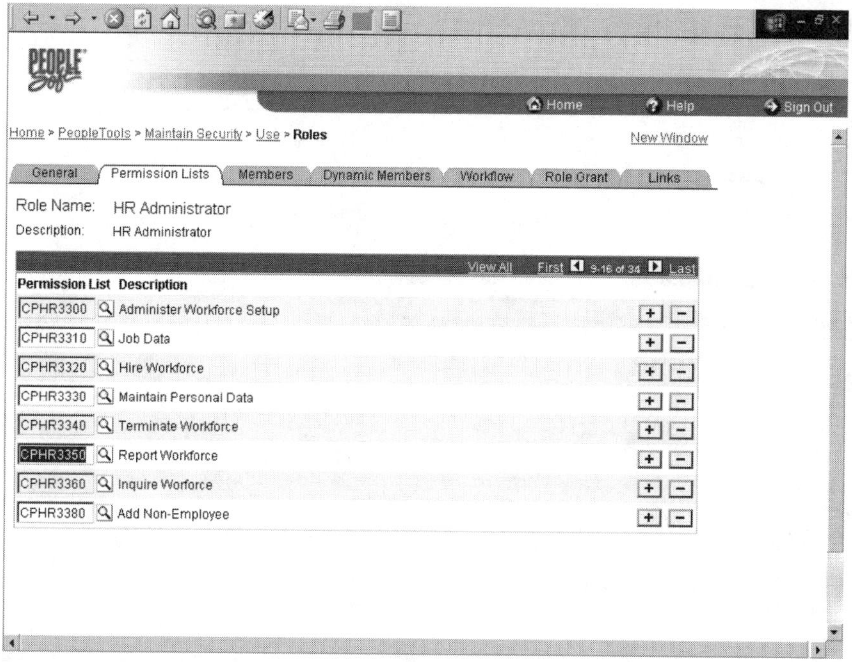

Figure 23.33 Identifying the permission lists to be used

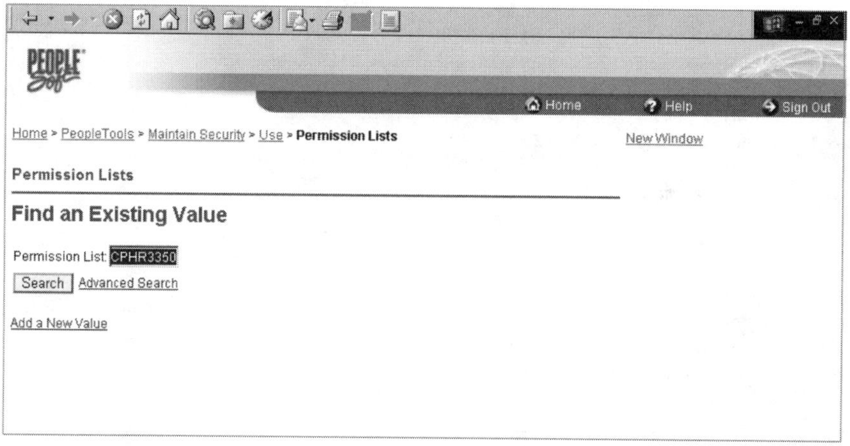

Figure 23.34 Selecting permission list for CPHR3350

Press the Enter key and switch to the Pages tab (figure 23.35).

The Edit Components link (figure 23.35) will bring you to the list of all the components within the Administer Workforce GBL menu (figure 23.36). On this page, not all of the components have a check mark on their left. Only the checked components are

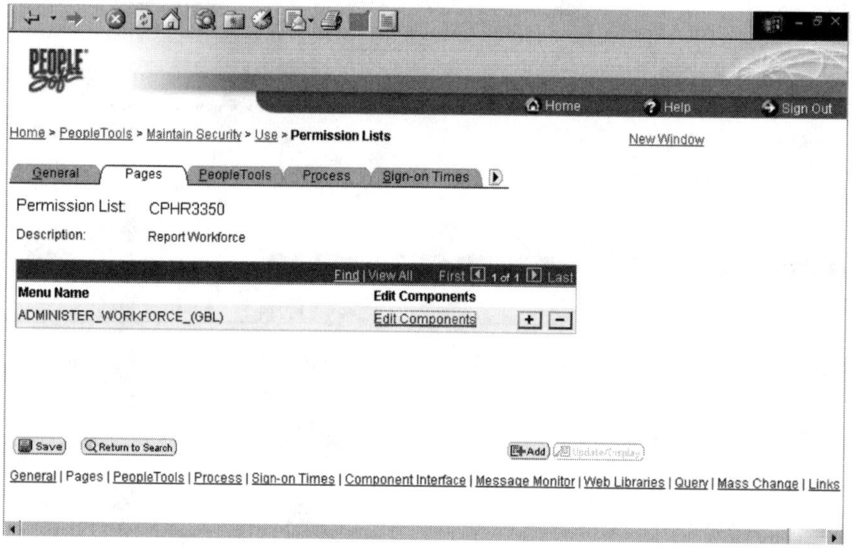

Figure 23.35 Reviewing the Pages tab

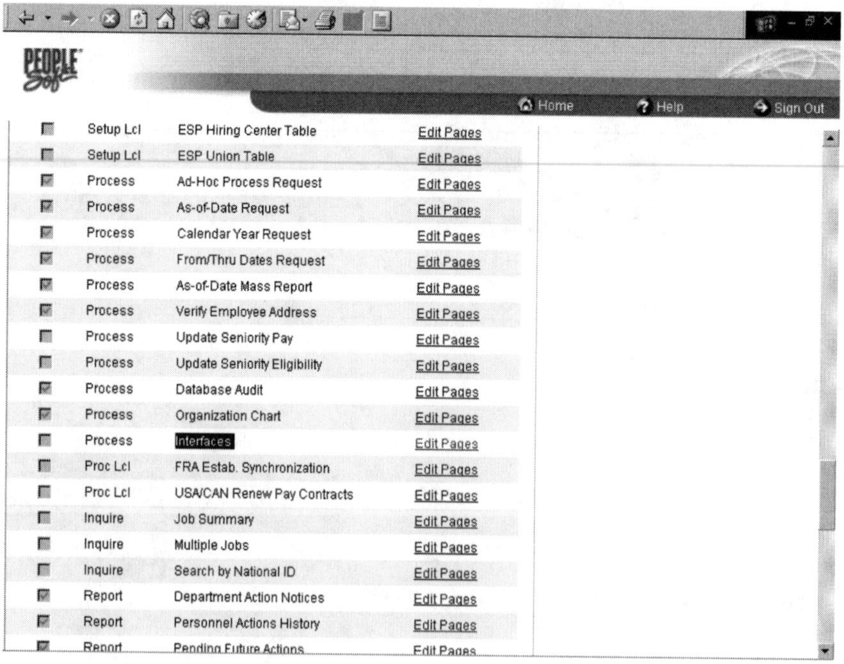

Figure 23.36 Finding our new component (Interfaces) in the list of all components for the Administer Workforce GBL menu

the ones that are authorized for user access. Our new component, Interfaces, does not have a check mark, and therefore, is not authorized.

Now, let's click on the Edit Pages link next to our new component, Interfaces (figure 22.36). This brings us to the Page Permissions screen (figure 23.37).

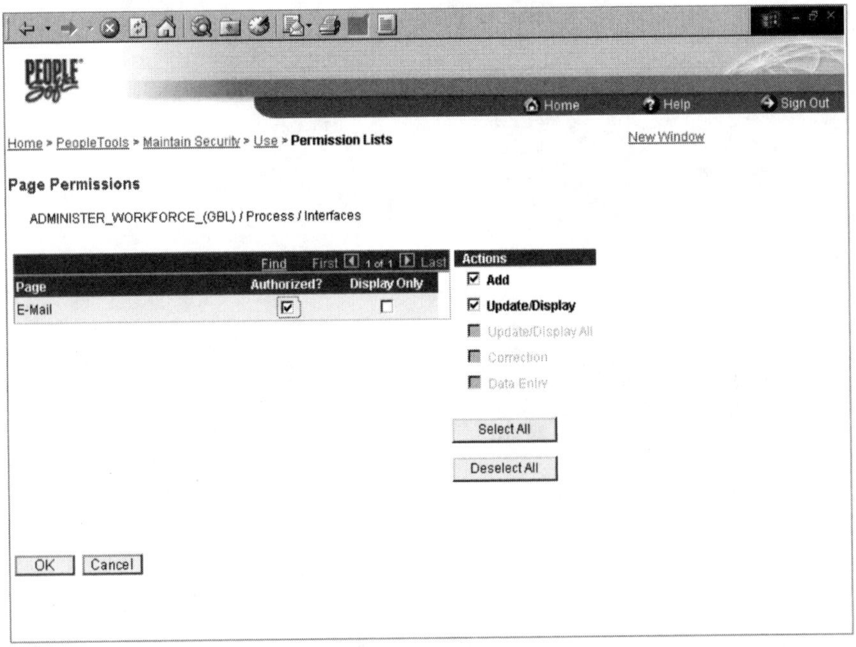

Figure 23.37 Authorizing access to the E-Mail page

On this page we specify the user actions, choose between the Display Only and full access, and decide whether to authorize each page of the component. Please note that the Authorized and Display Only options apply to each individual page in the component. On the other hand, the actions apply to the whole component. Remember that these actions will tell the system to add or reuse the Run Control record when selecting the Run Control page.

Let's click on Add and Update Display and Authorized check boxes. Then click the OK button. This will bring us back to the Permission Lists page. But this time we can see our new component marked as authorized (figure 23.38).

In order to finish the component update, scroll down and click the OK button.

This brings us to the very last step of saving of our modifications, as shown in figure 23.39.

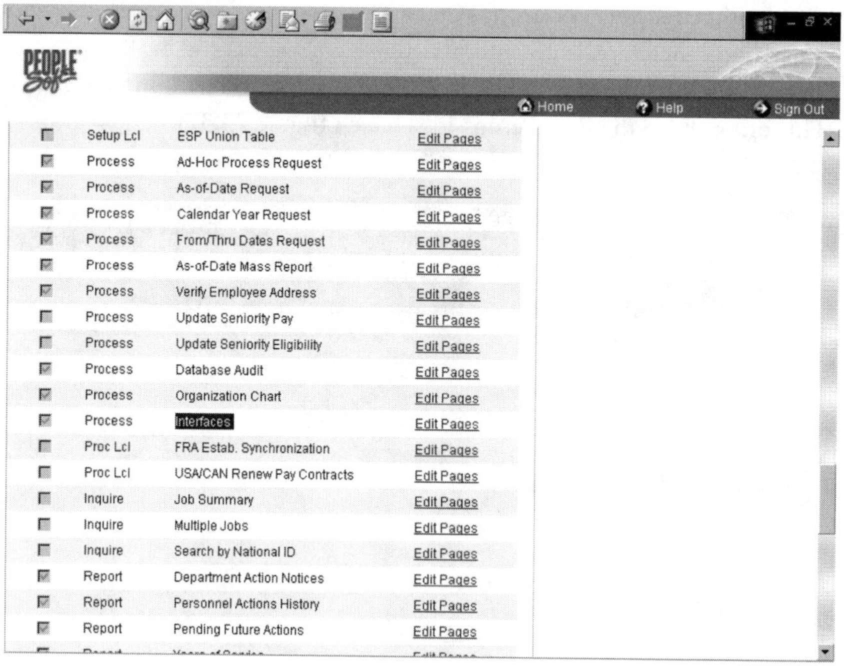

Figure 23.38 The Interfaces component is authorized

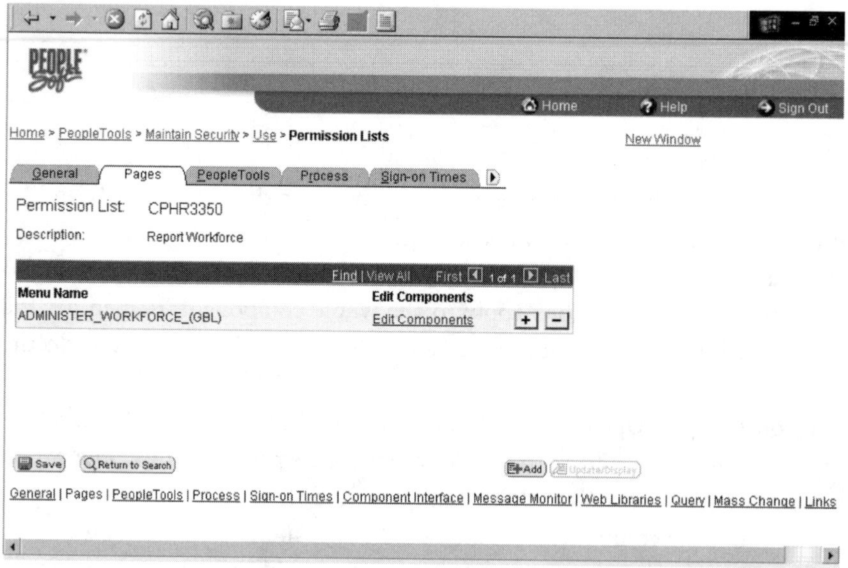

Figure 23.39 Saving the permission list update

After the Save button is clicked (figure 23.39), our permission list is modified, and should include the proper access to our new objects: menu, component, and page.

Before we start testing our new menu item, let's recall what objects we modified to grant our users access to our new objects. If we look back, we'll notice that we only modified the permission list. In order to find the right permission list, we did some research to make sure that the User ID PS is in fact linked to that permission list via the HR Administrator role. But what if some other users are also linked to the CPHR3350 permission list? Well, as we warned you before, all users that are linked to this permission list will be able to execute our E-Mail Interface program. In our particular case it is a valid solution. But when this is not the case, we would need to create a new permission list, and a new role. And then link this role to all users that will be responsible for our E-Mail Interface. Next are the steps you have to take in order to add a new permission lists and/or role.

Step1. Add a new permission list

Navigation: Home ➠ PeopleTools ➠ Maintain Security ➠ Use ➠ Permission List

1.1. Click on Add a New Value
- Specify a new permission list name, for example, HRINT
- Click Add

1.2. General tab
- Enter description: HR interfaces

1.3. Page Tab
- Click on the Prompt button and enter the Administer Workforce(GBL) menu
- Select Edit Component on the right to the Menu name. This will bring you to the Component Permission screen
- Select Edit Pages
- Click Select All, OK, and OK again on the next page

1.4. Save the permission list

Step 2. Add a new role:

Navigation: Home ➠ PeopleTools ➠ Maintain Security ➠ Use ➠ Roles

2.1. Select Add a New Value
- Enter role name: HR Interfaces
- Click Add

2.2. Select General tab
- Enter description: Manage HR Interfaces
- Click Save. The role is created

2.3. Select Permission List tab

- Enter the permission list name created in the Step 1, HRINT, press the Tab key
- Click Save. The permission list is linked to the HR Interfaces role

Step 3. Add a role to a user profile:

Navigation: Home ➟ PeopleTools ➟ Maintain Security ➟ Use ➟ User Profiles

3.1. Enter User ID: PS

3.2. Select Roles tab
- Click on (+) to add a new row
- Enter: HR Interfaces and press the Tab key
- Click Save. User PS is assigned to the HR Interfaces role that has permissions to execute our new interface, E-Mail Interface.

No matter what method we used to grant the appropriate access to the PS User ID, we are now ready to test the new menu item (figure 23.40).

Navigation: Home ➟ Administer Workforce ➟ Administer Workforce (GBL) ➟ Process >Interfaces

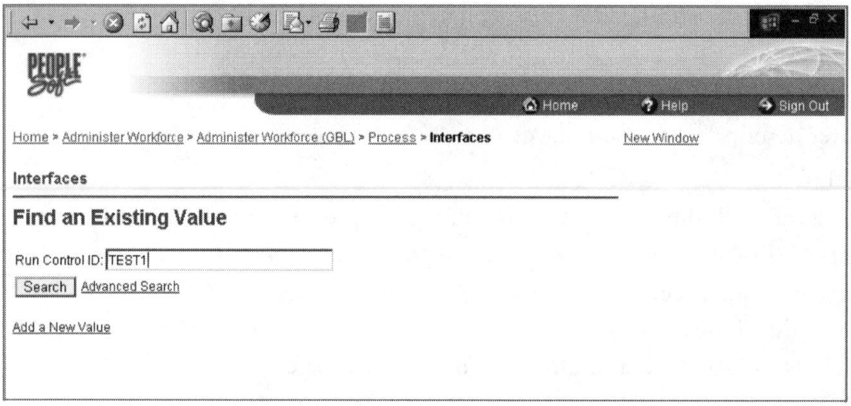

Figure 23.40 Selecting the Run Control ID to use in the Run Control page

Enter the TEST1 Run Control ID and press the Enter key. This will bring us to the Interfaces Run Control page (figure 23.41).

After the page is selected we can execute our process. Let's give it a try. Selecting the Run button (figure 23.41) should bring us to the Process Request page. Take a close look at figure 23.42. We see a Process Scheduler Request page with no process attached. What happened? The answer is simple. We haven't yet created a Process definition for our process.

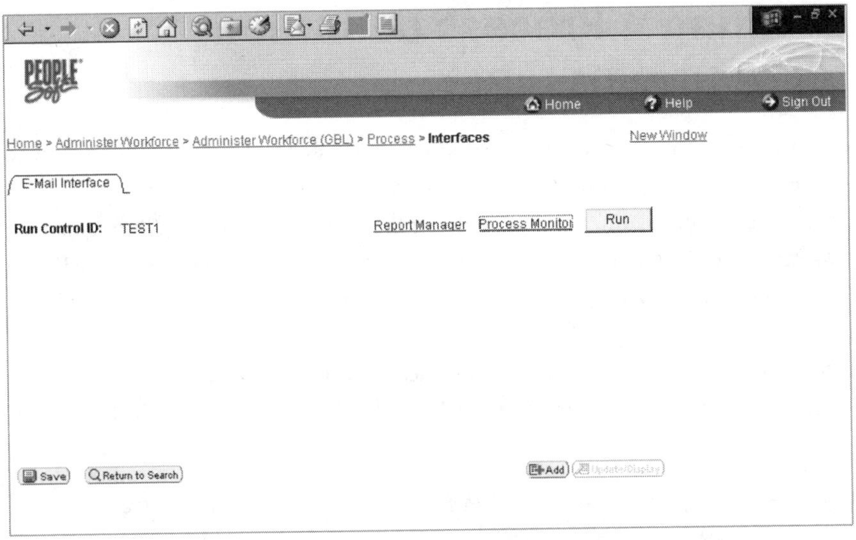

Figure 23.41 The Application Run Control page for the Interfaces menu item

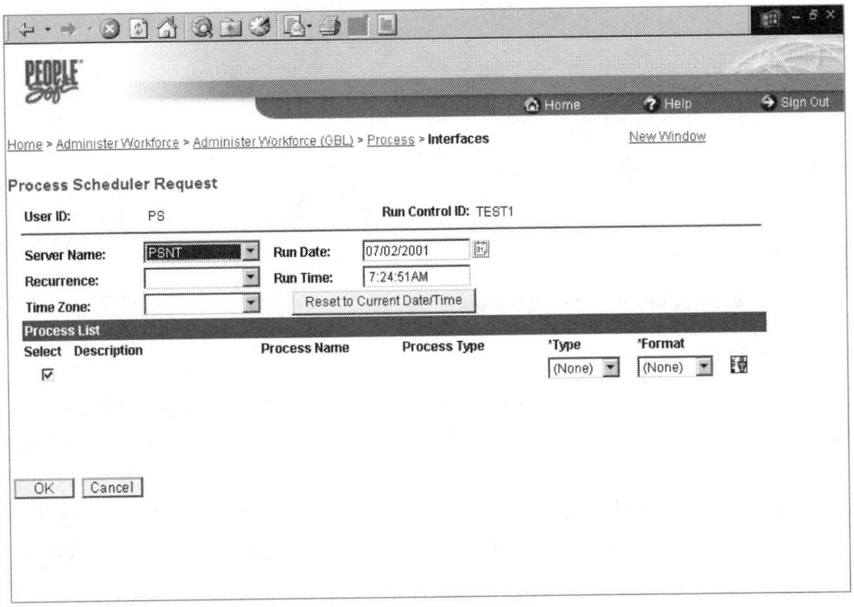

Figure 23.42 The Process Scheduler Request page with no Process definition attached

Our next step should be clear: we need to create a Process definition for our new process and attach it to the newly created component.

23.9 Creating a Process definition for your program

Every process run under the PeopleSoft Process Scheduler needs a Process Definition to specify the process attributes and link the process to the appropriate component.

To create a Process definition, we will be using the Process Scheduler Manager. This component of PeopleTools, similar to the Maintain Security tool, is accessed via PIA.

Navigation: Home ➠ PeopleTools ➠ Process Scheduler Manager ➠ Use ➠ Process Definitions

The system displays the Process definitions search dialog (figure 23.43). Since we are going to create a new Process definition, click on the Add a New Value link.

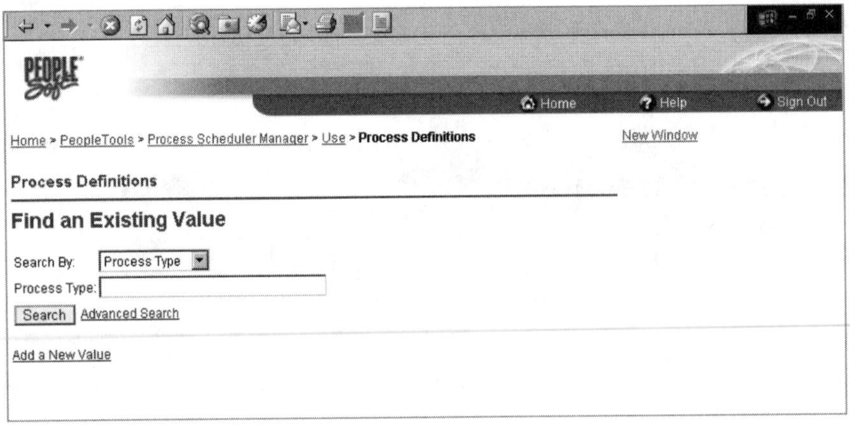

Figure 23.43 The Process definitions search dialog

As you can see from figure 23.44, we have to select the proper type for our process. Please note that the valid type for our process is SQR Report, not SQR Process. If you select SQR Process, the Process Scheduler will not pass the Operator ID and Run Control ID to your program and the program will not work correctly unless you specify Operator ID and Run Control ID as additional parameters. (Please refer to the PeopleTools technical manuals for additional information about process types.)

The Process Name must be the same as your program name: `Test17A`. Note that the `.sqr` extension is not needed (figure 23.45).

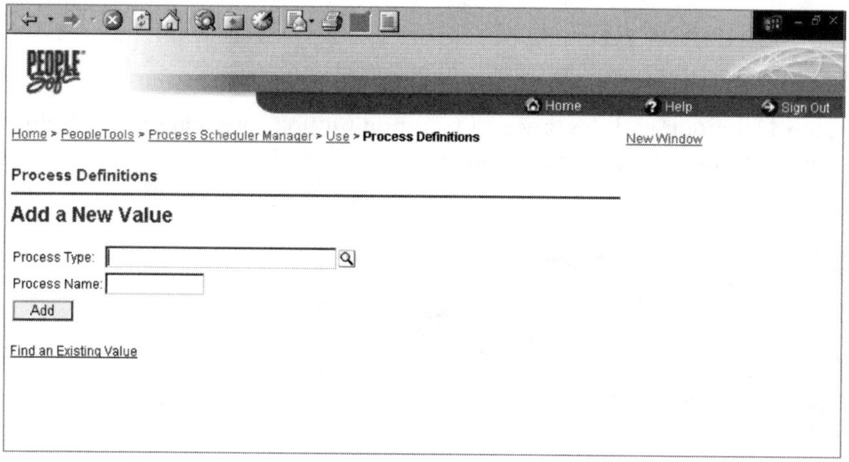

Figure 23.44 Adding a new Process definition

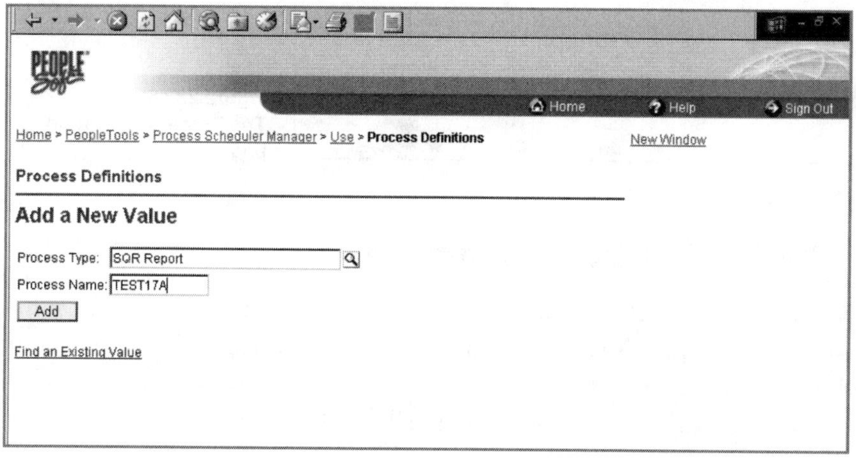

Figure 23.45 No extension is needed when entering the program name.

After you have pressed OK and assigned the type to your process, the system displays the Process Scheduler Process definitions component (figure 23.46). This component consists of the following six pages:

- Process Definition
- Process Definition Options
- Override Options
- Destination

- Page Transfer
- Notification

The Process Definition and the Process Definition Options pages are the only ones you have to fill in; the other four pages are optional.

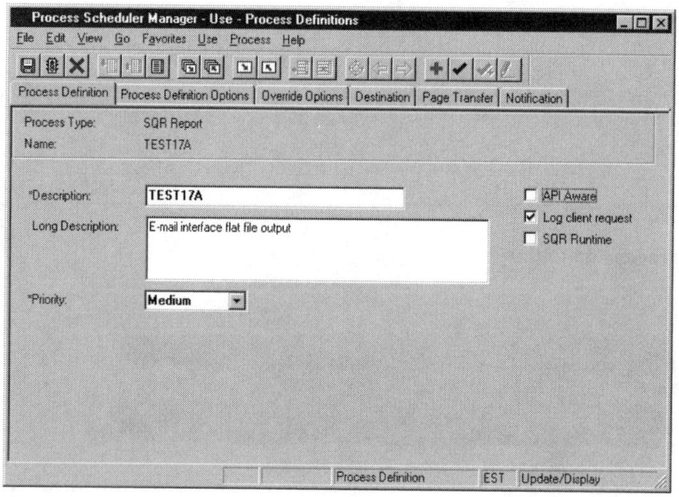

Figure 23.46
The Process Definition page

23.9.1 The Process Definition page

After the system displays the Process definition component, you have to enter the information about your process. It is very important to input the correct information and to understand the meaning of every field. If your definition is not correct, your process will stay Queued or Initiated forever. Let's look at all the fields on the page shown in figure 23.47.

- The Description will later appear along with your process name on the Process Request Scheduler page, so make it meaningful.
- The Long Description (Optional) is used for your process description.
- The Priority can be set to Low, Medium, or High. If several processes are queued on a particular server, the system will be using this priority to decide which process should be initiated first. This parameter is applicable for processes that run on a server only.
- An API Aware process is a process that updates the Process Request table (PSPRCS-RQST) with the process run status (`Error`, `Success`, etc.), completion code, message set, and message number. This allows the system to perform Commit or

Rollback, depending on the run status. Based on the process execution results, the system displays a standard or custom message on the Process Monitor's Process Request Detail page. Not every program is API Aware, you have to add certain logic to your SQR program to make it API Aware. Turning the API Aware flag `On` does not automatically make the process API Aware. We'll discuss the process of making an SQR program API Aware in detail in the next chapter, but please note that, if your program is not API Aware, the flag must be turned `Off`.

For our current program, you have to turn this setting off, since we did not place any special code to make our program API Aware—yet. (We'll cover this in the next chapter.)

- The Log Client Request is `On` by default for all API Aware processes. If turned on, every time the process is run on the client, the system logs the request on the Process Request table. This is useful as an audit trail. Note that, for all server run requests, logging is always performed.
- The SQR Runtime is checked when you want the system to append the `.sqt` extension to the process name (used for pre-compiled SQR programs). It will use the `SQT` working directory. For our E-Mail Interface program, this option should be turned off.

After all fields in the Process Definition page are filled, the page will look like the one in figure 23.47.

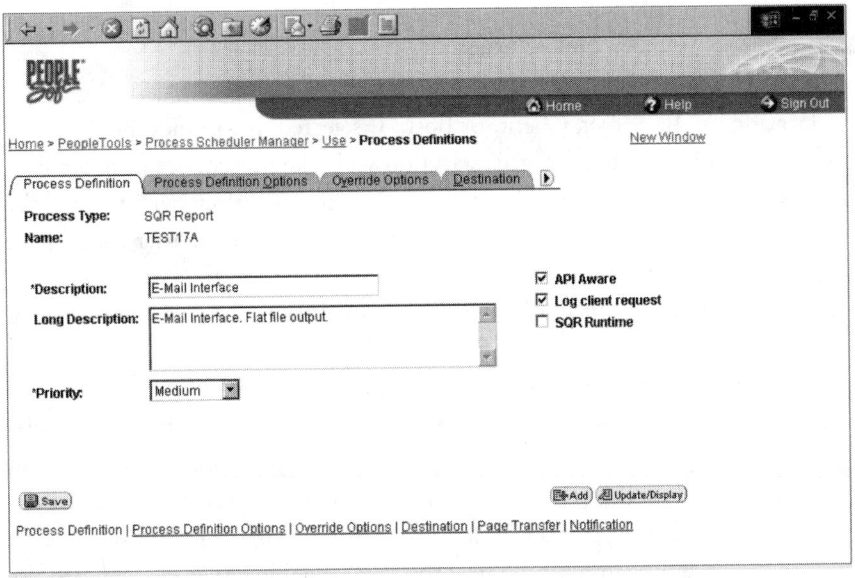

Figure 23.47 The Process Definition page for the E-Mail Interface process

23.9.2 Process Definition Options

Let's switch to the next tab on the Process Definition component, the Process Definition Options page, as shown in figure 23.48.

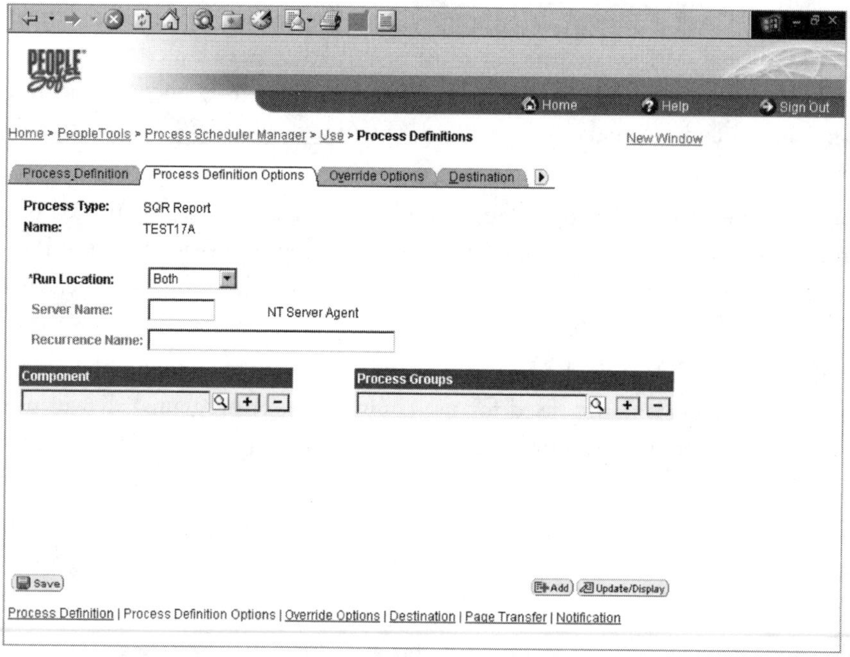

Figure 23.48 The Process Definition Options Page

The run location can be Server, Client, or Both. If selected, it specifies the run location for your process request. Note that this selection will take precedence over the Process Scheduler Request specification. This means that, if you select Server here, the process will be scheduled to run on Server only, regardless of what the user specifies in the Process Scheduler Request dialog.

Note that Client processes can not be run from your Internet Browser application, but only from the File, Run menu on your Windows client.

The Server Name (Optional) is specified if you always have to run your process on a particular server. If you do not want to be so restrictive, leave it blank. If, for example, you have both the UNIX and the NT Server available to run your process, and you do not specify the server name on this page, the users will be able to select the server of their choice on the Process Request page. If a user leaves the server name blank on the Process Request page, the system will automatically find the first available server that can process the request for this process class. The server name can be specified only if the run location is Server.

The Recurrence Name (Optional) can be selected only for processes that run on a server. The recurrence definitions are created in the Process Scheduler Manager, Use menu. All previously created definitions are shown in the lookup list for the `Recurrence Name` field. Note: if you enter the `Recurrence Name` here, this does not mean that the process will automatically start and run according to the specified recurrence definition. It has to be started manually for the first time.

The component is used to specify the component from which you want to run your process. In our case, it is the Interfaces component because we created this component to run the E-Mail Interface program. Note that, in order to link your process to a component, this component has to be created prior to creating the Process Definition. It is important to enter the correct component name. PeopleSoft does not edit this field: if you misspell it, users will not be able to run your process. To avoid the problem, you can search for a valid component. The system will display a list of all available components.

If you do not remember the name of the component, you need to find it. Go to PeopleTools, Application Designer, File, Open, Menu, Administer_Workforce (GBL). Find the Interfaces menu item, highlight it, select View and View Definition (see figure 23.49). You will see the name of the component (Interfaces).

You can optionally specify more than one component for your process. In this case, the process will appear on all selected components.

The process groups must be entered to identify which operators have permission to submit this process. At least one process group must be specified. You can allow multiple process groups to run your process. You have to specify the process groups that belong to

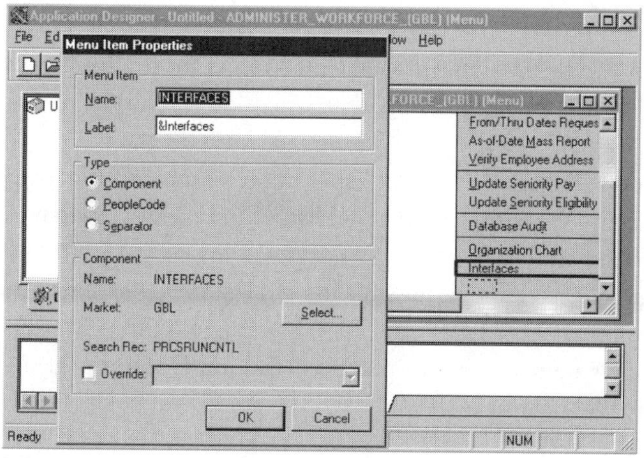

Figure 23.49
Finding the name of a component

your user. If you specified a process group here, but did not give a permission to some operators to use this group, the process will not be visible to these operators.

Please remember that the process groups must be linked to a permission list. Users can run only those processes through Process Scheduler that belong to process groups assigned to their role. Let's select the HRALL process groups (figure 23.50) and then verify our selection.

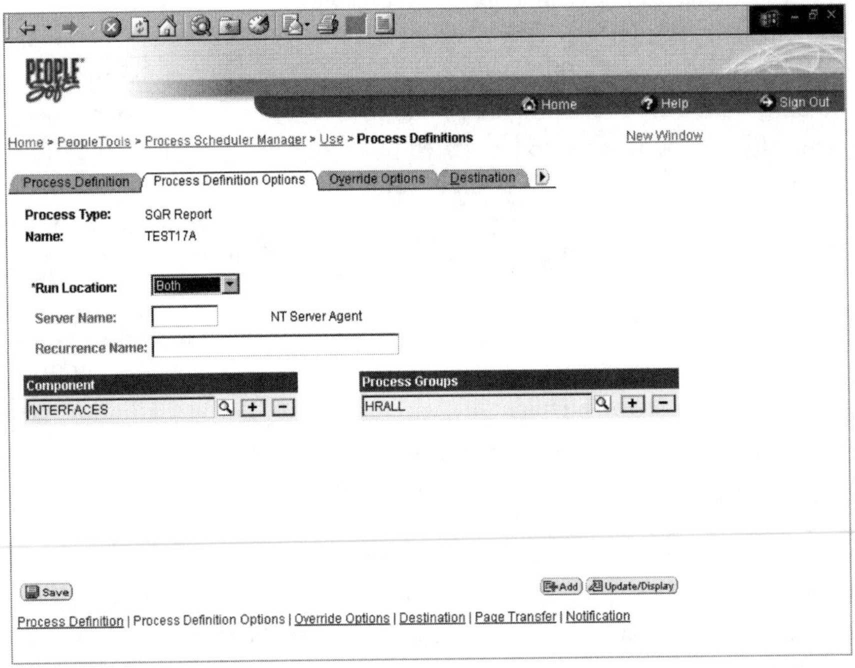

Figure 23.50 The Process Definition Options Page for the E-Mail Interface process

We need to make sure that the permission list we selected to use for the Interfaces menu item has the right process groups permissions that will allow execution of our E-Mail Interface process.

Click on the New Window hyperlink in the upper right corner of the page (figure 23.50), and open the Report Workforce permission list, (CPHR3350). Switch to the Processes tab as shown in figure 23.51.

As you can see from figure 23.52, our permission list allows one to execute the HRALL process group processes.

Now we can be sure that the parameters in our process definition Options page are valid and linked properly to the PS operator ID.

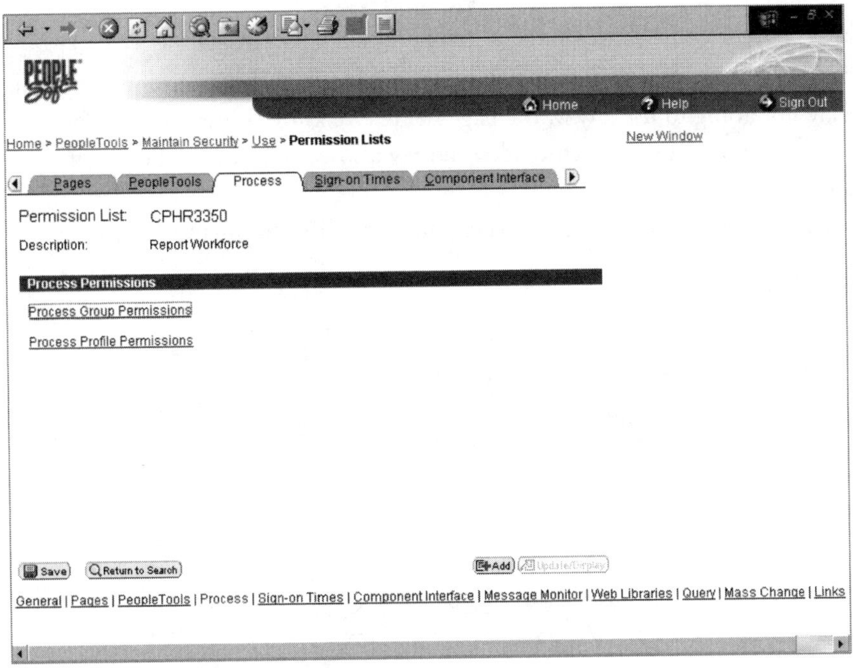

Figure 23.51 Verifying the process groups permissions

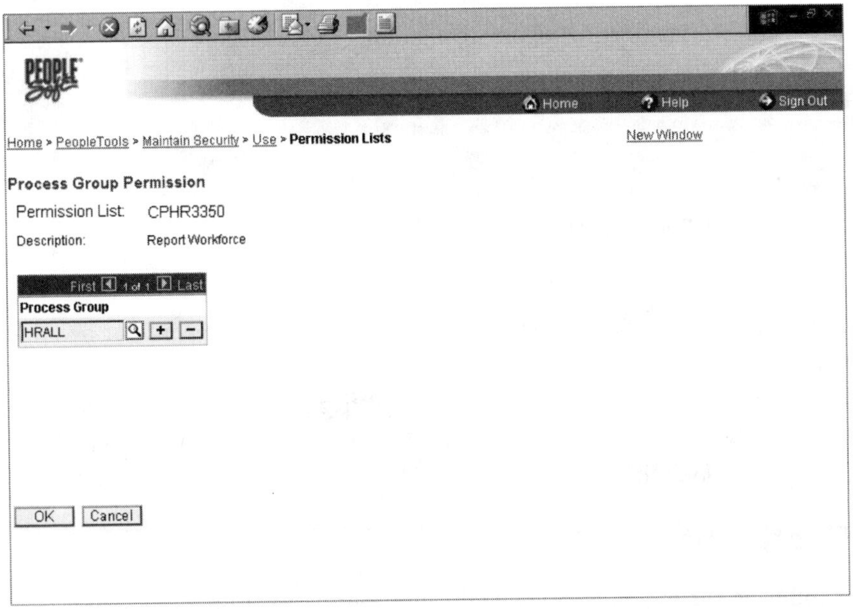

Figure 23.52 HRALL is assigned as a process group for Report Workforce permission list

23.9.3 Override Options page

The third page on the process definitions component (figure 23.53) is optional. For our process, we are not going to use any of the page fields. We know, however, that you may be curious about the meaning of each field. You may also wonder when the use of these fields could be helpful.

This page is used to modify the process parameter list, command line, or working directory.

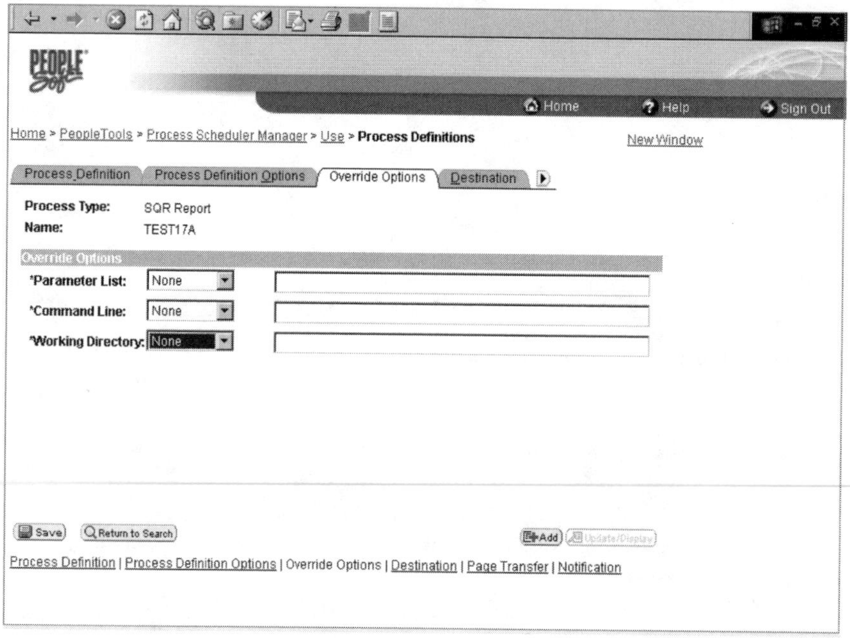

Figure 23.53 The Override Options page

The drop-down lists for each parameter allow you to preface, append, or override each parameter for your process.

For example, if you would like to add the `-A` SQR flag to append the output file to an existing output file of the same name and also define `-DebugXYZ` flags, your Override Options page may look like that in figure 23.54.

23.9.4 Destination page

The Destination page allows you to control which output destination a user may select. Setting source to User Specified permits users to provide an output destination at run

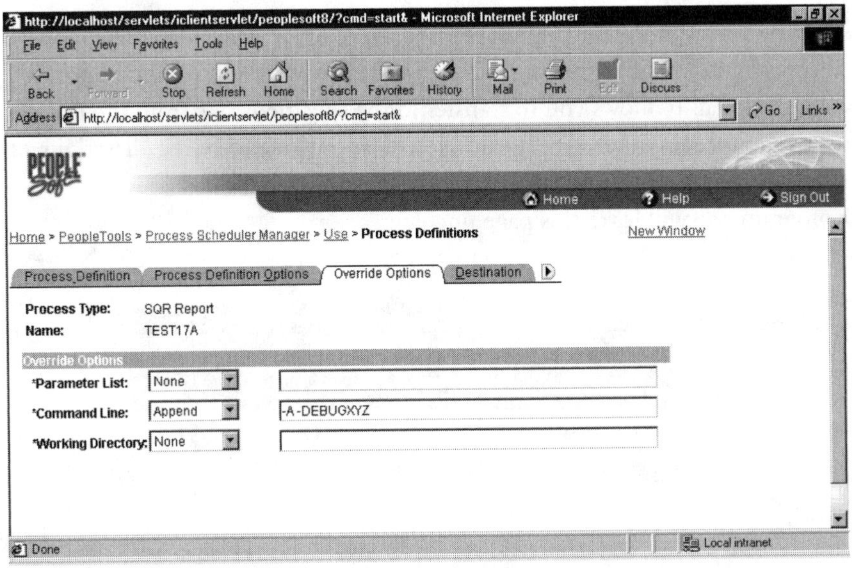

Figure 23.54 An updated Process Definitions Options page

time. For SQR processes, the Destination Source should be set to User Specified as shown in figure 23.55.

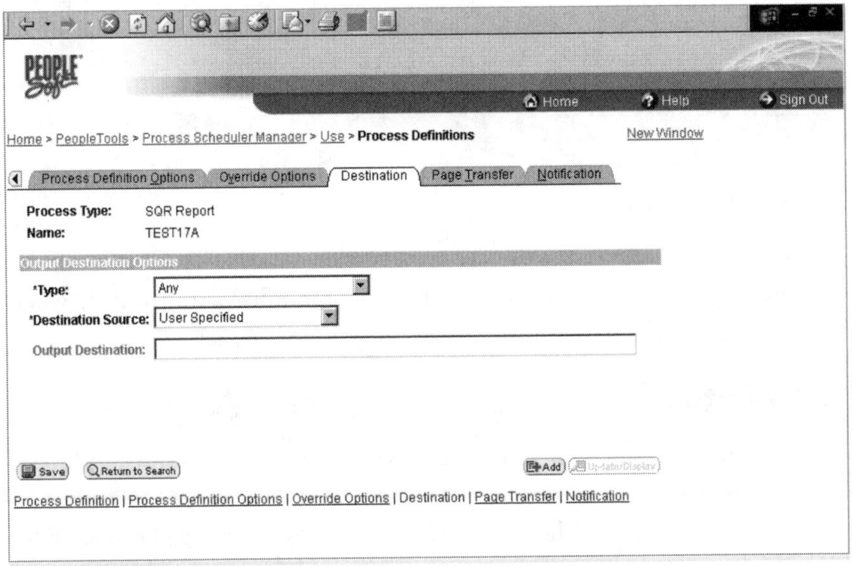

Figure 23.55 The Destination page

23.9.5 Page transfer

The page shown in figure 23.56 is the fourth page in the process definitions component. This page is also optional. It allows you to transfer to the specified page from the Process Monitor after your process is successfully completed. You can specify the directions of transfer and the menu actions in this page.

For our program, we will leave this page unchanged.

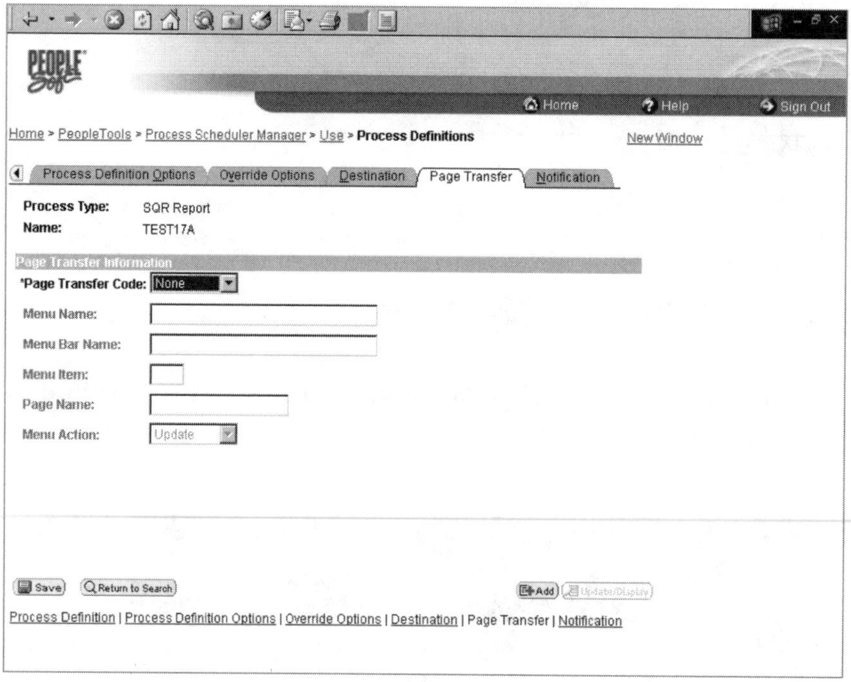

Figure 23.56 The Page transfers page

Please note that parameters on this page will not be modified automatically when you change your menu or page definitions in the Application Designer.

23.9.6 Notification page

This page allows you send messages to your users based on the results (error or success) of your process execution.

The messages can be sent to either a group of people by selecting the role as ID Type or to individual users by selecting User in the ID Type drop-down field.

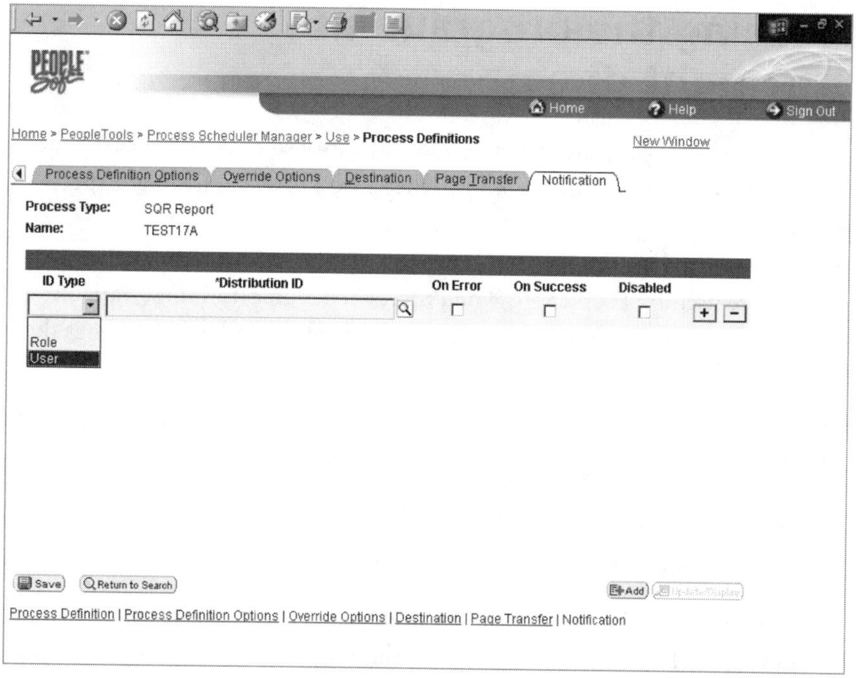

Figure 23.57 Notification page

You can also select multiple ID Types as shown in figure 23.58.

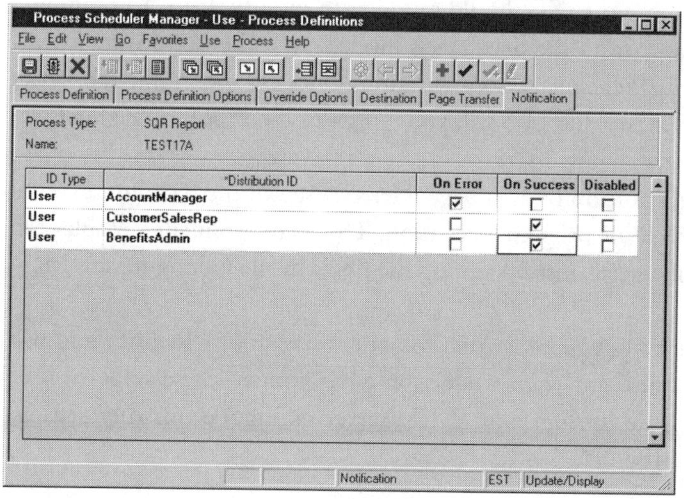

Figure 23.58 Notifying multiple users about the process completion status

23.10 Placing the program into the right directory

Your last task is to place your program into the right directory so that the Process Scheduler will be able to run it. But how do we know where the Process Scheduler expects to find the program?

SQR reports are located on the file server on your network. There are four environment variables that are used by PeopleSoft. The Process Scheduler uses these variables to search for your SQR program. PeopleSoft recommends using the following settings during development:

- %PSSQR1%—your workstation user SQR directory
- %PSSQR2%—your workstation PS delivered SQR directory
- %PSSQR3%—network file server user SQR directory
- %PSSQR4%—network file server PS delivered SQR directory

While developing and testing your program it is convenient to keep your program files on your workstation. If you use these settings, the Process Scheduler will first look at your workstation directory and then will search on the network file server. After your program is tested and ready for production, you can then move it to the file server's user SQR directory (%PSSQR3%).

If you execute your program in a two- or three-tier developer's mode (but not from PIA), the PeopleSoft Configuration Manager will help you to find out the right directories where your SQR program source file should reside or to modify them. You can only access Configuration Manager from the developer's mode. From the Administer Workforce GBL menu, select Edit/Preferences/Configuration. Click on the Profile tab, select the profile and then click on the Edit button. If you switch to the Process Scheduler tab, you'll see a page like the one in figure 23.59.

Take a look at the SQR portion on this page. Here we see all the flags and directories that are used during the SQR program execution. These environment variables can be easily customized for your needs just by editing the fields in the Configuration Manager page.

Please note that the settings will be written to your workstation's Registry and will only apply to your workstation. For your production environment, these values will be supplied by the settings made during your Batch Server configuration. Any settings made here will not apply to the PIA.

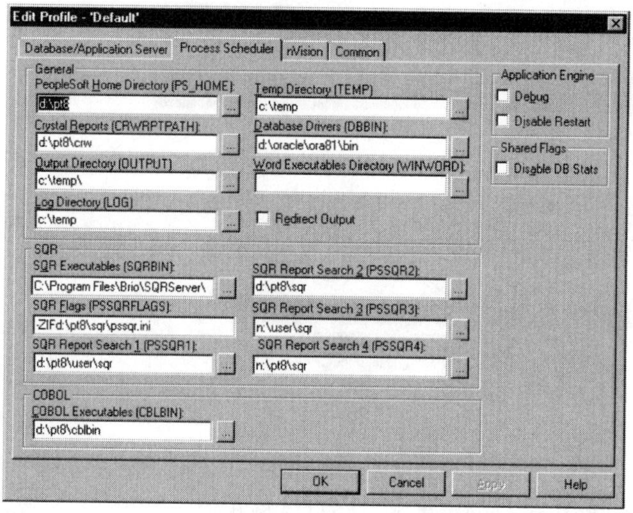

Figure 23.59
The Process Scheduler tab in the Configuration Manager

23.11 Testing your Process Definition

We performed a lot of object manipulations in this chapter. Let's retrace our steps in attaching our E-Mail Interface program to the PeopleSoft Process Scheduler:

1. Selected the PRCSRUNCNTL record as our Run Control Record
2. Selected the PRCSRUNCNTL page as our Run Control page
3. Created the new component: Interfaces and added our page to this component.
4. Added the new menu item: Interfaces to Administer_Workforce_(GBL), Processes menu.
5. Granted security access to the Component.
6. Created the Process Definition `Test17A` for our SQR program `Test17A.sqr`

Now we are ready to run our SQR program. In the PIA mode, go to the Administer Workforce (GBL), Process, Interfaces menu. Select TEST1 as the Run Control and click on the Run button. You'll get a Process Scheduler Request page with our `TEST17A` SQR process attached (fig. 23.60).

Select the PSNT server and click OK to submit the `TEST17A` process for execution. Click on the Process Monitor hyperlink and check the Run Status. As you can see from figure 23.61, the Run Status indicates that the process run status is Error.

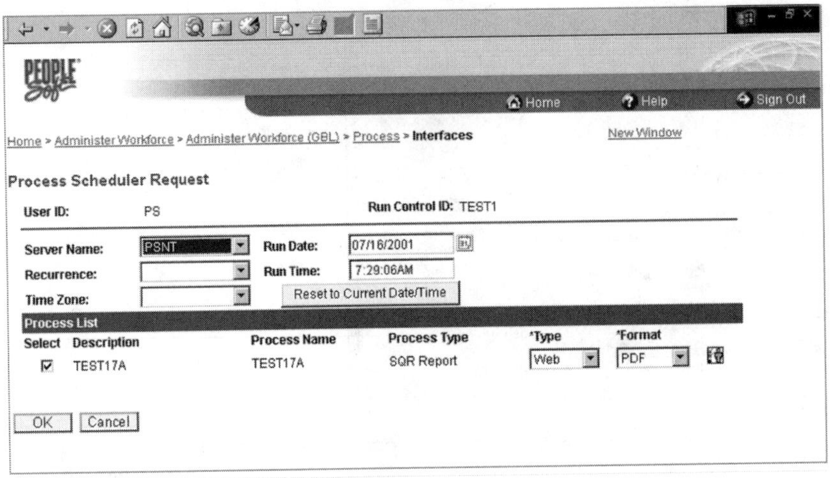

Figure 23.60 The Process Scheduler Request page with our TEST17A.SQR attached

Let's click on the Details link (figure 23.61) in order to find out what caused the error. This will bring us to the next page (Figure 23.62).

Now we can examine the Message Log file. Click on the Message Log link under the Actions group (Figure 23.62), and then on the Explain button (figure 23.63).

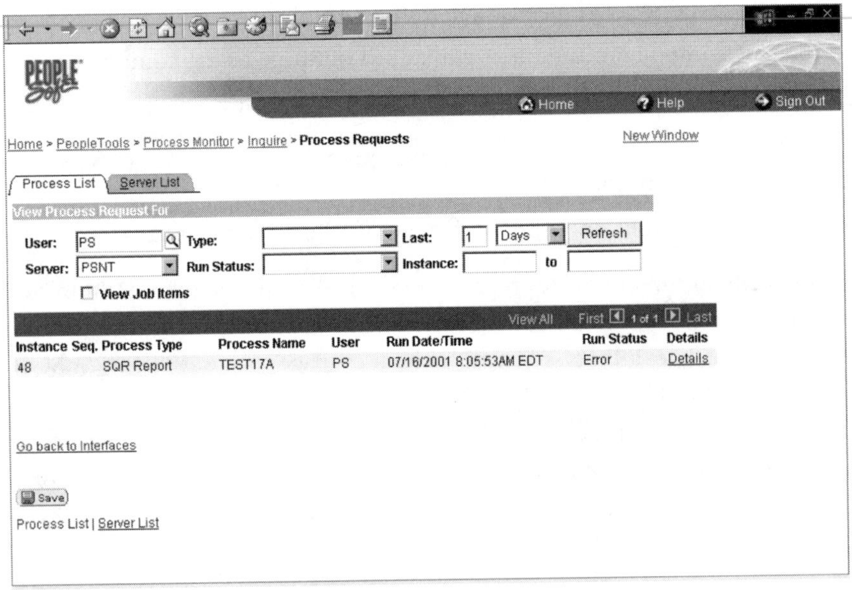

Figure 23.61 Viewing the Process Request run status

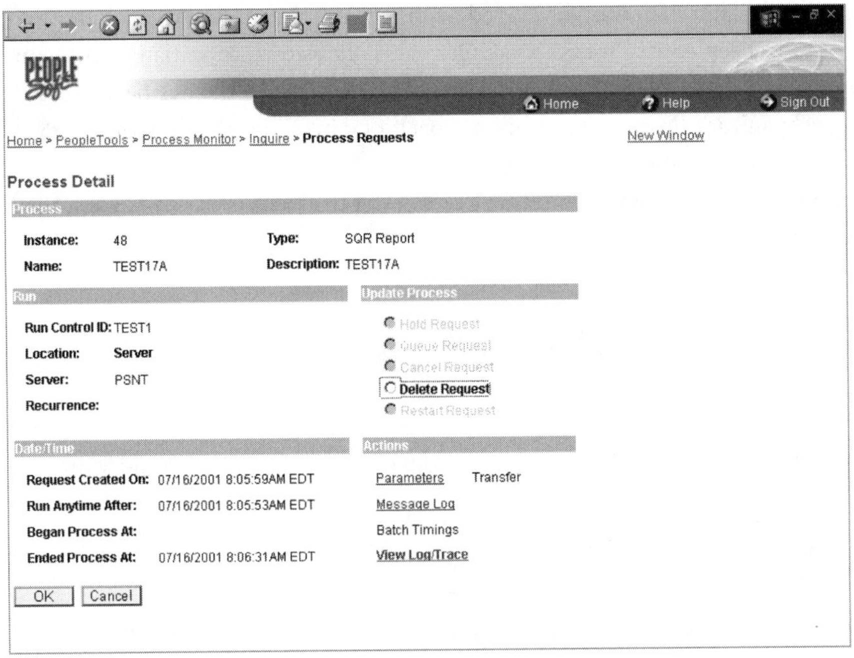

Figure 23.62 The Process Detail page

The description of the problem (figure 23.63) shows exactly what happened. Our process failed to update the status in the Process Request table. Remember, that we just

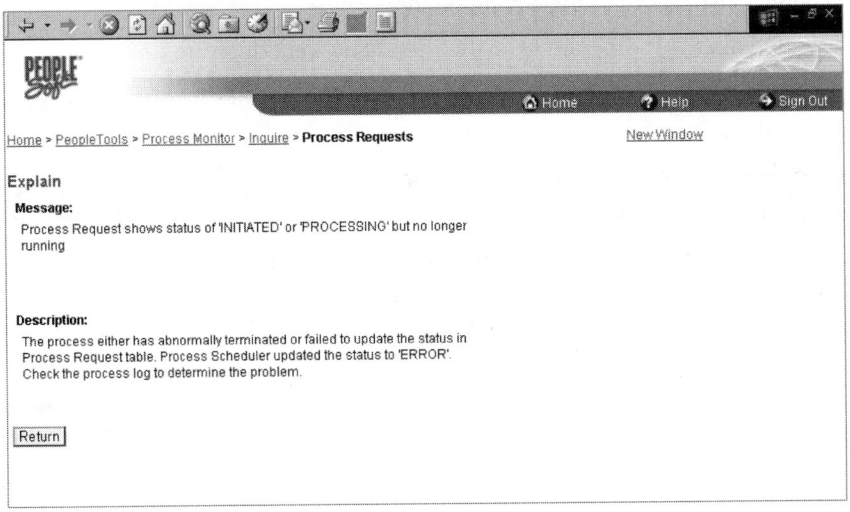

Figure 23.63 Reviewing the Message Log

took our SQR program that was developed with no PeopleSoft interface code, and plugged it into the PeopleSoft Process Scheduler. This allowed us to initiate and to run the program from the PeopleSoft page. Even the E-Mail Interface file has been created, but the Process Monitor's Process Status has not been updated, and therefore, PeopleSoft has no idea about the return code of this process.

In the next chapter, you will learn how to solve the problem by making your SQR program API Aware.

KEY POINTS

1. PeopleSoft delivers a number of records and pages that can be reused for your custom processes.
2. Any Run Control record must have the `Operator Id` and the `Run Control Id` as its key fields.
3. A Run Control record may contain additional fields that are not used in your program.
4. A Run Control page should be specific to your application and should contain (or display) only the fields that you want your user to enter. The same Run Control page may be used by many processes as long as they share the same input parameters.
5. A component acts as a link between a Run Control page and a menu. There may be multiple pages in a single component.
6. You can add your SQR program to an existing menu item or create a new one.
7. The appropriate security access must be granted to allow all users to see the new menu item.
8. Each PeopleSoft user has an individual profile, called User Profile which is linked to one or more roles.
9. Permission lists control access to menu, components, and pages for each role. Roles act as links between User Profiles and permission lists.

KEY POINTS (CONTINUED)

10 An API Aware process updates the Process Request (PSPRCSRQST) table with the process run status, completion code, and message parameters.

11 In order to make your SQR program run under the Process Scheduler, the following PeopleSoft objects have to be created, modified, or reused:

i. Application-specific Run Control record

ii. Application Run Control page

iii. Component

iv. Menu Item

v. Security access to the new component

vi. Process definition

C H A P T E R 2 4

Making an SQR program API Aware

IN THIS CHAPTER

- PeopleSoft-delivered `SQC` files
- How does SQR program know that it was invoked from the Process Scheduler?
- API variables as communicators between the program and the Process Scheduler
- The Process Scheduler and error situations

In the previous chapter we discussed the process of attaching an SQR program to a PeopleSoft online page as well as ways to run this program under the PeopleSoft Process Scheduler. You also learned that, in most cases, SQR programs run under PeopleSoft need certain changes. While any SQR program can be executed by the Process Scheduler, only programs that include special code are capable of communicating their status back to the Process Scheduler. In order to allow the Process Monitor to reflect your program status, you have to make your program API Aware.

Making an SQR program API Aware involves adding a program code to update the Process Request table (PSPRCSRQST) with the program run status (`Error`, `Success`, etc.), completion code, error message set, and error message number.

24.1 Using PeopleSoft-delivered SQC files

PeopleSoft provides a number of routines that handle the communication between SQR programs and the Process Scheduler. In order to make your SQR program API Aware, you have to use the `#Include` operators to add the `STDAPI.sqc` and `SETENV.sqc` files to your program. The `STDAPI.sqc`, in turn, uses the nested `#Include` operators that refer to other important API files (figure 24.1). Let's look at two of these files: `PRCSDEF.sqc` and `PRCSAPI.sqc`.

The `PRCSDEF.sqc` file includes the `Define-Prcs-Vars` procedure. This procedure initializes all the fields used in API. The `PRCSAPI.sqc` file includes two procedures: `Get-Run-Control-Parms` and `Update-Prcs-Run-Status`. The first procedure `Get-Run-Control-Parms` retrieves the input parameters (`Process Instance`, `Operator Id`, and `Run Control Id`) and updates the run status of the process request to `'Processing'`. Another procedure in `PRCSAPI.sqc`, `Update-Prcs-Run-Status`, is designed to update the Process Request table (PSPRCSRQST) upon the program completion.

When you run your program from the Process Scheduler, the control parameters that identify your process (Database Name, Process Instance, Operator ID and Run Control ID) are passed as a part of the command line. The application-specific input parameters are not passed to the program—these parameters are saved in the `Run Control` table. (In the next chapter you will learn how to retrieve parameters from the `Run Control` table.) When you run the same program from the SQR dialog box or from the command line rather than from the Process Scheduler, the `Get-Run-Control-Parms` API procedure will not detect any input values and will instead identify the process as being run from outside the Process Scheduler.

Figure 24.1 lists PeopleSoft delivered API `SQC` files and procedures and also shows the location of each API procedure and `SQC` file.

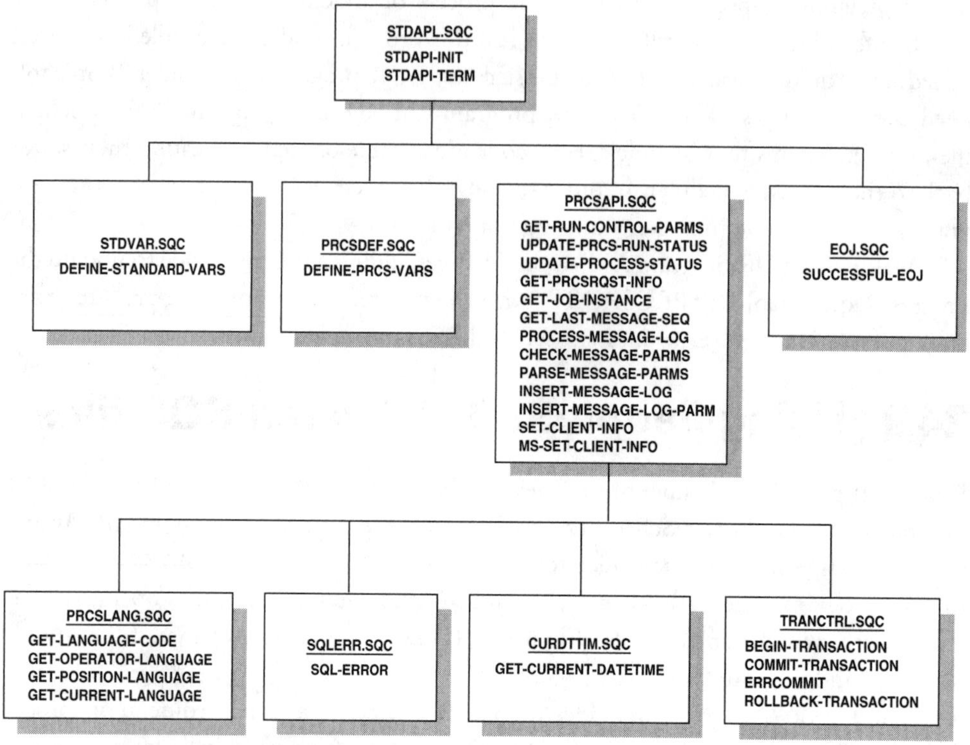

Figure 24.1 The Process Scheduler API SQC files and procedures

24.2 Incorporating SQC files into your program

To make our E-Mail Interface program API Aware, let's add the SQC files we just discussed to the program code. (The updated program will be called `Test24A.sqr`):

```
!TEST24A.SQR
!Making the E-Mail Interface program API Aware
!E-Mail Interface
#Include 'setenv.sqc'      !Set environment

!********************
Begin-Program
!********************
   Do Stdapi-Init
   Let  $FileName='c:\book\Employee.dat'
   Open $FileName As 1 For-Writing Record=100 Status=#OpenStat
```

The `Stdapi-Init` procedure in `STDAPI.sqc` calls `Define-Prcs-Vars` and `Get-Run-Control-Parms` to initialize API variables, gets control parameters from the command line and updates the run status to `'Processing'`

```
    If #OpenStat != 0
      Show 'Error Opening ' $FileName
    Else
      Do Process_Employees
      Close 1
    End-If

    Display 'Total records exported: ' Noline
    Display #Tot_Recs 999,999,999

    Do Stdapi-Term
End-Program
!*********************************************
Begin-Procedure Process_Employees
!*********************************************
Move 0 to #Tot_Recs
Begin-Select
A.Emplid
A.Deptid
B.Name
B.Phone
   Do Write-Output-Record
From PS_Job A, PS_Personal_Data B
Where   A.emplid=B.emplid
   And A.Empl_Rcd=0
   And A.Empl_Status = 'A'
   And A.Effdt = (Select Max(Effdt)
                  From    Ps_Job
                  Where   Emplid     = A.Emplid
                  And     Empl_Rcd  = A.Empl_Rcd
                  And     Effdt    <= Sysdate)
   And A.Effseq =  (Select Max(Effseq)
                    From      Ps_Job
                    Where     Emplid     = A.Emplid
                    And       Empl_Rcd   = A.EmpL_Rcd
                    And       Effdt      = A.Effdt)
End-Select
End-Procedure

!**********************************
Begin-Procedure Write-Output-Record
!**********************************

 Write 1 From
  &A.Emplid ','
  &A.Deptid ','
  &B.Name ','
  &B.Phone
  Add 1 to #Tot_Recs
```

The `Stdapi-Term` procedure in `STDAPI.sqc` calls the `Successful-Eoj` procedure from `EOJ.sqc` which updates the run status to `"Successful"`

```
End-Procedure
!**********************************
                                             This SQC file includes all
                                                  necessary API code.
#Include 'datetime.sqc'  !Routines for date and time formatting
#Include 'stdapi.sqc'   <-
```

At the program start, the `STDAPI-Init` procedure is invoked. This procedure is a part of the PeopleSoft-delivered `SQC` file `STDAPI.sqc`. `Stdapi-Init`, invokes two more procedures in turn. The first one, named `Define-Prcs-Vars`, is located in `PRCSAPI.sqc`. Its job is to initialize all API variables. The second procedure, `Get-Run-Control-Parms`, determines whether the program is called from the Process Scheduler and, if yes, promotes the run status from `'Initiated'` to `'Processing'`.

If you are curious how the `Get-Run-Control-Parms` procedure knows that the program is invoked from the Process Scheduler, take a look at the procedure source code shown in the following example.

We'll list just a portion of the `Get-Run-Control-Parms` procedure of `PRCSAPI.SQC` that deals with input parameters.

```
begin-procedure Get-Run-Control-Parms
...
input $database_name
 'Database Name (Optional, Press ENTER to continue)'
input $prcs_process_instance
 'Process Instance (Optional, Press ENTER to continue)'
   if not isnull($prcs_process_instance)
       let #prcs_process_instance = to_number($prcs_process_instance)
        input $prcs_oprid
         'Operator ID (Optional, Press ENTER to continue)'

        input $prcs_run_cntl_id
         'Run Control (Optional, Press ENTER to continue)'
   else
        let #prcs_process_instance = 0
   end-if

   if #prcs_process_instance > 0
        let #prcs_first_time = {True}
        do Get-Language-Codes
        do GetTimeZones
        let #prcs_run_status = #prcs_run_status_processing
        do Update-Prcs-Run-Status
        let #prcs_run_status = #prcs_run_status_successful
   end-if
```

As you can see the procedure code contains four `Input` commands with request to supply values for the following variables: Database Name, Process Instance, Operator ID and Run Control ID. All these values are optional. The program instructs you to Press Enter to continue. This is actually done to accommodate two different modes for your program execution: from the command line or SQRW window and from the Process Scheduler. If the program is invoked from SQRW or command line (which usually happens during the program's testing), the operator will receive the prompts and as instructed will press the Enter key. The Process Instance variable (`$PRCS_PROCESS_INSTANCE`) will then be populated with NULL value, which works as an indicator to the code that this program is being executed outside of the Process Scheduler.

If the program is invoked from the Process Scheduler, the `$prcs_process_instance` variable receives its value from the parameter list string passed from the Process Scheduler. The parameter list string, besides the `Process Instance` value, also includes the `Database Name Operator Id`, and the `Process Run Id`. Figure 24.2 shows the Process Request Parameters page for the Employee Birthdays program. You can see the program parameters on the page in the command line. You can also see that for this particular program run, the `Database Name` is HR8DMO, the `Process Instance` equal to `76`, the `Operator Id` is `PS`, and the `Process Run Id` is `Test1`.

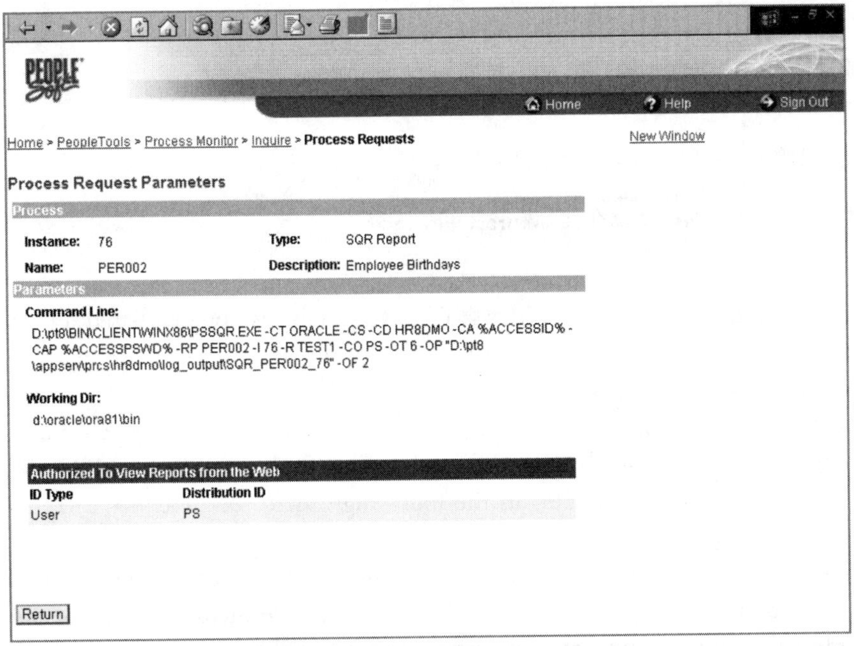

Figure 24.2 Run Control parameters passed to an SQR program

Let's return to `Test24A.sqr`. At the end of the main section, the program calls the `Stdapi-Term` procedure, which is a part of `STDAPI.sqc`. The purpose of this procedure is to update the PSPRSCRQST table with the Process Run Status, Message Parameters, and Return Code. The program logic in `Stdapi-Term` may seem a bit convoluted. The chart in figure 24.3 will help you figure out how this procedure communicates the program status to the Process Scheduler.

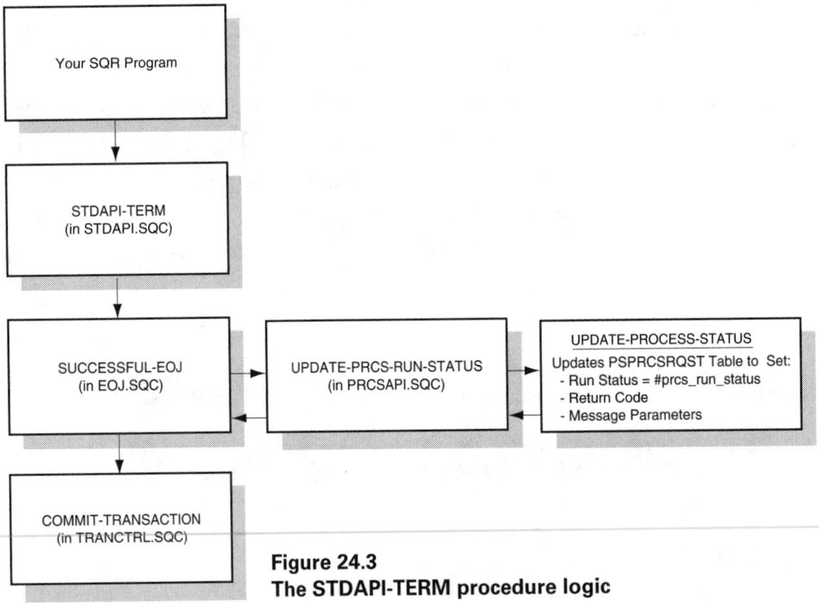

Figure 24.3
The STDAPI-TERM procedure logic

As you can see, the `Run Status` in the `PSPRCSRQST` table is updated based on the `#prcs_run_status` variable value. This variable determines the `Run Status` that you can see on the Process Monitor page.

It is important to remember that in case of an error, the value of the `#prcs_run_status` variable must be updated by the application program. In a normal run, PeopleSoft promotes the process `Run Status` in the following order: `'Queued'`→`'Initiated'`→`'Processing'`→`'Success'`.

Please note that `#prcs_run_status` is a numeric variable. It cannot be assigned the above-discussed text values directly. The `PRCSDEF.sqc` file includes a number of predefined numeric status variables that can be used to assign the `#prcs_run_status` variable the right status value (table 24.1).

Table 24.1 Predefined numeric Run Status variables

Predefined Variable Name	Numeric Value	Status
#prcs_run_status_error	3	Error
#prcs_run_status_processing	7	Processing
#prcs_run_status_successful	9	Success
#prcs_run_status_unsuccessful	10	Used in PRCSAPI.sqc to set the proper error message
#prcs_run_posting	14	Posting

As soon as your program is scheduled to run, the Process Scheduler sets the run status on the Process Monitor to `Queued`. Next, if all parameters in the `Process Definition` are resolved, and the appropriate `Server Agent` is up and running (for server processing only), the Process Scheduler changes the status to `Initiated`. If your program fails to get through the compilation stage, the status on the Process Monitor panel will depend on where the program runs. If your program runs on client, the status will remain `Initiated`. If it runs on server, the status will be changed to `Error` by the SQR invocation script.

The `Stdapi-Init` procedure (which must be called in the beginning of every API Aware program) changes the status to `Processing`, and updates the `PSPRCSRQST` table. At this moment, you will see the status set to `Processing` on the Process Monitor page. The `Stdapi-Init` procedure then sets the `#prcs_run_status` variable to `Success` (`#prcs_run_status_successful`) in the program memory only, but will hold on to the `PSPRCSRQST` table update until either the `Stdapi-Term` or `Sql-Error` procedure is called. Therefore, you will still see the `Processing` status on the Process Monitor page.

If your SQR program runs to the end, and then calls the `Stdapi-Term` procedure as shown in figure 24.3, this procedure will update the `Process Status` to `Success`. In case of an error, it is your program's responsibility to call a PeopleSoft-delivered error-handling routine `SQL-Error` or to code a similar logic in your program. Otherwise, the status on the Process Monitor will either remain set to `Processing` if your program aborted during execution or, worse yet, will be set to `Success` if the program ran to the end and called `Stdapi-Term` regardless of the error situation.

If your program uses a PeopleSoft-delivered error handling routine (part of which is shown in the example below), you do not have to worry about updating the API variables in an error situation. If, however, your program uses its own error processing logic, the program must include a code to set all the API variables to the proper values and update the Process Request table PSPRCSRQST. An example of the PeopleSoft-delivered SQL error-handling procedure is shown below:

```
!A part of the SQL Error
!procedure in SQLERR.SQC
#include 'sqlstat.sqc'
       if #prcs_process_instance > 0
        let #prcs_message_set_nbr = #prcs_msg_set_nbr
        let #prcs_message_nbr = #prcs_msg_nbr_sql_error
        let #prcs_run_status = #prcs_run_status_error
        let #prcs_rc = #sql-status
        let $prcs_message_parm1 = $sql-error
        let #prcs_continuejob = 0
        do Rollback-Transaction
        if $prcs_in_update_prcs_run_stat <> 'Y'
          do Update-Prcs-Run-Status
          do Commit-Transaction
        end-if
      end-if
        let #return-Status = 1
      stop
```

This procedure is usually referenced in the `On-Error` parameter of the `Begin-Sql` statement.

Updating API variables

Updating the `PSPRCSRQST` table

As you can see, the error processing logic in an API Aware program should include updating a set of API variables and calling the `Update-Prcs-Run-Status` procedure that updates the `Process Request` table for your program. After the `Process Request` table is updated, the `Commit-Transaction` function makes this table change permanent.

Later in this chapter we will show you how to create your own error handling routine similar to the one above.

A process request with an output destination type of Web will have several different statuses. As soon as the program successfully finishes its execution, the Process Scheduler Distribution agent will attempt to transfer the files to the Report Repository. The process Scheduler Server Agent will set the Run Status to `Posting` at this moment. If all files are successfully transferred to the Report Repository, the Run Status is changed to `Success` while the Distribution Status in Report Manager is changed to Posted. If Distribution Agent failed to transfer file to the Report Repository and hasn't reached the Maximum Transfer Retries the status remains set as `Posting`. But when The Distribution Agent failed to transfer files to the Report Repository and had used up the Maximum Transfer Retries the Run Status will be changed to `Not Posted`. As you can see, it is very important to understand how the system works. It will help you in troubleshooting the errors. Your program may run to success, but if something is blocking the way to transfer the files, the status may not be successful at all. Please refer to table 22.2 in chapter 22 for the complete list of the Process Monitor and Report Manager Statuses.

24.3 Testing your changes

Now that you better understand how an API Aware SQR program interacts with the Process Scheduler, let's run our program from the Interfaces menu created in chapter 23.

Before we start testing, we need to make one more change. Since our program name has changed from `Test17A.sqr` to `Test24A.sqr`, a new Process definition will have to be created as we did in chapter 23. Just remember that this time our process must be marked as API Aware (see figure 24.4).

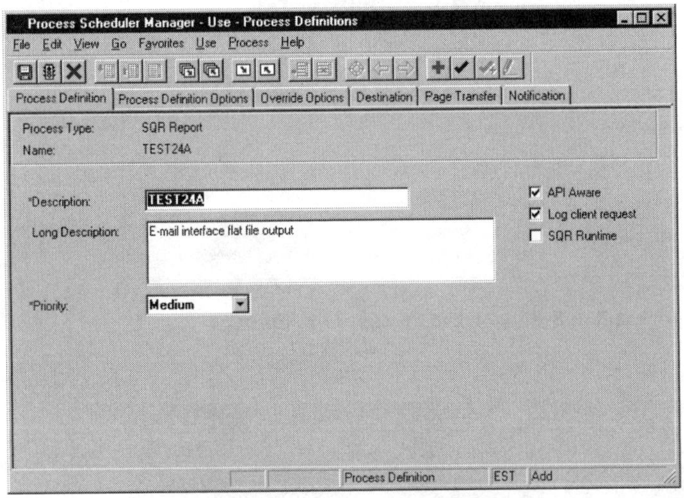

Figure 24.4 Creating the Process definition for the E-Mail Interface program

Now we are ready to execute our program. In the Web mode, let's go to the Interface Menu item, and select the TEST1 Run Id. Then click on Run and select our process from the Process Scheduler Request page (figure 24.5).

As you can see, we now have two processes under the same menu item. Our old TEST17A and the new one, TEST24A, which is changed to become an API Aware process. Select the second process and then click on the OK button. Let's then click on the Process Monitor hyperlink to examine the process run status (fig 24.6).

At this point, you may want to ask, Is Success always a success? In other words, does the fact that the Run Status field on the Process Monitor page is set to Success mean that the process finished successfully? The best way to verify the program run results is to check the program's log and trace files. Figure 24.7 shows the answer to our questions.

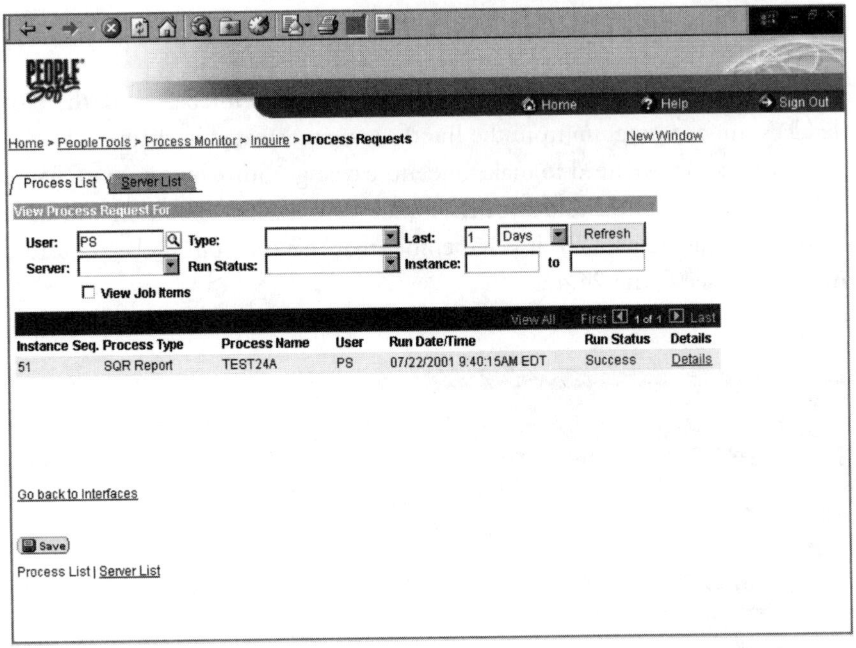

Figure 24.6 Examining the process Run Status on the Process Monitor page

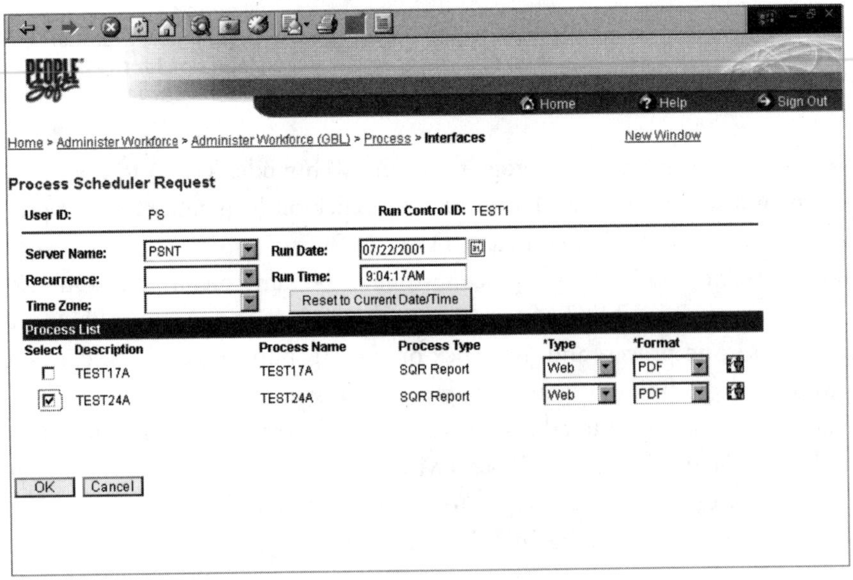

Figure 24.5 Selecting the API Aware process to run

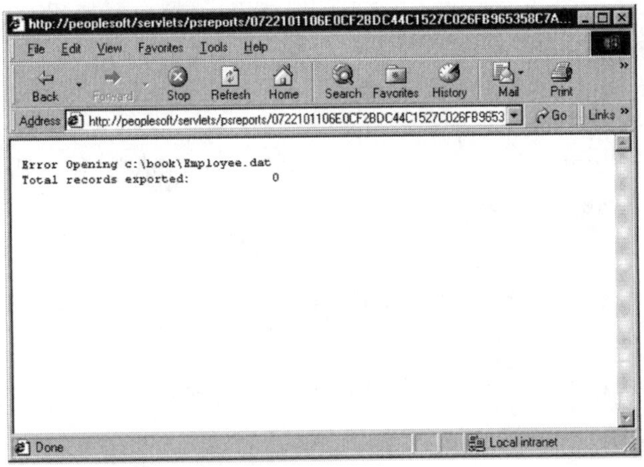

Figure 24.7
The Test24A.SQR Trace file

How can the Process Monitor say `Success` when the program hasn't yet written a single record to the output file? The `Success` in the `Status` field can sometimes be misleading.

Apparently, the program isn't communicating its status back to the Process Monitor. Why not? You will find the answer in a moment.

24.4 Communicating errors back to the Process Scheduler

Let's reexamine our program again and see if we missed any of the error situations. One point of concern is the output file opening code shown here:

```
!The E-Mail Interface program code
!with no comprehensive error handling
Do Stdapi-Init
   Let  $FileName='c:\book\Employee.dat'
   Open $FileName as 1 For-Writing Record=100 Status=#OpenStat
   If #OpenStat != 0
     Show 'Error Opening ' $FileName
    Else
     Do Process_Employees
     Close 1
    End-If
    Display 'Total records exported: ' noline
    Display #tot_recs 999,999,999
    Do Stdapi-Term
...
```

Upon the error, the program called the Stdapi-Term procedure, but offered no clue that the program failed.

By now, you probably have realized that we did not do a good job in error handling. The program sent an error message to the log file, but failed to inform the Process Scheduler about the output file opening error. The Process Scheduler had no way of knowing the status of our process. The best way to correct the situation is to clone the PeopleSoft-delivered code in the `SQL-Error` procedure, and to modify this code according to our program logic. Here is one way to do this:

```
!TEST24A.SQR
!The E-Mail Interface program with enhanced error handling
Do Stdapi-Init
   Let  $FileName='c:\book\Employee.dat'
   Open $FileName as 1 For-Writing Record=100 Status=#OpenStat
   If #OpenStat != 0
     Let $Error_Text=Rtrim('Error Opening ' ||$FileName,' ')
     Let #Ret_Code=#OpenStat
     Do File-Error
   Else
   Do Process_Employees
   Close 1
   End-If
   display 'Total records exported: ' noline
   display #tot_recs 999,999,999
   Do Stdapi-Term
...
!**********************************
Begin-Procedure File-Error
!**********************************
if #prcs_process_instance > 0
   Show $Error_Text
   Print $Error_Text (+1,1)
   let #prcs_message_set_nbr = #prcs_msg_set_nbr
   let #prcs_message_nbr = 30    !set to blank
   let #prcs_run_status = #prcs_run_status_error
   let #prcs_rc = #Ret_Code
   let $prcs_message_parm1 = $Error_Text
   let #prcs_continuejob = 0
End-if
End-Procedure
```

In this portion of code, the error-related information is moved to the appropriate API fields and is made available to the Process Scheduler.

Let's incorporate this code into our `TEST24A.SQR`. We will use the same program name to avoid unnecessary PeopleSoft changes. Now we can execute the program. You will see the improvement right away (figure 24.8).

Yes, the Run Status is now shown as Error. And what about the error log message? Click on the Detail hyperlink and select to view the Message Log (figure 24.9).

Our error message is shown on the PeopleSoft Process Request Message Log page.

Now you know that, should an error situation occur, your program will not only send the error messages to the program log file, but will also communicate the error

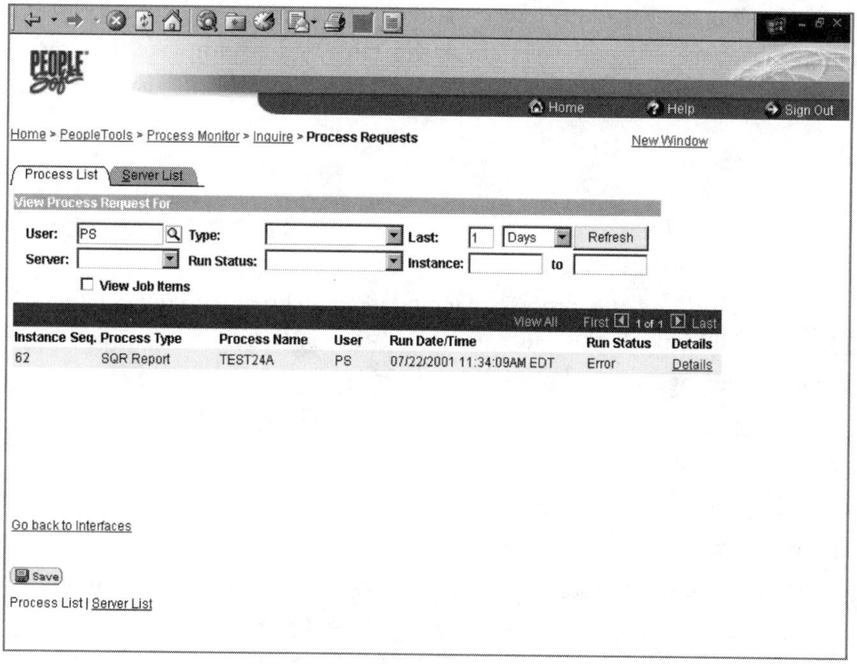

Figure 24.8 The Run Status is changed to Error

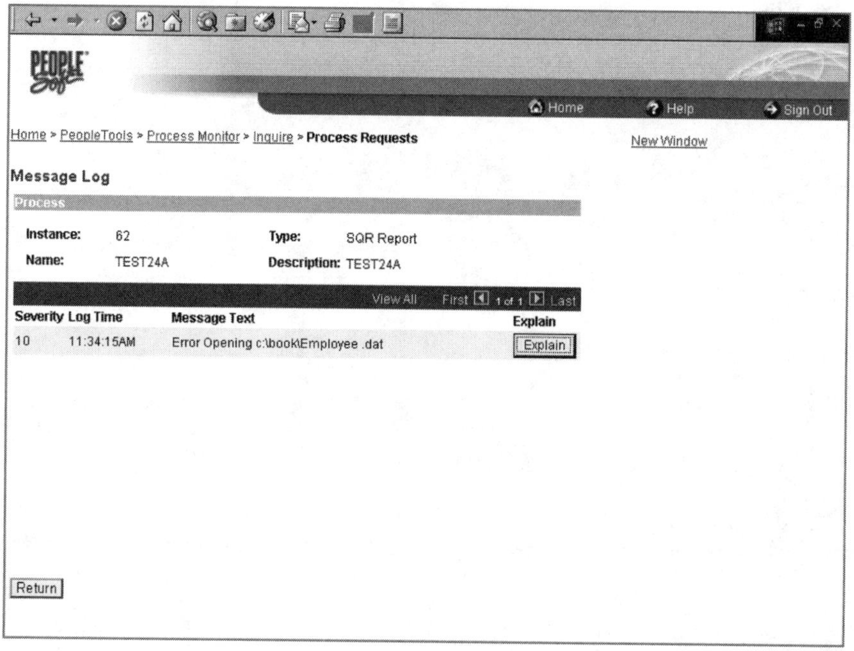

Figure 24.9 The Error message is displayed on the Process Request Message Log page

information to the Process Scheduler by updating the proper fields in the `Process Request` table. The Process Monitor will check this table and both update the process status and display the program's error message on the Process Request Message Log page.

KEY POINTS

1. An API Aware process is a process that updates the Process Request table (PSPRCSRQST) with the process run status (`Error`, `Success`, etc.), completion code, message set, and message number.
2. PeopleSoft-delivered `SQC` file `STDAPI.sqc` helps you to make your SQR program API Aware.
3. The `Define-Prcs-Vars` procedure in `PRCSDEF.sqc` initializes all the fields used in the API.
4. The `Get_Run_Control_Parms` procedure in `PRCSAPI.sqc` retrieves input parameters: `Database Name`, `Process Instance`, `Operator Id`, and `Run Control ID`.
5. It is your SQR program's responsibility to communicate errors back to the Process Scheduler.

CHAPTER 25

Accepting input parameters from PeopleSoft pages

IN THIS CHAPTER

- Using the PeopleSoft-delivered SQC files to accept input parameters
- Creating your own SQC files or modifying the existing SQC files
- Changing an SQR program to work with SQC files
- Creating your own Run Control records and pages
- Testing your changes

In chapter 24 you learned that the PeopleSoft-delivered SQC files can help SQR programs in accepting the Run Control parameters from the Process Scheduler and in keeping the Process Scheduler informed as to what is going on with the programs.

There is, however, another level of communication between PeopleSoft and an SQR program: accepting application-specific parameters from PeopleSoft. In PeopleSoft, users enter application-specific parameters via Run Control pages. In chapter 23, we discussed how the Process Scheduler passes input parameters to processes. You learned the difference between the PeopleTools Run Control records and the Application Run Control records. Now you will learn how an SQR program accepts and handles application-specific parameters from PeopleSoft Run Control pages.

25.1 Using application-specific SQC files to obtain input parameters

PeopleSoft delivers a number of application-specific SQC files that are used to read input parameters from Application Run Control records. Usually, two SQC functions are involved in reading the parameters: one function selects the input parameters while another one formats the selected parameters and moves them to the designated SQR program variables. You can either use the PeopleSoft-delivered SQC files or develop your own, depending on the parameters your SQR program needs to accept.

Let's first learn how PeopleSoft-delivered SQR programs work with input parameters. Later, you will learn how to use a similar approach in your program. Let's take a look, for example, at the PeopleSoft-delivered Temporary Employees report and examine how this program works. This program accepts As-Of-Date as its input parameter.

25.1.1 How the Temporary Employees program accepts its input parameters

The name of the program that generates the Temporary Employees report is Per007.sqr. If you open Per007.sqr, and scroll down to the end of the program code, you will see that it uses the following SQC files:

```
!SQC files that are used to obtain input parameters in the
!Temporary Employees report
#include 'hrrnctl1.sqc'  !Get run control parameter values
#include 'hrgetval.sqc'  !Get values mask routines
#include 'askaod.sqc'    !Ask As Of Date input
```

This is how the input parameter read section of Per007.sqr looks:

```
!Procedures used in reading input parameters in PER007.sqr
```

```
begin-procedure Init-Report
  move 'PER007' to $ReportID
  do Stdapi-Init
  if $prcs_process_instance = ''
     do Ask-As-Of-date
  else
     do Select-Parameters
  end-if
...
end-procedure
```

Check if ran from the Process Schedule. If yes, call Select-Parameters; otherwise call the `Ask-As-Of-date` procedure.

```
begin-procedure Get-Values
   let $language_cd = $PRCS_LANGUAGE_CD
   do Get-As-Of-Date
end-procedure
```

This procedure is called from the `Select-Parameters` procedure.

In the previous chapter, you learned that the `Stdapi-Init` procedure initializes `API` variables and obtains the Process Scheduler command line parameters (if any). Next, the program determines the method of its invocation: it may be initiated by the Process Scheduler or invoked some other way (submitted via the SQR dialog box, executed from the command line, or called by another application). Based on this check result, the program calls the proper subroutine to obtain the application-specific input parameters.

If the program is not run under the Process Scheduler, the `$prcs-process-instance` variable remains empty and the regular SQR `Input` command is used in the `Ask-As-Of-date` subroutine to read the input parameters from user input. The `Ask-As-Of-date` code is located in the `Askaod.sqc` file.

If the program is invoked by the Process Scheduler, the `$prcs-process-instance` variable is assigned the process instance number value, and the `Select-Parameters` subroutine is called to retrieve the input parameters from a specific application `Run Control` table. In case of the Temporary Employees report, the program is designed to work with the Run Control table named `PS_RUN_CNTL_HR`, but the procedure logic is a typical example of the communication between an SQR program and a PeopleSoft Run Control page.

Let's examine the `Select-Parameters` procedure. The procedure code is located in the `HRRNCTL1.sqc` file:

```
!A typical input parameters read procedure in HRRNCTL1.SQC
begin-procedure select-parameters
BEGIN-SELECT

RUN_CNTL_HR.OPRID
RUN_CNTL_HR.RUN_CNTL_ID
RUN_CNTL_HR.ASOFDATE
RUN_CNTL_HR.FROMDATE
RUN_CNTL_HR.THRUDATE
```

```
RUN_CNTL_HR.CALENDAR_YEAR
RUN_CNTL_HR.SERVICE_YEARS
RUN_CNTL_HR.AD_STEP
RUN_CNTL_HR.AD_STEP_ENTRY_DT
RUN_CNTL_HR.AD_COMPRATE
RUN_CNTL_HR.AD_HOURLYRT
RUN_CNTL_HR.AD_MONTHLYRT
RUN_CNTL_HR.AD_ANNUALRT
 !...
 !...
RUN_CNTL_HR.AD_CHANGEAMT
RUN_CNTL_HR.AD_CHANGEPCT
RUN_CNTL_HR.EEO_REPORT_TYPE

  do Get-Values

from PS_RUN_CNTL_HR RUN_CNTL_HR

where RUN_CNTL_HR.OPRID = $prcs_oprid
  and RUN_CNTL_HR.RUN_CNTL_ID = $prcs_run_cntl_id
end-select
end-procedure
```

If your program includes the `HRRNCTL1.sqc` file, a procedure named `Get-Values` should be coded within your program.

In this procedure, developed by PeopleSoft, the application-specific input parameters are selected from the PS_RUN_CNTL_HR table for a given combination of `Operator ID` (`$prcs_oprid`) and `Run Control ID` (`$prcs_run_cntl_id`). As you learned in the previous chapter, these two variables came from the Process Scheduler parameter list. An important and not-to-be-missed part of the `Select-Parameters` procedure is a call to the `Get-Values` procedure. This procedure moves and edits the selected input parameter values to the designated variables in an SQR program. If your program uses the `HRRNCTL1.sqc` file, the name of the input parameter edit subroutine must be `Get-Values`. If you code the input parameter retrieval logic yourself, the name of this subroutine (if any) can be different.

In case of the Temporary Employees report, a subroutine named `Get-Values` is a part of the `Per007.sqr` code. You can see this subroutine in our previous example depicting procedures used to read input parameters. Because the `Per007.sqr` program accepts only two application-specific parameters, `Language Code` and `As Of Date`, the `Get-Values` subroutine in this case is very simple: it moves the `Language Code` value to its designated program variable and calls the `Get-As-Of-Date` procedure to format `As Of Date` and to move it to its designated variable:

```
begin-procedure Get-As-Of-Date

  let $AsOfDate = RTRIM(&RUN_CNTL_HR.asofdate, ' ')

  if $AsOfDate = ''
```

```
    move $AsOfToday to $AsOfDate
  end-if

end-procedure
```

The flow-chart shown in figure 25.1 will help you to better understand how the Temporary Employee program (`Per007.sqr`) retrieves its application-specific input parameters.

25.1.2 Changing your SQR program to accept from and thru dates as input parameters

Now that we reviewed how a PeopleSoft-delivered program retrieves its application-specific input parameters, let's apply this knowledge to the E-Mail Interface program. One problem exists: this program accepts no input parameters. It can be modified, however. For example, the employee selection can be limited to the effective dates

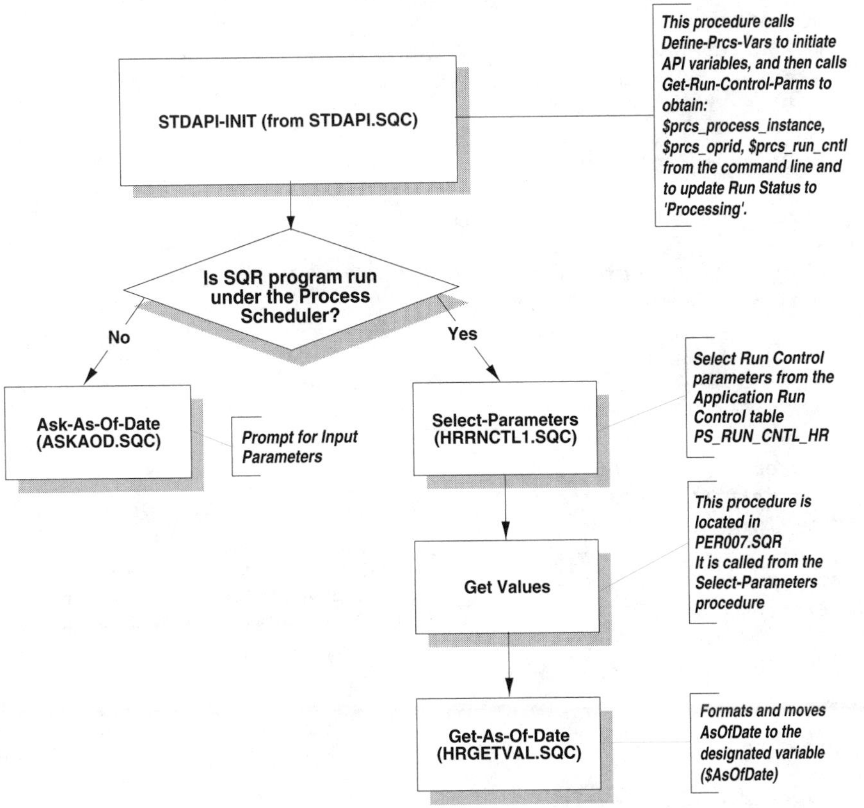

Figure 25.1 Using SQC files to obtain input parameters in the Temporary Employees report

within a user-specified date range. Assuming that the date range is defined by two parameters—`FromDate` and `ThruDate`—our program can use the PeopleSoft-delivered Application Run Control record `PS_RUN_CNTL_HR`, which includes the two necessary parameters. This will make our task much simpler. (Later, you will learn how to create your own Application Run Control records). The changed E-Mail Interface program is named `Test25A.sqr`:

```
!TEST25A.SQR
!The E-Mail Interface program modified to accept the
!From and Thru dates as input parameters
!E-Mail Interface
#include 'setenv.sqc'      !Set environment

!*******************
Begin-Program
!*******************
Do Init-Report
   Let  $FileName='c:\book\Employee.dat'
   Open $FileName as 1 For-Writing Record=100 Status=#OpenStat
   If #OpenStat != 0
     Let $Error_Text=Rtrim('Error Opening ' ||$FileName,' ')
     Let #Ret_Code=#OpenStat
     Do File-Error
   Else
     Do Process_Employees
     Close 1
   End-If

   Display 'Total records exported: ' Noline
   Display #Tot_Recs 999,999,999

   Do Stdapi-Term
End-Program

!*******************************
Begin-Procedure Init-Report
!*******************************
Do Stdapi-Init

If $prcs_process_instance = ''
   Do Ask-From-Thru-Date
 Else
   Do Select-Parameters
 End-if

End-procedure

!*****************************
Begin-Procedure Get-Values
!*****************************
```

Check if run from the Process Scheduler. If yes, then call `Select-Parameters`; otherwise call the `Ask-From-Thru-Date` procedure (in `ASKFTD.SQC`).

```
   Do Get-From-Thru-Date
End-Procedure
```

Call **Get-From-Thru-Date** from HRGETVAL.SQC

```
!**********************************
Begin-Procedure File-Error
!**********************************
if #prcs_process_instance > 0
   Show $Error_Text
   Print $Error_Text (+1,1)
   Let #prcs_message_set_nbr   = #prcs_msg_set_nbr
   Let #prcs_message_nbr       = 30                    !Set to blank
   Let #prcs_run_status = #prcs_run_status_error
   Let #prcs_rc = #Ret_Code
   Let $prcs_message_parm1 = $Error_Text
   Let #prcs_continuejob = 0
End-if
End-Procedure

!********************************
Begin-Procedure Process_Employees
!********************************
Move 0 to #Tot_Recs
Begin-Select
A.Emplid
A.Deptid
B.Name
B.Phone
   Do Write-Output-Record
From PS_Job A, PS_Personal_Data B
where  A.emplid=B.emplid
   And A.empl_Rcd=0
   And A.Empl_Status = 'A'
   And A.Effdt = (Select Max(Effdt)
           From   PS_JOB
           Where    Emplid  = A.Emplid
           And      Empl_Rcd = A.Empl_Rcd
           And      Effdt Between $FromDate and $ThruDate)
   And A.Effseq =  (Select Max(Effseq)
        From     PS_JOB
        Where    Emplid     = A.Emplid
        And      Empl_Rcd = A.Empl_Rcd
        And      Effdt      = A.Effdt)
End-Select
End-Procedure
```

Select the dates between the From and Thru dates.

```
!********************************
Begin-Procedure Write-Output-Record
!********************************

 Write 1 from
 &A.Emplid ','
 &A.Deptid ','
```

```
   &B.Name ','
   &B.Phone
   Add 1 to #Tot_Recs

End-Procedure
!********************************** *

#include 'datetime.sqc'   !Routines for date and time formatting
#include 'stdapi.sqc'
#include 'hrrnctl1.sqc'   !Get run control parameter values
#include 'hrgetval.sqc'   !Get values mask routines
#include 'askftd.sqc'     !Ask From-Thru Date input
```

Make sure to include additional SQC files.

As you can see from the program source code, the changes make the input retrieval parameter logic look very similar to that in `Per007.sqr`. The only difference is that `Per007.sqr` accepts `As Of Date` as its input parameter, whereas our program accepts `From` and `Thru` dates. Therefore, the program uses `Get-From-Thru-Date`, and `Ask-From-Thru-Date` in place of `Get-As-Of-Date` as well as a different PeopleSoft-delivered SQC file: `Askftd.sqc`.

25.1.3 Adding unique input parameters to your SQR program

In the previous example, an application program uses input parameters that are already present in one of the PeopleSoft-delivered Application Run Control records. We take advantage of this fact and reuse the PeopleSoft-delivered input parameter retrieval code. Our only problem involves finding a code that will handle the input parameters your program needs to use. If your program uses some parameters that are not included in any existing Run Control record, however, you have to develop your own record, or modify an existing one.

Let's consider a situation where an input parameter in your program cannot be found in any PeopleSoft-delivered Run Control record. For example, let's add another input parameter to the E-Mail Interface program: the name of the program output file. As a result, the program will have three input parameters: `FromDate`, `ThruDate`, and `FileName`. There are several different approaches to accomplish this.

One solution is to add the new field to an existing Run Control record and an existing Run Control page and change the input parameter retrieval code in all related SQC files. This solution is the quickest one from a development point of view. If you consider the future release upgrades, however, it may not be the wisest one since, in this case, you would have to reapply all your customizations to all the PeopleSoft objects you have changed. Also, if you are going to change a PeopleSoft-delivered page, you have to keep in mind that this same page may be used by another application, and, therefore, additional PeopleCode statements will have to be added to the related records either to hide the existing fields your application does not need or to hide the new field when the page is used in other applications.

Another solution is to create a new Run Control record and a new Run Control page and to write a code to retrieve and process the input parameters, optionally placing this code in your SQC files. This approach will require a little bit more work, but it will pay off when it comes to the future release upgrades. You might also be able to use the newly created record for other custom programs by adding the required fields to it. We recommend and will be using the second approach for our task.

25.2 Creating your own Run Control records and pages

The easiest way to create your own Application Run Control record is to find a similar record and save it under a different name, allowing you to modify the record by adding the new fields and deleting the fields your program does not need.

Since we already know that the RUN_CNTL_HR Run Control record contains both the FromDate and ThruDate fields, we will clone this record.

If you do not know which record to clone, you can browse all records with names that start with "Run," or, better yet, use Object Reference to find all records that contain the FromDate and ThruDate fields. Here is how you do this: Click on File, Open and specify Field as the object type in the Application Designer panel. Type FromDate in the Selection Criteria box and press Select. Select Edit, Find Object References. You will get the screen shown in figure 25.2 listing all PeopleSoft objects that use the FromDate field.

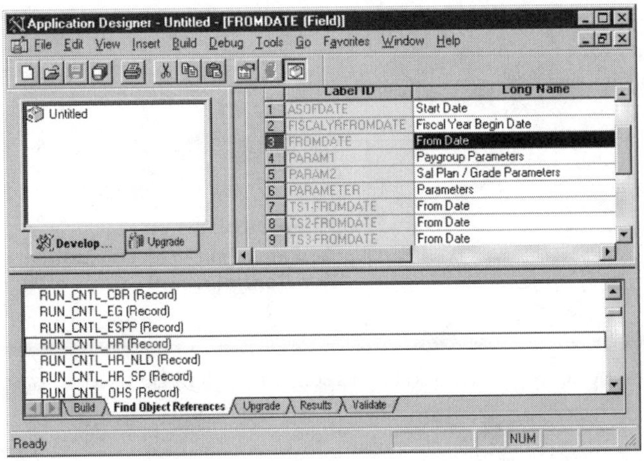

Figure 25.2 Selecting a Run Control Record that contains the FromDate field

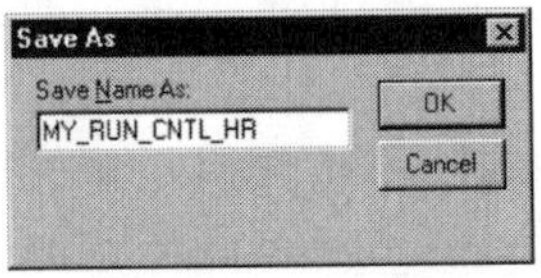

Figure 25.3 Creating a new Application Run Control record as a clone of RUN_CNTL_HR.

Assuming that the `RUN_CNTL_HR` Run Control record is the right one to be cloned, let's open this record and save it as `MY_RUN_CNTL_HR` (figure 25.3).

In this record you must keep the key fields: `OPRID` and `RUN_CNTL_ID`. Another pair of fields you will need are `FromDate` and `ThruDate`. Let's also leave the `Language_Cd` and `AsOfDate` fields for potential future use. All other fields can be deleted. If, in the future, you need more fields, you will always be able to add them.

Note Fields that are used in PeopleSoft records are not defined within the scope of each record. Each field is defined globally throughout the entire database and, therefore, can be used in many records.

After deleting the unnecessary fields, you can add an additional field, `FILENAME`, to store the value of the respective input parameter. You can either create a field or reuse the existing one if the field attributes of your field are identical to the existing field. Keep in mind that each field definition's properties are common across the entire database.

For our task, we'll use the existing field `FILENAME`, and add it to our record using the Insert Field menu option (see figure 25.4).

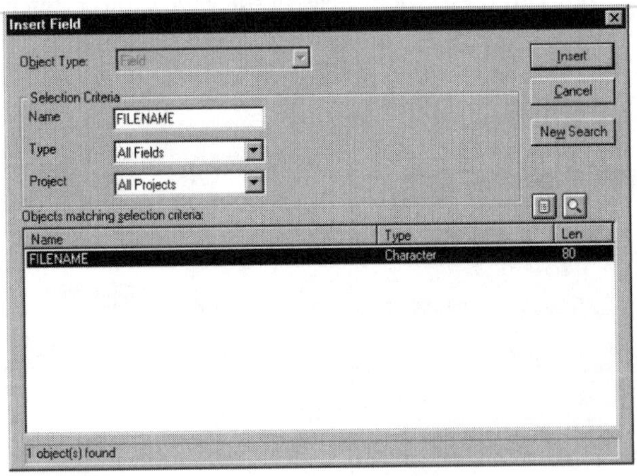

Figure 25.4 Adding a field to an Application Run Control record

We now have built a new Application Run Control record that will be used to pass input parameters to the E-Mail Interface program. After you select File, Save, there is another step to take.

But before that, we should not forget to add our newly created object to the Project. The Projects are used in PeopleSoft to keep track of all customizations and to promote your modifications to other databases. You can press the F7 key or select Insert Current Object into Project. You can also instruct the system to do it automatically by selecting Tools, Options, and clicking Insert Object into Project when Object is modified and saved. Let's use this option as shown in figure 25.5

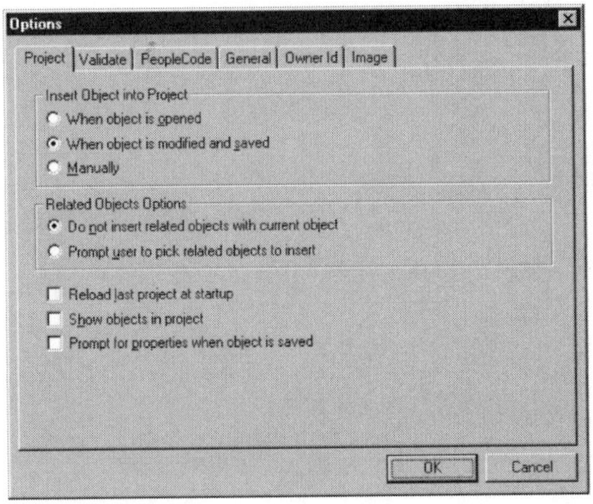

Figure 25.5
Keeping track of all system modifications

After our first custom object, the record definition, is saved to a project, let's save the project as `MY_PROJECT` (figure 25.6)

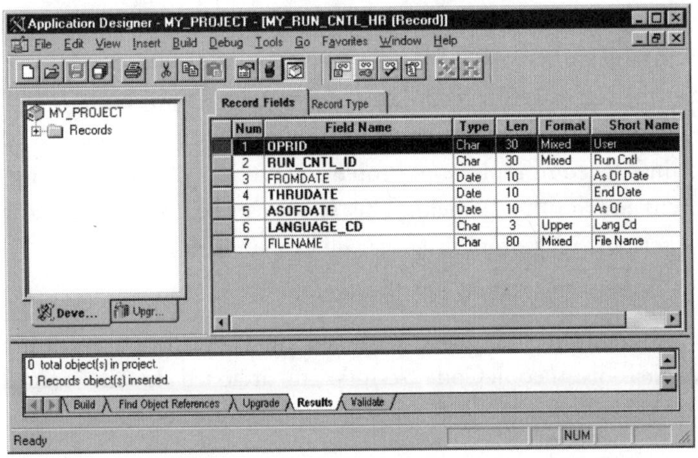

Figure 25.6 Saving our custom object into the MY_PROJECT project

So far, we have just created a Record definition of the new Run Control record, sometimes called a *PeopleTools-level record*. Now, you will have to create a physical table. Sometimes this step is called creating a *database-level record*. Let's select Build, Current Object as shown in figure 25.7 and build the new MY_RUN_CNTL_HR table.

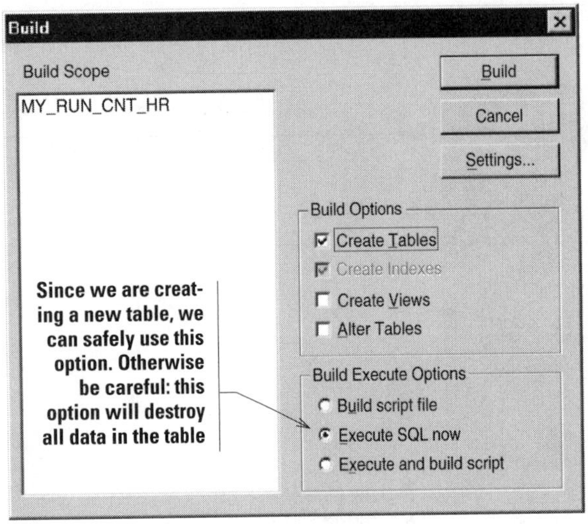

Figure 25.7 Creating a database-level MY_RUN_CNTL_HR record

As you can see from figure 25.7, we request the system to create the MY_RUN_CNTL_HR table. The key of the newly created table is a combination of the `Operator Id` and the `Run Control Id`. When the E-Mail Interface program is run under the Process Scheduler, the operator can select either `New` or `Update/Display` option (see, for example, figure 22.3 in chapter 22). When `New` is selected, a new record is inserted into the MY_RUN_CNTL_HR table, otherwise, an existing record is updated.

When creating your own Run Control record, do not forget to mark both `OPRID` and `Run_Cntl_Id` as key fields. You must also make sure that the `Operator Id` will be stored in the record by adding the commonly used PeopleCode script which will be triggered by the `RowInit` event for the `OPRID` field. This script can be copied from any Run Control record. (The script is very simple and we will explain it shortly.)

Note PeopleCode is a programming language designed by PeopleSoft specifically for use with PeopleTools. PeopleCode scripts are attached to the record fields, and are triggered by specific events. Please refer to the PeopleCode manual for more information.

The PeopleCode script in the RowInit event for the OPRID field moves the operator ID to the OPRID field in our record. You access this script from the Application Designer panel, by opening the MY_RUN_CNTL_HR record, double-clicking on the OPRID field, and selecting View PeopleCode. Figure 25.8 shows the script.

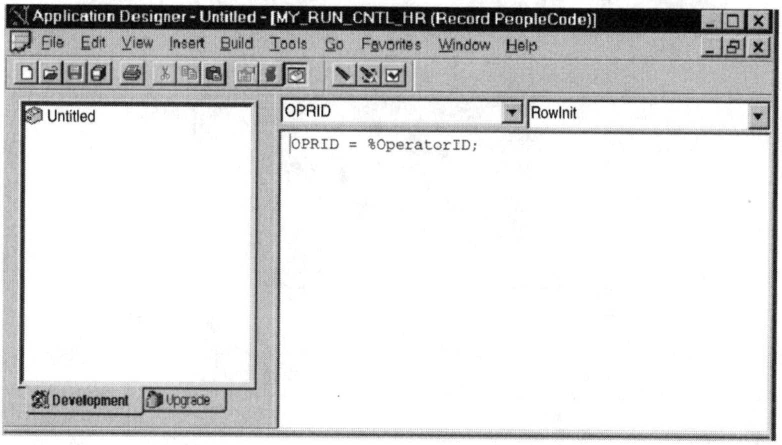

Figure 25.8 The PeopleCode script in the RowInit event for Oprid moves the Operator Id from the system variable %OperatorId to the OPRID field in the record.

The code shown in figure 25.8 will be executed when the operator selects the MY_RUN_CNTL page from the Interfaces menu. It places the Operator ID into the OPRID field of the MY_RUN_CNTL_HR record.

25.2.1 Building a custom Run Control page

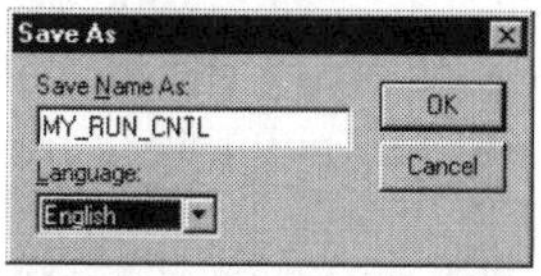

Figure 25.9 Creating a new Run Control page by cloning an existing page

As in the case with the Run Control record, we need to find a suitable Run Control page for use as a new page template. In chapter 23, we discussed different methods of selecting the appropriate page. You can look for pages that use specific Run Control records or specific fields within the records, or simply select pages by the page name. Since our program's input parameters are: FromDate, ThruDate, and File Name, the PeopleSoft-delivered RUNCTL_FROMTHRU page will be ideal to clone. Let's open it and save this page as MY_RUN_CNTL (figure 25.9).

Now we can change the page by adding the FILENAME field to it. PeopleSoft pages can have different types of visual objects: radio buttons, check boxes, drop-down lists, edit boxes, etc. In our case, an edit box is the most suitable because it allows users to

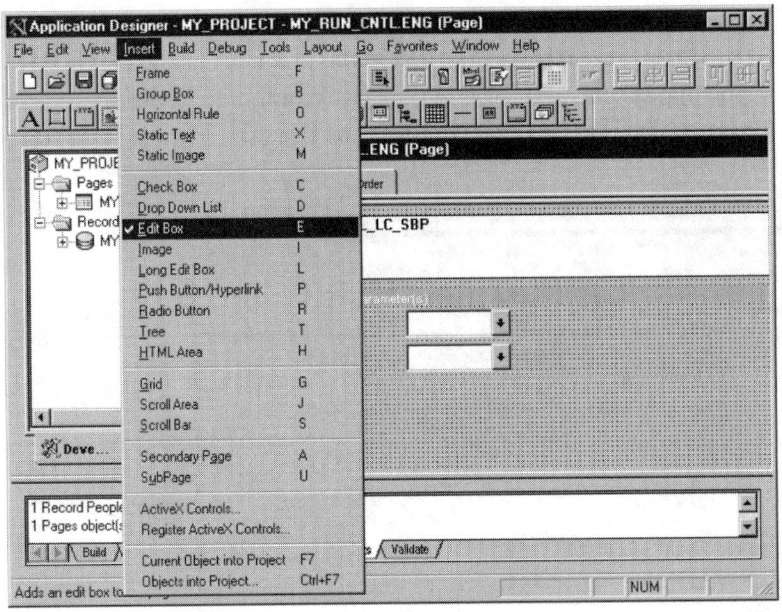

Figure 25.10 Adding a new field to MY_RUN_CNTL panel

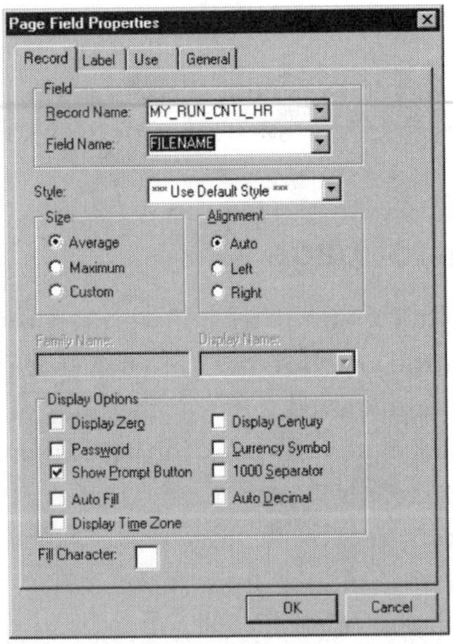

Figure 25.11 Associating a panel field with a field in a Run Control record

enter the program output file name. Select Insert, Edit Box from the Application Designer page (figure 25.10).

After the newly created edit box is added to the page, it is still a dummy field with no connection to any Run Control record. We need to associate this dummy object with our record. Click on the page field and select Edit, Page Field Properties from the Application Designer menu (or merely click the right mouse button while pointing to the field) to get the Page Field Properties page shown in figure 25.11. Select MY_RUN_CNTL_HR record as `Record Name`, and FILENAME as `Field Name` (figure 25.11).

After you click `OK`, our new page will contain the new field: `File Name` (figure 25.12).

Do not forget that you created the new Run Control page by cloning an existing page, RUNCTL_FROMTHRU. The RUNCTL_FROMTHRU page's two existing fields, `FROMDATE`

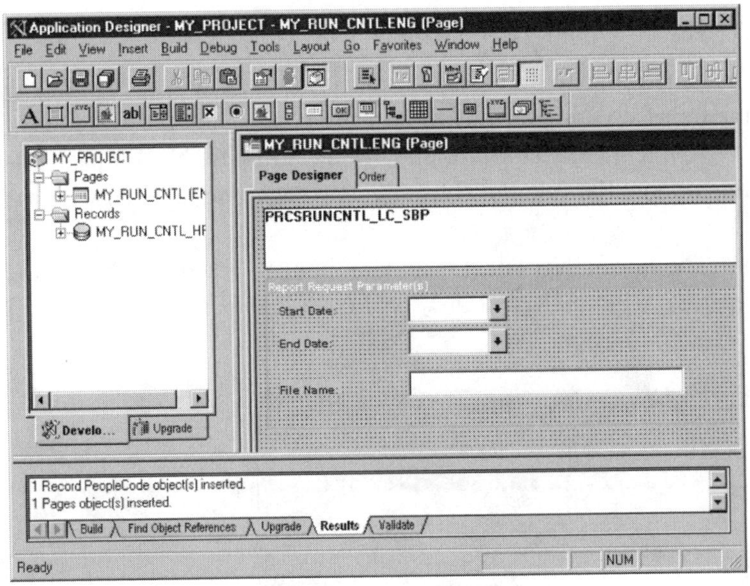

Figure 25.12 Modifying the MY_RUN_CNTL_HR page

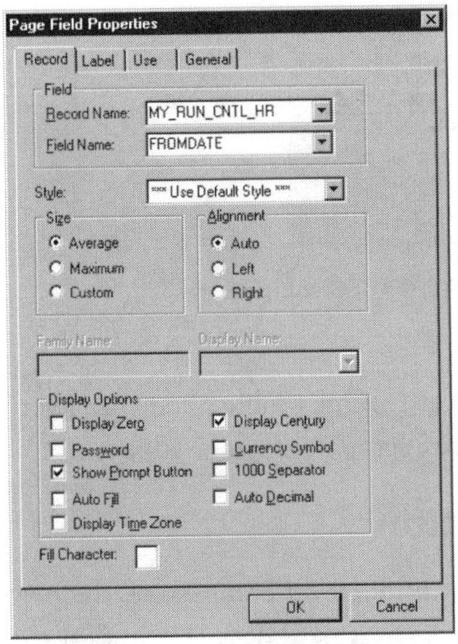

Figure 25.13 Changing the relationship between a panel field and a Run Control record

and THRUDATE, are attached to the RUN_CNTL_HR Run Control record. After cloning, these two fields remained attached to the same record. Now you will have to attach both fields to the new record, MY_RUN_CNTL_HR. You can do this by clicking on each of the fields, selecting Edit, Page Field Properties, and reassigning the field to MY_RUN_CNTL_HR. Let's start with FROMDATE. Click on this field and select Edit, Page Properties. The system will display the Page Field Properties dialog window. Replace the old record name by selecting MY_RUN_CNTL_HR in Record Name (figure 25.13).

Repeat the same procedure to update the field properties for the THRUDATE field.

Our new page has been built. It has all the input parameters that your modified application program will need. Let's save this page.

25.2.2 Modifying the component

If you want the newly created page to become accessible from the Interfaces menu, you will have to modify the Interfaces component. You will also have to link the MY_RUN_CNTL page to this component. Remember, originally the PRCSRUNCTL page was linked to this component. The PRCSRUNCTL page now has to be replaced with the new one.

In the Application Designer, select File, Open, Component, Interfaces. Delete the old page name and replace it with the MY_RUN_CNTL page name (figure 25.14).

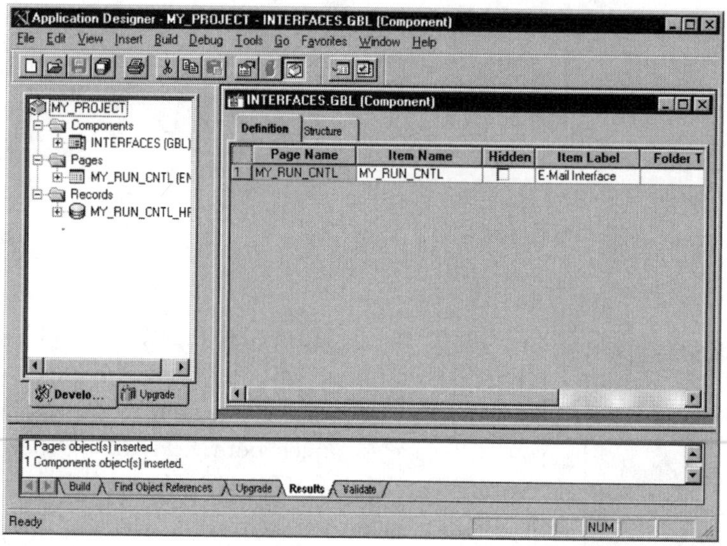

Figure 25.14 Attaching the MY_RUN_CNTL page to the INTERFACES component

Are you ready to run the program now? Well, almost … One problem remains: Every time a component is changed, the corresponding security setup needs to be adjusted.

25.2.3 Creating the Process definition

Since our program has been modified and we saved it under a different name, the new Process definition has to be created. Simply create a TEST25B Process Definition the very same way you created the Process definition for `TEST25A.SQR`.

25.2.4 Granting Permissions

In chapter 23, we recommended to use the Internet mode login in order to grant the security access to the new menu, component, and page. But you can use your developer's two- or three-tier mode to do it as well. Since we already logged into the PeopleSoft in developer's mode, let's change the security this way. Our goal is to authorize our new page in the CPHR3350 (Report Workforce) Permission list.

Navigation: Go ➟ PeopleTools ➟ Maintain Security ➟ Use ➟ Permission Lists ➟ Pages

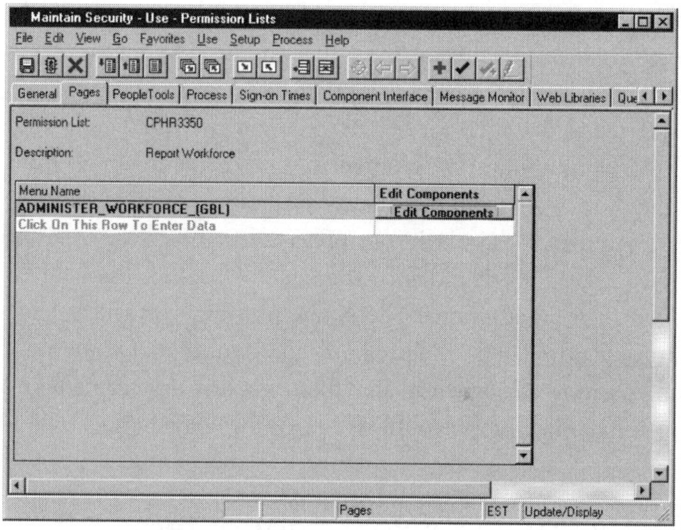

Figure 25.15 Selecting the Report Workforce Permission List

Click on Edit Components and scroll down to Process Interfaces. Click on Edit Pages. Select Authorized as shown in figure 25.16

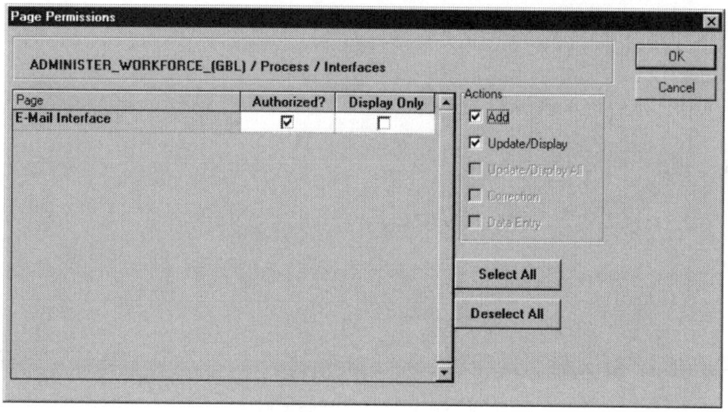

Figure 25.16 Authorizing the E-Mail Interface page

Press OK, OK, and then save the permission list changes.

You now are done with all the online changes. The next step is to create all the necessary SQC files and to modify the E-Mail Interface program accordingly.

25.3 Creating your own SQC files

In order to create new application-specific `SQC` files, we will be using our proven technique of cloning the existing `SQC` files. You already know that you need to have one `SQC` file to select the input parameter values from the appropriate `Run Control` record and another one to format the selected values and move them to designated variables in your program. Keeping in mind that your application program should retain an ability to be executed from the SQR dialog box or the command line, you have to provide the code to prompt the user for input parameters as well. In our previous examples, we used the `Askaod.sqc` and `Askftd.sqc` files, which provided the code to prompt users for As Of Date and From-Thru Date. For an additional File Name prompt, you will have to create an `SQC` file or place the code directly in the program. Please note that you do not have to place all input parameter retrieval logic into `SQC` files. It is just a convenient and modular way to read the input parameters. You could also place this logic in the application program.

25.3.1 Creating an SQC file to select parameters from the Run Control record

To create a new input parameter retrieval `SQC` file, we'll clone the existing `HRRNCTL1.sqc` file. Let's bring this file in, save it as `MYRNCTL.sqc`, and change the file to make it work with the MY_RUN_CNTL_HR Run Control record:

```
!**********************************************************************
! MYRNCTL.SQC:  Retrieve Run Control parameters
!**********************************************************************

begin-procedure select-parameters

BEGIN-SELECT

MY_RUN_CNTL_HR.OPRID
MY_RUN_CNTL_HR.RUN_CNTL_ID
MY_RUN_CNTL_HR.ASOFDATE
MY_RUN_CNTL_HR.FROMDATE
MY_RUN_CNTL_HR.THRUDATE

   do Get-Values

from PS_RUN_CNTL_HR MY_RUN_CNTL_HR
```

```
where MY_RUN_CNTL_HR.OPRID = $prcs_oprid
  and MY_RUN_CNTL_HR.RUN_CNTL_ID = $prcs_run_cntl_id
end-select
end-procedure
```

25.3.2 Creating an SQC file to format selected input parameters

We will use the existing `HRGETVAL.sqc` file as a basis when creating the new input parameter formatting file `MYGETVAL.sqc`. All you will need to do is to delete the commands that format unused input parameters, add logic to format, and save the new `File Name` parameter. The changed program saved as `MYGETVAL.sqc` is:

```
!**********************************************************************
! MYGETVAL.SQC:  Mask Run Control Value                               *
!**********************************************************************

!----------------------------------------------------------------------!
! Procedure:     Get-As-Of-Date                                        !
! Description:   Get the entered as of date.                           !
!----------------------------------------------------------------------!

begin-procedure Get-As-Of-Date

  let $AsOfDate = &MY_RUN_CNTL_HR.asofdate

  if $AsOfDate = ''
     move $AsOfToday to $AsOfDate
  end-if

end-procedure

!----------------------------------------------------------------------!
! Procedure:     Get-From-Thru-Date                                    !
! Description:   Sets the defaults for the From and Thru Dates.        !
!----------------------------------------------------------------------!

begin-procedure Get-From-Thru-Date

  let $FromDate = &MY_RUN_CNTL_HR.fromdate
  let $ThruDate = &MY_RUN_CNTL_HR.thrudate

  do Century-Begin-Date

  if $FromDate = ''
     move $Century_Begin_Dt to $FromDate
  end-if

  if $ThruDate = ''
     move $AsOfToday to $ThruDate
```

```
   end-if

end-procedure

!-----------------------------------------------------------------!
! Procedure:     Century-Begin-Date                                !
! Description:   Sets century begin date to '1900-01-01'          !
!-----------------------------------------------------------------!

begin-procedure Century-Begin-Date

   do Format-DateTime('19000101',$Century_Begin_
Dt,{DEFCMP},'','native')

end-procedure

!-----------------------------------------------------------------!
! Procedure:     Get-File-Name                                     !
! Description:   Get the entered file name                         !
!-----------------------------------------------------------------!
begin-procedure Get-File-Name
let $FileName = Rtrim(&MY_RUN_CNTL_HR.FileName,' ')
end-procedure
```

As you can see, the modified program includes the changed names of the column variables for `AsOfDate`, `FromDate`, and `ThruDate`. In addition, a new `Get-File-Name` procedure is added to get the additional parameter, `File Name`. The E-Mail Interface program will be using only two procedures in `MYGETVAL.SQC`: `Get-From-Thru-Date` and `Get-File-Name`. The other two procedures are left in the file for future use.

25.4 Changing your SQR program to accept parameters from the Run Control record

Finally, the last program change! The change will include a few modifications to the E-mail Interface program to make it work with the newly created Run Control record and to include the new SQC files: `MYRNCTL.sqc` and `MYGETVAL.sqc`. Let's save the modified program as `Test25B.sqr`:

```
!TEST25B.SQR
!The E-Mail Interface program with customized SQC files
!E-Mail Interface
#include 'setenv.sqc'     !Set environment

!********************
```

```
Begin-Program
!*******************
Do Init-Report
Open $FileName as 1 For-Writing Record=100 Status=#OpenStat
  If #OpenStat != 0
   Let $Error_Text=Rtrim('Error Opening ' ||$FileName,' ')
   Let #Ret_Code=#OpenStat
   Do File-Error
  Else
   Do Process_Employees
   Close 1
  End-If

  Display 'Total records exported: ' Noline
  Display #Tot_Recs 999,999,999

  Do Stdapi-Term
End-Program

!******************************
Begin-Procedure Init-Report
!******************************
 Do Stdapi-Init

 If $prcs_process_instance = ''
   do Ask-From-Thru-Date
   do Ask-File-Name
 Else
   do Select-Parameters
 End-if

End-procedure

!******************************
Begin-Procedure Get-Values
!******************************
   Do Get-From-Thru-Date
   Do Get-File-Name
End-procedure

!**********************************
Begin-Procedure File-Error
!**********************************
If #prcs_process_instance > 0
      Show $Error_Text
      Print $Error_Text (+1,1)
      Let #prcs_message_set_nbr      = #prcs_msg_set_nbr
      Let #prcs_message_nbr          = 30                !Set to blank
      Let #prcs_run_status = #prcs_run_status_error
      Let #prcs_rc = #Ret_Code
      Let $prcs_message_parm1 = $Error_Text
      Let #prcs_continuejob = 0
```

`$FileName` is the new input parameter.

Check if run from the Process Scheduler; If yes, call Select-Parameters; otherwise, call the `Ask-From-Thru-Date` and `Ask-File-Name` procedures.

Located in `MYRNCTL.sqc`

Call the `Get-From-Thru-Date` and `Get-File-Name` procedures from `MYGETVAL.sqc`.

```
End-If
End-Procedure
!*********************************
Begin-Procedure Process_Employees
!*********************************
Move 0 To #Tot_Recs
Begin-Select
A.Emplid
A.Deptid
B.Name
B.Phone
   Do Write-Output-Record
From PS_Job A, PS_Personal_Data B
Where   A.emplid=B.emplid
   And A.Empl_Rcd=0
   And A.Empl_Status = 'A'
   And A.Effdt = (Select Max(Effdt)
                 From    PS_JOB
                 Where   Emplid  = A.Emplid
                 And  Empl_Rcd = A.Empl_Rcd
                 And  Effdt Between $FromDate and $ThruDate)
   And A.Effseq =  (Select Max(Effseq)
                   From       PS_JOB
                   Where      Emplid    = A.Emplid
                   And        Empl_Rcd = A.Empl_Rcd
                   And        Effdt     = A.Effdt)
End-Select
End-Procedure
!**********************************
Begin-Procedure Write-Output-Record
!**********************************
 Write 1 From
  &A.Emplid ','
  &A.Deptid ','
  &B.Name ','
  &B.Phone
  Add 1 To #Tot_Recs
End-Procedure
!***************************************
Begin-Procedure Ask-File-Name
!***************************************
Input $FileName Maxlen=8 Type=Char 'Please enter File Name'
End-procedure

#include 'datetime.sqc'  !Routines for date and time
#include 'stdapi.sqc'
#include 'myrnctl.sqc'  !Get run control values
#include 'mygetval.sqc'  !Get values mask routines
#include 'askftd.sqc'    !Ask From-Thru Date input
```

Restrict the date range between the `From` and `Thru` dates.

Prompt for the user input if not run under the Process Scheduler.

Include the new SQC files.

To summarize, the following steps were undertaken to allow our E-Mail Interface program to accept input parameters from the Process Scheduler:

1 The `MYRNCTL.sqc` file was created to read the program input parameters from the MY_RUN_CNTL_HR table record.

2 The `MYGETVAL.sqc` file was created to format the input parameters, and to move them into the designated program variables.

3 The `E-mail` program was changed to:
   - include the `MYRNCTL.sqc` and `MYGETVAL.sqc` files
   - add the `Ask-File-Name` procedure to get program input from the SQR dialog box or the command line if the program is not executed from the Process Scheduler
   - modify the `Init-Report` and `Get-Values` procedures to reflect the new `SQC` functionality
   - change the output file opening code to open a file with a name that was accepted as an input parameter
   - alter the `Where` clause in the `Process_Employees` procedure to select records with the effective dates between the `From` and `Thru` dates

25.5 Testing your SQR program

Now, with all the changes, you are ready to test your program. Before we start testing, let's list all the objects that were created or modified to make the `E-mail` program accept input parameters from the Process Scheduler:

- A new Run Control record, MY_RUN_CNTL_HR, was created
- A new Run Control page, MY_RUN_CNTL, was built
- The `INTERFACES` was modified to replace the old panel name with the MY_RUN_CNTL page
- The `INTERFACES` menu security was restored
- The `MYRNCTL.sqc` file was created to select input parameters from the MY_RUN_CNTL_HR record
- The `MYGETVAL.sqc` file was created to format the selected parameters and to move them to the designated program variables
- The E-Mail Interface program `Test25B` was modified
- A new Process definition for `Test25B` was created.

The next step is to create a test plan to outline the order of testing and to specify how each object will be tested:

Table 25.1 The E-Mail Interface program test plan

Test Step	Object	Method of Testing
1 Test the updated menu	INTERFACES menu	Make sure that the menu appears in the right place and is visible for operators who are allowed to access it
2 Test the new page	Run Control page: MY_RUN_CNTL	Make sure all the fields are in place, enter parameters, and save.
3 Test the new Run Control record	Run Control record: MY_RUN_CNTL_HR	Run the following query: `SELECT OPRID, RUN_CNTL_ID, FROMDATE, THRU-DATE, ASOFDATE, LANGUAGE_CD, FILENAME FROM PS_MY_RUN_CNTL_HR WHERE OPRID='PS' AND RUN_CNTL_ID='MyTest'.` If the record is not found, verify the record name and rebuild it, specifying: Execute SQL Now. Repeat step 2. Make sure that all the input values for your OPRID and RUN_CNTL_ID are saved correctly. Pay attention to OPRID. If it's not what you entered, or it is set to spaces, check if your Run Control record has the correct PeopleCode statement.
4 Test the new Process Definition	`Test25B` Process Definition	After selecting on the Run Control page, your Process Request page should appear with the `Test25B` process attached. If it's not there, make sure that the process definition points to the correct component. Also, verify that the Process Definition name is same as your SQR program name.
5 Test the E-Mail Interface program	`Test25B.sqr` program	Inspect all output and log files.

Now let's execute our test plan. Select Administer_Workforce (GBL), Process, Interfaces. Add `Run Control Id: MyTest`. The system will display the newly created MY_RUN_CNTL dialog page shown in figure 25.17.

On the page, enter the values for `FromDate`, `ThruDate`, and `FileName`. Let's save the values and execute the SQL `SELECT` statement described in step three to verify our Run Control record (figure 25.18).

Once we see that our Run Control record is populated correctly, we can run our SQR program. From the Run Control page, click the Run button. The system will display the already familiar Process Request page (figure 25.19).

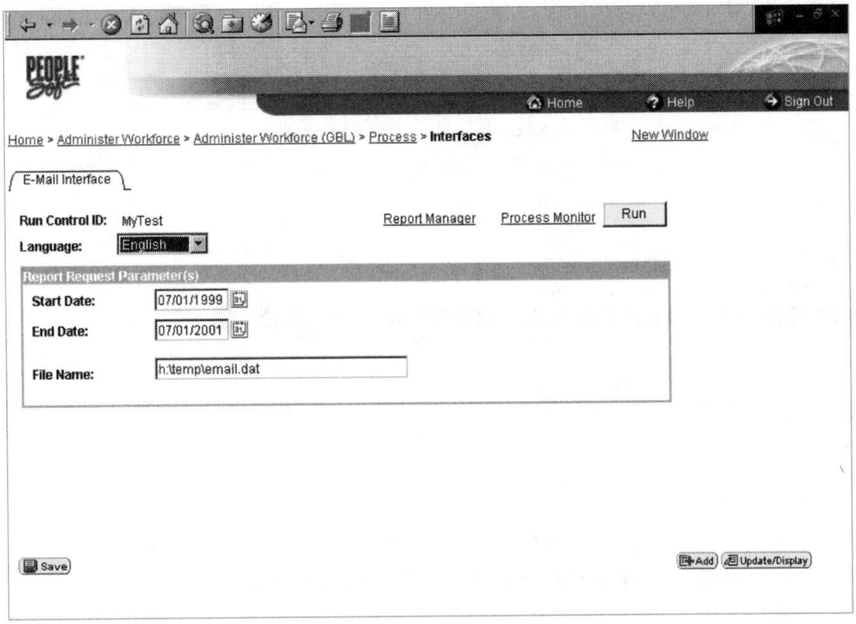

Figure 25.17 Entering the application-specific parameters for the E-Mail Interface program.

Figure 25.18 Selecting the fields from the MY_RUN_CNTL_HR Run Control record

Click the OK button, and our program is up and running! Let's check the program run status.

As you can see from figure 25.20, the program run status is `Success`. This is a good sign and a necessary condition to consider our test successful, but it is not sufficient. You still need to check to see if the file in the specified directory was created and, also, to make sure that the file output meets the specified business requirements.

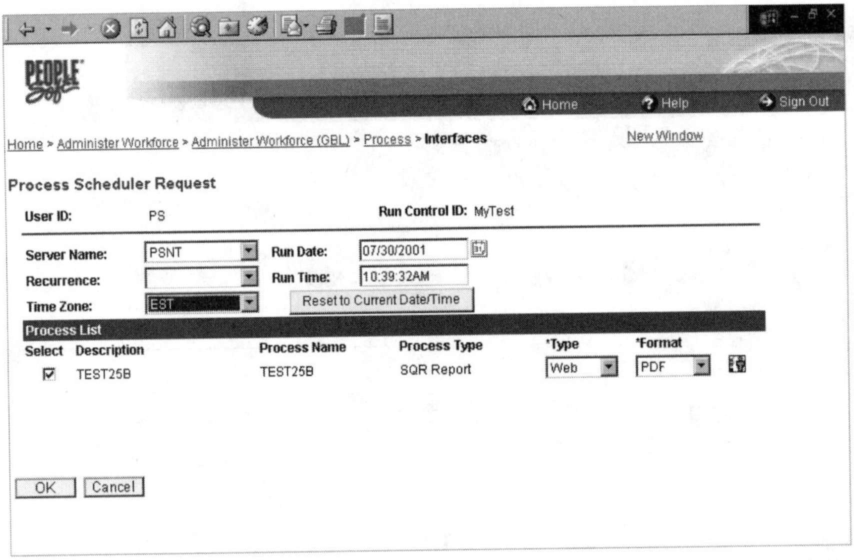

Figure 25.19 The Process Request page for the modified E-Mail Interface program

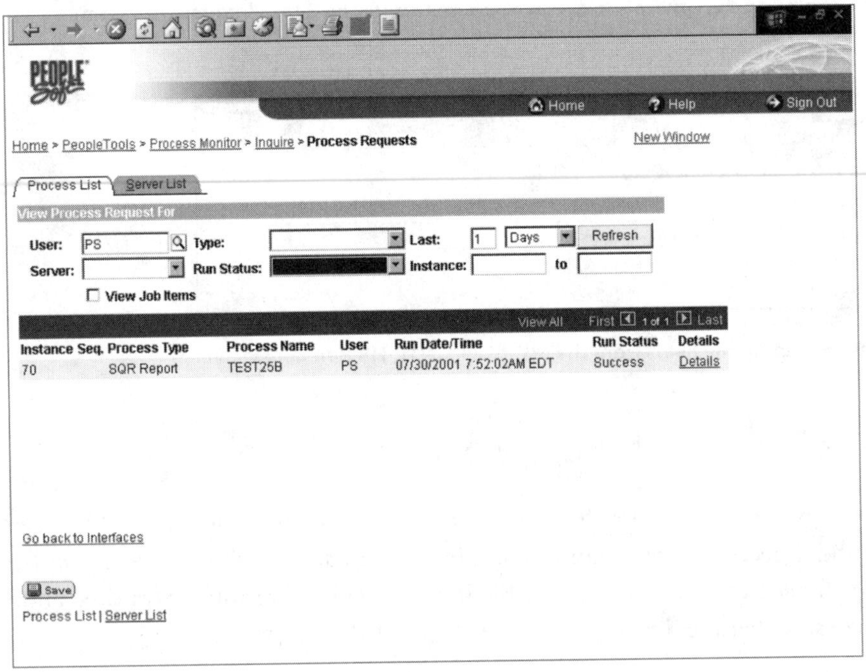

Figure 25.20 Checking the E-Mail Interface program run status

KEY POINTS

1 To accept input parameters from PeopleSoft online pages, you can either use the existing PeopleSoft-delivered `SQC` files or develop your own, depending on the parameters your SQR program needs to accept.

2 Your program should support both types of input parameter retrieval logic: retrieving the parameters from the Process Scheduler, or accepting them from the SQR Dialog Box, or the command line.

3 Usually, there are two `SQC` files involved in accepting program input parameters from a PeopleSoft online page. One file should contain a procedure to select all required fields from the proper Run Control record. Another one should include procedures to edit the selected fields and place them into designated SQR variables.

4 Your SQR program must be changed to include the proper `SQC` files, and a code to call the input parameter retrieval procedures.

5 A Run Control page that contains all the input parameters should be developed, or an existing page should be used or customized.

6 The changed SQR program has to be thoroughly tested to make sure that the input parameters are passed and accepted correctly.

C H A P T E R 2 6

Using process recurrences and job streams

IN THIS CHAPTER

- Creating a recurrence definition
- Scheduling programs for execution on a recurring basis
- Creating job streams that contain multiple processes

During the course of this book we discussed the execution of PeopleSoft-delivered and custom processes under the PeopleSoft Process Scheduler. We demonstrated how to create a Process Definition to execute SQR programs, and how to monitor the status of process execution. You also learned how your program can communicate with the Process Scheduler via the API programs. However, there are some other important aspects of the PeopleSoft Process Scheduler that we did not cover.

26.1 Recurrence definition

When you execute your programs on the server, you can schedule them to run at predefined intervals. A special Recurrence definition has to be created and assigned to the process. When the Recurrence definition is created, it may be assigned to the process through its Process definition or from the Process Request Dialog page at runtime.

Let's see, for example, how we can schedule our custom program `TEST25B.SQR` for execution every day at 9:00 PM.

As we already mentioned, starting from release 8 PeopleSoft moved the creation of Recurrence definitions to the Process Scheduler Manager.

Navigation: PeopleTools ➠ Process Scheduler Manager ➠ Use ➠ Recurrence Definition

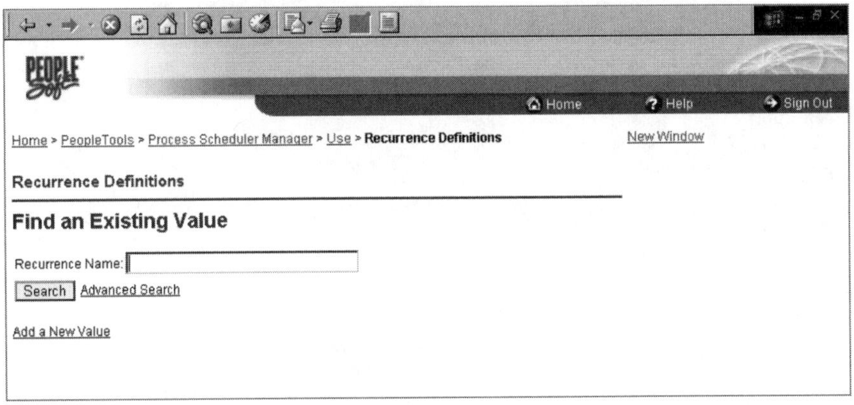

Figure 26.1 Recurrence Definitions page

This page (figure 26.1) allows us to add a new recurrence or reuse an existing one. Let's create our own Recurrence Definition. Click on the Add a New Value link. Then choose a meaningful name for your process. Since our goal is to execute the `TEST25B.SQR` every day, let's call it `TEST25B_DAILY` as shown in figure 26.2.

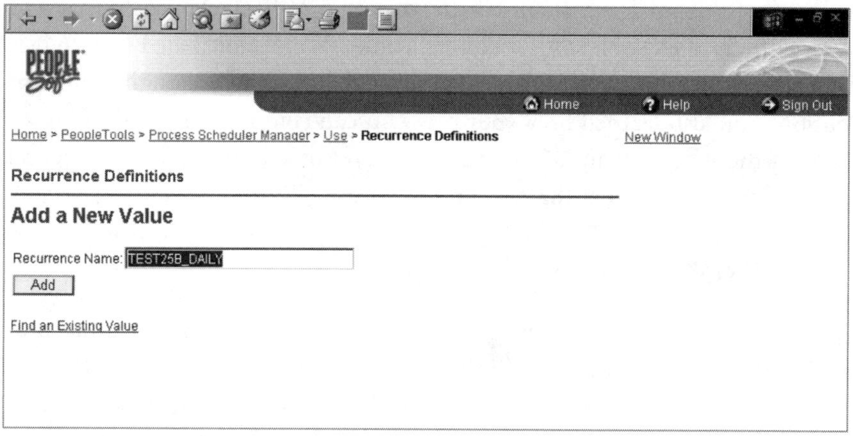

Figure 26.2 Adding a new Recurrence Definition, TEST25B_DAILY

Click on the Add button (figure 26.2). This brings us to the Recurrence Definitions page (figure 26.3).

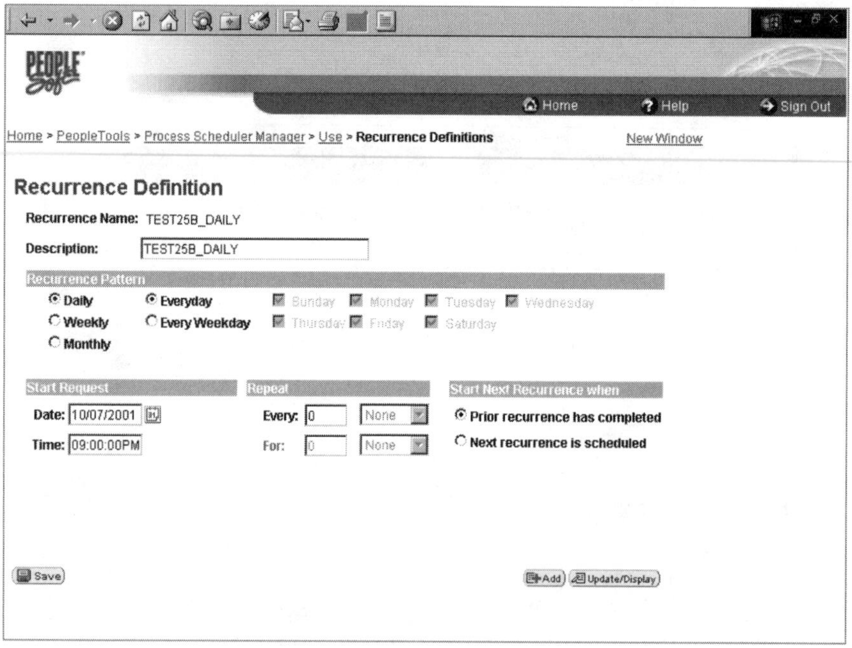

Figure 26.3 Setting up the Recurrence Definition page

In the page shown in figure 26.3, we added a `Description` to our process recurrence, clicked on Daily to specify the Recurrence pattern, then selected the starting day and time of the cycle under the Start Request column. The Repeat column indicates how many times the process will repeat within the For timeframe. For example, you could specify that the process should run every 15 minutes within an hour.

We also selected the option to `Start Next Recurrence` when the `prior recurrence` has completed. This means that the next process will be queued only when the previous process completed successfully. If you would like it to run regardless of the completion of prior runs, click on the Next Recurrence is Scheduled option.

Also note that we selected to run our process every day by clicking on the Everyday check box. There is another option that we could have utilized if needed, that is to execute our process every weekday. In this case if we click on the Every weekday check box, the system would automatically select days Monday thru Friday.

We can also execute our report weekly as shown in figure 26.4.

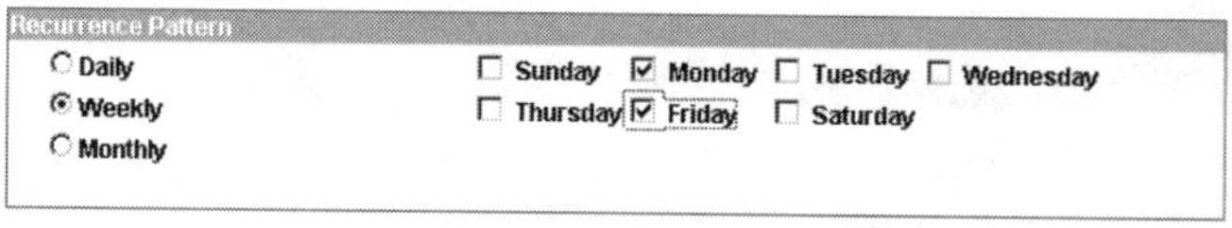

Figure 26.4 Selecting the Weekly pattern

In this case the system allows us to mark the days of the week we want to execute our report on. In the example shown in figure 26.4, the report will be executed every Monday and Friday.

We can also select the Monthly option (figure 26.5).

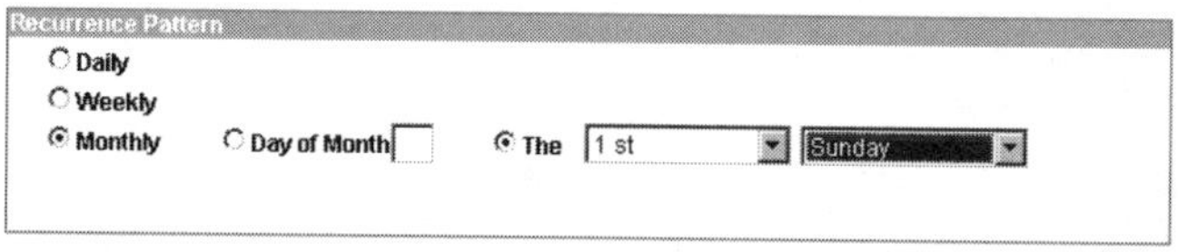

Figure 26.5 Selecting the 1st Sunday every month pattern

When selecting Monthly, the system allows us to set a specific date every month or you can set a recurrence of the 1st, 2nd, 3rd, 4th, or Last Day of the month. The Day can also be any day of the week. For example, in figure 26.5 we selected our process to run every 1st Sunday of the month.

Let's have our process run daily at 9:00 PM and click Save.

Our new Recurrence definition is created. But in order to utilize it properly, we will need to go through a few more steps discussed in the next subchapter.

26.2 Scheduling programs for execution on a recurring basis

We just created a Recurrence definition for our `TEST25B.SQR` process requesting that our process needs to be scheduled for execution every day at 9:00 PM. Our next step is to assign this Recurrence definition to the process. There are two ways of doing this. The Recurrence definition may be assigned to the process through its Process Definition or from the Process Request page at runtime.

Let's use the first method.

Navigation: PeopleTools ➡ Process Manager ➡ Use ➡ Process Definitions

Select the TEST25B Process Definition and switch to the Process Definition Options page, as shown in figure 26.6.

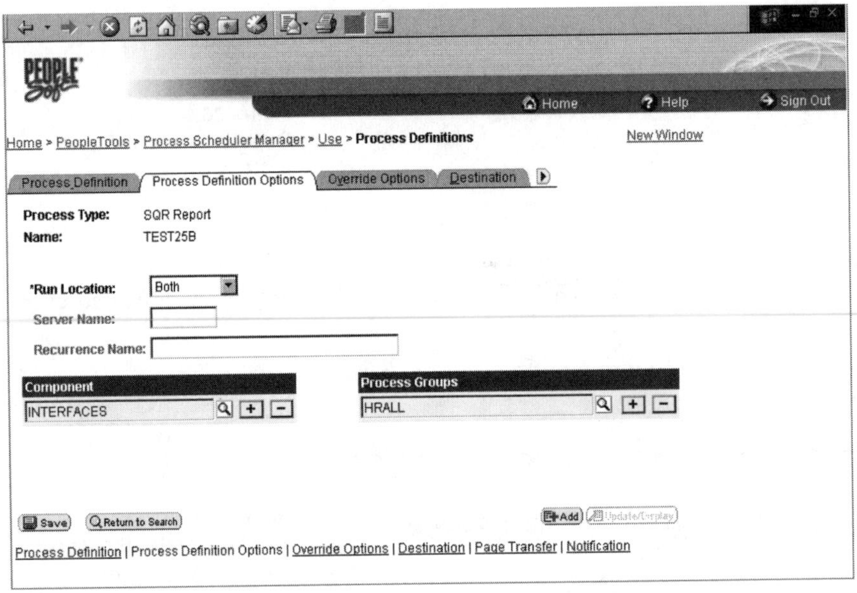

Figure 26.6 Process Definition Options page with Recurrence name grayed-out

Now we can type in our Recurrence definition name into the Recurrence Name field on the Process Definition page (figure 26.6). The only problem is that this field is grayed-out. The system does not allow us to specify the Recurrence. Why? The answer is simple. A program can only be scheduled for a recurrence execution if it is run on Server. Let's change the Run Location from Both to Server, and then enter or search for a valid Recurrence definition (figure 26.7).

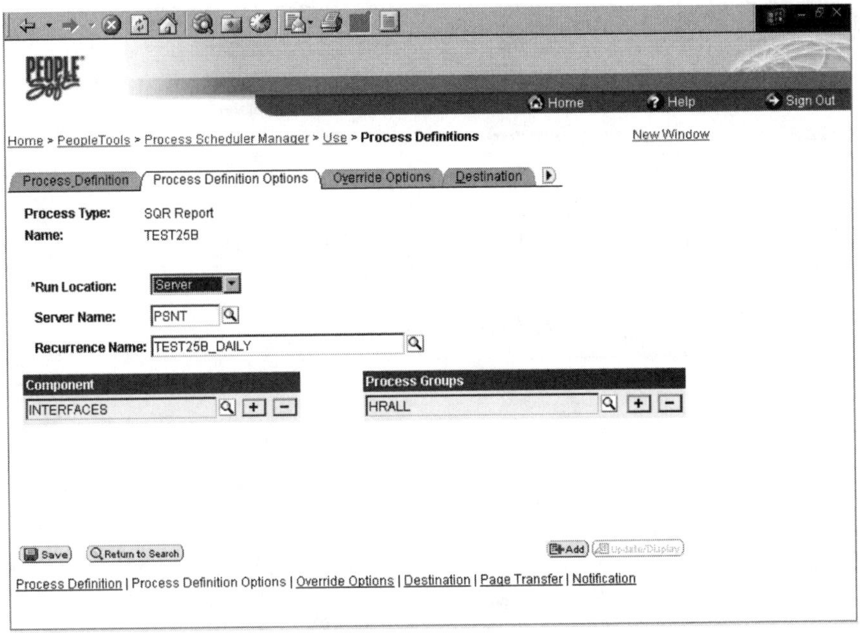

Figure 26.7 Assigning a Recurrence Definition to TEST25B

Now we can save our modified Process definition and start testing.

Navigation: Administer Workforce ➡ Administer Workforce (GBL) ➡ Process

Select any existing Run Control ID, and fill in the Run Control page with your input parameters as shown in figure 26.8.

Let's examine our Run Control page again (figure 26.8). Since we are planning to schedule this process for execution every day, we have to supply the appropriate parameters to our SQR program every time the program runs. In our case, the parameters are: Start Date, End Date, File Name. When the program is executed manually, users enter the parameters when they submit the process for execution, as we just did in figure 26.8. We need to find a way to automatically fill in our Run Control table. There are several methods you can use depending on your business needs. The simplest one is to use the System date as the Start Date/End Date parameters. The standard method is to make your program default to System date if the date in the Run Control record is blank. If the System date technique is not applicable to your process, you would have to develop your own custom method to automatically supply the correct date to your program at each program execution. The third parameter, File Name, can be entered only once, and the Run Control record will retain its value for all subsequent runs.

For our test, we'll leave the Start Date and the End Date as is. Let's click now on the Run button. This will bring you to the Process Scheduler Request page (figure 26.9)

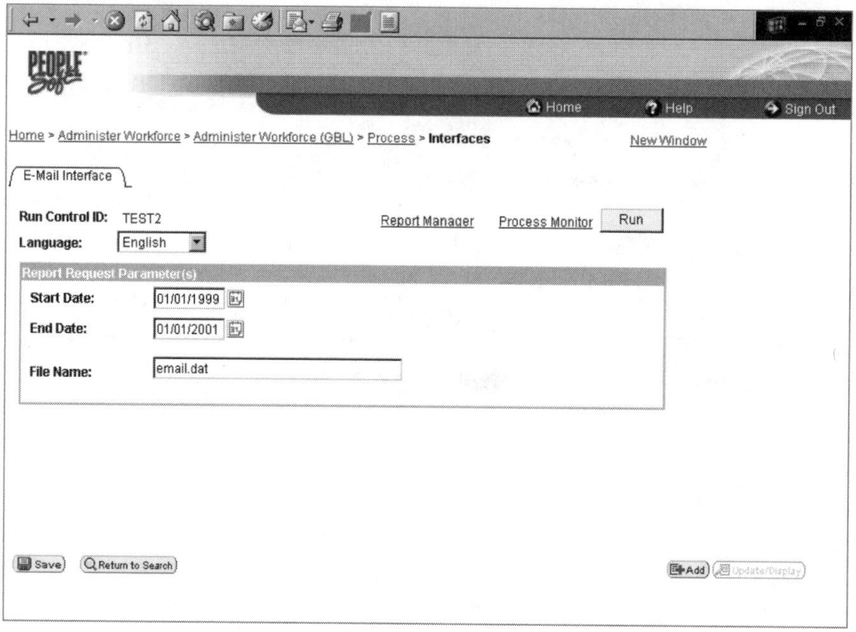

Figure 26.8 Filling in the Run Control page

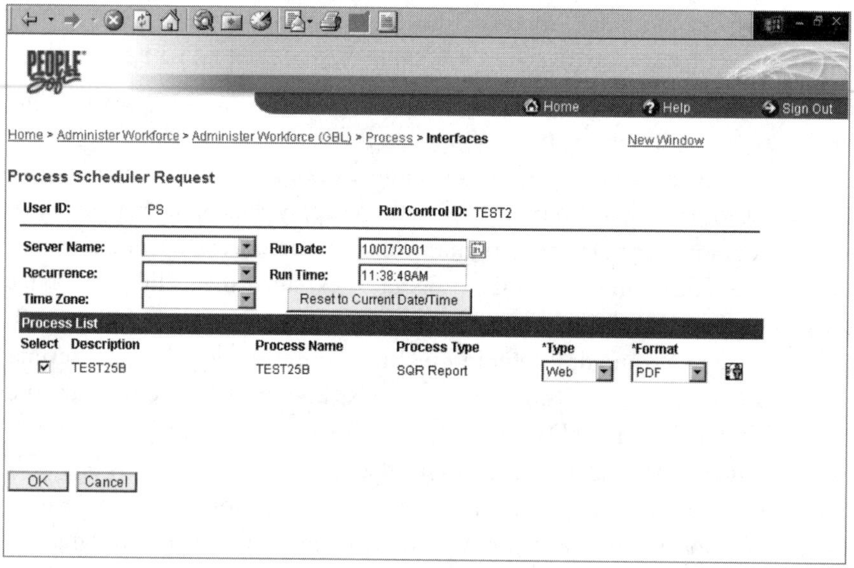

Figure 26.9 Process Scheduler Request page

Notice that here we do not have any Recurrence specified. Let's leave the Server and the Recurrence fields blank and see how the system will schedule our process. Remember that even though we haven't selected any Recurrence definition here, we still have the Recurrence attached to our Process Definition. Let's submit our process by clicking on the OK button, the system will bring you to the Process List tab on the Process Requests page shown in figure 26.10.

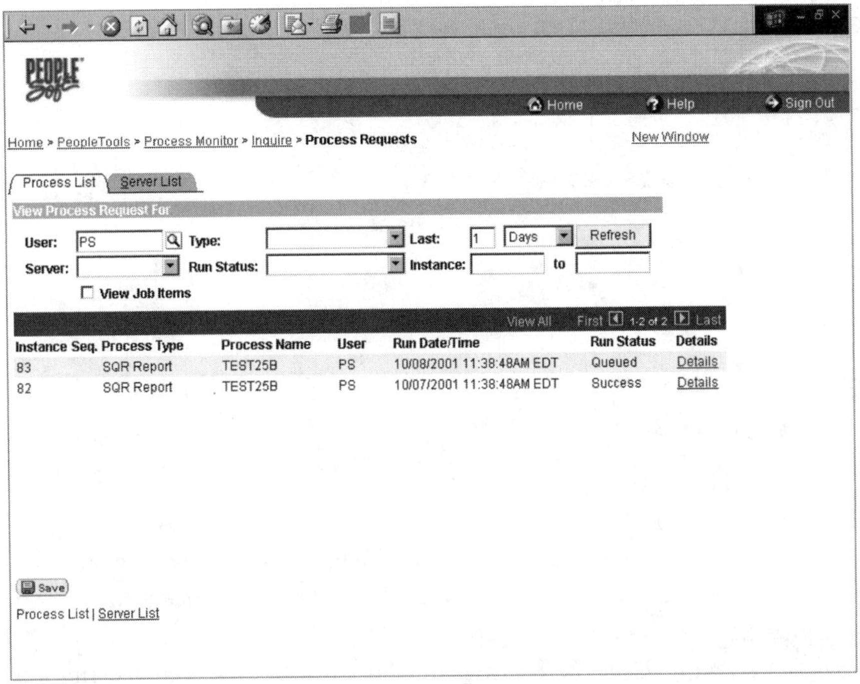

Figure 26.10 Submitting TEST25B for execution automatically schedules same process execution on the following day

Notice that we only submitted the process with instance number 82. As soon as this process has been successfully executed, the next process with instance number 83 is queued for the future execution.

Let's click on the Details link next to the queued process. This will bring you to the Process Request Details page (figure 26.11)

On this page we can see that the Process Scheduler used the Recurrence definition TEST25B_DAILY and therefore, has already scheduled our process for the next day execution. Also notice that even though our process had been queued for next day execution, the time of the next day run is not 9:00 PM as we would expect. Take a look at the

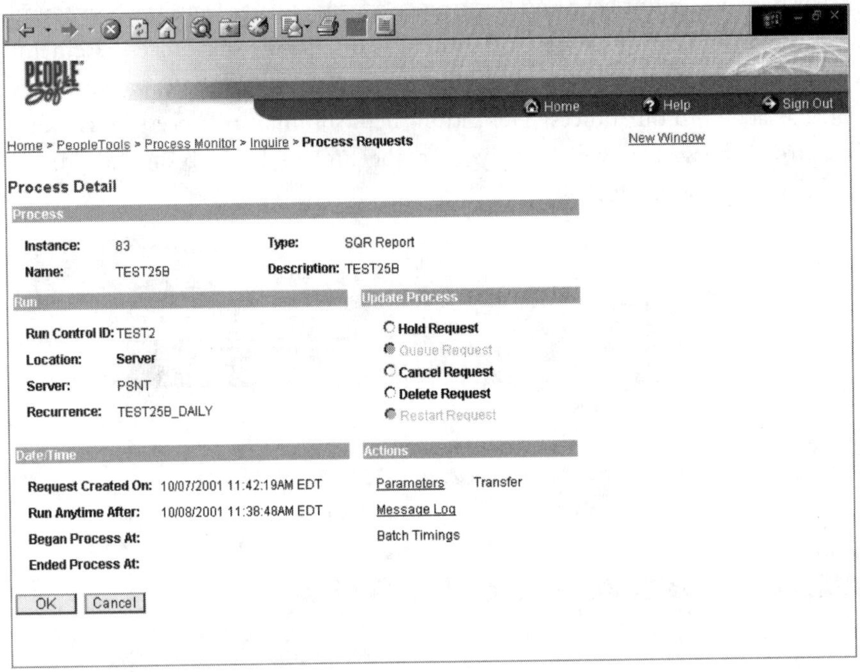

Figure 26.11 Verifying the Process Request details

Process Request page in figure 26.9. The Run Time parameter specified on this page is exactly the time that the process is scheduled to run. We have our answer now. In order to schedule the process at the right time, we need to specify the Recurrence definition on the Process Request page. Let's do this.

For our next test, we'll fill in the Recurrence field with the Recurrence definition that we prepared before as shown in figure 26.12.

Notice that as soon as we selected the Recurrence definition, the Run Time field became grayed-out. Click on the OK button to submit the process.

As you can see from figure 26.13, our process has been scheduled for execution at 9:00 PM. This is exactly what we specified in our recurrence definition.

We've done lots of experimenting here. What have we learned so far?

- In order to schedule a process for recurrent executions, a Recurrence Definition has to be created.
- If a Recurrence Definition is attached to a Process Definition, then as soon as this process is submitted for execution, the next recurrence is created. Note that this will happen even if the Recurrence is not specified on the Process Request page. In this case the time of execution will be the time specified on the Process Request page.

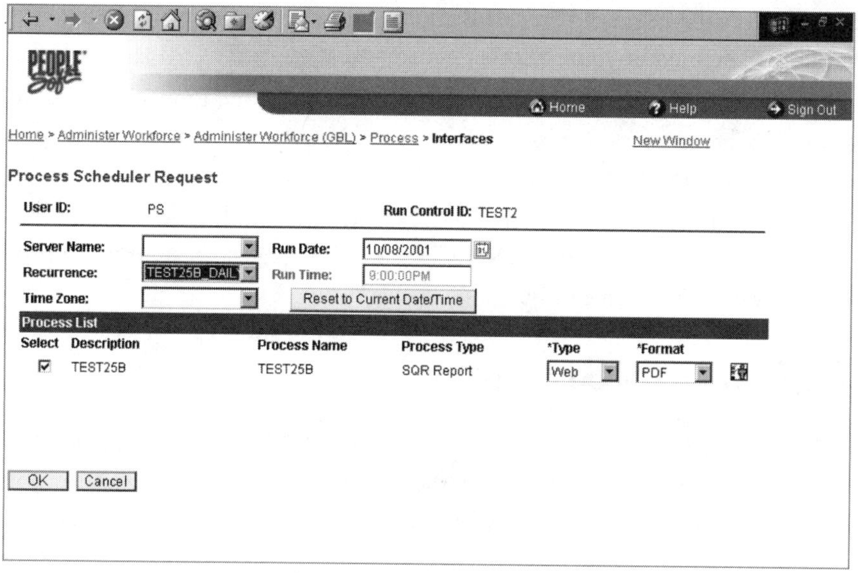

Figure 26.12 Specifying the Recurrence definition on the Process Request page

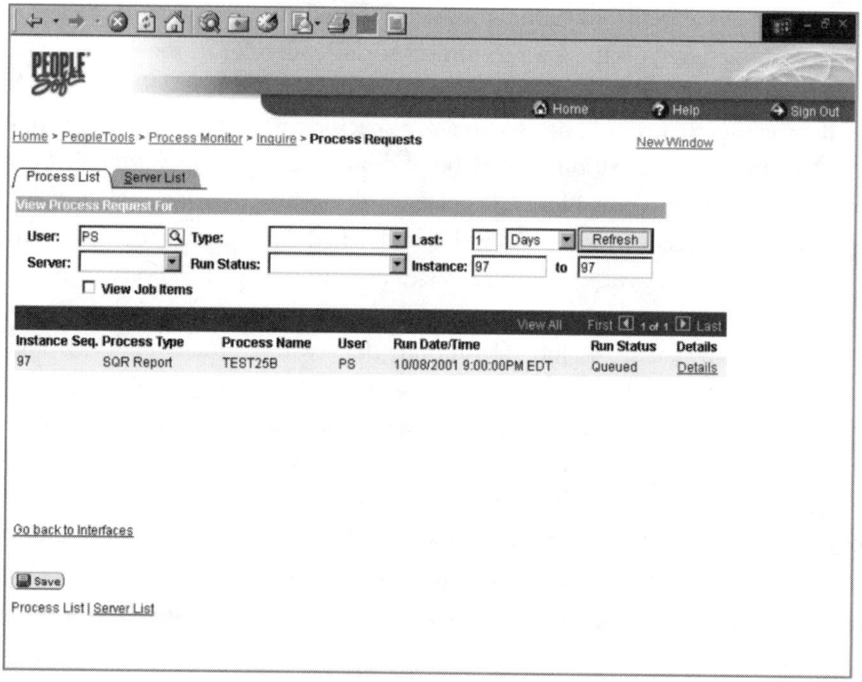

Figure 26.13 The process has been queued for execution at 9:00 PM

- If you specify Recurrence on the Process Request page, the time of your process execution will be as defined in your Process Recurrence.
- You do not have to always attach a Recurrence definition to the Process definition. You do it only when you want to protect the execution of a particular process on a recurrent basis from any user modifications.
- In order to submit a process for recurrent executions, simply select the proper Recurrence definition on the Process Scheduler Request page and submit the process manually for the first time only.

26.3 Using Job Streams

So far in this book we have been executing single processes from the PeopleSoft Process Scheduler. Oftentimes, your business requires the execution of multiple processes one after another or in parallel. PeopleSoft allows you do this if you run your processes on a Server. The Job definition is used to accomplish this task.

A Job (or Job stream) in PeopleSoft usually consists of two or more processes. You can combine your SQR and Cobol programs into one Job to be executed in a parallel or serial mode. When scheduling your Job to run in a serial mode, all processes within the Job will be executed sequentially, one after another. Otherwise, they will be executed in parallel mode without any specific order. Similar to an individual process, you can schedule a Job to run at a later time or on a recurring basis. It is always a good approach to combine all processes that should be executed at a specific time into a Job stream, and schedule this Job stream for execution at predefined time intervals (e.g., every night).

Let's take, for example, one of the PeopleSoft delivered processes, the Refresh Employees Application Agent process (PER099) and schedule it to run together with our Email interface (`TEST25B.SQR`). Both processes need to be executed every night.

In order to schedule any Job for execution, a Job definition has to be created. In our case, we will need to create a Job Definition that will contain PER099 and `TEST25B.SQR`. As we already know, when executing a process from the Process Scheduler, the process accepts its input parameters from the on-line pages. A Process definition is linked to a specific page through a Component. Likewise, the Job definition also requires a Component to be specified. Therefore, all processes in your Job stream will accept input parameters from this particular Component that may consist of several pages. To illustrate this point, let's create a Component for our Job stream.

26.3.1 Creating a Component for a Job stream

Since both processes in our Job stream are already designed to run under the Process Scheduler, our task is very simple. We just need to combine their Run Control pages into one Component.

Let's find out what pages are used as Run Control pages for `PER099.SQR` and `TEST25B.SQR`. Log in to the developer's environment.

Navigation: Go ➡ Define Business Rules ➡ Administer HR System ➡ Process ➡ Refresh PS_Employees Table ➡ Update/Display

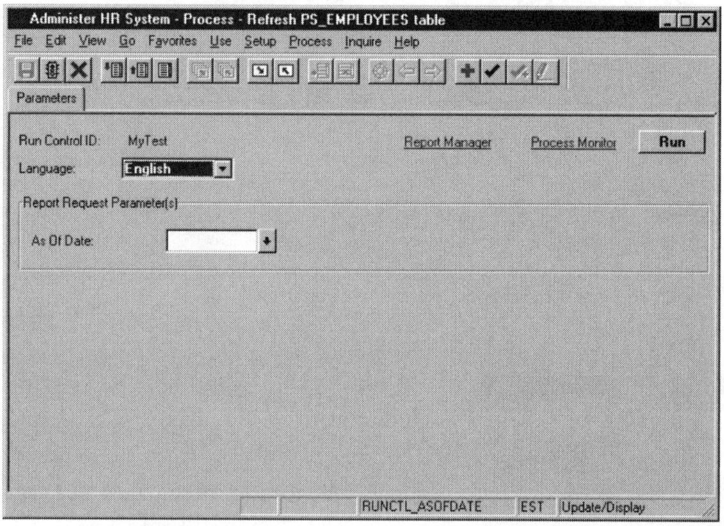

Figure 26.14 Finding the name of the Run Control Page for the Refresh PS_Employees Table process

You can see the name of the run control page at the bottom of the window (figure 26.14). If you don't see the page name, click on `View` ➡ `Page Name` from the menu. The Run Control page that is used to run the Refresh Employees Table process is `RUNCTL_ASOFDATE`. When scheduling this program for execution in a Job stream, we obviously want to preserve all the functionality of the job's components, including the input parameters processing. Therefore, we need to include this page into our new component.

We know from the previous chapter that the name of the Run Control page for our Email process is MY_RUN_CNTL.

That's all we need to know in order to create our job Component.

Let's now create our new Component.

Navigation: Go ➡ PeopleTools ➡ Application Designer ➡ New ➡ Component

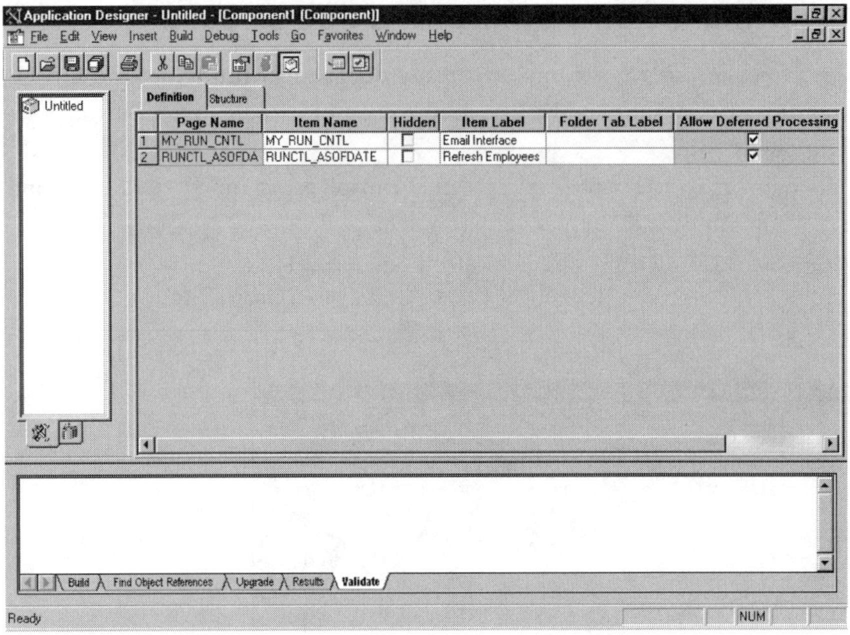

Figure 26.15 Creating a new Component for a Job Stream

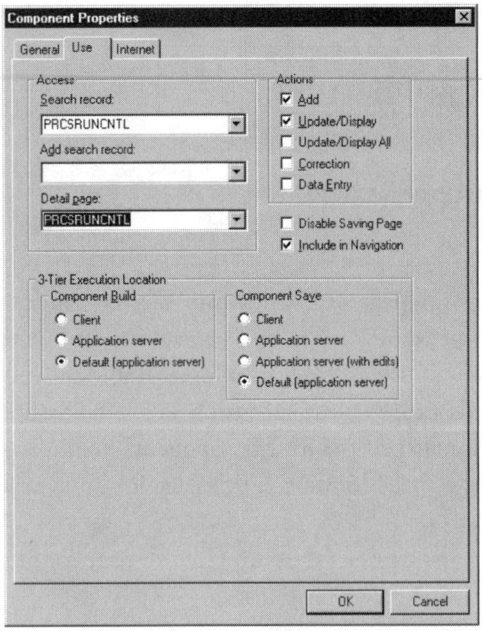

Figure 26.16 Specifying Component Properties for our Job stream

Our new Component should include both the MY_RUN_CNTL and RUNCTL_ASOFDATE run control pages. After inseting these pages and typing in some meaningful labels for each page in the Item Label fields, we need to specify the Component's Properties (figure 26.16).

The Search record and the Detail page for our Run Control Component should be the same as that for a Component in a single process.

Figure 26.17 Saving Component for new Job Stream

Now, we save the new object as MY_HR_NIGHTLY (figure 26.17). Do not forget to add your new object to the Project by clicking on F7 function key on your keyboard. After clicking on the OK button, we are ready to add our job to a Menu.

26.3.2 Creating a Menu Item for our new Job stream

In order for our users to access a Run Control page, we need to attach this page to the proper Menu Item via a Component. Let's use the existing Administer HR System menu, and create a new menu bar, named Job Stream, and use it to add our new Job stream menu item and for all future Job streams related to HR tasks.

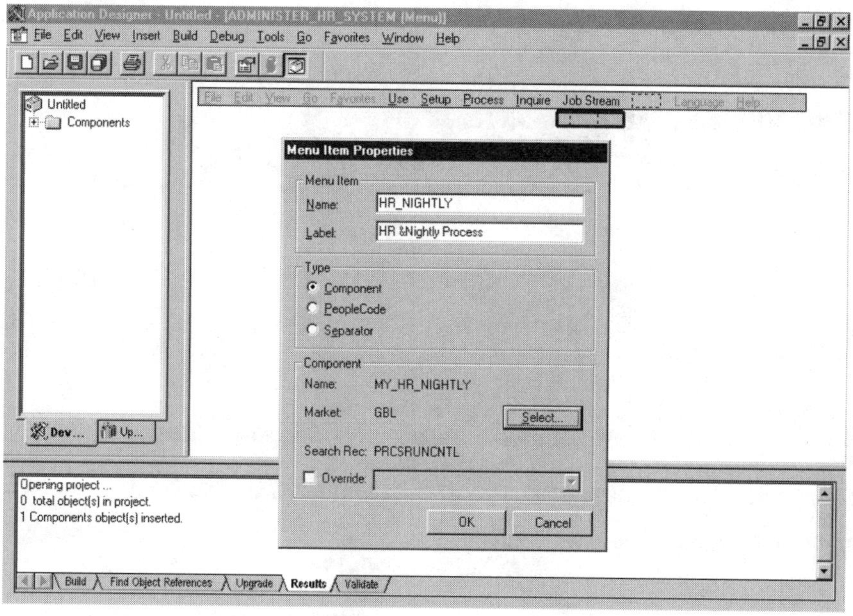

Figure 26.18 Creating a new Menu Bar and Menu Item

As you can see in figure 26.18, we created a new menu bar, Job Stream. Then, just by clicking on an empty rectangle under this Menu Bar, we created a new menu item, HR Nightly, and linked our MY_HR_NIGHTLY Component to this Menu Item.

After clicking on the OK button, we will modify the security to allow access to our new Menu item.

26.3.3 Granting security access to the new objects

Instead of adding our new items to the existing Permission Lists as we did before, let's follow the steps described in chapter 23.8 and create a new Permission List.

Navigation: Home ➡ PeopleTools ➡ Maintain Security ➡ Use ➡ Permission List

Let's click on Add a New Value and specify the new Permission List name as `HRJOBS`. Click on the Add button. After specifying the description of our new Permissions, switch to the Pages tab and select the Administer_HR_System menu as shown in figure 26.19.

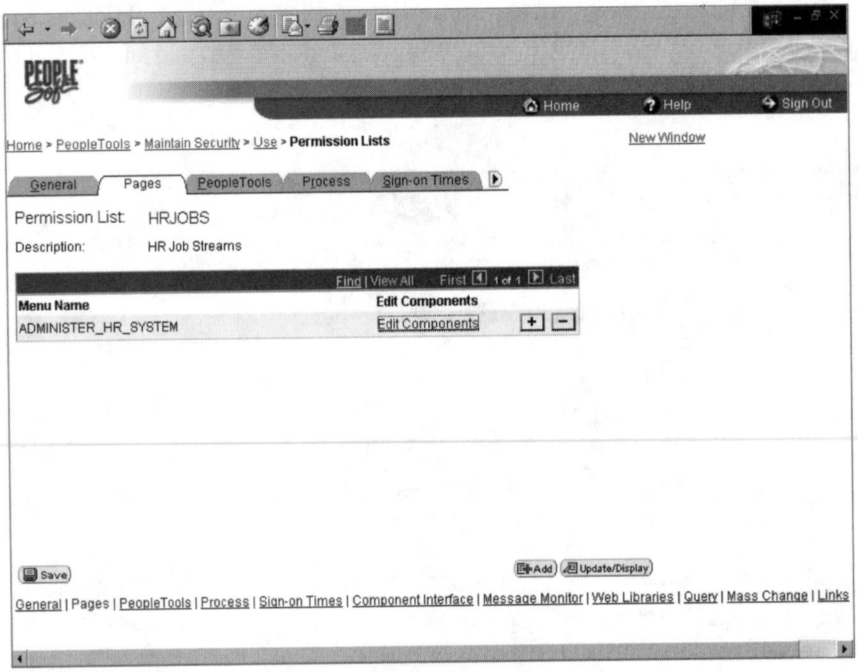

Figure 26.19 Adding a menu to the new Permission list

Let's select Edit Component to the right of the Menu name. This brings us to the Component Permission screen. Scroll down and find our new component, Job Stream. Select Edit Pages next to the Job Stream Component.

Click on Select All and then OK as shown in figure 26.20. Click on the OK button again and save our new Permission List.

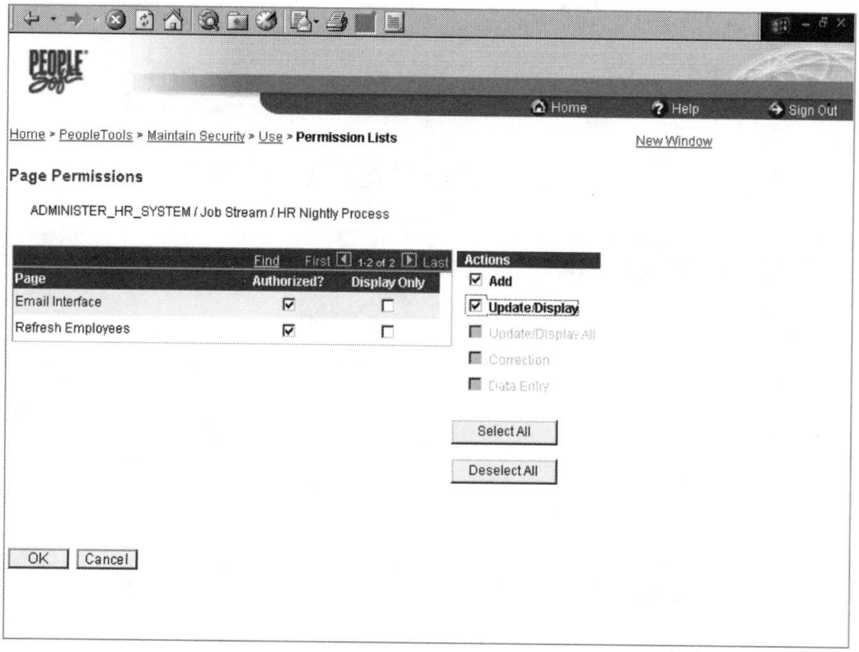

Figure 26.20 Authorizing our new component and pages within it

The new Permission list HRJOBS has been created. We need to attach it to the existing Role or create a new Role. Let's create a new Role. Again, we can follow the steps described in chapter 23.8 of this book.

Navigation: Home ➞ PeopleTools ➞ Maintain Security ➞ Use ➞ Roles

Let's select Add a New Value and enter a new Role Name, My HR Role. Click on the Add button. After entering the role's description on General tab, click on the Save button. The Role is created.

Switch to the Permission List Tab and enter the Permission List name, HRJOBS created in the previous step as shown in figure 26.21. Click on Save.

The Permission List is now linked to My HR Role (figure 23.21). Our next step is to add the newly created role to the user profile.

Navigation: Home ➞ PeopleTools ➞ Maintain Security ➞ Use ➞ User Profiles

Let's modify our profile to test the application, and then we will do the same for all users who are going to use our new objects. Enter User ID as PS and switch to the Roles tab. Scroll down the page and click on the (+) sign to add a new row. Enter: `My HR Role` and press the tab key (figure 26.22).

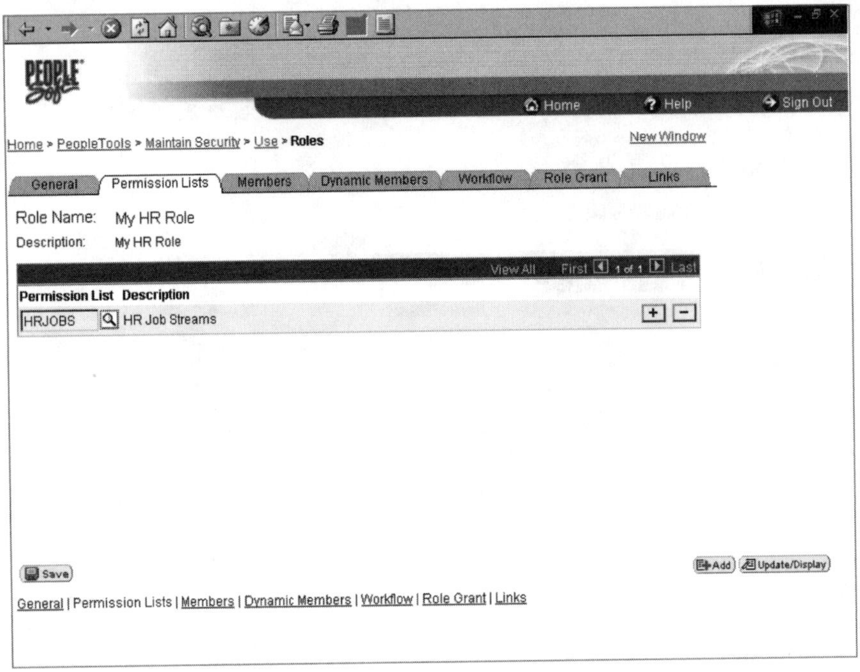

Figure 26.21 Creating a new Role, MY HR Role

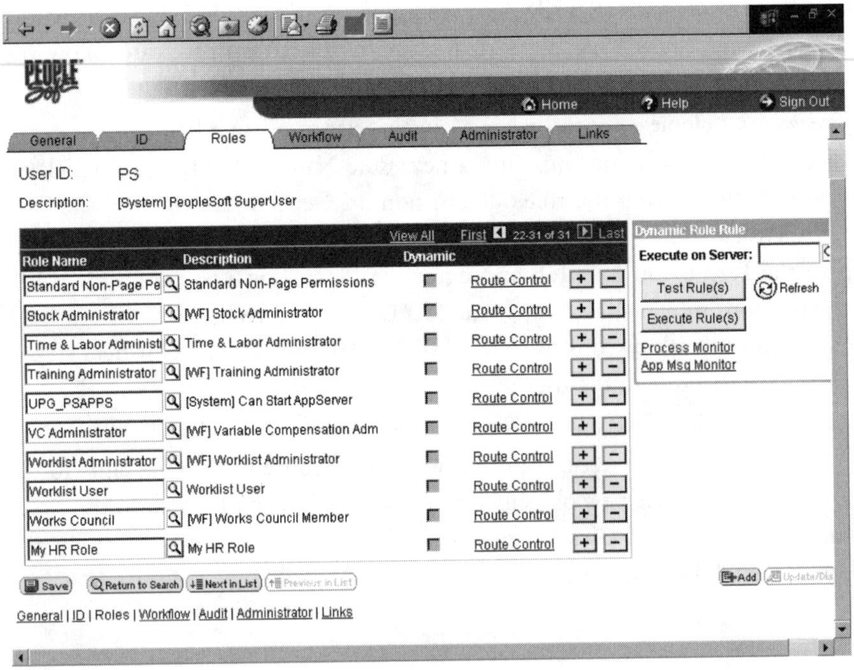

Figure 26.22 Adding a role to a User Profile

Let's save our changes. User PS is assigned to My HR Role that has permissions to execute our new job stream.

Now, we can test our new menu.

Navigation: Home ➡ Define Business Rules ➡ Administer HR System ➡ Job Stream

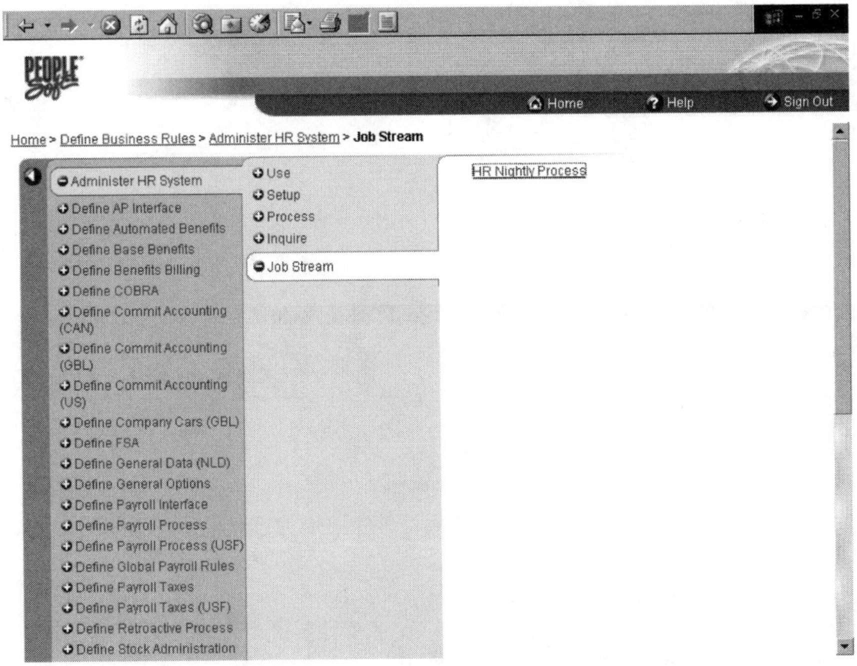

Figure 26.23 The new menu bar and menu item are created for our job stream

Are we ready to run our job? Not yet. We need to create a Job Definition first.

26.3.4 Creating a Job definition

When creating a new Job definition, use a unique Job definition name across Process definition names and Job definition names. PeopleSoft does not allow the same names within both definition, i.e.; Process definitions and Job definitions.

Navigation: Go ➡ PeopleTools ➡ Process Scheduler Manager ➡ Use ➡ Job Definitions

Click on Add A New Value and add MYHRJOB. Unlike the process definition creation, when you add a new job definition, the job name does not have to match any of your processes. You can give any name to your job.

The process of creating a Job definition is similar to that of creating a Process definition. Let's take a close look at what is involved in this process, and discuss the meaning of each field in the Job definition (figure 26.24).

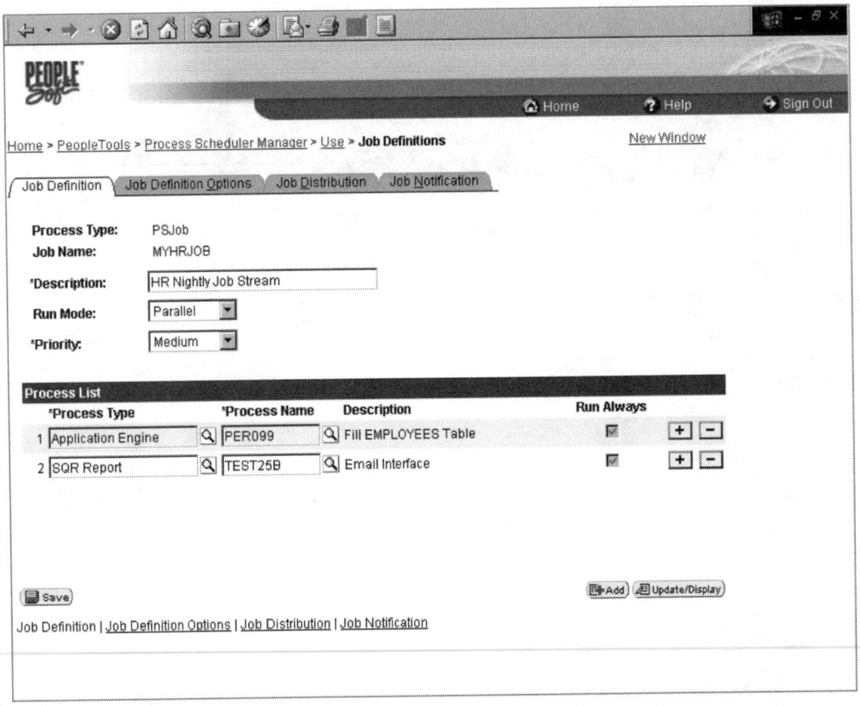

Figure 26.24 Creating a Job definition

In *Job description*, you specify the Job definition description that will be displayed on the Process Scheduler Request page.

Run mode can be either Serial or Parallel. If you want all processes in your job run sequentially, select Serial mode, otherwise, use Parallel. We will run our processes in a Parallel mode since the second process does not depend on the first process execution.

Job priority can be High, Medium, or Low. This information is used by the Process Scheduler to initiate jobs with higher priorities first. We'll specify our job priority as Medium.

In the lower portion of your Job Definition page, below Process List, enter the processes that will be included into your job. If you've selected a Serial mode your processes have to be listed in the order they will be executed, otherwise, list them in any order.

You should turn On the Run Always flag if you want your processes to be executed even if one of the previous processes failed. Since we selected to execute our process in

Parallel mode, this field is not available for edits. The system automatically turns this flag On if the processes are run in a parallel mode. Also note that users can not run the Job's individual processes if the Run Always flag is set to On.

Let's switch to the next tab, Job Definition Options (figure 26.25).

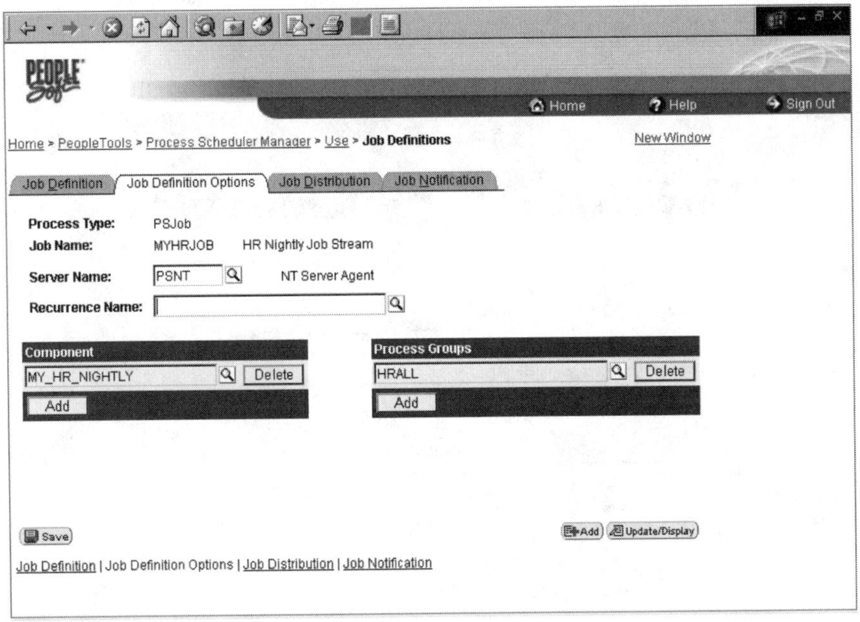

Figure 26.25 The Job Definition Options tab

Recurrence Name is used to specify a recurrence schedule that you previously set up. This parameter is optional, and can also be specified for your Job on the Process Scheduler Request page.

We need to specify a Component your Job should be attached to. For our Job we will specify the name of the MY_HR_NIGHTLY Component that we previously created to run this Job.

For each component you specify Process Groups for users who should be allowed to run your job.

Now we can save our job definition. There are two more optional pages in this group, the Job Distribution and Job Notification pages. We'll not use these pages for our test.

Our Job Definition is created. Let's save it and see how we can submit our Job for execution.

26.3.5 Scheduling a Job for Execution

Let's add a new Run Control for our job, MYJOB. The Run Control Component appears. It consists of two pages, one for each process. Let's enter the input parameters for each process. (figure 26.26).

Navigation: Home ➡ Define Business Rules ➡ Administer HR System ➡ Job Streams ➡ HR Nightly Process

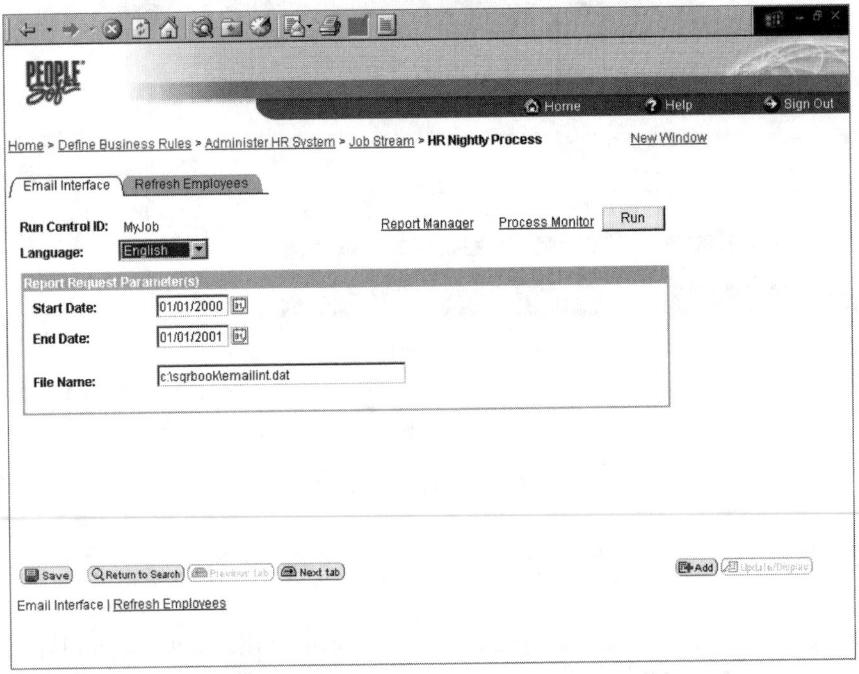

Figure 26.26 Populating the Run Control page with required parameters for Email Interface

Note that the first page in our component is the Email interface page and the second one is the Refresh Employees Process run control page. Does this mean that if you have ten processes in your job definition you would need ten pages in your Run Control Component? Not necessarily. Some of your processes may not even require any input parameters and, therefore, would not need additional Run Control pages. Others may need the same input parameters, and in this case one page can be used for several processes. It all depends on the records your processes are using to get the input parameters from.

Let's take, for example, the Years of Service program. It accepts two parameters: As of Date and Years of Service. If you have a job that includes this program and another one that only needs As of Date as its input parameter (for example the Pending Future

Actions report), you can use the same page to run both reports. This is all, of course, under a condition that both programs are using the same Run Control record.

In the second page of our Component, the Refresh Employees Process Run Control page, we also use the As of Date input parameter. But since the run control records for both our processes are different, you have to include both pages in our Component (figures 26.26 and 26.27.)

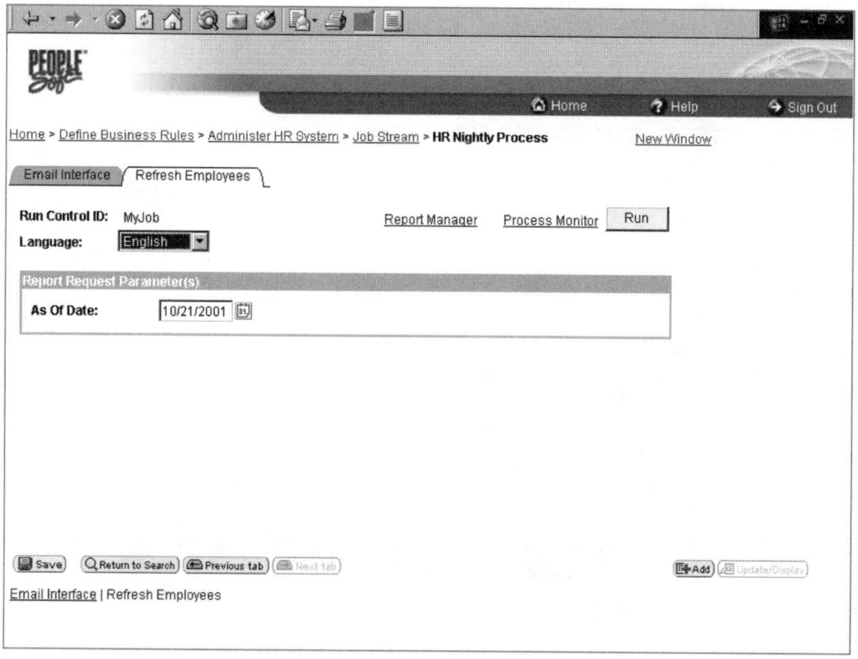

Figure 26.27 Entering input parameters for the Refresh Employees process

After all parameters in the Run Control pages are entered, we are ready to execute our job. Click on the Run button to submit the job (figure 26.28)

As you can see in figure 26.28, as soon as the job is submitted for execution, a number of process instances are created. In this case, there are three process instances: 206, 207 and 208. If you click on the Process Monitor, you will see why the system created three unique process instance numbers (figure 26.29).

On the Process Request page click on the View Job Items check box. The page will display the job process instance (206) and all process instances within it (207, 208). As you can see, all the processes in our job successfully finished their execution.

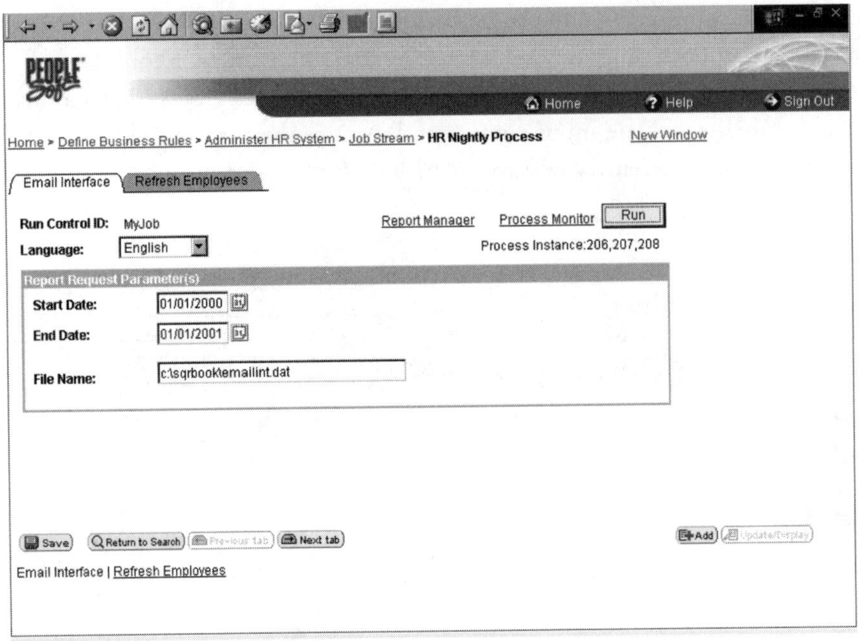

Figure 26.28 Submitting our job for execution

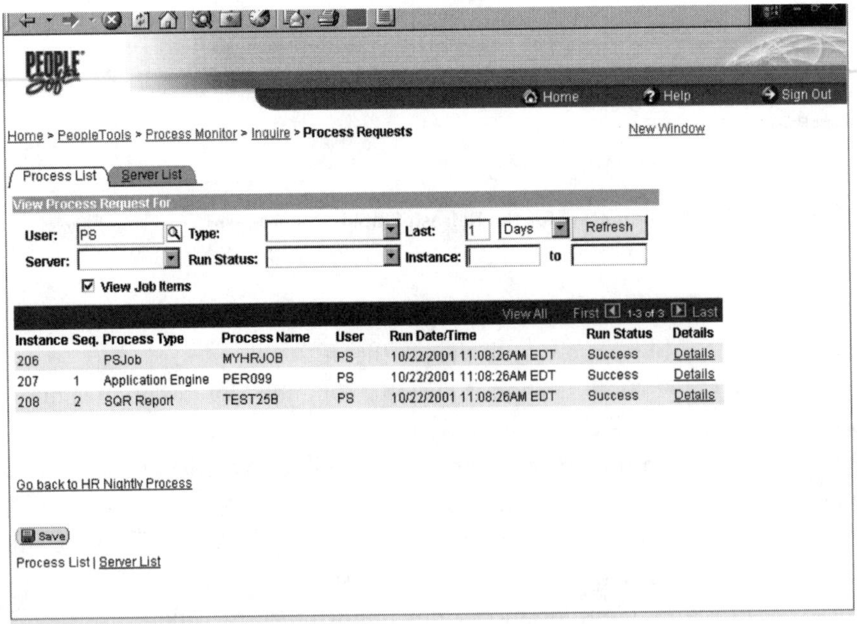

Figure 26.29 Process Request page

In many cases jobs are created to run automatically on a recurrent basis. We can schedule our nightly job for a recurrent execution the same way as we did for individual process in the beginning of this chapter.

KEY POINTS

1. You can schedule your programs that run on Server for execution on a recurring basis.
2. A job (or job stream) may include one or more processes.
3. In order to schedule a job for execution, a Job definition has to be created. Like a Process definition, a Job definition needs to be associated with a Component.
4. You can include processes of different types (SQR program, COBOL, Application Engine) into one job.
5. You need to create a page in the job's Component for each run control record used by a process in the job.
6. If you want your processes to be executed sequentially, you should select the Serial mode on your Job Definition page, otherwise, use the Parallel mode.

C H A P T E R 2 7

Implementing security in SQR

IN THIS CHAPTER

- Why SQR needs security
- Preventing SQR from executing outside the Process Scheduler
- Implementing row-level Security in SQR

27.1 Why SQR needs security

In chapter 23 of this book we already discussed the importance of building and maintaining data security. We learned how PeopleSoft Security Maintenance tools could help us to accomplish this task. At that point we were concerned with online security, and particularly with user security. Based on certain permissions, our users were able to access the menu, component and page that we created in order to execute our SQR report. As we already mentioned, PeopleSoft provides many different levels of security. Let's discuss now why we need SQR security.

Let's say, we developed an SQR program that prints salary information for all employees in the corporation. This corporation, as many others, consists of different departments. The department managers are allowed to see their respective department information. Also, a head of the HR department is allowed to see the entire report output. When we developed the report, we placed it under a certain menu item and allowed access to this report to all department and HR managers, so they can execute it whenever the need arises. But how can we make sure that data from different departments are visible only to their respective managers and the head of the HR department? For tasks like this, the row-level security is the answer.

Row-level security is used to control access to specific rows of data in the database. PeopleSoft delivers applications with row-level security. PeopleSoft uses security search views to provide on-line row-level security when accessing pages and via PS Queries. These views are also used in some of the PeopleSoft-delivered SQR programs. The security search records are, in fact, regular SQL views designed with security in mind. You can design your own security search views or use the PeopleSoft-delivered ones. After such a view is created, PeopleTools lets you attach the view to the corresponding PeopleSoft record and component. PeopleSoft delivers different security search mechanisms based on the application. For example, the built-in Department security is delivered with PeopleSoft HRMS package, while PeopleSoft Financial applications secure financial transactions by business units and ledgers. In the following sub-chapters we will learn how to use and implement row-level security in custom-made SQR programs.

Before we jump into the details of implementing the row-level security in SQR, let's look at another security aspect: how to prevent SQR program execution outside the PeopleSoft Process Scheduler.

27.2 Preventing an SQR from running outside the Process Scheduler

SQR program can be submitted in different ways: from the Process Scheduler, from the SQRW dialog box, or from the command line. If you are running your program from the Process Scheduler, its execution is controlled by various levels of PeopleSoft security. First, you must be an authorized PeopleSoft user to login to the PeopleSoft system. Second, the menu security is in place to prevent unauthorized access to a particular menu or page. Third, when creating a Process definition, you must specify authorized process security groups, thus restricting the execution of a particular program to a specific group or groups of users. All these guards, stand between a user and SQR. Once the user passes through the PeopleSoft online checkpoints, the system, in most cases, will run SQR using SYSADM as user ID, which means that your program will have full, unrestricted access to data. In order to prevent this, you need to implement the row-level security in your SQR program.

If your SQR program is not run under the Process Scheduler, your security is at a much bigger risk: the database access password alone is not sufficient to maintain the proper security.

In order to prevent SQR execution outside the PeopleSoft Process Scheduler, PeopleSoft offers now a simple and efficient solution. This technique is used in most PeopleSoft delivered SQR programs for HRMS application. Let's take a look, for example at the Emergency Contacts report, PER004.SQR:

```
!Part of the PER004.SQR that restricts the SQR execution outside
!the Process Scheduler
...
begin-procedure Init-Report
  #define Year4 '1'
  move 'PER004' to $ReportID
  do Stdapi-Init
  if $prcs_oprid=''       <----- If the value of $prcs_oprid is Null,
                                 SQR detects that it is not executed from
                                 the Process Scheduler
     display ''
     display 'REPORT CAN NOT BE EXECUTED OUTSIDE OF PEOPLESOFT,PLEASE
USE PROCESS SCHEDULER.'
     display ''
    goto last1
  end-if

  do Security-Param

  if $prcs_process_instance = ''
    !No Prompt
  else
    do Select-Parameters
  end-if
  do Init_Printer
  do Init_Report_translation ($ReportID, $language_cd)
  do Append_Report_Translation ('HR')
LAST1:
end-procedure
```

As you can see from the `Init-Report` procedure of the `PER004.SQR`, the program checks the `$prcs_oprid` variable, which is populated by the API code (in the `Get-Run-Control-Parms` procedure) only if the report was initiated from the Process Scheduler. If the value of `$prcs_oprid` is Null, SQR displays an error message and exits the program.

This simple code can be easily implemented in any custom program, thus ensuring program execution under the PeopleSoft Process Scheduler only.

27.3 Using PeopleSoft Security views in SQR to implement row-level security

PeopleSoft incorporated row-level security in some of the HRMS application programs. Let's examine how SQR security is implemented, for example, in the Emergency Contacts program, `PER004.SQR`.

```
!The excerpt from PER004.SQR that deals with Security
...
begin-procedure Init-Report
  #define Year4 '1'
  move 'PER004' to $ReportID
  do Stdapi-Init
  if $prcs_oprid=''
     display ''
     display 'REPORT CAN NOT BE EXECUTED OUTSIDE OF PEOPLESOFT,PLEASE
USE PROCESS SCHEDULER.'
     display ''
    goto last1
  end-if

  do Security-Param        <-- Call the Security-Param procedure from HRSECTY.SQC

  if $prcs_process_instance = ''
    !No Prompt
  else
    do Select-Parameters
  end-if
  do Init_Printer
  do Init_Report_translation ($ReportID, $language_cd)
  do Append_Report_Translation ('HR')
 LAST1:
 end-procedure

 begin-procedure Get-Values
 let $language_cd = $PRCS_LANGUAGE_CD
 end-procedure

 begin-procedure Process-Main
```

```
begin-SELECT DISTINCT
A.NAME        (+1,1,39)  on-break level=1
A.DEPTNAME    (0,41,30)  on-break level=1
...
FROM  PS_EMPLOYEES A,
PS_EMERGENCY_CNTCT B,
PS_FAST_PERSGL_VW2 SCRTY              <---  Join with security search record
WHERE B.EMPLID = A.EMPLID
[$SecurityClause]    <---  Use dynamic condition defined in hrsecty.sqc
AND A.EMPLID = SCRTY.EMPLID
ORDER BY [$qualifier], B.PRIMARY_CONTACT DESC, B.CONTACT_NAME ASC
end-SELECT
end-procedure Process-Main
...
#include 'hrrnctl1.sqc'  !Get run control parameter values
#include 'hrgetval.sqc'  !Get values mask routines
#include 'hrsecty.sqc'   !Get SQR Security parameters
...
```

As you can see in the above excerpt from the PER004.SQR program, the program calls the Security-Param procedure. This procedure is located in the hrsecty.sqc include file. The Security-Param procedure builds the $SecurityClause variable that is used to augment the Where clause in the main select. Basically, this procedure selects the Row Security Operator Class of the operator that executes our PER004.SQR program. It also looks at the Installation table and uses the Override Row Security Class from it, in case if it is specified there to override the operator's security class. The next listing shows how this simple procedure prepares all the necessary components that could be then used in many SQR programs.

```
begin-procedure Security-Param
  Show 'This Report is using Fast Security. If no data is selected,
please have your'
  Show 'Security Administrator verify that the Fast Security View(s)
have been created'
  Show ' '
BEGIN-SELECT
A.ROWSECCLASS
  LET $OverrideClass = RTRIM(&A.ROWSECCLASS,' ')
FROM PS_INSTALLATION A
END-SELECT

BEGIN-SELECT
B.ROWSECCLASS

  LET $OpridClass = RTRIM(&B.ROWSECCLASS,' ')

FROM PSOPRDEFN B
WHERE B.OPRID = $prcs_oprid
```

```
END-SELECT

if $OverrideClass = ''
 let $RowSecClass = $OpridClass
else
 let $RowSecClass = $OverrideClass
end-if
Let $SecurityClause =
 ' AND SCRTY.ROWSECCLASS = '''
 || $RowSecClass || ''''

end-procedure
```

$SecurityClause can be used in the Where clause in any program that calls this routine and selects from the Security view

After the procedure is executed, the program's main select procedure can utilize the variables that where built in the Security-Param procedure. You can see that a new view, PS_FAST_PERSGL_VW2, is added to the SQL join. This is the fast department security view developed by PeopleSoft. This view is joined with the Employees table by EMPLID. In addition, the ROWSECCLASS which is a key field in the security view, is matched with ROWSECCLASS for $prcs_oprid. In other words, the Select statement only selects records of the employees that the operator ($prcs_oprid) is authorized to access.

The fast security view PS_FAST_PERSGL_VW2 is an alternate fast search record for PS_PERS_SRCH_GBL. In order to use this view, the Fast Security functionality delivered by PeopleSoft must be implemented. Fast Security uses the Application Engine to populate special security tables that were created to support search views with faster performance. Instead of the PS_FAST_PERSGL_VW2 record, the PS_PERS_SRCH_QRY1 search record can be used. Fast security is an optional feature of PeopleSoft, if it is implemented in your organization, you can take advantage of it. Similarly, if your program selects from the Job table, you can join with PS_FAST_EMPGL_VW2 or EMPLMT_SRCH_QRY.

Let's summarize now what we learned about implementing security in SQR and what practical steps have to be undertaken to support this security.

- Add code to your program to make sure your SQR is executed from the Process Scheduler by verifying the $prcs_oprid variable
- Include hrsecty.sqc in your SQR program
- Call the Security-Param procedure to select and build the security clause
- Add a Security Search record to your Main Select to restrict access to non-authorized data

Now, that we know how simple it is to implement security in SQR, can we go ahead and incorporate it in all our custom programs? The process may not always be as simple as it seems. You need to know your data and choose a correct search record for your data selection procedure. If your goal is to limit the employee selection by authorizing operators only based on the department security implemented in your system, you can use either the fast security records or the query search records. Both these views utilize the department security. If your SQR program selects neither employees nor departments, you would need to use some other alternatives based on your specific needs.

KEY POINTS

1. In order to prevent an SQR program execution outside the PeopleSoft Process Scheduler, check the value of the `$prcs_oprid` variable.
2. Row-level security is used to control access to specific rows of data in the database. PeopleSoft delivers applications with row-level security.
3. PeopleSoft uses security search view records to provide on-line row-level security.
4. Build your own security views when you cannot use the PeopleSoft-delivered ones.

CHAPTER 28

Working with effective-dated tables

IN THIS CHAPTER

- Selecting the current rows
- Selecting the top rows to include both the current and future rows
- Working with both the current and prior rows
- Identifying prior rows based on certain selection criteria
- Finding orphan rows in the parent-child table relationship
- Calculating date intervals between different events

In this chapter we will discuss effective-dated tables. Working with these tables presents certain challenges to SQR programmers, and we will consider a few sample solutions to a number of frequently used tasks.

28.1 Understanding effective-dated records

In PeopleSoft, most applications are built around the concept of effective dates. This approach facilitates managing data changes over time and keeping track of all changes. It also allows for creating future-dated information and making these data effective only on the appropriate date. In order to accomplish this task, some PeopleSoft tables contain a special field: `Effdt`—effective date. A table that contains the effective date as a part of the table key, is usually called an *effective-dated table*, and the data rows of such tables are called *effective-dated rows.*

PeopleSoft relates all effective-dated rows to one of the following three categories:

- historical data rows
- the current data row
- future data rows.

The best way to better understand this concept is to relate each record to the current date. The *current data row* is the most recently entered row, whose effective date comes closest to today's date without exceeding it. For a given search criteria, there can be only one current data record within a particular table. The *future data rows* are rows with effective dates that are greater than today's date. All other rows are considered *historical rows.* The historical data rows include rows with effective dates that are less than the current row's effective date, as well as the rows with the effective date equal to the current row effective date if these rows were entered into the system prior to the current row.

As an illustration, consider the following example. A table has the following key structure: `Company Code`, `Effdt`. As time goes by, users change some of the characteristics about the companies. They would like to keep track of all the changes. Some of the table rows are entered ahead of time to take effect in the future. Table 28.1 will help you better understand historical, current, and future records:

As you can see, the row with the effective date 06/01/1997 is the current row in this table even if its effective date is less than today's date (01/01/1998).

In PeopleSoft, if the effective date is present in a table record, it is always a part of the table's key. When records in effective-dated tables are selected for processing or viewing, these tables are usually sorted by the effective date in descending order to keep the future and most recently entered rows on the top.

Table 28.1 **Future, current, and historical data rows in an effective-dated table**

Today's Date	Effective Date	Category
01/01/1998	02/01/1998	Future
01/01/1998	06/01/1997	Current
01/01/1998	04/01/1997	Historical
01/01/1998	01/01/1996	Historical

28.2 Multiple records with the same effective date

In many cases, you need to insert multiple rows with the same effective date into an effective-dated table. Let's consider an example of the effective-dated table `PS_Job` that belongs to the PeopleSoft HRMS system. This table contains employee job history records. An employee may have several events that can occur on the same date. Most of these events are registered in the employee's job history. The first event, for example, may take place when an employee is transferred to another location, while a second event might happen when this employee gets a promotion. Although these two different events may occur on the same date, your HR department would like to register them as separate records. To handle situations like this, PeopleSoft provides another key field: Effective Sequence (`Effseq`). When piared with `Effdt`, this key combination allows one to enter more than one unique row with the same effective date.

In table 28.2, the `Job` table records, in addition to the employee Id and effective date, include one more key field: effective sequence:

Table 28.2 **An effective-dated table with multiple records with the same effective date**

Today's Date	Job Effdt	Job Effseq	Category
10/01/1998	01/01/1999	0	Future
10/01/1998	01/01/1997	1	Current
10/01/1998	01/01/1997	0	Historical
10/01/1998	04/01/1996	0	Historical
10/01/1998	01/01/1996	0	Historical

As you can see, the concept of having only one current record for a given employee remains unchanged. Two records exist with the effective date of 01/01/1997, but only one of them, the one entered last on this date, is considered current.

28.3 Different techniques of selecting data from effective-dated tables

The concept of effective date-driven data gives users a great deal of flexibility in tracking historical data, as well as pre-recording future events. At the same time, this approach adds a certain degree of complexity to the application development process. A clear understanding of and ability to visualize the effective-dated data is particularly important when SQR programs are developed in the PeopleSoft environment.

There are many ways of selecting effective-dated records in conjunction with specific business requirements. As is always the case in programming, the same goal can be achieved by using different SQL queries. In this chapter, we will discuss a few of the most common techniques used in PeopleSoft application development. While it is impossible to foresee all tasks and challenges that await you down the road, the examples presented here may lay a good foundation for mastering the subject. It is a good habit to build programs using already-tested SQL queries, since it lowers the cost of both application development and maintenance.

28.3.1 Selecting the current data row

Selecting the current data row from effective-dated tables is a fundamental part of nearly all queries. Depending on the key of the table you are working with, the task of selecting the current record may be accomplished by using a sub-query.

In the following example we will show you a commonly used technique of selecting the current row from an effective-dated table using the `PS_Company_Tbl` table as an example. The key structure of this table includes the `Company` and `Effdt` columns. The query below selects the current row for a given company:

```
!TEST28A.SQR
!Selecting the current data rows
#Include 'setenv.sqc'
Begin-Program
Do Get-Current-DateTime

Begin-Select
A.Company      (+1,1)
A.Effdt        (,+1)
A.Eff_Status   (,+1)
From  PS_COMPANY_TBL A
Where      A.Company     = 'CCB'
And A.Effdt = (Select Max(Effdt)
          From    PS_COMPANY_TBL
          Where   Company= A.Company
          And   Effdt     <= $AsOfToday)
```

```
End-Select
End-Program

#Include 'datetime.sqc'
#Include 'curdttim.sqc'
```

In the example above, the sub-query results in selecting (for a given company) the maximum effective date that is less than or equal to the today's date stored in the `$AsOfToday` variable. This fits our definition of the current date: it is not just the maximum date because the future records should not be included. The main query simply selects the row with the effective date equal to the date returned from the sub-query.

Please note that the today's date is obtained by calling the PeopleSoft-delivered procedure `Get-Current-DateTime` located in the `Curdttim.sqc` file. This procedure retrieves the server system date and places this date into the `$AsOfToday` variable. It is a good practice to use this variable instead of, for example, Oracle's `Sysdate`, since it makes your program database independent.

Let's add some complexity to our example: this time, we need to select the current records for a list of companies. We only want current records with an effective status equal to `Active`. Here is the modified query:

```
!TEST28B.SQR
!Limiting the current row selection to
!only records with the active status
#include 'setenv.sqc'
Begin-Program
Do Get-Current-DateTime

Begin-Select
A.Company    (+1,1)
A.Effdt      (,+2)
A.Eff_Status (,+2)
From  PS_COMPANY_TBL A
Where A.Company in ('CCB','CCA','CIA')
And A.Eff_Status = 'A'
And A.Effdt = (Select Max(Effdt)
             From   PS_COMPANY_TBL
             Where  Company= A.Company
             And    Effdt  <= $AsOfToday)
End-Select
End-Program

#Include 'datetime.sqc'
#Include 'curdttim.sqc'
```

The above example selects only the active current rows for a given list of the company Ids. Please note that the sub query does not include the `Eff_Status` column in its

WHERE clause. This is the right way to build the query. Placing this column into the sub query (as shown in TEST28C.SQR) will result in an incorrect selection.

```
!TEST28C.SQR
!An improperly built WHERE clause brings an incorrect result set
#Include 'setenv.sqc'
Begin-Program
Do Get-Current-DateTime

Begin-Select
A.Company          (+1,1)
A.Effdt            (,+2)
A.Eff_Status       (,+2)
From   PS_COMPANY_TBL A
Where A.Company in ('CCB','CCA','CIA')
And A.Effdt = (Select Max(Effdt)
              From   PS_COMPANY_TBL
              Where  Company = A.Company
              And    Eff_Status = 'A' ! INCORRECT
              And    Effdt <= $AsOfToday)
End-Select
End-Program

#Include 'datetime.sqc'
#Include 'curdttim.sqc'
```

Moving the effective status check to the sub-query results in incorrect selection.

What's wrong with the query in Test28C.sqr? This query selects the most current among all active records instead of the current active records. See the difference? Take a look at table 28.3.

Table 28.3 Records with Effective Date and Effective Status

Today's Date	Company	Record Effective Date	Eff_Status
01/01/1998	Comp1	06/01/1997	I
01/01/1998	Comp1	04/01/1997	A
01/01/1998	Comp1	01/01/1996	A
01/01/1998	Comp2	01/01/1999	I
01/01/1998	Comp2	01/01/1998	A
01/01/1998	Comp2	01/01/1997	A

The correct result from Test28B.sqr is as follows:

```
Comp2          01/01/1998                    A
```

This result is correct.

The incorrectly written program Test28C.SQR selects the following rows:

```
Comp1          04/01/1997          A <——  This result is incorrect.
Comp2          01/01/1998          A
```

Now you see the difference between the two queries: the status of the current record for company `Comp1` is set to "`I`" (Inactive). The correctly built query should not have returned this record because all we wanted was the current active records.

28.3.2 Selecting the current data row from a table which includes multiple records with the same effective dates

We have already discussed tables that may include multiple records with the same effective dates. The common method of maintaining table row uniqueness in these tables is to add a sequence number to the table key that is unique for any given effective date. Conceptually, the basic query algorithm is similar to the one presented in `Test28A.sqr`. However, because the table key includes both the effective date and the sequence number, selecting the current row now involves using two sub-queries instead of one: one for the effective date, and another for the sequence number.

The following example will show you how to select, for a given company, the current row for each employee in the PeopleSoft `Job` table.

```
!TEST28D.SQR
!Selecting the current record from the Job table
#Include 'setenv.sqc'

Begin-Program
Do Get-Current-DateTime

Begin-Select
J.Emplid     (+1,1)
J.Company    (,+1)
J.Effdt      (,+1)
J.Action     (,+1)
  Show &J.Emplid
From PS_JOB J
Where      J.Company='CCB'
  And      J.Effdt  =(Select Max(J1.Effdt)
              From PS_JOB J1
              Where  J1.Emplid   = J.Emplid
              And    J1.Empl_Rcd = J.Empl_Rcd
              And    J1.Effdt    <= $AsofToday)
  And J.Effseq =(Select Max(J2.Effseq)
```

```
                From PS_JOB J2
                Where J2.Emplid        = J.Emplid
                And J2.Empl_Rcd        = J.Empl_Rcd
                And J2.Effdt           = J.Effdt)
End-Select
End-Program

#Include 'datetime.sqc'
#Include 'curdttim.sqc'
```

To understand the above example, let's assume for a second, that the query in the example does not have the second sub-query. This will result in returning more than one row if multiple events took place on the current record, but there should not be more than one current record for a given employee.

The second sub-query, for any given effective date, selects only the record with the maximum effective sequence. As a result, the entire query returns only one row for each employee: the current row.

Sometimes, business requirements call for selecting the record with the lowest effective sequence, that is, the record reflecting the first event of the day. In that case, the second sub-query in `Test28D.sqr` can be easily modified by using the `Min` aggregate function in place of the `Max` function.

28.3.3 Using the Loops parameter in the Select paragraph to limit the number of selected rows

Suppose we need to select all active employees and, for each selected record, find out whether this employee is currently enrolled in a medical plan. This task can be accomplished by employing the above described current record search technique. This time, however, when the program finds the current record for an employee, it retrieves the current health benefit record for this employee:

```
!TEST28E.SQR
!Using the Loops parameter to select the current record
#Include 'setenv.sqc'
Begin-Program
Do Get-Current-DateTime
Do Main
End-Program

Begin-Procedure Main
Begin-Select
J.Emplid     (+1,1,11)
J.Empl_Rcd (,+2,3)
P.Name       (,+2,15)
J.Company    (,+2,10)
J.Effdt      (,+2,10)
```

```
    Do Select_Health_Ben
    If $Found = 'Y'
       Print &B.Benefit_Plan (,+2)
    End-If
From PS_JOB J, Ps_Personal_Data P
Where   J.Company        ='CCB'
And     J.Emplid         = P.Emplid
And     J.Empl_Status    ='A'
And     J.Effdt=(Select Max(J1.Effdt)
                From PS_JOB J1
                Where J1.Emplid     = J.Emplid
                And J1.Empl_Rcd     = J.Empl_Rcd
                And J1.Effdt       <= $AsOfToday)
And     J.Effseq =(Select Max(J2.Effseq)
                From PS_JOB J2
                Where J2.Emplid     = J.Emplid
                And J2.Empl_Rcd     = J.Empl_Rcd
                And J2.Effdt        = J.Effdt)
End-Select
End-Procedure

!*******************************************
Begin-Procedure Select_Health_Ben
!*******************************************
Let $Found = 'N'
Begin-Select Loops=1
B.Emplid
B.Plan_Type
B.Benefit_Plan
 Let $Found='Y'
 Show 'Selected ' &B.Emplid ' ' &B.Plan_Type
From PS_Health_Benefit B
Where
     B.Emplid     =&J.Emplid
And  B.Empl_Rcd   =&J.Empl_Rcd
And  B.Effdt      <=$AsOfToday
And  B.Plan_Type ='10'
And  B.Coverage_Elect = 'E'
Order By B.Emplid,B.Effdt Desc
End-Select
End-Procedure

#Include 'datetime.sqc'
#Include 'curdttim.sqc'
```

`Loops` = 1 parameter tells SQR to retrieve only one record and then exit the `Select` loop.

Since the records are sorted by `Effdt`, the first retrieved row will be the current record.

Note how the main procedure selects the current data row for each active employee who belongs to the 'CCB' company. For each selected employee, we need to find the current record from the `Health_Benefit` table with `Plan_Type = '10'` (Medical) and `Coverage_Elect` flag `= 'E'` (Enrolled). The task is achieved by calling the `Select_Health_Ben` routine for each row selected in the main routine. Since the

Health_Benefit table is an effective-dated table, we could have used the same "Max (Effdt)" technique but, in this case, considering that we need to select only one record for each employee, it will be much more efficient to use the Loops=1 parameter in the Begin-Select command. The Loops=1 parameter actually tells SQR to retrieve only one record that satisfies the Where clause and, then, exit the Select loop. Since we sort the selected records by the effective date in descending order, the first selected row will be the current record we are looking for. As you can see, limiting the query result set in the Select_Health_Ben routine made the program simpler and more efficient.

28.3.4 Selecting the top row from an effective-dated table

As we already mentioned, the top row in an effective-dated table is not always the current row. It may be one of the future rows. In certain cases, you need to select only the top records for employees, without checking to see whether or not the records are the current records or the future records.

Selecting the top records involves only a slight modification of the query presented in Test28D.sqr. Here is how it looks now:

```
!TEST28F.SQR
!Selecting the top row for each employee within a given company
#Include 'setenv.sqc'

Begin-Program
Do Get-Current-DateTime

Begin-Select
J.Emplid          (+1,1,11)
J.Company         (,+2,3)
J.Effdt           (,+2,10)
J.Action          (,+2,5)
 If &J.Effdt > $AsofToday
   Print 'Future' (,+2)
   show  'Future ' &J.Emplid
 Else
   Print 'Current' (,+2)
   Show 'Current ' &J.Emplid
 End-If
From PS_JOB J
Where J.Company='CCB'
And   J.Effdt=(Select Max(J1.Effdt)
            From PS_JOB J1
            Where J1.Emplid     = J.Emplid
            And   J1.Empl_Rcd   = J.Empl_Rcd)
And   J.Effseq =(Select Max(J2.Effseq)
            From PS_JOB J2
            Where J2.Emplid     = J.Emplid
```

The sub-select does not include additional restrictions on the effective dates.

```
                And    J2.Empl_Rcd    = J.Empl_Rcd
                And    J2.Effdt       = J.Effdt)
End-Select
End-Program

#Include 'datetime.sqc'
#Include 'curdttim.sqc'
```

The query in the example above selects only the top record for each employee. For some employees, this may be the current record, for others, the query may return the most recent future records. An additional `If-Then` SQR statement in the main query prints the appropriate label ("Future" or "Current") for each selected record.

28.3.5 Selecting the current and prior rows

Now we are going to tackle a somewhat more complex task. Often a need arises to first select a record using certain criteria and, then, based on the results of the first selection, select the prior historical record. For example, when working with employee benefits, you often need to know whether the benefit plan an employee is enrolled in has changed, or whether the employee's dependents dropped their coverage. In Human Resources, you may want to know the action code in the prior row if, for example, the current record action is termination. There may be lots of other business reasons to retrieve the prior record. Let's take a look at some techniques which may be helpful.

This task now is more complex than previous ones. Using just plain SQL might prove to be rather difficult (although we will show you how to do this), but the strength of SQR lies in its ability to combine the power of SQL with the flexibility of procedural logic. Now is the time to take advantage of this fact.

In our first example, we will utilize SQR's ability to perform logical operations on each selected row. For each row selected in the main procedure, the program will call another select procedure which will, in turn, use the data selected in the main procedure as bind variables:

```
!TEST28G.SQR
!Selecting both the current and the prior rows
#Include 'setenv.sqc'

Begin-Program
Do Get-Current-DateTime
Do Main
End-Program

Begin-Procedure Main
Begin-Select
J.Emplid        (+1,1)
J.Empl_Rcd      (,+1)
```

```
J.Company      (,+1)
J.Effdt        (,+1)
J.Effseq       (,+1)
J.Action       (,+1)
   Print 'Current Row' (,+1)
   If &J.Effseq > 0
     Do Select_Prior_Seq
   Else
     Do Select_Prior_Row
   End-If
From PS_JOB J
Where    J.Company='CCB'
And      J.Empl_Status='A'
And      J.Effdt=(Select Max(J1.Effdt)
             From PS_JOB J1
             Where J1.Emplid     = J.Emplid
             And J1.Empl_Rcd     = J.Empl_Rcd
             And J1.Effdt        <= $AsOfToday)
  And    J.Effseq =(Select Max(J2.Effseq)
             From PS_JOB J2
             Where J2.Emplid     = J.Emplid
             And J2.Empl_Rcd     = J.Empl_Rcd
             And J2.Effdt        = J.Effdt)
End-Select
End-Procedure
!*******************************************
Begin-Procedure Select_Prior_Row
!*******************************************
Begin-Select
JP.Emplid       (+1,1)
JP.Company      (,+1)
JP.Effdt        (,+1)
JP.Effseq       (,+1)
JP.Action       (,+1)
   Print 'Prior Effdt Row' (,+1)
   Show &J.Emplid ' ' &J.Effseq ' ' &J.Effdt ' ' &Jp.Effdt ' '
      &Jp.Effseq
   Add 1 To #Count_Prior
From PS_JOB JP
Where    JP.Emplid    =&J.Emplid
And      JP.Empl_Rcd  =&J.Empl_Rcd
And      JP.Effdt     =(Select Max(J1P.Effdt)
               From PS_JOB J1P
               Where J1P.Emplid = JP.Emplid
               And J1P.Empl_Rcd = JP.Empl_Rcd
               And J1P.Effdt < &J.Effdt)
And     JP.Effseq    =(Select Max(JP2.Effseq)
               From PS_JOB JP2
               Where JP2.Emplid = JP.Emplid
               And JP2.Empl_Rcd = JP.Empl_Rcd
               And JP2.Effdt = JP.Effdt)
End-Select
```

```
End-Procedure
!****************************************
Begin-Procedure Select_Prior_Seq
!****************************************
Begin-Select
JS.Emplid       (+1,1)
JS.Company      (,+1)
JS.Effdt        (,+1)
JS.Effseq       (,+1)
JS.Action       (,+1)
 Print 'Prior Effseq Row' (,+1)
From PS_JOB JS
Where    JS.Emplid   = &J.Emplid
And      JS.Empl_Rcd  =&J.Empl_Rcd
And      JS.Effdt    = &J.Effdt
And      JS.Effseq   = (Select Max(JS2.Effseq)
               From PS_JOB JS2
               Where JS2.Emplid = JS.Emplid
               And JS2.Empl_Rcd = JS.Empl_Rcd
               And JS2.Effdt = JS.Effdt
               And JS2.Effseq < &J.Effseq)
End-Select
End-Procedure

#Include 'datetime.sqc'
#Include 'curdttim.sqc'
```

To better understand the algorithm of `Test28G.sqr`, let's take a look at some data samples.

Suppose the current record, selected in the query of the main procedure, contains 01/01/1998 as the effective date and 03 as the effective sequence. Let's also assume that the prior record has 01/01/1998 as its effective date and 02 as its effective sequence. In the algorithm above, after selecting the current row, we check to see if the effective sequence is greater than zero. If yes, we know that the prior row should have the same effective date, but a lower effective sequence. Therefore, we call the `Select_Prior_Seq` routine. If the record selected in the main procedure query has a zero effective sequence, then we know that the prior row should have a lower effective date and call the `Select_Prior_Row` routine.

Another method of solving the same problem is to use the just-discussed `Loops` parameter to limit the number of prior records to be selected:

```
!TEST28I.SQR
!Using Loops=1 to select the prior row
#Include 'setenv.sqc'

Begin-Program
Do Get-Current-DateTime
Do Main
```

```
Show '#Count_Prior=' #Count_Prior
End-Program

Begin-Procedure Main
Begin-Select
J.Emplid       (+1,1)
J.Empl_Rcd     (,+1)
J.Company      (,+1)
J.Effdt        (,+1)
J.Effseq       (,+1)
J.Action       (,+1)
   Print 'Current Row' (,+1)
   Do Select_Prior_Row

From PS_JOB J
Where    J.Company='700'
And      J.Empl_Status='A'
And      J.PayGroup='WE1'
And      J.Effdt=(Select Max(J1.Effdt)
             From PS_JOB J1
             Where J1.Emplid  = J.Emplid
             And J1.Empl_Rcd  = J.Empl_Rcd
             And J1.Effdt     <= Sysdate)
And      J.Effseq =(Select Max(J2.Effseq)
             From PS_JOB J2
             Where J2.Emplid  = J.Emplid
             And J2.Empl_Rcd  = J.Empl_Rcd
             And J2.Effdt     = J.Effdt)
End-Select
End-Procedure
!*****************************************
Begin-Procedure Select_Prior_Row
!*****************************************
Begin-Select Loops=1
JP.Emplid       (+1,1)
JP.Company      (,+1)
JP.Effdt        (,+1)
JP.Effseq       (,+1)
JP.Action       (,+1)
   Print 'Prior Effdt Row' (,+1)
   Add 1 To #Count_Prior
From PS_JOB JP
Where     JP.Emplid     =&J.Emplid
And       JP.Empl_Rcd   =&J.Empl_Rcd
And       ( JP.Effdt    < &J.Effdt
            Or  (JP.Effdt = &J.Effdt And JP.Effseq < &J.Effseq) )

Order By JP.EMPLID,JP.Effdt Desc, JP.Effseq Desc
End-Select
End-Procedure

#Include 'datetime.sqc'
#Include 'curdttim.sqc'
```

As you can see, the `Order By` clause in the `Select_Prior_Row` routine sorts the selected rows by the effective date and the effective sequence in descending order, thereby ensuring that the query returns the prior rows with the most recent one on top. The `Loops=1` parameter limits the query result set to the top selected row only.

We promised to demonstrate how to select prior rows by using only SQL with no SQR procedure calls. You can do this by joining the `Job` table with itself. The key to this technique is to think of the second `Job` table as if it were a different table. Another important point of this algorithm is that it uses a concatenation of the effective date and the effective sequence.

If we convert the effective date into the "YYYYMMDD" format and concatenate this string with the effective sequence, the resulting string will be a combination of both fields. Assuming that the current effective date is 01/01/1998 and the current effective sequence is 03, the string will look like this: "1998010103". Now, we know that the combination of the effective date and effective sequence for any prior record must be less than "1998010103". For example, if the effective date in the prior record is 01/01/1998, and the effective sequence of the prior record is 02, the combination will be "1998010102". What if the effective sequence of the current record is zero? In that case, our string will look like "1998010100", and the prior record will have a lower effective date. As a result, regardless of the prior record's effective sequence, the combination of the effective date and effective sequence for this record will have a lesser value than that for the current record. For instance, the prior record's effective date may be 12/31/1997 and the effective sequence may be 05. The string "1997123105" is lower in value than "1998010103".

> ***Note*** This logic is valid only if you include the century in the year. Be careful!

The following code will show you how to implement the technique described above:

```
!TEST28J.SQR
!Using Self-Join to select the current
!and the prior rows of data in one query
#Include 'setenv.sqc'

Begin-Program
Do Get-Current-DateTime
Show $AsOfToday
Do Main
Show 'Count=' #Count
End-Program

Begin-Procedure Main
Begin-Select
J.Emplid        (+1,1)
J.Empl_Rcd      (+1,1)
```

```
J.Company      (,+1)
J.Effdt        (,+1)
J.Effseq       (,+1)
J.Action       (,+1)
  Print '->'   (,+1)
JP.Effdt       (,+1)
JP.Effseq      (,+1)
JP.Action      (,+1)
   Add 1 To #Count
   Show &J.Emplid ' ' &J.Effseq ' ' &J.Effdt ' ' &Jp.Effdt ' '
       &Jp.Effseq
From PS_JOB J, PS_JOB JP
Where   J.Company='CCB'
And     J.Empl_Status='A'
And     J.Effdt=(Select Max(J1.Effdt)
           From PS_JOB J1
           Where J1.Emplid = J.Emplid
           And J1.Empl_Rcd = J.Empl_Rcd
           And J1.Effdt <= $AsOfToday)
And J.Effseq =(Select Max(J2.Effseq)
           From PS_JOB J2
           Where J2.Emplid = J.Emplid
           And J2.Empl_Rcd = J.Empl_Rcd
           And J2.Effdt = J.Effdt)
 And    JP. Emplid = J.Emplid
 And    JP.Empl_Rcd = J.Empl_Rcd
 And    JP.Effdt = (Select Max(J1P.Effdt) From PS_JOB J1P
           Where J1P.Emplid = JP.Emplid
           And J1P.Empl_Rcd = JP.Empl_Rcd
           And   To_Char(J1P.Effdt,'YYYYMMDD')
              ||to_char(J1P.EFFSEQ,'99')
              < To_Char(J.Effdt,'YYYYMMDD')||to_char(J.EFFSEQ,'99'))
 And    JP.effseq = (Select Max(J2P.Effseq) From PS_JOB J2P
           Where J2P.Emplid = JP.Emplid
           And J2P.Empl_Rcd = JP.Empl_Rcd
           And J2p.Effdt=Jp.Effdt
           And   To_Char(J2P.Effdt,'YYYYMMDD')
              ||to_char(J2P.EFFSEQ,'99')
              < To_Char(J.Effdt,'YYYYMMDD')||to_char(J.EFFSEQ,'99'))

Order By J.emplid, J.effdt

End-Select
End-Procedure

#Include 'datetime.sqc'
#Include 'curdttim.sqc'
```

Here we use a combination of the self-join technique and a concatenation of two columns `Effdt` and `Effseq` to avoid the need to invoke extra queries. The code in this example is really efficient. This example contains one drawback, however. There are situations in which the query will not print any rows. Can you guess when? It will happen in the case in which the prior record does not exist. The remedy to this problem (if we still want to do everything in one select procedure) is to use the outer join. You will have to make sure that your database supports outer joins. In many cases, not printing records may perfectly fit your business needs if you do not need to select any rows anyway. Regardless, you should definitely keep the above-mentioned in mind.

28.3.6 Using Exists in the Where clause to check for prior rows

Often you need to select records only when the prior record with specific characteristics exists.

Suppose you would like to select the current records of all active employees who were promoted prior to a specified date. Our SQR code may look like the following:

```
!TEST28K.SQR
!Using the Exists operator to check if there is at least one record
!for this employee whose Action='PRO' (promotion)
...
Do Get-Current-Date-Time
...
Begin-Procedure Main
Begin-Select
J.Emplid        (+1,1)
J.Company       (,+1)
J.Effdt         (,+1)
J.Effseq        (,+1)
J.Action        (,+1)

From PS_JOB J
Where  J.Company=$Comp1
And    J.Empl_Status='A'
And    J.Effdt=(Select Max(J1.Efdt)
          From PS_JOB J1
          Where J1.Emplid = J.Emplid
          And J1.Empl_Rcd = J.Empl_Rcd
          And J1.Effdt <= $AsofToday)
 And    J.Effseq =(Select Max(J2.Effseq)
          From PS_JOB J2
          Where J2.Emplid = J.Emplid
          And J2.Empl_Rcd = J.Empl_Rcd
          And J2.Effdt = J.Effdt)
And Exists
 (Select 'X' From PS_JOB JP
 Where    JP.Emplid   = J.Emplid
 And      JP.Empl_Rcd = J.Empl_Rcd
 And      JP.Effdt    < $InputDate
 And      JP.Action   = 'PRO')
```

If this sub-select returns at least one record, then the `Exists` statement will return `'True'` and the current record will be selected; otherwise, the conditions in the `Where` clause are not satisfied, and the record is not selected.

```
 End-Select
End-Procedure
...
#Include 'curdttim'
```

The `Exists` operator checks for any records with the effective date less than the `$InputDate`. It does not actually care if the selected record is current or historical record. If you don't want to include the current record in this selection, just add the following to the `Exists` operator in the `Where` clause:

```
And To_Char(JP.Effdt,'YYYYMMDD')
   ||JP.EFFSEQ < To_Char(J.Effdt,'YYYYMMDD')||J.EFFSEQ
```

28.4 Other frequently used operations with effective-dated tables

28.4.1 Identifying orphan rows

When dealing with parent-child relationships in database processing, it is important to make sure that all logically related tables are kept synchronized. When deleting parent records, all child records of this parent have to be deleted as well. In database design, this is called *referential integrity*. It can be enforced by RDBMS, but, for a number of reasons, PeopleSoft chose not to enforce referential integrity on the Human Resources Management System (HRMS) core tables. Therefore, it becomes the programmer's responsibility. Good housekeeping should not permit "orphan" rows (rows without their respective parents), however, there are often situations in which orphan rows are created during conversions or due to some other reasons. In order to delete orphan rows, they have to be identified first. The following example demonstrates a simple technique of identifying orphan rows in the `Health_Dependnt` table.

```
!TEST28L.SQR
!Identifying orphan rows
...
Begin-Select
A.Emplid            (+1,1)
A.Empl_Rcd          (,+1)
A.Cobra_Event_Id    (,+1)
A.Plan_Type         (,+1)
A.Benefit_Nbr       (,+1)
A.Dependent_Benef
   Do Delete-Orphan-Record
From PS_HEALTH_DEPENDNT A
 Where
 A.Emplid NOT IN
       (Select Emplid from PS_Health_Benefit
```

The `PS_Health_Benefit` table is a parent to the `PS_Health_Dependnt`. Therefore, a parent should exist for each row in the child table.

```
        Where   Emplid              =   A.Emplid
        And     Empl_Rcd            =   A.Empl_Rcd
        And     Cobra_Event_ID      =   A.Cobra_Event_ID
        And     Plan_Type           =   A.Plan_Type
        And     Benefit_NBR         =   A.Benefit_NBR
        And     Effdt               =   A.Effdt)
   End-Select
End-Procedure
...
```

28.4.2 Calculating date intervals between events

Working with different applications, especially with HRMS, often requires that various operations be performed on date intervals. For example, you may be asked to create a report with all employees' anniversary dates. Another example is when you need to calculate the length of time that has passed since a specific event in an employee's history, or to alert an HR administrator that an employee review is past due.

Once the specified records are selected, there are many different ways to perform the actual date calculations. Most databases provide a number of date arithmetic and date conversion functions that could be used for date operations. In order to create database independent programs, you should avoid using database-specific functions and use the similar SQR functions instead (see chapter 4). If you use date interval calculations in the `Where` clause, you have to use database-specific functions: SQR commands and functions cannot be used in the `Where` clause. We will demonstrate different techniques using both database-specific date functions and SQR database-independent functions, leaving it up to our readers to decide which method to use, based on their own specific system requirements.

28.4.3 Calculating time difference in years since employee's last promotion

Suppose our task is to select all presently active employees for a specific company, who have stayed with the company for at least a year, and, for each selected employee, to print the employee Id, hire/rehire date, company name and length of time that has passed since the employee's last promotion. For those employees who had not had their promotions yet, print a string of asterisks to identify a potential problem. Also, mark all employees who did not have a single promotion for more than five years.

```
!TEST28M.SQR
!Calculating the length of time that has passed since the
!employee's last promotion
#Include 'setenv.sqc'
!**********************************************
Begin-Setup
```

```
!*************************************************
Declare-Variable
  Date     $Serv_Dt
  Date     $AsOfToday_Dt
End-Declare
End-Setup
!*************************************************
Begin-Program
!*************************************************
Do Get-Current-DateTime                 ! Get $AsOfToday
Do Main
End-Program
!*************************************************
Begin-Procedure Main
!*************************************************
Begin-Select
J.Emplid
J.Empl_Rcd
J.Company
J.Effdt
E.Hire_Dt
E.Rehire_Dt

     If &E.Hire_Dt > &E.Rehire_Dt
       Let $Serv_Dt=&E.Hire_Dt
     Else
       Let $Serv_Dt=&E.ReHire_Dt
     End-If

   Let $AsOfToday_Dt = strtodate($AsOfToday, 'YYYY-MM-DD')
   Let $Years_Worked=datediff($AsOfToday_Dt,$Serv_Dt,'year')

     If $Years_Worked >='1'
       Print &J.Emplid       (+1,1,11)
       Print &J.Empl_Rcd     (,+1,2)
       Do Select_Promotion_Row
       If $Found='Y'
         Let #Diff=datediff($AsOfToday_Dt,&JP.Effdt,'year')
         Move #Diff To $Diff1 99.99
         Print  $Diff1 (,+1,5)
         If #Diff > 5
           Print '*' (,+1)
         End-If
       Else
         Print ' '     (,+7,10)
         Print '*********' (,+1)

       End-If
     End-If

 From PS_JOB J, PS_Employment E
 Where  J.Company='CCB'
```

```
And    J.Empl_Status    ='A'
And  J.Effdt    =(Select Max(J1.Effdt) From PS_JOB J1
            Where J1.Emplid  = J.Emplid
            And J1.Empl_Rcd  = J.Empl_Rcd
            And J1.Effdt     <= $AsOfToday)
And  J.Effseq   =(Select Max(J2.Effseq) From PS_JOB J2
            Where J2.Emplid  = J.Emplid
            And J2.Empl_Rcd# = J.Empl_Rcd#
            And J2.Effdt     = J.Effdt)
 And   E.Emplid        =J.Emplid
 And   E.Empl_Rcd      =J.Empl_Rcd
 End-Select
End-Procedure

!**************************************************
Begin-Procedure Select_Promotion_Row
!**************************************************
Let $Found='N'
Begin-Select
JP.Effdt
     Let $Found='Y'
     Print &JP.Effdt (,+1,10)

From PS_JOB JP
Where   JP.Emplid      = &J.Emplid
And     JP.Empl_Rcd    = &J.Empl_Rcd
And     JP.Company     = &J.Company
and     JP.Effdt       = (Select Max(J1P.Effdt) From PS_JOB J1P
                 Where J1P.Emplid      = JP.Emplid
                 And J1P.Empl_Rcd      = JP.Empl_Rcd
                 And J1P.Action        = 'PRO'
                 And J1P.Effdt         <= $AsOfToday)
  And   JP.Effseq      = (Select Max(J2P.Effseq) From PS_JOB J2P
                 Where J2P.Emplid      = JP.Emplid
                 and J2P.Empl_Rcd      = JP.Empl_Rcd
                 And J2P.Effdt         = JP.Effdt)
End-Select
End-Procedure

#Include 'datetime.sqc'
#Include 'curdttim.sqc'
```

Note that the `Action` is checked in the sub-query, not in the main query.

In `Test28M.sqr`, we accomplish our task by using a two-step process. In the first step, we select all active employees for a given company. Then, for each selected employee record, we check to see if the employee had been with the company for more than a year, and, if so, we call a separate procedure named `Select_Promotion_Row`. In this procedure, we only select records with `Action = 'PRO'` (promotion). Please note that the check for promotion is located in the `Where` clause of the sub-query, not in the main query because our task is to select the latest record among all the records with

Action = 'PRO'. If we had placed this check into the main query, the selection would be limited only to the promotion records that happen to be in the top row. This mistake is fairly common.

In our main procedure, based on the result from the Select_Promotion_Row procedure, we either calculate the date difference using the SQR datediff() function, or print a string of asterisks if no records with Action = 'PRO' have been found. We also calculate the difference between the today's date and the last promotion date, and, if this difference is greater than five years, print an asterisk next to this field.

The code presented in Test26M.sqr uses only SQR date functions and, therefore, is database independent. The next example will demonstrate a somewhat more efficient technique, but performance in this case is achieved at the expense of database independence.

In the previous example, the query in the Main procedure selects all current rows, regardless of the employee promotion history. If we wanted to limit the number of rows selected in the Main procedure, we could have included a check for the number of years in service in the Where clause. This approach will certainly increase efficiency. However, because SQR commands cannot be placed in the Where clause, we can use only database-specific functions to calculate the difference between the dates. As a result, our program will become database-specific. To demonstrate this technique, let's rewrite the previous example using Oracle functions in date difference calculations:

```
! TEST28N.SQR
!Using the Oracle functions to calculate date differences
...
Begin-Procedure Main
Begin-Select
J.Emplid
J.Effdt
   Print &J.Emplid       (+1,1,11)
   Print &J.Empl_Rcd     (,+1,2)
   Do Select_Promotion_Row
   If $Found='Y'
      Let #Diff=DateDiff($AsOfToday_Dt,&JP.Effdt,'year')
      Move #Diff to $Diff1 99.99
      Print  $Diff1 (,+1,5)
      If #Diff > 5
         Print '*' (,+1)
      End-If
   Else
      Print ' '    (,+7,10)
      Print '*********' (,+1)
   End-If
From PS_JOB J, PS_Employment E
Where    J.Company='CCB'
And      J.Empl_Status    ='A'
And      J.Effdt     =(Select Max(J1.Effdt)
```

```
                From PS_JOB J1
                Where J1.Emplid      = J.Emplid
                And J1.Empl_Rcd      = J.Empl_Rcd
                And J1.Effdt         <= $AsofToday)
And    J.Effseq    =(Select Max(J2.Effseq)
                From PS_JOB J2
                Where J2.Emplid       = J.Emplid
                And J2.Empl_Rcd       = J.Empl_Rcd
                And J2.Effdt          = J.Effdt)
And   E.Emplid          =J.Emplid
And   E.Empl_Rcd        =J.Empl_Rcd
And  (Months_Between(Sysdate,decode
 (A.ReHire_Date,A.Null,A.Hire_Dt,ReHire_Dt))) >= 12

End-Select
End-Procedure
```

Placing the date difference calculation in the Where clause makes the program database-dependent.

In Test26N.sqr, we use the Months_Between Oracle function to calculate the difference between the system date and the hire or rehire date. We also use another Oracle function, Decode, when deciding which date should be used in the calculation: Hire_Date or Rehire_Date. As you can see, the program becomes smaller and more efficient since, instead of selecting all current records, we select only ones that satisfy the Where clause. But speed comes with a price tag: the program loses database independence.

28.4.4 Producing an employee fifth anniversary list

In the following example, we will show you how to generate a list of employees who are eligible to receive the Fifth Anniversary Award. The program in the example runs once a year as of January 1 and produces a list of all employees who will receive the award during the run year. We will use the Oracle date calculations functions in this example:

```
! TEST28O.SQR
!Creating an employee fifth anniversary list
...
Begin-Procedure Main
Begin-Select
A.Emplid         (+1,1)
A.Hire_Dt        (,+1)
A.Rehire_Dt      (,+1)
J.Empl_Status    (,+1)

From PS_Employment A, PS_Job J
Where   A.Emplid          =J.Emplid
And      A.Empl_Rcd       =J.Empl_Rcd
And      J.Empl_Status     = 'A'
And    (Months_Between(Sysdate,decode(A.ReHire_Dt,Null,
       A.Hire_Dt,A.ReHire_Dt)) / 12) > 4
And    (Months_Between(Sysdate,decode(A.ReHire_Dt,Null,
       A.Hire_Dt,A.ReHire_Dt)) / 12)<= 5
```

Placing the date difference calculation in the Where clause makes the program database-dependent.

```
And       J.Effdt    =(Select Max(J1.Efdt)
               From PS_JOB J1
               Where J1.Emplid     = J.Emplid
               And J1.Empl_Rcd     = J.Empl_Rcd
               And J1.Effdt        <= $AsofToday)
And       J.Effseq   =(Select Max(J2.Effseq)
               From PS_JOB J2
               Where J2.Emplid     = J.Emplid
               And J2.Empl_Rcd     = J.Empl_Rcd
               And J2.Effdt        = J.Effdt)
End-Select
End-Procedure
...
```

As you can see, the program uses Oracle-specific functions. If we want to make our program database independent, we would have to break the above selection into two steps: select all active employees in the main procedure, and, then, for every selected employee, calculate the time difference between their hire or rehire date and today's date, using the `datediff()` SQR function.

KEY POINTS

1. Placing effective dates in table records allows for managing and tracking data changes over time.
2. Tables that contain the effective date columns are usually called the effective-dated tables.
3. PeopleSoft relates all effective-dated rows to one of the three categories: historical rows, current row, or future rows.
4. There can be only one current record for a particular table key.
5. In PeopleSoft, if the effective date is present in a table record, it is always a part of the table key.
6. The effective sequence fields, when paired with the effective date fields, allow for entering more than one row with the same effective date.

KEY POINTS (CONTINUED)

7 The `Max` SQL aggregate function can be used to select the current rows from an effective-dated table.

8 You can improve performance when selecting the current records by sorting the table by the effective date and sequence and using `Loops=1` to limit the output of sub-queries to only one record.

9 You can select both the current and prior rows from an effective-dated table.

10 You can use the `Exists` SQL operator to select only specific prior rows.

11 Date intervals between events can be calculated using either SQR date functions or database-specific functions. Avoiding database-specific functions makes your programs database-independent.

appendix A

Sample database

In this appendix we will discuss the sample database that was used to run the SQL-related examples throughout the book.

When creating this database, we used the PeopleSoft HRMS database as a model to make our test examples as close to real life applications as possible. At the same time, our database is different from the PeopleSoft database. We included only tables that were used in our test programs and examples. This does not mean that other tables are not important, we simply did not use them in our book. When creating our tables, we included only those columns that were essential to run our examples. We assigned the columns the same names as their PeopleSoft counterparts' names to avoid confusion and to make our examples closer to those in real business experiences. (In certain cases, we had to simplify the table structure by including only one of several related columns. For example, we included only the `Address1` column into the `Personal_Data` table instead of the four address columns: `Address1`, `Address2`, `Address3`, and `Address4`.)

In order to emphasize the difference between the PeopleSoft database and the database used in the SQR-related chapters (parts 1 and 2), our tables do not have the `PS_` prefix in their names. When running the PeopleSoft-related examples (part 3 of this book), we had to use the PeopleSoft database to take advantage of many existing PeopleSoft objects and `SQC` files. In these examples, the table names are prefixed with `PS_`.

Figure A.1 displays the sample database, its tables, and the relationships between these tables. This figure is identical to the one included in chapter 2.

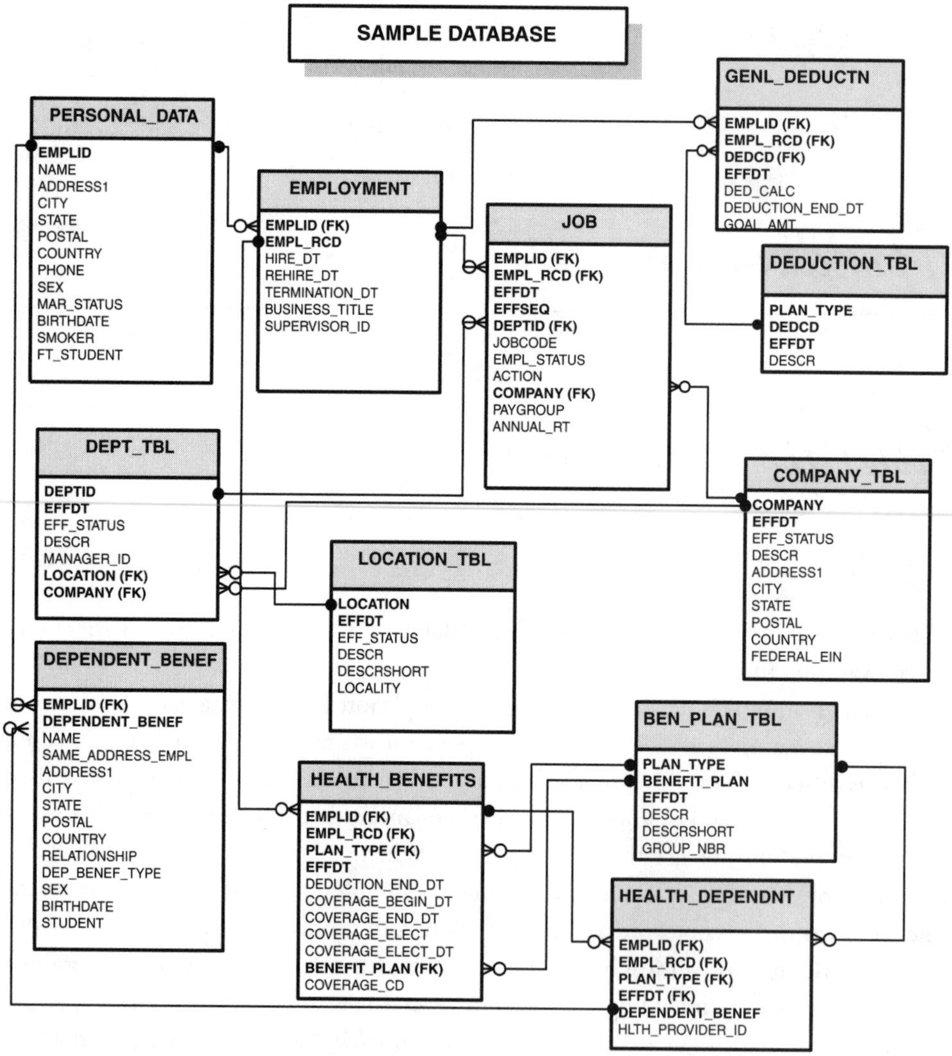

Figure A.1 Sample database tables

The `Personal_Data` table is the anchor table in the database. It contains personal information about each employee: name, address, phone, sex, marital status, etc. and is used to record data that do not tend to change. The table has one record per each employee. Its primary key is `Emplid`.

Column Name	Format	Description	Note
Emplid	`Char`	Unique employee ID	Primary key
Name	`Char`	Employee name	
Address1	`Char`	Employee address	
City	`Char`	Employee's city of residence	
State	`Char`	Employee's state of residence	
Postal	`Char`	Employee ZIP code	
Country	`Char`	Employee country	
Phone	`Char`	Employee home phone	
Sex	`Char`	Employee sex	
Mar_Status	`Char`	Employee marital status	
Birthdate	`Date`	Employee birth date	
Smoker	`Char`	Smoker char Smoker flag (Y/N)	
FT_Student	`char`	Full-time student flag (Y/N)	

The `Employment` table is one of the most important tables in the database. It contains each employee's job-related information that does not tend to change. The table has one record per each employee's employment assignment. This table is not designed to store historical information. (For example, if an employee's business title changes, the new title replaces the old one.) Its primary key is a combination of `Emplid` and `Empl_Rcd`. Its parent is the `Personal_Data` table.

Column Name	Format	Description	Note
Emplid	`Char`	Employee ID	Part of primary key
Empl_Rcd	`Number`	Employment record number. Used to differentiate between different jobs	Part of primary key
Hire_Dt	`Date`	Hire date	
Rehire_Dt	`Date`	Rehire date	
Termination_Dt	`Date`	Termination date	
Business_Title	`Char`	Business title	
Supervisor_Id	`Char`	Supervisor ID	

The `Job` table is also one of the most important tables in the database. It contains each employee's job-related information that changes over time. The table has one record per event that occurs in the course of employment. This table is designed to store historical information about different events. Its primary key is a combination of `Emplid`, `Empl_Rcd`, `Effdt`, and `Effseq`. Its parent is the `Employment` table.

Column Name	Format	Purpose	Note
Emplid	`Char`	Employee ID	Part of primary key
Empl_Rcd	`Number`	Employment record number. Used to differentiate between different jobs	Part of primary key
Effdt	`Date`	Effective date of an event	Part of primary key
Effseq	`Number`	Effective sequence: used to control multiple events that may occur on the same effective date	Part of primary key
Deptid	`Char`	Department ID	Foreign key to Dept_Tbl
Jobcode	`Char`	Job code	
Empl_Status	`Char`	Employee status, e.g., "A" (active), "T" (terminated), etc.	
Action	`Char`	Action, e.g., "PRO" (promotion)	
Company	`Char`	Company	Foreign key to Company_Tbl
Paygroup	`Char`	Paygroup	
Annual_Rt	`Number`	Annual rate	

The `Dept_Tbl` table contains information about each department. This table is designed to store historical information. Its primary key is a combination of `Deptid` and `Effdt`.

Column Name	Format	Description	Note
Deptid	`Char`	Department ID	Part of primary key
Effdt	`Date`	Effective date	Part of primary key
Eff_Status	`Char`	Effective status	
Descr	`Char`	Department description	
Manager_Id	`Char`	Manager ID	
Location	`Char`	Location code	Foreign key to Location_Tbl
Company	`Char`	Company ID	Foreign key to Company_Tbl

The `Location_Tbl` table contains information about each location. This table is designed to store historical information. Its primary key is a combination of `Location` and `Effdt`.

Column Name	Format	Description	Note
Location	`Char`	Department ID	Part of primary key
Effdt	`Date`	Effective date	Part of primary key
Eff_Status	`Char`	Effective status	
Descr	`Char`	Location description	
Descrshort	`Char`	Short description	
Locality	`Char`	Locality	

The `Company_Tbl` table contains information about each company. This table is designed to store historical information. Its primary key is a combination of `Company` and `Effdt`.

Column Name	Format	Description	Note
Company	`Char`	Company ID	Part of primary key
Effdt	`Date`	Effective date	Part of primary key
Eff_Status	`Char`	Effective status	
Descr	`Char`	Company description	
Address1	`Char`	Company address	
City	`Char`	City	
State	`Char`	State	
Postal	`Char`	ZIP code	
Country	`Char`	Country	
Federal_EIN	`Number`	Federal Employer ID Number	

The `Dependent_Benef` table contains information about each employee's dependents. The table has one record per each employee's dependent. This table is not designed to store historical information. Its primary key is a combination of `Emplid` and `Dependent_Benef`. Its parent is the `Personal_Data` table.

Column Name	Format	Description	Note
Emplid	Char	Employee ID	Part of primary key
Dependent_Benef	Char	Dependent code	Part of primary key
Name	Char	Dependent name	
Address1	Char	Dependent address	
City	Char	Dependent's city of residence	
State	Char	Dependent's state of residence	
Postal	Char	Dependent's ZIP code	
Country	Char	Dependent's country	
Relationship	Char	Relationship to employee	
Dep_Benef_Type	Char	Dependent beneficiary type	
Sex	Char	Dependent's sex	
Birthdate	Date	Dependent birth date	
Student	Char	Student indicator (Yes/No)	

The `Health_Benefits` table contains information about each employee health benefits. This table is designed to store historical information. Its primary key is a combination of `Emplid`, `Empl_Rcd`, `Plan_Type`, and `Effdt`.

Column Name	Format	Description	Note
Emplid	Char	Employee ID	Part of primary key
Empl_Rcd	Number	Employment record number	Part of primary key
Plan_Type	Char	Plan type code	Part of primary key
Effdt	Date	Effective date	Part of primary key
Deduction_End_Dt	Date	Deduction end date	
Coverage_Begin_Dt	Date	Coverage begin date	
Coverage_End_Dt	Date	Coverage end date	
Coverage_Elect	Char	Coverage election code	
Coverage_Elect_Dt	Date	Coverage election date	
Benefit_Plan	Char	Benefit plan	Foreign key to Benef_Plan_Tbl
Coverage_Cd	Char	Coverage code	

The `Health_Dependnt` table contains information about each employee's dependent health benefits. This table is designed to store historical information. Its primary key is a combination of `Emplid`, `Empl_Rcd`, `Plan_Type`, `Effdt`, and `Dependent_Benef` columns.

Column Name	Format	Description	Note
Emplid	`Char`	Employee ID	Part of primary key
Empl_Rcd	`Number`	Employment record number	Part of primary key
Plan_Type	`Char`	Plan type code	Part of primary key
Effdt	`Date`	Effective date	Part of primary key
Dependent_Benef	`Char`	Dependent code	Part of primary key
Hlth_Provider_Id	`Char`	Health provider ID	

The `Ben_Plan_Tbl` table contains information about available benefit plans. This table is designed to store historical information. Its primary key is a combination of `Plan_Type`, `Benefit_Plan`, and `Effdt` columns.

Column Name	Format	Description	Note
Plan_Type	`Char`	Plan type	Part of primary key
Benefit_Plan	`Char`	Benefit plan	Part of primary key
Effdt	`Date`	Effective date	Part of primary key
Descr	`Char`	Plan description	
Descrshort	`Char`	Short plan description	
Provider	`Char`	Plan provider	

The `Genl_Deductn` table contains information about each employee's payroll deductions. This table is designed to store historical information. Its primary key is a combination of `Emplid`, `Empl_Rcd`, `Dedcd`, and `Effdt` columns.

Column Name	Format	Description	Note
Emplid	`Char`	Employee ID	Part of primary key
Empl_Rcd	`Number`	Employment record number	Part of primary key
Dedcd	`Char`	Deduction code	Part of primary key
Effdt	`Date`	Effective date	Part of primary key
Ded_Calc	`Char`	Deduction calculation routine	
Deduction_End_Dt	`Date`	Deduction end date	
Goal_Amt	`Number`	Goal amount	

The Deductn_Tbl table contains information about different types of payroll deductions for each plan type. This table is designed to store historical information. Its primary key is a combination of Plan_Type, Dedcd, and Effdt columns.

Column Name	Format	Description	Note
Plan_Type	Char	Plan type	Part of primary key
Dedcd	Char	Deduction code	Part of primary key
Effdt	Date	Effective date	Part of primary key
Description	Char	Plan type description	

appendix B

SQR command line flags

SQR command line flags can be entered in the report argument portion of the SQR Dialog Box, or as a part of the SQR command line of the SQR Execute command line, or the SQR Print command line. SQR, SQR Execute, and SQR Print use different sets of flags.

In the following table, all SQR command line flags are listed alphabetically. The table includes all SQR flags. Three separate table columns indicate which SQR product uses each specific flag.

Flag	Dialog Box	SQR Command Line	SQR Execute	SQR Print	Description
-A	Y	Y	Y	Y	The program output will be appended to an existing output file. If the file does not exist, a new one will be created. This option is not allowed for PDS files (MVS).
-Bnn	Y	Y	Y	N	(Oracle, Sybase CT-Lib) The size of a buffer to hold retrieved rows each time data is retrieved from the database. The default is ten rows. You can enhance performance by increasing the number of rows in the buffer. Regardless of the setting, all rows are retrieved. When used on the command line, `-B` controls the setting for all `Begin-Select` commands. Within a program, each `Begin-Select` command may also have its own `-Bnn` flag for further optimization.
-BURST:{*xx*}	Y	Y	Y	Y	This flag is used when either the `-PRINTER:HT` or `-PRINTER:EH` flag is specified (for Internet enabling). Using this flag allows you to divide your HTML output into smaller files for faster load time or to generate only certain portions of the entire report. `-BURST:T` generates the Table of Contents file. `BURST:S[i ]` generates the report output according to the symbolic Table of Contents entries. *i* is the level at which to burst upon (as defined in the `TOC-ENTRY` command) `-BURST:P [ i, s [, s] . . . ] ]` where *i* is the number of logical report pages in each `.htm` file and s is the page to burst upon
-C	Y	Y	Y	N	(Windows) The Cancel dialog box will appear while the program is running so you can terminate the program execution.
-CB	Y	Y	Y	N	(Windows) Forces the communication box to be used (the default setting)

Flag	Dialog Box	SQR Command Line	SQR Execute	SQR Print	Description
-D*nn*	N	N	Y	Y	(non-Windows) The program output report will be displayed on the terminal while it is being written to the output file. *nn* is the maximum number of lines to display before pausing. If no maximum number of lines is specified, the display will scroll down continuously. The printer type must be LP or the display will be ignored
-DB *database*	N	Y	Y	N	(SYBASE) The database name. This flag will override any `Use` command in the program.
-DEBUG [*xxx*]	Y	Y	N	N	When this flag is specified, all source code lines preceded by "`#Debug`*Y*" will be compiled. *y* is any character among *xxx* or space. Without this flag, these lines are ignored.
-DNT:[*xx*]	Y	Y	N	N	Specifies the default behavior for numeric variables. The value for xx can be `Integer`, `Float`, `Decimal`, or `V30`. If V30 is specified, all numeric variables are considered float. To specify a precision for `Decimal`, append it with a colon delimiter (:)—for example, `DNT:Decimal:20`. Can be overridden by the `Default` parameter in the `Declare-Variable` command.
-E[*file*]	Y	Y	Y	Y	Causes SQR error messages to be directed to the named file. The default file is your program name with the `.err` extension. If no errors occur, no file is created. If this flag is specified, all SQR-generated errors (not the output of the `Display` or `Show` commands) will be directed to this file instead of the `LOG` file. You should either specify the fully qualified file name or no file name (do not specify the flag and the directory).

Flag	Dialog Box	SQR Command Line	SQR Execute	SQR Print	Description
-EH_APPLETS:*dir*	Y	Y	Y	Y	This flag is used only when either the –PRINTER:EP or –PRINTER:EH flag is specified. It specifies a directory where the Enhanced HTML applets reside. The default directory is where the GIF files used by the Navigation Bar reside.
-EH_BQD	Y	Y	Y	Y	This flag is used only when either the –PRINTER:EP or –PRINTER:EH flag is specified. When specified, SQR generates a BQD (Brio Query Format) file (with the name equal to your report name and the .BQD extension) and a BQD icon in the Navigation Bar.
-EH_BQD:*file_name*	Y	Y	Y	Y	This flag is used only when either the –PRINTER:EP or –PRINTER:EH flag is specified. When specified, SQR associates the BQD icon with the specified file.
-EH_BROWSER:*browser_code*	Y	Y	Y	Y	This flag is used only when either the –PRINTER:EP or –PRINTER:EH flag is specified. This flag specifies the target HTML browser. When browser_code is set to BASIC, SQR generates HTML suitable for all browsers. When browser_code is set to ALL, SQR generates a Java script which senses which browser is installed on the user's machine. When browser_code is set to IE, SQR generates HTML designed for Internet Explorer. When browser_code is set to NETSCAPE, SQR generates HTML designed for Netscape Navigator.
-EH_CSV	Y	Y	Y	Y	This flag is used only when either the –PRINTER:EP or –PRINTER:EH flag is specified. When specified, SQR generates a CSV (Comma Separated File) file (with the name equal to your report name and the .CSV extension) and a CSV icon in the Navigation Bar.

Flag	Dialog Box	SQR Command Line	SQR Execute	SQR Print	Description
-EH_CSV:*file_name*	Y	Y	Y	Y	This flag is used only when either the –PRINTER:EP or –PRINTER:EH flag is specified. When specified, SQR associates the CSV icon with the specified file.
-EH_CSVONLY	Y	Y	Y	Y	This flag is used only when either the –PRINTER:EP or –PRINTER:EH flag is specified. When specified, SQR generates a CSV file and a CSV icon in the Navigation Bar without generating an HTML file.
-EH_FULLHTML: *level*	Y	Y	Y	Y	This flag is used only when either the –PRINTER:EP or –PRINTER:EH flag is specified. This flag specifies the level of the Enhanced HTML code. Possible values are 30, 32, 40, TRUE (equivalent to 40), or FALSE (equivalent to 30).
-EH_ICONS: *dir*	Y	Y	Y	Y	This flag is used only when either the –PRINTER:HT or –PRINTER:EH flag is specified. This flag specifies the directory for the icons used in the HTML.
-EH_IMAGES: *dir*	Y	Y	Y	Y	This flag is used only when either the –PRINTER:EP or –PRINTER:EH flag is specified. This flag specifies the directory for the GIF files used by the Navigation Bar.
-EH_KEEP	Y	Y	N	N	This flag is used in conjunction with the –EH_ZIP flag and only when either the –PRINTER:EP or –PRINTER:EH flag is specified. When specified, SQR keeps its output files after copying them to the specified ZIP file.
-EH_LANGUAGE: *language*	Y	Y	Y	Y	This flag is used only when either the –PRINTER:EP or –PRINTER:EH flag is specified. This flag specifies the language used for the HTML Navigation Bar. Possible values are ENGLISH, FRENCH, GERMAN, PORTUGUESE, SPANISH.

Flag	Dialog Box	SQR Command Line	SQR Execute	SQR Print	Description
-EH_PDF	Y	Y	Y	Y	This flag is used only when either the –PRINTER:EP or –PRINTER:EH flag is specified. When specified, SQR generates an Adobe PDF file (with the name equal to your report name and the .PDF extension) and a PDF icon in the Navigation Bar.
-EH_SCALE[:*nnn*]	Y	Y	N	N	This flag is used in conjunction with the –EH_ZIP flag and only when either the –PRINTER:EP or –PRINTER:EH flag is specified. Sets the scaling factor for the report body from 50 to 200.
-EH_XML: *file_name*	Y	Y	N	N	This flag is used only when either the –PRINTER:EP or –PRINTER:EH flag is specified. When specified, SQR associates the XML icon with the specified file.
-EH_ZIP[: *file_name*]	Y	Y	N	N	This flag is used only when either –PRINTER:EP or –PRINTER:EH flag is specified. When specified, SQR moves the output files to the specified file or to your_report_name.ZIP if no file name is specified.
-F[*file* | *directory*]	Y	Y	Y	Y	Overrides the default output report `LIS` file name. If this flag is not specified, the output file will be created in the same directory in which the source program file resides. The default file name is your program name with the `.lis` extension. To use the current directory, specify `-F` without an argument. If the file name does not include a directory, the file will be created in the current directory. For multiple report programs, you can use multiple `-F` flags.
-G file_mode	N	N	Y	Y	(VM) specifies the file mode to use when the report output file is created. See the VM C library manual "`afopen`" function, for a complete description of all the valid keywords and values.

Flag	Dialog Box	SQR Command Line	SQR Execute	SQR Print	Description
-G *file_attributes*	N	N	Y	Y	(VMS, Open VMS) Specifies the file attributes to use when the report file is created. See the VAX C library manual, "`create`" function for a complete description of all the valid keywords and values.
-GPRINT =YES|NO	N	N	Y	N	(MVS) `-GPRINT=YES` causes SQR report file to have ANSI control characters written to the first column of each record of the file.
-ID	N	N	Y	Y	Causes the copyright banner to be displayed on the console
-I*dir_list*	Y	Y	N	N	Specifies the list of directories that SQR will search when processing the `#Include` directive if the include file does not exist in the current directory. The directory names must be separated by either commas (,) or semicolons (;).
-KEEP	Y	Y	Y	N	Causes SQR to create `SPF` output in addition to `LIS` output
-LL{s|d} {c|i}	Y	Y	N	N	The sorting method to be used in the `Load-Lookup` command: s = SQR sorts data, d = database sorts data, c = case sensitive sort, i = case insensitive sort.
-LOCK {RR|CS |RON | RL | XX}		Y	Y	N	(SQLBase) Defines the types of locking (isolation level) for the session
-M*file*	Y	Y	N	N	Defines a startup file containing sizes to be assigned to various internal parameters for large or complex reports
-NOLIS	Y	Y	Y	N	Causes SQR to create `SPF` output and suppress LIS output
-NR	N	Y	Y	N	(SQLBase) No Recovery mode is used when connecting to the database.
-O[*file*]	Y	Y	Y	Y	Directs log messages to the specified file. If `-O` with no file is specified, the log file name will be your program name with the `.log` extension. By default, the file `SQR.log` is created in the current working directory

Flag	Dialog Box	SQR Command Line	SQR Execute	SQR Print	Description
-P	N	N	Y	Y	(VM) Directs the output to the printer device
-PB	N	Y	Y	N	(Informix) Causes column data to retain trailing blanks
-Proleid [rolepass]	N	Y	Y	N	(Ingres) The role identifier used to associate permissions with SQR
-PRINTER: xx	Y	Y	Y	Y	Causes printer type xx to be used when creating all `LIS` files. Available printer types: LP (Line Printer), HP (HP LaserJet), HT (HTML), EH (Enhanced HTML), EP (Enhanced HTML/PDF), PD (PDF), PS (PostScript), WP (Windows default printer). The WP parameter sends the output to the default Windows printer. All other extensions send the output to the `LIS` file.
-RS	Y	Y	N	N	Saves the program in a pre-compiled file. The program is scanned and checked for correct syntax. Queries are validated. Then, the executable version is saved in a file with the name equal to your source program name and the `.sqt` extension. The `Ask` command variables are not prompted for after compilation. You can either use -RT flag to execute a pre-compiled program or the `SQR Execute`.
-RT	Y	Y	N	N	Executes pre-compiled files saved with the `-RS` flag. All syntax and query checking is skipped and processing begins immediately. The `Ask` command variables are not prompted for after compilation. Another way to run pre-compiled SQR programs is to use the `SQR Execute`.

Flag	Dialog Box	SQR Command Line	SQR Execute	SQR Print	Description
-S	Y	Y	Y	N	Requests that the status of all cursors be displayed at the end of the report run. Status includes the text of each SQL statement, number of times each was compiled and executed, and the total number of rows selected. This information can be used for debugging SQL statements and enhancing performance and tuning.
-SORT*nn*	N	Y	Y	N	(SQLBase) Specifies the size of the sort buffer in characters
-T*nn*	Y	Y	Y	N	Specifies that you want to test your report for the first *nn* pages only. All `ORDER BY` clauses in `SELECT` statements are ignored to save time during testing. In multiple report programs this flag causes SQR to stop when the specified number of pages for the first report have been output.
-T {BZ|BZ|ZB}	N	Y	Y	N	(MVS) Prevents SQR from removing trailing blanks and zeros from database columns. `-TB` will prevent the trimming of blanks from character columns. `-TZ` will prevent the trimming of trailing zeros from the decimal portion of floating columns. `-TBZ` or `-TZB` will prevent both.
-U*username*	N	Y	Y	N	(Ingres) Specifies the user name. This overrides the user name specified in the connectivity string.
-V*server*	N	Y	Y	N	(SYBASE) Uses the named server
-XB	Y	N	Y	Y	(non-Windows) Suppresses the SQR banner and the "SQR ... end of Run" message
XC	N	Y	N	N	Suppresses the database Commit when the report has finished running.
-XCB	Y	Y	Y	N	Suppresses the SQR communication box. Requests for input will be made in Windows dialog boxes.

Flag	Dialog Box	SQR Command Line	SQR Execute	SQR Print	Description
-XI	Y	Y	N	N	Prevents user interaction during a program run. If the `Ask` or `Input` command requires user input, an error occurs.
-XL	Y	Y	Y	N	Prevents SQR from logging on to the database. Programs run in this mode cannot contain any SQL statements. You still must supply a forward slash (/) on the command line as a placeholder for the connectivity information.
-XLFF	Y	Y	N	N	Prevents trailing form feed.
-XMB	Y	Y	Y	N	Disables the error message display so that a program can be run without interruption by error message boxes. Error messages will only be sent to an `.err` file.
-XNAV	Y	Y	Y	N	Prevents SQR from generating the "Navigation Bar" in generated `.htm` files. This will occur when only a single `.htm` file is produced. Multiple `.htm` files generated from a single report will always contain the "Navigation Bar".
-XP	N	Y	Y	N	(SYBASE DBLib) Prevents SQR from creating temporary stored procedures
-XTB	Y	Y	Y	Y	Preserves the trailing blanks in a `.lis` file
-XTOC	Y	Y	Y	Y	Prevents SQR from generating the Table of Contents for the report. This flag is ignored when `-PRINTER:HT` or `-PRINTER:EH` is also specified.
-ZIF*file*	Y	Y	Y	Y	Overrides the default directory for the SQR initialization file, `SQR.ini`
-ZIV	Y	Y	Y	N	Invokes the `SPF Viewer` after generating SPF output. In case of multiple output files, only the first report file will be passed to the `SQR Viewer`.

Flag	Dialog Box	SQR Command Line	SQR Execute	SQR Print	Description
-ZMF*file*	Y	Y	Y	Y	Specifies the full path and name of the SQR error message file, `SQR-err.dat`
-ZRF{*file_name*}	Y	Y	Y	Y	Specifies the full name of an alternate `registry.properties` file. This file lists data sources that SQR server can access.

appendix C

Built-in functions

SQR built-in functions are used in expressions in the `Let` command and in logical expressions in the `If [ Else]` and `While` operators.

SQR offers more than 50 different built-in functions. In addition, you can write your own functions in `C` using the supplied source file `Ufunc.c` (see chapter 18 for details).

All SQR built-in functions can be divided into the following five categories:

- numeric functions
- file-related functions
- date functions
- string functions
- miscellaneous functions.

In this appendix, we grouped all the functions by the above categories and listed the functions along with their descriptions, syntax, and examples of usage.

Numeric functions

abs()

Description	Returns the absolute value of its argument
Syntax	*target_var* = `abs` ({ *num_value* | *num_expression* })
Arguments	A decimal, float, or integer literal, column, or expression
Returns	The type of the returned value is same as the function's argument type

Example

```
Let #Diff = abs( #Plan - #Actual)
```

acos(), asin(), atan()

Description	Returns the arccosine, arcsine, or arctangent value of its argument
Syntax	*target_var* = `acos` ({ *num_value* | *num_expression* }) *target_var* = `asin` ({ *num_value* | *num_expression* }) *target_var* = `atan` ({ *num_value* | *num_expression* })
Arguments	A decimal, float, or integer literal, column, variable, or expression between -1 and 1 for `acos()`, `asin()`, and between 0 and high value for `atan()`
Returns	A float numeric in radians between 0 and π for `acos()`, or a float numeric in radians between -π/2 and π/2 for `asin()` and `atan()`

Examples

```
Let #Num1 = acos( 0 )
Let #Num2 = asin(#var2)
Let #Num3 = atan(#tan3 / 2)
```

cos(), sin(), tan()

Description	Returns the cosine, sine, or tangent value of its argument
Syntax	*target_var* = `cos` ({ *num_value* | *num_expression* }) *target_var* = `sin` ({ *num_value* | *num_expression* }) *target_var* = `tan` ({ *num_value* | *num_expression* })
Arguments	A decimal, float, or integer literal, column, variable, or expression in radians
Returns	A float numeric between -1 and 1 for `cos()` and `sin()`, or a float numeric between 0 and high value for `tan()`

Examples

```
Let #Cos = cos( 0 )
Let #Sin = sin(#var2)
Let #Tan = tan(#Var1 + #Var2)
```

cosh(), sinh(), tanh()

Description	Returns the hyperbolic cosine, sine, or tangent value of its argument
Syntax	*target_var* = `cosh` ({ *num_value* | *num_expression* }) *target_var* = `sinh` ({ *num_value* | *num_expression* }) *target_var* = `tanh` ({ *num_value* | *num_expression* })
Arguments	A decimal, float, or integer literal, column, variable, or expression
Returns	A float numeric

Examples

```
Let #Cosh = cosh(#Var1)
Let #Sinh = sinh(#Var2)
Let #Tanh = tanh(#Var3)
```

ceil(), floor()

Description	For `ceil()`, returns the smallest integer that is greater than or equal to the value of its argument. For negative arguments, returns a negative integer with an absolute value that is less than or equal to the absolute value of its argument for `floor()`, returns the largest integer that is less than or equal to the value of its argument. For negative arguments, returns a negative integer with an absolute value that is greater than or equal to the absolute value of its argument
Syntax	*target_var* = `ceil`({ *num_value* | *num_expression* }) *target_var* = `floor`({ *num_value* | *num_expression* })
Arguments	A decimal, float, or integer literal, column, or expression
Returns	The type of the returned value is same as the function's argument type

Example

```
Let #Ceil = ceil(#Var1)
Let #Floor = floor(#Var2)
```

deg(), rad()

Description	For `deg()`, converts degrees to radians For `rad()`, converts radians to degrees
Syntax	*target_var* = `deg`({ *num_value* | *num_expression* }) *target_var* = `rad`({ *num_value* | *num_expression* })

Arguments	A decimal, float, or integer literal, column, or expression
Returns	A float numeric

Example

```
Let #Degrees = deg(#Radians)
Let #Radians = rad(#Degrees)
```

e10(), exp()

Description	Returns the value of 10, or e raised to its argument
Syntax	*target_var* = `e10`({ *num_value* | *num_expression* }) *target_var* = `exp`({ *num_value* | *num_expression* })
Arguments	A decimal, float, or integer literal, column, or expression
Returns	A float numeric

Example

```
Let #Dec_Value = e10(#Var1)
Let #Exp_Value = exp(#Var2)
```

log(), log10()

Description	Calculates the natural or base-10 logarithm of its argument
Syntax	*target_var* = `log`({ *num_value* | *num_expression* }) *target_var* = `log10`({ *num_value* | *num_expression* })
Arguments	A decimal, float, or integer literal, column, or expression
Returns	A float numeric

Example

```
Let #Nat_Log = log(#Var1)
Let #Base10_Log = log10(#Var2)
```

mod()

Description	Returns the fractional remainder of a division of its first argument by its second argument
Syntax	*target_var* = `mod`({*num_value-X* | *num_expression_X*},{*num_value-Y* | *num_expression_Y*})
Arguments	A decimal, float, or integer literal, column, or expression. The second argument must not be a zero
Returns	The arguments are promoted to the type of the greatest precision and the function returns a value of that type

Example

```
Let #Rem = mod(#VarX, #VarY)
```

power()

Description	Returns the value of its first argument raised to the power of its second argument
Syntax	*target_var* = `power`({*num_value-X* | *num_expression_X*},{*num_value-Y* | *num_expression_Y*})
Arguments	*First argument*: a decimal, float, or integer literal, column, or expression *Second argument*: a decimal, float, or integer literal, column, or expression
Returns	A float numeric

Example

```
Let #Power_Var =power(#VarX, #VarY)
```

round(), trunc()

Description	`round()` rounds its first argument to the number of decimal places determined by its second argument `trunc()` truncates its first argument to the number of decimal places determined by its second argument
Syntax	*target_var* = `round`({*num_value-X* | *num_expression_X*},{*num_value-Y* | *num_expression_Y*}) *target_var* = `trunc`({*num_value-X* | *num_expression_X*},{*num_value-Y* | *num_expression_Y*})
Arguments	*First argument*: a decimal, float, or integer literal, column, or expression *Second argument*: an integer literal, column, or expression
Returns	A value of the same type as the first argument

Example

```
Let #Round_Result =round(#VarX, #PrecisionX)
Let #Trunc_Result =trunc(#VarY, #PrecisionY)
```

sign()

Description	Returns -1, 0, or +1 depending on the sign of its argument
Syntax	*target_var* = `sign`({*num_value* | *num_expression*})
Arguments	A decimal, float, or integer literal, column, or expression
Returns	-1, 0, or 1

Example

```
Let #Sign = sign(#Var1)
```

`sqrt()`

Description	Calculates the square root of its argument
Syntax	*target_var* = `sqrt`({*num_value* | *num_expression*})
Arguments	A non-negative decimal, float, or integer literal, column, or expression
Returns	A float numeric

Example

```
Let #Sqrt_Val = sqrt(#Var)
```

File-related functions

`delete()`

Description	Deletes the specified file
Syntax	*status_var* = `delete`(*file_name*)
Arguments	A string literal, column, or expression
Returns	Zero, if the file was deleted or an operating system specific return code if the file was not deleted

Example

```
Let #Result = delete($File_Name)
```

`exists()`

Description	Determines if the specified file exists
Syntax	*status_var* = `exists`(*file_name*)
Arguments	A string literal, column, or expression
Returns	Zero, if the file was found or an operating system specific return code if the file was not found

Example

```
Let #Exists = exists($File_Name)
```

`rename()`

Description	Determines if the specified file exists
Syntax	*status_var* = `rename`(*file_name*)

Arguments	A string literal, column, or expression
Returns	Zero, if the file was renamed or an operating system specific return code if the file was not renamed

Example

```
Let #Renamed = rename($File_Name)
```

Date functions

dateadd()

Description	Adds the specified number of date/time units to the function's first argument and returns the result of addition
Syntax	*target_date* = `dateadd`(*source_date* , *date_unit* , *quantity*)
Arguments	*First argument*: a date literal, column, or expression *Second argument*: a string literal, column, variable, or expression. Specifies the type of the date/time unit. Valid units are: `'YEAR'`, `'QUARTER'`, `'WEEK'`, `'MONTH'`, `'DAY'`, `'HOUR'`, `'MINUTE'`, `'SECOND'` *Third argument*: a numeric literal, column, variable, or expression. Specifies the number of date units to be added
Returns	A date

Example

```
Let $Fifth_Anniversary_Dte = dateadd(&Hire_Dte,'YEAR',5)
```

datediff()

Description	Calculates the difference between the specified dates expressed in the specified number of date/time units
Syntax	*date_diff* = `datediff`(*date_1* , *date_2* , *date_unit*)
Arguments	*First argument*: a date literal, column, or expression *Second argument*: a date literal, column, or expression *Third argument*: a string literal, column, variable, or expression. Specifies the type of the date/time unit. Valid units are: `'YEAR'`, `'QUARTER'`, `'WEEK'`, `'MONTH'`, `'DAY'`, `'HOUR'`, `'MINUTE'`, `'SECOND'`
Returns	A float numeric

Example

```
Let #Date_Diff = datediff($Eff_Dte, $Curr_Dte, 'DAY' )
```

datenow()

Description	Returns the current local date and time from the client machine
Syntax	*curr_date* = `datenow ( )`
Arguments	None
Returns	A date

Example

```
Let $Curr_Dte = datenow()
```

datetostr()

Description	Converts a date to a string with optional editing
Syntax	*target_string* = `datetostr` (*source_date* , [*edit_mask*])
Arguments	*First argument*: a date variable or expression *Second argument (optional)*: a string literal, column, variable, or expression specifying the edit mask. If not specified, the `SQR_DB_DATE_FORMAT` setting will be used. If the setting is not specified, the database-dependent format will be used
Returns	A string

Example

```
Let $Date_String = datetostr(datenow(), 'DD-MM-YY' )
```

strtodate()

Description	Converts a string to a date with optional editing
Syntax	*target_date* = `strtodate` (*source_string* , [*edit_mask*])
Arguments	*First argument*: a string literal, column, variable, or expression *Second argument (optional)*: a string literal, column, variable, or expression specifying the edit mask. If not specified, the `SQR_DB_DATE_FORMAT` setting will be used. If the setting is not specified, the database-dependent format or the database-independent format `'SYYYYMMDD[HH24[MI[SS[NNNNNN]]]]'` will be used
Returns	A date

Example

```
Let $Date = strtodate(&Eff_Dte, 'MON-DD-YYYY' )
```

String functions

`edit()`

Description	Formats the source string using the specified edit mask
Syntax	*target_string* = `edit` (*source_string* , *edit_mask*)
Arguments	*First argument*: a string literal, column, variable, or expression
	Second argument: a string literal, column, variable, or expression specifying the edit mask
Returns	A string

Example

```
Let $SSN= edit(&SSN, 'xxx-xx-xxxx' )
```

`instr()`

Description	Returns the numeric position of the specified sub-string within a string. The search begins at the specified position (starting from 1) within the string
Syntax	*position* = `instr` (*source_string* , *substring* , *position*)
Arguments	*First argument*: a date or string literal, column, variable, or expression
	Second argument: a string literal, column, variable, or expression specifying the searched sub-string
	Third argument: an integer literal, column, variable, or expression specifying the starting position
Returns	A float numeric

Example

```
Let #Pos= instr($Full_Name, 'Mary', 1 )
```

`instrb()`

Description	(Double-byte version of SQR only) Works similarly to `instr()` except that the starting point and returned value are expressed in bytes rather than in characters
Syntax	*position* = `instrb` (*source_string* , *substring* , *position*)
Arguments	*First argument*: a date or string literal, column, variable, or expression
	Second argument: a string literal, column, variable, or expression specifying the searched sub-string
	Third argument: an integer literal, column, variable, or expression specifying the starting position in bytes
Returns	A float numeric

Example

```
Let #Pos= instrb($Full_Name, 'Mary', 1 )
```

isblank()

Description	Returns a value of 1 if its argument is an empty string or composed of only whitespace characters; otherwise, returns a zero value
Syntax	*target_var* = `isblank` (*source_string*)
Arguments	A date or string literal, column, variable, or expression
Returns	0 or 1

Example

```
Let #Blank_Flag= isblank(&Full_Name )
```

isnull()

Description	Returns a value of 1 if its argument is `NULL`; otherwise, returns a zero value
Syntax	*target_var* = `isnull` (*source_string*)
Arguments	A date or string literal, column, variable, or expression
Returns	0 or 1

Example

```
If isnull(&Eff_Dte )
   Do Print_Error
Else
   Do Print_Detail
End-If
```

length()

Description	Returns the number of characters in its argument
Syntax	*length* = `length` (*source_string*)
Arguments	A date or string literal, column, variable, or expression
Returns	A float numeric

Example

```
Let #Length= length($Input_String )
```

`lengthb()`

Description	(Double-byte version of SQR only) Works similarly to `length()` except that the return value represents the number of bytes, rather than the number of characters
Syntax	*length* = `lengthb` (*source_string*)
Arguments	A date or string literal, column, variable, or expression
Returns	A float numeric

Example

```
Let #Length= lengthb($Input_String )
```

`lower(), upper()`

Description	Converts its argument to lower (upper) case. Does not convert special characters
Syntax	*target_string* = `lower` (*source_string*) *target_string* = `upper` (*source_string*)
Arguments	A date or string literal, column, variable, or expression
Returns	A string

Examples

```
Let #Lower_Case_String= lower($Input_String )
Let #Upper_Case_String= upper($Input_String )
```

`lpad(), rpad()`

Description	Pads its first argument on the left (right) to the length specified in its second argument using the value specified in its third argument
Syntax	*target_string* = `lpad` (*source_string* , *length* , *pad_value*) *target_string* = `rpad` (*source_string* , *length* , *pad_value*)
Arguments	*First argument*: a date or string literal, column, variable, or expression *Second argument*: a decimal, float, or integer literal, column, variable, or expression specifying the length of the sub-string to be padded *Third argument*: a string literal, column, variable, or expression specifying the substituting sub-string
Returns	A string

Examples

```
Let #Left_Padded_String= lpad($Input_String, #Length, ' ' )
Let #Right_Padded_String= rpad($Input_String, 5, '/' )
```

ltrim(), rtrim()

Description	Trims its first argument from the left (right) until a character specified in its second argument is not found
Syntax	*target_string* = `ltrim` (*source_string* , *trim_value*) *target_string* = `rtrim` (*source_string* , *trim_value*)
Arguments	*First argument*: a date or string literal, column, variable, or expression *Second argument*: a string literal, column, variable, or expression specifying the sub-string to be trimmed
Returns	A string

Examples

```
Let #Left_Trimmed_String= ltrim($Input_String, ' ' )
Let #Right_Trimmed_String= rtrim($Input_String, $Trim_Char )
```

replace()

Description	Scans the contents of source_string and replaces all occurrences of *from_string* with *to_string.*
Syntax	*target_string* = replace (*source_string, from_string, to_string*)
Arguments	*First argument:* a date or string literal, column, variable, or expression *Second argument:* a string literal, column, variable, or expression *Third argument:* a string literal, column, variable, or expression
Returns	A string.

Example

```
$New_Phone_Number = Replace($Old_Phone_Number,'-','/')
```

roman()

Description	Converts its argument to lower case roman numerals
Syntax	*target_string*= `roman` (*source_numeric*)
Argumenst	A decimal, float, or integer literal, column, variable, or expression
Returns	A string

Example

```
Let $Roman_Chapter_Number= roman(#Chapter_Number )
```

substr()

Description	Extracts the specified number of characters from its first string argument. The extraction begins at the specified position (starting from 1) within the string
Syntax	*target_string* = `substr` (*source_string* , *position*, *length*)
Arguments	*First argument*: a date or string literal, column, variable, or expression *Second argument*: a decimal, float, or integer literal, column, variable, or expression specifying the starting position of extraction *Third argument*: a decimal, float, or integer integer literal, column, variable, or expression specifying the number of extracted characters
Returns	A string

Example

```
Let #Substring=substr($Input_String, 1, #Length )
```

substrb()

Description	(Double-byte version of SQR only) Works similarly to `substr()` except that the position and length are expressed in the number of bytes, rather than in the number of characters
Syntax	*target_string* = `substrb` (*source_string* , *position*, *length*)
Arguments	*First argument*: a date or string literal, column, variable, or expression *Second argument*: a decimal, float, or integer literal, column, variable, or expression specifying the starting position of extraction in bytes *Third argument*: a decimal, float, or integer integer literal, column, variable, or expression specifying the number of extracted bytes
Returns	A string

Example

```
Let #Substring=substrb($Input_String, 1, #Length_In_Bytes )
```

to_char()

Description	Converts its argument from numeric to string using maximum precision
Syntax	*target_string* = `to_char(` *source_numeric*)
Arguments	A decimal, float, or integer literal, column, variable, or expression
Returns	A string

Example

```
Let $My_String= to_char(#My_Number )
```

`to_multi_byte()`

Description	(Double-byte version of SQR only) Converts its argument from single-byte format to double-byte format. Any occurrence of a double-byte character that also has a single-byte representation (numerals, punctuation, roman characters, and katakana) will be converted
Syntax	*target_string* = `to_multi_byte(` *source_numeric*)
Arguments	A date or string literal, column, variable, or expression
Returns	A string

Example

```
Let $Multi_Byte_String= to_multi_byte($Single_Byte_String )
```

`to_single_byte()`

Description	(Double-byte version of SQR only) Converts its argument from double-byte format to single-byte format. Any occurrence of a single-byte character that also has a multi-byte representation (numerals, punctuation, roman characters, and katakana) will be converted. It will also convert a sequence of kana characters followed by certain grammatical marks into a single-byte character which combines the two elements
Syntax	*target_string* = `to_single_byte(` *source_numeric*)
Arguments	A date or string literal, column, variable, or expression
Returns	A string

Example

```
Let $Single_Byte_String= to_single_byte($Multi_Byte_String )
```

`to_number()`

Description	Converts its argument from string to float numeric
Syntax	*target_numeric*= `to_number(` *source_string*)
Arguments	A string literal, column, variable, or expression
Returns	A float numeric

Example

```
Let #My_Number= to_number($My_String )
```

`translate()`

Description	Inspects the string specified in its first argument and converts the characters specified in the second argument into the corresponding characters specified in the third argument
Syntax	*target_string* = `translate(` *source_string* , *from_set*, *to_set* `)`

Arguments	*First argument*: a date or string literal, column, variable, or expression *Second argument*: a string literal, column, variable, or expression specifying the character set to be translated *Third argument*: a string literal, column, variable, or expression specifying the resulting character set
Returns	A string

Example

```
Let $From_Set = ',-'
Let $To_Set = ' /'
Let #Translated_String=translate($Input_String, $From_Set , $To_Set )
Let $New_Date = translate($Old_Date,'/','-')
```

Miscellaneous functions

array()

Description	Returns a pointer to the starting address of the specified array field. The returned value can only be used in user-defined functions
Syntax	*target_string* = `array(` *array_name* , *field_name* `)`
Arguments	*First argument*: a string literal, column, variable, or expression specifying the array name *Second argument*: a string literal, column, variable, or expression specifying the array field name
Returns	A string containing the pointer value

Example

```
! In this example, a user-defined ConvertToHex() function is used
Let #Hex_String=ConvertToHex(array('Employees', 'Employee_Id'), #Length)
```

ascii()

Description	Converts the first character of its argument to ASCII
Syntax	*target_ascii*= `ascii(` *source_string*`)`
Arguments	A date or string literal, column, variable, or expression
Returns	A float numeric

Example

```
Let #Ascii= ascii($My_String )
```

chr()

Description	Converts its argument from ASCII to character
Syntax	*target_char*= `chr(` *source_numeric*`)`

Arguments	A decimal, float, or integer literal, column, variable, or expression
Returns	A string

Example

```
Let $Char= chr(#My_Ascii )
```

cond()

Description	If the first argument is non-zero, returns the second argument; otherwise returns the third argument
Syntax	*target_variable* = `cond(` *x_value* , *y_value* , *z_value*)
Arguments	*First argument*: a decimal, float, or integer literal, column, variable, or expression *Second argument*: a date, string or numeric literal, column, variable, or expression *Third argument*: a date, string or numeric literal, column, variable, or expression If the second argument is numeric, the third argument must also be numeric If either the second or the third argument is a date, the function returns a date
Returns	The format depends on the function's second or third argument (whichever is returned)

Example

```
Let #Average_Salary=#Total_Salary / cond(#Number_Of_Empl,
     #Number_Of_Empl, 1)
```

getenv()

Description	Returns the value of the specified environmental variable
Syntax	*target_stringr* = `getenv(` *variable_name*)
Arguments	A string literal, column, variable, or expression
Returns	A string

Example

```
Let $Full_Name= getenv('PATH' ) || $File_Name
```

nvl()

Description	If the first argument is `NULL`, returns the second argument; otherwise returns the first argument
Syntax	*target_variable* = `nvl(` *x_value* , *y_value*)

Arguments	*First argument*: a date, string, or numeric literal, column, variable, or expression *Second argument*: a date, string or numeric literal, column, variable, or expression If the first argument is numeric, the second argument must also be numeric; otherwise date and string arguments are compatible
Returns	The format depends on the format of the returned argument

Example

```
Let $Address1=nvl( &Adress1, '          N/A                    ' )
```

range()

Description	Returns 1 if the the first argument value is between the second and third argument values; otherwise returns zero
Syntax	*target_variable* = `range(` *x_value* , *y_value, z_value*)
Arguments	*First argument*: a date, string, or numeric literal, column, variable, or expression *Second argument*: a date, string or numeric literal, column, variable, or expression *Third argument*: a date, string or numeric literal, column, variable, or expression If the first argument is numeric, the other two arguments must be numeric. If the first argument is string, the other two arguments must be string. If the first argument is a date, the other two arguments can be dates or strings
Returns	0 or 1

Example

```
Let #Flag = range(#Hourly_Rte, #Min_Rte, #Max_Rte)
```

wrapdepth()

Description	Returns the number of print lines for a wrapped string
Syntax	*number_lines* = `wrapdepth(` *source_string* , *width* , *line_height* , *break_chars* , *strip_chars*)

Arguments	*First argument*: a string literal, column, variable, or expression specifying the string to be wrapped *Second argument*: a decimal, float, or integer literal, column, variable, or expression specifying the maximum paragraph width in characters *Third argument*: a decimal, float, or integer literal, column, variable, or expression specifying the number of lines to skip between each line of the wrapped data *Fourth argument*: a string literal, column, variable, or expression specifying which characters will force a wrap to occur. Will accept regular characters plus non-display characters whose ASCII values are surrounded by angled brackets *Fifth argument*: a string literal, column, variable, or expression specifying which characters will be converted to spaces before the wrap occurs. Will accept regular characters plus non-display characters whose ASCII values are surrounded by angled brackets
Returns	A decimal, float, or integer numeric

Example

```
Let #Number_Lines= wrapdepth(&Desc, 25, 2, '<13>', '/\@-' )
```

appendix D

SQR command syntax

In this appendix, we will provide our readers with SQR command syntax, including operands, parameters, and options. We split all SQR commands and operators into the following categories:

- Program sectioning
- Compiler directives
- File input/output operators
- Operations on string, date, and numeric variables
- Logic operators
- Interacting with databases
- Compile-time and run-time dialog commands
- Print control commands
- Working with arrays

- Interacting with host operating systems
- Miscellaneous commands

Syntax conventions

We will use the following conventions:

Bold	SQR commands and command arguments, e.g., **Next-Column At-End=New-Page**
italic	information to be substituted with a variable name, value, or other data, e.g., *printer_type*.
{ }	indicates a set of alternative values, e.g., **Border = {Yes | No }**
|	alternative value separator
X (underlined)	default value, e.g., **3D-Effects = {Yes | No }** (No underlined)
[ ]	indicates optional item(s), e.g., **Begin-Select [Distinct]**
( )	arguments or values must be enclosed in parentheses, e.g., **(** *column* , *line* **)**
...	preceding parameter(s) can be repeated, e.g., **(***report_name1***[**, *report_namei***] ...)**

Example

```
Declare-Variable [Default-Numeric = {Decimal [(nn)] | Float | Integer}]
                                [Decimal [(nn)] name1 [(nn)] [namei[(nn)] ]...]
                                  [Float name1 [ namei ] ... ]
                                  [Integer name1 [ namei ] ... ]
                                  [Text name1 [ namei ] ... ]
                                  [Date name1 [ namei ] ... ]
End-Declare
```

Program sectioning

Begin-Program, End-Program

Purpose	To declare the beginning or the end of the **Program** section
Syntax	**Begin-Program** **End-Program**
Arguments	None
Notes	In SQR versions prior to version 4, the **Program** section was also called the **Report** section and the **Begin-Report** and **End-Report** commands were used. These commands are still valid, but may be obsolete in the future.
Refer to	Chapter 5

Example

```
Begin-Program
! SQR statements
End-Program
```

Begin-Heading, End-Heading

Purpose	To declare the beginning or the end of the **Heading** section
Syntax	**Begin-Heading** *lines* **[For-Reports =** **{ (***report_name1***[**, … *report_namei***]** … **)** | **(All) }]** **[For-Tocs = (** *toc_name1* **[** , … *toc_namei* **]** … **)]** **[Name** = heading_name **]** **End-Heading**
Arguments	*lines* The number of lines allocated for the heading. Only numeric literals can be used *report_namei* The name of the report(s) the heading is applied to. The report name is defined in the **Declare-Report** statement. If no report name or **(All)** is coded, the heading will be applied to all reports in the program. *toc_namei* The name of the table of contents (HTML only). When coded, the heading is applied to the specified table of contents. *heading_name* This argument cannot be used if For-Reports or For-Tocs is specified. This name is used in conjunction with the Alter-Report command.
Notes	SQR generates the heading and footing after the body of the page has been filled.
Refer to	Chapter 5

Example

```
Begin-Heading 3 For-Reports(Detail_Rpt Total_Rpt)
Print 'Summary Report' (1,1) Center
End-Heading
```

Begin-Footing, End-Footing

Purpose	To declare the beginning or the end of the **Footing** section
Syntax	**Begin-Footing** *lines* **[For-Reports = { (***report_name1* **[**, … *report_namei***]** … **)** | **(All) }]** **[For-Tocs = (** *toc_name1* **[** , … *toc_namei* **]** … **)]** **[Name =** footing_name **]** **End-Footing**
Arguments	*lines* The number of lines allocated for the footing. Only numeric literals can be used *report_namei (optional)* The name of the report(s) the footing is applied to. The report name is defined in the Declare-Report statement. If no report name or (**All**) is coded, the footing will be applied to all reports in the program.

	toc_namei The name of the table of contents (HTML only). When coded, the footing is applied to the specified table of contents. *footing_name* This argument cannot be used if `For-Reports` or `For-Tocs` is specified. This name is used in conjunction with the `Alter-Report` command.
Notes	SQR generates the heading and footing after the body of the page has been filled.
Refer to	Chapter 5

Example

```
Begin-Footing 2 For-Reports(Detail_Rpt Total_Rpt)
Page-Number (1,50) 'Page '
End-Footing
```

Begin-Procedure, End-Procedure

Purpose	To declare the beginning or the end of the `Procedure` section
Syntax	**Begin-Procedure** *name* **[Local | (***arg1***[,** … *argi* **]** … **)]** **End-Procedure**
Arguments	*name* The name of the procedure **Local** Indicates that the procedure is local *argi* Input and output procedure arguments. Input arguments can be variables, SQR columns, or literals. Output arguments can only be variables. Output argument names must be preceded by a colon.
Notes	If a procedure has no arguments and no **Local** is specified, the procedure is considered global. If arguments are specified, the procedure is considered local When global variables are referenced inside a local procedure, the variable names must be preceded by an underscore.
Refer to	Chapter 5

Example

```
Begin-Procedure Calc_Average (#Total_Amt, #Empl_Number, :#Average_Amt)
! SQR statements
End-Procedure
```

In this example, the procedure **`Calc_Average`** is considered local because it uses arguments: two input arguments, **`#Total_Amt`**, **`#Empl_Number`**, and one output argument, `#Average_Amt`.

Begin-Setup, End-Setup

Purpose	To declare the beginning or the end of the `Setup` section
Syntax	**Begin-Setup** **End-Setup**
Arguments	None

Notes	The **Setup** section must be the first section in the program. The **Setup** section is processed during the program compilation stage before actual program execution.
Refer to	Chapter 5

Example

```
Begin-Setup
  Declare-Variable
      Date $As_Of_Date
  End-Declare
End-Setup
```

Begin-Select, End-Select

Purpose To declare the beginning or the end of the **Select** paragraph

Syntax

Begin-Select [Distinct] [-C*nn***] [-B***nn***] [-XP] [NR] [-SORT***nn***]**
[-LOCK {RR | CS | RO | RL | XX}]
[{-Db*database* **| -Db***connect_string* **}] [Loops =** *nn* **]**
[On-Error = *proc_name* **[(***arg1* **[,** ... *argi***]** ... **)]]**
End-Select

Arguments

Distinct Eliminates duplicate rows from the query output

-C*nn*:

- (Oracle, SQLBase, Ingres) Query buffer size. If not specified, the default size is used
- (Sybase DB-Lib) Logical connection number. Used in the **Load-Lookup** and **Execute** commands

-B*nn* (Oracle, Sybase CT-Lib) Number of rows to be retrieved at one time. Used for performance purposes only. The default value is 10 or the value specified in the **-B** SQR command line flag.

-XP (Sybase) Prevents the creation of a stored procedure for this SQL. If your program uses bind variables and dynamic query variables in the same query, this parameter may improve the program performance.

-NR (SQLBase) No Recovery mode is used when connecting to the database.

-SORT*nn* (SQLBase) The size of the sort buffer

-Lock (SQLBase) Type of locking (isolation level): **RR-** repeatable read, **CS-** cursor stability, **RO-** read-only, **RL-** release locks, **XX-** no default isolation level. The default is **RR**

-DBdatabase (SQLBase) Default database name

-DB*connect_string* (ODBC) ODBC connection string

-Loops = ***nn* If this parameter is specified, the **Select loop stops after the number of retrieved rows riches *nn*. Can be used for debugging purposes to limit the query outputs.

On-Error = *proc_name* The name of the SQL error handling procedure

Notes

You can place SQR commands in the **Select** paragraph anywhere between the column names and the **From** keyword.
SQR commands in the **Select** paragraph must be indented.
You must list all the selected columns in the **Select** paragraph: **Select *** is not allowed.

	The print position parameters next to a table column in the **Select** paragraph cause the column value to be printed without using the **Print** command.
Refer to	Chapter 6

Example

```
Begin-Select Loops = 100
Emplid    (+1,1)
Name      (,+2)
City      (,+2)
State     (,+2)
     Do Print_Dependents
From Personal_Data
Where City = 'New York'
End-Select
```

Begin-SQL, End-SQL

Purpose	To declare the beginning or the end of the **SQL** paragraph. **SQL** paragraphs allow you to use native SQL statements (other than SQL Select) in SQR
Syntax	**Begin-SQL [-C***nn***] [-XP] [NR] [-SORT***nn***]** **[-Lock {RR | CS | RO | RL | XX}]** **[{-Db***database* | **-Db***connect_string* **}]** **[On-Error =** *proc_name* **[(***arg1* **[,** ... *argi***]** ... **)]]** (in non-**Setup** section) **[On-Error = { Stop | Warn | Skip }]** (in **Setup** section) **End-SQL**
Arguments	**-C***nn* (Oracle, SQLBase, Ingres) Query buffer size. If not specified, the default size is used. **XP** (Sybase) Prevents the creation of a stored procedure for this SQL. If your program uses bind variables and dynamic query variables in the same query, this parameter may improve the program performance. **-NR** (SQLBase) No Recovery mode is used when connecting to the database. **-SORT***nn* (SQLBase) The size of the sort buffer **-Lock** (SQLBase) Type of locking (isolation level): **RR-** repeatable read, **CS-** cursor stability, **RO-** read-only, **RL-** release locks, **XX-** inhibit default isolation level. The default is **RR** **-DB***database* (SQLBase) Default database name **-DB***connect_string* (ODBC) ODBC connection string **On-Error =** *proc_name* The name SQL error-handling procedure if SQL paragraph is used in other than Setup section. If no procedure name is specified, SQR displays an error message and aborts the program. **On-Error** If SQL paragraph is used in the Setup section, specifies an action to be taken in case of an SQL error (the default is Stop): • **Stop** abort the program • **Warn** display a warning message and continue to run • **Skip** ignore the error and continue to run.

Notes	If there is more than one SQL statement in one SQL paragraph, each statement except the last one must be terminated by a semicolon. Oracle PL/SQL can also be used in the SQL paragraph. In this case, you have to add an extra semicolon at the end of each PL/SQL statement.
Refer to	Chapter 7

Example

```
Begin-SQL On-Error=SQL_Error
Update Personal_Data
  Set Postal = $New_Zip
  Where Postal = $Old_Zip;
Delete From Temp_Empl
End-SQL
```

Begin-Document, End-Document

Purpose	To declare the beginning or the end of the **Document** paragraph
Syntax	**Begin-Document (** *X* **[,** *Y* **])** **End-Document**
Arguments	*X, Y* The line and column positions of the document on the page. Can be absolute or relative positions
Notes	SQR commands are not allowed within the **Document** paragraph.
Refer to	Chapter 15

Example

```
Begin-Document (+1, 1)
...
End-Document
```

Compiler directives

#Include

Purpose	To insert an external source file into an SQR program
Syntax	**#Include** '*name*'
Arguments	*name* The name of the file to be inserted into the program. The name must include the file name extension.
Notes	**#Include** is processed during the compile stage SQR supports nested inclusions (up to four levels)
Refer to	Chapters 18, 19, 21

Example

```
#Include 'my_header.dat'
```

#Debug

Purpose	To execute a specified SQR command in the debugging mode
Syntax	**#Debug [** *x* ... **]** *SQR_command*
Arguments	*x* Any letter or digit
Notes	The **#Debug** directive is activated by using the **-DEBUG** SQR command line argument. When this command line argument is used, any SQR command preceded by **#Debug** will be executed. The **-DEBUG** flag can be suffixed by up to 10 letters or digits. These characters are then used in the **#Debug** command to match the suffix to the **-DEBUG** command line flag characters. Commands without suffixes always match.
Refer to	Chapter 20

Example

If the value **-DEBUG12** was one of the SQR command line arguments, this can be used in the following commands:

```
#Debug Show 'Start processing' ! This command is executed
                               ! regardless of any suffix
#Debug1 Display #Empl_Total    ! This command is executed
                               ! because it matches suffix '1'
#Debug2 Display #Comp_Total    ! This command is executed
                               ! because it matches suffix '2'
! But #Debug3 Display 'Nothing' will be ignored because
!it does not match any suffix in the -DEBUG12
```

#If, #Else, #End-If / #EndIf

Purpose	To change the way SQR compiles the specified pieces of source code, depending on the specified substitution variable value
Syntax	**#If** *subs_variable comparison_operator value* SQR commands **[#Else** SQR commands **]** **#End-If**
Arguments	*subs_variable* These variables can be obtained from user input with the help of the **Ask** command or defined by the **#Define** directive. *comparison_operator* Any valid SQR comparison operator, e.g., "=" or ">=" *value:* a string or numeric literal
Notes	The **#If [#Else]** directives can be nested (up to 10 levels), each **#If** command must have a matching **#End-If**. **#EndIf** is a synonym of **#End-If**
Refer to	Chapter 20

Example

```
Begin-Setup
    Ask mode 'Debugging mode? (Yes, No)'
End-Setup
Begin-Program
#If {mode} = 'Yes'
     Show 'Main section'
#Else
    ! ...
#End-If
! ...
End-Program
```

#IfDef, #End-If
#IfNDef, #End-If

Purpose	**#IfDef** To check if the specified substitution variable was declared and, if yes, compile the SQR commands placed between **#IfDef** and **#End-If** **#IfNDef** To check if the specified substitution variable was declared and, if no, compile the SQR commands placed between **#IfNDef** and **#End-If**
Syntax	**#IfDef** *subs_variable* SQR commands **#End-If** **#IfNDef** *subs_variable* SQR commands **#End-If**
Arguments	*subs_variable* These variables can be obtained from user input with the help of the **Ask** command or defined by the **#Define** directive. They are also created automatically when the **-DEBUGx** command line argument is used. In this case, SQR assigns the substitution variables special names like **debug[x]** where '*x*' is one of the suffixes used in the **-DEBUGx** command line argument.
Notes	**#EndIf** is a synonym of **#End-If**
Refer to	Chapter 20

Example

1 When debugging the piece of code below, one can control which `Show` command will be executed by entering **-DEBUGa** or **-DEBUGb** in the SQR command argument line:

```
#IfDef debuga
   Show 'Get_Empl_Name started'
#Else
 #IfDef debugb
   Show $Empl_Name
 #End-If
#End-If
```

2 The substitution variable **debug_mode** is defined with the help of the **#Define** command:

```
#Define debug_mode yes
#IfDef debug_mode
     Show 'Executing in a debug mode'
     Show 'Program started'
#End-If
```

#Define

Purpose	To declare a substitution variable and to assign the variable a value
Syntax	**#Define** *subs_variable value*
Arguments	*subs_variable* The substitution variable name *value* The substitution value
Notes	Each substitution variable is declared with a separate **#Define** directive. Substitution variables can be defined in an external source file.
Refer to	Chapter 11

Example

```
#Define col_emplid      12
#Define col_empl_name   30
#Define col_sep          2      !Column Separator
! ...
Print 'Emplid'              (0,1,{col_emplid})
Print 'Name   '             (0,+{col_sep},{col_empl_name})
```

File input/output operators

Open

Purpose	To open a sequential file for subsequent processing
Syntax	**Open** *file_name* **As** *file_number* **{For-Reading | For-Writing | For-Append}** **{ Record** = *length* **[:Fixed | :Fixed_Nolf | :Vary] }** **[Status** = *status* **]**
Arguments	*file_name* The file name. Can be a string variable, SQR column, or literal *file_number* A file identification number which later will be used in other file processing commands. Can be any positive number less than 64,000. Can be coded as a numeric variable, SQR column, or literal **For-Reading** The file will be used for sequential read only. **For-Writing** To create a new file **For-Append** If the file already exists, all new records will be placed at the end of the file. If the file does not exist, a new file will be created. **Fixed** A fixed-length record file with no line feed characters. Can be used for both character and binary data

	Fixed_Nolf A fixed-length record file with no line feed characters. Can be used for both character and binary data **Vary** A variable-length record file with no line feed characters. Can be used for character data only. This is the default record type. *length* The file record length. For variable-length record files, it is the maximum record size. *Status* This is a numeric variable which is set to zero if the **Open** command was successful and to -1 if there was a problem with **Open**.
Notes	SQR works only with sequential files. A maximum of 256 files can be opened at one time. If record type is not specified, the default is **Vary**. When appending to an existing file, the record length and type of the appended file must match that of the existing file.
Refer to	Chapter 17

Example

```
Open 'daily_accum.dat' As 1 For-Append Record=50
Open $File_Name As #File_Handle For-Writing Record=100:Fixed Status =
     #Status
```

Read

Purpose	To read the next record of a sequential file
Syntax	**Read** *file_number* **Into {***io_area* **:** *length* **} … [Status** = *status* **]**
Arguments	*file_number* A file identification number previously specified in the **Open** command. Can be a numeric variable, column, or literal *io_area* One or more variables to hold the record data after **Read** is complete. The variables can be of the string, date, or numeric format. *length* The length of each *io_area* **Status** This is a numeric variable which is set to zero if the **Read** command was successful, or a system-specific error number if an error occurred.
Notes	If a field in the input record holds a date variable, it may be read into a date or string variable. The date variable in the record must be in one of the following formats: • **SQR_DB_DATE_FORMAT** setting • database-specific format • database-independent format **'SYYYYMMDD[HH24[MI[SS[NNNNNN]]]]'**. If a field in the input record is a binary number, it must be read into a numeric variable of the proper length. On end-of-file, the SQR reserved variable **#end-file** is set to `1`; otherwise, it is set to zero. This variable must be checked after each **Read** operation. If the input record has variable length, you can use one *io_area* to read the entire record in and the **Unstring** command to parse the record into separate fields. In this case the *length* must be the maximum record length.
Refer to	Chapter 17

Example

```
While Not #end-file
   Read #File_Handle Into $Empl_Id:4 $Empl_Name:25
$Empl_Address:50 Status=#Read_Stat
   If #end-file
     Break
   End-If
   If #Read_Stat <> 0
     Do Read_Eror(#Read_Stat)
   Else
     Do Process_Input_Record
   End-IF
End-While
Close #File_Handle
```

Write

Purpose	To write a record to a file from the program memory
Syntax	**Write** *file_number* **From {** *io_area* **: [** *length* **] } … [Status** = *status* **]**
Arguments	*file_number* A file identification number previously specified in the **Open** command. Can be a numeric variable, column, or literal *io_area* One or more variables to hold the data to be written to the file. The variables can be of the string, date, or numeric format. *length* The length of each *io_area* **Status** This is a numeric variable which is set to zero if the **Write** command was successful, or a system-specific error number if an error occurred.
Notes	If length is not specified, the current length of the variable will be used, but if the variable is numeric, the length is required. If a field program memory holds a date variable, the date will be converted to a string using the format specified by the **SQR_DB_DATE_FORMAT** setting or the database-specific format. When writing binary data, the file must be open using the **Fixed** or **Fixed_Nolf** parameters. This file may not be portable between different platforms. Files opened for writing are treated as having variable-length records. To use fixed-length records, specify a length for each variable in the **Write** command.
Refer to	Chapter 17

Example

```
Write #File_Handle From $Empl_Id:4 $Empl_Name:25 $Empl_Address:50
```

Close

Purpose	To close a sequential file
Syntax	**Close** *file_number*
Arguments	*file_number* A file identification number previously specified in the **Open** command. Can be a numeric variable, column, or literal

Notes	The file must be previously opened using the **Open** command.
Refer to	Chapter 17

Example

```
Close 1
Close #File_Handle
```

Operations on string, date, and numeric variables

Date-Time

Purpose	To obtain the current date/time. Depending on the syntax used, the date/time can be printed or stored in a column variable.
Syntax	**Date-TIme ([Y, Y]) [*format* [*column*]]**
Arguments	**X,Y** The line and column positions of the date and/or time field on the page. Can be absolute or relative positions *format* A date format mask *column* Causes SQR to store the retrieved date/time in the specified SQR column instead of printing
Notes	The **Date-TIme** command may be discontinued in the future releases. It is recommended that the **datenow()** function or the **$current-date** reserved variable be used instead. If the column name is specified, the current date and time will be retrieved each time the command is executed. Otherwise, the date and time are retrieved at program start and do not change during the program execution. If no date format mask is specified, the following default formats will be used (for databases with two default formats, the first format will be used for date/time printing, the second one will be used for placing date/time into an SQR column. DB2: **YYYY-MM-DD-HH:MI** **YYYY-MM-DD-HH:MI:SS.NNNNNN** Informix: **YYYY-MM-DD HH:MI** **YYY-MM-DD HH:MI:SS.NNN** Ingres: **DD-MON-YYYY HH:MI** **DD-MON-YYYY HH:MI:SS** Oracle: **DD-Mon-YYYY HH:MI:PM** SQLBase: **DD-Mon-YYYY HH:MI:PM** Sybase: **DD-Mon-YYYY HH:MI**
Refer to	Chapter 4

Example

```
Date-TIme (+1,4-0) MM/DD/YYYY  ! In this example, the current date is
printed.

! In this example, the current date and time are placed into
! &C_Date,&C_Time
Date-Time ( ) MM/DD/YYYY &C_Date
Date-Time ( ) HH:MI &C_Time
```

Declare-Variable

Purpose	To explicitly declare a variable. In most cases, SQR variables do not have to be explicitly declared in the program; when a variable appears the first time, SQR assigns this variable its type and initial value (based on the first character of the variable's name).
Syntax	**Declare-Variable** **[Default-Numeric = {Decimal [(*nn*)]** | **Float** | **Integer}]** **[Decimal [(*nn*)]** *name1* **[(*nn*)] [*namei*[(*nn*)]] ...]** **[Float** *name1* **[** *namei* **] ...]** **[Integer** *name1* **[** *namei* **] ...]** **[Text** *name1* **[** *namei* **] ...]** **[Date** *name1* **[** *namei* **] ...]** **End-Declare**
Arguments	*namei* The name of the variable to be declared. The name must include the proper prefix: "**#**" or "**$**". *nn* Precision qualifier (for decimals only). This is not the number of decimal places! Can range between 1 and 38. The default value is 16. **Default-Numeric** Defines the default type for all numeric variables in the program. Overrides the default numeric type in the `SQR.ini` file **Decimal** Specifies that the numeric variables must be used as decimals. The precision qualifier can be assigned to all variables that follow the argument or to each individual variable. **Float** Specifies that the numeric variables must be used as double precision floating point variables **Integer** Specifies that the numeric variables must be used as integers with a range between -2,147,483,648 and +2,147,483,647 **Text** Specifies that the string variables must be used as text variables **Date** Specifies that the date variables may contain dates
Notes	Available starting from version 4. Can only be used in the **Setup** section or as the first statement of a local procedure. In SQR for DDO, list variables can not be declared using this command.
Refer to	Chapter 4

Example

```
Begin-Setup
Declare-Variable
   Default-Numeric = Decimal(12)
   Decimal(16) #Dec1 #Dec2 #Dec3
   Integer #Sub1 Sub2
   Date $As_Of_Date
End-Declare

End-Setup
```

Move

Purpose	To move the contents of one field to another field with optional editing
Syntax	**Move** *source_name* **To** *target_name* **[[:]** *edit_mask* | **Number** | **Money** | **Date]**
Arguments	*source_name* The source field name. Can be a variable, an SQR column, or a literal *target_name* The target field name. Can only be a variable *edit_mask* The edit mask (if editing is required). The edit masks are described in chapter 4 and 9. **Number** Specifies that after the move, the target field will be edited using the **Number-Edit-Mask** **Money** Specifies that after the move, the target field will be edited using the **Money-Edit-Mask** **Date** Specifies that after the move, the target field will be edited using the **Date-Edit-Mask**
Notes	The source and target fields in the **Move** command can have different formats. In this case, the command performs the necessary conversion. Date and numeric variables are not compatible. The edit mask can be a literal or a string variable. When a string field is moved to a date variable, or when using a date format mask, or when the keyword `Date` is used, the source must be in one of the formats specified by: • **SQR_DB_DATE_FORMAT** setting • database-specific format • database-independent format **'SYYYYMMDD[HH24[MI[SS[NNNNNN]]]]'**.
Refer to	Chapter 4

Example

```
Move '(xxx)bxxx-xxxx' To $Phone_Mask
Move '1231234567' To $Phone :$Phone_Mask
```

In the above example, the value of `$Phone_Mask` is used as the target field edit mask. After the move, the `$Phone` field will contain `(123) 123-4567`.

```
Move 100000 To #Salary
Move '$,$$$,$$$V99' To $Salary_Mask
Move #Salary To $Salary :$Salary_Mask
```

In the above example, the last `Move` command performs a numeric-to-string conversion and edits the target field using an edit mask. After the move, the `$Salary` field will contain `$100,00000`.

```
Let #Sub = 5
Move #Sub To $Display_Sub
```

In the above example, the `Move` command performs a numeric-to-string conversion using the default numeric edit mask. After the move, the `$Display_Sub` field will contain `005.000000`.

```
Move '19980615' To $Run_Date
Move $Run_Date To $Display_Date Day,bMONTHbDD,YYYY
```

In the above example, the `$Run_Date` is a previously declared date format field. The first `Move` command converts a string literal to the date format. The second `Move` command converts the date format field `$Run_Date` back to the string format using a date edit mask. After the move, the `$Display_Date` field will contain `Monday, JUNE 15,1998`.

Let

Purpose	To assign the value of an expression to a variable
Syntax	**Let** *target_name = expression*
Arguments	*target_name* The name of the variable to which the value of the result of the expression is assigned. Can be a variable or an array field *expression* The expression to be calculated or evaluated
Notes	An SQR expression may include operands, operators, and functions Operands of different types can be combined in one expression
Refer to	Chapter 4

Example

```
Let #Amount = #Quantity * #Price
Let $Print_Date = strtodate(&Eff_Dte, 'DD/MM/YYYY')
```

Concat

Purpose	To append the contents of one field to the end of another field with optional editing
Syntax	**Concat** *source_name* **With** *target_name* **[[:]** *edit_mask* **]**
Arguments	*source_name* The name of the source field to be appended to the end of the target field. Can be a variable, an SQR column, or a literal. The source field must be of the string or date format. *target_name* The name of the target field. The target field will contain the result of the concatenation. Can only be a variable *edit_mask* The edit mask (if editing is required). The edit masks are described in Chapters 4 and 9.
Notes	The edit mask can be a literal or a string variable. If the source field is a date variable or column and no edit mask is specified, SQR will convert the date to a string based on the format specified by **SQR_DB_DATE_FORMAT**, or if not specified, to the database-specific format.
Refer to	Chapter 4

Example

```
Move $First_Name To $Full_Name
Concat ' ' With $Full_Name
Concat $Last_Name With $Full_Name
Concat $Apt With $Disp_Apt bxx
Concat $Run_Date With $Quote_Id MMDDYYYY
```

Extract

Purpose	To extract a portion of a string into another string
Syntax	**Extract** *target_name* **From** *source_name start_position length*
Arguments	*target_name* The name of the target field. The target field will contain the result of the extraction. Can only be a variable *source_name* The name of the source field from which the string is extracted. Can be a variable, an SQR column, or a literal. The source field must be of the string or date format. *start_position* The starting position of the extracted sub-string. The starting positions are counted from left to right starting from position zero. *length* The length of the extracted sub-string
Notes	The starting position and length can be literals or numeric variables If the source is a date variable or column, SQR will convert the date to a string before the extraction based on the format specified by **SQR_DB_DATE_FORMAT**, or if not specified, to the database-specific format. If the target is a date variable, the extracted portion must be in one of the formats specified by: • **SQR_DB_DATE_FORMAT** setting • database-specific format • database-independent format **'SYYYYMMDD[HH24[MI[SS[NNNNNN]]]]'**
Refer to	Chapter 4

Example

```
Extract $Area_Code From $Phone_Number 0 3
Extract $Reg_Date From $Input_Record  #Pos  #Length
```

Find

Purpose	To find the starting position of a sub-string within a string
Syntax	**Find** *search_argument* **In** *source_string start_position location*
Arguments	*search_argument* Specifies the sub-string to be searched for. Can be a variable, an SQR column, or a literal. This field must be in a string or date format. *source_string* The name of the source field to be searched. Can be a variable, an SQR column, or a literal. The source string must be of the string or date format. *start_position* The starting position of the search. The starting positions are counted from left to right starting from position zero. *location* Specifies the field where SQR will place the position of the sub-string (if found)
Notes	If the sub-string is not found, SQR moves `-1` to the location. The starting position can be a literal or a numeric variable. The location must be a numeric variable. If the source is a date variable or column, SQR will convert the date to a string before the search based on the format specified by **SQR_DB_DATE_FORMAT**, or if not specified, to the database-specific format.
Refer to	Chapter 4

Example

```
! Assuming $Full_Name contains last name, comma, first name, space:
Find ',' In $Full_Name 1 #Location
If   #Location <> -1
     Let #Start_Loc = #Location + 1
     Find ' ' In $Full_Name  #Start_Loc  #End_Loc
     Let #Length = #End_Loc - #Start_Loc
     Extract $First_Name From $Full_Name #Start_Loc #Length
End-If
```

Encode

Purpose	To place a sequence of special characters onto a string variable. The special characters can be displayable or non-displayable characters. Can be used to send a string of special characters or escape characters to an output device.
Syntax	`Encode source_string Into target_name`
Arguments	*source_string* A string of characters to be encoded. Non-displayable characters are coded as numbers between <001> and <255>. *target_name* A string variable to hold the result of encoding.
Refer to	Chapter 4

Example

```
Encode '<27>L11233' Into $Bold
Encode '<128>' Into $Euro
Print $Bold ()
Print $Euro (+1,20)
```

Lowercase, Uppercase

Purpose	To convert a string variable to lowercase or upper case
Syntax	**Lowercase** *string* **Uppercase** *string*
Arguments	*string* The string to be converted. Can be only a variable
Notes	These two commands use the same field as source and target. Neither **Uppercase** nor **Lowercase** change the case for non-alphabetic characters.
Refer to	Chapter 4

Example

```
Lowercase $Input
Uppercase $Name
```

String, Unstring

Purpose	To build a string from a list of sub-strings To break a string into a list of sub-strings
Syntax	**String** *substring* ... **BY** *delimiter* **Into** *target_string* **Unstring** *source_string* **BY** *delimiter* **Into** *substring* ...
Arguments	For the **String** command: *substring* One or more fields to be concatenated, separated by the specified delimiters, and placed into the target string. A sub-string can be a variable, an SQR column, or a literal. Can be of the string or date format . *delimiter* One or more characters to be inserted as sub-string separators. Can be a variable, an SQR column, or a literal *target_string* The name of a string variable to hold the result of the concatenation For the **Unstring** command: *source_string* The string to be taken apart. A source string can be a variable, an SQR column, or a literal. Can be of the string or date format *delimiter* One or more characters to be used as sub-string delimiters. Can be a variable, an SQR column, or a literal *substring* One or more string variables to hold the result of the operation
Notes	If the source is a date variable or column, SQR will convert the date to a string before the **String** or **Unstring** operations, based on the format specified by **SQR_DB_DATE_FORMAT**, or, if not specified, to the database-specific format. Use a null delimiter in the **String** command when no delimiter between sub-strings is needed. If the **Unstring** command specifies more target sub-strings than can be found in the source string, the remaining sub-strings will be set to NULL. If the **Unstring** command specifies fewer target sub-strings than can be found in the source string, the extra source sub-strings will not be processed.
Refer to	Chapter 4

Example

```
String $First_Name $Mid_Initial $Last_Name By ':' Into $Empl_Name
Unstring $Empl_Name By ':' Into $First_Name $Mid_Initial $Last_Name
String &Company &Paygroup &Emplid By '' Into $Paycode
```

Mbtosbs

Purpose	To convert a double-byte string to its single-byte equivalent. Any occurrence of a double-byte character that has a single-byte presentation (numerals, punctuation, roman characters, and katakana) is converted.
Syntax	**Mbtosbs** *string*
Arguments	*string* The string to be converted. Can be only a variable
Notes	This command is available for the double-byte SQR mode only.
Refer to	Chapter 21

Example

```
Mbtosbs $My_String
```

Sbtombs

Purpose	To convert a single-byte string to its double-byte equivalent. Any occurrence of a single-byte character that has a double-byte presentation (numerals, punctuation, roman characters, and katakana) is converted.
Syntax	**Sbtombs** *string*
Arguments	*string* The string to be converted. Can be only a variable
Notes	This command is available for the double-byte SQR mode only.
Refer to	Chapter 21

Example

```
Sbtombs $My_String
```

Add, Subtract, Multiply, Divide

Purpose	To perform addition, subtraction, multiplication, or division operations on numeric fields with optional rounding
Syntax	**Add** *source_field* **To** *target_field* **[Round =** *nn* **]** **Subtract** *source_field* **From** *target_field* **[Round =** *nn* **]** **Multiply** *source_field* **Times** *target_field* **[Round =** *nn* **]** **Divide** *source_field* **Into** *target_field* **[On-Error = {High | Zero}]** **[Round =** *nn* **]**
Arguments	*source_field* A numeric variable, SQR column, or literal *target_field* A numeric variable which will hold the result of the operation **Round =** *nn* (decimal and float variables only) Rounds the result to the specified number of digits to the right of the decimal point **On-Error** If coded, the result of a zero-division will be set to either the highest value or to zero. If not coded, SQR stops processing when a zero-division occurs.
Notes	To avoid small inaccuracies when working with money fields, it is recommended to use decimals rather than float variables.
Refer to	Chapter 4

Example

```
Add #Salary To #Salary_Total
Subtract 1 From #Counter
Multiply #Hours Times #Rate Round=2
Divide #Employee_Number Into #Average_Salary Round=2 On-Error=Zero
```

Logic operators

Do

Purpose	To invoke an SQR procedure
Syntax	**Do** *procedure_name* **[(** *arg1* **[,** *argi* **] …)]**
Arguments	*procedure_name* The name of the procedure to be invoked *argi* zero, one, or more arguments to be passed to the procedure
Notes	The arguments must be passed in the order listed in the **Begin-Procedure** statement of the invoked procedure. String arguments can be passed to procedure string or date arguments. Date arguments can be passed to procedure date or string arguments. Numeric arguments can be passed to procedure numeric arguments, but the numeric subtypes (**Decimal**, **Float**, or **Integer**) do not have to match: SQR will automatically convert numeric values to the proper subtype.
Refer to	Chapter 5

Example

```
Do Get_Company_Name
Do Calc_Average (#No_Employees, &Company, #Avg_Salary)
```

If, End-If, Else

Purpose	To transfer program control depending on the value of a logical expression
Syntax	**If** *logical_expression* SQR commands **[Else** SQR commands] **End-If**
Arguments	*logical_expression* A valid SQR logical expression
Notes	The **If [Else]** commands can be nested, each **If** command must have a matching **End-If**. The logical expression value is evaluated with a non-zero value considered TRUE. When a date variable or column is compared to a string, SQR performs a chronological comparison, not a string comparison. To support a chronological comparison, the string must be in one of the formats specified by: • **SQR_DB_DATE_FORMAT** setting • database-specific format • database-independent format **'SYYYYMMDD[HH24[MI[SS[NNNNNN]]]]'**.
Refer to	Chapter 8

Example

```
If  #Count
  Show 'Number of rows processed = ' #Count
Else
  Show 'There were no rows found'
```

```
End-If

If (&A.Claim_Dte >= $Policy_Eff_Dte And &A.Claim_Dte <= $Policy_Exp_Dte)
    Do Process_Reg_Claims
Else
   If (&A.Claim_Status = 'S')
     Do Process_Special_Claims
   Else
     Do Print_Error
   End-If
End-If
```

Evaluate, End-Evaluate, Break

Purpose	To evaluate the value of a variable, column, or literal and to execute the proper sequence of SQR commands, depending on the result of the evaluation

Syntax	**Evaluate {** *variable1* | *column1* | *literal1* **}**
	  When *comparison_operator* **{** *variable2* | *column2* | *literal2* **}**
	    SQR commands ...
	    [Break]
	  [When *comparison_operator* **{** *variable2* | *column2* | *literal2* **}**
	    SQR commands ...
	    [Break]]
	  [When-Other
	    SQR commands ...
	    [Break]]
	End-Evaluate

Arguments	*variable1* | *column1* | *literal1* A variable, column, or literal to be used in the evaluation. Can be of the string, date, or numeric format *comparison_operator* Any valid comparison operator, e.g., ">," "=," ">=," etc. *variable2* | *column2* | *literal2* A variable, column, or literal to be used in the comparison. Can be of the string, date, or numeric format **When** Starts the comparison/action block. If the result of the comparison is TRUE, all SQR commands in the block are executed. If the expression is FALSE, the next **When** is evaluated. **Break** Is used to specify an immediate exit from the entire **Evaluate** command. If not coded, the next **When** block will be evaluated **When-Other** Specifies the default actions when all previous **When** statements yielded a FALSE result
Notes	The **Evaluate** commands can be nested, each **Evaluate** command must have a matching **End-Evaluate**. When a date variable or column is compared to a string, SQR performs a chronological comparison, not a string comparison. To support a chronological comparison, the string must be in one of the formats specified by: • **SQR_DB_DATE_FORMAT** setting • database-specific format • database-independent format **'SYYYYMMDD[HH24[MI[SS[NNNNNN]]]]'**.
Refer to	Chapter 8

Example

```
Evaluate  $Claim_Status
  When = 'A'
    Do Process_Active_Claims
    Break
  When='P'
  When='R'
      Do Process_Pending_RunOff_Claims
    Break
  When-Other
    Do Process_Unknown_Status
    Break
End-Evaluate
```

While, End-While, Break

Purpose	To create a logical loop which is used to process the body of the loop for a number of times until the specified condition is FALSE
Syntax	**While** *logical_expression* SQR commands ... **[Break]** SQR commands ... **End-While**
Arguments	*logical_expression* A valid SQR logical expression **Break** Is used to specify an immediate exit from the entire **While** loop
Notes	When the logical expression is evaluated, a zero result is considered FALSE; any non-zero result is considered TRUE. The **While** loops can be nested.
Refer to	Chapter 8

Example

```
While  1
      Read 1 Into $Employee_Record:80
      If   #end-file = 1
           Break
      End-If
      Add 1 To #Record_Count
   Do Process_Input
End-While

While $Empl_Status = 'A' And $Company_Code = &Company
         Do Get_Employee_Name
         While $Emplid = $Save_Emplid
             Do Read_Creadit_Record
             If #Total_Amt > 0
                   Do Adjust_Total
             End-If
         End-While
End-While
```

Goto

Purpose	To transfer program control to the specified label
Syntax	**Goto** *label*
Arguments	*label* An SQR program label
Notes	SQR program label names must end with a colon. The **Goto** command can use labels only within the same section or paragraph.

Example

```
Goto  Error_Routine
! ...
Error_Routine:
  Show 'Errors found'
  Stop
```

Interacting with databases

Connect

Purpose	To disconnect the current database connection and to connect under a new user Id
Syntax	**Connect** *id/password* **[On-Error =** *proc_name* **[(** *arg1* **[, ...** *argi* **] ...)]]**
Arguments	*id/password* User name and password. Can be stored in a string variable or column *proc_name* The name of a procedure to be invoked if **Connect** fails
Notes	**Connect** is an SQR command, not an SQL command After each **Connect**, SQR sets its reserved variable **$username** to a new value. **Connect** causes all cursors and logons to be closed before its execution. **Connect** should not be issued within a **Select** or **SQL** paragraph.

Example

```
Let $Connect_String = 'jsmith/mypword'
Connect $Connect_String On-Error = Connect_Error
```

Commit

Purpose	To perform a database commit (Oracle, SQLBase, Rdb, Ingres)
Syntax	**Commit**
Arguments	None
Notes	**Commit** is an SQR command, not an SQL command. Should not be used within an SQL paragraph For Sybase, use **Commit Transaction** and, if necessary, **Begin Transaction** The **Commit** command cannot be used in SQR for **Informix**.
Refer to	Chapter 7

Example

```
If #SQL-count = #Insert_Count
   Commit
End-If
```

Rollback

Purpose	To perform a database rollback to the last commit point (Oracle, SQLBase, Rdb, Ingres)
Syntax	**`Rollback`**
Arguments	None
Notes	**`Rollback`** is an SQR command, not an SQL command. Should not be used within an SQL paragraph For Sybase, use **`Rollback Transaction`** and, if necessary, **`Begin Transaction`**. The **`Rollback`** command cannot be used in SQR for **`Informix`**.
Refer to	Chapter 7

Example

```
If #SQL-error <> 0
   Rollback
End-If
```

Exit-Select

Purpose	To exit a **`Select`** paragraph immediately
Syntax	**`Exit-Select`**
Arguments	None
Notes	Use **`Exit-Select`** when you need to end a query before all rows have been retrieved.
Refer to	Chapter 7

Example

```
Begin-Select
Emplid
SSN
Name
City
State
     Do Write_To_Output
     If  #Write_Error
          Exit-Select
     End-If
From Personal_Data
End-Select
```

Load-Lookup

Purpose
: To build a table array in the program memory and populate this array with data from a database table

Syntax

```
Load-Lookup Name = lookup_table Table = database_table
                  Key = key_column Return_Value = data_column
                  [ Rows = initial_row_number ] [ Extent = extent ]
                  [ Where = where_clause ]
                  [ Sort = sort_mode ]
                  [ Cursor = connection_number ] [ Quiet ]
```

Arguments

lookup_table The name assigned to the table array

database_table The name of the database table to be used as the data source. You can use multiple tables

key_column The name of the database table column to be used as a key when searching in the table array. This column must have unique values in the table. No NULL values are allowed. Can be database-supported expressions

data_column The name(s) of the column(s) or expression(s) to be retrieved using the value of *key_column* as the key. It may be just one table column or a combination of several table columns. In case of a column combination, the columns must be concatenated in accordance to your database rule, e.g., with the help of "||" for Oracle.

initial_row_number The initial number of rows in the lookup array table (default is 100)

extent The number of rows to add to the array table when it becomes full (default is 25%)

where_clause The **Where** clause to be used when the database table rows are retrieved

sort_mode The sorting method to be used when ordering elements in the table array:

- **DC** sorting by database, case-sensitive sort
- **DI** sorting by database, case-insensitive sort
- **SC** sorting by SQR, case-sensitive sort
- **SI** sorting by SQR, case-insensitive sort

connection_number (Sybase DB-Lib) The connection number to use. The connection number is defined in the **Begin-SQL** statement

Quiet Is used to suppress the message "Loading lookup array..." when the **Load-Lookup** command is executed

Notes

The lookup array table built by **Load-Lookup** is to be used by one or more Lookup commands.

The number of lookup tables and their sizes are limited only by the amount of available memory.

Refer to

Chapter 6

Example

```
Begin-Setup
!**************
Load-Lookup Name=Client_Name_Address
            Rows=500
            Table=Clients
            Key=Client_Id
```

```
            Return_Value='Client_Name||''-''||Client_Address'
    Where=State='NY'
End-Setup
```

Lookup

Purpose	To search a table array created and populated by the **Load-Lookup** command
Syntax	**Lookup** *lookup_table key_value return_value*
Arguments	*lookup_table* The name of a lookup table previously defined by the **Load-Lookup** command *key_value* A key value to be used for the search. Can be a variable, column, or literal. *return_value* A string variable to hold the search result
Notes	If no match is found, the return value is set to NULL
Refer to	Chapter 6

Example

```
! This example is used in conjunction with the example for the Load-Lookup
! command
Lookup Client_Name_Address  &Client_Id  $Name_Address
Unstring $Name_Address By '-' Into $Name $Address
```

Use (Sybase and Microsoft SQL Server only)

Purpose	To use the specified database instead of the default database associated with your user id
Syntax	**Use** *database*
Arguments	*database* The name of the database to use
Notes	Can be used only in the **Setup** section prior to any query Cannot be used within an SQL paragraph Can be overridden by the **-DB** command line flag

Example

```
Begin-Setup
   Use testbase
End-Setup
```

Execute (Ingres, Sybase, Microsoft SQL Server)

Purpose	To execute a stored procedure
Syntax	Ingres **Execute** *proc_name* **[(** *parm_name* **=** *parm1* **[,** *parmi* **] …)]** **[On-Error =** *proc_name* **[(** *arg1* **[,** *argi* **] …)]]** **[** *status* **]**

Sybase, MS SQL Server:

Execute [-C*nn*] *proc_name*
  [[*@parm1* **=]** *value1* **[OUT[PUT]] [, [***@parmi* **=]** *valuei*
    [OUT[PUT]]…]
  [On-Error = *proc_name* **[(** *arg1* **[,** *argi* **] …)]] [***@status* **=]**
  [*@status_var* **=]**
  [Do = *do_proc_name* **[(** *do_arg1* **[,** *do_argi* **]) …]**
  [Into *column1 type1* **[(** *length1***)] [,** *columni typei*
  [(*lengthi***)]] …]**
  [With Recompile]

Arguments *proc_name* The name of the stored procedure

parmi Optional arguments to be passed to the stored procedure. The arguments can be passed with or without names. If used without names, must be passed in the same sequence as defined in the stored procedure.

On-Error The procedure name to be invoked if an error occurs. If not coded, SQR will halt program execution when an error occurs.

status The name of a numeric variable which will hold the procedure return code.

-C*nn* The logical connection number (defined in the Begin-Select or Begin-SQL statement).

do_proc_name The name of the procedure to be invoked for each row selected in the query.

do_argi Optional arguments to be passed to the procedure invoked for each selected row.

OUT[PUT] Indicates the the parameter will receive a value from the stored procedure

Into Lists the names, types, and lengths of columns where the rows retrieved from the stored procedure will be stored. If the stored procedure has more than one `Select` query, only the first query result will be stored. Rows from subsequent queries will be ignored

With Recompile Causes the query to be recompiled each time the stored procedure is invoked.

Example

```
 ! Ingres:
Execute  On_Update(Tblname=$Department_Tbl, Key=$Deptid) #Rtn_Status=

! Sybase, MS SQL Server
Execute On_Update(@Tblname=$Department_Tbl, @Key=$Deptid) @#Rtn_Status
```

Declare-Connection

Purpose To define the data source logon parameters prior to logon. Can be used to override the default connection logon parameters.

Syntax

Declare-Connection *connection_name*
  Dsn = *datasource_name*
    [User = *user* **]**
  [Password = *password* **]**
    [Parameters = *keyword_list* **]**
  [No-Duplicate = {True | <u>False</u> }]
End-Declare

Arguments	`connection_name` The name of the connection. Can be referred to in the *Alter-Connection* command. `datasource_name` The logical datasource name as recorded in the DDO registry. Can be coded as a string variable or literal in the program body or as a string literal in the `Setup` section. *user* user id Can be coded as a string variable or literal in the program body or as a string literal in the `Setup` section. `password` password Can be coded as a string variable or literal in the program body or as a string literal in the `Setup` section. `keyword_list` A connection string as required by the data source. The string is a list of keyword-value pairs. **No-Duplicates=True** prevents SQR from creating additional logins to data sources that may be busy handling a previous query.
Notes	This command can be coded in the `Setup` section or in the program body. Do not wrap the lines in the parameters line.

Example

```
Declare-Connection MYCONNECTION
    Dsn = $Dsn
    User = $Userid
    Password = $Password
    No-Duplicate = True
End-Declare
```

Alter-Connection

Purpose	To alter the data source logon parameters prior to logon. Can be used to override the default connection logon parameters.
Syntax	**Alter-Connection Name** = *connection_name* **Dsn** = *datasource_name* [**User** = *user*] [**Password** = *password*] [**Parameters** = *keyword_list*] [No-Duplicate = {True | False }]
Arguments	`connection_name` The name of the connection defined in the `Declare-Connection` command. `datasource_name` The logical datasource name as recorded in the DDO registry. Can be coded as a string variable or literal. `user user id` Can be coded as a string variable or literal. `password` password Can be coded as a string variable or literal. `keyword_list` A connection string as required by the data source. The string is a list of keyword-value pairs. **No-Duplicates=True** prevents SQR from creating additional logins to data sources that may be busy handling a previous query.
Notes	This command cannot be coded in the `Setup` section. Do not wrap the lines in the parameters line.

Example

```
Alter-Connection Name = MYCONNECTION
    Dsn = $Dsn
    User = $Userid
    Password = $Password
    No-Duplicate = True
Parameters = 'logon.client=600;logon.ashost=star;logon.language=EN;'
```

Begin-Execute, End-Execute

Purpose To get a data row from various relational or non-relational datasources. The exact syntax depends on the datasource specifics.

Syntax

```
Begin-Execute
      [ Connection = connection_name ]
   [ On-Error = error_procedure[(arg1[,argi]... )] ]
      [ Rsv = row_number ]
   [ Status = status_var ]
      [ Schema = schema ]
   [ { Procedure = procedure_name
      [       Parameters = (parm1[{In|Inout|Null}]
                  [,parmi[{In|Inout|Null}]]...)]
      | Command = command_line
      | Getdata = getdata_line }]
   [ Begin-Select
      [ Before = before_select[(arg1[,argi] ...)]]
      [ After = after_select[(arg1[,argi] ...)]]
      col_name1 = {Char|Text|Number|Date  [ edit_mask]} [On-Break]
     ,col_namei = {Char|Text|Number|Date [edit_mask]} [On-Break] ...
      From { Rowsets = ( {m, -n, n-m, m- | All } ) |
          Parameter = parm_list }
      End-Select ]
     [ Properties = keyword_list ]
    End-Execute
```

Arguments

`connection_name` The name of the connection defined in the `Declare-Connection` command.

`error_procedure` The name of a procedure to be invoked if an error occurs.

`row_number` A global numeric variable containing the number of the retrieved row set.

status_var A variable to receive the status of the stored procedure. Can be coded as a list variable, numeric variable or string variable.

`schema` Identifies the datasource, e.g., a name of an OLAP datamart. Must be registered in the DDO directory. Can be coded as a string literal or variable.

`procedure_name` The name of the stored procedure. If the datasource is SAP/R3, the procedure must be a BAPI. Can be coded as a string literal or variable. Cannot be coded with the `Command` or `Getdata` arguments. The parameter list may include list variables, numeric variable or string variables, literals or columns. All parameters required by the stored procedure must be coded in the order the procedure will receive them. If you want to pass a null value for one of the parameters, use the Null qualifier.

command_line A text string that is passed to the datasource without any modification. Cannot be coded with the `Procedure` or `Getdata` arguments. Can be coded as a string literal or variable.

getdata_line supports the DDO GetData paradigm. This argument is used to read data from various non-relational datasources, e.g., CVS, XML, OLAP. Cannot be coded with the `Procedure` or `Command` arguments. Can be coded as a string literal or variable.

Begin-Select, End-Select define the names and, optionally, formats of retrieved columns, SQR procedures to be invoked before and/or after retrieval, on-break processing options, rowsets from which to retrieve the column values, and so on. The `Before` and `After` Procedures are not invoked unless at least one row is returned.

From Rowsets Defines the rowsets from which to retrieve the column values. This argument can be used with all datasource types, including SAP R/3 and JDBC. If more than one rowset is specified, use identical column names and types. You can specify specific rowsets or ranges of rowsets, e.g., (1, 3-5, 8-). Rowset numbers can be coded as numeric literals or variables.

From Parameter This argument can be used only with SAP R/3. Names an output parameter containing one or more rows from which the column values are retrieved. Use only in conjunction with the `Procedure` argument.

keyword_list A list of keyword-value pairs that represent modifications to the *Parameters* argument in the `Declare-Connection` or `Alter-Connection` command. The difference between the `Begin-Execute` command and `Declare-Connection` and `Alter-Connection` commands is that this argument alters the properties of returned information as opposed to the login properties.

Notes: This command cannot be coded in the `Setup` section.
The column names in the `Begin-Select` construct should not be indented.

Examples

```
Begin-Execute
  Connection = OLAPCONNECT
  Schema = 'FoodMart'  ! Must be registered in the DDO registry
  Getdata = 'Sales'
Begin-Select Before = Print_Header After = Print_Total
Month_Year         (+1,1) Type=Date Edit 'MM/YYYY'On-Break
Product            (,10)  Type=Char
Measure.Quantity   (,30)  Type=Number Edit '999,999'
Measure.Sales      (,30)  Type=Number Edit '$$$,$$$.99'
Measure.Profit     (,30)  Type=Number Edit '$$$,$$$.99'
From Rowsets = (#Rowset)
End-Select
End-Execute
```

Set-Members

Purpose	Returns the set of members in a dimension, level, or hierarchy at the specified level (OLAP DDO).
Syntax	**Set-Members=(** *dimension_1,hierarchy_1* **[**,*dimension_i,hierarchy_i*,**...])**
Arguments	*dimension_i* Specifies the dimension *hierarchy_i* Specifies the hierarchy of the dimension

Example

```
Set-Members = ('sales','gross sales.toys.toys under 5',
               'time','2000.Q1.Week1',
               'region','North East')
```

Set-Generations

Purpose	Specifies dimension hierarchy in previously declared dimensions (OLAP DDO).
Syntax	**Set-Generations**=(*dimension_1,hierarchy_1* **[**,*dimension_i,hierarchy_i,***...])**
Arguments	*dimension_i* Specifies the dimension *hierarchy_i* Specifies the hierarchy level

Example

```
Set-Generations = ('sales', 3,'time', 1)
! Returns Sales, Toys, Toys Under 5
! Returns Year only
```

Set-Levels

Purpose	Extends the levels in previously declared dimension hierarchies (OLAP DDO). If used only with the previous `Set-Members` command, returns all members under the product hierarchy and the next *`level_i`* generations. If used with the previous `Set-Members` and `Set-Generations` commands, returns all members for generation levels from the level specified in the `Set-Generations` command.
Syntax	**Set-Levels=(***dimension_1,level_1* **[**,*dimension_i,level_i,***...])**
Arguments	*dimension_i* Specifies the dimension *level_i* Specifies the level

Example

```
Set-Levels = ('sales', 1)     ! Returns Sales, Toys
```

Compile-time and run-time dialog commands

Input

Purpose	To read user input into the program memory
Syntax	**Input** *name* **[Maxlen =** *nn* **] [** *prompt_text* **]** **[Type = { Char | Text | Number | Integer | Date }]** **[Status =** *status_code* **] [Noprompt] [Batch-Mode]** **[Format =** *format* **]**

Arguments *name* The name of the variable to be populated from user input. Can be of the string, date, or numeric format

nn The maximum length of user input

prompt_text The prompt text to be displayed. If omitted, the default prompt will be used

Type If specified, SQR performs automatic type checking of user input. If a type mismatch is found, an error message is displayed and the **Input** command is reissued

status_code: a numeric variable to hold the completion code of the Input command:

- 0 Successful
- 1 Type mismatch detected
- 2 Input length error
- 3 Nothing entered

Noprompt Do not display a prompt text

Batch-Mode If specified and there are no more arguments in the command line, the status code is set to 3 and the user is not prompted for input

format date edit mask. Used for dates only.

Notes The **Input** command is executed at run time.

When entering a date, use one of the following formats:

MM/DD/YYY [BC|AD] [HH:MI[:SS[.NNNNNN]] [AM|PM]]
MM-DD-YYY [BC|AD] [HH:MI[:SS[.NNNNNN]] [AM|PM]]
MM.DD.YYY [BC|AD] [HH:MI[:SS[.NNNNNN]] [AM|PM]]
SYYYYMM [H24 MI[SS[NNNNNN]]]

When coding the **Format** keyword, use any date edit mask or the keyword **Date**.

Refer to Chapter 11

Example

```
Let #Input_Error = 1
While #Input_Error = 1
  Input $State_List  Maxlen=80 Type=Char Status=#Input_Status
        'Enter a list of comma separated state codes (ex. NY,CT,MI)'
  Let $State_List=Rtrim($State_List,' ')
  If $State_List = '' Or #Input_Status <> 0
    Show 'Incorrect Input'
    Let #Input_Error = 1
  Else
    Let #Input_Error = 0
  End-If
End-While
```

Ask

Purpose To obtain the value of a substitution variable from user input, command line argument, or command argument file entry

Syntax **Ask** *name* **[** *prompt_text* **]**

Arguments *name* The substitution variable name

prompt_text An optional prompt text string if user input is used

Notes	**Ask** assigns values to its substitution variables at compile time. The **Ask** command can be used only in the **Setup** section prior to any substitution variable references.
Refer to	Chapter 11

Example

```
Begin-Setup
Ask Array_Size   'Enter Array Size '

Create-Array Name=My_Array  Size={Array_Size}
  Field = Emplid:char
  Field = Name:char
  Field = Zip:char
End-Setup
```

Print control commands

Declare-Report

Purpose	To declare a report in a multiple-report program
Syntax	**Declare-Report** *report_name* **[Layout =** *layout_name* **]** **[Printer-Type = {HT|HP|PS|LP|HTML|HPLASERJET |POSTSCRIPT|LINEPRINTER}]** **[Toc =** *toc_name* **]** **End-Declare**
Arguments	*report_name* The name of the report. This name is used in the **Declare-Procedure** and **Use-Report** commands *layout_name* The name of the layout to be used in the report. Layouts are defined by the **Declare-Layout** command. If not specified, the default layout is used **Printer-Type** Defines the printer type for this report. The default is **LINE-PRINTER** *toc_name* The name of the table of contents (HTML only)
Notes	The **Declare-Report** command can be used only in the **Setup** section Multiple reports are written into different report files. When multiple reports are printed, the report file names can be specified in the **-F** command line flag. If not specified, the report naming will be controlled by the **OUTPUT-FILE-MODE** environmental variable. If **OUTPUT-FILE-MODE** is set to **SHORT**, the first report file name is *program_name*.**lis**, additional report names are *program_name*.**L***nn* , where *nn* is a number between 01 and 99 in the order in which the reports are declared. If the **-KEEP** or **-NOLIS** command line arguments are used, the first report file's name is *program_name*.**spf**, the additional report names are *program_name*.**S***nn*, where *nn* is a number between 01 and 99 in the order in which the reports are declared. If **OUTPUT-FILE-MODE** is set to **LONG**, the first report file is *program_name*.**lis**, additional report names are *program_name_nn*.**lis**, where *nn* is a number between 01 and 99 in the order in which the reports are declared. If the **-KEEP** or

	-NOLIS command line arguments are used, the first report file name is *program_name*.**spf**, the additional report names are *program_name_nn*.**spf**, where *nn* is a number between 01 and 99 in the order in which the reports are declared.
Refer to	Chapter 13

Example

```
Begin-Setup
Declare-Report Employee_List_US Layout=US_Layout
End-Declare
Declare-Report Employee_List_EU Layout=EU_Layout Printer-Type=POSTSCRIPT
End-Declare
End-Setup
```

Alter-Report

Purpose: To change the current report's heading or footing sections while the report is running.

Syntax:

Alter-Report
  [**Heading** = *heading_name*]
  [**Heading-Size** = *heading-size*]
  [**Footing** = *footing_name*]
  [**Footing-Size** = *footing-size*]

Arguments:

heading_name The name of heading specified in the `Begin-Heading` command. Can be coded as a string variable, column or literal.

heading_size The number of lines the heading will occupy in the page. Can be coded as a numeric variable, column or literal. If no *heading_name* is coded, this value applies to the current heading section.

footing_name The name of footing specified in the `Begin-Footing` command. Can be coded as a string variable, column or literal.

footing_size The number of lines the footing will occupy in the page. Can be coded as a numeric variable, column or literal. If no *footing_name* is coded, this value applies to the current footing section.

Notes:

The `Alter-Report` command does not switch to another report: it only changes the current report's heading or footing characteristics.

If the `Alter-Report` command is issued within a `Heading` or `Footing` section, and the current page has not been completed, the changes to heading or footing take effect immediately; otherwise the changes take effect on the next page.

If *heading_name* or *footing_name* is set to 'NONE', this heading or footing section is disabled for the current report.

If *heading_name* or *footing_name* is set to 'DEFAULT', this heading or footing section will revert to whatever was in effect when the current report was initiated.

Refer to: Chapter 5

Example

```
Begin-Setup
Begin-Heading 3
   Name = Domestic
   Print ' North American ' (1,1,0) Center
   Print $current-date (1,50) Edit MM/DD/YYYY
```

```
End-Heading

Begin-Heading 3
   Name = International
   Print ' International ' (1,1,0) Center
   Print $current-date (1,50) Edit DD/MM/YYYY
End-Heading
! . . .
End-Setup

Begin-Program
! . . .
   Alter-Report
      Heading='Domestic'
      Heading-Size=5
! . . .
   Alter-Report
      Heading='International'
      Heading-Size=4
End-Program
```

Use-Report

Purpose	To switch between reports in a multiple report program
Syntax	**Use-Report** *report_name*
Arguments	*report_name* The name of the report to become the current report. Can be a string variable, column variable, or literal. This name must be defined in a **Declare-Report** command
Notes	After the **Use-Report** command is issued, all subsequent **Print** commands direct their output to the specified report until the next **Use-Report** is issued.
Refer to	Chapter 13

Example

```
 Begin-Procedure Print_My_Report
  Use-Report My_Report

    Print 'My Report ' (1,1)
End-Procedure
```

New-Report

Purpose	To close the current report output file and open a new one with the specified file name
Syntax	**New-Report** *file_name*
Arguments	*file_name* The new report file name. Can be a string literal, variable, or column variable

Notes	When this command is used, the internal page and line counters are initialized. When issued in a multiple-report program, changes the current report file name. After this command execution, the SQR reserved variable **$sqr-report** is updated.
Refer to	Chapter 13

Example

```
Input $File_Name 'Enter a name of the report file'
New-Report $File_Name
```

Declare-Procedure

Purpose	To declare procedures to be invoked when the specified report-related events occur
Syntax	**Declare-Procedure** **[For-Reports = (** *report1* **[,** *reporti* **] …)]** **[Before-Report =** *procedure_name1* **[(** *arg1* **[,** *argi* **] …)]]** **[After-Report =** *procedure_name2* **[(** *arg1* **[,** *argi* **] …)]]** **[Before-Page =** *procedure_name3* **[(** *arg1* **[,** *argi* **] …)]]** **[After-Page =** *procedure_name4* **[(** *arg1* **[,** *argi* **] …)]]** **End-Declare**
Arguments	**For-Reports** Specifies one or more reports that use the specified procedures. If not specified, the procedures will be invoked for all reports **Before-Report** Specifies a procedure to be invoked at the beginning of the report creation (e.g., first **Print** command) **After-Report** Specifies a procedure to be invoked at the end of the report **Before-Page** Specifies a procedure to be invoked at the beginning of every report page **After-Page** Specifies a procedure to be invoked before every page is written to the output file
Notes	The **Declare-Procedure** is a compile-time command and can be used only in the **Setup** section. You can issue multiple **Declare-Procedure** commands. The last command takes precedence; therefore, it is recommended to place common **Declare-Procedure** commands first and report-specific **Declare-Procedure** commands second.
Refer to	Chapter 10

Example

```
Begin-Setup
Declare-Procedure
    For-Reports = (Employee_List_US, Employee_List_EU)
    Before-Report = Empl_List_Heading
    After-Report = Empl_List_Totals
    Before-Page = Empl_List_Page_Header
End-Declare
End-Setup
```

Use-Procedure

Purpose	To change procedures to be invoked when the specified report-related events occur
Syntax	**Use-Procedure** **[For-Reports = (** *report1* **[,** *reporti* **] …)]** **[Before-Report =** *procedure_name1* **[(** *arg1* **[,** *argi* **] …)]]** **[After-Report =** *procedure_name2* **[(** *arg1* **[,** *argi* **] …)]]** **[Before-Page =** *procedure_name3* **[(** *arg1* **[,** *argi* **] …)]]** **[After-Page =** *procedure_name4* **[(** *arg1* **[,** *argi* **] …)]]**
Arguments	**For-Reports** Specifies one or more reports that use the specified procedures. If not specified, the procedures will be invoked for all reports **Before-Report** Specifies a procedure to be invoked at the beginning of the report creation (e.g., first `Print` command) **After-Report** Specifies a procedure to be invoked at the end of the report **Before-Page** Specifies a procedure to be invoked at the beginning of every report page **After-Page** Specifies a procedure to be invoked before every page is written to the output file
Notes	The **Use-Procedure** command is a run-time equivalent of the compile-time command **Declare-Procedure**. You can issue multiple **Use-Procedure** commands. The next command supersedes the previous command settings.
Refer to	Chapter 10

Example

```
Begin-Procedure My_Procedure
Use-Procedure
  For-Reports = (Employee_List_US, Employee_List_EU)
  Before-Report = Empl_List_Heading
  After-Report = Empl_List_Totals
  Before-Page = Empl_List_Page_Header
End-Procedure My_Procedure
```

Declare-Printer

Purpose	To override the printer default settings for the specified printer type
Syntax	**Declare-Printer** *printer_name* **[For-Reports =** **(** *report1* **[,** *reporti* **] …)] [Type =** *type* **]** **[Init-String =** *init_string* **]** **[Reset-String =** *reset_string* **]** **[Color = {Yes | No}] [Point-Size =** *nn* **] [Font =** *nn* **]** **[Font-Type = { PROPORTIONAL | FIXED}]** **[Symbol-Set =** *set* **] [Startup-File =** *file_name* **]** **[Pitch =** *nn* **] [Before_Bold =** *before_bold_string* **]** **[After_Bold =** *after_bold_string* **]** **End-Declare**

Arguments *printer_name* A printer type name to be reserved for the declared printer type
reporti the name(s) of report(s) which use this printer definition. Not used for single-report programs
Type = {HT|HP|PS|LP|HTML|HPLASERJET|POSTSCRIPT|LINEPRINTER}
init_string A sequence of characters to be sent to printer at the beginning of the report
reset_string A sequence of characters to be sent to printer at the end of the report
Color Yes—for color printers, **No**—for non-color printers
Point-Size The starting size of the selected font. The default is 12. Does not apply to **LINEPRINTER**
Font the font number
Font-Type Is used for **HPLASERJET** only
Symbol-Set Is used for **HPLASERJET** only. The default value is 'OU' for the ASCII symbol set. See the printer manual for a complete list of symbol sets.
Startup-File is used for **POSTSCRIPT** only. The default is **POSTSCRI.str**.
Pitch the pitch size in characters/inch. Is used for **HPLASERJET** only
Before_Bold, After-Bold Is used for **LINEPRINTER** only. Specifies the character string to turn the **Bold** on and off

Notes Every printer type has a set of defaults. The **Declare-Printer** command overrides these defaults. You can use multiple **Declare-Printer** commands, one per each printer type to be overridden.
The **Declare-Printer** command can be used only in the Setup section. If you need to change this command setting later, use the **Alter-Printer** command.

Refer to Chapter 13

Example

```
Declare-Printer Alternate-HP
    For-Reports=(Empl_List_US, Empl_List_EU)
    Type=HPLASERJET
    Font=3
End-Declare
```

Alter-Printer

Purpose To override printer type parameters at run time

Syntax **Alter-Printer**
[Point-Size = *nn* **] [Font-Type = { PROPORTIONAL | FIXED}]**
[Font = *nn* **] [Symbol-Set =** *set* **] [Pitch =** *nn* **]**

Arguments **Point-Size** The new font point size
Font-Type Is used for **HPLASERJET** only
Symbol-Set The new symbol set. Is used for **HPLASERJET** only. See the printer manual for a complete list of symbol sets.
Font The new font number
Pitch The new pitch in characters/inch

Notes	The **Alter-Printer** command is a run-time command and should not be used in the `Setup` section. This command changes the default attributes of the current printer type associated with the current report. Use the **Use-Report** command to change the current report and the **Use-Printer-Type** command to change the current printer type.
Refer to	Chapter 13

Example

```
Alter-Printer
    Point-Size = 12
    Symbol-Set = 0U
```

Use-Printer-Type

Purpose	To set the printer type to be used for the current report
Syntax	**Use-Printer-Type** *printer_type*
Arguments	*printer_type* The printer type to be used for the current report. Must be a valid printer type
Notes	This command must be issued before the first output is written to the report.
Refer to	Chapter 13

Example

```
Use-Printer-Type LINEPRINTER
```

Declare-Layout

Purpose	To define the layout of a report
Syntax	**Declare-Layout** *name* **[Paper-Size = ({** *size_code* | *width* **[** *units* **] ,** *length* **[** *units* **] }) [Formfeed = { Yes** | **No }]** **[Orientation = { PORTRAIT** | **LANDSCAPE }]** **[Left-Margin =** *nn* **[***units***] [Top-Margin =** *nn* **[***units***]** **[{Right-Margin =** *nn* **[***units***]** | **[Line-Width =** *nn* **[** *units* **]** | **Max-Columns =** *nnn* **}]** **[{Bottom-Margin =** *nn* **[***units***]** | **[Page-Depth =** *nn* **[** *units* **]** | **Max-Lines =** *nnn* **}]** **[Char-Width =** *nn* **[***units***] [Line-Height =** *nn* **[***units***]** **End-Declare**
Arguments	*name* The name of the layout. This name can be referenced in the **Declare-Report** command. **Paper-Size** The size of the page. Can be specified as size code (**LETTER** | **LEGAL** | **A4** | **EXECUTIVE** | **B5** | **COM-10** | **MONARCH** | **DL** | **C5**) or by specifying actual page dimensions. *units* Units of measure (**dp** | **pt** | **mm** | **cm** | **in**) **Formfeed** Specifies whether formfeeds are to be placed at the end of each page **Orientation** page orientation. The default is **PORTRAIT**.

Left-Margin The amount of blank space at the left side of the page
Top-Margin The amount of blank space at the top of the page
Right-Margin The amount of blank space at the right side of the page
Line-Width The length of the page line
Max-Columns The maximum number of columns on a page line
Bottom-Margin The amount of blank space at the bottom of the page
Page-Depth The depth of the page
Max-Lines The maximum number of lines on the page
Char-Width The size of each character column. The default is 7.2 pt.
Line-Height The size of each line on the page. The default is 12 pt.

Notes — The **Declare-Layout** command is a compile time command and can be used only in the `Setup` section.
If no **Declare-Layout** command is coded, a default layout named **Default** is created.
You can define multiple layouts.

Refer to — Chapter 5, 13

Example

```
Declare-Layout Special_Layout
    Paper-Size = (5 in, 12 in)
    Left-Margin = 20 mm
    Top-Margin = 35 mm
    Orientation = LANDSCAPE
    Formfeed = No
End-Declare
```

Declare-Chart

Purpose — To define a chart to be displayed using the **Print-Chart** command

Syntax —

```
Declare-Chart chart_name
  [ Data-Labels = {Yes | No}
  [ Color-Palette = palette_name ]
  [ Item-Color = (chart_item , {color_name | (rgb)}) ]
  [ Chart-Size = ( nn , mm ) ] [ Title = title ] [ Sub-Title = subtitle ]
  [ Fill = { GRAYSCALE | COLOR | CROSSHATCH | NONE } ]
  [ 3D-Effects = { Yes | No } ] [ Border = { Yes | No } ]
  [ Point-Markers = { Yes | No } ]
  [ Type = {LINE|PIE|BAR|STACKED-BAR|100%-BAR|
          OVERLAPPED-BAR|FLOATING|BAR|HISTOGRAM|AREA|STACKED|
          AREA|100%-AREA|XY-SCATTER-PLOT|HIGH-LOW-CLOSE} ]
  [ Legend = { Yes | No } ] [ Legend-Title = { None | legend_title } ]
  [ Legend-Placement = {CENTER-RIGHT|CENTER-LEFT|
                        UPPER-RIGHT|UPPER-LEFT|UPPER-CENTER|
                        LOWER-RIGHT|LOWER-LEFT|LOWER-CENTER} ]
 [ Legend-Presentation = {INSIDE|OUTSIDE}
  [ Pie-Segment-Quantity-Display = { Yes | No } ]
  [ Pie-Segment-Percent-Display = { Yes | No } ]
  [ Pie-Segment-Explode = {NONE|MAX|MIN|USE-3RD-DATA-COLUMN} ]
```

```
[ X-Axis-Label = x_axis_label ]
[ X-Axis-Min-Value = {AUTOSCALE | nnn} ]
[ X-Axis-Max-Value  = {AUTOSCALE | nnn} ]
[ X-Axis-Scale = { LOG | LINEAR } ]
[ X-Axis-Major-Tick-Marks = { Yes | No } ]
[ X-Axis-Minor-Tick-Marks = { Yes | No } ]
[ X-Axis-Major-Increment = { AUTOSCALE | nnn } ]
[ X-Axis-Minor-Increment = { AUTOSCALE | nnn } ]
[ X-Axis-Tick-Mark-Placement = {INSIDE|OUTSIDE|BOTH} ]
[ X-Axis-Grid = { Yes | No } ]
[ Y-Axis-Label = x_axis_label ]
[ Y-Axis-Min-Value = {AUTOSCALE | nnn} ]
[ Y-Axis-Max-Value = {AUTOSCALE | nnn} ]
[ Y-Axis-Scale = { LOG | LINEAR } ]
[ Y-Axis-Major-Tick-Marks = { Yes | No } ]
[ Y-Axis-Minor-Tick-Marks = { Yes | No } ]
[ Y-Axis-Major-Increment = { AUTOSCALE | nnn } ]
[ Y-Axis-Minor-Increment = { AUTOSCALE | nnn } ]
[ Y-Axis-Tick-Mark-Placement = {INSIDE|OUTSIDE|BOTH} ]
[ Y-Axis-Grid = { Yes | No } ]
End-Declare
```

Arguments *chart_name* The name of the chart to be referenced in the **Print-Chart** command
Chart-Size The size of the chart in lines and columns
Title The title to be displayed on the chart
Sub-Title The sub-title to be displayed on the chart below the title
Legend-Title If coded, will be displayed as the title for the chart legend
data_labels If set to '**Yes**', SQR prints the numeric values above the individual data points.
palette_name The name of the color palette used to color individual data points in a chart. The name of the palette is defined in the Create-Color-Palette command.
chart_item An individual item in the chart that needs a special color. The list of possible items includes: ChartBackground, ChartForeground, HeaderBackground, HeaderForeground, FooterBackground, FooterForeground, LegendBackground, LegendForeground, ChartAreaBackground, ChartAreaForeground, PlotAreaBackground.
color_name The name of a color.
rgb Color value in the RGB (red green blue) units. Each color component value can be between 0 and 255.

Notes The **Declare_Chart** command is a compile-time command and can be used only within the **Setup** section
Chart attributes defined by the **Declare-Chart** command can be later overridden by the **Print-Chart** command
Only POSTSCRIPT printer or HP LASERJET 3 printers and higher will be able to support all these chart characteristics.

Refer to Chapter 16

Example

```
Declare-Chart Employees_By_Region
              Chart-Size = ( 20 , 25 )
```

```
            Title = 'Number of US Employees'
            Sub-Title = ' By Region '
            Fill = COLOR
            3D-Effects = Yes
           Type = PIE
End-Declare
```

Create-Color-Palette

Purpose	To create a color palette to be used in the `Declare-Chart` or `Print-Chart` command.
Syntax	**Create-Color-Palette** **Name** = *palette_name* **Color_1** = **({***color_name1* | *r1g1b1***})** **[Color_i** = **({***color_namei* | *rigibi***})** **...]**
Arguments	*palette_name* The name of the color palette. *color_namei* The name of a color. Can be coded as a string variable, column or literal. *(rigibi)* Color value in the RGB (red green blue) units. Each color component value can be between 0 and 255 and can be coded as a numeric variable, column or literal.
Notes	You can create an unlimited number of color palettes. You can define up to 64 colors in each palette. This command is used in conjunction with the `Declare-Chart` or `Print-Chart` command. The colors defined in each palette are used to color individual data points in a chart, for example, bars, sectors, etc. The order of colors corresponds to the data areas of a chart. If there are more data points in a chart than the number of colors in the palette, SQR resets the palette from color 1. No gaps are permitted in the palette.
Refer to	Chapter 16

Example

```
Create-Color-Palette Name = 'My_Palette'
    Color_1 = (255,156,74)
    Color_2 = (255,255,198)
    Color_3 = ('blue')
    Color_4 = ($My_Color)
```

Declare-Image

Purpose	To define an image to be displayed using the `Print-Image` command
Syntax	**Declare-Image** *image_name* **[Type = { EPS-FILE|HPGL-FILE|GIF-FILE|JPEG-FILE|BMP-FILE }]** **[Image-Size = (** *nn* **,** *mm* **)** **[Source** = *file_name* **)]** **End-Declare**
Arguments	**Image-Size** The width and the height of the image **Source** The name of the image file. The file must be in the `SQRDIR` directory, otherwise you must specify the full path.

Notes	The **Declare-Image** command is a compile-time command and can be used only within the **Setup** section. Image attributes defined by the **Declare-Image** can be later overridden by the **Print-Image** command.
Refer to	Chapter 16

Example

```
Declare-Image ABCD_Logo
     Type = BMP-FILE
     Source = 'abcd_logo.bmp'
End-Declare
```

Columns

Purpose	To define logical columns for the **Print** command. The logical columns can be later used by the **Next-Column** and **Use-Column** commands
Syntax	**Columns** *column1* **[** *columni* **]** ...
Arguments	*columni* Specifies the left position of column *i* within the page
Notes	The **Columns** command defines one or more logical columns and makes the first column of the group the current column.
Refer to	Chapter 9

Example

```
!  This command defines three logical columns
!  at positions 10, 20, 30 and sets
!  the current column position at 10:
Columns 10 20 30
!  This command prints starting from position 2 relative to the current
!  position which makes the printing position equal to 11.
Print 'ABCD' (+1, 2)
```

Next-Column

Purpose	To switch from the current logical column to next logical column. The logical columns are defined by the Columns command
Syntax	**Next-Column [At-End = { Newline | Newpage }]** **[Goto-Top =** *nn* **] [Erase-Page =** *mm* **]**
Arguments	**At-End** Specifies an action to be taken when **Next-Column** is applied to the last logical column defined **Goto-Top** Sets up the new current line after switching to the next logical column. *nn* can be a numeric literal, variable, or column variable **Erase-Page** Specifies where to begin erasing the page when **At-End = Newpage** occurs
Refer to	Chapter 9

Example

```
Next-Column At-End=Newpage
```

Use-Column

Purpose	To switch from the current logical column to specified logical column. The logical columns are defined by the **Columns** command.
Syntax	**Use-Column** *nn*
Arguments	*nn* The new logical column number. Can be a numeric literal, variable, or column variable
Notes	Specifying **Use-Column = 0** causes switching from logical column printing mode to normal printing mode.
Refer to	Chapter 9

Example

```
Use-Column 2
```

New-Page

Purpose	To write the current page and open a new one
Syntax	**New-Page [** *nn* **]**
Arguments	*nn* If specified, causes erasing the old page starting from this line otherwise the entire old page gets erased
Notes	There is no need to issue the **New-Page** command if a page overflow normally occurs. In tabular reports, use **Next-Listing** instead of **New-Page**. After each **New-Page** command, a form feed character is written to the output file unless **Formfeed = No** is specified in the **Declare-Layout** command.
Refer to	Chapter 9, 10, 17

Example

```
! The current page is written to the output file and then the page
! buffer is erased starting from line 3 to prepare for a new page
New-Page 3
```

Page-Number

Purpose	To print the current page number
Syntax	**Page-Number ([***X* **[,** *Y* **]]) [** *pre_text* **[** *post_text* **]]**
Arguments	*X, Y* The position where the entire current page numbering statement will be placed *pre_text* A text string to be printed before the current page number *post_text* A text string to be printed after the current page number
Refer to	Chapter 5

Example

```
Page-Number (+1, 30) 'Page '  '. '
```

Last-Page

Purpose	To print the number of the last page in a report
Syntax	**Last-Page ([***X* **[,** *Y* **]]) [** *pre_text* **[** *post_text* **]]**
Arguments	*X, Y* The position where the entire last page numbering statement will be placed *pre_text* A text string to be printed before the last page number *post_text* A text string to be printed after the last page number
Notes	When this command is used, SQR does not print all report pages but rather accumulates them until the last page number is known. When this command is used, SQR generates an SPF file to temporarily store the program output report. The file is erased after the program finishes.
Refer to	Chapter 5

Example

```
Last-Page (, 25) 'Total of '  'pages.'
```

Next-Listing

Purpose	To end the current detail group and start another one in a tabular report
Syntax	**Next-Listing [No-Advance] [Skiplines =** *nn* **] [Need =** *mm* **]**
Arguments	**No-Advance** Suppresses line movement when no printing has occurred since the previous **New-Listing** or **New-Page**. If not specified, the line position will advance even if nothing was printed. **Skiplines** The number of lines to be skipped before starting another detail group. Can be an integer literal, variable, or SQR column **Need** Tells SQR to begin a new page if there are less than *mm* lines left on the current page. Can be an integer literal, variable, or SQR column
Notes	When the **Next-Listing** command is used, the SQR reserved variable **#current-line** holds the actual line number within the page.
Refer to	Chapter 9

Example

```
Begin-Select
Company   (1,1)
Descr     (2,1)
Address   (3,1)
      Next-Listing Skiplines = 1 Need = 3
From Company_Table
End-Select
```

Position

Purpose	To set the current position on a page
Syntax	**Position ([***X* **[,** *Y* **]]) [** *@document_marker* **[Columns** *col1* **[** *coli* **] …]]**
Arguments	*X, Y* The position on a page *@document_marker* If coded, the position specifies the location of the specified document marker in a document **Columns** The columns beginning at the location of the document marker. The columns are defined relative to the document marker.
Notes	When **Columns** are used, the entire command must be coded in one line.
Refer to	Chapter 9, 15

Example

```
Position ( ) @employee_name Columns 1 20
Position (+1)
```

Page-Size

Purpose	To set the page size in a report
Syntax	**Page-Size** *nn mm*
Arguments	*nn* Page depth in lines *mm* Page width in columns
Notes	This command may be discontinued in a future release. Use the **Max-Lines** and **Max-Columns** parameters of the **Declare-Layout** command. The default page size is 62 lines by 132 columns.
Refer to	Chapter 19

Example

```
Begin-Setup
  Page-Size 55.60
End-Setup
```

Graphic

Purpose	To draw a box or line, or to change a font
Syntax	**Graphic (** *X* , *Y* , *Z* **) BOX** *depth* **[** *rule_width* **[** *shading* **]]** **Graphic (** *X* , *Y* , *Z* **) HORZ-LINE [** *width* **]** **Graphic (** *X* , *Y* , *Z* **) VERT-LINE [** *width* **]** **Graphic ( ) FONT** *font_number* **[** *point_size* **[{ 1 | 0 } [** *pitch* **]]]**
Arguments	*X, Y* The location of the graphical object on a page The meaning of other command arguments depends on the command type: BOX *Z* The width of the box in character columns *depth* The depth of the box in page lines

rule_width The box rule width in decipoints (there are 720 decipoints per inch). The default is 2.

shading The shading percentage between 1 (very light) and 100 (black)

HORZ-LINE

z The length of the line in columns

width The line width in decipoints. The default is 2.

VERT-LINE

z The length of the line in lines

width The line width in decipoints. The default is 2

FONT

font_number The font number

point_size The point size

1 Indicates a proportional font; **0** indicates a non-proportional font

pitch Pitch in characters per inch

Notes: The **Graphic Font** command may be discontinued in a future release. Use the **Declare-Printer** and **Alter-Printer** commands instead.

Refer to: Chapter 16

Example

```
Graphic (+1, 5, 50) BOX 20 15         ! Draw a shaded box 50 columns wide
                                      ! 20 lines deep
Graphic (+1, 5, 50) HORZ-LINE  6      ! Draw a 50 character long
                                      ! 6 decipoint wide
                                      ! horizontal line
Graphic (+1, 5, 50) VERT-LINE 4       ! Draw a 50 character long
                                      ! 4 decipoint wide vertical line
Graphic ( ) Font 3 12 0
```

Print

Purpose: To print data at a specified position

Syntax: **Print** *name* **([[{+|-}]** *x* **] , [[{+|-}]** *y* **] [, [***z* **]])**
[*format_command* **[** *format_parameters* **] ...] ...**

Arguments: *name* A variable, SQR column, or literal. Can be of the string, date, or numeric format

x Page line number. If used with the plus or minus sign, indicates a relative to the current line number; otherwise, an absolute line number. If omitted, the current line number is used. Can be a numeric literal or variable

y Page starting column number. If used with the plus or minus sign, indicates a relative to the current column number; otherwise, an absolute column number. If omitted, the current column number is used. Can be a numeric literal or variable

z The number of print positions allocated to the output. If omitted, SQR will calculate the number of positions based on the variable length, type, and the format command(s) used

Arguments (continued)

format_command One or more of the following formatting commands:

- **Background** = **(**{*color_name* | *rgb*}**)**—specifies a background color as color name or color value in the RGB (red green blue) units. Each color component value can be between 0 and 255
- **Bold**—prints the output in bold type
- **Box**—prints a graphical box around the printed area
- **Center**—prints the output in the center of the line. The column parameter is ignored
- **Code-Printer = {HT|HP|PS|LP|HTML|HPLASERJET|POSTSCRIPT LINEPRINTER}**
- **Date**—prints the output using the **Date-Edit-Mask** from the current locale
- **Edit**—edit_mask edits the output before printing using the specified edit mask (Edit masks are discussed in chapters 4 and 9). Can be used only with string or date fields
- **Fill**—fills the output with the spedified character or string
- **Foreground** = **(**{color_name | rgb}**)**—specifies a foreground color as color name or color value in the RGB (red green blue) units. Each color component value can be between 0 and 25.
- **Match**—compares a field to a list of key values and if a match is found, prints the corresponding string. (Please see an example in chapter 9)
- **Money**—prints the output using the **Money-Edit-Mask** from the current locale. Can be used with numeric fields only
- **Nop**—suppresses the printing
- **Number**—prints the output using the **Number-Edit-Mask** from the current locale. Can be used with numeric fields only
- **On-Break**

  [Print = {Always | Change | Change/Top-Page | Never}]—specifies an action when the value of the printed field changes

  [Skiplines = *nn* **]**—causes SQR to skip *nn* lines when the value of the printed field changes

  [Procedure = *procedure_name* **[(***arg1* **[,** *argi***]** ... **)]**—specifies the procedure to be invoked when the value of the printed field changes

  [After = *procedure_name* **[(***arg1* **[,** *argi***]** ... **)]**—the procedure to be invoked after the value of the printed field changes

  [Before = *procedure_name* **[(***arg1* **[,** *argi***]** ... **)]**—the procedure to be invoked before the value of the printed field changes

  [Save = *nn* **]**—the name of a string variable to hold the previous value of the break field

  [Level = *nn* **]**—the break level for multiple break reports

  [Set = *nn* **]**—assigns a number to the set of leveled breaks with more than one set of independent breaks

  Note: The **On-Break** command is discussed in detail in chapter 10
- **Shade**—prints a shaded graphical box around the printed area
- **Underline**—underlines the printed area
- **Wrap**—wraps the printed text (please see an example in chapter 9

Notes: The **On-Break** format command can be used only with string or date fields. The **Before** and **After** qualifiers can be used only within a **Select** paragraph.

Refer to: Chapters 9, 10

Example

```
Print &B.Company   (,1,7)  On-Break Level = 1 Before=Company_Name
        After=Company_Totals  Skiplines = 1
```

```
Print &B.Paygroup  (,10,8) On-Break Level = 2 After=Paygroup_Totals

Print $Emplid      (,+2,8)

Print #Annual_Rt   (,+2,12) Edit $,$$$,$$$.00
```

No-Formfeed

Purpose	To prevent form feed characters from being written to the output file
Syntax	**No-Formfeed**
Arguments	None
Notes	This command may be discontinued in a future release. Use the **Formfeed** parameter of the **Declare-Layout** command.

Print-Chart

Purpose: To print a chart. The chart may be previously defined using the **Declare-Chart** command.

Syntax:

```
Print-Chart [ chart_name ] ( X [, Y ] )
      Data-Array = array_name
      Data-Array-Row-Count = nn
      Data-Array-Column-Count = mm
    [ Data-Array-Column-Labels = { NONE|array_name|
    (label1 [ , labeli ] ...) ]
    [ Data-Labels = {Yes | No}
    [ Color-Palette = palette_name ]
    [ Item-Color = (chart_item , {color_name | (rgb)}) ]
    [ Chart-Size = ( nn , mm ) ] [ Title = title ]
    [ Subtitle = subtitle ]
    [ Fill = { GRAYSCALE | COLOR | CROSSHATCH | NONE } ]
    [ 3D-Effects = { Yes | No } ] [ Border = { Yes | No } ]
    [ Point-Markers = { Yes | No } ]
    [ Type = {LINE|PIE|BAR|STACKED-BAR|100%-BAR|OVERLAPPED-BAR|
     FLOATING|BAR|HISTOGRAM|AREA|STACKED|AREA|100%-AREA|
     XY-SCATTER-PLOT|HIGH-LOW-CLOSE} ]
    [ Legend = { Yes | No } ] [ Legend-Title = legend_title ]
    [ Legend-Placement = {CENTER-RIGHT|CENTER-LEFT|
                          UPPER-RIGHT|UPPER-LEFT|UPPER-CENTER|
                          LOWER-RIGHT|LOWER-LEFT|LOWER-CENTER} ]
    [ Legend-Presentation = {INSIDE|OUTSIDE}
    [ Pie-Segment-Quantity-Display = { Yes | No } ]
    [ Pie-Segment-Percent-Display = { Yes | No } ]
    [ Pie-Segment-Explode = {NONE|MAX|MIN|USE-3RD-DATA-COLUMN} ]
    [  X-Axis-Label = x_axis_label ]
    [ X-Axis-Min-Value = {AUTOSCALE | nnn} ]
    [ X-Axis-Max-Value  = {AUTOSCALE | nnn} ]
```

```
[ X-Axis-Scale = { LOG | LINEAR } ]
[ X-Axis-Major-Tick-Marks = { Yes | No } ]
[ X-Axis-Minor-Tick-Marks = { Yes | No } ]
[ X-Axis-Major-Increment = { AUTOSCALE | nnn } ]
[ X-Axis-Minor-Increment = { AUTOSCALE | nnn } ]
[ X-Axis-Tick-Mark-Placement = {INSIDE|OUTSIDE|BOTH} ]
[ X-Axis-Grid = { Yes | No } ]
[ Y-Axis-Label = x_axis_label ]
[ Y-Axis-Min-Value = {AUTOSCALE | nnn} ]
[ Y-Axis-Max-Value = {AUTOSCALE | nnn} ]
[ Y-Axis-Scale = { LOG | LINEAR } ]
[ Y-Axis-Major-Tick-Marks = { Yes | No } ]
[ Y-Axis-Minor-Tick-Marks = { Yes | No } ]
[ Y-Axis-Major-Increment = { AUTOSCALE | nnn } ]
[ Y-Axis-Minor-Increment = { AUTOSCALE | nnn } ]
[ Y-Axis-Tick-Mark-Placement = {INSIDE|OUTSIDE|BOTH} ]
[ Y-Axis-Grid = { Yes | No } ]
```

Arguments *chart_name* The name of the chart defined in the **Declare-Chart** command. If not specified, all required chart attributes must be specified in the **Print-Chart** command.

X, Y The row and column position of the left upper corner of the chart

Data-Array The name of the array containing the data to be plotted. The name of the array must be defined in the **Declare-Array** command.

Data-Array-Row-Count The number of rows in the array referenced in **Data-Array**. If the array has more rows than specified in this parameter, only the first *nn* rows will be included.

Data-Array-Column-Count The number of columns in the array referenced in **Data-Array**. If the array has more columns than specified in this parameter, only the first *mm* columns will be included.

data_labels If set to 'Yes', SQR prints the numeric values above the individual data points.

palette_name The name of the color palette used to color individual data points in a chart. The name of the palette is defined in the `Create-Color-Palatte` command.

chart_item An individual item in the chart that needs a special color. The list of possible items includes: ChartBackground, ChartForeground, HeaderBackground, HeaderForeground, FooterBackground, FooterForeground, LegendBackground, LegendForeground, ChartAreaBackground, ChartAreaForeground, PlotAreaBackground.

color_name The name of a color.

rgb Color value in the RGB (red green blue) units. Each color component value can be between 0 and 255.

Notes The **Print-Chart** command is a run-time command and cannot be used within the **Setup** section.

Only POSTSCRIPT printers or HP LASERJET 3 printers and higher will be able to support all these chart characteristics.

Refer to Chapter16

Example

```
Print-Chart Employees_By_Region (1, 5)
            Data-Array = Employee_Stat
```

```
Data-Array-Row-Count = 5
Data-Array-Column-Count = 2
3D-Effects = No
Type = PIE
```

Print-Bar-Code

Purpose	To print bar codes
Syntax	**Print-Bar-Code (** *X* **[** , *Y* **]) Type =** *type* **Height =** *height* **Text =** *text* **[Caption =** *caption* **] [Checksum = { Yes | No }]**
Arguments	*X, Y* The position of the upper left corner of the bar code *type* The type of the bar code (see the SQR manual for valid barcode types) *height* The height of the bar code in inches. Must be between 0.1 and 2 inches *text* The text to be encoded in the bar code *caption* An additional text to be printed under the bar code. In most cases, it repeats the text in the **Text** argument. **Checksum** Specifies whether an optional checksum needs to be included into the bar code. The default is **No** *data_labels* If set to 'Yes', SQR prints the numeric values above the individual data points. *palette_name* The name of the color palette used to color individual data points in a chart. The name of the palette is defined in the `Create-Color-Palette` command. *chart_item* An individual item in the chart that needs a special color. The list of possible items includes: ChartBackground, ChartForeground, HeaderBackground, HeaderForeground, FooterBackground, FooterForeground, LegendBackground, LegendForeground, ChartAreaBackground, ChartAreaForeground, PlotAreaBackground. *color_name* The name of a color. rgb Color value in the RGB (red green blue) units. Each color component value can be between 0 and 255.
Notes	After the command is executed, the current position is returned to the upper left corner of the bar code. **Caption** is not valid for ZIP+4 Postnet. If coded, will be ignored. The number of characters and type of the text to be encoded depend on the bar code type.
Refer to	Chapter 16

Example

```
Let $Bar_Code_Text = '12345678910'
Let #Bar_Code_Type = 1  ! UPC-A
Print-Bar-Code ( +1, 5)
          Type = #Bar_Code_Type
          Height = 0.5
          Text = $Bar_Code_Text
          Caption = $Bar_Code_Text
```

Print-Image

Purpose	To print an image. The image may be previously defined using the `Declare-Image` command.
Syntax	`Print-Image` **[** *`image_name`* **]** **(** *`X`* , *`Y`* **)** **[Type = { EPS-FILE|HPGL-FILE|GIF-FILE|JPEG-FILE| BMP-FILE }]** **[Image-Size = (** *`nn`* , *`mm`* **)** **[Source =** *`file_name`* **)]**
Arguments	*`image_name`* The name of the image defined in the **`Declare-Image`** command. If not specified, all required image attributes must be specified in the **`Print-Image`** command *`X, Y`* The row and column position of the upper left corner of the image. Document markers are not allowed. **`Image-Size`** The width and the height of the image **`Source`** The name of the image file. The file must be in the `SQRDIR` directory, otherwise you must specify the full path.
Notes	The **`Print-Image`** command is a run-time command and cannot be used within the **`Setup`** section. After the image is printed, the current position is returned to the upper left corner of the image.
Refer to	Chapter 16

Example

```
Print-Image ABCD_Logo (+1, 2)
     Image-Size = (10, 5)
```

Print-Direct

Purpose	To print into the output file without accumulating the page in memory
Syntax	**`Print-Direct [ Nolf ]`** **`[ Printer = {LINEPRINTER|POSTSCRIPT|HPLASERJET|HTML|LP|PS|` **`HP|HT} ]`** *`text`*
Arguments	**`Nolf`** No line feed character is needed **`Printer`** The type of printer *`text`* The text to be printed. Can be a literal, variable, or column
Notes	The **`Print-Direct`** command is a run-time command and cannot be used within the **`Setup`** section. The **`Print-Direct`** command is used in special cases when the regular way of accumulating entire print pages in the memory is not applicable.

Example

```
Let $My_Text = 'Print direct'
Print-Direct Nolf Printer = HP $My_Text
```

Printer-Init

Purpose	To define a sequence of characters to be sent to printer at the beginning of the report
Syntax	**Printer-Init** *init_string*
Arguments	*init_string* A sequence of characters to be sent to printer at the beginning of the report
Notes	This command may be discontinued in a future release. Use the **Init-String** parameter of the **Declare-Printer** command.

Printer-DeInit

Purpose	To define a sequence of characters to be sent to printer at the end of the report
Syntax	**Printer-DeInit** *reset_string*
Arguments	*reset_string* A sequence of characters to be sent to printer at the end of the report
Notes	This command may be discontinued in a future release. Use the **Reset-String** parameter of the **Declare-Printer** command.

Declare-Toc

Purpose: To declare a table of contents in an HTML-enabled program

Syntax:

```
Declare-Toc toc_name [ For-Reports = ( report_name1
  [ , report_namei ] … ) ]
  [ Dot-Leader = {Yes | No } ] [ Indentation = indent ]
  [ Before-Toc = proc_name [ ( arg1 [, argi ] … ) ] ]
  [ After-Toc = proc_name [ ( arg1 [, argi ] … ) ] ]
  [ Before-Page = proc_name [ ( arg1 [,  argi ] … ) ] ]
  [ After-Page = proc_name [ ( arg1 [, argi ] … ) ] ]
  [Entry = entry-procedure ]
End-Declare
```

Arguments:

toc_name The name of the table of contents. This name can be referenced in the **Declare-Report**, **Begin-Heading**, or **Begin-Footing** commands.
report_name The name of the reports which use this table of contents. Reports are defined by the **Declare-Report** command.
Dot-*Leader* Defines whether or not a dot leader will precede the page number
indent The number of spaces that each level will be preceded by
Before-Toc Name of the procedure to be invoked before the t.o.c. generation
After-Toc Name of the procedure to be invoked after the t.o.c. generation
Before-Page Name of the procedure to be invoked at page start
After-Page Name of the procedure to be invoked at page end
entry_procedure Name of the procedure to process each t.o.c. entry instead of standard SQR processing. When this procedure is invoked, the following SQR reserved variables are passed to the procedure: `#Sqr-Toc-Entry` contains the entry level, `$Sqr-Toc-Text` contains the entry text, `#Sqr-Toc-Page` contains the page number.

Notes: The **Declare-Toc** command can be used only in the **Setup** section.

Refer to: Chapter 19

Example

```
Begin-Setup
   Declare-Toc Employee_List_Toc
      For-Reports = (Employee_List, Dependent_List)
      Before-Page = Open_Table_Proc
      After-Page = Close_Table_Proc
   End-Declare
End-Setup
```

Toc-Entry

Purpose	To specify an entry in a table of contents in an HTML-enabled program
Syntax	**Toc-Entry Text =** *text* **[Level =** *level* **]**
Arguments	*text* The text to be placed in the table of contents *level* The level to which the text belongs
Notes	The **Declare-Toc** command can be used only in the **Setup** section.
Refer to	Chapter 19

Example

```
Begin-Setup
 Toc-Entry       Text = $Heading Level = 2
End-Setup
```

Declare-Color-Map

Purpose	To define colors in an SQR report
Syntax	**Declare-Color-Map** *color_name1* = **(r1g1b1)** [color_namei = (rigibi) ...] **End-Declare**
Arguments	*color_name* A symbolic color name. *(rgb)* Color value in the RGB (red green blue) units. Each color component value can be between 0 and 255. The default colors defined in the SQR.INI file are: black = (0,0,0), white = (255,255,255), gray = (128,128,128), silver = (192,192,192), red = (255,0,0), green = (0,255,0), blue = (0,0,255), yellow = (255,255,0), purple = (128,0,128), olive = (128,128,0), navy = (0,0,128), aqua = (0,255,255), lime = (0,128,0), maroon = (128,0,0), teal = (0,128,128), fuchsia = (255,0,255).
Notes	This is a compile-time command and can be used only in the **Setup** section. You can define or redefine as many colors as you want.
Refer to	Chapter 9

Example

```
Begin-Setup
  Declare-Color-Map
    Orange = (255,156,74)
    Pale_Yellow = (255,255,198)
    End-Declare
End-Setup
```

Alter-Color-Map

Purpose	To dynamically redefine colors in an SQR report

Syntax	**Alter-Color-Map**
	    Name = color_name
	    Value = color_value

Arguments	*color_name* A symbolic color name. Can be coded as a string variable, column or literal. *color_value* A color value in the RGB (red green blue) units. Each color component value can be between 0 and 255 and can be coded as a numeric variable, column or literal.
Notes	This is a run-time command and can be used wherever the Print command is allowed. You can only redefine a previously defined color. See SQR default color definitions in the `Declare-Color-Map` command.
Refer to	Chapter 9

Example

```
If $Check_Printing_Fl='Y'
  Alter-Color-Map ! Make color brighter
    Name=Pale_Yellow Value=(255,255,146)
End If
```

Get-Color

Purpose	To dynamically obtain the current background and foreground colors

Syntax	**Get-Color**
	   [Print-Text-Foreground = **(**foreground_color_var**)]**
	   [Print-Text-Background = **(**background_color_var**)]**

Arguments	*foreground_color_var* A string variable to hold a symbolic name for foreground color. *background_color_var* A string variable to hold a symbolic name for background color.
Notes	This is a run-time command and can be used wherever the Print command is allowed. The color name "none" is returned if no color is associated with the specified area. If no symbolic name is assigned for the current color associated with the specified area, the color name is returned as "RGBredgreenblue", for example, RGB123123123. See SQR default color definitions in the Declare-Color-Map command.
Refer to	Chapter 9

Example

```
If $Check_Printing_Fl='Y'
  Get-Color Print-Text-Foreground =($Save_Foreground)
    Print-Text-Background = ($Save_Background)
  Set-Color Print-Text-Foreground = ($Check_Foreground)
    Print-Text-Background = ($Check_Background)
    Do Print_Check
  Set-Color Print-Text-Foreground = ($Save_Foreground)
    Print-Text-Background = ($Save_Background)
End If
```

`Set-Color`

Purpose	To set the current background and foreground colors
Syntax	**`Set-Color`** **`[Print-Text-Foreground`** = **`({`***`foreground_color_name`* | *`rgb1`***`})]`** **`[Print-Text-Background`** = **`({`***`background_color_name`* | *`rgb2`***`})]`**
Arguments	*`foreground_color_name`* A symbolic color name for foreground. Can be coded as a string variable, column or literal. *`rgb1`* Color value for foreground in the RGB (red green blue) units. Each color component value can be between 0 and 255 and can be coded as a numeric variable, column or literal. *`background_color_name`* A symbolic color name for background. Can be coded as a string variable, column or literal. *`rgb2`* Color value for background in the RGB (red green blue) units. Each color component value can be between 0 and 255 and can be coded as a numeric variable, column or literal.
Notes	This is a run-time command and can be used wherever the `Print` command is allowed. Use the color name "none" to turn off color associated with the specified area. See SQR default color definitions in the `Declare-Color-Map` command.
Refer to	Chapter 9

Example

See the example for the `Get-Color` command.

Working with arrays

`Create-Array`

Purpose	Create an SQR array in the program memory
Syntax	**`Create-Array Name`** = *`array_name`* **`Size`** = *`nn`* **`Field`** = *`name`* : *`type`* **`[:`***`occurs`***`]`** **`[`** = *`initial_value`* **`]`** ...
Arguments	*`array_name`* Name of the array *`nn`* The number of rows in the array **`Field`** Defines each field in the array. A field definition includes the field's **name**, and **type**. The following types can be specified: • **`Char`** (or **`Text`**) for character strings • **`Number`** for default numeric type fields • **`Decimal[(p)]`** for decimal numbers with an optional precision qualifier **`p`** • **`Float`** for double precision floating point numbers • **`Integer`** for integers • **`Date`** for date variables. *`occurs`* For multiple-occurrence fields, the number of occurrences *`initial_value`* An initial value for the field. This value will be assigned to the field by the **`Create-Array`** command and will be re-assigned again by the **`Clear-Array`** command. The default values are zeroes for all numeric types, and `NULL`s for the string and date types.

Notes	SQR creates arrays in the compile stage before the program execution starts. When array's rows are referenced, the row numbers start from zero. When field's occurrences are referenced, the occurrence numbers start from zero.
Refer to	Chapter 12

Example

```
Create-Array Name=Paygroups Size=200
Field=Code:Char='999'
Field=Week_Total:Decimal(2):4
```

Clear-Array

Purpose	Reset each field of an SQR array to its original value
Syntax	**Clear-Array Name** = *array_name*
Arguments	*array-name* Name of the array
Notes	The **Clear-Array** command is used to re-initialize an SQR array. Each array's field is set to its initial value previously defined by the **Create-Array** command. If no initial value was specified for a field, the field is set to its default initial value: zeroes for all numeric types, and NULLs for the string and date types
Refer to	Chapter 12

Example

```
Clear-Array Name=Clients
```

Get

Purpose	Move data from an SQR array into program memory
Syntax	**Get** *variable_name* ... **From** *array_name*(*row_number*) [*field* [(*occurrence*)]] ...
Arguments	*variable_name* Name of the target variable in program memory. The variable can be of the numeric, string, or date type. SQR columns cannot be used as targets. *row_number* Indicates the row in which the source field(s) is (are) located. Row numbers start with zero. If no row number is specified, row number zero is used. *row_number* can be a numeric literal or a numeric variable *field* Defines each source field in the array. If no source fields are specified, the values are moved from the first *n* array fields where *n* is the number of target variables. *occurrence* For multiple occurrence fields only, indicates the occurrence in the source field. The occurrence numbers start from zero. If no occurrence is specified, occurrence number zero is used.
Notes	The target and source fields must have compatible formats: • numeric target fields can receive data from numeric source fields of the array • string target fields can receive data from character or date source fields of the array • date target fields can receive data from character or date source fields of the array.
Refer to	Chapter 12

Example

```
Create-Array Name=Paygroups Size=100
Field=Code:Char='999'
Field=Week_Total:Decimal(2):4
```

Put

Purpose	Move data from program memory into an SQR array
Syntax	**Put** *variable_name* | *literal* ... **Into** *array_name*(*row_number*) [*field* [(*occurrence*)]] ...
Arguments	*variable_name* Name of the source variable or literal in program memory. The variable or literal can be of the numeric, string, or date type. SQR columns can also be used as sources. *row_number* Indicates the row in which the target field(s) is (are) located. Row numbers start with zero. If no row number is specified, row number zero is used. *row_number* Can be a numeric literal or a numeric variable *field* Defines target source field in the array. If no target fields are specified, the values are moved to the first *n* array fields where *n* is the number of source variables. *occurrence* For multiple occurrence fields only, indicates the occurrence in the target field. The occurrence numbers start from zero. If no occurrence is specified, occurrence number zero is used.
Notes	The target and source fields must have compatible formats: • numeric target fields in the array can receive data from numeric source • string target fields in the array can receive data from character or date source fields • date target fields in the array can receive data from character or date source fields.
Refer to	Chapter 12

Example

```
Put '01' Into Dependents(5)
```

Array-Add, Array-Subtract, Array-Multiply, Array-Divide

Purpose	Perform arithmetic operations on one or more fields in an SQR array. Depending on the operation performed, the values of the source fields in program memory are added to, subtracted from, multiplied times, or divided into the target fields in the array. The result of each operation is stored in the target fields.
Syntax	**Array-Add** *variable_name* [...] **To** *array_name* (*row_number*) [*field* [(*occurrence*)]] ... **Array-Subtract** *variable_name* [...] **From** *array_name* (*row_number*) [*field* [(*occurrence*)]] ... **Array-Multiply** *variable_name* [...] **Times** *array_name* (*row_number*) [*field* [(*occurrence*)]] ... **Array-Divide** *variable_name* [...] **Into** *array_name* (*row_number*) [*field* [(*occurrence*)]] ...

Arguments	*row_number* Indicates the row in which the target field(s) is (are) located. Row numbers start from zero. If no row number is specified, row number zero is used. *row_number* can be a numeric literal or a numeric variable. *field* Defines the target field in the array. If no target fields are specified, the first n array fields will be used where *n* is the number of source variables. The target fields must be numeric. *occurrence* For multiple occurrence fields only, indicates the occurrence in the target field. The occurrence numbers start from zero. If no occurrence is specified, occurrence number zero is used.
Notes	In case of a zero-division situation, SQR displays a warning message and continues processing without changing the target field. Refer to chapter 12.

Example

```
Array-Add  #Count  to Clients(#i) Count
Array-Subtract  1 from Books(500) Books_Received
Array-Multiply #Incr1 #Incr2 #Incr3 Times Empl(1)  Rate(0) Rate(1)
Rate(2)
Array-Divide  5  Empl(#M)
```

Interacting with host operating systems

Call, Call System

Purpose	To issue an operating system command or to call an external subroutine written in another language
Syntax	**Call** *subroutine* **Using** *input_parm output_parm* **[** *parm_string* **]** **Call System Using** *command status_var* **[{ Wait | Nowait }]**
Arguments	*subroutine* The name of your subroutine *input_parm* The input parameter to be passed to the subroutine. Can be a text or numeric variable, column variable, or literal *output_parm* A text or numeric variable into which the called subroutine will place the result of its execution *parm_string* An optional alphanumeric string to be passed to the subroutine *command* The host operating system command to be executed. Can be a sting literal, variable, or column variable *status_var* A numeric variable to hold the status returned by the operating system. The status values are system-dependent. **Wait (Windows NT, VMS)** Indicates that SQR will suspend its execution until the called command returns control back to SQR **Nowait (Windows NT, VMS)** Indicates that SQR will continue its execution after issuing the called command
Notes	**Call** is used to invoke an external subroutine written in another language. **Call System** is used to issue an operating system command. **Call** is available in all SQR environments except SQR Workbench. For SQR Workbench, use **Call System** instead.
Refer to	Chapter 18

Example

```
Call myprog Using #Inparm #Outparm
Call System Using 'sort file1.dat>file2.dat'  #Status
```

Miscellaneous commands

Show

Purpose	To display one or more literals, variables, or columns on the screen
Syntax	**Show [(** *X* **[,** *Y* **])] [{ CLEAR-SCREEN | CS | CLEAR-LINE | CL }]** **[** *name* **] [{ Edit** *edit_mask* **| Number | Money | Date }]** **[Bold] [Blink] [Underline] [Reverse] [Normal]** **[Beep] [Noline] …**
Arguments	*X, Y* The starting position on the screen (not on the report page). Can be literals or variables. Use only positions within the screen boundaries. **CLEAR-SCREEN** or **CS** To clear the screen and set the starting cursor position to the left upper corner **CLEAR-LINE** or **CL** Clears the line from the current cursor position to the end of the screen line *name* The information to be displayed. Can be a literal, variable, or column variable **Edit** Causes SQR to format the output using the edit mask specified **Number** Causes SQR to format the output using the default numeric mask. Cannot be used with date variables **Money** Causes SQR to format the output using the default money mask. Cannot be used with date variables **Date** Causes SQR to format the output using the default date mask. Cannot be used with numeric variables **Bold**, **Blink**, **Underline**, **Reverse** Causes SQR to change the display of characters on terminals that support these special effects **Normal** Turns off all special display characteristics **Beep** Issues an audio beep **Noline** To eliminate the line feed characters in the output
Notes	The **Show** command can display multiple variables. Do not intermix the **Show** and **Display** commands when referencing relative cursor positions.
Refer to	Chapter 20

Example

```
Show CLEAR-SCREEN (5, 1) 'Department total:' #Dept_Total Edit $$$,$$$,$$$.00
```

Display

Purpose	To display the specified literal, variable, or column on the screen
Syntax	**Display** *name* **[{ [:$]** *edit_mask* **| Number | Money |** **Date | }] [Noline]**

Arguments	*name* The information to be displayed. Can be a literal, variable, or column variable *edit_mask* Causes SQR to format the output using the edit mask specified **Number** Causes SQR to format the output using the default numeric mask. Cannot be used with date variables **Money** Causes SQR to format the output using the default money mask. Cannot be used with date variables **Date** Causes SQR to format the output using the default date mask. Cannot be used with numeric variables **Noline** To eliminate the line feed characters in the output
Notes	The **Display** command does not provide for screen position control. Use the **Show** command to control the screen positioning.
Refer to	Chapter 20

Example

```
Display $Employee_SSN xxx-xx-xxxx Noline
```

Alter-Locale

Purpose	To select or change the locale parameters. A locale is a set of preferences for language, currency, and the presentation of money, dates, and numbers
Syntax	see below

```
Alter-Locale [ Locale = { locale_name | DEFAULT | SYSTEM } ]
  [ Number-Edit-Mask = { number_mask | DEFAULT | SYSTEM } ]
  [ Money-Edit-Mask = { money_mask | DEFAULT | SYSTEM } ]
  [ Date-Edit-Mask = { date_mask | DEFAULT | SYSTEM } ]
  [ Input-Date-Edit-Mask = {input_date_mask | DEFAULT | SYSTEM } ]
  [ Money-Sign = { money_sign | DEFAULT | SYSTEM } ]
  [ Money-Sign-Location = { LEFT | RIGHT | DEFAULT | SYSTEM } ]
  [ Thousand-Separator = { thousand_separator | DEFAULT | SYSTEM } ]
  [ Decimal-Separator = { decimal_separator | DEFAULT | SYSTEM } ]
  [ Date-Separator = { date_separator | DEFAULT | SYSTEM } ]
  [ Time-Separator = { time_separator | DEFAULT | SYSTEM } ]
  [ Edit-Option-NA = { edit_option-na | DEFAULT | SYSTEM } ]

  [ Edit-Option-AM = { edit_option-am | DEFAULT | SYSTEM } ]
  [ Edit-Option-PM = { edit_option-pm | DEFAULT | SYSTEM } ]
  [ Edit-Option-BC = { edit_option-bc | DEFAULT | SYSTEM } ]
  [ Edit-Option-AD = { edit_option-ad | DEFAULT | SYSTEM } ]
  [ Day-Of-Week-Case = { UPPER | LOWER | EDIT | NO-CHANGE |
     DEFAULT | SYSTEM } ]
  [ Day-Of-Week-Full = ( day1 ... day7 ) ]
  [ Day-Of-Week-Short = ( day1 ... day7 ) ]
  [ Months-Case = { UPPER | LOWER | EDIT | NO-CHANGE |
     DEFAULT | SYSTEM } ]
  [ Months-Full = ( month1 ... month12 ) ]
  [ Months-Short = ( month1 ... month12 ) ]
```

Arguments

`locale_name` The name of the locale. The name must be specified in the **SQR.ini** file. If the name is omitted, the current locale will be used. SQR stores the name of the current locale in the reserved variable **$sqr-locale**.

Number-Edit-Mask The default edit mask to be used when the keyword **Numeric** is specified in the **Print**, **Move**, **Show**, or **Display** command.

Money-Edit-Mask The default edit mask to be used when the keyword **Money** is specified in the **Print**, **Move**, **Show**, or **Display** command.

Date-Edit-Mask The default edit mask to be used when the keyword **Date** is specified in the **Print**, **Move**, **Show**, or **Display** command, or in the functions `datetostr` or `strtodate`.

Input-Date-Edit-Mask The default date format to be used with the **Input** command.

Money-Sign The character(s) which will replace the dollar sign in in edit masks

Money-Sign-Location Where the money sign character(s) will be placed

Thousand-Separator The character which will replace the comma edit character

Decimal-Separator The character which will be used to separate the decimals portion

Date-Separator The character which will be used to separate day, month, and year in dates

Time-Separator The character(s) which will be used to separate the colon in date/time fields

Edit-Option-NA The character(s) which will be used to substitute "NA"

Edit-Option-AM The character(s) which will be used to replace 'AM' in time fields

Edit-Option-PM The character(s) which will be used to replace 'PM' in time fields

Edit-Option-BC The character which will be used to replace 'BC' in date fields

Edit-Option-AD The character which will be used to replace 'AD' in date fields

Day-Of-Week-Case Specifies what case (upper or lower) must be used for the day portion when printing date fields:

- **UPPER** or **LOWER**—the output will be in the upper or lower case regardless of the mask specified
- **EDIT**—the case will be defined in the edit format mask
- **NO-CHANGE**—SQR will use the case specified in the `Day-Of-Week-Full` and **Day-Of-Week-Short** parameters
- **Default**—the parameter value will be retrieved from the "default" locale
- **System**—the parameter value will be retrieved from the "system" locale

Day-Of-Week-Full The full names of the seven days of the week starting from Sunday

Day-Of-Week-Short The short names of the seven days of the week starting from Sunday

Months-Case Specifies what case (upper or lower) must be used for the month portion when printing date fields:

- **UPPER** or **LOWER**—the output will be in the upper or lower case regardless of the mask specified
- **EDIT**—the case will be defined in the edit format mask
- **NO-CHANGE**—SQR will use the case specified in the **Months-Full** and **Months-Short** parameters
- **Default**—the parameter value will be retrieved from the "default" locale
- **System**—the parameter value will be retrieved from the "system" locale

	Months-Full The full names of the twelve months of the year starting from January **Months-Short** The short names of the twelve months of the year starting from January
Notes	The "system" locale is a set of locale parameters corresponding to the SQR versions prior to Version 4 The "default" locale settings are defined in the **[Default-Settings]** section of the **SQR.ini** file
Refer to	Chapter 21

Example

```
Alter-Locale
  Date-Edit-Mask = 'Mon DD YYYY'
  Input-Date-Edit-Mask = 'MM/DD/YY'
  Money-Sign = 'FF'
  Date-Separator = '-'
  Time-Separator = '.'
```

Stop

Purpose	To halt SQR
Syntax	**Stop [Quiet]**
Arguments	**Quiet** If coded, SQR stops with the "SQR: End of run" message instead of aborting with an error message.
Notes	The **Stop** command halts SQR and causes the **Rollback** command to be issued (not in Sybase, Microsoft SQL Server, or Informix). All accumulated page buffers are flushed; no headers or footers are printed, and the **After-Page** and **After-Report** procedures are not invoked.

Example

```
Stop Quiet
```

bibliography

"Administration Tools." *PeopleTools 8.12 PeopleBook*, Pleasanton, CA: PeopleSoft Inc., 2000.

Aronoff, Eyal, Kevin Loney, and Noorali Sonawalla. *Advanced Oracle Tuning and Administration.* Berkeley, CA: Osborne McGraw-Hill, 1997.

Barkakati, Nabe. *The Waite Group's Microsoft C Bible*. Indianapolis, IN: Sams, 1992.

DeLia, Tony, Galina Landres, Isidor Rivera, Prakash Sankaran, *Essential Guide to PeopleSoft Development and Customization*. Manning Publications, 2001.

"Development Tools." *PeopleTools 8.12 PeopleBook*, Pleasanton, CA: PeopleSoft Inc., 2000.

Gruber, Martin. *Understanding SQL*. Alameda, CA: Sybex, 1996.

"Integration Tools." *PeopleTools 8.12 PeopleBook*, Pleasanton, CA: PeopleSoft Inc., 2000.

Loney, Kevin, George Koch, *Oracle 8i: The Complete Reference*. Osborne/McGraw Hill, 2000.

Quigley, Ellie. *UNIX Shells by Example*. Upper Saddle River, NJ: Prentice Hall PTR, 1997.

"Reporting and Decision Support Tools." *PeopleTools 8.12 PeopleBook*, Pleasanton, CA: PeopleSoft Inc., 2000.

SQR Language Reference Version 6. Brio Technology, Santa Clara, CA, 2000.

SQR User's Guide Version 6. Brio Technology, Santa Clara, CA, 2000.

index

C

D

E

F

G

H

I

J

K

L

M

N

O

P

S

T

U

W

X

Z